HOUSE OF PSYCHOTIC WOMEN

AN AUTOBIOGRAPHICAL TOPOGRAPHY OF FEMALE NEUROSIS
IN HORROR AND EXPLOITATION FILMS

KIER-LA JANISSE

HOUSE OF PSYCHOTIC WOMEN

AN AUTOBIOGRAPHICAL TOPOGRAPHY OF FEMALE NEUROSIS IN HORROR AND EXPLOITATION FILMS

First published July 2012
2nd pressing April 2014, 3rd pressing December 2016, 4th pressing December 2018
This 5th pressing September 2020

FAB Press Ltd.
2 Farleigh, Ramsden Road,
Godalming, Surrey,
GU7 1QE, England, U.K.

www.fabpress.com

THE AUTHOR WISHES TO EXPRESS HER THANKS TO:
Adele Hartley, Harvey Fenton, Francis Brewster, Chandra Mayor, Janelle Ionn, Sam McKinlay, David Bertrand, Katie East, Naben Ruthnum, Iain Banks, Ralph Bakshi, Charles Bernstein, Mike Malloy, Federico Caddeo, Matthew Rankin, Frank Labonte, Daniel Bird, Lara Simms, Caelum Vatnsdal, tamara rae biebrich, Cam Bush, Monica Lowe, crys cole, Douglas Buck, Rita Romagnino, Mike Gingold, Paul Corupe, James Burrell, Fabio Vellozo, Nathaniel Thompson, Sean Smithson, David Blyth, Chris Alexander, Blake Etheridge, Shade Rupe, Rodney Perkins, Matthew Kiernan, Pete Tombs, Atom Leborgne, Ariel Esteban Cayer, Valerie Hudson, Dan Yates, Melissa Howard, Karim Hussain, Craig Ledbetter, Mitch Davis, Lars Nilsen, Zack Carlson, Tim & Karrie League, Robin Bougie, Dave Alexander, Stuart Andrews, Simon Laperriere, Melinda Michelak, K.K. Celine, Matthew Garrett, Jonathan Culp, Greg Sonier, Kristen Bell, Brendan Sloane, Charles Smith, Andrew Parkinson, Mike White, Mark Savage, Michael Raso, Sarah Bradley, Stephanie Llewellyn, Alexander Dafoe, Jay Slater, Kelly Hughes, Ariel Gordon, Jordan Janisse, Teresa Cooper, Rob Jones, Michel Janisse, Andrea Morse, Virginia Offen, Ivo Scheloske, Patricia Gardner, Mike Josephson, Clint Enns, Leslie Supnet, Aaron W. Graham, Donato Totaro, Marc Morris, Sean Hogan, Mitch Putnam, and many others without whose support this book would never have been completed.

Written with the generous support of the City of Winnipeg through the Winnipeg Arts Council.

 WINNIPEG ARTS COUNCIL

Edited by Harvey Fenton.
Page layout by Harvey Fenton, after an original design idea by Kier-La Janisse.

Front cover illustration, hardcover: Artwork originally used in the promotion of Andrzej Zulawski's **Possession** (1981)
Front cover illustration, paperback: Montage of images from **Let's Scare Jessica to Death** (1971) with thanks to Silver Ferox (www.silverferoxdesign.com)
Back cover illustrations: **Possession** (1981), **Carrie** (1976), **Black Swan** (2010)
Frontispiece illustration: Asia Argento in Dario Argento's **The Stendhal Syndrome** (1996)
Contents page illustration: **The Last Exorcism** (2011)

Stills and illustrations in this book are copyright © the respective copyright holders and are reproduced in the spirit of publicity, with due acknowledgement to the following organisations and individuals: Alpha Films, American International Pictures, Anahuac S.A., Anolis Entertainment, Arte Cinema de Mexico, S.A., Audubon Films Inc., Avco Embassy Pictures, Avis Ascot, BCP, Border Film Productions (London) Ltd., Capitol International, Catfish Studios, C.C.C. Film Gmbh, Chris Releasing Corp., Cine 2000, Cinecrest Films Inc., Cinema International Corporation, Cinematografica S.A., Cinerama Releasing, City Lights Pictures, CJLJ Film, Classic Film Industries, Cockney Rebels Specials, Code Red, Columbia-EMI-Warner Distributors, Columbia Pictures, Columbia Tristar, Comflik Associates, Commonwealth United, Compton, Condor Films, Cox Broadcasting Corporation, Dark Vision Pictures, Dyna-Mite! Entertainment, Dzen Film, El Entertainment, E.Sanchez Ramade, E Tube Entertainment, Fastigium Films, Fetter Productions, Fortissimofilms, Gloria Film, Golden Harvest, Goldwyn Entertainment Company, Harbor Productions Inc., Headway Films Inc., Hispamex Films, S.A., IIF, Imagination Worldwide, Independent-International, Izaro Films, Jennings Lang, Julie D'Amour-Léger, Lionsgate, LMG, Lopert Films Inc., Malpaso Company, Maron Films Ltd., MCI, Medusa Film, Mercurio Films S.A., Metro-Goldwyn-Mayer, Miracle Films, Navaron Films, Network Releasing, New Line Cinema, Niles International, Odyssey, Palomar Pictures International Inc., Paramount Pictures, Polfilm, Portland Film Corporation, Producciones Filmicas Maynat, S.A., Profilms, S.A., Ram, Rank Organisation, Raro Video, Realart, Reluctant Pictures, RKO Radio Pictures Inc., Roadshow Distributors, Rochelle Films Inc., Salient Media, Scimitar Films, Scotia International Films Inc., Seda Spettacoli Rome, Selznick International, Seven Arts, Stormlight Films, Strike Entertainment, Studiocanal, Thorn EMI, Tigon, Titanus Films, Tobis Filmkunst, Twentieth Century-Fox, Unisphere, United Artists, United Film Distribution Co., United International Pictures, United Producers, Universal Pictures, VCL, Warner Bros., Warner-Columbia, William Mishkin Motion Pictures, Inc., Wingnut Films, World Film Services Ltd.

hardcover: ISBN 978 1 903254 68 4
paperback: ISBN 978 1 903254 69 1

**FOR ADELE, JANELLE and CHANDRA
and JUDITH ANNE MORSE**

CONTENTS

INTRODUCTION: "HAVE YOU GOT A MAGNIFICENT PROBLEM?"

"[*Red Desert*] shows with almost clinical precision how, to the deeply neurotic mind, everything in life is levelled to the problem: not only love in its various forms but family responsibility, work, friendship, even simple mechanical tasks like driving a car. The details are perfectly rendered, the metonyms hauntingly real and physical... No less palpable are [Giuliana's] longings – to have everyone and everything she has loved around her to form a wall against the terror... Yet Antonioni also shows that behind all the fears there are sharply aggressive feelings. What makes Giuliana more apprehensive than anything is how close she feels to violence."
– Seymour Chatman, *Antonioni, or the Surface of the World*

"I wanted to find the fool who invented 'closure' and shove a big closure plaque up his ass."
– James Ellroy, *My Dark Places*

It all started with *Possession*. Zulawski's film, formally speaking, is perfection – its deep blue hues, its labyrinthine locations, the hypnotic cinematography of Bruno Nuytten. But that's not what drew me to return to it again and again. There was something terrible in that film, a desperation I recognized in myself, in my inability to communicate effectively, and the frustration that would lead to despair, anger and hysteria.

My relationship with this film caused me to look at what kinds of warnings – or in some cases reinforcements – I was getting out of other films in which disturbed or neurotic women figured greatly. Over the past ten years I started keeping a log of these films, accompanied by rambling, incoherent notes and occasionally wet pages. I have drawers full of these scribblings; they're spilling out of manila envelopes in my closet, and they're all pieces of a puzzle that I have to figure out how to put together. But my starting point was a question, and that question presented itself easily: I wanted to know why I was crazy – and what happens when you feed crazy with more crazy.

As with most female horror fans, people love to ask me what it is I get out of horror. I give them the stock answers: catharsis, empowerment, escapism and so on. Less easy to explain is the fact that I gravitate toward films that devastate and unravel me completely – a good horror film will more often make me cry than make me shudder. I remember someone describing their first time seeing Paulus Manker's *The Moor's Head* as so devastating they had to lie on the sidewalk when they exited the theatre. Now, *that*'s what I look for in a film.

Cinema is full of neurotic personalities, but I decided to focus on women because this is what I know. And again, I decided to focus on horror and exploitation films because this is what I know. Everything in my early existence – the Creature Feature double bills of old Hammer and AIP films, the Alice Cooper records and stage shows, *Scooby-Doo*, *The Devil and Daniel Mouse* and *The Hardy Boys Mysteries* – shaped me for this particular future. I was chauffeured into this dark terrain by my parents, but I stayed there because of something in myself. And that 'something' was decidedly female.

opposite: Isabelle Adjani in Andrzej Zulawski's **Possession** (1981).

The concept of female neurosis that proliferated in 19th century literature and extended into 20th century cinema became such a self-fulfilling prophecy that well-adjusted, secure and good-humoured female characterization was seen as an appealing but improbable alternative to reality. From the roots of *fin de siecle* culture grew the stereotype of female emotional and mental development that we would encounter again and again throughout cinematic history: the weak, swooning girls of *The Cabinet of Dr. Caligari* and the Universal monster shows; the masochistic death-wish of Louise Brooks in *Pandora's Box*; the crippling paranoia of Hitchcock's *Rebecca* and her counterpart in *The Horrible Dr. Hichcock*; the desperate loneliness of *Carrie* and *May* (and conversely, the demented bonds of the girls in *Don't Deliver Us from Evil* and *3 Women*); the repression of *Mademoiselle* and *A Lizard in a Woman's Skin*; the dangerous obsessiveness of *Trance*; the hysteria of *Possession*.

Unlike her comparatively-lauded male counterpart – 'the eccentric' – the female neurotic lives a shamed existence. But the shame itself is a trap – one that is fiercely protected by men and women alike.

The feminist movement's fervour waned in the late 1970s and 1980s as individual excess and consumerism replaced any strong sense of female solidarity. Like any organized movement, Women's Lib ignored the tendency toward individualism and free thought. Where the militancy of the feminist movement was to some extent accepted – and necessary – in the 1960s, the social advances it facilitated were taken for granted by the 1980s, and fewer and fewer women felt compelled to vigorously tout its banner. The movement seemed stunted, and as it struggled to regain its cultural foothold, literature and cinema – particularly pornography and genre cinema – started to come under attack. Female genre fans were guilt-tripped into feeling like 'traitors to the cause', and it seems that much feminist horror theory was born out of the need for a defensive response. Just as the Women's Lib movement originated amongst women in higher education, it was within this milieu that new concepts of femininity – and how they related to horror and exploitation cinema – started to percolate by the end of the 1980s.

Admittedly, hyperbolic responses to the 'emancipated woman' were ever-present in early '70s horror, and men's fears either materialized as murderous, lust-filled females, or found relief in the reinforcement of pre-existing 'woman as helpless victim' stereotypes. But just as men struggled to adapt to this practical exercise in equality of the sexes, so did women, many of whom were opposed to the feminist movement from the outset, or were at least comfortable enough in their existing lifestyles to find it a distinct threat. After all, feminism was critical of them. It accused them of being complacent, mindless, dependent upon men for both money and self-worth. It saw them as weak and shameful.

When I first started edging into film writing in the mid-'90s, I was all about girl-power; how horror films (even slasher films) were empowering to women, how most horror films were about men's anxieties concerning the nature of femininity and female sexuality, gender relations, castration anxiety – all this great, meaty stuff. I saw positive female representation in everything, no matter how ostensibly reprehensible the film's politics. For a female horror/exploitation film fan, that's a great place to start; certainly much more productive than denouncing the genre altogether as some counter-revolutionary, misogynist exercise in populist entertainment. But I often found myself generalizing, and the brevity of magazine articles allows for that, even encourages it. I wanted to explore neurotic characterization as comprehensively as I could, but I also didn't want to write a dense book of horror theory, as my interest in academic writing has diminished significantly over the years. I also knew that if I started leaning too much on Freud and Lacan I'd be out of my depth. I needed to focus on what I know: namely, that the films I watch align with my personal experience in that every woman I have ever met in my entire life is completely crazy, in one way or another. Whether or not that's a disparagement is part of what I aim to explore in this book.

Naturally, my interests extend beyond conventional genre boundaries, but for the most part I'll be concentrating on horror and violent exploitation films. That said, exploitation cinema, like any other, does not exist in a vacuum, and there has been constant interplay and cross-pollination over the decades between 'legit' cinema and genre cinema. Directors of pedigrees as varied as Roman Polanski and Andy Milligan have plumbed the depths of female neurosis because it's such fertile ground. You could say that the entire catalogue of rape-revenge films are descended from Bergman's *The Virgin Spring* (1960) and the medieval folk tales that inspired it, and that many of the characters in this book owe a certain debt to those created by directors as diverse as Michelangelo Antonioni, Richard Lester and Yasuzo Masumura.

Monica Vitti's character Giuliana in Antonioni's *Red Desert* (1964), for example, has been labelled "the neurotic personality of our time".[1] While *Red Desert* lies outside the genre scope of this book, the detailed manifestation of female neurosis would have an impact on many filmmakers featured here. And while Antonioni once said that his films frequently featured female protagonists because "woman is the more subtle filter of reality"[2] there is nothing subtle about the women you'll meet in the following pages.

I myself have been the subject of a film – Ashley Fester's *Celluloid Horror* (2003) – and while I was a reluctant subject and have often voiced my embarrassment regarding the film's portrayal of my life and relationships at the time, I now recognize the benefit of this alternative perspective on what were clouded

issues for me. While ostensibly focused on the CineMuerte Horror Film Festival, which I created and nurtured throughout its 7-year history (1999-2005 inclusive), the documentary delved into some uncomfortable subject matter: my adolescent propensity for physical violence, my history in group homes, foster homes and detention centres, and the years of involuntary therapy that only encouraged my rebellion further. Most painful of all, it captured the disintegration of my brief marriage.

My constructive participation in genre film exhibition and promotion over the years has curbed my (often misdirected) aggression to a great degree. As my own neurosis became more subdued I found myself unconsciously drawn to female characters who exhibited signs of behaviour I had recognized in myself: repression, delusion, jealousy, paranoia, hysteria. But these issues didn't magically disappear; they just became buried beneath business and activity, and came back to sideswipe me at inopportune moments.

We have more patience, or perhaps even empathy, for fictional characters than we do their real-life counterparts. Faced with neurosis in film or literature, we want to investigate rather than avoid. If watching horror films is cathartic because it provides a temporary feeling of control over the one unknown factor that can't be controlled (death), then wouldn't it make sense to assume a crazy person would find relief in onscreen histrionics?

As I sit down now to rewrite this book for the umpteenth time, my life is enveloped by chaos, and all the old ghosts are back. Unresolved issues weigh heavily on me: feelings of failure, sabotaged relationships, blinding anger. Amidst this sea of dangerous emotions I came to focus again, thankfully, on this project. I am determined to have a different ending to my story than the one that keeps presenting itself.

This book follows my own personal trajectory. While it examines cinematic patterns as thoroughly as possible, and goes in and out of film synopses and critiques, it's still, at the end of the day, a book about my life. My recollections have been criticized by family members who remember things differently, and who question the credibility of my own memories. But any person who has witnessed or experienced traumatic events knows that it is often difficult to retain a full, clear picture of these events. They present themselves in fragments and pieces that come together to form a truth that is sometimes unique to that person, but no less relevant.

So hopefully the outcome of this writing, of the commonalities that present themselves between the events of my own life and those that unfold onscreen will be a weird celebration of the colourful, challenging and surprisingly funny history of female neurosis – both real and imagined.

above: Monica Vitti and Richard Harris in Michelangelo Antonioni's **Red Desert** (1964).

PART ONE:
WOUND GATHERERS

Winnipeg is an isolated city in the dead centre of Canada known for its long, harsh winters and its citizens' tragic propensity for alcoholism and violent crime. This is where I was born. It was October of 1972, and my biological mother was a redheaded teenager from an outlying rural town, whose boyfriend – a year her junior – split when she became unexpectedly pregnant. The rural prairies were not then – as they likely remain – an accommodating climate for either single mothers or the quick-fix alternative of abortion, and so I was put up for adoption at the Women's Hospital in Winnipeg, now known as the Health Sciences Centre.

I was adopted by Merrill (who I refer to as 'Oates' because he looks like the great character actor Warren Oates) and Julie Janisse, a couple nearly ten years into a rocky marriage who had managed to have one son of their own despite several preceding miscarriages and stillbirths. During the adoption interview, Julie was excited and hopeful, while Oates was characteristically sardonic (when asked if he had a happy childhood, he said "Well I only had one, so I have nothing to compare it to.") My adoption was meant to be a renewed focal point for their marriage, which was slowly disintegrating as the sexual revolution became an accepted reality and Oates was looking towards younger, greener, and more numerous pastures.

But their wishful thinking didn't pay off; instead of providing a means by which to strengthen the marriage, my presence only added further strain. My father's questionable extracurricular activities resulted in violent opposition from my mother, who inevitably came to realize that further investment was hopeless.

When I was two years old, my mother took my brother and I back to her hometown of Windsor, Ontario, where she would have the support of her family, and pursued life as a single mom in a townhouse complex called Columbia Court, under her maiden name of Julie Smith. I was too young to grasp the significance of her divorce, to understand how adult relationships worked, and I would constantly pester her to marry someone new. Since my world was limited to my immediate family, my first choice for a new dad was my Uncle Jack, her younger teenaged brother, and if that failed, my own brother would do. She would laugh off these absurd suggestions, trying to explain while I looked on quizzically that aside from her disinterest in marrying either of them, it would also be illegal.

Like my biological mother, Julie was also a redhead, a small-framed feisty woman with a cackling laugh who was always smiling and dancing to hide what was certainly a crushing heartbreak. I remember her singing into a spatula while Shaun Cassidy played on the turntable, twirling around clumsily while making breakfast for my brother and I. But for me, these memories would come later. My first memory of living in that Windsor townhouse with my newly-compacted family is less cheerful.

above: My mother and me, November 1972.

opposite: Barbara Hershey in Sidney J. Furie's **The Entity** (1982).

As a means of illustrating my early predilection for horror films, I have always told people that my first awareness of being alive is of watching the Granada/Benmar co-production *Horror Express* (1972) starring Peter Cushing and Christopher Lee as rival anthropologists stuck on a Trans-Siberian train with a recently-reanimated alien life form, and, perhaps more unnervingly, Telly Savalas. *Horror Express* would play a pivotal role in my development, and watching it is likely my first fully-formed cognitive memory. But my very first memory is more fragmented, more abstract, and it would be over a decade before its meaning would become apparent. Knowing what I know now, it doesn't make for pleasant conversation, which is why *Horror Express* has usurped its place in all pre-existing interviews or documentation on my formative years.

My earliest memory is of waking up in a dark apartment at night with a start, after hearing a strange noise. I get up to investigate, but I'm locked in my room from the outside (my mother later told me there was a latch on the outside of my door due to my violent temper tantrums as a child). Next there's a flurry of shadows and distorted noises and a distinct feeling of fear. My mother sweeps me up in her arms and we sit on my windowsill while she tells me everything is going to be okay, but her voice is shaking and I don't quite feel comforted.

The meaning of this episode would be reluctantly explained to me years later, when I was in my early teens, by an aunt. My mother had sworn her to secrecy, but my aunt felt that knowing the truth might help me have more compassion for this woman I had come to despise and mistrust through the intervening years. It was a mistake – I was always looking for new ways to humiliate my parents, and the elucidation of what I had always thought was just a weird, recurring dream gave me ample ammunition.

My mother was an attractive woman and a generous caretaker – she was a registered nurse and throughout my childhood worked at various nursing homes taking care of elderly people in varying stages of dementia – but outside of an obsessive need to clean, she was hopeless around the house. This was compensated for by the landlord's stable of recovering drug addicts from the halfway house down the street, who were frequently sent over to deal with minor plumbing or electrical problems. My brother, who was 5 or 6 at the time, often stayed over at my grandmother's house, and that's where he was when one of these guys put a jam in the lock on the window after fixing the sink.

From what I'm told, the noise that awoke me that night was the sound of my mother being raped. She heard me banging on my door trying to get out of my room, followed by a loud crack as the latch outside the door ripped off and I came running down the hallway toward them. Her room was dark, and she was pinned on the floor beneath her much larger assailant. As I appeared in her doorway, my mother begged the man to leave, convincing him that she hadn't seen his face and couldn't identify him. But if I were to turn on the light, he would have two witnesses.

This tactic worked, and the man left. I wasn't tall enough to even reach the light switch, but no matter – in my mother's eyes, I had saved her life. She picked me up and barricaded us in my room. At one point she got up and went to the door, hearing a rustling downstairs that turned out to be the attacker returning momentarily for his cigarettes. My mother cradled me in the nook of my windowsill and told me everything was going to be okay, but I knew that something was horribly wrong. I was sent to stay with an aunt for a short time afterwards, because my mother tried to kill herself.

This episode undoubtedly created a weird imbalance in our relationship. While she considered it lucky that I'd been around to cause a diversion, I later got the feeling that she never recovered from the embarrassment of the whole thing; that she somehow held it against me that I'd been witness to the most traumatic experience of her life. Resentment bounced back and forth between us, well, forever. Actually, a mix of resentment and pity.

This wasn't the first time, and wouldn't be the last, that my mother would experience physical violence in her own home. Over time I think she came to expect it, or perhaps even to believe she deserved it.

When I was about ten years old I remember overhearing her talking about a new film that disturbed her greatly, although I don't know if she actually saw it or just read about it somewhere. The film was shrouded in controversy, so I don't doubt that a newspaper article may have prompted her reaction. As a teenager I would eventually see the film, and I understood why it upset her, just as it upset many women at the time. It was Sidney J. Furie's *The Entity*.

The film, released in 1982, explores the domestic abuse/woman-as-masochist stereotype by veiling it as a supernatural horror film. But what made the film's uncomfortable hypothesis impossible to dismiss was that it was based on a true story.

Culver City, California, 1974: UCLA Parapsychologists Dr. Kerry Gaynor and Dr. Barry Taff were approached in a bookstore by a woman who claimed she had a ghost in her house. During a two-hour preliminary interview the woman (whose real name was Doris Bither) admitted that the ghost had beaten and raped her. The doctors were hesitant to believe her until several of her friends independently verified the phenomena. Bither claimed that there were in fact three apparitions – the primary assailant, and two others who would hold her down as she was raped by the first. During one of the attacks, Bither's teenage son was hurled across the room and his arm broken (strangely, the actor who played her son in the film also had his arm broken while shooting the

scene based on this event). While Gaynor and Taff frequently saw physical evidence of brutal beatings, the most they ever witnessed personally were strange light formations that they managed to photograph (and which appeared in *Popular Photography* magazine[3]). Nonetheless, Gaynor and Taff served as technical advisors when *The Entity* was being filmed.

In the movie, Carla Moran (Barbara Hershey) is a single mother whose struggle to get by is aggravated by the presence of an extremely violent, foul-smelling and distinctly masculine ghost. The entity threatens her body as much as her sanity; it repeatedly and brutally rapes her, in one instance in front of her children, and another while she is fast asleep. Her boyfriend Jerry (Alex Rocco) is talked about more than seen; he is away on business trips for most of the film. As the entity's attacks intensify, Carla assumes the role of the abused housewife, which is especially fitting since the absence of a patriarch in the home leaves room for the entity itself to function as a sort of drunk, violent husband. Furthermore, the entity attacks her in a friend's home, and in her car, which causes her to retreat into the physical and emotional isolation that is characteristic of many victims of domestic abuse. Close-ups of her increasingly vacant, detached gaze signify her resignation to the violence.

After the attack in her car, Carla goes to see a psychiatrist named Dr. Sneiderman (Ron Silver) who insists that the attacks are the product of her imagination. "I've seen cases of hysteria that have raised welts, caused blindness, loss of hearing…" he explains, while calmly filling out a prescription for tranquilizers. He coaxes her to tell him about her childhood, believing, like any good Freudian, that therein lies the key. "As a kid I experienced every cliché in the book", she admits, "I was scared of the dark, I was afraid of my father. He was a minister… when he held me it wasn't in the way a father should hold a daughter." So at the age of 16 she ran away, married a teenager who got her pregnant almost immediately, and things went downhill from there.

above: Barbara Hershey in **The Entity** (1982).

Her young husband started drinking and popping pills excessively and got himself killed in a motorcycle accident before the baby was born. She turned to a man three times her age, but that relationship didn't last either.

The psychiatrist's role in the film is pivotal, because he is the one character close to Carla who views her predicament symbolically. While her children, her boyfriend, and a team of parapsychologists all concur without doubt that something is living in the house with her that is not just the product of her own delusions, Dr. Sneiderman's opposing stance resulted in the dismissal of the film by many viewers who felt that it appeared to advocate – or at least validate – the myth of therapeutic rape.

The attack while she is asleep (which boasts incredible FX by the late Stan Winston that show her breasts being manipulated by invisible fingers) is made all the more painful by Carla's subsequent admission to the sceptical Dr. Sneiderman that she had an orgasm during the experience. This admission only serves to strengthen his theoretical resolve. His interviews with her mirror the interrogation heaped upon abused women when they finally turn to someone for help: they are suspected of fabrication, provocation, even seduction. Sneiderman believes

she has brought on the attacks herself; that she is not the victim of a demonic external entity, but of her own repression and secret need for abuse. He subscribes to Freud's assertion in *Beyond the Pleasure Principle* (1920) that the unconscious seeks to return to the major unresolved traumas of childhood in an attempt to master the conflict. He believes that Carla has to be saved from herself; and for the most part, she agrees: "I do need your help", she confides, "I really do. And I won't fight you. If it's really me creating all this, if I'm that sick, then I have to be stopped." She wants to believe him. After all, if the source of the problem is in her, then so is the solution.

As the film continues, Carla's response to the entity alternates between resignation and determination. Still, she doesn't seem especially hopeful; when Sneiderman reaches out to her, and suggests that she needs to maintain contact with someone in the outside world who cares about her, she says, "I don't want to make that contact." Again, she exhibits the behaviour of the masochistic woman who repeatedly returns to an abusive lover. In a sense, it's traumatic bonding – the abuse only strengthens the ties between the abused and her abuser, because it is a shameful secret that is shared between them.

Dr. Sneiderman puts her before a panel of psychiatrists who agree with his prognosis that the attacks are mounted from within, that she is acting out some adolescent masturbation fantasy and repressing the desire to have intercourse with her son, who is the spitting image of her dead husband. She is analyzed as having a fear of sex bred into her by a strict Christian upbringing, and as 'imagining' her father to have had incestuous designs on her. Any chance of having a normal, healthy relationship with a man is sabotaged by her need to have 'safe sex', meaning sex through which she derives no real pleasure; so she creates a destructive fantasy to intervene. But the panel's observations don't sit right with her; these people are objectifying her, and are insensitive in their accusations. A female psychiatrist on the board cuts to the chase: "Would it be a reflection on you as a woman if [the entity] left you, if you were cured?"

But self-blame is no less destructive; it's an easy out that only feeds the negative cycles of abuse. After the events that led to her divorce, and bolstered by the incident at Columbia Court (which my father Oates – a psychologist – refused to believe ever occurred), my mother remarried, and this new relationship would bring its own challenges in the form of an ill-tempered stepfather whose behaviour would be tolerated because my mother felt to do otherwise made her a failure. If one views Carla's situation in *The Entity* as the equivalent of domestic violence, Sneiderman's assessment is not far off the mark: women who cyclically pair up with or return to abusive partners are more often than not re-enacting residual experiences, constantly returning to the source of trauma in an attempt to master it, to get it right.

In *The Entity*, Carla is eventually driven from her home; but as the film's closing credits indicate, the entity follows her, and the attacks on her real-life counterpart were supposedly still occurring after the film had been made. If the film had provided some sort of closure – if Carla Moran had somehow defeated her spectral assailant – perhaps the film would have been received more favourably. Any misogynist elements would have been softened by the triumph of the woman at the end. But Carla doesn't win. She remains the victim.

The more recent film *Paranormal Activity* (2007 – which since this writing has gone on to spawn a successful franchise), while less fraught with controversial sexual politics than *The Entity*, deals with a similarly recurring haunting. A young couple (Kate and Micah) invest in a home video camera to record the nightly paranormal occurrences that have been plaguing them since they moved in together: banging and scratching sounds coming from the walls and the hallways, the movement of small objects, an odorous breath coming from an invisible source. But as Micah becomes more fascinated with the possibility of capturing a haunting on tape, Kate becomes increasingly agitated and fearful that the camera is antagonizing the entity and inviting more intense attacks.

Her trepidation is reinforced by a psychic who visits them and asserts that there is indeed a demonic presence in the house that is specifically interested in Kate, and that any tension between Kate and Micah, any tangible strain on their relationship, will only extend a further invitation to evil forces. The seeds of discord are certainly there, and increase as the couple suffers from sleep deprivation that heightens their mutual sense of anxiety. Kate objects to her boyfriend's liberal use of the camera around the house – which acts as a buffer obscuring their personal communication – and his increasingly macho attitude about handling the problem himself, without the assistance of a professional demonologist. He challenges and taunts the entity even as Kate begs him to stop inviting more horror upon her.

Micah thinks it's a game though, and to emphasize this, he brings a Ouija board into the house, to Kate's furious objection. With the Ouija board left alone during an argument that takes the couple out of the room, the camera records the movement of the planchette across the board, spelling out a word that appears to be the name 'Diane' before spontaneously bursting into flames.

It is revealed that Kate is no stranger to these incidents; they've been happening to her intermittently since she was a child, and ended when her house suddenly caught fire and burned down with no apparent cause that the fire department was ever able to concretely determine. As Micah scours the internet looking for related information, he comes across a mirroring case a generation earlier, involving a young woman named Diane who suffered a haunting as a child, which ended when her home also burned to the ground. But Diane was also revisited by the entity as a young adult – and she didn't survive its return. Kate sees much of herself in this girl

Diane, and the precedent convinces her that it is the work of the same demon, which transferred its abuse from one victim to the next. She feels herself headed towards the same fate as the girl who came before.

However, Micah offers little emotional support. It becomes apparent that his defiant refusal to accommodate Kate's wishes stems from a passive-aggressive resentment over the fact that she neglected to mention these hauntings before they moved in together. He feels that, by withholding this information from him, she made her choice – and now he has the right to deal with the situation in his own way, stating "You're *my* girlfriend, and I'll handle this *myself*." Kate becomes listless and withdraws into emotional vacancy, resigning herself to a lack of control as her boyfriend and the demon engage in a dangerous battle of wills over her life. As in *The Entity*, the woman is only a pawn, being objectified, interrogated and ultimately silenced.

In Peter Tscherkassky's experimental shorts *Outer Space* (1999) and *Dream Work* (2001) – whose images are derived from *The Entity* – the filmmaker's hands themselves become the entity, prodding, breaking and doubling her image with sadistic detachment. But unlike *The Entity*, *Paranormal Activity* doesn't delve too deeply into Kate's history or how the haunting may have affected her psychologically, other than illustrating an associated

sense of shame that lends to her evasiveness as an adult. These kinds of films, in which an invisible antagonist returns again and again to an increasingly defeated victim – while operating superficially as ghost stories – are almost always analogous to other psychological issues, most notably the repression of traumatic memories and the cyclical acceptance of abuse.

The notion of a haunting coming back intermittently is something that has always interested me, based on the fact that many of the traumatic events of my own life have patterns of reappearance. A haunting is very much like a memory, as Barry Curtis noted in his book *Dark Places: The Haunted House in Film* (2008): "The experience of being haunted is accompanied by a crisis of objectivity and demands a process supplementing unreliable vision with other kinds of knowledge."**4** As she grew older, my mother would wrestle with unwanted memories and delusional visions, just as I struggled with identical, recurring nightmares for most of my childhood, followed by a hysterically violent adolescence that repeated much of what my stepsister had gone through before. No one in that house was okay. We mistrusted and manipulated each other, creating an epic drama in which the unreal became real, the foundation of which has been lost over time.

When my mother remarried, I was thrilled. I loved my new stepfather Adam and his two teenage daughters, one of whom – Karen – would be coming to live with us in a large house that had previously belonged to Adam's parents. Karen seemed the perfect big sister to me: she was ten years my senior, she had platform shoes and Black Sabbath records, and she looked just like Suzi Quatro's character on *Happy Days*, Leather Tuscadero.

But Karen was less excited about the new setup; she and my mother held each other in reserved suspicion, competing for Adam's attention and creating conflict that soon erupted into physical violence. My mother won out, and my stepfather's frustration turned to Karen. He would hurl accusations at her; she would respond with typically teenage nihilistic vitriol; he would lose patience and start talking with his fists. My brother Burl would retreat, hiding in his room until it was over. But I would come rallying to my sister's defence: I remember my stepfather dragging her down the stairs by her legs, and I jumped on his back – a mere 5 years old – punching and kicking to try to get him to stop hurting her. Karen ran away from home shortly thereafter, and it would be years before I saw her again.

She woke me up the night she ran away to tell me that all the belongings she was leaving behind were now mine. As a kid there was no person I idolized as much, and for years her room remained untouched; it was like a silent monument to her rebellion, Led Zeppelin and Alice Cooper records strewn everywhere, dirty underpants still stuffed beneath the bed. I hung out in there a lot, trying on lip gloss, prancing about in platform heels several sizes too big that boasted names like KISS and BAD COMPANY written in black magic marker along the cork wedges.

She attained mythological status in my mind once she fled the domestic scene, especially since I only heard about her in whispers for the next several years. I would think of her when watching Disney's sole venture into horror territory, *The Watcher in the Woods* (1980) in which 'Karen' was the name of the missing daughter who haunted the forest from a parallel dimension. Karen's room always figured heavily in my

above: Peter Tscherkassky's **Outer Space** (1999).

dreams; except in my dreams it was *my* room, which I took to be an unconscious wish to be her. I didn't become my sister, but I soon filled the same role in our house.

My stepfather was easily agitated and often in a bad mood; he didn't like his job or his boss, and he had a chronic mysterious pain in one of his legs that he refused to see a doctor about. The events with Karen had created an atmosphere of trepidation in the house, and my brother and I were instructed not to bother my stepfather unless he initiated conversation. I could never tolerate this. I didn't see how, as a young child, it was my fault if he chose to stay in a job he didn't like, or to not get a prescription for whatever his ailment was. So while my brother would stay out of sight, I insisted on being front and centre. I would push my stepfather's buttons even though I knew it wouldn't end well.

The most extreme incident of physical abuse, for me, came in the year following Karen's departure. It was Saturday morning and my father was reading the paper while I sat beside him at the table eating cereal, and waiting for my toast to brown in the toaster-oven. Not looking up from the paper, he told me to stop chewing with my mouth open. It was a habit I'd never grown out of, and I probably managed to stop for a minute or two before I started up again. The paper went slamming down on the table and my father arose quickly and grabbed my toast out of the toaster oven and slammed it into my mouth, its crisp edges cutting my lips as he shouted, "You want to be a pig?! I'll teach you how to eat!" He went to the freezer and grabbed a box of frozen shrimp, opened it, and began hurling the tiny rocks at my face with a force that raised red welts on my cheeks and forehead. I ran from behind the table towards my parents' room, where my mother was still sleeping after working a late shift, but he grabbed me and dragged me toward the basement. I went flying down the stairs to the dark bottom as he yelled, "Stay down there and don't move – and if you turn on the light I'll come down and break your fingers off!"

I was afraid of the dark, and stayed down there for what seemed an eternity before I heard the sound of my mother getting up from her room to go to the bathroom. I bolted up the stairs to the bathroom door and began pounding on it, screaming for my mother's attention. She opened the door and looked at me, a mess, welts on my face and blood lining my kneecaps and the corners of my mouth. She stood there for a moment before saying "I can't deal with this", and then went back into her room and closed the door, ignoring my continued pleas for her help.

This would become the familiar response whenever my stepfather lost his temper with me, although it would never again reach the same level of physical violence. Over the years, my mother would refuse to address this issue, as would any relatives – including my father in Winnipeg – to whom I would readily protest.

The fights continued well into my teens, although there were moments of respite and bonding. Despite everything I was probably closer to my stepfather than anyone else in my immediate family. Both possessed of volatile tempers, he and I would engage in brutal, noisy, violent altercations that would have everyone else in the house hiding from a flurry of projectiles. After a particularly vicious fight, the routine was always the same: my stepfather would wake me up in the middle of the night for the late-night creature feature on some Detroit station, bowl of popcorn in hand, and say, "Remember this next time you get mad at me." In other words, my tolerance for real-life violence was rewarded with horror films.

The police were at our house frequently, although I never knew who called them. I loved the attention, the tension, the probing questions, knowing full well that if I said the right thing, my stepfather might go to jail. But I didn't want him to go to jail. I just wanted him to stop being in a bad mood all the time.

Part of me must have thrived on the drama of the violence, otherwise I would have adopted my brother's seemingly neutral stance instead of engaging in what now seems to me deliberate sabotage. My mischievous nature made it easy for me to be blamed for everything, while my brother sailed through any threat of punishment just by keeping his mouth shut. In retrospect I think he had the right idea. But there was something attractive about being able to endure the violence, and it wasn't just the popcorn and horror movies I would get afterwards. As I mentioned, my mother tolerated it because she felt to do otherwise made her a failure. Why I put up with it was for a totally different reason: I knew it made my *parents* failures, and the more I could take, the more morally superior I felt.

It makes sense to me in hindsight why my mother loves made-for-TV movies so much. She's a sucker for cheap melodrama, an inclination she passed on to me. *The Burning Bed, Deadly Intentions* – my mother, the eternal victim, had found the perfect small-screen reflection of her own anxieties, and she buried her troubles in the comfort of the prime-time ritual – commercial breaks meant a refill on beer, a few pills, a bathroom detour, and back to the ABC movie of the week. Until I moved into foster homes as a teenager I had no idea it wasn't normal for a tiny woman to down a case of beer each day. But my childhood was only the beginning of her problems.

I'm tempted to say she never had a chance, but we all have a chance. We all make choices. Barbara Hershey in *The Entity*, Florinda Bolkan in *Footprints*, Mimsy Farmer in *The Perfume of the Lady in Black*, Daliah Lavi in *The Whip and the Body*, Daria Nicolodi in *Shock*, Seo Won in *Bad Guy* – they all make choices. But what choices do they make and why do they make them?

PART TWO:
BROKEN DOLLS

"You know what you are? You're a schizo."
"You just don't understand women, that's all."
– Robert Altman's *Images*

Like most kids who have imaginary friends or custom-made boogeymen, I had a tall, dark-haired man living in my closet.

Before my mother remarried – I must have been only 3 or 4 years old – I remember sitting on the floor in the back living room at my grandmother's house playing with my toys and watching television intermittently. We got all the Detroit stations in Windsor, and the *Saturday Afternoon Creature Feature* was on. I didn't catch the movie title at the time, but later – as a young adult who trawled the horror section at the local video store almost daily – I eventually discovered it to have been *Horror Express*. What stood out wasn't Christopher Lee or Peter Cushing – although the gentleman Cushing would become something of an obsession further down the line – but the possessed Russian priest with glowing zombified eyes, played by eurotrash staple Alberto de Mendoza. He was transformed through my hyperactive imagination into 'The Man with Green Eyes', and would become the primary fixture of my sleeping life for almost a decade.

The dream was always the same: I would be woken up by a scratching sound coming from the inside of the closet. I would sit up in bed and stare at the closet door in the darkness, trying to discern shapes in the shadows. Eventually the closet door would slowly open, a bony white hand gripping it from the inside. The Man with Green Eyes would step partially out, still holding tight to the door, and beckon me to the closet. I would always go. When I reached the door, he wasn't there; instead, there was a long staircase going down into the bowels of the closet, and he would be standing at the bottom with his long arms outstretched in a grotesquely welcoming manner. Someone would push me from behind, and I would go flying down the stairs toward him. Just as he was about to catch me, my face only inches from his giant toothy smile, I would wake up. I had this dream (among others) every night until I was 12 years old, and it took me a long time to recognize its purpose.

above: Alberto de Mendoza (aka The Man with Green Eyes) in Eugenio Martín's **Horror Express** (1972).

opposite: Mylène Jampanoï in Pascal Laugier's **Martyrs** (2008).

My relationship with my stepsister – even though it was often imaginary – was integral to the problems I would have with my mother and stepfather, as well as providing the impetus for the impossible loyalty I would demand in future female friendships. In her absence I posited myself as a stand-in (not wholly unconsciously), and functioned dually as a young, naïve child – who could entertain myself for hours in my room playing with Barbies or creating entire three-dimensional villages out of leftover Smurfs wallpaper – and a rebellious teenage counterpart who wasn't afraid to sneak out, take hand grenades to school, or respond to my parents and teachers with self-righteous insolence. The notion of diametrically opposed siblings is a common enough scenario in films: one's good, one's bad; one commits a crime, the other covers it up. Occasionally it's difficult to tell which one is which.

I started to disassociate from an early age; I would often imagine that I was one of those changeling children I read about in fairy stories, a substitute for a real child that had been stolen away because it was more perfect. My veneration for my missing sister wasn't the only factor in this belief; undoubtedly it was fed also by my jealousy of my brother – the 'real' son of the parents who adopted me. I wanted to be loved and accepted, but the shadow my sister cast over our family was too great, and my sense of identity was constantly shifting. As I stepped further into the role of the disturbed child, I was full of hatred, and was hated in return. Even in my sister's absence, I bonded closer to her.

(519) 944-2544

K.K. (Kier-la) Janisse
4345 Pleasant Place
Windsor, Ontario, Canada
N8Y 2E9

ARTS AND CRAFTS TEACHER

It's often commented that Antonioni's *L'avventura* (1960) is unique in that it is defined by absence – that its plot is dominated by a person who is not there. The character of Anna goes missing at the film's outset, and the remaining characters are fuelled entirely by their reaction to her absence, her ghost hanging over them through every decision and misstep. For me, these ghosts were my sister (physically absent) and soon after, my mother (emotionally absent). I filled these vacancies with many things, ranging from mildly damaging (over-achieving) to completely damaging (anger, spite, sabotage, violence); even as a child, and in the midst of turmoil, I would come home with excellent grades and would initiate an abundance of extracurricular projects (I recently found a business card I made at age 10 proclaiming myself to be an "arts and crafts teacher"). I was constantly – then as now – struggling with the dilemma of whether to give up completely, or to succeed as a form of revenge against those who habitually abandoned me.

My mother and sister also struggled with a fear of abandonment – both were afraid my stepfather would pick one over the other – and their relationship, for the short time we all lived together, was rife with mean-spiritedness from both sides. In the midst of all this, even as my mother adapted to her new re-married life, she still frequently voiced resentment towards Oates back in Winnipeg, who had in the meantime set himself up in a swinging '70s bachelor pad with a hi-fi stereo system, Japanese minimalist décor, and an endless queue of much younger girlfriends.

The emotional volatility in our house was heightened by certain triggers that could make things go out of control very quickly; triggers that would cause me to free-associate between seemingly unconnected incidents, or between real life and onscreen fiction. It's still amazing how devastated I can get at an onscreen image that is actually six steps removed from the thing that really upsets me, just through the weird connections my brain makes. In all families, roles are reversed, subverted and substituted, and triggers – whether a word, a colour, a sound, a storm – also substitute fictional experiences for real ones.

In Juan Antonio Bardem's *The Corruption of Chris Miller* (1973), Ruth Miller (Jean Seberg) lives with her exotic-looking stepdaughter Chris in an isolated country house. Chris is recovering from a recent stay in an institution, and the dynamic between them is immediately set up as one of oppression and mistrust. Abandoned by Chris's father, Ruth spouts her hatred for the male gender at frequent intervals ("Men don't love… they possess. They injure, they invade. Always cruelty and violence."), while Chris has no choice but to listen and absorb.

Ruth veils her own possessiveness in a guise of concern for Chris's welfare; Chris suffers from fits of hysteria whenever it rains and can't be trusted not to hurt herself or others, but Ruth's means of caring for her are suspect from the outset. On rainy nights, Ruth dresses in seductive nightclothes and rushes to Chris's side like a lover, kissing her all over to calm her down. Eventually Chris is quieted and lies there in a catatonic state while her stepmother molests her. But for someone who experiences violent flashbacks whenever it rains, they've certainly

above: My childhood 'business card'.

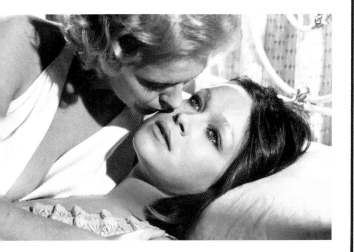

chosen a rainy region to settle down in, and that's only one of many clues that something's seriously wrong in this household. The move was a conscious decision: Ruth likes the girl's dependence on her.

When Ruth finds a handsome young vagrant crashed out in the barn one morning, she invites him in for morning sex and coffee, then puts him to work doing odd jobs around the house. He immediately notices the strained relationship between Ruth and Chris:

> Man: "What do you ladies do all day, stuck in a place like this?"
> Chris: "Ruth designs, I ride and sunbathe. For amusement we spy on each other – don't we Ruth? We wait for someone who never arrives. We don't know whether we love or hate each other."

The two women plot to use the man against each other; however, he has his own agenda – and it's not romance. His role in their hermetically sealed drama is that of a catalyst for a drastic role-reversal, wherein Ruth must admit her dependence on Chris to validate her own feelings of anger and betrayal:

> Ruth (to Chris): "It's true, I wanted to corrupt you, to destroy you… but now… I need you more than you need me."

Ruth has allowed herself to be destroyed by a man – by Chris's father who abandoned them both years before. Now she lives only for revenge, happy to isolate herself in a cocoon of man-hating security that has manifested itself as an obsession with Chris, who she sees simultaneously as an opportunity and a threat. According to her own deluded logic, she can achieve her pitiful 'revenge' on Chris's father by effecting Chris's psychological ruination. But as Chris grows older and shows signs of independence, Ruth's anger becomes warped and misdirected; it loses its focus. Now there is only Chris to hate. Now there is only Chris to abandon her. And that abandonment is inevitable.

top left: Jean Seberg and Marisol in Juan Antonio Bardem's **The Corruption of Chris Miller** (1973).

top right: U.S. theatrical poster for **The Corruption of Chris Miller**.

The female characters in Carlos Aured's *The Blue Eyes of the Broken Doll* (aka *House of Psychotic Women*, 1973) are similarly bound to each other by a fear of abandonment. The film stars – and was co-written by – the late horror maestro Paul Naschy (who passed away just as I was writing this chapter) who plays the part of Gilles, a drifter hitchhiking through the Spanish countryside looking for work and hiding from a distressing past. He gets a lift from a busty but stern redhead named Claude, who has a badly scarred arm and a fake hand, which she attempts to hide when she notices him staring at it. She offers him a job tending to the house and garden at the remote mountaintop home she shares with her two sisters: the nymphomaniac Nicole (also a redhead); and Ivette, who is wheelchair-bound after a mysterious accident – the same accident that likely caused Claude's disfigurement.

When a temporary home-care nurse confides in their long-time doctor her concern that the three women are "not normal", he offers that, "these three women are frustrated individuals. To some degree they all suffer some sort of neurosis. Only Claude has some balance, and she sacrifices everything for her sisters' sakes. I don't know a lot about their parents, but their mother died insane and the father committed suicide, overtaken by a sickly melancholy." The doctor also believes Ivette's paraplegia to be psychosomatic – like the murderess in *A Candle for the Devil* (1973), her neurosis is the result of having been abandoned at the altar years before. Her fiancée, it turns out, left her for her best friend.

The relationship between the three women is one of obligation – all three maintain that they are 'stuck' together, and complain frequently about being shut away from the rest of the world (the nympho Nicole being literally locked in her room at times by the jealous Claude), but none of them will do anything about it. Instead they play manipulative games, vying for male attention (which has included a rotating stable of groundskeepers), sneaking around and spying on each other. Claude has assumed a matronly role in the house – her beauty is not immediately apparent due to her severely pulled-back hair and a permanent scowl – and the doctor urges her to seek out a normal life away from her sisters and their neuroses; his insistence that she is the most 'balanced' of the three sisters is belied by the fact that she refuses to acquire a more modern artificial limb, even though she laments that her current one is "hideous and disgusting". For Claude, there is safety in ugliness, but Claude's predicament is symptomatic of a larger problem: change is frightening and inconvenient. This was the defining factor explaining why I idolized my sister conversely resenting my mother; my mother fabricated excuses as to why she had to

top left: Poster for Carlos Aured's **The Blue Eyes of the Broken Doll** (1973), re-titled for North American release.

top right: Spanish poster for **The Blue Eyes of the Broken Doll**.

remain in an unhappy situation while Karen – by running away from home – made the statement that she would never put up with anything less than she felt she deserved. Little did I know that years later Karen would prove to be just as complacent. As with most people who refuse to remove themselves from damaging situations, Claude feels more comfortable blaming her loneliness on her family obligations and her mild physical handicap than on her own unwillingness to take steps toward fulfilment. Even when Gilles makes advances towards her, she protests: "No one can like me. I can only be disgusting."

Nicole, the most physically healthy and sex-crazed of the three sisters, jumps on Gilles as soon as he arrives at the remote homestead, trumpeting her 'normalcy' over the disfigurement of her two sisters. However, Gilles asserts that he finds them both attractive, despite their perceived handicaps. Nicole doesn't get it. "You're the same as me," he tells her, "A wretched failure looking for love to feel important. But we're nothing. Nothing."

The prominent plotline concerning the three neurotic sisters incorporates the presence of a serial killer in their midst – someone is killing all the blonde, blue-eyed women in their small community. Although the police immediately suspect the drifter Gilles, the audience is driven, through the film's less-than-subtle female characterization, to suspect one of the three women. This is especially interesting for a female viewer: although the women appear to be contending for male attention, their real issues are with each other, and with the integrity issues that they create for each other. There is an apparent mistrust between women, a lack of empathy, a fear of betrayal. Woven through this mistrust and suspicion are identity issues that are common among siblings and other family members alike.

My mother and sister in particular had struggled with the identities being shaped for them by the new familial arrangement: Karen was used to doing whatever she wanted due to my stepfather's lack of parenting skills, and my mother was too busy nursing some serious emotional wounds to deal with Karen's confrontational nature. My mother felt pressure to control a situation that she was not equipped to handle, and so she sought small victories: I would be grounded frequently for stupid things like saying the word 'excellent' too much, and on one occasion was sent to my room just because the *Quincy* 'punk' episode terrified my mother so much she just didn't know what else to do. Eventually my punishments required playing outside, once my mother figured out that I actually preferred being alone in my room.

Our familial bonds and roles were tested from the outset; we had a patchwork family – adoptions, step-parents/siblings – no one felt grounded. This was especially true for me, since I didn't have a single biological connection to anyone in this bizarre configuration. So the concept of family is something I've always looked at from a distance, making those films that emphasize the posturing inherent in family constructs especially interesting.

top: Eva León in **The Blue Eyes of the Broken Doll**.

bottom: Diana Lorys in **The Blue Eyes of the Broken Doll**.

In common with *The Corruption of Chris Miller*, the roles in Nikos Nikolaidis's *Singapore Sling* (1990) are substitutive and contrived (and both films end the same way, which I won't disclose here). A man searching for his lost love stumbles upon an isolated villa where two women play out a perverse identity game. We don't know the precise relationship between these women – who have assumed a mother/daughter dynamic – only that it's a dangerously co-dependent one. Barely conscious upon arrival, he is quickly adopted into the fold as both plaything and patriarch. The film is a depraved take on Otto Preminger's 1944 film noir *Laura*, and the lush black and white cinematography by Aris Stavrou recalls the esteemed work of Welles staple Gregg Toland even amid the sea of nauseating decadence and spiritual corruption that it enthusiastically puts on display.

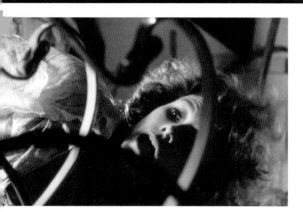

The secluded house in *Singapore Sling* is a sticky arena for masturbation, paedophilic obsession, gluttony and erotic regurgitation, vivified more confusingly by remarkable performances that would have been Oscar-worthy in any other kind of film. But in the cinematic landscape, *Singapore Sling* lives in a place entirely its own.

While the man doesn't speak a word of dialogue throughout the whole film, his off-screen narration guides us through the basic elements of his past that have led him here, as well as his internal struggle to make sense of the situation in which he now finds himself. The actresses, on the other hand, address the camera directly, constantly reminding us that this twisted scenario is playing out for our benefit. Substitution, and the role-playing that results from it, is discernible everywhere in *Singapore Sling*. The two women act out their mother/daughter fantasy – wherein they are lovers as well as kin – and the younger woman also confesses to having a sexual relationship with her absent 'father' before the two women killed him. At the heart of the film and its bizarre trajectory of torture and manipulation is the visiting man's belief that the younger woman is actually his missing girlfriend, Laura. He is willing to endure physical, mental and sexual humiliation in an attempt to save her, but he appears already too broken to save anyone, including himself. Instead he succumbs to the pretence they subsist on, assuming multiple roles that blend into one big, messy Freudian nightmare.

The interloper in these films often acts only to illuminate the complex dynamic of its primary characters – in this case the two women. He is the character who leads us into the story, but the story is not his own.

As in *Singapore Sling*, the family in the 1970 Freddie Francis feature *Mumsy, Nanny, Sonny & Girly* (based on Maisie Mosco's stage play *Happy Family*) are living in a semi-permanent state of infantilism – they exist in a Victorian fantasy world and speak in what Nigel Burrell (in *Ten Years of Terror: British Horror Films of 1970s*) calls "playground patois".[5] Sonny and Girly are teenagers, but dress and act like oversexed 5-year-olds. The teens habitually pick up strangers (all uniformly named "New Friend") and bring them to the house for deadly games. British stage and television actor Michael Bryant plays the latest New Friend – a male prostitute who is lured into their role-playing game and held prisoner until the time when he will inevitably be "sent to the angels". The lethal Lolita Girly is the film's aesthetic centre (thus the shortening of the title in the U.S. to just *Girly*), but the household is run by a female autocracy – the bedroom-sharing Mumsy and Nanny. All three women are equally mad, despite Girly's assertion that, "We're not mad – we're happy! We're a happy family!" But when Girly discovers the sociopathic Mumsy bedding down with New Friend, she gets inexplicably flustered

top left: Panos Thanassoulis in Nikos Nikolaidis's **Singapore Sling** (1990).

centre left: Meredyth Herold in **Singapore Sling**.

everyone
is
dying
to
meet

Girly

she drives men to her knees

and tries to win New Friend over by offering to play a game with him called "Mothers and Fathers". But New Friend soon realizes that their infantilism is his means of escape – their lack of perspective has left them open to manipulation and confusion. He starts fuelling Girly's increasing need for independence. Girly shares a room with her brother Sonny (complete with an oversized crib with railing and canopy), but she starts bending the rules and wanting things of her own, even though Mumsy says, "in happy families it's nicer to share." So they come to an agreement whereby they can share New Friend's affections on alternating days. However, this arrangement doesn't last long before Girly's budding sexuality and increasing jealousy lays waste to the whole perverse family unit.

Most families are dysfunctional to some extent, and most like to keep their dysfunction hidden. They don't want their dirty laundry aired to the whole neighbourhood. But this kind of enforced repression inevitably breeds resentment and individual neuroses that will continue to affect a person as they try to embark upon adult relationships in later life. In genre films, familial dysfunction is often characterized as overt monstrosity: either homicidal behaviour or physical monstrosity like lycanthropy or vampirism. The interloper – that character who comes into the narrative to shake things up – is a witness who seeks to expose the family. Likewise, any person in the family who tries to draw attention to these problems by voicing anguish or distress is themselves seen as 'the problem', and they become the focus of the family's vitriol. In my family, this person was me.

above: Detail from U.S. poster for Freddie Francis's **Mumsy, Nanny, Sonny & Girly** (1970).

My insistence on openly addressing problems in our house – which usually revolved around my stepfather's erratic mood-swings – was especially bothersome for my brother. He never understood why I couldn't just keep my mouth shut. Every time I spoke out, it disrupted his life – his resentment of me hitting a high point when Children's Aid recommended that we go into family therapy. He maintained that we had no problems in our family except the ones that I fabricated to get attention. My relationship with my brother, while relatively normal as young children – we had mutual neighbourhood friends and would frequently engage in elaborate block-spanning outdoor games of our own concoction (including my favourite game, 'Bloody Murder', a reversal of hide-and-seek in which the person who's 'it' hides in the darkness and waits to entrap the other players) – became very strained as we hit adolescence. Our fundamental character differences became more apparent; I was driven and easily troubled, while he was seemingly self-satisfied and saw no need to go beyond the confines of what was expected of him as a member of the family. I saw problems in everything, whereas for him the only problem was my insistence on making those problems everyone else's business.

Staten Island filmmaker Andy Milligan's *The Rats Are Coming! The Werewolves Are Here!* centres on the Mooneys, an eccentric family living in a decrepit Victorian household who are stricken with hereditary lycanthropy. Although the family has a dying patriarch as their focal point, the men in the family (including middle brother Mortimer and youngest son Malcolm) are subject to the whims of the three distinctly-typed females: Phoebe, the eldest sister and self-appointed 'mother' figure; Monica, the sadistic and attention-starved middle sister; and Diana, the youngest and only educated sister, who is also the most emotionally stable, and born of a different mother than the others. Sent to medical school abroad so that she could continue her father's delicate genetic experiments, any hope of cleansing the family bloodline lies in her hands.

Given its predetermined fate on the grindhouse circuit, and produced by renowned exploitation kingpin William Mishkin (who fronted the funds for most of Milligan's pictures), *Rats…* is more expertly-written than might be expected. Milligan's admitted obsession with Jean Cocteau is manifest in the female characterizations – even Diana, the level-headed one of the bunch, reveals herself to be just as manipulative and murderous as her sisters.

Rats… is ostensibly a werewolf film (the rat subplot only existing as a half-baked attempt to cash in on the then-recent success of *Willard*, which even gets a nod in the form of blatant on-screen references) but is actually a thinly veiled examination of repression and inbreeding. The family lives together, feeds together, kills together, and they will die together. They are suspicious of outsiders, and – bound by a dire family curse – they have reason to be. They are not especially trusting of one another either, but given that they cannot fraternize freely with others, they have no choice but to maintain a volatile familial loyalty.

Like *Singapore Sling*, *Rats…* takes place exclusively on an antiquated family estate. Milligan loved Victorian settings and they act as the perfect backdrop for his wordy and histrionic dramas. But more pointedly, the house provides the domestic environment that seems to go hand-in-hand with any horror film predominantly concerned with female characters. Because the woman's sphere of influence was traditionally limited to the home – certainly in Victorian times – it is the most believable setting for any exercise in female agency. It is also, by extension, the setting in which a woman's natural talents for manipulation could have the most resounding success; certainly a prerequisite for Milligan, an admitted misogynist.

Considering Phoebe's acknowledged sexual relationship with her father, and the emphasis on cleansing the bloodline through extracurricular breeding, it's obvious that the film's werewolf premise is allegorical. The Mooneys' real affliction then, the cause of their mutual dementia and Malcolm's permanently arrested development, is likely to be inbreeding. Despite Diana's attempts to find a scientific means of escaping the cycle, continued inbreeding is only reinforced further by the repression associated with harbouring such a grim secret.

In family-melodrama horror there is always one family member (in this case Diana) trying to escape the confines of their limited existence, or an outsider coming into the narrative poised to steal them away. Their only social interaction – which sometimes encompasses sexual intercourse – is with their siblings, but something happens that awakens them to the possibilities of the outside world. They may even make sincere attempts to escape, but as we have learned from a century of such films, the family always comes first, a reconciliation takes place, and the would-be escapee is forced to recognize their inherent nature and the fact that they belong with their family – especially when they are concealing a secret that would render them socially unacceptable to the outside world. They retreat to the familiarity of the only people who accept them for who they are. Again: traumatic bonding.

Repression was a subject Milligan would return to with some frequency in films such as *The Degenerates* (1967), *Seeds* (1968) and *The Body Beneath* (1970), and in literature and film lycanthropy is traditionally linked with repression, notably in *Dr. Jekyll and Mr. Hyde* or other famous doppelganger stories. In *The Rats Are Coming! The Werewolves Are Here!* – as in *Singapore Sling* – roles are convoluted and perverted: every daughter becomes a mother, a wife, a killer – they are interchangeable substitutes for the absent mother figures who came before.

In addition to its Victorian setting, Milligan's film is also notable for its fundamental religious sensibility. Repression is a keystone of Catholicism, and countless horror films – most notably European ones – rely on Catholic concepts of sin and punishment as plot propellers. Perhaps this is what has drawn me to the Italian films so often: my parents were church-going Catholics, and the grotesque imagery and dirge chants associated with the faith would inspire horrible dreams, coupled with a crippling sense of guilt that still plagues me to this day (that The Man with Green Eyes was a religious figure is of no small importance). Catholicism loves its suffering, and teaches that real love and loyalty always involve a tremendous amount of anguish as proof of one's dedication.

When I was about 8 years old I had a dream that I woke up in my sister's bedroom. I walked across the hall to the den (where we watched TV), but the door normally leading into the den was not there. Going further down the hall, I went to the big storage closet where my mother kept all her gaudy flower-power gear – so that she would be ready if it ever came back in style – and pushing apart the clothes hanging there, I discovered a tiny door at the back of the closet. I crawled through the door and emerged from behind an altar into a dark room illuminated by liturgical candles. This was our den, but in a different configuration; in reality, the TV loomed where the altar stood in my dream. When I told my mother about the dream she confirmed that there was such a passageway behind the television, and when I went into the closet, there it was – a little door that opened up behind the TV in the other room. Brushing off what I took to be a totally creepy psychic occurrence, my mother explained that my step-grandparents who lived there before us used

above: Hope Stansbury in Andy Milligan's **The Rats Are Coming! The Werewolves Are Here!** (1972).

the den as a secret praying room, and that I surely must have known about that somehow. Even then the irony of the television replacing the altar was not lost on me – I suppose it makes sense that watching films became my substitute for religious experience.

Even though the altar had been removed, there was another sort of shrine in our house: my sister's bedroom, a hallowed place in my mind. My sister, the expelled martyr – in reality just a mouthy teen, but no matter – was immortalized in fictional form by the sanctity I imposed upon this room. There was a narrative here, and though it had run its course from beginning to end, the shrine made sure that it would never be forgotten.

French director Pascal Laugier's ambitious and controversial *Martyrs* (2008) is a heady fusion of sibling and doppelganger horror. While far from a perfect film, *Martyrs* goes full-throttle into hypotheses of guilt and religious transcendence, but with consequences that are *far* more grim than anything in Andy Milligan's Gothic melodrama.

A tidy synopsis would describe *Martyrs* as a tale of long-term revenge with a metaphysical twist, but – for better or worse – it's more complex. It is the tale of two abused children who grow up haunted: Lucie, a young woman determined to murder the strangers who tortured her as a child, dogged by the spectre of a fellow victim who never made it out; and Anna, Lucie's protector and enabler. The two women met at a home for orphans and disturbed children, following Lucie's escape from her captors. Visibly traumatized, Lucie is reticent and secretive, and only Anna knows about Lucie's nightly visits from the grotesque, crawling, white-skinned woman that functions equally as a physical manifestation of her guilt over having abandoned another child in escaping, and as a doppelganger that fills her with homicidal rage.

Both Lucie and Anna grow into beautiful young women, not physically dissimilar (further echoing the doppelganger element), but even as she matures outwardly, Lucie is still being followed by the doppelganger, and she believes the only way she can get rid of it is to seek revenge on the people who captured and tortured her almost 20 years earlier. The black-clad Lucie arrives at the strangers' house with a loaded shotgun and Anna in tow, and things quickly spiral from a simple revenge story into a morass of substitutive relationships and abject horror.

Martyrs (as with Laugier's 2004 film *Saint Ange*) is also strangely preoccupied with 19th century psychological, domestic and spiritual concerns. This is not unfamiliar in a genre context considering that *fin-de-siècle* culture created the neurotic stereotypes of female psychological development that would come to be the crux of much cinematic horror. But while *Martyrs* revels in its protagonists' neuroticism, it also allows them to transcend it in disturbing fashion.

As indicated by its title, the final act of the film takes a sharp turn in another direction, one whose contrast of graphic physical torture and spiritual cultism divided many audiences. The strangers' house is revealed to be a meeting place for a sinister cult that tortures women until they reach a state of 'grace' or 'martyrdom', hoping that they may be able to provide a key into the afterlife. Most of these women and children 'fail' their torturers by dying like pathetic, whimpering dogs, without ever reaching this state of spiritual perfection. But Anna, who has accompanied Lucie on her homicidal mission, is different – she has given her life in the service of others, sacrificing her own sanity and safety in the process. She is practically a saint already.

In the 19th century there was a popular belief that being close to people on the verge of death brought one closer to God, hence people would congregate around the sick and dying hoping to experience a vicarious flicker of divinity – this would later be called 'The Cult of Invalidism', and is only one component of *Martyrs*'s weird Victorian ethic (although the director of *Martyrs* came to know of this historical precedent only after making his feature). The film also posits women as more suitable 'martyrs' than men, a notion that

above: Morjana Alaoui in Pascal Laugier's **Martyrs** (2008).

is prominent not only in Victorian and Edwardian literature but (most infamously) in Japanese cinema as well: the woman sacrifices and endures, ultimately transcending humiliation and debasement to emerge as a noble and revered creature.

Despite its religious overtones, at the heart of *Martyrs* is the neurotic bond between Anna and Lucie. Laugier's focus on the intimacy of this relationship causes the film to be both emotionally and physically insular, facilitated by the delusions of its protagonists: Lucie's that she can end the mental terror by killing, and Anna's that she is helping Lucie by allowing her to unravel. Even as a child though, Anna made a decision about what her role would be in Lucie's life: she is all things to Lucie: mother, sister, and – it is suggested – lover. When Lucie is killed, Anna's loyalty is transferred to another character with equal fervour: a grotesque, white-skinned woman who is discovered deep in the ground beneath the captors' house, unable to speak or see after years of continuous torture. It's no mistake that the white woman bears a remarkable resemblance to the creature that haunted Lucie at night for all those years – in this film, one woman is very like another. All are equally damaged, but as with any doppelganger film, coexistence isn't possible for long – one always has to die so that another can live.

The fractured personalities that result from the adoption of different roles, faces or personas are one of the most prominent aspects of sibling- or family-centric horror films; the relationship between the siblings (or pseudo-siblings, as in the case of *Martyrs*) is often such that one functions as a reflection of the other; they're not quite doppelganger films but they dabble in the doppelganger lexicon. Otto Rank's notion of the doppelganger, or 'double' in his 1914 book *Der Doppelgänger* is the template for all subsequent doppelganger studies, stating that, "all instincts and desires that don't fit the 'ideal' image are rejected and cast out of the self, repressed internally, and inevitably return externally personified in the double, where they can be at once vicariously satisfied and punished."[6] It was a concept that would be revisited again and again throughout the history of horror fiction.

Robert Altman made four films that are generally referred to as his 'Feminine Quartet': *That Cold Day in the Park* (1969); *Images* (1972); *3 Women* (1977); and *Come Back to the Five and Dime, Jimmy Dean, Jimmy Dean* (1982), two of which – *3 Women* and the earlier *Images* – deal specifically with manufactured familial relationships and the concept of the double (both also bear striking similarities to Ingmar Bergman's 1966 feature *Persona*). It would be safe to say that this period is Altman's darkest hour in terms of exposing the frailties of identity and the inconsistencies of emotion, and these two films are the closest Altman would come to making an outright horror film (*That Cold Day in the Park* was a more subtle approach to the psychosis that would be full-blown in its two successors). *Images* is the more self-referential of the two, thrashing about between chaos and tranquillity, between light and dark, expression and repression – all the while returning to the literal puzzle "with so many missing pieces" that functions as an analogy for the film as a whole.

Susannah York stars as Cathryn, a children's writer with a husband, two houses, and a split personality. The film opens with her reciting her newest book in her head, as she will often do throughout the film (whether or not she actually writes children's books increasingly appears to be a possible delusion – a clever twist being that Susannah York herself wrote the children's book that the film uses as her character's story). The atmosphere and setting are nothing short of brilliant; the eerie score by John Williams is randomly interrupted by sharp, alarming sounds (courtesy of Japanese musician Stomu Yamashta), and the house itself is host to deliberately inconsistent architecture and decor – half of the house is old and dark, the other bright and contemporary. This certainly

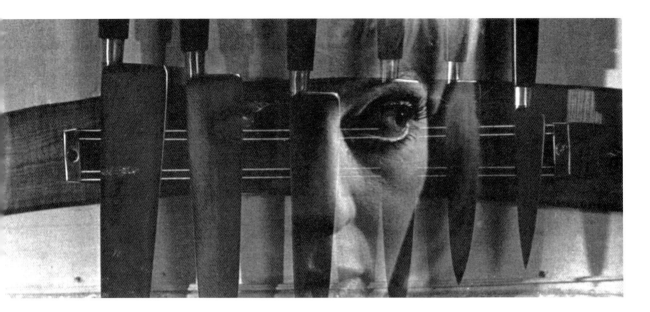

hearkens back to the Gothic notion of the house being representative of its owner's mental state (i.e. *The Fall of the House of Usher*, Miss Havisham's Satis House in *Great Expectations*), and is emphasized by the fact that Cathryn has two homes, one apparently in the city, the other in the country in a magical valley that she loves dearly, almost – revealingly enough – as if it is not real.

Her disconnection from the world outside of her own mind is conveyed straight away by means of her phone call with her friend Joan; she puts the phone down and wanders away, disinterested in what her friend has to say, and when she returns to the conversation there is an alien voice on the line – that of an aggressive, malicious woman who claims to be with Cathryn's husband. When her husband returns home, Cathryn questions him furiously as to his previous whereabouts, and when he tries to comfort her – their faces disappearing into the darkness of a kiss – he emerges transformed into another man, and Cathryn is thrown into a fit of hysteria. This becomes a common occurrence throughout the film: things will transform into other things, voices change, and yet Cathryn will grow accustomed to it and cease to respond as if a change has even taken place. In Freudian dream-logic – and the film does largely function according to this logic – things, or the illusion of things (i.e. images) 'condense'. Condensation, or 'compression', occurs in dreams so that many truths can be conveyed to us in a short period of time. This also relates to the puzzle that appears throughout the film as a recreational activity; a dream is like patchwork, with parts that are lost or missing (but really only forgotten), and when a transformation takes place it is evidence of a mental short cut.

A further complexity of the film, and one connected to the dream-process of condensation, is the appearance of a double. If the existence of a double is attributed to guilt over the difference between one's ideal self and one's actual self, then in Cathryn's case, the double exists as an outlet for her adulterous desires. There are two Cathryns (often distinguished by black/white costuming), just as there are two homes, and the camera will follow one and then the other without warning, so that the viewer comes to accept the simultaneous existence of both. The teenage daughter of her husband's friend can be seen as a double as well, as the physical similarity between the two is mentioned more than once, and the younger girl tells Cathryn that she wants to be "just like her". As further evidence of Altman's deliberate doubling, the two actresses have interchangeable names – Susannah York plays 'Cathryn' while Cathryn Harrison plays 'Susannah'.

My determination to have a sister who was "just like me" (while simultaneously rationalizing her physical absence) had some bizarre manifestations: at one point in my childhood I went with my parents to a yard sale in Belle River, a small town about half an hour outside of Windsor. I fixated upon a portrait of a little girl, painted in a late 19th century style, and used my allowance to buy it. I put it on a shelf at the foot of my bed so that I could always see it. At night, in the darkness, I thought I could see its lips move, and I would lie awake, staring at it for hours, trying to figure out what it was saying. I told my friend Kerri-Lynn about the

above: Susannah York in Robert Altman's **Images** (1972).

picture, and Kerri was so scared she wouldn't come over again until I got rid of it. But I chose this new fictional friend over a real one: like the haunted narrator of Charlotte Perkins Gilman's *The Yellow Wallpaper* (which remains the prototype for the modern madwoman), I was certain that something was going on with this picture, a life beneath the façade of the paint. I imagined that the little girl told me a story, of drowning in Belle River just after this portrait was commissioned, and that her spirit was now trapped in the painting. I started to bring candy and place it on the shelf at the foot of the picture. But when the candy didn't disappear, I started to feel rejected and eventually frightened. I brought more candy, toys, costume jewellery, to no avail. The girl in the picture stopped talking to me. I was convinced she was planning something; that she was going to steal my soul while I was sleeping. So I asked my mother to put the painting in the basement, where it still resides to this day.

A drowned girl, a painting in the basement; it doesn't take a genius to detect my typical childhood habit of alternately confronting and expelling. There was always something narcissistic in my fictional siblings – their darkness was mine, and I perceived this even as a child. The doppelganger is there and not there; it comforts and threatens simultaneously. There is an inherent push-pull aspect to the doppelganger, and it is this kind of frenetic confusion that sees Cathryn completely disintegrate by the end of Altman's *Images*.

The concept of the double is also prevalent in *3 Women*, except in this case we are dealing with more than a single woman's madness; there is something far more primordial about *3 Women*. With powerhouse performances by Shelley Duvall and Sissy Spacek (neither of whom is a stranger to horror territory), *3 Women* is a film whose provocative schizophrenia is both gripping and contagious.

Spacek plays Pinky Rose, the obtuse new girl working at a surreal geriatric water-therapy centre where she meets her soon-to-be room-mate Milly Lammoreaux (Duvall). Milly is everything Pinky isn't: glamorous, confident, in Pinky's words, "perfect", but Milly's projected confidence is in opposition to the reality that shuts her out, even if it can't shut her up. In Pinky, Milly finally receives the captive audience she needs in order to keep up her illusion of social adeptness, and Pinky gets a role model, however questionable. The psychic sisterhood between the two women is made apparent even before they move in together – Pinky is fascinated by the twins who also work at the spa, and obviously draws a parallel between their symbiotic relationship and her ensuing connection with Milly. The twins have a certain mythological resonance as well; in the middle ages, twins were feared as an affront to nature, and would often be exposed to the elements at birth, left to die – largely because of the 'problem of identification' that they pose. The recurrent image of the twins foreshadows the transformational shift of identity that will occur later in the film.

While Pinky gradually fabricates a personality that emulates that of Milly, Milly's own personality is equally false, based on fashion magazines and advertisements that tell her what a successful woman is supposed to be like. Milly desperately seeks male attention to validate her existence, and when she finally receives it in the form of her lecherous landlord Edgar, Pinky is harshly ejected from the apartment so that the cavorting couple can have some privacy. Pinky is distraught; as she stares into the pool outside, she is bewitched by the bizarre murals that cover its floor and is compelled to leap to her death.

above: U.S. one-sheet poster for **Images**.

While her suicide is unsuccessful, by jumping into the pool Pinky has wandered into the psychic space of the third woman, the pregnant Willie (Janice Rule), whose emotionally distant husband Edgar is in bed with Milly. Willie's presence in the film is a silent one in all but the mythopoeic murals she fixedly paints, which operate as her voice. Peter Nicholls has argued that the erotic, chaotic murals Willie paints have a "serpentine femaleness that pervades the whole film",[7] but any assessment of the figures as exclusively female ignores the fact that several of the intertwined figures are clearly sporting huge phalluses, and it seems more likely that they represent the transcendence of gender and personality more than alluding to one sex in particular (an idea similarly explored in Altman's *Come Back to the Five and Dime Jimmy Dean, Jimmy Dean*). Just as Willie's painting 'summoned' Pinky into the pool, it is Willie who first arrives on the scene, and it is at this point that we hear her voice for the first time, when she screams for Tom, one of the tenants of the building.

When Pinky recovers from the resultant coma (this and the pool water signifying the archetypal 'trip to the underworld'), she is a changed woman. She rejects the people Milly has tracked down in the belief that they are Pinky's long-lost parents, insists that her name is not Pinky but 'Mildred', and becomes a picture-perfect self-absorbed horror of a person, leaving Milly to shrink into a state of nervousness and inferiority. It has been maintained by certain critics that Milly's 'invisibility' of character becomes apparent only after Pinky's recovery from her coma, but in fact, Milly has been visible *only* to Pinky up until now – the other characters have never wanted anything to do with her. But it is Pinky's acceptance into the ranks of 'popularity' that causes Milly's ineffectualness to become more debilitating.

Just as there is a change in Pinky (or 'Mildred'), there is a corresponding one in Milly; out of genuine concern, she dutifully visits Pinky in the hospital every day while she is in her coma. Her motive may be largely due to guilt over Pinky's 'accident', but she has nevertheless taken responsibility for Pinky, and for her behaviour towards her. It comes as a shock to her then, when Pinky awakens from her previous passivity to become a violent, demanding woman. She is, in fact, what Milly's idealized self has been up to this point – sexually confident, attractive and interesting to others, and popular enough to warrant behaving like a self-absorbed bitch. Pinky's behaviour finally tarnishes what Milly had previously thought of as signifying the model contemporary American woman.

When Willie's male child is stillborn, another role-reversal takes place: Pinky once again becomes the passive child and Milly assumes a maternal role, but this time Pinky has acquired the twin she so desperately sought at the beginning of the film, in the form of Willie, who was previously the film's maternal figure. With the final transformation in place, we see the three women functioning as a self-contained archetypal unit existing without men (the male child died at birth, and Willie's husband Edgar was 'accidentally' killed somehow, although we are not privy to the details).

above: U.S. theatrical poster for Robert Altman's **3 Women** (1977).

Although equally complex in their portrayal of the feminine realm, what ultimately distinguishes *3 Women* from the earlier *Images* is the female characters' relation to the real world that surrounds them. The female characters in *3 Women* become something separate from social reality; they have transgressed the laws of identity and exist as three parts of the same mind. Nevertheless, they can still function within the framework of 'society', even if only in a rudimentary fashion – after all, they are still running the bar that Willie and Edgar operated before the three women amalgamated. The real world can come and visit (e.g. the travelling salesman who appears at the end), but it has no resonance for them. In *Images*, Cathryn's schizophrenia is dangerously out of control; although Altman spares us her fate, it can only follow that the outside world will intervene, and that her imaginary world will have to become a permanent edifice rather than a mere flickering mask of contradictory images if she is to survive.

It's not uncommon for kids to fantasize about being someone else, or to fashion fictional relationships that fulfil a desire for affection. Kids can become attached to people who shower them with attention pretty quickly, and are let down just as easily. My reliance on an idealized version of my sister once she was gone from my life, and my adoption of traits that I associated with her – from her rebelliousness to her feathered hair – was an attempt to avoid feelings of abandonment. While this type of fabrication presents its own set of problems, in genre films the convergence of fantasy and reality is downright dangerous.

In Brian De Palma's *Sisters* (1973), Margot Kidder plays Danielle, one half of a pair of French Canadian Siamese twins, who submerges herself in pills and alcohol to escape from a terrible secret. When she first meets Philip (Lisle Wilson) on a game show called 'Peeping Tom' she invites herself along to dinner with him and proceeds to get roaring drunk, talking about the aesthetic differences between Quebec and New York, and how she's "not a feminist" because she doesn't hate men. She can tell herself this, but we'll find out otherwise soon enough.

Danielle mentions in passing to Philip that she has had trouble bonding with people since her sister "went away", but the morning after their romantic tryst in her apartment he overhears Danielle arguing in the other room with a woman that Danielle claims to be her "visiting" sister Dominique. It's their birthday, and Dominique wants them to spend the day together, without the male intruder. Philip attempts to reconcile this by bringing them a joint birthday cake, and when he returns with it, he is viciously stabbed and killed by a maniacal, spasming woman who is the spitting image of Danielle, minus the coquettish charm.

above: Sissy Spacek in **3 Women**.

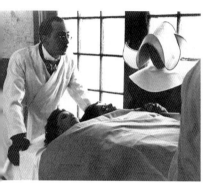

When Danielle's creepy ex-husband (played by De Palma regular William Finley) Emil shows up at the door, Danielle answers, apparently unaware that a murder has just taken place in her apartment. But Emil, who quickly establishes himself as her ritual caretaker, rushes to clean everything up as Danielle asserts that her sister Dominique – who is now gone – must have done something unspeakable.

Jennifer Salt (who ironically went on to be a writer and producer for the plastic surgery show *Nip/Tuck*) plays Grace Collier, the disheartened, tomboyish reporter for the Staten Island paper who witnesses the murder from her window across the street. She immediately phones the police and barges into Danielle's apartment with them, but only after arguing against their apathy concerning the situation. They are hesitant

top left: Margot Kidder in Brian De Palma's **Sisters** (1973).

centre left: William Finley plans a separation in **Sisters**.

right: U.S. poster for **Sisters**.

to investigate, partially because Grace has been critical of the police in her newspaper column, but also because the victim was a black man – and as one of the cops says, "these people are always stabbing each other" (only one indicator of the film's peripheral criticism of racial prejudice). As they search Danielle's apartment, Grace is fascinated by the sets of matching clothes that line Danielle's closets and asks outright if Danielle has a twin, which the latter denies vehemently. With the body neatly hidden away and no evidence of a crime, Grace is left to investigate on her own, with the help of a private investigator (played with humorous panache by Charles Durning).

Danielle and Grace are instantly paralleled by their relationships with men – both are treated with condescension, and encouraged to submit to traditional behavioural modes of femininity. Grace is constantly criticized by her mother for putting her "little job" ahead of any ideas of marriage, and when she gets riled up about the murder she just witnessed, her mother responds with, "Are you taking diet pills again?" Even Danielle pokes at Grace's solitary life in an attempt to disparage her accusations of murder, pointing out with contrived empathy that isolation can lead to flights of fancy. Throughout the film the 'aloneness' of people is emphasized in order to elevate the bond between twins.

Soon, Grace's investigation turns up an old film reel that reinforces her suspicions that Danielle has a twin: Danielle and Dominique Blanchion were famous Siamese twins who spent a long time under supervision at the Loisel Institute in Canada. Danielle was the feminine, submissive sister, and Dominique her belligerent 'other'. Doctor Pierre Milius, being interviewed for the reel about the psychological challenges faced by twins, explains that while most of his colleagues "think Dominique is the truly disturbed one, I think they will find that Danielle, who is so sweet, so responsive, so normal as opposed to her sister, can only be so because of her sister."

The unexpected coda to this revelation is that Dominique has been dead for some time, as a result of a botched attempt to separate the twins. Propelled further to find out the truth behind Danielle, her slimy husband Emil, and the murder she knows she saw, Grace follows the couple to a sprawling house in the country – which she discovers (too late) to be a private mental clinic run by none other than Emil himself. Grace has stumbled into a trap: Emil convinces the staff that she is a recently admitted patient with delusions of being a reporter. She is drugged and put under hypnosis, and led into the film's climactic horrifying flashback sequence wherein she is posited as a stand-in for the long-dead Dominique, the unwanted sister. She was a burden to Danielle, who only wanted to be normal, get married and have babies. But Danielle is *not* normal, and her longing for normalcy is what has caused her most debilitating emotional aberration. She thinks that to get rid of Dominique is the answer, but even the separation surgery – deliberately played out like a grotesque castration (and mirrored in the literal castration of the men in the film) – cannot dispose of the monstrosity that Dominique represents to the seemingly perfect Danielle.

"The only way I can save you is to separate you from Dominique", Emil says, but he could not have predicted the outcome of this tragic operation: Danielle could never let go of Dominique. She compensated for the immense void by imagining Dominique to still be alive, by *becoming* her in ferocious spurts that could only be subdued by a constant reliance on medication. The tagline for the film was, "What the Devil hath joined together let no man cut asunder." But any evil here is relative. The beauty of the doppelganger film is that it celebrates the necessity of darkness.

When I was a teenager, my sister Karen returned for visits more regularly after she had a child that my parents tentatively adopted. I babysat for her occasionally and tried to be girlish and sisterly, but our relationship was never the same as the one that had always existed in my head. We were nothing alike after all, even though I long held onto this notion that she was instrumental in shaping me. I still remember my disappointment when we went on a road trip as adults, and I brought out CDs of the old albums she had left behind for me all those years ago – The Sweet, Alice Cooper, Stories, Black Sabbath – only to have her not recall any of the songs. As much as I looked at them as emblematic of our psychic connection, they had meant nothing to her. In her absence I had created a fictional sibling, just as I had created 'The Man with Green Eyes' out of an Argentinean bit-part-player bearing little resemblance to the monster in my closet. When I finally saw *Horror Express* again as a teenager, and realized it was the film that had spawned my nightmares, I was surprised to learn that the monster's eyes were *red*, not green. A conversation with my mother provided the reason for my confusion: I had seen the film on a black and white television. His eyes were only green in my imagination. A fertile place, indeed.

above: Alberto de Mendoza in **Horror Express**.

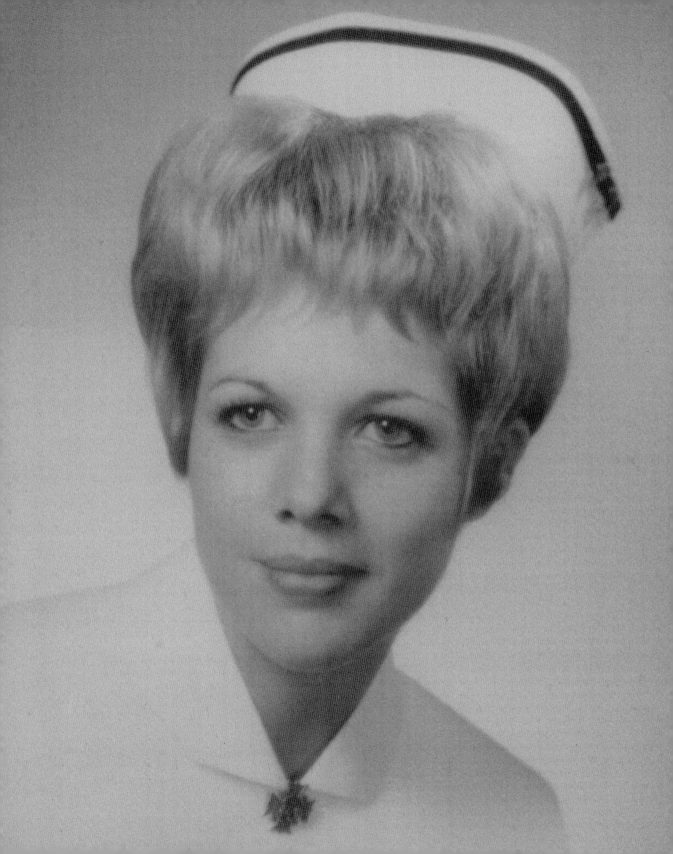

PART THREE:
ALL SAFE AND
DEAD

My mother was asleep for much of my childhood. I always thought it was due to her work schedule, but that's not entirely true. She worked the graveyard shift at an old folks' home, and I have many memories of getting her to sign notes, half-asleep, that I could bring to school saying it was okay for me to stay inside at recess, to read books from the library meant for the older kids, or to skip class altogether. I also remember being run over by a car and not being able to wake her up to take me to the hospital. I had been playing on my Big-Wheel in the driveway of the Kavanaugh's house, which was cater-corner to ours. A large hedge obscured the sightlines of the next driveway, and I ripped around the corner just as the neighbour's car was pulling out. I was low to the ground and she ran right over me, not realizing until I was half under the car that she had hit something. I was fine – I think I had a minor cut on my head – but everyone around me was hysterical. My brother and I went home to tell my mother but we couldn't get her to wake up. So we just went back out and played.

She was a registered nurse, and got pills from work to help her sleep during the day, but the habit soon expanded to a cupboard full of multi-coloured pill bottles with a high turnover rate. The bathroom was a step away from her bedroom door, and the wear of the carpet formed a visible pathway between the two. But she wasn't completely unlike many other mothers; after all, she loved her kids, she hid her problems using pills and alcohol, and she called in sick the night JR got shot.

But she came of age at a confusing time; social mores changed around her on a daily basis. Unlike the recent 'Naptime is the New Happy Hour' hipster-mom fad, in the immediate post-war period, female alcoholism started to come under attack in the media, with the boozing, pill-popping housewife emerging as a stock character in news stories, literature and films. Female alcoholics proliferated as social drinking – in moderation – became acceptable for women. But many of these women, knowing that female alcohol abuse was especially taboo, and not wanting to be associated with the stereotype being propagated in the media, continued to drink in isolation, hiding their increasing dependency from their families and friends. In the 1950s, doctors estimated that 25% of American alcoholics were female, but because female alcoholism was relatively invisible, we have no way of knowing how accurate the statistics are. Add to this the free-flowing psychotropic prescriptions that flourished in the 1950s and '60s – billed as 'happiness pills' – as a means of treating depression among largely female patients, and you have the makings of domestic cataclysm. Studies undertaken during the 1960s also showed that nurses, like my mom, represented a large proportion of female pill addicts.

Early on in the movies, female drinking was tied to some kind of sexual pathology, and female alcoholics were portrayed as loose, public women – nightclub singers, hostesses, barflies – with marriage and domesticity seen as the answer to their evasive fulfilment. But by the 1960s, this had reversed – alcoholism came into the home, and the domesticity itself was seen as its cause. As Norman K. Denzin points out in the book *Hollywood Shot By Shot: Alcoholism in American Cinema*, the film *Smash-Up: The Story of a Woman* (1947) saw the perfect intersection of these two stereotypes when a socially-boozing singer gives up her career for marriage, only to be driven to full-fledged alcoholism through boredom and increasing feelings of low self-worth.[8] Mainstream films showing the ugly side of female alcoholism proliferated as the '60s wore on – *Days of Wine and Roses* (1962), *Who's Afraid of Virginia Woolf?* (1966), *The Graduate* (1967) – often linking these problems to the boredom of upper-class housewives, or the blotting out of feelings that one's identity was being compromised by the act of marriage in and of itself.

opposite: My mother's nursing graduation photo, 1960s.

In horror films, alcoholism wouldn't always be front and centre in the plot, but the signs of habitual substance abuse – prominently placed and well-stocked bar-carts, prescription pill bottles – were there. Likewise, the issues I associated with excessive drinking from my experiences with my mother – withdrawal, loneliness, boredom, fear, escape – were ever-present in domestic horror. Just as alcoholism and drug abuse were now problems within the home, so the concept of 'home' itself became a problem as women became conflicted over the role of marriage in their lives. Husbands were now suspicious characters trying to keep their wives' ambitions under wraps while they themselves cavorted freely through the sexual revolution's exploratory offerings.

Eloy de la Iglesia, the director of Cannibal Man, also wrote and directed the effective Spanish giallo The Glass Ceiling (1971), which starred Carmen Sevilla as Martha, a loyal housewife whose husband goes away on business far too often, leaving her isolated and alone with her imagination. Her attempts to ease her boredom by being sociable are commonly misinterpreted – a delivery boy invited up for some milk makes a move on her, and when spurned, retorts, "don't think you're the only woman in this predicament. There are millions of women who are bored... almost as bored as you." Indeed, her boredom is what leads her to eavesdrop on her neighbours and speculate on what their lives are like – and on what it means when she hears a loud thump in the middle of the night followed by scurrying footsteps.

When she notices the extended absence of Victor, the man upstairs, she comes to the conclusion that his wife Julie (stunning Euro-starlet and Barbara Steele-lookalike Patty Shepard) and an alleged lover murdered him. She becomes obsessed with the idea, and her days are filled with trying to solve the 'mystery' of Victor's disappearance. Her only friend is the landlord/sculptor Richard (the fact that nubile teenager Emma Cohen keeps exposing herself to him is supposed to indicate that he's hunky), who proposes that she's a voyeur: "Have you ever heard of voyeurism?" he asks, "Voyeurs are people who get a kick out of spying on the most intimate, the most personal secrets of other people... and like you said – snooping, for instance, is this instinct we all have." Prompted by the suggestive tone of his analysis, they share an illicit kiss, which leaves Martha feeling guilty and suffering from nightmares involving grotesque images of infidelity and murder.

Even when she's absolutely convinced a murder has taken place and her life is in grave danger, she takes no steps to make herself safe; instead she sits in her apartment in silence, ruminating on every accentuated sound, and she starts coming apart. But she's not crazy – a murder has taken place, and the murderers – including her absent husband Michael – make every assurance that she be completely unhinged by the time it is her inevitable turn to die. So while she's neurotic, her neurosis is fuelled exclusively by external factors; before a murder was carried out within earshot of her, she was bored and uninspired, but hardly crazy.

1970s horror films abound with marriage-phobia (and the corresponding paedophobia), but nowhere is the medicated wife or girlfriend more visible than in the Italian giallo film. Although the hallmark of the giallo is its misogynistic violence, these movies tend to incapacitate women by medicating them just as often as by killing them. The characters' skewed subjectivity (heightened by the abuse of alcohol and medication) creates tension for the spectator and also allows for the tangential lapses of logic characteristic of most gialli.

In the cinematic world, alcohol abuse is fuelled by aesthetic considerations, especially in giallo films, where J&B whisky bottles are as much a deliberate part of the production design as giant pop art paintings. The lifestyle depicted in most gialli is one of leisure; women are seen lying down – wearing muumuus, lingerie or other items of lounging attire that imply that they don't leave the house much – more than they are seen standing up. They are either independently wealthy or married to rich men. Their apartments vary between tacky baroque and black and white '70s minimalism, complete with shag carpets, oversized cushions and furniture made in bizarre geometric shapes. There is an element of fantasy in these rooms; they mirror the decadence of the sexually liberated, and no attempt is made to model them after the bedrooms of reality. That said, Oates's house would have been a great giallo set: a white split-level bungalow complete with minimalist chrome-and-glass furniture, bright, psychedelic wallpaper, hi-fi stereo and various imported Japanese accoutrements.

Throughout these films there is a certain 'cult of laziness' being propagated. The giallo wives and girlfriends, with their booze, pills and ethereal blankness become almost a perverted counterpart to the 19th century 'Angel in the House', an ideal of womanhood popularized by poet Coventry Patmore (and later to be famously criticized by writers such as Virginia Woolf and Charlotte Perkins Gilman). In this scenario, the perfect wife was devoted and submissive, passive and powerless, and – contrary to the sexually pathological giallo women – morally incorruptible.

Sergio Martino is a prolific Italian exploitation film director celebrated for his work in both the giallo (Torso, 1973) and crime genres (The Violent Professionals, 1973). Taking its cues from Rosemary's Baby in the supernatural department, All the Colors of the Dark (1972) is a unique entry in Martino's oeuvre and easily the most hallucinatory of all his films. After perfecting the giallo with The Strange Vice of Mrs. Wardh (1971), Martino took his regular stable of actors (Edwige Fenech, Ivan Rassimov and George Hilton) and threw them into his most perverse narrative yet. Rassimov has never looked more stunning, or more threatening. Fenech has never looked more crazy.

Fenech plays Jane, a woman teetering on the brink of a nervous breakdown and constantly medicated accordingly by her long-time boyfriend Richard (Hilton). Left alone much of the time, her dangerously active imagination is free to wander, and when asleep she is haunted by violent nightmares that somehow connect to an incident in her past that she has repressed. When she wakes up from a nightmare, sweaty and exasperated, she reaches for her boyfriend on the bed beside her, but he – as usual – is not there. He comes home to find her in the shower, fully clothed. He shakes his head in disappointment: "You didn't take your pills again, huh?" Instead of rushing into his arms for comfort, she stands alone in the shower, looking ridiculous and shrinking in shame.

He makes her take her pills and tells her to go to sleep, but once she passes out, he undresses and starts fondling her. She reacts accordingly, gripping him passionately in a drug-induced half-sleep – but their lovemaking is interrupted by the haunting images that invade her sleep each night, and she thrusts him away, screaming. We are given the impression that their sex life has followed this routine for some time.

When Jane's sister inquires about the pills Richard constantly plies her with, insisting that he is not a doctor and that Jane should refuse anything not prescribed by a shrink or a physician, Jane immediately comes to Richard's defence: "They're just concentrated vitamins, but when I take them I always throw up... but Richard would never do anything to harm me."

When Jane visits a psychiatrist against Richard's wishes, she discloses to him that the various images from her dream – a pregnant woman, a witchy, toothless *Baby Jane* lookalike, a menacing pair of crystal blue eyes, a hand stabbing, the motion of a car crashing into a tree – relate directly to the loss of her own unborn child in a car accident, and to the murder of her mother as a child. She has never told Richard about the latter, claiming that he would "never believe her". But in asserting that

centre right: Edwige Fenech and Marina Malfatti in Sergio Martino's **All the Colors of the Dark** (1972).

bottom right: Edwige Fenech and George Hilton in **All the Colors of the Dark**.

COMME CHAQUE NUIT LE REVE SE TERMINE PAR UN HURLEMENT DECHIRANT, CELUI DE LA MÈRE.

JEANNE SE REVEILLE, ELLE EST COUVERTE DE TRANSPIRATION.

ELLE N'EN PEUT PLUS, ELLE SE SENT DEVENIR FOLLE!

Seulement trois heures du matin!

Cela ne peut plus durer!

EN TITUBANT, ELLE SE REND DANS LA SALLE DE BAIN.

LE MIROIR LUI RENVOIT L'IMAGE D'UN VISAGE PALE, CREUX, AUX YEUX CERNES.

the story is hard to believe, she is in a sense saying that she herself doesn't believe it; that she questions the reliability of her own memory. The psychiatrist mistrusts Richard, and urges Jane to stop taking the pills he gives her – insisting that her real problem is loneliness, but this doesn't account for the creepy man with shocking blue eyes (Ivan Rassimov) who has been following her all around town – a man identical to the attacker in her dream.

Lonely and frightened, Jane is pleased when a new woman named Mary (Marina Malfatti) moves into her creepy building, and proves as friendly as she is beautiful. When Fenech admits to her new friend that she suffers from bouts of depression and frequent nightmares ("I'm almost certain that someone is after me, someone from my past, from something that happened in my childhood"), Mary urges her to stop seeing the psychiatrist and to come see 'her friends' instead. When Jane asks who these friends are and what they do, Mary responds enigmatically, "They don't like to be questioned."

Mary leads her to a giant secluded mansion, into a dark basement full of people in bizarre make-up and either naked or clothed in robes bearing occult symbols. "Drink this and you will be free", orders the high priest, handing her a goblet of fresh dog's blood (Only in a giallo film would a woman be convinced to join a Satanic cult to cure her psychological ailments). After she is forced to imbibe, the cultists descend upon her in an orgiastic frenzy, paralleling the earlier scene of Richard drugging and mounting her. Thus Jane is bounced around from one controller to the next, all these people – her boyfriend, her sister, Mary, the psychiatrist, and the Satanists – who want her to just obey them without hesitation. Just shut up, take your pills, go to sleep, don't question.

As Jane is increasingly terrorized on all fronts, she comes to realize that the Satanists – like the man who has been following her – are connected to her mother's murder years before.

In a later sequence, the man following her reveals his purpose: he is a murderer sent by the Satanists to visit retribution upon those who have forsaken them. "You have renounced us just like your mother!" he hisses.

above: Excerpt from a 60-page French photostory of **All the Colors of the Dark**.

While no back-story is given on Jane's mother (other than an apparent Satanic affiliation), there are clearly efforts to deprive women of their individuality. Jane is made out to be a crazy woman as a means of keeping her dependent, of convincing her that she is incapable of making decisions on her own. The one concrete decision she has made without the influence of others is to not officially marry her long-time boyfriend Richard. While she lives out all the trappings of an unhappy marriage, tolerating his constant absence and even succumbing to his amateur prescriptions, she has denied him legal control over her. But men are not her only problem. Even the other women in the story want to stop her from being independent: the two women who urge her to defy Richard's wishes also betray her. By the end of the film, with several people dead and a mountain of secrets exposed, she is no better off than she was at the start. Her last words are words of despair: "Oh darling, help me."

When my mother was in her first marriage to Oates, she discovered early on that he was cheating on her. Not with one woman, but several, and he openly flaunted his affairs to her and her family members, even – according to one of my aunts – bringing a girlfriend to the hospital the night my brother was born. He was condescending and emotionally manipulative, and when one of my uncles confronted my father, asking why he didn't just divorce my mother if he found marriage so restrictive, my father said, "Oh that would be too easy", continuing on to admit that he looked forward to driving my mother crazy. Supposedly he even went so far as to enlist someone to lurk outside the windows of the house when my mother was home alone, in an attempt to scare her out of her wits. He would have been a perfect giallo husband.

The Italian title for Sergio Martino's *Gently Before She Dies* (aka *Excite Me*, 1972) translates directly as '*Your Vice Is a Locked Room and Only I Have the Key*' – a line from the previous Ernesto Gastaldi/Sergio Martino collaboration *The Strange Vice of Mrs. Wardh*. In a script freely adapted from Edgar Allan Poe's *The Black Cat*, *Gently Before She Dies* stars Anita Strindberg as Irina, the anorexic, humiliated and abused wife of philandering failed writer Oliviero (Luigi Pistilli) who gets caught up in a murder rap.

Irina lives in a state of unrelenting nervousness as the target of her husband's sadism; she takes sleeping pills frequently and seems to just live in wait for the next display of hostility. The opening sequence depicts a wild party at their large country house (it should be pointed out that party scenes in giallo films are always a hotbed for sleazy and hilarious academic musings) in which Oliviero physically forces Irina to drink a boozy mixture from a giant bowl in a room full of jeering hipsters. The more she sputters and coughs, the more pleasure he derives from the situation, and the more inexplicable her own submissive behaviour becomes, given the context of the liberated early '70s; but marriage provides its own context that seems to stay locked in time. "Nowhere are the effects of the historical and cultural forces that predispose women toward masochism more keenly realized than in marriage", says Natalie Shainess in her book *Sweet Suffering: Woman As Victim*. "The husband has the fantasy of destroying the wife, and that fantasy will give him potency."[9] In *Gently Before She Dies* Oliviero's potency manifests itself literally as well as figuratively: it is in those moments when his loathing of Irina is at its apex that he finds himself aroused enough to rape her.

Oliviero becomes the prime suspect when his young mistress is brutally murdered, and when his maid turns up dead as well, he convinces the unstable Irina to wall up her corpse in the cellar to avoid further suspicion. While he denies having anything to do with the murders, he frequently extols the virtues of murder to the anxious Irina, caressing her throat as he purrs, "Maybe this will be my first one." His homicidal designs on her are no secret, but Oliviero's campaign to destroy his wife is not limited to physical violence; it is much more calculated. He doles out various punishments – verbal abuse, neglect and dismissal, frequent beatings, the flaunting of extramarital affairs – and is increasingly disgusted with her for putting up with them.

When Oliviero's promiscuous niece Floriana (Edwige Fenech, sporting a sharp bob haircut) shows up to stay with them, Irina is thrown even more off guard by the girl's sexual advances and suggestions that she bump off her loutish husband. "He's a brute, an alcoholic and a drug addict", Floriana insists, pointing out that he's also rumoured to have slept with his own mother. When Floriana suggests that Irina should leave him, Irina says he would never allow it: "To lose his plaything, his victim? Never." Their relationship, however abusive, is co-dependent. Like the couples in Ingmar Bergman's *From the Life of the Marionettes* (1980) or Pasquale Festa Campanile's *Hitch-Hike* (1977), each is reliant on the responses of the other for a reinforcement of their own identity. The self-confidence

above: Anita Strindberg in Sergio Martino's **Gently Before She Dies** (1972).

of Oliviero, the sadistic husband, is fuelled by the denigration of his wife. The further she sinks, the more powerful he feels, but he forgets that it takes two to play this game, and he makes the mistake of denying Irina the affection that motivates her compliance, which will prove his own undoing.

The Italian horror film, the giallo in particular, often features female neurosis as an adjunct to the husband's moral deficiency and/or mental illness, which is often a catalyst for the wife's own mental disturbance. Due to the patriarchal nature of marriage however, the husband's mental instability is not seen as the problem, even though it may have been the primary instigator – he is allowed to drive his wife crazy, and she suffers domestically and socially as a result.

Throughout my childhood, there was constant interplay between my mother's physical and mental well-being. Because my father was a psychologist, he had professional validation for dismissing my mother's health problems (and problems with their marriage) as unfounded anxiety. Certain members of my mother's family were onto him, but he just filed away their grievances as stemming from the same neurotic source. To return to Gilman's *The Yellow Wallpaper*, in which an anxious female writer is driven mad by her husband's insistence that she give up writing and stay in bed:

> "John laughs at me, of course, but one expects that in marriage. John is practical in the extreme. He has no patience with faith, an intense horror of superstition, and he scoffs openly at any talk of things not to be felt and seen and put down in figures. John is a physician, and perhaps – (I would not say it to a living soul, of course, but this is dead paper and a great relief to my mind) – perhaps that is one reason I do not get well faster. You see he does not believe I am sick! And what can one do? If a physician of high standing, and one's own husband, assures friends and relatives that there is really nothing the matter with one but temporary nervous depression – a slight hysterical tendency – what is one to do?"[10]

Whereas the husband in *The Yellow Wallpaper* is just the ignorant product of an earlier time in medical history, Oates, like the giallo husbands, should have known better. Even my own perception of my mother's various illnesses is filtered through the conflicting stories of various family members… "She's sick, she's not sick, she's faking it, she's on drugs, she's an alcoholic, she's a victim, poor thing…"

In Dino Risi's *Anima persa* (*Lost Soul*, 1977) – written by the frequent Fellini collaborator and writer of Argento's *Profondo rosso*, Bernardino Zapponi – Vittorio Gassman and Catherine Deneuve are stately couple Fabio and Sofia, who live in Sofia's crumbling ancestral home in Venice. The arrival of their teenage nephew, who is staying with them while he attends art school, brings their dysfunctional relationship to light: Sofia is a nervous wreck for undisclosed reasons, and her domineering husband clearly detests her. The revelation that Fabio's insane brother lives shut in an attic room is unnerving enough – but that's only the beginning of the horrors that await the young art student. Evidence of a child's one-time existence in the house prompts him to ask questions that bring forth uncomfortable and contradictory answers. Sofia maintains that she once had a young daughter, Beba, whose beauty entranced Fabio's entomologist brother to the point of driving him insane and prompting the young girl to leap to her death in the canals. Fabio tells a different story: when he married Sofia, she was a widow with a ten-year-old daughter whom he loved as though she was his own. Jealous of their innocent affection for each other, Sofia allowed the child to die when she was struck by bronchitis – an easily treated illness in childhood.

With the couple's mistrust and hatred of each other clearly laid out, there is still one more twist to their already convoluted (but believably played-out) tale: there is no stately husband and wife; there is only an insane

above: Luigi Pistilli and Anita Strindberg in **Gently Before She Dies**.

entomologist and his child bride, who he came to detest when she grew out of innocence and into womanhood. Concocting a phony death for his lover and a bland identity for himself as an engineer with a rich wife, he had hoped to keep his passion and grief locked away in a room upstairs, where he could periodically act out the role of the crazy brother with his wagging tongue and broken dolls, and then re-emerge with the straightened, hair combed, and id in check. Sofia, the broken doll in question, plays along, as she's never known any other way; she's been with this man since pre-pubescence (although how that initially came to be – once we know there's no wife – remains unexplained). She also has a double life: alternating between being the ageing woman who's mostly bedridden and has a drink problem, and the little girl in ribbons and baby-doll dress that she regresses to when required by her sick lover. "Do you know why they're locked up?" Fabio asks his nephew as they drive past an asylum, "Because, like children, the insane know the truth. And people fear the truth."

The truth, and the threat it poses, can be too overwhelming to bear, and for many women in the aftermath of the sexual revolution, the truth was that their experiences were being dismissed by the men in their lives. Although many of the women in the films of this period are clearly meant to be schizophrenic, sociopathic or downright psychotic, the underlying implication (and there always is one in horror films) is that these 'illnesses' come in at the break between the woman's experience and the man's experience of the same situation – and what is 'true' or 'right' is often whatever the man says it is. Many horror films dealing with mental illness are deliberately ambiguous: we are left to form our own conclusions as to whether the protagonist is insane, or whether we believe that supernatural forces are indeed at work.

One of the most subtle masterpieces of '70s genre cinema is John Hancock's moody, ethereal *Let's Scare Jessica to Death* (1971), starring Zohra Lampert as a young woman recently released from a mental institution. As in Mario Bava's *Shock* (1977), the husband's bright idea is to move to a new home so that his wife can "get better" – in this case an imposing, labyrinthine house on an isolated apple farm, far removed from New York City. Before the film even gets going we know that this is probably a bad decision on his part: he has spent everything they had buying this house, leaving them financially as well as socially cut adrift. He has brought along his pal Woody, and Jessica likes Woody just fine – as she does everyone – but there is no escaping the fact that her husband has brought her into a very limited environment in which she has to be dependent solely upon him. Even her doctor is miles away in New York, and they have no financial contingency should Jessica feel the need to contact him. The nearby townspeople – all hostile and intimidating old men wearing weird bandages – will prove no help to Jessica either.

The house itself is a gorgeous piece of Victorian architecture, with a large turret and winding staircases – including one set of stairs in the front yard that leads nowhere. As Jessica perches on this staircase, negotiating with the voices in her head, we are given a striking, tangible image of her mental state.

top right: Vittorio Gassman and Catherine Deneuve in Dino Risi's **Anima persa** (1977).

bottom right: Zohra Lampert in John Hancock's **Let's Scare Jessica to Death** (1971).

When they first enter the house, she sees a woman at the top of the stairs, and thankfully her husband sees her too, making Jessica sigh and laugh with relief. The pale redheaded stranger introduces herself as Emily, a drifter who has been crashing out in what she thought was an abandoned house. Jessica invites her to stay with them, happy to have a female companion, but Emily – like most strangers who intrude upon a family unit in genre films – will prove the catalyst for Jessica's complete mental breakdown.

Jessica is fascinated by rumours in the town about the house's previous inhabitants, the Bishop family, whose 20-year-old daughter Abigail drowned, wearing her wedding dress, in the cove behind the house. Abigail's body was never recovered, and the townsfolk believe that she is still alive, roaming the country as a vampire. These vampiric myths intertwine with Jessica's increasing view of Emily – a spitting image of the 'missing' Abigail Bishop – as a predator who wants to steal away her husband and keep Jessica a prisoner on the farm. "Duncan's mine now", she hears the voices whispering, "You want to die... Stay with me... forever."

As Jessica's visions intensify, and Emily/Abigail gets more aggressive with both Jessica and the men in the house, she finds it harder and harder to maintain any front of normality. Zohra Lampert, a stage actress who once went out with director John Hancock, is incredible in her portrayal of Jessica's struggle to hold herself together. Her credibility is repeatedly called into question, not only by the other members of her mock-family, but by Jessica herself. She sees things, and talks herself out of revealing them to the others for fear of chastisement. She feels that her mental state has caused her husband to be sexually disinterested in her, and consequently encouraged his budding fascination with the hippie girl who's come into their fold. Even for the viewer, there is confusion between which off-screen voices are Jessica's own, and which are those of the supernatural forces with which she is apparently attuned. Jessica compensates by being over-friendly, over-generous and goofy. But this goofiness soon transforms into hysteria.

When everyone around her is dead, Jessica dissociates completely. As she says in the film's opening, and again in its closing moments, drifting peacefully in a boat out in the cove:

> "I sit here and I can't believe that it happened. And yet I have to believe it. Dreams or nightmares, madness or sanity. I don't know which is which."

Jessica's attempts to rebuild her life failed. The illness was too strong, the ghosts too overbearing. Her guilt over not being able to 'act normal' only exacerbated her awkwardness and invited the kind of self-hatred that would unravel her. The same was true in my own home; my mother wanted a perfect life, to erase painful recollections of her past – and when it didn't materialize by the mere act of remarrying, she felt that, again, she had somehow failed. But failure begat failure, and my mother shrunk away from uncomfortable situations by trying to convince herself that they didn't exist. Repression and guilt are the most weighty contributors to the alcoholism endemic to many of these films; women self-medicate to repress traumatic memories, the lingering reminders of horrible deeds committed either by them or unto them.

Suppose you knew who you had been in your previous life. Where you had lived...whom you had loved and how you had died. What then?

MAX EHRLICH
AUTHOR OF THE BEST SELLER

The Reincarnation of Peter Proud

NOW
AN ELECTRIFYING
MOTION PICTURE

BCP presents
The Reincarnation of Peter Proud
starring **Michael Sarrazin** **Jennifer O'Neill**
Margot Kidder
Cornelia Sharpe
Screenplay by Max Ehrlich from his novel Executive Producer Charles A. Pratt
Produced by Frank P. Rosenberg Directed by J. Lee Thompson
Music by Jerry Goldsmith Panavision® Technicolor
BCP a service of Cox Broadcasting Corporation
From Cinerama / An American International Release

top left: Zohra Lampert in **Let's Scare Jessica to Death**.

bottom right: U.S. poster for J. Lee Thompson's **The Reincarnation of Peter Proud** (1975).

In J. Lee Thompson's bizarre and morally disturbing *The Reincarnation of Peter Proud* (1975), Michael Sarrazin plays the title character, who is haunted by recurring dreams that convince him he is reliving scenes from a past life. The images lead him to a small lakeside town in Massachusetts, where 30 years earlier he was murdered by his wife Marcia (Margot Kidder) in a staged drowning incident. However, the more he delves into his past life the more he realizes what a reprehensible character his 1940s counterpart was – aside from myriad adulterous indiscretions, he sexually humiliates his wife. When she confronts him about his extracurricular love life he rapes her, muttering clichéd comments such as, "you know you want it…" (even his name seems to reflect his macho self-righteousness), but Marcia's struggling eventually gives way to rapture and she clutches at him hungrily, only to have him immediately spring from the bed afterwards saying that he's going for a late night swim, "to wash her stink off" – thus prompting the 'accident'.

Years later, Marcia's traumatic memories come flooding back, prompted by the sudden appearance of the suspicious stranger in her (their) daughter's life, who is the spitting image of her dead husband. Marcia is visibly disturbed, and her routine drinking – which has been a problem since the time of her husband's death, and was explained away by a psychiatrist as "typical middle-aged female alcoholism" – intensifies, and she frequently hides away in her room. On one such occasion, curled up defensively in the bathtub, the memory of her rape starts to excite her – at first her hands go toward her crotch defensively, but slowly they start to move back and forth… Complicating things further is the fact that Peter appears to be courting her (their) daughter, which she perceives as a deliberate transgression on his part, to further torment her. Early on in the film Peter bemoans not being able to have "normal Freudian dreams", elaborating with, "why can't I just dream of killing my father and raping my mother?" His flippant wish to be governed by easily recognizable Freudian tropes comes true, which is effectively squirm-inducing for the audience. As his "dreams" dissipate with the integration of his old life into his new reality, he is still haunted by the last image of being murdered in the lake – an image that will only leave him once he has re-enacted the scene. While he is acting out of a need to satisfy his own curiosity, his former wife (Marcia) is coming apart – being forced, with no choice in the matter, to relive the most unpleasant episode of her life. And like Carla Moran in *The Entity*, she struggles with the concept of blame, believing that she deserves the torment because of her inability to reconcile her need for individuality and respect with her apparent sexual appetite toward an abuser. She has a reason to feel guilty – she has, after all, murdered her husband – but one gets the sense that the murder is not what she feels guilty about.

Guilt ran through 1970s genre films like a parasite, eating away at the psyches of female characters, who oscillated between domestic responsibility and the desire for autonomy. A perfect, devastating example of this cinematic guilty conscience can be found in Richard Loncraine's *The Haunting of Julia* (also known as *Full Circle*, 1977), which sees Mia Farrow as the titular distraught mother of a child she has accidentally killed while performing an emergency tracheotomy.

When Julia emerges from the hospitalisation that ensues, she immediately leaves her husband Magnus (Keir Dullea) and goes looking for a house of her own, to be alone with her grief. Julia explains to her sister-in-law Lily (Jill Bennett) that her marriage had been on the rocks for some time, and says, "Now that Katie's gone… there's no reason to try." However, Lily and Magnus are both dependent on Julia's trust fund, and make increasingly aggressive attempts bordering on personal terrorism to convince her to return to her marriage. Augmenting this pressure is the fact that Julia's new home is the kind of immense, sinister house that undoubtedly fuels nightmares and paranoia.

She tries to go through the motions of a new life, but is isolated by a debilitating guilt over her daughter's death. She laughs one minute and cries the next. "It's like stepping out on a window ledge and feeling so alive because any second you could jump", she says. "Sometimes I feel I've already jumped."

Though she occasionally socializes with her bohemian friend Mark, Julia is unwavering in her decision to work through her grief alone. Therapy is not an option – after all, if you go to therapy, people might think you're crazy. But there are a million things that can drive you crazy, and ruminating in solitude is one of them.

When my mother was a teenager, she was involved in a drowning accident in which one of her best friends died. A group of her school friends were out swimming in a lake. A wicked storm blew in, and they were forced to form a circle and clasp hands to stay afloat. One of the girls went down, and my mother let go of the chain in order to save her. And save her she did – but in letting go of another girl's hand, the second girl drowned. My mother was put into therapy, but was not allowed to talk about it. Somehow, even though she had saved another girl's life, she became the shame of the family because of her incapacitating emotional response to the incident. One lingering effect of that terrible event is that my mother had difficulty making decisions ever after.

Guilt would continue to plague my mother throughout her life: guilt over her friend's death, the failure of her marriage, remarrying out of fear, subjecting her children to an abusive stepfather, and excessive drinking – and guilt over the latter would just fuel more of the same. She was determined to punish herself.

Come take your place in the circle... if you dare!

full Circle

MIA FARROW
in
"FULL CIRCLE"
starring
KEIR DULLEA
Tom CONTI · Jill BENNETT

PRODUCERS PETER FETTERMAN
ALFRED PARISER
DIRECTOR RICHARD LONCRAINE
EXECUTIVE PRODUCER JULIAN MELZACK

A CLASSIC FILM INDUSTRIES ·
FETTER PRODUCTIONS PRESENTATION

Like my mother, Julia has a hard time sleeping, and spends her nights self-medicating while the days pass in a vacant haze. As she explores her new neighbourhood, she goes to the park and sees a child that she thinks is her daughter, but when she approaches, the girl disappears, and what's left behind in the sand is a mutilated animal and a bloody knife. Julia picks up the knife and is unhinged again. To make matters worse, a nearby mother and child witness her holding the dead animal and chastise her as a nut. She runs off home, and for the third time in the film, she has to wash blood off her hands.

At night, Julia hears sounds in and around the house, which may or may not be Magnus trying to scare her into returning to her loveless marriage. Lily sees fit to bring a group of whack-jobs over to Julia's new pad for a séance – a move so insensitive that it only proves further that Magnus and his sister are trying to drive Julia insane in order to get her declared incompetent and thus take over management of her trust fund. Julia's reliable best friend Mark – who is secretly in love with her – thinks the same thing. The séance turns sour when the medium is scared witless and makes vague pronouncements that something "wicked" is in the house, and another guest inexplicably goes plummeting down the stairs.

Julia decides to investigate the former inhabitants of the house, and discovers that a little girl named Olivia once lived there, a girl so beautiful that she could get away with anything – including the murder of another child. After hearing the gruesome tale of a young boy mutilated by Olivia and her pack of devoted schoolmates, Julia self-medicates to go to sleep, and has a visit in the night from the child, who touches her face and hands in an exploratory (and from what we know, threatening) manner, but Julia is not threatened; she identifies with the child's murderous guilt, playing the roles of both child and the child's redeemer. She is going to help the terrible child find peace.

In a madhouse in Wales, Olivia's ageing mother, Mrs. Rudge, is visited by the increasingly obsessed Julia, who asks her about the child's death. "Not dead", protests Mrs. Rudge, "I'm the one who is dead. All safe and dead... all safe and dead. Have you ever seen evil, Mrs. Lofting? I have. I'm safe though. Evil is not like

above: Poster for Richard Loncraine's **The Haunting of Julia** (1977) under its alternative title **Full Circle.**

ordinary people – evil never dies. She's not dead – and you're not safe. You killed your daughter… like I killed mine… she choked, she choked on her own wickedness."

After she visits Mrs. Rudge and hears it voiced aloud that she "killed her daughter" (thereby confirming what she's been feeling all along), she goes home and faces Olivia (who she sees as a reflection of her own guilt) and finds her redemption… in suicide. Mirroring the revelation at the end of Mario Bava's haunted-woman film *Shock*, the ghost's murderous hands are in actuality the protagonist's own.

In the book *American Nightmare: Essays on the Horror Film*, Richard Lippe has pointed out that Julia's sense of guilt is intensified by the fact that her daughter's death allowed her to escape from an unhappy marriage.[11] It is fitting then, that the dead girl 'haunting' her killed and castrated a male child, symbolically reflecting Julia's resentment toward her own husband.

My mother had some brewing resentment of her own. Not only had she endured an emotionally abusive first marriage, but her new marriage offered little solace either, due to my stepfather's frightening temper. As my battles with my stepfather became more frequent, my mother was increasingly absent and emotionally distant. It was hard to know if she was ever happy, if maybe their marriage would have had a chance without me in the equation. But an incident when I was a teenager provided the answer to that. After a particularly gruesome argument my mother went to my Grandma Peggy's house a few blocks away to spend the night away from my stepfather. Grandma Peggy lived in Florida for half the year, and my parents looked after her apartment while she was gone.

My mother would often go and hide out there when things were strained between her and my stepfather. This time however, we got a call from the police: there had been a fire. My mother drank herself into a blackout with a pizza in the oven. A fire started, and she was clinically dead for several minutes from smoke inhalation. I remember the day my stepfather brought her home wrapped in a blanket from the hospital, and the look on her face was horrifying. I had never seen her so full of spite and venom. My mother rarely swore, but on this day she had lost all sense of propriety. My greeting to her was met with, "You should have left me alone! Why couldn't you have let me die?! I was in heaven! YOU TOOK ME OUT OF HEAVEN! I FUCKING HATE ALL OF YOU!!!"

above: Mia Farrow in **The Haunting of Julia**.

PART FOUR: SECRET CEREMONIES

While Edgar Allan Poe stories and Hammer Films were an indispensable part of my childhood that inevitably set me apart from other kids, there were certainly things about me that were more conventional. Like any pre-pubescent girl, I loved playing with Barbies. My Barbies lived in a perfect world filled with dream pools, dream houses, dream pets (although the Afghan that stood in as Barbie's breed of choice was a far cry from what I considered to be the perfect dog) – even their own McDonalds with tiny plastic Big Macs. What this perfect world lacked was a male counterpart. My first choice as a mate for Barbie was Paul McCartney, but my incessant letters to Mattel demanding a line of Barbie-sized Beatles dolls went unanswered. The obvious runner-up was Ken.

My mother curiously ignored my pleas for a Ken doll for several years. But one fateful day she came home with a surprise. I held my breath as she unsheathed from a Sears bag what I supposed would be the answer to Barbie's prayers. But to my horror, what appeared before my eyes was... a Jimmy Osmond doll. Not even a Donny Osmond doll – a *Jimmy* Osmond doll. And he was a good inch shorter than Barbie. Didn't mother know that women couldn't date men they blatantly dwarfed in height? I threw Jimmy to the floor and ruminated on what possible role this glittery plastic midget could have in Barbie's life.

Jimmy sat collecting dust for many years, forgotten among the Weebles, Strawberry Shortcake dolls and rotten sandwiches that lined the inner reaches of my closet. Years passed, until I was much too old to be playing with Barbies, but still secretly did. One day I was thumbing through the HBO guide and noticed a movie listed that I'd been anticipating ever since seeing the ads earlier that year: *Extremities* (1986). *Extremities* was a regular feature of the Barbie Drive-In theatre I made out of cardboard (there were two screens back-to-back: one was always playing *Extremities* and one was always playing *Christine* (1983)). I was a fan of *The Burning Bed* (1984) and this looked like more of the same: Farrah Fawcett, perfect-hair-in-peril.

Fawcett's coif aside, the character that really made an impression on me was James Russo as the thug that tries to rape the former Angel only to have the tables turned on him and end up bound and gagged in the fireplace. In retrospect, *Extremities* amounts to little more than a mediocre adaptation of a stage play, with production values that reek of movie-of-the-week. But to my young mind it would operate as a gateway into harder drugs – namely movies like *The Last House on the Left* (1972), *I Spit on Your Grave* (1978), *Ms.45* (1981), *Lipstick* (1976 – which is unique in its assertion that listening to electronic music is a factor in the perverted tendencies of rapists!), *Last House on the Beach* (1978), *Poor Pretty Eddie* (1975), *Dirty Weekend* (1993) and *Thriller: A Cruel Picture* (aka *They Call Her One Eye*, 1974). But that would all come later. The immediate consequence of watching *Extremities* was a new vocation for my unwanted Jimmy Osmond doll: RAPIST.

The scenario was always the same: Barbie and friends would head out in the Barbie dream camper for a picnic in the country. Barbie would have to go to the bathroom, and since there aren't any toilet facilities in Barbie's Dream World (sinks, showers, bathtubs, yes – toilets, no), Barbie would excuse herself to go urinate behind a bush. With Barbie in this vulnerable state, Jimmy would lunge out from behind an adjacent bush and ravage her.

There was no revenge in this scenario, just Barbie's subjugation to Jimmy's perverse desires again and again. There would be no augmenting of this familiar storyline, no deviation in the form of a hero, a sudden burst of female agency or just plain good luck. Barbie didn't even have an immediate response to the incident – she wouldn't cry, wouldn't tell anyone. The story would just end and start again at the beginning. The rape itself was always the fulfilment of the story. I hadn't yet learned how rape can be used most effectively as a narrative tool – namely, as fuel.

opposite: Mimsy Farmer in George Lautner's **Road to Salina** (1970).

Female audiences often complain about the presence of rape scenes in films. These scenes are cited as exploitive and their directors labelled misogynists. But they don't realize that a rape scene is the single greatest justification for anything else in the film that follows – no matter how illogical, unbelievable, sadistic, misanthropic, graphic or tortuous. The audience will accept any direction the story takes because, culturally, rape is worse than death.

While many manifestations of neurosis are triggered by external factors, rape is especially tragic in that it *always* results in neurosis. Despite eventual 'renormalization', no woman ever fully recovers from being raped. Even when a woman is able to emotionally detach herself from the occurrence, that detachment itself is often accompanied by a cynicism that will negatively affect all her future relationships.

Their sense of moral assertion and vigilante justice is probably the primary factor that led to my interest in rape-revenge films. It's been said a million times that horror films are meant to be cathartic, and that we put ourselves through the terror as a means of symbolically overcoming something we're afraid of. And for a

woman, we're taught that nothing is more terrifying than the ever-present threat of rape. So it seems natural to me that I would love rape-revenge films, especially when the revenge is particularly sadistic or creative, or when the female protagonist is completely transformed as a consequence. Even more exciting than the revenge is preparing for the revenge: buying a gun, learning martial arts, setting booby traps, the symbolic cutting of hair – all set to a pounding, anticipatory soundtrack.

As a teenager watching rape-revenge films more consciously, *The Last House on the Left* was probably the first I saw, followed by the inflammatory *I Spit on Your Grave* (which has inspired more commentary than it deserves). The standard trajectory of a rape-revenge film is this: a woman is raped; she retreats inward, often cutting her hair short or erasing other discernible signs of femininity; she gets angry and starts learning about hand to hand combat, weapons and covert surveillance; she exacts a violent revenge – and then the film ends abruptly. In many cases, if the victim is killed or incapacitated by catatonia, a friend or family member takes her place as the avenger. Of course there are variations in plot or the characters' emotional responsiveness – in Mario Andreacchio's *Fair Game* (1986) star Cassandra Delaney is remarkably undeterred by the Aussie gang of outback hooligans who are systematically terrorizing her, and in *Poor Pretty Eddie*, Leslie Uggams is indignant but not sufficiently motivated to take extreme action against her oppressors (instead being rescued by Ted Cassidy in a Peckinpah-esque slo-mo shootout) – but a female revenge film (as with any revenge film) tends to follow a similar structure because it's been proven to wind up the audience and gain their empathy.

The film that had the biggest impact on me, and which sealed any doubt I had about being a rape-revenge fan, was Abel Ferrara's *Ms.45* (aka *Angel of Vengeance*). I'd seen clips of it watching *Terror in the Aisles* (1984) – a popular horror compilation that also first introduced me to Gary Sherman's amazing *Vice Squad* (1982) – and the image of a young girl in a nun's habit blessing each bullet with a kiss before putting it into the magazine of her weapon immediately set me on a hunt for the film. I would not be disappointed. *Ms.45* is the most enjoyable and fulfilling rape-revenge film that follows the standard genre trajectory.

above: Zoë Tamerlis in Abel Ferrara's **Ms.45** (1981).

Other rape-revenge films are notable for their innovations: *The Accused* (1988) sees its revenge in court, *The Ladies Club* (1986) in a clandestine operating room, and *Irreversible* (2002) turns the established pattern on its head. But among the countless rape-revenge films that enjoy a similar structure, *Ms.45* remains the finest of its ilk.

The film stars Zoë Tamerlis, the doe-eyed beauty who would go on to co-write Ferrara's *Bad Lieutenant* (1992) before dying of drug-related lung and heart failure in 1999. Tamerlis stars as Thana (her name rooted in the Greek word for 'death'), an innocent mute girl who works as a seamstress at an independent fashion studio in NYC's garment district. Her innocence is stressed through her relationship with others: her nosy landlady checks in on her; her boss pats her on the head; her co-workers look out for her – they all see her muteness as a "severe handicap" but seem intent on helping her make a productive life for herself. But all in all she is looked upon more as a child than a woman. She will become a woman through the course of the film – not by being 'deflowered', but through the act of survival.

She is raped not once but twice by *two* unconnected assailants as she returns home from work (the first played by director Ferrara). She kills the second in her apartment, severs his limbs and deposits suspicious paper bags in random dumpsters around town. The murder weapon is ironically an iron – her primary tool at work. As such, her anxiety is constantly triggered and she becomes irritable and subject to flashbacks of the event. She starts to lack concentration, stops short of finishing tasks and gets in trouble for inattentiveness. Her response, scrawled on a notepad to a co-worker: "I wish they would all leave me alone."

After the incident(s), Thana suddenly becomes hyper-aware of male aggression and machismo – it seems to be everywhere. She becomes suspicious of others' concerns for her and is averse to being touched. She knows she's alone and has to take care of her problem alone. She can't even look at her own body in the mirror without visualizing her assailants in the room with her. There's no therapy for Thana – but there is disassociation, withdrawal and revenge.

It must be pointed out that Zoë Tamerlis inhabits this role with such believability that her performance really is at the heart of why this film continues to hold up. She goes from genuinely terrified to genuinely demented with remarkable emotional agility. It is obvious that the silence of many rape victims is represented and emphasized by her character's muteness, but it's suggested through a dream sequence that she was raped as a child, and that her muteness is not biological. Muteness is the most prevalent psychosomatic manifestation of post-traumatic stress disorder – also used to great effect in Umberto Lenzi's *Knife of Ice* (1972) – but Thana's solitary existence, her need to survive mute and alone in a dangerous city, is far more sympathetic than most similar portrayals. Thana's gun becomes her voice and it's a loud voice that's been waiting a long time to be heard.

Psychologists assert that there are three stages to rape trauma syndrome – the acute stage (where everything is hyper-intensified and extreme shock or hysteria may occur), the outer adjustment stage (an attempt to create the illusion of normalcy despite lingering inner turmoil), and the re-normalization stage, wherein the rape stops being the central focus of the victim's life, and feelings of shame and guilt subside. Rape-revenge films don't exactly follow this pattern, especially since the genre requires that revenge take the place of re-normalization. After the initial period of intense nervousness, Thana skips the second phase of rape aftermath – which in films is usually signified by dressing dowdy, the cutting of long hair, the general

above: Abel Ferrara and Zoë Tamerlis in **Ms.45**.

denial of womanhood – in favour of the third (cinematic) phase: the Vamp (Dario Argento's *Stendhal Syndrome* (1996) is probably the most concrete example of all three phases at work). The sleazy score by frequent Ferrara collaborator Joe Delia, with its repetitive bursts of obnoxious sound, simulates the rushing of adrenaline as Thana's mission becomes clear. Thana herself becomes the hunter, actively seeking out scumbags to dispatch. She goes out into the park late at night and is circled by a group of thugs (one of whom has nunchakus!) and the typical spatial relationship is illustrated: the woman's movement is restricted by male desires. There are places a woman can't go – her world is smaller than a man's because she is forced to retreat inward as men move forward, constantly invading her space. In real life, instead of asserting their right to access certain places, women are forced to avoid them, to give them over to men: a notion similarly expressed in Auli Mantila's female vigilante film *The Geography of Fear* (2000). However, Thana goes to these places deliberately; she puts herself in dangerous situations and reinforces her womanhood by coming out alive.

above: Abel Ferrara and Zoë Tamerlis in **Ms.45**.

If survival defines a woman, her methods of survival are what set one woman apart from another. Thana's diminished responsiveness to the social world and her workplace is addressed frequently, and her lack of hesitation in gunning down any semi-threatening male can be attributed to a sense of foreshortened future or fatalism. It's common for a rape victim to feel as though their life cannot revert to what they knew before, that they have no future, and that nothing matters any more. This makes considering the consequences of their actions difficult.

In most rape-revenge films, when the woman is avenged, the film ends. Reality doesn't impede this superficial sense of fulfilment with a coda about how the woman was later tried and convicted for her crimes, as would happen in real life. Because that would be depressing. And from my perspective, it seems that rape-revenge films are meant to be strangely triumphant.

Ms.45 dares to deglamorize its female protagonist and her agenda. The film does a more thorough job than usual in showing the consequences of giving in to revenge – Thana sabotages her own future, her career, a circle of supportive friends who are themselves outspoken women who could have helped her. This gives the film a sense of sadness and regret not always encountered in the standard rape-revenge films, which are more centred on how the male assailants have ruined their victims' lives, and not how the women contribute to the ruination of their own lives. Thana may be triumphant briefly, but she loses out in the end.

Playing out rape scenarios with my Barbies also got me into trouble with my mother; I remember being grounded more than once for Barbie-related transgressions. There was no talking-to, just punishment. My mother expected me to know what it was I had done wrong. At the time I wouldn't have known about, or consciously remembered, what had happened in the townhouse all those years ago, so enacting these games wouldn't have been a way of exploring my mother's experience. And she, although unable to express constructively how psychologically dangerous this kind of play was, knew only how to extend her own repression of the trauma into wilful oppression.

I was adamantly shielded from sexual expression by my mother, who allowed me to watch any kind of violence but was against profanity (if I concentrate hard enough, I can still taste the soap) and showed visible revulsion any time a sex scene unfolded onscreen. Because my horror movie watching went relatively unmonitored, the first penis I ever saw (in anything other than a drawing) was at the end of the 1983 slasher movie *Sleepaway Camp* – and it was on a *woman*. Anyone who's seen that film can understand how traumatic this must have been.

My mother's attitudes about sex, and specifically her views on monogamy, were thrust upon me from a very young age, and it's been tangled emotional terrain for me ever since. When I was about 6 years old, we were at a garage sale, and I saw a paperback copy of Peter Benchley's *Jaws* for 25 cents. I desperately wanted to read it, having seen the incessant television commercials for the movie, and I begged my mother for a quarter to buy it. She conceded, with the caveat that she be allowed to read it first, to make sure it was "acceptable reading" for a child my age. I expected this. What I didn't expect was to get the book back marked up with ballpoint pen, words changed, and entire pages scribbled out. I still think this book is my mother's masterpiece of repressive zeal.

My favourite word substitution came on page 106. The original sentence reads: "He lay on his back, staring at the ceiling and feeling his erection dwindle." In mother's amended text, this sentence became: "He lay on his back, staring at the ceiling and feeling his mind dwindle." But the main casualty of this censorship was Hooper and Ellen's affair in the book. It wasn't just the sex that offended my mother – even the scenes depicting their courtship were blackened out (Ellen's pill-popping on the other hand, wasn't deemed worthy of creative removal). Of course, the ink didn't deter me: if I held the pages up to the light I could read through it. Like all things buried, these dirty truths come to the surface one way or another.

I've always thought that if my mother had a giallo counterpart, it would be Mimsy Farmer – a small, short-haired blonde who specialized in playing frigid, twitchy women repressing the memory of some debilitating psychological distress, but the back-catalogue of this professional headcase has quite a bit of me in it too: absent fathers, alcoholic mothers, and a blatant refusal to grow up.

One almost forgets that American-born Mimsy Farmer ever played anything *other* than 'the nervous girl with a past'. Her lighter roles are all but sublimated to those now-defining ones in Barbet Schroeder's *More* (1969), Dario Argento's *Four Flies on Grey Velvet* (1971), Armando Crispino's *Autopsy* (1975), and Francesco Barilli's oppressive and atmospheric *The Perfume of the Lady in Black* (1974), as well as Fulci's beautiful, if poorly-received *The Black Cat* in 1981. Even in the comparatively innocuous *Riot on Sunset Strip* (1967) she is a secretive teenager, hiding away an alcoholic mother.

A slender, androgynous and frail-looking woman with an expression that could alternate seamlessly between vacant and homicidal, Mimsy Farmer was a unique fetish object in the horror world, like an edgy eurotrash counterpart to Mia Farrow. Her best films present her as pallid and sickly-looking, with that beautiful ethereal glow reserved for tuberculosis patients. After appearing in a trio of low-budget films made during 1967:

Hot Rods to Hell, Devil's Angels and the aforementioned Riot on Sunset Strip – films she was less than thrilled about – Farmer took a short sabbatical from her burgeoning film career and went to work in Canada, "in a hospital where they were doing experiments with LSD", as she recounted in Luca Palmerini's book Spaghetti Nightmares.[12]

LSD experiments were rampant in the 1950s and '60s, and not just by those immersed in the emerging counterculture: in Saskatchewan they were doing studies in the '50s using LSD as an antidote to alcoholism, with both provincial support and the endorsement of Alcoholics Anonymous; at the Allen Memorial Institute in Montreal, Dr. Ewen Cameron conducted his controversial brainwashing experiments from 1957 through 1964 in what was known as 'the sleep room', using a mixture of LSD, electroshock, repeating subliminal messages, isolation and sleep inducement.

Farmer was first a patient, and then a counsellor at a hospital in Vancouver where LSD therapy experiments were being undertaken. Her job: to sit in a room with patients as they were tripping, playing records and taking notes. Certainly fitting employment for a woman who would go on to play Oscar-worthy mental-hospital material.

Soon after quitting the hospital (when a patient became hostile and co-workers didn't come to her aid as they'd assured), she starred in the Roger Corman vehicle The Wild Racers (1968) and then the film that would provide the mould for the upcoming Italian thrillers – More. Barbet Shroeder's directorial debut sees Farmer as a magnetic and enigmatic junkie who captivates a German traveller named Stefan; he follows her across the continent to Greece, where she gets him hooked on the heroin she gets from her sugar-daddy. This role, along with her part in Georges Lautner's Road to Salina soon after (1970) must have been the deciding factors behind her casting as Nina Tobias in Argento's Four Flies on Grey Velvet, and the typecast was set.

Four Flies is worth talking about here if only because it's part of a larger trend in Farmer's career. To summarize – and the discussion requires that I give the murderer away – Roberto Tobias (Argento look-alike Michael Brandon) plays an emotionally vacant drummer in a (jaw-droppingly terrible) Italian prog rock band. Upon discovering that he's being followed by sinister fellow in a trenchcoat, Roberto confronts the man and accidentally stabs him, only to be photographed in the act by a witness wearing an androgynous plastic face mask. Reluctant to report the incident to the police, lest he be jailed for murder, Roberto goes home and tries to ignore what happened. We first see his wife Nina (Mimsy Farmer) facing away from him in bed, asleep, as he struggles with the day's events and fades in and out of a bad dream involving a public execution. When she goes out the next morning, her goodbye to him goes unanswered, which establishes the lack of affection and distance in their relationship.

Still, when Roberto is attacked at night in his home by the same masked perpetrator who had photographed him earlier, he has no alternative but to confide in Nina, who urges him to go into hiding somewhere with her. He refuses, and instead turns to his friend God (Italo staple Bud Spencer), God's bible-quoting hobo pal, a charming gay private detective, and Nina's nubile young cousin Dalia (French Canadian actress Francine Racette), who apparently has no qualms about playing house with Roberto once Nina takes off to be safe among other relatives. As the investigation gets closer to a revelation and witnesses threaten to come forward, the bodies start to pile up. Roberto, still convinced that going to the police isn't an option, becomes a prisoner in his own home, waiting in the dark with a gun pointed at the door.

The murderer is revealed by means of a fictional scientific process: at the turn of the last century it was commonly believed that the retina retained the image of the last image a person saw as they died. Thus, an examination could reveal key clues in cases of foul play – including the murderer's identity. In the case

top left and centre left: Mimsy Farmer and Michael Brandon in Dario Argento's **Four Flies on Grey Velvet** (1971).

of *Four Flies*, such an examination reveals an image of four flies – which Roberto discovers at the film's denouement to be the pendant hanging around his wife's neck.

Roberto is understandably confused: "Why?" he pleads, as she trains a gun on him and smiles maniacally. We've been given snippets of this story throughout the film as the investigation proceeded, but Nina lays it all out in a confessional monologue: "I wanted so badly to see you die slowly... painfully. Because you're so much like him." She shoots him in the arm – a simultaneous close-up of her mouth, the piercing sound of her laughter and the bullet flying towards Roberto recalling Thana in *Ms.45*: after a silence that has lasted too long, the gun acts as her voice. As Roberto winces with the pain, Nina continues: "It hurts. I know what it's like. I've suffered too. My pig father – he made me suffer! Do you know he brought me up as a boy? He treated me like a boy – he beat me. He beat me! He said I was crazy. My mother – she died in an asylum. He brought me there too. Then my father died – before I could kill him! When I met you, I couldn't believe it. It was like a miracle. You look just like him. I knew I would kill you."

An earlier interview with a doctor at an insane asylum now makes sense: Nina had been admitted as a paranoid homicidal maniac, stemming from her father's resentment of her ("I wanted a boy! Not a weakling like you!"), but when the father died, all symptoms disappeared and the doctors found her to be completely cured. Then the interview ends with a loaded statement that is never addressed again in the film: "We suspected that the man was not the patient's real father."

Interpreting the meaning of this statement can only be speculative, but it does add to the film's staggering layers of substitution and imitation. Maitland McDonagh pointed out in her book about Argento's films, *Broken Mirrors/Broken Minds*, that the desire to marry the twin of her father acts as some kind of incestual wish-fulfilment on Nina's part,[13] but I think that – like many of the characters in this book – the issue is more one of approval, acceptance and encouragement. Sadly Roberto is not a nurturing character, and any chance he had of reversing Nina's trauma with affection is undermined by his own obliviousness.

Nina Tobias is a murderer, and she's clearly intensely disturbed, but Roberto Tobias is a despicable jerk. He ignores her, he cheats on her, and nothing in the film suggests that he has any conscience whatsoever. As a female viewer of the film, I too wanted to see him die slowly and painfully. Throughout the film Nina

expertly feigns concern for him, calling all their mutual friends to check up on him, to convince him to turn himself in, or to go somewhere safe. He shrugs off her suggestions and builds a wall between himself and everyone around him. We don't know yet that she's a killer, so all we see is a talentless philanderer who has no consideration whatsoever for his beautiful, caring wife. The interesting thing about how *Four Flies* operates is that even when Nina is revealed to be the killer, my sympathies are still with her. I don't know if this was Argento's intent.

When Roberto first finds out that it's Nina who's behind the blackmail, emotional torture and multiple murders, he suddenly stops being afraid. After all, she's just a girl – she's powerless to him. He slaps her twice across the face, knocking her to the ground, as though punishing her for some domestic transgression. He fails to realize that not only is she dangerous, but also that he has contributed to her paranoid mania by being so dismissive of her. Like her father, Roberto associates femininity with weakness, and sadly, Argento is equally dismissive: he doesn't allow Nina either redemption or revenge. But he does allow her the film's most beautiful death.

Armando Crispino's 1975 feature *Autopsy* (the Italian title of which translates literally as 'Sun Spots') starts off with a montage of infrared images of the burning sun intercut with a rash of suicides, all set to a pounding score. Mimsy Farmer plays a forensic pathologist finishing her master's degree. Her thesis: defining the difference between authentic suicides and simulated ones. The subject matter is admittedly getting to her – she immediately starts experiencing hallucinatory episodes at work, imagining that the dead are popping up from their beds and fornicating with each other. This is the first of many indicators that, in poor Mimsy's mind, there is something inseparable about sex and death, some crossed wires in her past that have traumatized her. Both are presented in vulgar fashion, but Mimsy is admittedly more unnerved by sex than by even the most haunting, graphic blow-ups of gore and viscera. Like my mother, who also worked hands-on in an intimate, sometimes gory medical environment, she exhibits a tangible revulsion toward sexual intimacy.

A beautiful young girl shows up at her door one night, claiming to be crashing at the apartment upstairs (which happens to be the abode of Mimsy's dashing oft-absent father) and in need of an envelope. She notices a display of disturbing photos laid out on Mimsy's coffee table and picks one up with trepidation. "You get your kicks from this stuff?" she asks, to which Mimsy replies – in a sinister tone that almost sounds sarcastic – "My interest is purely professional." It's only ten minutes into the movie and we can already surmise otherwise.

It is obvious before Mimsy's father even shows up on the scene that he's the source of her sexual neurosis. Despite the fact that he seems well adjusted and probably did nothing to facilitate it, Mimsy is suffering from a crippling Electra complex (effectively the female equivalent of the Oedipal complex). At lunch, when he informs her that he's getting married, she becomes hostile and interrogatory. "You have the instincts of a wife – or worse – a mother in law!" he says, "It's a good thing you have no time for men." In an unsuccessful attempt to bait him, she offers: "That may no longer be the case."

Her boyfriend, spritely photographer Ray Lovelock, plays the clown – he's a practical joker, yet she is utterly humourless. Nevertheless, he's extremely patient with her; every time they are about to have sex, she starts envisioning grinning corpses popping out of their body bags, which prematurely interrupts their activities. Mimsy is devastated. "I want to change", she pleads, "Can you help me? Or don't you think the art of seduction would have any effect on me?" They try different speeds, different approaches, but nothing works. He shows her pornographic Parisian slides (which are blown-up onscreen and are interchangeable with the death photos elsewhere in the film) and she tries to emulate the women in them, but gives up mid-blowjob: "Oh, this is absurd."

When the envelope girl shows up dead in Mimsy's lab the next day – another alleged suicide – Mimsy's thesis is put to the test; she does not believe the girl committed suicide, based primarily on the fact that the fatal wound was in her face. Good-looking girls tend to like to leave good-looking corpses. The girl's brother, a young priest (played by Barry Primus) agrees. He knows his sister was murdered because of some information she held. Discovering the exact nature of this information becomes the film's primary mandate from here on.

The priest has a past of his own – he was once a temperamental professional racing driver who ran off the track and fatally wounded 15 spectators. He retired, turned to the cloister, and now tries desperately to control his violent mood swings. Mimsy is drawn to him, but can't yet figure out why.

When her father is paralyzed from the waist down in an accident, Mimsy is devastated – but not for the reasons she thinks she is. Her father signifies everything virile and sexual to her, and his emasculation mirrors her frigidity.

Mimsy comes to realize that she's in love with the priest; she can visualize having sex with him without the ghosts of her profession intruding. But it's safe sex, because it will never happen. He confesses that her feelings are reciprocated, but that he will never break his vows. They both have scarred psyches, and both are frozen in a perversely determined inactivity. Mimsy has only shifted her impossible love from one man (her father) to another; she's not 'cured' by any means.

Mimsy's sexual neurosis has nothing to do with the film except to make her a pawn and a temporary suspect; once the physical mystery is solved, the emotional mysteries of the film are abandoned. This is a typical giallo move (a tactic also exploited in Lucio Fulci's *A Lizard in Woman's Skin*), and one of the reasons giallo films

stand out as so different from American mysteries: it is just assumed in giallo films that everyone is neurotic. Still, it made for an interesting tagline: "She is the girl who knows more about death than about love. And he is the man who will teach her about both."

The father-daughter relationship that forms the basis of her neurosis in this film duplicated itself throughout this part of her career – *Four Flies*, *Autopsy* and *The Perfume of the Lady in Black* all have a similar (sub)plot. Like many female genre characters – Thana in *Ms.45* and Catherine Deneuve's character Carol in Polanski's *Repulsion* (the 1965 film considered to be the mother of all 'neurotic women' horror movies) – Mimsy's most unhinged roles have a paternal figure at the heart of their psychoses.

In Francesco Barilli's *The Perfume of the Lady in Black*, Farmer stars as Silvia, a well-paid and workaholic scientist who lives alone in a large apartment in Italy. Her boyfriend of four months (Dirk Benedict-lookalike Maurizio Bonuglia) is a geologist named Roberto who is often out of town on work assignments. Despite his own occupational commitments, he has no patience for hers, and childishly threatens to dump her whenever she puts her work before him. After one such argument, she goes to his house to apologize and is frightened by an apparition in the mirror: a dark-haired woman in black (later identified as her long-dead mother) spraying herself with perfume. She screams for Roberto, but when he arrives the apparition is gone. Later she spies a familiar flower vase in a store window that prompts an unwelcome flashback of a brutish man having sex with her mother as she looks on.

Later, Silvia cuts her hand playing tennis, and keeps repeating "Silvia's hurt herself... Silvia's hurt herself..." in a child's voice (and in the third person). This, combined with her collection of old toys and figurines, is the first indication that she is living in a state of arrested development due to unresolved trauma from her childhood. Silvia's father was a sailor who left his wife and child for long stretches, and one day just didn't come home. Her resultant idolization of her absent father was reinforced when her mother took up with "a terrible man", a new stand-in paternal figure who terrorized and raped the young Silvia, which her mother either didn't notice or wilfully ignored. Emotional distance and resentment mounted until Silvia turned to extremes, pushing her mother over a balcony to her death.

As these memories intensify, mirrors start to become an omnipresent set piece – with reflections duplicated, distorted or broken – their purpose revealed one stormy night by the sudden appearance of a little girl at Silvia's door who is the spitting image of herself as a child. Unnerved and desperate, Silvia begs the little girl to go away, to no avail. As the storm intensifies, lights flickering and thunder cracking loudly outside, Silvia's feelings of entrapment are palpable; she knows this little girl is herself (the well-worn copy of *Alice Through the Looking Glass* by her bedside is an equally unsubtle hint of doppelganger theory at work). They fight over a music box that each claim as their own, the little girl finally spitting, "You're old! You're old! What do you want it for? You're too old!" But Silvia can't accept this – because she only goes through the motions of being 'old', or 'grown up', as though sleepwalking.

top right: Mimsy Farmer in Armando Crispino's **Autopsy** (1975).

centre right: Italian DVD cover for Francesco Barilli's **The Perfume of the Lady in Black** (1974).

overleaf: Mimsy Farmer features in this montage image, sourced from a fotobusta for **Autopsy**.

Silvia's relationship with her boyfriend is especially telling; she is made to feel bad for having her own career, and whenever she opens up to him, he harshly dismisses her feelings. She desperately needs to be loved, but everything around her tells her that she can't be loved and be independent at the same time; for Silvia, independence comes with isolation and delusion. When she confesses to Roberto that she's had a fatal run-in with the man who abused her all those years ago, he responds with condescension, which immediately causes her to retreat back into a mode of defensiveness. "Don't touch me!" she shouts. "I'm not yours! I'm not yours!"

Her sex with Roberto – which in itself does not seem troubled – is flanked by images of her mother wantonly having sex with a man who would just as soon have sex with a child. She doesn't want to grow up if it means being like her mother. She keeps repeating to herself as everything starts to crumble around her: "Only Silvia's good... only Silvia's good..." Maybe so on one side of the mirror – but on the other she's a damaged, homicidal child.

There are a lot of elements from my own life playing themselves out in this film. Silvia's crazy work ethic, her independence, her collection of toys and other signifiers of stunted emotional development, her idolization of an absent father, her abuse at the hands of a substitute father-figure, and her consequent demonization of her mother for allowing it all to happen. And yet, as I've mentioned, physically Mimsy Farmer resembles my mother in her youth, making identification with her character rather emotionally charged for me.

My mother, like so many women in horror films, was irreparably damaged by her experiences with men, and I know she was only trying to spare me from making the same mistakes by shielding me from the emotional sinkhole she associated with sexual relationships. But the 'men' her traumatic experiences came from were usually 'fathers' to me, and so my own issues with men as I grew older would inevitably be coloured by the issues my mother had with the men who raised and shaped me.

It didn't help things that my sister Karen was convinced that Oates was actually my real father, and that the adoption story was a scam meant to cover up his infidelities. Karen believed that my mother was forced to adopt me when Oates got one of his students pregnant. This has since been confirmed as an ill-founded rumour, but it shows the level of manipulation and mistrust that exists within my extended family.

I always viewed my mother's relationship with my stepfather as sexless; while I'm sure it wasn't, my stepfather perpetuated this notion as much as she did. Their lives were very separate in a way, and not just due to opposite working hours. My mother had her TV movies and night-time soaps, and my stepfather busied himself with his ever-growing collection of military paraphernalia that occupied a crowded room in the basement, filled with badges, medals, uniforms and weapons. This collection became a means of bonding for my stepfather and I; not only was I the only one of the kids who had ever shown any interest in it, but I would also travel with him to Detroit frequently on weekends to go to gun shows where he would meet up with like-minded collectors. Each time, he would let me pick out something I wanted, and then afterwards I would wait in the car with my new present while he went in to a little downtown bar called The Old Shaleighleigh, where he would presumably be greeted like a friendly regular.

So, aside from those loud, argumentative spurts, I viewed the relationship between my mother and stepfather as rather conventional for a married couple; each compromised a part of themselves in order to stay true to a greater ideal, one that nevertheless was fraught with unhappiness for both of them. But I also knew from an early age that this wasn't the life I wanted when I grew up. I found Oates's bachelor lifestyle far more exotic, worldly and exciting – feelings that were also tinged with guilt because of the Catholic morality that had been foisted upon me by my mother and stepfather.

Despite my mother's best intentions, she couldn't protect my brother and I when we went to visit Oates in Winnipeg, with his well-worn copy of The Joy of Sex openly displayed on the coffee table, his liberated girlfriends and the ridiculously short kimono he would wear around the house. Compared to the cultural squareness of my primary home environment, visiting Oates was like going to the Playboy Mansion. But any confusion about the dichotomy in parental concerns was met with an easy answer: our father was an adulterer. We were not to listen to anything he said.

MAR /82

above: Oates and brother Burl, March 1982.

In 1970 the Court of Queen's Bench of Manitoba (the highest trial court for the province) awarded my father with nearly twenty boxes of pornography on which to conduct psychological 'research'. Pornography was still illegal in Canada at the time, and this huge lot had been seized from a local convenience store. My father, being a psychologist, was given the task of finding whether the material had any sociological, educational or scientific merit. He never did the research (as far as I know), so the boxes languished away in the cubbyhole (a vast expanse of storage space beneath the house) awaiting my pre-pubescent curiosity. Needless to say, once I turned about 10 or 11, I spent a lot of time in the cubbyhole during my visits. As such, my sexual education came courtesy of the illustrious Grove Press, Black Cat Press, Ophelia Press, Cameo Press, Pendulum Press, and other dime-store porn novels disguised as educational materials (most containing a framing device whose cinematic equivalent is known as 'the square-up'). For some reason, there was rarely any straight 'loving' in these books, but gay/lesbian sex, teenage prostitution, incest, S/M and even necrophilia figured heavily.

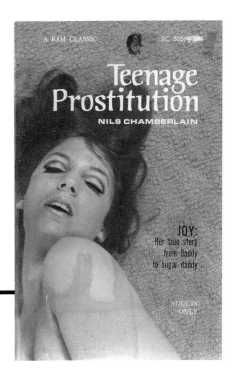

The presence of these books, combined with the always young, beautiful girlfriends and his active social life (he had frequent dinner parties with colleagues, while my parents back home only invited relatives over as dictated by a holiday of some sort) inevitably created an awareness of my father as a charismatic and sexual creature. Still, I never looked upon him as my own sexual ideal, as is often the case with little girls in genre films. But there are commonalities between all types of trauma – whether talking about victims (or witnesses) of rape, incest or domestic violence, neglect or bullying, or even the experiences of combat veterans, political prisoners and the like. These stories bleed into one another. I related to these kinds of films insofar as the absent father contributes greatly to the neurosis of the characters, because his absence allows for a fantasy version of him to fill the void. And in genre films, these fantasies are often morbidly unfettered.

Where to begin with *Toys Are Not for Children*? One of the most revered exploitation films of the '70s among true trash connoisseurs, Stanley Brasloff's 1972 *Toys* is a thoroughly demented Electra complex tale with plenty of meat and no morals to speak of.

The film doesn't take long to get where it's going: in the opening moments, a teenage girl named Jamie is lying on her bed in the nude, rubbing a stuffed doll against herself in masturbatory fashion, panting "Daddy… Daddy…" over and over until interrupted by the intrusion of her mother, who chastises her for not only being a pervert, but also for being a pervert *just like* the father who abandoned them years earlier for a life of debauchery. The mother has nothing nice to say about her former spouse, and the woman's pinched face, unkempt appearance and vicious demeanour only reinforces Jamie's belief that her father was right to leave. The only indications that her father is alive and well somewhere in the world are the toys he routinely sends her at birthday time, unaware of the fact that she has grown from a child into a beautiful young woman in his absence.

When Jamie's mother kicks her out of the house, she gets a job at a toy store and moves in with a fellow employee named Charlie, whom she marries soon after. The honeymoon is short-lived however, when it suddenly dawns on the husband that he's not gonna get any action out of his new bride, who busies herself playing with her childhood toys and spurns his every advance. He confides in their employer of Jamie's all-consuming obsession with toys. "Of course she loves toys. Everybody loves toys", says the employer dismissively. But Charlie shakes his head: "I think she likes toys too much." Frustrated, he starts picking up chicks at a local dive for late-night fun, while Jamie becomes fascinated with an older woman named Pearl, whom she believes has a connection to her estranged father.

Soon, Jamie is making frequent trips into the city to visit Pearl, who we discover to be an ageing prostitute with a greasy Hispanic pimp half her age, who "has a thing for virgins". Seems old dad had a thing for the wild life, including partying with professional sex workers, and Jamie finds herself attracted to this seedy lifestyle that

above: A typical title from the cubbyhole stash.

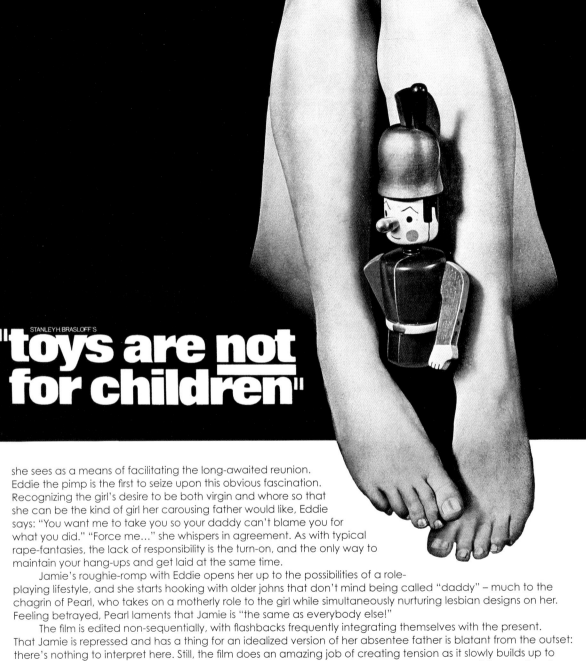

STANLEY H BRASLOFF'S

"toys are not for children"

she sees as a means of facilitating the long-awaited reunion. Eddie the pimp is the first to seize upon this obvious fascination. Recognizing the girl's desire to be both virgin and whore so that she can be the kind of girl her carousing father would like, Eddie says: "You want me to take you so your daddy can't blame you for what you did." "Force me…" she whispers in agreement. As with typical rape-fantasies, the lack of responsibility is the turn-on, and the only way to maintain your hang-ups and get laid at the same time.

Jamie's roughie-romp with Eddie opens her up to the possibilities of a role-playing lifestyle, and she starts hooking with older johns that don't mind being called "daddy" – much to the chagrin of Pearl, who takes on a motherly role to the girl while simultaneously nurturing lesbian designs on her. Feeling betrayed, Pearl laments that Jamie is "the same as everybody else!"

The film is edited non-sequentially, with flashbacks frequently integrating themselves with the present. That Jamie is repressed and has a thing for an idealized version of her absentee father is blatant from the outset: there's nothing to interpret here. Still, the film does an amazing job of creating tension as it slowly builds up to the inevitable climactic reunion with the estranged patriarch. The last ten minutes are some of the most squirm-inducing ever committed to celluloid.

above: Image adapted from the U.S. one-sheet poster for Stanley Brasloff's **Toys Are Not for Children** (1972).

There is no evidence in the film that Jamie was molested, or that her childhood relationship with her father was anything other than a loving one in the purest sense. The catalyst for his switch from caring family man to debauched womanizer is not made clear. We only hear from the mother (who is presented as a castrating, spiteful bitch) that he is a "pig", and from Pearl that he is "scum". In flashback however, the father-daughter imagery is only rendered disturbing by the daughter's subsequent fixation, and by the fact that the sounds of a pivotal sex scene are laid over these visuals.

Why Jamie's fixation is sexual is also not stated plainly, although one can guess that because her father left the domestic scene so early, she never got to grow emotionally past the point where little girls think they're going to grow up to marry their own fathers. She is socially awkward and needy in general, but her turn to prostitution isn't a means of getting approval or attention from random men in order to boost her self-esteem; she thinks it makes her closer to her father's ideal, and every john just temporarily takes his place. Her naivety is confounding: she is hardly shaken by her encounters with the various johns, as they're more than happy to accommodate her in her father-daughter role-play. When she asserts to Pearl that she "knows what she's doing", she explains it with a childlike smile: "A customer is called a john. Making love to a john is called turning a trick. And always get the money first."

An interesting component of the film is that it shows how easily people revert to the roles of the basic family unit. If we don't have those role models in our life, we will create them desperately. Every parent or child left behind finds themselves replaced – surrogates are easily adopted. It's been said more than once that the reason I befriend so many ageing horror directors and actors is that they are all surrogate fathers. I suspect there's some truth in this. It's the same as people who always dream of going back to high school: everyone just wants a chance to get it right.

In genre films, issues stemming from absentee husbands or fathers are usually tied to some sort of sexual pathology in mother and daughter alike; the absentee father is over-sexualized, and this virility is looked upon alternatively as an entirely admirable or despicable trait, depending on the film, or the character expressing the opinion. As with *Toys Are Not for Children*, in Joseph Losey's *Secret Ceremony* (1968), Peter Whitehead and Niki de Saint Phalle's *Daddy* (1973), and Matt Cimber's *The Witch Who Came from the Sea* (1976), the father is characterized as a "pervert", and rightly so.

In Losey's underrated *Secret Ceremony* (largely dismissed at the time due to what was seen as ham-fisted, overly histrionic acting) an ageing but still glamorous Elizabeth Taylor stars as Leonora, a prostitute grieving over the death of her daughter in a drowning accident. On the way to the graveyard for a visit one day, she is accosted on a city bus by a waifish weirdo named Cenci (Mia Farrow), who insists that Leonora is her 'missing' mother. Cenci's pleading eyes remind Leonora of her dead daughter, and she concedes to follow the girl to her giant London house, where she immediately spies a picture of the mother in question and understands the confusion – the two women are nearly identical. But in all the family photos, the image of the father is suspiciously blackened out.

Leonora sizes up the situation: a young girl alone in a big house who wants her dead mommy back, and a childless mother living in poverty who could get quite used to being doted on by a young daughter-figure and living a life of opulence. Within minutes the two are playing out a scenario of domestic damage, wherein Cenci recounts the events that led up to her father's absence: he was caught doing something 'scandalous' to Cenci in the kitchen, and the mother threw him out, erasing him from their mutual history. The only witnesses to Cenci's previous life are two batty aunts who routinely visit her under the guise of 'checking on her' but who really only use these occasions to pilfer furs, silver and jewels from the house to sell in their antique shop.

Leonora settles in easily to her new home, with her fabulous new clothes, assuming the roles of both matriarch and confidante to Cenci's stunted little girl, who takes to asking Leonora personal questions about the missing father: "Was daddy Albert a great lover? Was he stupendously gentle and also brutal? Did he make you give out... a sound?" The two women compare orgasm sounds and laugh, but Leonora is secretly disturbed by Cenci's sexual awareness, considering her obvious arrested development.

Eager for insight into Cenci's neurosis, Leonora decides to visit the thieving aunts – who are the sisters of Cenci's mother's long-dead first husband, Gustaf – claiming to be the mother's American cousin. She is shocked to discover that Cenci is in fact 22 years old. "Crazy people never look their age", the sisters say, dismissively, continuing on to reveal that Cenci was irreparably messed up from a childhood sexual affair with her stepfather Albert. "That's disgusting!" Leonora shrieks, "Why didn't you do something? You've all let her down – you've abandoned that child, all of you!"

When daddy Albert (Robert Mitchum, in his creepiest role since *The Night of the Hunter* in 1955) reappears, recently released from prison after a stint for child-molesting, he arrogantly and nonchalantly shows up at the house and immediately figures out that Leonora is after Cenci's money just like everyone else. But she's not; not entirely, anyway. Her maternal instincts (as well as feelings of guilt over her own

It's time to speak of unspoken things...

ELIZABETH TAYLOR
MIA FARROW more haunted than in "Rosemary's Baby"
in A JOHN HEYMAN PRODUCTION / JOSEPH LOSEY'S
"SECRET CEREMONY" IN TECHNICOLOR
and starring
ROBERT MITCHUM
Suggested For Mature Audiences

co-starring PEGGY ASHCROFT · PAMELA BROWN
Music by RICHARD RODNEY BENNETT · Based on the original short story by MARCO DENEVI · Screenplay by GEORGE TABORI · Directed by JOSEPH LOSEY · Produced by JOHN HEYMAN and NORMAN PRIGGEN A UNIVERSAL PICTURES LIMITED / WORLD FILM SERVICES LIMITED / PAUL M. HELLER Production

daughter's death) have kicked in and she is suddenly desperate to protect Cenci from all the people obviously out to exploit her naivety. Barely prompted, Albert tells Leonora about her predecessor in the house: "She never forgave me for treating her as though she were a woman", Albert says of his dead wife, chalking up her eventually fatal illness to "an unhealthy disrespect for sex." (For a prostitute, Leonora seems pretty uptight about sex herself.) He boasts about his relationship with Cenci, and when Leonora clarifies that it was *rape*, not a *relationship*, Albert retorts: "I make her feel like a woman. I've always made her feel like a woman. What do you make her feel like – a retarded zombie? If you don't let her go, she'll just keep getting smaller and smaller. At 25 or 30 you'll find her in a corner with a baby bottle!" Albert is wrong, though: Cenci will be a mess either way. Leonora knows she's indulging the girl's morbid fantasy by playing 'mother' to her, but sees a more positive potential outcome than leaving her to the whims and malicious reasoning of her paedophilic stepfather – a man who describes meeting Cenci at age 6 and saying to himself, "that's for me."

Finally realizing that all this delusion can't be good for anyone, Leonora resolves to talk to Cenci truthfully about their situation, but Cenci won't have any of it. Hermetically sealed in the giant house with the blackened photographs, Cenci knows only how to play games, and if she has to do it on her own, she's content to do that. Her game-playing is a thinly-veiled and poorly-executed distress signal: it calls attention to her neurosis while simultaneously aiming to deflect attention from it. To talk about the truth would be to admit being a victim, and she is somehow more comfortable being complicit in her sexual abuse.

above: U.S. half-sheet poster for Joseph Losey's **Secret Ceremony** (1968).

Like Cenci in *Secret Ceremony*, Molly's complacency in Matt Cimber's 1976 exploitation oddity *The Witch Who Came from the Sea* is equally accommodating to her abuser. Monte Hellman alumna Millie Perkins (most famous for playing the title role in George Stevens's 1959 adaptation of *The Diary of Anne Frank*) plays Molly, whose father was also a seafaring man who molested her repeatedly as a child. She loves her father desperately, and is acquiescent throughout the abuse out of love for him, even though she senses that what he is doing to her is wrong. As an adult she mythologizes him, telling her two young nephews tales of their sea captain grandfather, "a perfect, good man" who never swore or had tattoos (or a girl in every port), and who went missing at sea 15 years previous.

Molly's adamance concerning her father's moral perfection simply hides her deeply repressed anxiety over her his incestuous transgressions; she grows up to be an alcoholic, drinking excessively to quell the flashbacks that haunt her, even though her frumpy sister Cathy begs her to take better care of herself lest she turn out to be "a drunken bum" just like their father. "It's good for what ails you", Molly says flippantly. "But *what* ails you?" her sister pleads. Such queries are fruitless; it's clear there's no confidence shared between the two sisters, fuelled by divergent opinions about their dead father's moral character. Instead Molly lives a fantasy life in her head where she seduces and murders men, only to discover – in the wake of numerous homicides – that these fantasies might be intruding on her reality. That her targets are all large, strong men – football players and weightlifters – is an attempt to rectify the helplessness she felt as a little girl, trapped beneath the weight of her father. But that weight is also an emotional one.

Actress Millie Perkins's father was a sea captain in real life, and her husband, Corman writer Robert Thom (who sadly passed away in 1979) wrote the script for Cimber's film, integrating many elements of Perkins's personal life, including her own childhood obsession with the sea. The image of the sea is one that comes up again and again in these films, and in the case of *The Witch Who Came from the Sea* it's not just the symbolic connection between water and femininity that is of interest, but also the fact that the father is a seaman, like Silvia's father in *The Perfume of the Lady in Black*. In literature – from medieval mythology to Wilkie Collins to Yukio Mishima – seafaring men have always been outsiders: their life's work is typically to protect and uphold societal values, but they live outside of the structure that maintains those values. Both Molly and Silvia idolize their fathers for 'belonging to the sea', the only place where they are at home, and sympathetically liken the corruption associated with sailors on leave to being 'fishes out of water' – drinking and carousing excessively only to mask the pain of separation from the sea.

Consequently, both Molly and Silvia have difficulty adapting to reality, and instead long for a magical place where they will be safe to live out their delusions – for Molly, it's the sea, and for Silvia it's the other side of the looking glass. For both, living in the real world holds too many emotional triggers; most notably, people who keep telling them they're crazy. This push-pull relationship between the actual truth and the imaginary truths they've created in order to survive, and the conflict that naturally exists when people urge you to open up only to criticize and punish you when you do, often results in misplaced anger. In Molly, her anger is directed at her well-meaning sister, and at confident, beefy men – while her father's memory is spared. Revenge is carried out, but not always at the right time, to the right people, or for the right reasons.

While my father and stepfather were fundamentally different people, and their individual parental deficiencies might seem to cancel each other out, in actuality the schizophrenic contrast would cause both to bear the brunt of the other's faults. My relationship with my stepfather Adam was highly emotional and active; irrespective of his temper, our relationship was tangible and impossible to ignore. I never had to strive for his attention; despite everything, I knew that he cared about me. Oates, on the other hand, was distant and

above: U.S. theatrical poster for Matt Cimber's **The Witch Who Came from the Sea** (1976).

65

HOUSE OF PSYCHOTIC WOMEN

impenetrable. I tried everything to get a response out of him, some sign that I mattered at all. I always felt like I was running after him, and that he would elude my grasp at every turn. My anger at each of them would manifest in confusing ways as I careened into mid-adolescence: with Adam I grew condescending and critical, treating him as though he were some uncultured white trash hick, while with Oates I struck out with fists and knives. Neither could understand the rules of the respective games I was foisting upon them. I was punishing them for ancient crimes.

Filmmaker/writer/professional falconer Peter Whitehead both documented and personified the contradictions inherent in 1960s revolutionary counterculture. Whitehead and his onetime lover, sculptress Niki de Saint Phalle, collaborated on a bizarre sexual revenge picture called *Daddy* in 1973. I first saw stills of it in an old *Films and Filming* magazine spread, but it proved impossible to find, only resurfacing when Whitehead biographer Paul Cronin prompted an international retrospective of Whitehead's work in 2006. Whitehead and Saint Phalle's collaboration was originally meant to be a short film composed of Saint Phalle's childlike drawings of a father undergoing various stages of torment, all given flip titles like "Mummy eats Daddy", "Mummy Crucifys [sic] Daddy", "Poor Daddy" and so on. The film eventually morphed into a feature after some soul-searching by Saint Phalle revealed that she had some unexplored childhood trauma, but the drawings still made their way into the film as pseudo-chapter headings.

The film opens with Saint Phalle's character, a statuesque art-star, returning to her childhood chateau in France after receiving a telegram that her father has died. When she arrives for the funeral, she wanders around the grounds, dotted by large, surreal sculptures (created by Saint Phalle herself), and comes upon a coffin housing a giant plaster penis.

Saint Phalle starts to ruminate on her childhood, flashbacks revealing the game called 'Blindman' that she and her father used to play together in the garden. She would blindfold him, and he would try to chase her, and when he finally caught her, as he always would, he would frolic with her on the ground in a manner that was not wholly appropriate, urging her not to tell her mother about their secret game. At first, the little girl would laugh and giggle, but eventually she would start crying and try to run away. But the next day, she would be anxious to play the game again.

The Blindman game was a real memory from Saint Phalle's life, which she recounted to Whitehead in passing, but which he saw as emblematic of her subsequent development into a strong, determined woman: by symbolically blinding (i.e. castrating) her father, she was allowed to grow into the phallic woman herself. Whitehead likened it to the story of Oedipus, who was punished for "wanting to see everything": blind and feeble, he becomes dependent on his daughter Antigone to lead him through Hades. Likewise, Saint Phalle (or her character) was happiest when her father was bound to her. The symbolic castration was a means of making him stay put, but it wouldn't be until returning for the funeral years later that the character would make this association herself.

Obsessing over a relationship with one parent inevitably leaves another in the cold. In *Daddy*, all this attention on Saint Phalle's relationship with her father (who is subject to childlike temper tantrums of his own) – wanting his love, his devotion, his approval – estranged her from her mother, who saw the father as he really was. In flashbacks, the mother spouts vitriol about

top left: Niki de Saint Phalle in Peter Whitehead's **Daddy** (1973).

centre left: Niki de Saint Phalle holds court in **Daddy**.

bottom left: Mia Martin in **Daddy**.

Daddy, pointing out that while he's free to do what he wants, he expects his wife and daughter to play submissive, doting female roles. Saint Phalle imagines herself marrying a monster (literally – it's one of Saint Phalle's sculptures, looking eerily like Jerkbeast from the Seattle public access show of the same name), which sums up her feelings about marriage pretty succinctly.

As an adult, Saint Phalle's character aims to rectify the long term disconnect between her and her mother: she imagines them teaming up to mock, humiliate and reject the father – making him crawl on his hands and knees, using him as a tea-table, and tying him to a chair as a pubescent body-painted nymphette (played by Mia Martin) dances around suggestively in front of him, revealing him for the pervert he is.

As with *The Witch Who Came from the Sea* and the Mimsy Farmer films *Autopsy* and *The Perfume of the Lady in Black*, the father is a wanderer, which their daughters associate with virility. In their eyes, mobility and freedom are inextricably tied to sexual prowess. It makes sense then, that to blind such a man is tantamount to castrating him. "It was your eyes I wanted to kill, Daddy", Saint Phalle says. "Your eyes that looked at everything… and saw nothing."

As a kid I related to Oates with some trepidation; while I loved the freedom that would be implicit in any visit with him – restricted movies, no problem! – I always felt that his ties to my brother Burl were visibly stronger, and that I was just along for the ride out of obligation. I vied for his approval at every opportunity, even competing with my brother to see who could say "thank you" first when Oates gave us anything (my brother always won). He just seemed like a slippery character that I couldn't put my finger on, and like Saint Phalle's character in *Daddy*, I wanted the roving father to just stay put long enough to notice me. Oates is also known for his biting sense of humour, which invariably revolves around putting someone else down, usually the dumbest person in the room. Being the youngest, this would often mean *me*. At restaurants he would tell the waiters, "Don't mind my daughter, she's retarded", and delighted in pushing me down into snow banks.

But it wasn't all bad: he would let us tell jokes in his psychology classes at school, put us on a campus radio show in a skit that posited us as then-Prime Minister Joe Clark and his wife Maureen McTeer, and the revolving queue of girlfriends did result in at least one immortal quip: when I was teased in grade school for being flat-chested, Oates's girlfriend said: "next time they say that, just say 'I don't see no bulge in *your* pants!'"

But as Whitehead himself has pointed out, the revenge scenario in *Daddy* is not fuelled just by Niki de Saint Phalle's interpretation of her fictional father's transgressions during her childhood; it is revenge upon patriarchy itself. Like many horror and exploitation films with female protagonists, there is an ongoing dialogue between self and society, between how women are and how society wants them to be. We probably see this less in horror films nowadays, because a post-feminist landscape takes egalitarianism for granted. Until recently, subverting gender roles was still the predominant concern of horror subplots, but since everyone assumes that feminism has long since served its purpose, misogyny in contemporary horror films is especially empty, their female characters lacking in the kind of meaning we derived from their counterparts during the heyday of feminist horror criticism.

above: Niki de Saint Phalle with one of her phallic sculptures in **Daddy**.

Rape and rape-revenge is still a potent and oft-revisited subject for genre films, but while the remakes of *I Spit on Your Grave* (2010) and *The Last House on the Left* (2009) are deprived of the impact of their original context, the older films still seem theoretically meaty in comparison. Many of the latter are not just about a singular act; like *Daddy*, they are explorations of a larger societal problem wherein women are limited by historical and often subconscious oppressive structures. In these films, as in real life, female existence is affected by notions of propriety handed down to women by parents and educators and reinforced by the people who surround them every day – who have been shaped by their *own* parents and educators.

The values we inherit from our parents are often so insidious. We have the choice to break the cycle, but as with Cenci in *Secret Ceremony*, or Molly in *The Witch Who Came from the Sea*, we refuse to admit our own victimization, as though the admittance itself compounds our perceived weaknesses.

Sometimes there is strength in numbers, and counterbalancing those films in which women are isolated with their trauma are films in which women grab onto one another for support. But in genre films, this usually means collective vigilante justice – which is often a short-lived victory.

Based on Anja Kauranen's controversial bestseller *Pelon maantiede* (which in turn was based largely on the research done by Hille Koskela of the Department of Geography at the University of Helsinki), Auli Mantila's *The Geography of Fear* (2000) won best screenplay at Cannes in 2001, and further develops the theme of female violence that was explored in Mantila's earlier film *The Collector* (1997).

The film opens with the investigation of a drowned man whose body drifts ashore near Helsinki. Oili Lyyra is the forensic dentist assisting in the case, who discovers that the man's death may be connected to her sister Laura's new circle of friends – a group of radical female vigilantes. When Oili first meets her sister's friends, she is subject to hostile interrogation concerning her profession, which she describes as predominantly "reconstructing bite marks to assist in rape cases". Laura is clearly pleased at Oili's uncomfortable responses to questioning, as their relationship has been set up as one in which Oili is the older, judgemental counterpart to her flighty sister. Mirroring Oili's success is Laura's failure to achieve or comply, and their interpersonal dynamic is only one facet of Laura's overwhelming feeling of trepidation, of moving through a world that provides threat instead of reinforcement, "besieged by fear on a map that fits into a hand, though it should be the size of the earth."

Later that night, Laura is brutally raped and beaten as she walks home alone, through a grey terrain of concrete and fences. At the same moment, Oili is safe at home, in the shower, being proposed to by her loving boyfriend. Once she hears of Laura's predicament, Oili's relationship with her boyfriend changes dramatically. She begins to see things from her sister's point of view: that everything in the world has been constructed to instil in women a sense of restricted space. Maaru, the most outspoken and intimidating of Laura's vigilante friends, is a professional feminist lecturer. After Laura's attack, she appears on television, asserting that women have been conditioned to shrink their personal space; instead of staking out her turf, as men do, the woman retreats into herself. As the world becomes more threatening to women, they restrict their interaction with it rather than fighting against these societally-imposed restrictions – that women shouldn't walk alone, that they shouldn't go out after dark, that they shouldn't go to bars – or else they are 'asking for it'. "Instead of moulding our society, we have started moulding ourselves", Maaru says. "A line has to pass somewhere – and it'll pass exactly where it is drawn."

Oili is originally opposed to the radicals, seeing them as unkempt, uptight misanthropes with an anarchic programme of terrorizing men. "I'm not like you", she says, "I don't hate anyone." One of the vigilantes – who herself will be beaten and raped before the end of the film – disagrees: "No, you're just sad every day, and don't realize that sometimes it's the same thing."

top left and centre left: Tanjalotta Räikkä and Leea Klemola in Auli Mantila's **The Geography of Fear** (2000).

Juxtaposed with the story of Oili and her sister is a subplot concerning a chauvinistic driving instructor who sexually harasses his female students. He urges the students to avoid certain areas of town because they are sometimes subject to heavy traffic. When a female student asks how they are supposed to learn how to drive by merely avoiding challenges, the instructor responds harshly: "You are here, above all, to learn a healthy sense of fear – so that you won't go rushing into places you have no business going to." Another male instructor offers that women shouldn't learn to drive at all: "Women should stick to mass transportation", he says, "It's safer, and they won't be tempted to go too far." But in limiting women's geography we are transferring the threat from the attacker to the public space, as well as creating a false impression about those spaces where women are deemed "safe", such as their own homes. Women are forced to think strategically about where and when to travel.

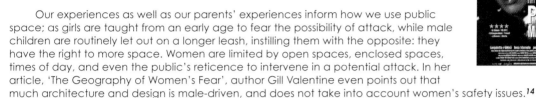

Our experiences as well as our parents' experiences inform how we use public space; as girls are taught from an early age to fear the possibility of attack, while male children are routinely let out on a longer leash, instilling them with the opposite: they have the right to more space. Women are limited by open spaces, enclosed spaces, times of day, and even the public's reticence to intervene in a potential attack. In her article, 'The Geography of Women's Fear', author Gill Valentine even points out that much architecture and design is male-driven, and does not take into account women's safety issues.[14]

I often walk alone at night, and usually with blaring headphones, which people are always admonishing me about. I figure I'm not very strong and I'm not very fast. If they're gonna get me, they're gonna get me. So I am constantly re-negotiating my right to public space, and I think my heavy diet of rape-revenge films informs that decision to a great degree. Instead of making me more afraid, they make me more determined, which runs contrary to the rapist's insistence that the woman be denied her self-determination.

"Rape is a form of mass terrorism, for the victims of rape are chosen indiscriminately", says author Susan Griffin, "but the propagandists for male supremacy broadcast that it is women who cause rape by being unchaste or in the wrong place at the wrong time – in essence, by behaving as though they were free."[15] It is no surprise then, that an entire subgenre exists in which women violently avenge themselves against such brutal societal restrictions, often in solidarity with one another. Through traumatic bonding, women who have survived personal violence are all members of a club in which the violence itself becomes inextricable from their sense of identity.

Janet Greek's *The Ladies Club* (1986) – released under the director's pseudonym 'A.K. Allen' due to a dispute over marketing tactics – deals in female vigilantism of a much more calculated sort: Diana Scarwid stars as an average housewife whose teenage sister is catatonic after being raped. After receiving over 100 letters from women who'd been raped, or whose friends or family members had been raped, Scarwid and her doctor (whose daughter had also been raped and murdered) form a support group. "After a while some things become pretty clear", says the doctor, "like how helpless we all are. How much we need to strike back. To regain control of our lives." Their mutual complaints all point to a single radical solution – systematic castration of all known rapists. Armed with case files of repeat offenders, the women divide into teams who patrol the city and dangerously offer themselves as bait. Once they've identified their 'targets', the offender is drugged and taken back to an impromptu operating room at the doctor's house to be castrated. The reprobate is then released back onto the street unconscious. The local police department gets a kick out of all the men who show up to report their 'stolen jewels', and the tables are turned on the men, who now find *themselves* the victims of an uncaring judicial system.

Female vigilantes also provide misguided justice in Todd Morris and Deborah Twiss's *A Gun for Jennifer* (1997), a film that disappeared in most territories shortly after its brief festival run due to music rights issues. It has resurfaced on European DVD but still remains largely unseen, which is unfortunate given that it is a powerful contribution to the genre.[16]

Deborah Twiss plays Allison, a young woman who is attacked by two men shortly after arriving at Port Authority in New York City. She is rescued by a group of gun-toting women who, as it turns out, have been systematically castrating and killing known rapists, pimps and child-sex traffickers. But the women are far from nurturing to the shaken Allison (who tells them her name is Jennifer); instead they are themselves like a group of hostile men, bullying and prodding her with questions and feminist rhetoric. She is quick to recognize them as "a crazy gang", but is prevented from leaving the fold lest she rat them out. Instead, she joins them as a waitress at the go-go strip joint they operate, which is owned by a former rape counsellor and feminist activist and serves as a front to their extracurricular outlaw activities.

above: Finnish DVD cover for **The Geography of Fear**.

The group – who engage in martial arts and weapons training under the tutelage of the somewhat maniacal gang leader Jesse – all come from abusive backgrounds where they were exploited by men in one fashion or another. One of the women tries to assert that their disdain for men is not indiscriminate, offering that: "there's nothing wrong with men. It's just the things that some people do..." but another of the women interjects: "If they think they can get away with something, they'll do it." Working at the strip club every day is simultaneously empowering and humiliating; despite owning the place and working for themselves, it only reinforces their hatred of men, who feel entitled to hurl sexist and verbally abusive remarks at them. When two obnoxious soap-opera actors prove to be exceptionally abusive customers, the women respond by locking the doors and making them strip onstage, berating the men for their somewhat 'lacking' manhood.

A female homicide detective hailing from the sex crimes division is certain that the murders are the work of female vigilantes, and quickly zeroes in on Jesse and her gang of not-so-merry gentlewomen. A background

top: Freida Hoops in Deborah Twiss and Todd Morris's **A Gun for Jennifer** (1997).

bottom left: The girls mock their male clients in **A Gun for Jennifer**.

check reveals that Jesse was the daughter of a military man who taught her to use guns from a young age, which she turned on him at age 14, killing him in revenge for molesting her and her younger sister Trish (who is also in the gang). Because of her father's heroic record, no one believed her, and she was shipped off to a home for disturbed children. After several escape attempts, fights with other inmates and the stabbing of one of the doctors, Jesse was sent to an adult correctional facility for women, which further hardened her resolve against the patriarchal society that allowed rapists like her father to go free. Likewise Allison – aka Jennifer – was the victim of domestic abuse, before killing her husband in self-defence and running off to New York incognito.

Like the women in *The Geography of Fear* and *The Ladies Club*, as well as individual women in other rape-revenge films, the vigilantes in *A Gun for Jennifer* have a hard time distinguishing between people who want to hurt them and people in general. Many innocent bystanders are killed in their shoot-outs, including other women who – as one gang member alleges – deserved to die because they "chose their friends poorly". Any one of the vigilantes could be accused of the same thing, which goes a long way to indicate their loss of humanity through their systematic programme of revenge.

When the women in *A Gun for Jennifer* or *Baise-moi* (2000) turn the tables on their sexist customers by humiliating them and making them 'the object of the gaze' so to speak, we cheer in solidarity. In theory female vigilantism is great; in reality things are a little different. Any genuine manifestation of mob mentality is something to be feared, discouraged and avoided. This is one reason so many rape-revenge films cut away to the credits immediately after the revenge is carried out – so as to avoid the heady issue of consequence, which would of course obliterate the pleasant notion of fantasy. In rape-revenge films what often begins as a sympathetic reaction against injustice transforms into severe anti-social behaviour, which has ill effects for friends and enemies alike. The disregard for (and violation of) the rights of others may be chronic in the male perpetrators at the centre of many of these films, but this lack of conscience sadly proves contagious. The once-victimized women become empowered through false self-aggrandizement; they become arrogant and self-righteous sociopaths, excessively opinionated while still managing to exude a superficial charm with which they can deceive or manipulate others.

In Mantila's film, in place of salvation – which never arrives – we have ongoing tribal warfare between men and women, or between order and chaos. Neither side fully wins. At best, characters have their eyes opened a little, and begin to see what their opponents see. The most tragic characters remain blind and singular. In a public statement about the film, Mantila concluded: "*The Geography of Fear* is a story about the choices of an individual and about the individual's right to make choices. It is also a story about the conflicts arising from one person's decision to use that right. The violent events in the film could happen when women get tired of yielding and tolerating."[17]

Stylistically pared-down – even to a complete lack of dialogue – Australian director Mark Savage's 2004 film *Defenceless* is a woman's revenge story brimming with vaginas and viscera – and is not for the weak of stomach. Genitals don't last long in this movie. Aside from the graphic and repeated castrations that colour the film, however, Savage also has some interesting things to say about female space.

The story is simple: an environmental activist (Susanne Hausschmid, who also co-produced) takes on some rather relentless and seemingly untouchable developers with horrific results. One by one, the most important things in her life are taken away from her – her husband, her lover, her child – and in mythological fashion, she is led to exact a primal, bloody revenge. While it's common for revenge films to follow a certain similar trajectory, it's the execution that counts. And with *Defenceless*, I mean that in more ways than one.

After a final run-in with the developers in which she is left for dead in the ocean, a supernatural metamorphosis takes place and becomes a turning point in the film. *Defenceless* is not strictly a rape-revenge film, because her revenge is fuelled by a succession of horrific acts of personal terrorism, although these do culminate in her own rape and murder. That said, there is an incredibly sexist tone in the developers' modes of harassment; it's clear the developers feel their entitlement to the land is more apparent because their adversary is a woman.

top right: Deborah Twiss and Rene Alberta in **A Gun for Jennifer**.

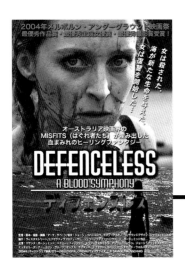

In a particularly gruesome rape scene, the three developers accost the woman while she's enjoying a day on a deserted beach with her young son. With her son watching, they rape her, and then brutally thrust a knife into her vagina before tossing her limp body into the sea. The Woman emerges from her watery grave as a feral child, with no real memory or conscious motivation outside of systematically cutting down her attackers. With her staggered movements and her childlike wonder at the bloody red mess she creates wherever she goes, Susanne Hausschmid effectively channels Françoise Blanchard from Jean Rollin's *The Living Dead Girl* (1982) in her portrayal of the post-metamorphosis woman. In between bloody trysts she curls up in a shallow pool by the ocean and waits.

"Susanne and I had many conversations about places to go, places to hide, places where The Woman is safe", explained Mark Savage in a 2006 interview I conducted with him upon the North American DVD release of *Defenceless*. "This imagery is effective because it is primal and sexual. Our secrets are safe when we are safe. The womb-like cavern is, almost literally, the womb of the earth, a haven. I must have walked fifty miles looking for that perfect pool. The film is filled with female power imagery and places of natural gestation. The Woman is destroyed and then she is recreated to become Nature's fury."**18**

After her initial 'reawakening' she is discovered by a little girl who has built a doll-cemetery by the seaside (inspired by the children in René Clément's *Forbidden Games*, 1952), where she hides from her abusive stepfather. The little girl keeps a chest buried there, her treasures ranging from family photos and letters to found objects (bolstering the notion that women bury things to keep them safe). The little girl 'adopts' The Woman, and tries to teach her to act human, and a weird mixture of pathos, grotesquerie and comedy ensues when The Woman finds the remains of her husband buried in the ground and she starts eating the decayed viscera, regurgitating it, and smearing it over herself. Initially nauseated at this horrific spectacle, the little girl eventually finds it funny, and the two women share a laugh over it. The Woman also eats the entrails and body parts of the men she kills – this ingestion providing another example of the woman 'burying' something.

Another effective image is that of 'the monster' walking into the sea once its purpose is fulfilled. Perhaps it started with Mary Shelley's *Frankenstein*, but it's such a creepy, sad, and ultimately triumphant image that has been used to great effect in countless films as varied as Woody Allen's *Interiors* (1978) and Hiroshi Teshigahara's *The Face of Another* (1966) – and to a certain extent, *The Witch Who Came from the Sea* and *Let's Scare Jessica to Death*.

Savage agrees: "I love the monster returning to the sea, returning to its home. It feels like such a natural step to do that. Jean Rollin does imagery like that well in such films as *The Living Dead Girl* and *Fascination*, and I loved the ocean imagery in Toshiharu Ikeda's *Mermaid Legend* [1984], one of my favourite films of all time. The sea purifies all that enters it. It embraces without exception."

The Woman's character, monstrosity aside, is also embraced by the other female characters in the film, who express unconditional solidarity with her. In the film's climax, The Woman shows up at the Developer's house, where he is hosting a party to celebrate the acquisition of the beachfront property she died trying to defend. The developer's wife has grown increasingly distant from him, aware and wholly disapproving of what he's done, but it's not until she sees The Woman that she decides to do the right thing and be complicit in her husband's murder and castration. As with *The Geography of Fear*, *A Gun for Jennifer*, *Baise-moi*, *The Ladies Club*, and countless others, female solidarity is a driving component of the film, and is ultimately expressed in vigilantism.

The concept of female solidarity is something I've always struggled with because of my relationships with the damaged women in my life. But sometimes the camaraderie I pine for (however guardedly) sneaks up on me, and it becomes apparent that watching these films, and writing about them, is an act of solidarity in and of itself; a provocative means of dispelling the threat their subject matter poses to us. I also think that my interest in them, and my determination to talk it out, is a vicarious means of revenge for what my mother experienced in front of me all those years ago. Like the little girl in *Defenceless*, the keeper of the secrets, I want to tell her that she's not a monster because something monstrous happened to her.

top left: Japanese poster for Mark Savage's **Defenceless: A Blood Symphony** (2004).

opposite: Susanne Hausschmid in **Defenceless: A Blood Symphony**.

PART FIVE:
AFTER SCHOOL SPECIAL

Writing fan letters was a major component of my after school activities. I copied fan club addresses out of the backs of the *TV Guide*, *Teen Beat*, *Tiger Beat* and other short-lived magazines and voraciously scribbled my declarations of love and friendship to stars like Kristy McNichol, Paul McCartney, Leif Garret, Shaun and David Cassidy (I was still writing letters to David Cassidy at 18!), Gary Coleman, John Ritter, Elton John, Christopher Atkins, Bruce Jenner, Dorothy Hamill, Mark Hamill, Nancy McKeon and countless others. I even wrote fan letters to people I wasn't familiar with, just because I had access to their fan club addresses, like Roberta Flack, Bob Geldof and Jethro Tull (the latter started out "Dear Jethro…"). I sent a sympathy card to Yoko Ono when John Lennon was killed, and sent my brilliant ideas to toy companies like Mattel and Kenner. None of my letters received a response.

One day I was reading the *TV Guide* and I saw an article about how a sick kid in the hospital had been visited by Michael Jackson. Suddenly it occurred to me that these celebrities, who I always thought to be on another plane of existence, could come to my house and visit me! As a kid I had many acquaintances with whom I went in and out of fashion, but what I really yearned for was a *best friend*, the kind of idealized best friend I saw in movies and TV shows, a kindred spirit who would be inseparable from me. I was certain that if Kristy McNichol met me, she would want to be my best friend.

I invited her, along with about 15 other famous actors and musicians, to my 9th birthday party. But the party was a bust: it was just me, my parents and my brother, and I got a pop-up book that told the story of Jesus. So depressing. But then a card came in the mail. It wasn't from Kristy McNichol, but it was my first-ever celebrity response: It was a birthday card from Mr. T, signed by the cast of *The A-Team*.

My fan-letter writing would morph over the following decades into a career of booking celebrity appearances at festivals, screenings and other events, and in hindsight seems like practice for the constructive application of my various obsessions that would come later in life. But at times it went the other way: into a life of escapism and delusion where real relationships are indistinguishable from manufactured ones.

Eckhart Schmidt's 1982 German film *Der Fan* (renamed *Trance* for its obscure Canadian and British video releases) remains one of the most chilling portrayals of female delusion I have ever witnessed onscreen. More art film that exploitation film, *Trance* is a deliberately paced but fascinating study of fan obsessiveness.

German television star Désirée Nosbusch (only 17 years old at the time) plays an alienated and uninvolved teenage girl whose only emotional attachment is to a new wave singing star known only as 'R' (played by Bodo Staiger of the real-life Krautrock band Rheingold, who also provide the soundtrack). She feverishly writes him letters that go unanswered, and considers suicide an alternative if he doesn't write back ("That will make me a part of him, and him a part of me – forever.") She assaults the mailman daily, who humours her as she rummages through his mailbag looking for the 'misplaced' letters from R. rationalizing R's

above: Me at Burger King for my 8th birthday party.

opposite: Sissy Spacek in Brian De Palma's **Carrie** (1976).

lack of response as the result of a conspiracy to keep them apart, she runs away from home to meet him. She is certain that he will recognize her as the girl of his dreams once their eyes meet.

She crashes the television station where he is recording a video (and where we get the pleasure of hearing the same inept song over and over again), and he clearly likes the look of this young girl with a hard-on for German pop – he zeroes in on her outside the studio and invites her in. R is a strange choice for a pop idol: he has all the charisma of a cardboard cut-out – so it makes sense that his video shoot sees him wearing a bald-cap and standing motionless among a group of nude mannequins. He is incredibly attentive to the girl, so much so that we question whether all this is filtered through her delusion. He props his arm around her and cuts out of the station early, much to the chagrin of his entourage, who need him to get to work on his next single. For once, she feels special, and her sense of fate is fortified.

After some boring sex at his apartment he gets up to leave, thereby obliterating her fantasy of living happily ever after ("But I thought you needed me?" she pleads. His reply: "I certainly did.") But it's not just the rejection that upsets her, it's that R doesn't live up to her idealized version of him. He's just a mechanical construct of the money-fuelled music business, and there's nothing remotely romantic about him. She decides that the fantasy R is preferable to the real one, and is determined to reinstate his perfection. In what has to be the most minimalist and distinctly German murder scene ever committed to celluloid, she bludgeons him with a statue, dismembers him with an electric carving knife, then cooks and eats him – all with a brilliant emotional detachment and only a few drops of blood. Her 'all-consuming' love takes on a whole new meaning. She shaves her head like a Manson acolyte (or more specifically, like R in his video shoot), and after grinding his bones to dust and scattering them, returns home. R's disappearance is all over the news, but she is hardly fazed:

"I know where you are. Don't worry – I'll never give you away. I missed my period. I shall give birth to you... we'll be very happy together."

Writing fan letters at a young age was, in a way, a means of reaching out for something better than what my real life offered me at home. I idealized the actors and musicians I liked, and saw them as better prospects for friendship than the people who surrounded me on a daily basis. As with most female horror fans, Stephen King's *Carrie* struck a chord with me from an early age. I read it over and over again, always amazed that King actually threw out the treatment for this book and that his wife rescued it from the trash. Throughout school *Carrie* was frequently the subject of book reports, right up to my graduating year, where I augmented the usual text criticism with a giant map of the town of Chamberlain, Maine, illuminated with red ink signifying Carrie's warpath. My English teacher kept the map, and it stayed up on the classroom wall for several years afterward.

I was never as relentlessly unpopular as Carrie, but my social standing was always unpredictably wavering. I could never figure out the girls in my class, who would shower me with compliments one day for my feathered hair and/or new Jordache jeans, and then the next day lock me in the girls' bathroom, pick fights with me, or put fake notes in my desk from boys I liked. This fluctuating popularity left me with a distinct feeling of strangeness throughout my school life, and consequently I grew increasingly paranoid, always certain that whenever someone was nice to me, it was a trick.

The protagonist of Lucky McKee's *May* (2002) is equal parts Carrie White and Travis Bickle, a coalescence of gender typical of '90s indie movies. There was a rejuvenated surge in American independent filmmaking in the early 1990s unmatched since the heyday of the 1970s, when producers hungry for a youth market had unquestioningly backed emerging directors like Martin Scorsese, Francis Ford Coppola and Monte Hellman. In the '90s, the 'New Independents', initiated by the success of films like Steven Soderbergh's *Sex, Lies, and Videotape* (1989) and the founding of the Sundance Film Institute/Festival, pushed for recognition from a competitive

top left: Désirée Nosbusch in Eckhart Schmidt's **Trance** (1982).

centre left: Désirée Nosbusch admires the likeness of 'R' in **Trance**.

theatrical system that had previously relegated them to the straight-to-video market – and they won. The horror genre too was swept up in this indie firestorm and, having suffered a creative drought in the previous decade, repositioned itself as the arena for political, philosophical and sexual allegory it had been in the '70s. As such, young talent and underground vets alike gravitated toward the genre as an affordable means of expression: we had Michael Almereyda's *Nadja* (1994) and *Trance* (aka *The Eternal*, 1998), Abel Ferrara's *The Addiction* (1995), Larry Fessenden's revisionist monster films *No Telling* (1991), *Habit* (1995) and *Wendigo* (2001), Douglas Buck's *Family Portraits* trilogy, Lodge Kerrigan's *Clean, Shaven* (1993), and later, JT Petty's *Soft for Digging* (2001).

The 1980s American horror films, with their tendency toward non-existent character development, juvenile humour and a fetishization of murder that many critics saw as plain misogyny, routinely posited women as fodder for a legion of faceless psychopaths. Even though the '80s slasher films almost invariably held true to Carol Clover's 'Final Girl' theory,[19] the 1990s ushered in an age where – whether as protagonist or antagonist – the woman was more often the central character. In stark contrast to the indie boom of the '70s, the '90s in general offered female characters substantially more screen time and meatier parts; no longer merely the wife, the mother, the girlfriend or the daughter, actresses had their shot at being the Gene Hackmans, the John Cazales, the Jack Nicholsons. The horror genre was all too willing to comply with the new rules, and congruent with this '90s trend, classic horror stories were increasingly being revisited from a female perspective.

May cleverly utilizes the emergent indie film tropes to great effect. There's the *Pretty in Pink* DIY costuming, the pop culture references, the Kim/Kelley Deal soundtrack, and the all-too-familiar angst of the main character. Actress Angela Bettis (who incidentally plays Carrie White in the 2002 TV remake of *Carrie*) is terrific, imbuing May with an almost autistic, socially-inept sweetness. That is, until a constant flow of rejection sets her on an empowering path of destruction.

May is a girl who doesn't fit in. Her trajectory to neurosis is fuelled by a damaging relationship with her mother, who is obsessed with perfection and passed her unattainable standards down to the impressionable and unassertive girl. As a result, May grows up socially isolated, over-analytical and awkward, detachedly scrutinizing people in search of the elusive 'perfection' her mother trained her to value. At one point in the film she offers that she "only likes parts of people", and then, reconsidering, realizes that she "doesn't like any parts at all."

Her lazy eye is covered by a patch as a child, which further sets her apart from the other children at school, who make fun of her for looking like a pirate. But the lazy eye is an interesting touch in more ways than one; it is a constant reminder of May's skewed perception of things. In literature, visual arts and film, one eye being different from the other typically signifies an altered perception, an ability to see things differently from how other people see them. In some stories it might be an indication of 'second sight' or psychic ability, but in others it denotes isolation, and the character's inability to convey what they see to others who don't share their point of view.

"Then she looked at him and he saw her eyes. The right eye was strangely clear; it was young, almost happy, and quite free. But her left eye, which saw nothing straight, her left eye was a different soul, a different nation pursuing a different course; it held things undreamed of, fragile, delicate longings circumscribed by anguish itself…"
– Halldór Laxness, *Independent People*[20]

Her mother's insistence on her covering up May's 'difference' is reinforced by her traumatic experiences with socialization. Friendless and outcast, May's mother gives her a homemade doll in a glass case with strict instructions to never take her out. "This was the first doll I ever made", her mother says in a spooky Stepford Mom kind of way, further commenting that, "if you can't find a friend, make one!" This advice will prove almost a mantra to May later in the film. The act of creation – the mother's doll, May's handmade clothes – is a distinct component of the film's femaleness. The notion of her making her own clothes ties in with the whole 'Frankenstein' theme of the movie, but also provides the film with a great aesthetic, and one that lends May a sense of the Victorian 'affected woman' (with the mix of Victorian and indie-rock sensibilities, May also recalls musician/illustrator Dame Darcy).

May's upbringing fed into the cult of romance, which sees male approval and marriage as a woman's true vocation, and her notions of perfection are equally antiquated. She has also been indoctrinated into 'girl culture', what author Simon Frith referred to as "a culture of the bedroom, the place where girls meet, listen to music and teach each other make-up skills, practice their dancing, compare sexual notes, criticize each other's clothes and gossip",[21] but her 'best friend' is the doll handed down by her mother, with whom she shares secrets and exchanges advice. Still, the occasional excursion with her father as a child gave her an appreciation for tomboyish activities that she has a hard time reconciling with the perfect 'girly' daughter her mother needs her to be.

May works as a veterinarian's assistant, and much of the film's humour revolves strangely around harm coming to animals in bizarre ways – limbs falling off, accidental bludgeoning, sutures ripping open – and by May's unaffected reaction to these events, and all things revolting. Her strong stomach wins her the favour of Adam

(Jeremy Sisto) – the mechanic she's been stalking – who's an avid horror fan and is attracted by May's naïve weirdness. Temporarily, that is; director McKee calls Adam's bluff. When May proves too intense – emotionally, sexually, violently – Adam backs off dramatically, preferring to get his horror fix from fictional situations.

Resorting to the false safety of the company of women, May falls into a rebound relationship with a sultry co-worker named Polly (Anna Faris) – who fittingly calls her "doll" throughout the film – but soon finds herself playing second fiddle to a leggy blonde.

She signs up as a volunteer at a blind children's centre, hoping that their innate difference will somehow equalize hers. When she brings the doll – "her best friend" – to class, the kids violently grab at it, trying to feel it, and the case smashes to pieces on the floor. The kids still keep after it, cutting themselves on the glass. It is a horrifying spectacle from which May will not recover. When she is rejected even by the 'outcasts', she is driven over the edge and makes a decision that creates an impermeable barrier between herself and the world. She plucks out her lazy eye – the thing that makes her see things she doesn't want to see – and starts looking at the world with a singular, focused vision, however questionable that focus may be.

Taking her mother's advice to heart, May decides to "make" a friend by combining the "perfect" parts of all the people who've rejected her – Adam's hands, Polly's neck, the obnoxious blonde's notable gams – into her very own Frankenstein's monster. After her first killing, May completely detaches herself from social reality, and becomes more confident as a result – a feeling of euphoria common in short-term murderers. This is because there has been a drastic shift in self-concept; she has accepted the stigma of 'otherness', and has abandoned trying to achieve other people's standards of perfection.

It's apparent that *May*'s most direct references are *Carrie* and *Frankenstein*, but this misfit character – and the devotion with which the character is written and acted – fits neatly with the character studies that comprise many of *May*'s fellow indie films, regardless of genre. Films like *Buffalo '66* (1998) *Gummo* (1997), *Sling Blade* (1996), *Bad Boy Bubby* (1993) – all these films derive from the same tradition: that of reconciling the world to the (dangerously) disenfranchised and alone.

Granted, *May* is a bit more garish than your average indie character study, and its self-referential humour is decidedly less subtle, but director Lucky McKee's admitted fascination with Argento films – whose violence and baroque colour schemes are definitely hit upon here – could easily have led to a very different final product. *May* is also reminiscent of Curtis Harrington's oeuvre, with its rich colours, smothering matriarch, murderous female protagonist and the betrayal of a woman by another woman. All are essential themes present throughout Harrington's work. But it is the American indie M.O. that infuses *May* with its humanity.

Deviant behaviour is not a meaningless pathology; it is a valid attempt to solve the problems faced by a group or isolated individual. May's is the kind of path any of us could easily take with the right circumstances. The denial of love and social acceptance have led to violent outbursts with alarming regularity throughout history (especially well-documented throughout the last century). This category of neurosis really hits home because it can be very easily triggered by uncontrollable external factors. "We're all odd in some way or another," actress Angela Bettis said in an interview,[22] "but May just doesn't have a 'freak zone'" – meaning, that thing that keeps us from going over the line.

Like May, I had been handed down ideals of friendship and loyalty, and was consistently disappointed by my friends' inability to live up to these ideals. My mother had indirectly taught me that to be disloyal was a despicable trait (one of the reasons she put up with my stepfather's grouchy demeanour for so long was that he was as loyal as they come), and so I was constantly on the lookout for that person who would be my platonic better half.

Auli Mantila's debut thriller *The Collector* (1997) is an uncompromising glimpse into the mind of a disturbed young woman and her violent response to feelings of social invisibility. In this Finnish counterpart to Barbet Schroeder's *Single White Female* (1992), celebrated Scandinavian theatre actress Leea Klemola (who also appears in Mantila's follow-up film, *The Geography of Fear*, as Maaru) plays the awkward, tomboyish Eevi with chilling credibility; as she desperately strives for approval and love, her frightening aggression leads to one rejection after another, and to violently unpredictable behaviour through which she alienates herself from her peers, and from society at large. When her sister ejects her from their shared apartment so that her lover can move in, the expulsion takes on a cataclysmic significance for the obsessive-compulsive Eevi, and after trying to set fire to the apartment she hits the road for a 'holiday' that entails petty theft, kidnapping and murder. She behaves like a serial killer, but

above: Angela Bettis in Lucky McKee's **May** (2002).

leaves her victims alive – taking from them instead their identities, their possessions and their relationships. There is a disarming sentimentality in the relationship between the two sisters, but what sinister secrets they may share are never divulged. We only know that their relationship is burdened by a certain co-dependence, and as Eevi makes her way through the film it is clear that what she is looking for is a surrogate for the sister who abandoned her.

I was always a bit of an odd one at school, but as I approached adolescence, this strangeness became more pronounced. My strained relationship with my parents started to take a toll on my school and social life as strangeness turned into social deviance and I found it harder to make or keep friends who were on the same wavelength. I bounced around from one friend to the next, as each failed to show me the devotion I wanted.

My obsession with Stephen King's *Carrie* resulted in me adopting her name once I hit grade ten. In class, I wouldn't answer to 'Kier-La', and I can only imagine how ridiculous this must have seemed to my classmates, who nevertheless accommodated me. Even more ridiculous was the week-long period during grade nine when I insisted on wearing a shoulder-length blonde wig to school, thinking that no one would notice I'd had short hair the day before. Luckily my new nickname, 'Wiggy', died down after a few weeks. But going to a Catholic uniformed high school, I was determined to assert my individuality in one way or another, often at my own expense.

I swapped social groups with alarming regularity – alternating between preppy kids in Benetton and Kettle Creek clothes, deadbeats who got high at lunchtime in the Projects, Goths (who were then referred to as 'Scaries'), hip-hop kids, slutty girls, comic book nerds, and headbangers who hung out in a basement arcade near my school. Each group was suspicious of me for having friends in competing camps, and subsequently I was never really accepted by any of them. Through all this my reputation was worsening because my domestic problems had caused me to be put in a group home, which – to my friends' parents – made me a dangerous pariah.

At the group home (which was called 'The Inn' – and supposedly my stepsister Karen had once lived there too), I quickly learned that everything was structured to keep you off balance: no one was assigned the same bedroom or room-mate for more than a month before being moved to another room, no one was allowed to be in their room except at bedtime (which meant no time to oneself), and it was by nature a very transient place. If anything, it just reinforced the girls' feelings that we had nothing to hold onto. To combat this, I made up a soap opera called *Bridges and Borders* (which I suppose had to do with growing up in a border town) and wrote a new 'episode' of it every day, which I would read out loud to the other girls. They would eagerly crowd into the dining room to listen to the latest instalment of the convoluted, melodramatic story, and everyone had a favourite character (to aid with identification I had cut out pictures from the Sears catalogue and made a collage of the different 'characters'). For a while, it was the only thing that made life tolerable for me there.

In grade ten I started hanging out regularly with a girl named Allie, and I quickly latched onto her as my new 'best friend'. She was popular, funny, interested in a lot of the same music as me (which at the time consisted of The Cure, The Clash, The Smiths and various '60s throwback groups) and – most importantly – didn't seem fazed by my domestic problems. For a while we were inseparable, and I was blissfully devoted to her. She lived outside of Windsor in the small town of Belle River, but was driven in everyday for school by her parents, who worked in the city.

I was in and out of the group home as I tried to work things through with my parents. Usually our attempts at reconciliation would end the same – with me running away and being picked up and put back in the group home again. During one of these reconciliation periods, I went with my parents to our vacation trailer at Rochester Place (a 45-minute drive from Windsor), only to get in a massive fight and take off within an hour. Allie's house in Belle River was close to the trailer park, but not really close enough to walk – it took me about two hours to get there.

When I eventually arrived I was visibly upset, and as Allie's parents weren't home, we got into the liquor cabinet and downed the Tequila. When her parents came home we tried to hide our drunkenness by pretending we were tired and going to bed, but really I went to bed while Allie talked to her new boyfriend for an hour on the phone. Incidentally this new boyfriend lived down the street, and before long Allie was bugging me to sneak out and go to his place with her. I didn't want to go – contrary to my reputation, I didn't go out of my way to get in trouble with other people's parents, and I had no interest in sitting in her boyfriend's living room watching TV while he and Allie made out in the other room. However, sucker that I am, this is exactly what I ended up doing. After what seemed an eternity, I eventually demanded that we go back so that I could go to sleep. Allie reluctantly obliged, but when we snuck back in the basement window, Allie's mom was sitting on her bed waiting for us. Busted. "I'll talk to you two in the morning", Allie's mother said calmly, although I knew there was some serious trouble brewing.

The next morning when I woke up, Allie was already gone from the room. Her mother came in and informed me that my stepfather was there to get me. After our fight the previous day, he was the last person I wanted to see – and when I got to the front door and saw his face, I felt both ashamed and afraid. As I stood there, sheepishly putting my shoes on and trying to avoid my stepfather's eyes, Allie's mother confronted me: "I don't want to see your face again", she said, "Allie told me how you made her sneak out so that you could

go see your boyfriend. Since you've been coming around you've done nothing but get my daughter into trouble. Now get out of here and don't talk to Allie again!" I looked up the staircase and saw Allie hiding around the corner, watching as her mother scolded me. She'd sold me out. My father grabbed my arm forcefully and dragged me out to the car. My protestations were futile: it would be years before he would believe my side of the story. As my sister had lamented years before, what was the point of trying to be good, when everyone around you was convinced that you were an asshole?

It's strange how people don't comprehend the weight of their actions sometimes. I'm sure to Allie this story is a footnote in her life, if she even remembers it at all. But it was devastating to me. It would inform the blatant mistrust of women that I have carried and struggled with ever since. Of course the betrayal started with my mother, but I wasn't yet conscious of this. For me it all started with Allie.

I don't think I was ever a true delinquent until after this episode. I didn't get along with my parents, and ran away from home frequently (which was what had landed me in group homes), but up until then I was still just a kid trying to maintain some sense of normalcy in my life – and if I wasn't going to get it from my family, I sought it out in friendships. But those friendships were always short-lived, and brought with them their own contests and betrayals.

My isolation from my peers was exacerbated by increasingly poor performance at school (I scored a whopping 8% in Grade ten math, largely due to skipping class), and by a decision on the part of my high school principal (a physically abusive and crotchety priest named Father Zakoor) to kick me out of school unless I moved back in with my parents permanently. I was considered a bad influence on the other kids, and in short order I truly became one. I tried to coerce my schoolmates to sneak into former country bar Stanley's to see bands with me (I remember one in particular was Montreal-based garage band The Gruesomes, whom I adored), or to take the bus over to Detroit to visit the legendary St. Andrew's Hall (to see The Pogues being guest-fronted by Joe Strummer). No one I knew was brave enough to risk hell from their parents, and none would cave in to my accusations of conformist cowardice. So I looked for other kids who were more like me. Any idiot in a Ramones T-shirt would do. I was a bit of a lone wolf at this time, as I suppose I have always been, and so I related to movie characters who were left to wander through a frightening world by themselves, taking what they could from it.

above: Linda Manz in Dennis Hopper's **Out of the Blue** (1980).

Dennis Hopper's *Out of the Blue* (1980) was one of these films whose artistic centre was a knockout performance by such a character: Cebe Barnes (played by Linda Manz), who held the same iconic status in my eyes as Kristy McNichol. *Out of the Blue* was already in production when Dennis Hopper took over duties as director, and suffered from bad reviews on its first run, despite being nominated for the Palme d'Or at Cannes in 1980. Many reviewers have since changed their tune about it, and now see its improvisational realism as one of its greatest assets, rather than as the meandering laziness it had been suspected of previously. That said, the film is far from perfect, with a somewhat choppy script (co-written by Leonard Yakir, who directed the fantastic Canadian short film *Main Street Soldier* in 1972) and an abrupt ending that takes some time to sink in.

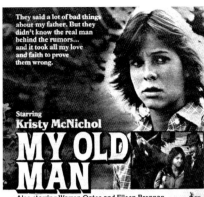

A young tomboy named Cebe turns to the chaotic dogma of punk rock when her hero Elvis dies. Her father (played by Dennis Hopper) is in jail and Cebe is left living with her promiscuous junkie mother. She doesn't have any friends, is constantly hit on by her mother's gross male companions and idealizes her relationship with her absent father.

The film was made in 1980, but the setting is a few years earlier – it starts on or shortly after 16 August 1977, the day Elvis died. The marketing campaign for *Out of the Blue* stressed its punk rock affiliations with the tagline "The only adult she admires is Johnny Rotten", but originally the film was about a girl, her dad and the death of The King. Any trappings of punk in the film were added upon shooting in Vancouver, when Hopper noted the cohesiveness of the punk scene there, and his young star's identification with it. So what you get as a result of meshing Neil Young's music (whose song was the film's namesake) with this adulation of Elvis and the Sex Pistols in the narrative is an interesting re-imagining of what punk is – alienation, nihilism, rebellion. If punk is all of these things, a response to one's environment as opposed to a musical era or genre, then it's not too crazy to see how these characters all fit together.

Cebe's love of Elvis comes from her alcoholic father, who's been in prison for five years after a drunk driving accident that caused the deaths of a busload of schoolchildren. Her father's chaotic leanings prove to be hereditary; she develops an interest in the burgeoning punk scene and its inherent sense of recklessness, but despite some gig posters adorning her walls (Teenage Head, The Dishrags, Subhumans [of Canada] and Public Enemy), her involvement is limited to the regurgitation of punk slogans: "Destroy. Disco Sucks. Kill All Hippies. Pretty Vacant. Subvert Normality." As with Kristy McNichol's traumatizing turn in *Little Darlings*, *Out of the Blue*'s teenage awkwardness comes across as very real. Cebe is constantly observing and assimilating, and there are times in the film when she seems genuinely happy, but her faith in people keeps being shaken by the shitty adults around her.

The punk showpiece of the film is a club scene featuring a live performance by the Pointed Sticks (who nevertheless go uncredited). Cebe runs away from her rural home and heads to the city to congregate with fellow punks, namely the Pointed Sticks' drummer Dimwit, who lets her bang away on his kit during a live rendition of their self-financed single 'Somebody's Mom'. Linda Manz had surprisingly few feature film roles to her credit considering her formidable natural talent – she was in *Days of Heaven* (1978) and *The Wanderers* (1979), but after an obscure 1983 West German film, she didn't resurface until Harmony Korine's *Gummo* in 1997.

My own emerging interest in punk music made my father's military collection suddenly very interesting to me. All the famous punks donned military garb, so I started swiping medals, badges and other ephemera from my dad's room in the basement to wear to school. I knew from the way it was covered in protective plastic that the real jewels in the room were the Nazi paraphernalia. Sid Vicious had a T-shirt with a swastika on it, and I wanted one too. Soon, iron crosses and swastikas were a regular part of my attire. In a strange attempt to bond with me, my stepfather gave me a gun – a Walther P-38 with Nazi insignia on the handle and the firing pin removed so that I couldn't actually use it. The principal's threat to kick me out of school finally came to pass when I was caught with the gun in my locker.

I was sent to live with my mom's younger sister Aunt Pam, who I'd always thought of as 'the cool aunt' until she become a born-again Christian after a traumatic event in her own life had prompted a need for some divine back-up. She had three young boys, as well as two little girls she babysat regularly, so the house was full of kids running around. One day I was wearing my swastika T-shirt and my aunt told me that the two girls were coming over, so I had better change. "Why?" I asked. "They're Jewish", she replied. I looked at her quizzically; I didn't know what she meant by this comment. "What does that have to do with anything?" She just shook her head

top right: My childhood idol Kristy McNichol, in an ad for a 1979 TV movie in which Warren Oates plays her absentee father.

and walked off; I suppose she thought I was being insolent. No one seemed to realize that we hadn't gotten to World War II in history class yet, and while I knew about Nazis, I didn't know about their racial programme. To me there was no difference between wearing Nazi insignia and singing about *Snoopy vs. The Red Baron*. Except that one seemed to piss people off more than the other – and as a juvenile delinquent, that was fine with me.

As I came and went from my primary home environment, things started to heat up between my mother and I. She grew increasingly exasperated with me, and I grew increasingly sadistic with her. The more she resigned, the more I stepped in to fill the space between us with vitriol. Worst of all, I remember telling her that if I could go back in time to the townhouse, I would just stay in my room and let that guy rape her. Just as Maaru says in *The Geography of Fear* that "a line has to pass somewhere, and it'll pass exactly where it is drawn", this is where my mother drew that line. Our relationship was officially irreparable.

With my outlook on life becoming increasingly nihilistic, what I really wanted was a friendship like that of the girls in Joël Séria's 1971 film *Don't Deliver Us from Evil* (proudly billed on the British quad poster as "The French Film Banned in France!") – a pair of anti-Catholic delinquents who would kill or die for one another. Inspired by the real life story of 1950s teenage murderesses Pauline Parker and Juliet Hulme (who also formed the basis for Peter Jackson's *Heavenly Creatures* in 1994), the girls in *Don't Deliver Us from Evil* are expert mischief-makers who spend their weekdays in a Catholic boarding school, and weekends and vacations with their oblivious parents in the French countryside. Anne, the more dominant of the two girls, gets a kick out of evil-doing, whether it's confessing to sins of impurity that she didn't commit just to embarrass the priest, reading dirty

top left: Jeanne Goupil and Catherine Wagener surround their prey in Joël Séria's **Don't Deliver Us from Evil** (1971).

bottom left: Hilarious British newspaper ad for **Don't Deliver Us from Evil**.

books, seducing simpletons, torturing animals, or spitting out her communion wafers to save them up for a Black Mass. Her sweet-faced companion Lore is less of a criminal mastermind, but enthusiastically partakes in Anne's campaigns to traumatize nearly everyone around them. Both are careful to feign innocence around their parents, lest they be forbidden from seeing one another.

Anne's family lives in a grand chateau, and it's a typical rich household, with servants and long dining room tables emphasizing the distance between family members. Her parents don't suspect their daughter is a hellraiser, but neither do they show her any real attention or affection. Instead, when she comes home for summer vacation, her parents elect to go out of town for two months, leaving her behind at the chateau with only the servants and the dim-witted gardener to monitor her activities. Lore, whose family lives nearby in a more modest abode, is thrilled. The next two months will be delinquent bliss.

With vestments stolen from the rectory and their stash of host wafers, they engage in secret Black Masses in the dilapidated chapel on the chateau grounds, not so much in commitment to 'Satanism' as to break the taboos upheld by the Church's regimen. Aside from their hatred of the Church – in particular what they see as its hypocrisies – the girls are also classist, targeting poor farmers and labourers for their disruptive activities. They set fires and kill beloved pets just so that they can watch as others suffer. They are both misanthropes, and live without conscience – typical of that age where no consequence seems especially threatening.

Their strength lies in their bond to one another – when Lore's family goes away for ten days taking Lore with them, the two girls are equally listless and lost. Anne kills one of the gardener's birds with her bare hands, and runs to the chapel crying; her evil resolve wavers without Lore there to bolster her. The two girls determine that they can never be apart again, and make a drastic decision that will keep them together in hell for eternity.

above: Gérard Darrieu in **Don't Deliver Us from Evil**.

Like the girls in *Don't Deliver Us from Evil*, the duo of Alucarda and Justine in Juan López Moctezuma's bloody and brazen *Alucarda* (1975) are co-dependent teens whose bond is filtered through Satanic frenzy.

When the despondent Justine is sent to live in a rural convent after the accidental death of her parents, she is immediately set upon by the frizzy-haired, black-clad Alucarda, a lonely girl who was abandoned there as a child. The convent is a strange place – dark and cavernous, decked-out with layer upon layer of crucified martyrs, and the home of nuns who wear costumes that look like bloody bandages (the bloodiest parts always at crotch-level, signifying that it may be menstrual blood). For a B-horror film, the creative aesthetics seem remarkably reminiscent of surrealist/Panic Theatre alumni Alejandro Jodorowsky's work, but aesthetics aside, the real showpiece here is the hysteric performance by Tina Romero as the title character; like a more histrionic version of *Carrie*'s Margaret White, Alucarda screams, spins and slaps out at invisible enemies, all while pledging allegiance to Satan and his various minions.

Justine is immediately intrigued by the bizarre girl in black, and within minutes they are out frolicking in the fields, Justine's recent tragedy all but forgotten. Alucarda shows her some small insects in the garden: "One is identical to the other, like an image in a mirror", she says, "Like you and me." The two make their way to an old crypt hidden away in the woods, and once inside Alucarda has the uncanny feeling she's been there before. It was, in fact, the place where she was born, the result of an unholy union between her now-dead mother and Satan himself. Once inside, Alucarda's behaviour becomes more aggressive: "Would you die for me?" she demands of Justine. "I love you so… you don't know how dear you are to me. The time is very near when you will love me as much as I love you. You will think me cruel and selfish, but love is always selfish. You don't know how jealous I am. You must love me to death!"

The girls' swift co-dependence is made all the more absurd by the fact that the whole film seems to take place in under a week, and on the night of their first meeting, they are already participating in an orgiastic blood ritual with the help of some local Satanic gypsies who live in the woods nearby. However, Alucarda is not the only woman in the convent obsessed with the newly-arrived Justine; intercut with the soul-selling sequence in the woods is an equally ecstatic prayer session by Sister Angélica, who prays for Justine's protection so fervently that she levitates and sweats blood.

Sister Angélica's prayers apparently don't work, because the next day in class, Alucarda and Justine loudly renounce God and proclaim Satan to be their lord and master. When sent to the confessional, Alucarda attacks the confessing priest through the grate, demanding that he "take off those filthy robes!" This sequence of sacrilegious events prompts a primitive exorcism that Justine doesn't survive. Alucarda's loyalty proves fickle, though – once Justine is gone she immediately turns her attention to the local physician's blind daughter. She is portrayed as a predatory lesbian, and, like Satan, she is seen as "the transgressor, the seducer, the enemy of virtue, the perpetual persecutor of innocence…"

The hysteric screaming in the film by the possessed girls – which is *abundant* – is paralleled by the religious ecstasy of the nuns as they pray and self-flagellate; one ceremony is very like the other. Setting up this lack of distinction between service to God and service to Satan posits the real issue here as being Alucarda's neediness and vengefulness over her own abandonment. Being put in a place where no love is given to her has made her cling fiercely to any new person in the hopes that they will be the one to show her unconditional love and stay with her forever.

Not surprisingly, given my erratic emotional and social patterns, my Christian Aunt Pam started to worry about my mental and spiritual well-being. After all, I was a sketchy juvenile delinquent with a gun living in the basement listening to *Anarchy in the UK* about a hundred times a day. One night, after all the kids had gone to bed, she and her weird friend Beth came down to my room to get me. They brought me into the living room and told me that they were going to save my soul with the help of Jesus Christ. I was really tired and asked if they could save my soul some other time. Not deterred, they made me sit on the couch and told me to stay still, while each kneeled down on either side of me and put their hands on my knees. And then they started speaking – in tongues.

This went on for several hours and I fell asleep sitting up on the couch. The next morning Aunt Pam was upset with me – supposedly the exorcism hadn't worked because I fell asleep. Thank God, I was still possessed.

After this incident, I ran away from my Aunt Pam's and ended up staying in a number of makeshift foster homes by convincing friends from school that their parents should take me in. None of these situations lasted long before I ran away or was kicked out. In one such self-placement, the foster parents treated me as a

opposite top: Tina Romero and Susana Kamini in Juan López Moctezuma's **Alucarda** (1975).

opposite bottom: Tina Romero, Claudio Brook and Susana Kamini in Juan López Moctezuma's **Alucarda**.

maid, making me do all the household chores while they secretly extorted money from my parents, claiming that I needed new clothes or other supplies that I never received. It was humiliating for me to have to clean up after my peers, and I resolved to run away – and to take their teenage son with me. As soon as we got to the city limits he chickened out and called his parents to pick us up. They came to get us, and told me that they'd called Children's Aid to take me away, because they "loved me too much" and were worried about getting too attached to me. Yeah, right. Too attached to my cleaning services, maybe.

I was picked up and put in a group home, where I had a blood- and piss-stained mattress on the floor with no blankets. I didn't last the night in that place. Although I didn't want to be at home, all this moving around left me with an increasing feeling of disposability; that I could be traded in whenever I stood up for myself or got too difficult to deal with. My old feelings of being a changeling came to the fore again.

Despite my yearning for that perfect friend who would support and accept me just as I was, my own loyalty left something to be desired: I had many friends in grade school – Chris and Kerri-Lynn Kavanaugh, Ryan Brown, Mora McIntyre – who I had drifted away from as high school drew near and the promise of a new life of excitement and popularity beckoned. But that popularity never came – if anything, high school just brought more uncertainty, more schizophrenic social behaviour and self-manipulation. And, of course, self-mutilation.

Neurosis and compulsive behaviour came early for me. Most notably, the uncontrollable ingestion of items other than food. I indiscriminately ate pencils, erasers, paper and other things small children come into contact with. Ironically, I was (and still am) an incredibly picky eater when it came to real food. I'd throw out my sandwiches and eat the paper lunch bag instead. Hospitalisation was frequent. It's been said I ate an entire plastic phone, had slivers extracted from my throat after eating my crib, and suffered a cardiac arrest after eating all my mother's cigarette butts out of the garbage. This compulsion has since transformed into a more olfactory one: now I just smell everything.

I was also injury-obsessed. I'd fashion fake splints out of plastic utensils and make up wildly imaginative stories about how I'd been on some adventure and narrowly escaped with my life. Eye patches, crutches, neck braces, band-aids, tensor bandages – they all got ample use, and were accompanied by elaborate fibs. Looking back, I'm sure no one believed a word I said, but I thought I was terribly convincing. My obsession was undoubtedly fuelled not only by my mother's profession but also the fact that she was a well-known hypochondriac. I always thought she was accident-prone, but some family members have contested that she faked many of her injuries.

Aside from my mother's neurosis rubbing off on me, I attribute my romanticizing of injury to the stills from Tod Browning's 1932 classic *Freaks* that graced every horror book I owned, and later, a French-Canadian film called *Kenny* (aka *The Kid Brother*, 1988). Although Kristy McNichol was the first love of my life, the feathered tomboy eventually gave way to a parade of half-bodied men, whose visages and stunted torsos graced my wall alongside John, Paul, George and Ringo.

As a child any deliberate self-injury was limited to scab-picking and other means of interfering with the natural healing process of wounds (not so abnormal), but adolescence brought the typical self-injurious behaviour – cutting, bruising, and consistently giving myself bad haircuts. I still maintain that the latter was the most damaging.

In hindsight, it's easy to see that my own masochistic behaviour – from eating things that were potentially harmful to me, to provoking physical violence from my stepfather or pretending to be injured – was fuelled by a need to feel I'd survived something that would incapacitate others, more than being borne out of low self-esteem.

The most common causal factor in female self-abuse is that women have been taught that it is 'unfeminine' to voice anxiety in an assertive way, so they tend to internalize it – and when it needs to find expression it tends to

top left and centre left: Kenny Easterday in action and with screen mom Caitlin Clarke in Claude Gagnon's **Kenny** (1988).

take the shape of self-directed violence. Women are always worried about being labelled hysterical, about 'blowing things out of proportion' and consequently having their perceptions devalued. As such, auto-aggressive women use physical pain to cancel out emotional pain, as a means of controlling it.

In Mark Savage's *Defenceless* (also discussed in part four of this book) dialogue is forfeited in favour of a story that exists solely on an emotional level; Savage wanted to internalize the woman's journey, to make the point of view completely specific to her. This female point of view is emphasized in every aspect of the film, and the sense of interiority becomes more pronounced the more threatened the protagonist feels. When her female lover is raped and killed, she locks herself in a bathroom (one of many typically female insular places the film inhabits) and turns a straight razor on her own crotch. "She mutilates herself because she is turning her pain and anger inward", Savage said In a 2006 interview I conducted with him for *Fangoria*. "She attacks her vagina first because they destroyed that part of her lover first. They destroyed her womanhood, so she turned on her own because she felt responsible for what had happened to her girlfriend. She had to obliterate before she could re-emerge. This scene is closure for her. She has regressed too, because she plays with her own blood like a child playing with its waste or saliva. She needs to journey through her life stages in order to return and be strong again."**23**

Both Douglas Buck's *Cutting Moments* and Marina de Van's *In My Skin* (2002) similarly explore the possibilities and meaning of cutting, albeit with differing agendas and conclusions. While both female protagonists engage in self-directed violence, their psychiatric profiles would be very different. *Cutting Moments* uses self-harm as a symbolic gesture that – although the film on the whole is grounded in realism – is meant to be somewhat fantastical. It is an overtly exaggerated externalization of one woman's inner pain. *In My Skin*, on the other hand, is more distinctly psychological – Esther's behaviour in that film can be diagnosed as a realistic and common type of neurosis. In both cases, the audience is encouraged to sympathize with their protagonists despite graphic bloodletting that would normally have them running from the theatre (and has, at some screenings, prompted fainting and/or vomiting).

Douglas Buck's shocking short film *Cutting Moments* took the festival circuit by storm in 1996, and went on to inspire a trilogy of horrific films about the dark face beneath the veneer of suburban society that were re-released theatrically in 2004, packaged together as a feature entitled *Family Portraits: A Trilogy of America*.

Inspired by an internship with the explosive cult director Abel Ferrara (*Ms.45*), and the PJ Harvey song *Rub Til It Bleeds*, Buck set out to make a film about female auto-aggression in a way that would not only horrify the audience but also incite empathy. He succeeded on both counts: gorehounds still speak of *Cutting Moments* as a milestone in horror FX, and film critics applaud Nicca Ray's incredibly sympathetic performance as the self-mutilating housewife, as well as Buck's careful writing of the characters.

The scene begins on an overcast day in what seems a typical suburban American household: the wife is in the kitchen preparing food, the husband is outside trimming the hedges, and the young son is on the grass playing out rape scenarios with his Power Rangers. The father's constipated expression betrays instantly that he is the source of the boy's early sexual aberrance. And that fact is no secret – the silent couple are just counting down the days until Child and Family Services comes to take the boy away.

The dialogue is deliberately spare, with long pregnant pauses to accompany the vast expanse of physical and emotional space between the characters. Superfluous noise is everywhere: overhead planes; a television baseball game; knives slice through vegetables and hit the cutting board with a deafening thud.

The woman's response – denial – is probably more typical than we know. She directs no anger toward her predatory husband, nor does she comfort her abused son. Outwardly she tries to act out her wifely role as though everything is the same – but everything has changed. The husband who once loved her now scorns her with every look. Her silence fuels resentment from both the husband and the son, and her zombie-like visage – dark circles under her eyes, waxy, pale skin – indicate that she's been eating away at herself from the inside for some time. She has adapted to their disdain, shrinking further into herself.

At night, the husband's side of the bed is empty, and she whispers to herself: "What have I done?" She blames herself for her son's abuse, but this too is irresponsible. By blaming herself, she creates some relief – because it gives the world in which she's living a sense of order. It makes the problem of neglect or abuse potentially correctable by her own efforts. Once she relocates the 'badness' from her husband onto herself, she can maintain the fantasy that her own efforts might repair the situation. Instead of recognizing that the primary problem is the husband's moral ineptitude, she believes she has not done enough to keep her husband's sexual attention fixed on herself. If only she tried harder, dressed up more, fixed her hair, put on shiny red lipstick…

So she does just that, and parades in front of her disinterested husband in what must be the most embarrassingly real display of sexual awkwardness ever captured on film: she stands there in a bargain-bin red dress with her arms outstretched in a welcoming gesture, while he stares at her with a mix of confusion and revulsion. Rejection is cemented with a single twitch of his furrowed brow. Her smile turns to a nervous frown, her arms fold across her chest, and she retreats to the bathroom to ruminate upon her imperfections.

As she stares at herself in the mirror, her anxiety increases and culminates in a sense of unreality that produces an emotional numbness and depersonalization. In order to combat this frightening loss of integral identity, she starts mutilating her face, first with steel wool, and then she picks up the scissors. She's surprised at how easy it is – how one pain so effectively blots out another. More surprising is her determination in doing it – she doesn't wince a single time. She's found the resolve that evaded her so often before. Buck maintains that she is so disassociated from herself that she doesn't feel the pain: "She had lost a perception of herself, and was really nothing more than a series of body parts."

She comes out of the bathroom, and parades in front of her husband again, in a grotesque re-enactment of the earlier scene. But this time, as Buck himself has pointed out, "she's wearing a different red dress". She is bathed in the blood haemorrhaging from her hacked and lip-less face. Like Conrad Veidt in *The Man Who Laughs* (1928), she's been disfigured so that, while her eyes are crying, her face wears a permanent smile. The mutilation of her mouth in particular is no accident; because she can't *articulate* her feelings, she carries out a horrific act aimed at making her husband *feel* those same feelings.

Her efforts do not go unnoticed – her husband sees her now, and for the first time acknowledges the pain he has caused. Through her sacrificial gesture, he is able to emotionally release his own pent-up self-hatred, which has been misdirected at his young son. He realizes what he has to do to make amends, and severs his penis with a pair of gardening shears. About the final bedroom scene, which is a Grand Guignol-esque inversion of a lovemaking scene, critic Douglas E. Winter says, "all her feminine attributes are being removed... she's being reduced to a pile of meat by her husband. They're finally reunited. Leaving only... their son."

Buck admits that while the husband's punishment is deserved, many viewers have questioned why the wife needs to also be obliterated. The notion that women will sacrifice part of themselves to serve an (often fictional) ideal is a popular one in literature and cinema, and is violently exaggerated in *Cutting Moments*.

Until the late '90s, France was not known as a hotbed for violent horror films (sex films are another story). Georges Franju's *Eyes Without a Face* (1959) – while controversial and shocking in its day – stood alongside Henri-Georges Clouzot's *Les diaboliques* (1955) as one of the few French psycho-thrillers of note (even Jacques Tourneur's major works were made outside of the country), and both quickly crossed over into the realm of academic interest. Even France's most prolific 'horror' auteur, Jean Rollin, made films that are more like Feuillade by way of Maya Deren. Alain Robak's *Baby Blood* (1990) was a bizarre anomaly that didn't succeed in spawning imitators – although the director's cut did become a hot item In North American collector's circles before the DVD explosion made everything so damned accessible.

French films are considered art films by default, but by the early '90s, things started to change. Gaspar Noé made the short film *Carne* (1991), followed by its feature-length sequel *I Stand Alone* (1998), and a whole new breed of violent French cinema was born, seemingly inspired by the confrontational aesthetic of Austrian director Michael Haneke's. Among the new slew of extreme French genre offerings were Noé's *I Stand Alone* (1998) and *Irreversible* (2002), Claire Denis's *Trouble Every Day* (2001), *The Piano Teacher* (2001, directed by the now-imported Haneke himself), Alexandre Aja's *Haute tension* (aka *Switchblade Romance*, 2003) and Fabrice Du Welz's French-language Belgian film *Calvaire* (aka *The Ordeal*, 2004). These films triggered a storm of controversy and had the art crowd up in arms, posing the question of just who they were made for. The movies were too violent for the crowd that had been blindly patronizing French films for the last half century, and seemed to appeal only to cult film audiences with more prurient interests in mind.

Marina de Van's *In My Skin* (2002) came at the height of this new wave of confrontational French horror, and like Claire Denis's bloody *Trouble Every Day* involved a female cannibal – of sorts.

In the opening credits of *In My Skin* a split screen displays a positive and negative of the same picture, which de Van related as "a desire to mutilate the image itself." Like many tales of female neurosis de Van's surprisingly beautiful take on auto-cannibalism and gory self-discovery shows a woman divided. On the surface she's ambitious and collected, but an unexpected accident leads her to literally cut herself open to find the identity inside.

above: The undoing of Nicca Ray in Douglas Buck's **Cutting Moments** (1996).

Lanky François Ozon regular de Van herself stars in her directing debut as the upwardly mobile marketing assistant who accidentally cuts her leg open while stumbling through the backyard at a business party. She walks into a series of obstacles in the dark yard, but, feeling no sensation of pain, thinks she's only ripped her trousers – until she notices the trail of blood staining the carpet behind her.

When she goes to the doctor (played by her real-life brother Adrien) for stitches, he marvels at her claims of not feeling anything, given the severity of the gash. "That's not normal", he says, "Are you sure it's *your* leg?" She responds with a startled look – because his flippant remark makes her question her relationship to her body. She starts to feel separate from it and grows hypersensitive to its functions, the texture and elasticity of her skin, the ease with which it can be cut open. She becomes fascinated with her wound and refuses to get corrective surgery for the tissue damage. Although she won't say it outright, she doesn't want the wound to heal.

She takes to probing the injured tissue, digging into her stitches in dark corners at work, in the bathroom, in restaurants. When she can't pick at her own body she substitutes it with peeling veneer off worn furniture, or exploring the grooves in dirty soap dishes. She confesses her deliberate actions to a co-worker, but tries to rationalize it as a natural response to office-job pressures. "I've been cooped up all day", she says as her friend looks on incredulously, "not even a lunch break. Then I cut myself in the storeroom. The storeroom, my office… the air conditioning, no windows open, can't breathe…"

She becomes more and more alienated from her own body (this sense of bodily dissociation recalling Buck's *Cutting Moments*); she wakes up one morning with her arm numb – a common enough occurrence – but the scene is played out incredibly so that the limb seems like it is really not her own. This notion of the 'rogue limb' is exaggerated to hilarious and horrifying effect when she goes for a business dinner with some important clients; in possibly the greatest awkward dinner scene ever her arm takes on a life of its own like a French art-film version of Ash's possessed hand in *Evil Dead 2*. As she struggles to hide her arm's independent transgressions she effectively ruins the business meeting. Her colleagues assume she's drunk. Indeed, her physical sensations are the same: dissociation, inability to verbalize, impaired balance, loss of muscle coordination, euphoria.

Realizing her newfound compulsion cannot co-exist with society at large, her work, her relationships, she gets a hotel room where she can self-mutilate in peace. Holed up in this room, free of judgement, she cuts, hacks, picks, pulls and eats her own skin. She smears the blood all over herself. She collects large flaps of skin so she can tan and preserve them. This is not just about hurting herself to obliterate a more emotional level of pain – this is about self-discovery more than self-destruction.

In an attempt to hide the cause of her new injuries, she pushes her car off the road to make it look like an accident (although she likes cutting, she still feels shame about it). She lies to her boyfriend (Laurent Lucas from *Calvaire*) and says she was driving drunk. He knows better. "Cut out the drinking and cut out the problem", he says, with emphasis on the word 'cut'.

She's making a big decision – her double life won't last forever, eventually the boundary will disintegrate and one will bleed into the other. This crisis becomes more pronounced with each scene. Even the most banal dialogue takes on additional meaning in this context, such as her boyfriend talking about some pending renovations at their flat: "The whole wall can't be load-bearing. We could cut it in half to feel less boxed-in. We can't knock it all down."

top right: Marina de Van in her film **In My Skin** (2002).

centre right: A rogue limb in **In My Skin**.

bottom right: Marina de Van re-integrates in **In My Skin**.

Soon her body starts reacting to the stress – her eyesight gets blurry, she becomes dizzy and disoriented. A final scene sees the split screen utilized again. "By wanting to look from too close, reality breaks apart and the body itself is no longer visible", de Van explained in an interview. "Esther's attention is splintered more and more, dispersed by peripheral gestures."[24] She is in the hotel room, supplies ready to camp out in a cutting frenzy. Half-naked and bloody, she poses for her camera as though she's part of a grotesque, Abramovic-like performance piece.[25] The next morning, she gets dressed for work, a mess of dried blood hidden beneath her clothes.

While a superficial reading of the film would characterize it as a social treatise about the rampant phenomena of female cutting (there are an estimated 3 million cutters in North America alone, almost exclusively female), de Van rejects what she sees as a facile interpretation. Like the other films discussed in this book, the fact that it is a fictional story allows for discrepancies in any sort of realistic character pathology – it is somewhere in between – but to say the film is more complex than 'just' a film about cutting is to oversimplify the motivation that stimulates cutting. De Van's film is also semi-autobiographical, so it does have its basis in her own pathology, which is transformed and exaggerated into what *The Guardian* facetiously referred to as "a sickening film… masquerading as existential self-exploration".[26]

In a press statement relating to the film, de Van related the story of a childhood accident wherein she was hit by a car and had her leg broken:

"I felt neither panic nor pain, when in fact I should have fainted. It was a very direct and rather violent way to experience this feeling of distance from one's body. I was watching my leg just like any other object, a deformed object. The wound only had a visual existence. My mother showed me the X-rays and a part of the bone was missing, the part that was crushed had been thrown into the garbage. It reinforced my feeling of strangeness, A part of me had been thrown into the garbage just like my torn clothes. Later on, at school, my scars became a source of games. My friends and I had fun by putting needles in them because the skin had become insensitive. I was proud but at the same time I felt that this insensitivity was frightening."

Unlike her childhood friends in real life, her friend in the movie is not interested in helping her explore this dark fascination. Instead, the friend and the boyfriend interpret her behaviour the only way they can – as the type of self-mutilation enjoyed by 'cutters'. Her boyfriend chalks it up to a self-esteem problem ("Don't you like your body?" he asks) and a need for attention. While it's obvious de Van was striving for something more philosophical than just a blanket psychiatric diagnosis, there's very little about Esther's behaviour that deviates from the development and practices of most cutters.

Often the compulsion in real life can be viewed just as philosophically as Esther's in *In My Skin*. Cutters use mutilation as a type of medicine or cure for other ills; they are re-focusing their pain into a type of pain that is easily controlled and negates the more resonant pain of emotional or societal pressures. Esther is going through major changes in her life at the time her cutting starts – a new job and subsequent promotion, a move into co-habitation with her boyfriend, the jealousy of her friend who resents Esther's quick advancement at work – and like many cutters, her actions are motivated by a feeling of mental disintegration and disassociation. "It is through my body that I am in the world, that I am connected with others", de Van relates in her press statement. "If I am no longer my body, what am I? Where does this desire come from to want to see what the body is, and if I am 'inside'? Self-mutilation is a way to reconnect with the present, the moment, and with sensation. A re-appropriation of the body comes with the pain."

Cutters are attached to their scars, even though shame and fear of social stigma causes the cutter to hide any evidence of self-harm. The scars signify some level of endurance that the cutter feels is unique to them: as Marina de Van said about the aftermath of her childhood accident, she felt proud that she had been able to tolerate something that would have been intolerable to others. The scars are simultaneously a source of self-esteem and of social trauma, which makes the experience of life hyper-intensified where before it had been numb, but cutting is addictive, and the cutter tends to be dysphoric – depressed and irritable – when not cutting. It releases endorphins, which fight anxiety, agitation and depression, and the body becomes addicted to the 'drugs' it self-manufactures.

The auto-eroticism inherent in Esther's actions – specifically her escape to the hotel, where she can be alone with herself as though she is sneaking off to be with a lover – is somewhat Cronenbergian in its pathology. That said, de Van has noted that her character's activities are more feral, almost pre-sexual and infantile. She is somewhere between depersonalisation disorder and fetishism.

I started cutting when I was about 13 years old. I don't remember an incident that prompted it, or where I might have gotten the idea from, or what I had hoped to accomplish by doing it, other than seeing it as an extension of the injury fixation I'd always had. Even the braces I'd worn for four years served as a badge of honour for me, and I actually liked going to the orthodontist and feeling the pain that would linger for the rest of the

day after my mouth had been torn and probed. My cuts were small and shallow, and always symmetrical, but like most cutters, I didn't go around showing off my scars. Instead, I pulled my sleeves down and was somehow happy knowing I had a secret. I couldn't keep it from my mother though, and she informed child and family services about it, resulting in an awkward and embarrassing lecture from my social worker. As with Esther in *In My Skin*, my family seemed less interested in knowing the source of the problem than they were shocked by the violence of it, and it was their own discomfort and embarrassment that they wanted accommodated in trying to get me to stop.

My mother was convinced that my cutting was practice for suicide. But that would come later, and razorblades weren't my method of choice. Cutting was a way of feeling present and alive at a time when my emotional outbursts were constantly being curtailed; voicing my opinion alone was seen as self-destructive by my family, friends, social workers and teachers. My thoughts and ideas were challenging and dangerous, and no one wanted to deal with me. As with many self-mutilators, I had trouble forming meaningful personal attachments, and so cutting was a means of limiting my disassociation.

The ages of 12 to 15 were incredibly inelegant; aside from experimenting with conflicting social groups, I also went through brief phases of superficial alteration that included wearing a wig, wearing an eye-patch, trying to dress like Molly Ringwald in *Pretty in Pink* (and failing miserably), changing my name and speaking with a bad Australian accent. None of these things lasted longer than a few months at most, and all of them were – not surprisingly – viewed as attempts at deliberate social alienation. Sensing that I was slipping away, my mother tried to bond with me by giving me the nickname 'Splatter' after the character in *Future Kill* (1985). The name stuck for a year or more and even appeared on my grade ten report card.

At one point I started hanging around with 'bad' kids who lived in various group homes and foster homes around town. I spent the night in cemeteries and hung around a downtown arcade verbally assaulting strangers to prove how 'punk rock' I was, but to my new friends I was still just a rich kid slumming, and no *Corrosion of Conformity* T-shirt was going to change that. One night the ringleader of the group – whose name, incidentally, was *Morticia* – turned on me and called me a poseur. Seeing the horrified look on my face she laughed: "Why don't you just go home and kill yourself!" So, that's what I did.

I went back to my parents' house. My mother was gone somewhere, probably at work, and my brother had recently moved to Winnipeg to live with Oates and go to University. But my stepfather was home, and started in on me about something or other. Overwhelmed with melodramatic teenage despair, I raided the medicine cabinet, my mother's pill bottles flying to and fro as I scoured for something sufficiently lethal. Not that it mattered: I didn't know the first thing about pharmaceuticals and wouldn't know Tylenol from Dilaudid. So I just took whatever I could shove down my throat, including Tylenol (which turned out to be the biggest mistake of all). I went to bed, happy knowing I wouldn't wake up the next morning.

When I woke up the next morning, the phone was ringing. I was incredibly drowsy and forgot all about downing so many pills the night before. I stood up to go get the phone and collapsed immediately onto the floor; my legs gave out from under me, and I couldn't feel them. I dragged myself to the phone and answered it; it was Sherri, one of the girls I'd been hanging out with the night before, being conciliatory about Morticia's comments to me. I suddenly felt nauseous and dragged myself down the hall to the bathroom to throw up. At some point I made it back to the phone and told Sherri that I'd taken a bunch of pills. *No, I didn't know what they were. No, I don't remember how many I took.* I don't remember hanging up the phone, but I do remember paramedics showing up and carrying me out of the house on a gurney to an ambulance that lay waiting in my driveway. As they carried me out, I looked around and saw all the neighbourhood kids I had ever babysat watching me being put in the ambulance. Shame washed over me and I lowered my eyes, unable to look at them. It was then that I realized my life had spiralled out of control. But it was going to get worse before it got better.

Anyone who's ever had their stomach pumped knows what a horrendous and humiliating experience it is. Giant tubes are stuffed up your nose and down into your throat, and then they make you drink charcoal to dilute the drugs in your system. Despite how nauseating the taste of the charcoal is, they chastise you if you puke it up. So while you are having a traumatizing physical experience, the doctors and nurses are also yelling at you at the same time. It just makes you want to die even more than you did in the first place.

My parents convened in the hospital room, including Oates, who had flown in from Winnipeg for the occasion. He would be taking me back to Winnipeg with him to be put into a treatment centre for wayward adolescents.

above: Marina de Van and Laurent Lucas in **In My Skin**.

PART SIX:
THE STRANGE PASSENGER

"Where I come from, there smiles are prized as highly as pathetic style."
– Henrik Ibsen, *Peer Gynt*

I settled into a basement room at my dad's house in Winnipeg, and quickly got to work spray-painting the walls with names of bands (The Clash, Ramones) and punk slogans like 'Anarchy' and 'The Rejected' – the latter the name of the gang from Penelope Spheeris's 1983 film *Suburbia*, which I rented so many times that the store up the street insisted on selling the VHS tape to me (it would be the first in an ever-burgeoning movie collection). I was put on a waiting list for the Manitoba Adolescent Treatment Centre (MATC), which we were told could last up to six weeks. My dad was not pleased: he had to go out of town on business, and the last thing he wanted was a juvenile delinquent left alone among his valuables (my brother lived there too, but he was rarely home). I spent my days lazing around the house – Tom Waits held court with Luther Campbell in my father's record collection, so aside from my own music there was plenty to discover – while my father neurotically watched me for any sign of deviant behaviour. With the waiting list still looming however, Oates had no choice but to go out of town and leave me to my own devices. Shortly afterwards, I noticed that he had left his credit card sitting on the kitchen table. This meant only one thing: shopping spree.

Armed with my father's credit card, I hit the mall and racked up a few hundred dollars in clothes and records. But buying things was not enough for me; I had acquired a new pastime: stealing. My favourite trick was to go into a store and grab a bunch of records, and then – holding them in plain sight – ask the clerk what time it was. After they told me, I would thank them and bid them a nice day, carrying the records right out of the store under their noses (this was the '80s, and security was much more lax than it is today).

Any shrink will tell you that recreational stealing is usually attributable to an emotional lack more than a monetary one. In Hitchcock's *Marnie* (1964) Tippi Hedren plays the title character, a compulsive thief, liar and identity swapper, whose ongoing MO is to get a job with a large firm, gain their confidence, and then raid the safe. With a new dye-job, a new social security number and a new name, she then moves onto the next job. Occasionally she reassumes her natural identity to visit her ailing, emotionally distant mother in Baltimore, and her beloved horse Foreo at a rural stable. The horse is her only real outlet for affection, and the only time she lights up emotionally is when she is riding him. Her mother, on the other hand, is a dour Christian woman who shows Marnie no affection whatsoever: when Marnie reaches for her, the mother pulls away. "Why don't you love me?" Marnie asks her mother, but the question just hangs in the air between them. Her mother won't even touch her, let alone answer the question. The one thing the mother does pass on to Marnie is her mistrust and repulsion towards men.

Staying still for too long means Marnie runs the risk of self-reflection, so she has little trouble bouncing from one role to the next, and finds it easy to conjure up fictional backstories as needed. She meets her match though, in the blue-blooded Mark Rutland (Sean Connery), her dashing new employer, who incidentally knows exactly who she

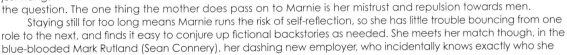

above: Tippi Hedren and Sean Connery in Alfred Hitchcock's **Marnie** (1964).

opposite: Linda Blair in Donald Wrye's **Born Innocent** (1974).

is and what she's up to. He's a former zoology major who sees Marnie as a beautiful, trapped animal, observing her as though studying predatory animal behaviour. He knows she's dangerous, but he wants to tame her, to solve her mystery. And as with all Hitchcock films, there is a mystery. Marnie has a recurring dream: a tapping on her bedroom door sometime during childhood, being roused from sleep and not wanting to get out of bed because of the cold, and then suddenly a struggle – someone is hurting her mother, there is a thunderstorm outside, and the colour red flashes before her. Marnie doesn't know the meaning of the dream, but she has residual panic attacks whenever a storm hits or she sees the colour red.

When Mark catches her in the act of robbing his business, he forces her to marry him, and traps her on a honeymoon cruise where she can't get away. When he makes conjugal advances, she shrieks, "I can't stand it, I'll die! Isn't it plain? I just cannot bear to be handled!" This statement provides an interesting contrast between the film's various relationships: Marnie desperately wants to touch her mother, and repeatedly tries, only to be spurned as though she's repulsive. But she, in turn, adopts this exact behaviour in her other relationships, instinctively refusing to cross a physical threshold while never understanding why. It's hard to imagine where the audience's sympathies were focused when the film came out in 1964; both characters are the stereotypes of what we've all 'been warned about': she's venomous, frigid, manipulative and hysterical; he's domineering, cocky, smug and self-righteous. But one gets the sense that Mark is meant to be seen as the hero of the picture, and he does, in the end, solve its mystery. Armed with the knowledge of his *Sexual Aberrations of the Criminal Female* textbook, he explains Marnie's pathology thus: "When a child – of any age – can't get love, it takes what it can get."

After my dad returned from his trip, I was suddenly stricken with guilt. I knew I had to own up to using his credit card, because he would find out sooner or later. So I spilled. He asked to see the stuff I bought, and I was reluctant to show him, certain that he would take it away from me. He convinced me that he had no intention of seizing it, that he just wanted to see what kinds of things I would buy. So, thinking that my father was just trying to get to know me better, I proudly brought out all the merchandise to show off what remarkable taste I had. But as soon as it was all in the open, he swiped it all up and ran upstairs into his room with it. I had been told never to enter his room, and I suppose he confused me with a child who actually obeyed such rules. As soon as I crossed the threshold into his room, he grabbed my arm and twisted it, causing me to get off balance and fall backwards into the closet, breaking the sliding door off its track.

I saw red. Literally – just a blinding red light. Suddenly, images of my violent fights with my stepfather rushed into my memory, and I confused the situation in my head. Oates had never laid a hand on me before, but no matter – to me, this was the last straw in a series of violent assaults. I ran down to my room, and he ran after me, probably to apologize – but before he had a chance to do so, I had reached under my pillow to grab the butcher knife that I customarily kept there, and swiped at him. I have never seen a grown man run so fast as he did then. He ran up the stairs, with me and my knife on his heels. I caught up to him in the kitchen and lunged at him again, just as the front door opened and my brother came in from school (he was actually whistling as he came in, punctuating the scene with even more absurdity, like a bad parody of *Twisted Nerve*). My brother ran at me and pinned me on the floor as my father made a phone call. The waiting list for MATC cleared up instantly. I was deposited there the next morning.

I was there for two weeks, undergoing daily IQ and Rorschach tests, as well as round-table therapy sessions with the other kids, most of whom were way worse off emotionally than I was. The doors to the building were open but you weren't allowed to go out unless accompanied by one of the staff. I was mostly well-behaved at MATC, with the occasional outburst that would land me in the rubber room – the stereotypical white padded room reserved for hysterics. They would take your shoes away before dumping you in there so that you couldn't hang yourself with your shoelaces.

On my 16th birthday I was supposed to get out. Some of the friends I'd made in MATC got out before me, and I made plans to meet them at a pool hall downtown. But when my social worker came to pick me up she told me that I wasn't getting out: I was getting moved. I protested that it was my birthday and I had plans, and she assured me that I just needed to check-in at the new place – called Seven Oaks – and then I could leave and meet my friends. I conceded, and we drove for what seemed an eternity out into the country, to a large building with an actual barbed wire fence around it. It looked like a prison. Once inside, we went through a series of locked doors to get to the 'cabin' where I would be staying (there were three wings, called 'cabins': one for girls; one for boys; and one that was co-ed, for lower-risk JDs). We were buzzed in and led into a large room with a pool table, a TV, an office at one end and concrete cells flanking the sides. There were about 20 girls there engaged in various activities; none of them acknowledged me as I came in. I was handed some bedding and pointed to the cell that would stand in as my new bedroom, which was maybe 7 feet long and 5 feet wide, with room for bunk beds and little else. My social worker left and I went about unpacking.

opposite: Tippi Hedren in **Marnie**.

SHE WAS BORN TO BE BRUTALISED ...

LINDA BLAIR
Star of 'THE EXORCIST'

BORN INNOCENT

The abuse and savage humiliation of a young girl in detention.

When I was finished, I went out into the common area and said aloud that I'd be back later. I tried to open the door to the hallway that led outside, but it wouldn't open, no matter how much I yanked on it. Frustrated, I kicked the door, and was suddenly set upon by several staff members who muscled me into my cell and locked the door. I spent the next six hours banging on the door and screaming to be let out, before finally giving up and sitting quietly. Eventually they opened up my cell and asked me why I had attempted AWOL.

"AWOL? What am I, in the Army?" I asked facetiously. "It's my birthday and I had plans to meet my friends!" They shook their heads: "This is lock-up. You can't leave." No amount of asserting that I'd been duped by my social worker would convince them: once you're categorized as a delinquent, nobody believes a word you say. I was allowed to make one phone call. I called my mother – but she refused to talk to me. I cried and cried, stating that dad had abandoned me in this horrible place on my birthday; that I had been tricked into what was essentially a juvenile prison. She just mumbled that she couldn't deal with this, and hung up.

I spent three months at Seven Oaks, eating only bread and butter, and learning how to avoid being beaten up. I may have been tough to my former school friends, but in here I was fresh meat. The first day I was there I was punched in the face by a girl named Anne. I had made the mistake of talking to her in the morning before she'd had a cup of coffee and two cigarettes. As long as you abided by this rule, she wasn't so bad.

I don't think the parents who send their kids to these places have any idea what life is like on the inside. They would have to be horrible people to know, and still sign the papers. In Donald Wrye's 1974 TV movie *Born Innocent*, Linda Blair plays Chris Parker, a 14-year-old soft-spoken runaway who is deposited in a state school for juvenile delinquents when her parents sign her over as a ward of the court. Interestingly, the sections of this school are called 'cottages', just as they are called 'cabins' at Seven Oaks. It's funny how they make it seem like the girls are all on vacation.

When one of the social workers (nicknamed "Mom") takes an interest in Chris, she is punished by the other girls – she is pinned down in the bathroom and raped with the handle of a toilet plunger. Not surprisingly, she attempts to run away, but doesn't get past the fence before she is caught and put in isolation. Only the one genre-typical 'understanding' social worker questions that a previously good student and socially balanced girl would suddenly turn antisocial and bolt – but the other workers have been in the system too long, and they're too jaded to care about questions. They just follow procedure – a girl runs, she gets put in isolation. No matter that when she comes out, she's a different girl.

When "Mom" visits Chris in isolation, the girl begs to be let out, to be allowed to go home. But the social worker pushes her for proof that it would be different this time. "If I was your mother", she offers, "what would you say to her right now?" Chris sobs: "Mom, I can't stay in that place any more. I need to be here with you. I'll be better. Try harder. And I'll stay out of dad's way." But going home is never idyllic; everyone acts weird and distant, her father has a temper and is easily irritated. Chris tries to share her experiences at the school with her mother, but her mother dismisses the topic: "Let's not talk about that place", she says, adding that the father's "not so bad" without Chris around. But Chris *is* around now, and it doesn't take long before the father (character vet Richard Jaeckel) starts making unfounded accusations and hitting her, causing her to run away again.

When she is put back in the reform school, no one acts surprised to see her back: that's because most social workers don't want you to succeed. They want you to be incorrigible so that it justifies their own behaviour toward you. As Chris sits there eating her daily prison mush, a pregnant cellmate tells her of her morning sickness. "First thing a kid does is make its mother sick", Chris muses. "I still make my mother sick."

The daily routine at Seven Oaks consisted of 'school' (and I use the term loosely), half an hour in the pen (the concrete yard in the back, from which we could look longingly at the highway on the other side of the barbed wire fence), shooting pool and watching movies on Friday nights. Each Friday a different kid was allowed to pick the movie. As long as it wasn't *The Lost Boys* – apparently the movie had been banned after the girls went around biting each other. When it was my turn, I picked *Rock 'n' Roll High School*. As we sat around the tube watching

above: British VHS cover art for **Born Innocent**.

the Corman-produced masterpiece from 1979, the girls erupted in riotous laughter. Not because the movie was so funny, but because they thought the Ramones were the most hilarious excuse for a rock band they had ever seen. I asserted that they were not only a *real* band, but they were also my *favourite* band, and this made the girls laugh all the more furiously. "I never realized you were so funny!" one of them said to me. "You're all right!"

One day a new girl arrived and she was assigned to my cell. Her name was Kim, and she was a 15-year-old Satan-worshipping prostitute. I had never met a real Satan-worshipper before (I still haven't), and I most certainly had never met a teenage prostitute. Once I realized she wasn't the type to get violent with me, I prodded her with questions. I'd seen *Angel* (1984) and read the book of *Christiane F.*, and while it wasn't really the life I wanted, I found something romantic in the street-level despair of it all.

The story of Christiane F. (Christiane Felscherinow) first came to the public eye in 1978, when a couple of writers for a German news magazine were interviewing her because she was a witness in a court case, testifying against a man who had paid underage girls with heroin for sexual favours. She was 15 at the time of the interview, and the initial two-hour session turned into several months of interviews that eventually became Christiane F.'s autobiography, *H: Autobiography of a Child Prostitute and Drug Addict*, which came out in 1979. Before the book was published, these reporters ran a series of articles about her in *Stern* magazine, so by the time her book came out she was already famous.

When I was a teenager, this book, along with *Go Ask Alice*, was pretty much required reading among delinquents. It's a first person tale of Christiane's decline from a mildly unhappy 12-year-old who did normal things like tobogganing and playing marbles, to a 13-year-old who used heroin and turned tricks at Berlin's notorious Zoo Station to support her habit. The book was a sensation around the world, and Christiane still supports herself from the royalties. There had been numerous books about drug addiction in the decades before this, many of them equally grim first person accounts, but *Christiane F.* came out at a time when there was an emerging war on drugs, which meant that kids like me were hearing about this book in school as a warning.

In 1981, Uli Edel (director of *Last Exit to Brooklyn* and *The Baader-Meinof Complex*) made the film version of the book. David Bowie, who was Christiane F.'s favourite performer throughout the time described in the book, appears in the movie as himself, and provided the soundtrack. The cast of the film is almost exclusively made up of youngsters – Natja Brunckhorst, who plays the title role, is only 14 in the film, which would never happen now given the part's severity and the fact that it contained nudity – and many of them never acted again. The kid who plays Detlef actually looks remarkably like his real life counterpart, but my favourite character was the androgynous Babsi, who died at the age of 12 – reportedly the youngest kid to OD in Berlin's history.

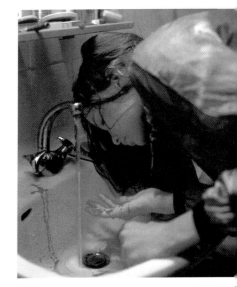

As with any tale set amidst seedy street life, these kids form a makeshift family to offset the neglect or abuse they encounter at home. But I was too young at the time of reading *Christiane F.* to realize that these bonds only exist out of desperation; each kid is still ultimately selfish. I was shocked years later to read in an interview with the real-life Detlef that he and Christiane had never been in love – they were only co-dependent because of their drug use. For me, this dispelled a lot of the story's romance. Not to mention that although Christiane was

top right: Natja Brunckhorst, the 14-year-old star of Uli Edel's **Christiane F.** (1981).

bottom right: Natja Brunckhorst in **Christiane F.**

HOUSE OF PSYCHOTIC WOMEN

clean when the book came out, she has struggled with heroin addiction throughout her life, and as recently as 2008 her son was taken away from her because she was caught using. I don't know whatever happened to my cellmate, but I hope she came to a better end than Christiane F.

Eventually I was picked up by a woman named Edna, who was to be my new foster mother. She had been a child of the system herself, and she looked like she'd been through the ringer. Edna was tough and intimidating – largely because I knew I couldn't easily manipulate her. Whatever I could do, she'd seen it all before, and *done* it all before. I knew there'd be no illusions of normal domesticity here, no pretending that she was going to treat me like a daughter. It was the first time I'd been in a foster home where there was no obfuscating the financial motivation. She made $1000 a month off each kid (there were four of us), and we got $7 a week in allowance – and had to buy our own shampoo and soap out of that money. I was a smoker, so I knew this arrangement wasn't going to work for me.

The first week I was there I was caught stealing tampons at the Safeway up the street. I had my $7, and a menstrual cycle and a smoking habit fighting for it. I slipped the tampons up my sleeve and went to the cash register to buy my cigarettes. When I got outside, I felt a hand on my shoulder, and a voice said – no joke – "hand over the Tampax please". I was dragged back into the store, with the security guard yelling "shoplifter!" just to make sure everyone got a good look at me, and then I was plopped down into a small, dark office and told to wait. I waited for what seemed like hours before two cops came in and asked me why I had stolen the tampons. "One guess", I said. They were not impressed. Neither was Edna, who showed up to get me shortly thereafter.

Life at Edna's was never dull. She was a heavy drinker, partied hard, and there was no shortage of drama between the four girls, each coming from disparate backgrounds: Blair, my room-mate and my favourite of the bunch (we borrowed each other's clothes), was a misunderstood snob from a well-off family; Tootie was inhumanly stacked and dumb as a post; and Natalie was a 15-year-old Portuguese psychopath (with a dumpy 30-year-old boyfriend). Adding to the depressing sordidness was the knowledge that the small Shih Tzu Mr. Muggs had been raped by one of the previous foster kids. But one day Edna came home with a surprise for us: we were all going to Mexico for a caveman vacation. Two weeks, no rules. It was like a Boaz Davidson movie come to life.

When we got to Mexico, the four girls shared a hotel room, while Edna stayed in a different hotel across the street. This experiment worked wonders for me – the more out of control my cohorts got (including Edna, who I found lying on the floor at a bar called Pancho's, yelling, "Luis! Luis! I love you!"), the more I clung to rules and structure. For all my anti-authoritarianism, I became the voice of reason on this trip, trying to keep us all from getting killed while still consuming as many Margaritas as I could without falling over – and since Pancho's had a street-team handing out coupons for free drinks everywhere we went, it wasn't long before I never wanted to see another Margarita ever again. Two of the girls had weird flings with much-older Mexican guys – both named Fernando – who worked at Pancho's, and these brief relationships would have bearing on the immediate future once we got back home.

above: Me, Tootie, Natalie and Blair in Mexico, 1988.

Upon our return, Blair ran away, but not before one of the Fernandos phoned her to say he had recently won the Mexican lottery. I came home from school one day to find the two Fernandos watching TV in our living room. Apparently they had come to claim their Canadian brides, and Edna welcomed them with open arms, going so far as to clean up the garage so that they could have an apartment in there. The whole situation seemed preposterous to me – not only did my foster-sisters have no intention of continuing these relationships (both already had boyfriends, for one thing), but I hardly thought that Child and Family Services would look kindly upon Edna harbouring two illegal aliens in the garage, but Edna decided to throw them a party, and invited all her gross biker friends over to celebrate their arrival in Canada.

As the alcohol flowed freely, the music blared and tempers flared. I sensed imminent disaster. I hid out in my room in the basement and called my dad, begging him to get me out of there. But as always, he didn't believe me. As I hung up I heard a loud crash and a scream. I ran upstairs to find that the glass kitchen tabletop had been toppled and broken, and Edna and her friend Kelly were on all fours looking for something on the floor. They were looking for part of Edna's toe – which apparently had been cut off when Kelly threw the glass table at her. I went back down into my room and waited it out. Eventually the two Fernandos were gone and things eased back into their previous state of 'normalcy'.

I got a weekend job at an all-night café called The Blue Note. I lucked into the job: The Blue Note was considered the coolest place in town, because beatniks and poets scribbled away by candlelight, they served cinnamon coffee and booze in the teapots after hours, the staff was rude and Rod Stewart got his jacket stolen there. I was the busgirl, and I worked there for two months before the owner even knew my name. One night The Gruesomes came in and I kept bussing their table needlessly, just hoping to be close to Bobby Beaton.

I still had few friends in Winnipeg by this point, and I fell in with a tight-knit group of hipster kids who hung out at The Blue Note and lived in a large house together. Hanging out there was a giant reprieve from the oppressive atmosphere of the foster home, where there was always drama. We'd smoke cigarettes until the wee hours, play guitar, have important teenage existential conversations; the usual. One of their peripheral friends was a freewheeling Deadhead named Thad who, for some reason I still can't comprehend, I decided was inconsequential enough to lose my virginity to. It was fairly unmemorable except for one fact: he loaned me his bike to get home the following morning and it was promptly stolen from beside Edna's house. I was distraught, and to make matters worse, when I told him, he was convinced that I'd sold it for the money. I soon found myself without all the friends I'd just made, and one of them gave me a stern talking-to in the Blue Note washroom, stressing that I was no longer welcome at their house – my pleas of innocence falling on deaf ears.

I later found out that Edna had noticed the bike sitting out and locked it away in the garage, worried that someone might steal it. I was so relieved; I immediately called Thad and told him it was all a mistake, but no matter: he was still certain that I'd sold it, and had somehow gotten it back out of guilt. Being a foster kid is tantamount to having the word 'thief' tattooed across your forehead.

Through all of this, I felt like the drifter in an old western story, rootless and bound to no one, but observing all the politics acutely. Watching films so frequently facilitated this; my choices in movie-watching always seemed to reflect my choices in life, and through them I was able to step outside of my situation to get a grip on where I was headed and where I wanted to go. From the ages of 12 to 16, I probably watched more JD movies than anything else – films like *Over the Edge*, *The Outsiders*, *Suburbia*, *Class of 1984* – each of them simultaneously validating my anger and offering a warning about what would happen if I didn't make some positive decisions and stick to them. Edna was also an influence in this regard: she was proof that nothing was going to come easy, and that mere survival was not enough. After we came back from Mexico and things settled down again, she started to take more of an interest in me. She could see that I was getting restless, and that like Blair, I could run away at any time. Knowing that I responded to movies, she would try to freak me out every once in a while by showing me a harrowing film about what happens to kids who make the wrong choices. One of these films was the documentary *Streetwise* (1984).

Directed collaboratively by Martin Bell, Mary Ellen Mark and Cheryl McCall, and based on the *Life* magazine photo essay 'Streets of the Lost' by Mark and McCall, the film is a vérité portrait of a group of kids who live on the streets in Seattle in the early '80s: among them Tiny, the sweet, spiky-haired 14-year-old prostitute; Rat, a gravelly-voiced little boy who knows every scam in the book; idyllic street-couple Patty and Munchkin; and DeWayne, the lanky pot-dealer who wants a normal family more than anything. DeWayne in particular doesn't get a happy ending.

The sense of freedom and independence the film initially posits as inherent in street life gradually dissipates into a palpable sense of imprisonment. All of these kids seem older than their years in terms of the practicalities of survival, but all are emotionally immature; they're no different from any other kid their age in their interactions with each other. Like the kids in *Christiane F.*, they are selfish and inconsiderate, petty, fickle and argumentative – but none of them have role models to show them any other way of doing things. The parents the film spends any time with are either alcoholics, sexually abusive, or serving time. The kids have delusional fantasies about being rich one day, about having meaningful romantic relationships and healthy children, but have no picture of how

to get to that point. Although I still struggle with the concept of responsibility, it was after I saw this film that I knew that the life I wanted wasn't going to just come to me. I was going to have to make it happen.

I told Edna and my social worker that I wanted to get on the Independent Living programme – essentially welfare for teenagers, where they get a stipend from the government each month to live on their own provided they go to school and have a part time job to supplement their income, which I did. The forces that be were reluctant, but just before my 17th birthday I got approved for Independent Living. After one night alone I realized I was scared by myself, so I invited my 15-year-old friend Hanna to come move in with me. Her parents agreed to it, provided we came over on Sundays to get a good meal and a load of laundry done, which seemed like a sweet deal to us. There was only one bedroom, so her bed went in the kitchen. We put all our money in a Tupperware container in the kitchen cupboard and had equal access to it, regardless of who had put in more. Somehow we seemed to always have money, despite the fact we went out nearly every night and I came home with at least 5 new records a week.

Helping our financial situation were two scams we had cooked up: firstly we made everyone who came over leave an item of food in a box by our front door, which we would sell back to them when they were stoned and hungry, and secondly we had a very good-looking 20-year-old friend who liked to publicly jerk off in front of junior high school girls, and he would give us a carton of cigarettes for every victim we found for him.

The most unexpected thing came with this new apartment and new job: popularity. I didn't really know how to take it. I liked it at first, especially having been deprived of it previously, but after a while I had to acknowledge that most of these people didn't even know my name – they just wanted a place to do hot knives, drink, or score. I floated on this popularity through the next year, until a couple of drug-related incidents resulted in a much-needed retreat.

When I was 17 I had a friend whose flustered psychiatrist would give him a prescription for nearly 200 pills every fortnight. By this time I was living in a dilapidated rooming house on the street with the highest murder rate per capita in all of Canada. Although only about ten people officially lived there, the house was always swarming with punk rock welfare cases, especially every second Wednesday, when my friend would come home with his giant bag of Librium, Ativan, Halcion and who knows what else. He was an unrepentant and uncontrollable drug addict, who asserted that if he did not hand out these pills liberally to the rest of us, he would just swallow them all himself in a single go. And we believed him; not that he was suicidal – on the contrary, he'd proved himself to be quite indestructible. He just loved pills. As did we all.

I was not new to the pleasures of pill-popping, but never before had such quality prescriptions been so openly accessible to me. I'd developed a taste for self-destructiveness and was hardly about to say no when offered a free trip of what I considered to be a 'safe' form of medication (most people in the house were also recreational users of heroin, a drug I vehemently steered clear of). I was given a handful of multi-coloured pills and took them without reservation. Ativan was my favourite because it was sublingual and feeling it dissolve under my tongue took me back to a more innocent time of fizz-poppers and penny candies. Impatient for the buzz to hit one Sunday afternoon, I kept dipping into the bag until I'd taken about 12 of each kind of pill, but after an hour or more I still felt nothing. Determined to not let the day be a total waste, I phoned my dad (Oates) to see if he could pick me up so I could do some laundry at his house. This was a mistake.

As soon as I closed the car door behind me, it hit. By the time the car pulled into my dad's driveway after what seemed an interminable drive out to the suburbs of St. Vital, I was an irreparable mess, and there was no hiding it. His friend Penny Finch – possibly his only platonic female friend – was over visiting, and I can't imagine the embarrassment I must have caused him. It was like an after school special come to life. I sat at the table, berating my father for everything from having no sense of humour (not true) to buying me shitty Christmas presents (probably true), while Penny Finch leaned across the table, asking in a calm, non-judgmental voice, "Are you on drugs right now?"

above: Teenage prostitute Tiny, in promo shots for Martin Bell, Mary Ellen Mark and Cheryl McCall's **Streetwise** (1984).

Fed up, my father threw me and my laundry out into the street. I woke up two days later, back at the rooming house, with no idea how I got there or what happened in between other than a few fleeting images: walking on the railing of the Marion St. Bridge; sitting in a dimly lit room with the (mostly) platonic friend I was in love with throughout my young life; arguing with my ex-room-mate at her parents' house in Norwood. From these memories I can surmise that I walked home from my father's house in St. Vital, through the Francophone district known as St. Boniface and back to my rickety fire-trap of a house on the edge of Wolseley. A distance of about 13 miles. Ironically, a later conversation with my ex-room-mate revealed our argument to have been caused by my indignation over what I considered to be her cavalier and excessive drug use.

A few years later I was listening to the radio at work and a news story came on about a guy who murdered his wife while under the influence of Halcion. They threw the case out because it had been discovered that Halcion caused both uncharacteristically violent behaviour and extensive memory loss, and has been consequently withdrawn from the market in many countries (Canada not being one of them). Ativan and Librium are also known for their amnesiac properties.

I'd never had a blackout before, nor have I had one since, but it's frightening to think that a shell of myself was walking around for two days doing god knows what. Although the standard definition of a blackout is a loss of memory caused by alcohol consumption, blackouts in films are often equally tied to self-medicating and/or repression. Brazilian actress Florinda Bolkan (the staunchest of eurotrash babes and rumoured to have been JFK's last lover) stars in two of the strongest giallo examples of the amnesiac subgenre: Lucio Fulci's *A Lizard in a Woman's Skin* (1971) and Luigi Bazzoni's *Footprints* (1975). Bolkan's screen presence – which is more castrating than arousing – diverges from the typical casting choices for 'weak and sickly' giallo girls, which makes her suspicions more believable, and her eventual breakdown of greater emotional import.

Just like *All the Colors of the Dark*, *A Lizard in a Woman's Skin* starts with a dream. A woman clad in a heavy fur coat (Bolkan) makes her way through a train corridor, which gets increasingly crowded with people before transforming into a long white hallway full of naked, cavorting partygoers. Her anxiety is apparent as she pushes her way past the flailing limbs and breasts, until she feels herself falling slowly into blackness. She emerges in a dark bedroom where a mostly nude beautiful blonde woman (Anita Strindberg, also of *Gently Before She Dies*) seduces her on a bed lined with red satin. Bolkan accepts the caresses but tellingly doesn't make eye contact with her seducer.

This is because Bolkan plays Carol, the prim, upright and repressed wife of an ambitious young lawyer who neglects and cheats on her, and the beautiful blonde is her slutty next door neighbour Julia, who Carol is secretly excited by despite her apparent disgust with Julia's excessively hedonistic lifestyle. She routinely attends therapy and discusses her dreams with a psychiatrist only too happy to interpret them as typical doppelganger fare: in her dreams, the neighbour becomes the depository for her shameful desires. When the dreams escalate to include the murder of the neighbour, the psychiatrist proclaims this to have been "a liberating dream… you killed the part of yourself that is attracted to degradation". But if the neighbour is a doppelganger, we know that means one thing: one of them is about to die for real.

Carol soon finds herself at the centre of a murder investigation, and her ability to distinguish between dream, memory and reality gradually crumbles. At one point, while being pursued by an attacker, she runs through a series of labyrinthine corridors and tunnels, and clenches her fists so tightly that her hands bleed – as though she is 'pinching herself' to see whether or not she is awake. She can no longer trust her own feelings of lucidity, especially since everyone close to her is so sceptical.

It's interesting how often dreams and memory cross over in genre films. Just as classic dream structure involves condensation and substitution – one person turns into another, spatial and temporal shifts are not navigated in a linear fashion – as well as wish-fulfilment, memories also sometimes shape themselves by filling in blanks from our subconscious. "Dreams have a short life in the memory", says Carol's therapist in *A Lizard in a Woman's Skin*. But if anything, I've come to realize that memories also have a short life in the memory.

top right: Florinda Bolkan and Anita Strindberg in Lucio Fulci's **A Lizard in a Woman's Skin** (1971).

"We interpret what we see, select the most workable of the choices", wrote Joan Didion in *The White Album*, "We live entirely, especially if we are writers, by the imposition of a narrative line upon disparate images, by the 'ideas' with which we have learned to freeze the shifting phantasmagoria which is our actual experience."[27] My own memories involve condensation and substitution, just as my dreams do, and wish-fulfilment would come in the form of fantastical lies I used to tell my schoolmates, which – when told enough times – became impossible to distinguish from the truth.

A profound but questionable memory I have (that could be easily proved or disproved with a little research) involves me and several of my schoolmates sitting beneath a tree next to the railroad tracks at recess. I'm not sure which grade it was, but it was elementary school and we were singing songs, as we did frequently. An old woman started walking across the tracks from the other side, where Jos. Janisse St. came to a dead end (strangely in Windsor everything is named "Janisse" this or that – it's the only place my surname is common). We'd seen her many times before; she was some crazy lady who seemed to wander around aimlessly every day near our schoolyard. But on this day she stopped dead in the middle of the tracks, and we heard the faint hum of a train coming.

We all bolted up and started yelling at her to get off the tracks, but she didn't even move. We assumed she must be deaf or something because she didn't react even slightly to the shouting and frantic waving of hands. There was a wire fence between us and her, and any one of us could easily have climbed over it. But none of us did. The next thing I remember is a paramedic prying my fingers off the fence and telling me I had the rest of the day off school.

My reaction to this traumatic event was to tell everyone that she had been cut into so many pieces they had to put her in six different body bags, and that they had forgotten one of her hands on the tracks – which was now rotting away amid the stones and weeds. For years afterwards, kids (myself included!) were afraid to cross the tracks on their way home lest 'The Green Hand' get them. That I made up the story of 'The Green Hand' is without doubt, but to this day I have yet to find anyone to corroborate that this train accident ever happened in the first place.

In *A Lizard in a Woman's Skin*, Carol even goes so far as to enlist witnesses in her dream – two hippies who look on from an upper loft as she murders her next door neighbour. When she asks the psychiatrist who these people are meant to be, he replies easily, "They were you as well". But if the hippies are also representations of her, then this might stand to mean that she is witnessing her own crimes from the outside, which gives her further insight into her transgressive activities.

In many women's horror films, loneliness and alienation lead to a complex fantasy life that exists in dreams and hallucinations, facilitated by self-medication or sometimes just an imagination working overtime. We fill in the gaps on one hand (saturating any emotional void with the love, excitement or personality traits we don't really have), but create gaps on the other (jumping from one reality to the next, and skipping over any truths we don't like). While the resolution to *A Lizard in a Woman's Skin* will negate its psychological preoccupations, its examination of repression and blackout psychology remains its most interesting facet.

In *Footprints*, Bolkan is again cast as a woman forced to re-evaluate her claim to sanity when events start to conspire against her. *Footprints* is one of only two gialli directed by Luigi Bazzoni, an unfortunate deficiency given that his two efforts far surpass many other examples of the genre (his other is the stunning *The Fifth Cord* (1971).

In both *A Lizard in a Woman's Skin* and *Footprints*, Bolkan is a woman alone – in *Lizard* because she is emotionally isolated from her husband and family, and in *Footprints* because she lives singularly in a perversely tidy apartment and spends most of her time immersed in her work. This detachment leads her to a life of social superficiality, and opens up an exaggerated internal fantasy life that includes alternate identities, false histories, and even murder.

In *Footprints*, Bolkan plays Alice, a well-paid translator living in Italy. Her memories of an old sci-fi movie that made "a terrible impression" on her in her youth inform her fantasy life in the present: images of a man abandoned on the moon as part of a sadistic scientific experiment, mirroring her own sense of isolation and longing for a firm sense of heritage and genealogy. Through her work as a translator, the languages of other cultures act as substitutes for any sense of her own ethnicity. Even though she is in Italy, she has no connection to the place – she was merely brought there for work. Similarly in real life, the Brazilian actress was cast in numerous Italian films but like most eurotrash leads, she is a foreigner – another of the giallo's continued obsessions.

Her adventure begins when – after waking from a bizarre nightmare inspired by a memory of the sci-fi film – she shows up for work and is reprimanded for having been absent the three days previous. Realizing she has no memory of this 3-day period, and assuming it must be due to an accidental overdose of the tranquilizers she routinely ingests due to general anxiety, she is nevertheless faced with a series of inexplicable tokens that hint at a forgotten adventure: an unfamiliar blood-stained dress in her closet; and a ripped up postcard from a place called Garma. A weird sense of urgency pulls her to the distant island of Garma in search of an explanation. There she meets a stable of odd strangers who claim to have seen her the previous Tuesday. One of them is Nicoletta Elmi, the creepy red-headed kid who showed up in every Italian exploitation of this period, who knows more about Bolkan's predicament than she is letting on.

While Bolkan's character has a certain strength and integrity about her, she is strange nonetheless, and almost accepts the mystery she is thrown into without question. Her new 'job' is to investigate her own disappearance – again positing herself in the third person, living her own experience from outside of it. As she stumbles through memory blocks looking for the truth, scenarios are subject to an increasingly frequent repetition, and in this manner the film recalls the mood evoked by Francesco Barilli's 1974 film *The Perfume of the Lady in Black* (it doesn't hurt that the same composer – Nicola Piovani – was employed for both features).

I don't profess to understand the conclusion of this convoluted film, but suffice to say Alice has some problems distinguishing fact from fiction, and memories from dreams. As such, the viewer too is a victim of the 'conspiracy'; the only thing we know for certain is that we can't trust our own perception.

The year between my 17th and 18th birthdays was a bridge of sorts: I was serious about reinventing myself, and I wanted to let go of my past and move on, but I didn't have anything to move on to. My struggles with identity persisted, and this entire year was spent placating the people around me so that my sudden 'popularity' wouldn't dissipate. However, a deep depression started to sink in. On a superficial level I finally 'fit in', but I was more lost than ever.

The desire to 'erase' one's painful past is the central theme of the subdued Korean sci-fi film *Nabi* (aka *The Butterfly*, 2001). Although not a wholly original science fiction concept, writer/director Moon Seung-wook uses it to examine issues of identity in Southeast Asian culture in general, and the emotional devastation of a young woman in particular.

A Korean woman named Anna arrives in Seoul after a long time abroad in Germany. Wandering around a desolate airport, she realizes she's lost her baggage; no matter, she won't need it where she's going. A young girl locates Anna and introducing herself as Yuki; she will be her guide through the "Oblivion virus" – an elusive virus that infests the city's

construction sites and promises a clean slate to all who catch it. While discovered inadvertently, it has become a popular industry, and 'travel agencies' have been set up to exploit the power the virus holds for those who want to permanently erase painful memories from their lives and start over.

What ensues is like a less comical *After Hours*: no matter what happens, Anna just can't get to the virus, or even to her hotel, whether it's because of the illegitimately pregnant Yuki, their driver K – who has his own agenda, trying to find the parents who abandoned him as a child – or the lethal acid rain which forces Anna to stop for antibiotic showers every time she gets stuck in a downpour. Although much of the film takes place in the car, it nevertheless has a completely chaotic feel to it that is emphasized by all the necessary science fiction elements that pervade the story.

Caught in a suddenly alien Seoul, Anna slowly develops an intense attachment to the two people whose job it is to lead her to Oblivion, and when her desire to lose her memory is mirrored by their desire to have

top right: Florinda Bolkan in Luigi Bazzoni's **Footprints** (1975).

centre right: Florinda Bolkan abducted by (imaginary) spacemen in **Footprints**.

bottom right: Florinda Bolkan struggling with her own perception in **Footprints**.

meaningful memories, and to have parents, friends, sisters or any semblance of permanence, she comes to question her decision. A bizarre situation becomes truly frightening when Anna discovers she may have already caught the Oblivion virus before.

Director Moon Seung-wook stated that the film is about the Asian experience of memory and the desire to emulate America, which serves as a virus upon that memory.[28] This is why the construction sites – where new mini-malls and fast food restaurants were being erected – were the sites of infestation. On a microcosmic level, at the centre of this story is a woman who must decide whether it is better to remember or to forget. It is never disclosed what catastrophic event, if any, prompted her to seek out the virus, let alone to seek it out more than once, but it is not important – she can't handle the baggage of memory, she can't use memory to inform a constructive direction in her life; instead it debilitates her.

On the other end of the spectrum is Jean Rollin's *La nuit des traquées* (aka *The Night of the Hunted*, 1980), which focuses on a group of people (including Rollin regular Brigitte Lahaie) who are being held in an experimental research facility. What these people have in common is their total loss of memory, requiring that their object of attention be directly in front of them at all times lest it be immediately forgotten. The surreal and desolate atmosphere of the facility at times recalls Cronenberg's early *Stereo* (1969) and *Crimes of the Future* (1970), as does the sense of mystery surrounding who these people are, and how they came to be in such a place. Rollin's film, while occasioned by overly sentimental dialogue and verging on the pornographic, explores those aspects of memory that we take for granted.

Most strikingly, it questions the possibility of an eternal present, of an existence without memory. The person who has no memory is seen as vulnerable (this is emphasized by the frequency with which the 'patients' are entirely unclothed), which stresses our past as essential to what we are now. Our personalities are reinforced by the things we have lived through, and to have no past, or to have none that we can recall, is to be somehow less human.

These people live in a constant state of anxiety that is only alleviated by the presence of other people, to whom they develop an immediate and intense attachment that more often than not, comes to fruition in the form of a lengthy sex scene (this is a Rollin film, after all). Rollin's pseudo-scientific explanation for what has happened to these people seems kind of tacked-on and unnecessary. Like its characters, the film has no firm grounding; it has a dreamy, ethereal quality about it that likens it to his earlier *Fascination* (1979) and *La rose de fer* (1973) or even

above: Brigitte Lahaie and Dominique Journet in Jean Rollin's **La nuit des traquées** (1980).

Werner Herzog's 1979 adaptation of *Nosferatu*. Interestingly, in Rollin's world, it seems memory loss could be seen as a cure for anti-social behaviour. But memory has its ways of persistence, of colouring every human transaction with the stains of the ones that came before.

My 18th birthday was a disheartening day: I was officially no longer a child, and the Independent Living Program's benefits were cut off. As I'd made no financial contingency plan, I was left with no choice but to apply for welfare. I lamented to my boyfriend at the time and he consequently broke up with me, stating that I was too depressing to be with. This didn't bother me so much as the terror of being in the wide open real world, now with the adult responsibilities I'd always wanted but was hardly prepared for.

My 18th birthday was also a turning point in another way. all my life I had been waiting for the day when I could legally register to meet my biological parents. I didn't know what I was going to do when I found them, and I didn't know how to register, other than going to the nearest Children's Aid office and telling them, "here I am – give me my parents!" So that's essentially what I did. I filled out a form, and they entered my information into the computer while I waited for it to match me up with my birth parents and any siblings. The social worker looked at the screen and sighed. "I'm afraid there's nothing here", he said. I stiffened. "What do you mean… nothing?" No one had registered to meet me, and with Manitoba adoption records closed up to a certain date, I was out of luck unless the request was mutual. I was devastated; it had never occurred to me that they wouldn't be waiting for me. I've never tried to find them since.

I moved around from one roommate to the next, while the welfare office forced me into a work placement programme called TRY (Training Resources for Youth). Through TRY I met a youth worker named Val, who would in short order become another pseudo-foster parent for me. Val was (and still is) one of the hippest women I'd ever met – she already had five kids of her own, many of whom she'd raised as a single parent, and she was funny, interesting, crafty and resourceful. And most importantly, she didn't think I was the loser that everyone else thought I was.

One of her kids was a 6-year-old girl named Erin, who I would be charged with babysitting from time to time. When I first met Erin she insisted that she was a cat, and would crawl around on all fours, eat food out of a dish on the floor, and rub up against people's legs, purring. Erin had a morbid sensibility, and I had great fun showing her films she was too young to watch, and regaling her with stories of cannibal killer Jeffrey Dahmer, who was heavily in the news at that time. Being the only girl in a family of male siblings, it was clear she wanted a big sister, just as I had at her age. She would draw me pictures of mutilated animals and I would proudly hang them on my refrigerator. I, in turn, gave her a *Hellraiser* T-shirt, which caused her to be sent home from school. Val didn't know about the movies her daughter had been privy to until one day Erin refused to go into the basement, fearing an attack from *The Cellar Dweller*. I was in trouble for about a week, but eventually Val had to give in and acknowledge that her kid just wasn't like all the others. Erin was the only kid I ever liked, and the only kid who ever liked me. And I'm proud to say she turned out to be a great adult.

A popular tradition in Winnipeg is something called a 'social': someone rents a community hall and throws a party for paid admission, usually as a sort of fundraiser for a wedding, school tuition or a trip overseas. While I was staying at Val's I went to a social high on mushrooms, along with my friends Sonja and Robin. As I moved through the crowd talking to people, the pleasure (and pride) of being familiar with everyone soon transformed into a bizarre physical sensation: I felt as though I was suspended in the air at a distance from everyone, and the closer I tried to get to them, the further away I would float. I sat like this for a while, observing everything from above, and it struck me that none of these people were my friends. There was no one in this room I would feel comfortable crying to, no one who would care or notice if I just disappeared.

I tried to tell Sonja and Robin that I was feeling socially anxious, but they just giggled to each other, compounding my anxiety. I had to get out of there. I convinced my friend Wolf's dad to drive me home, and I sat up all night in my room at Val's, trying to work out what to do with my life now that I figured I was completely friendless.

I told Val I was moving out, and I got a small basement apartment a few blocks away. I had no furniture, except for a pair of old couch cushions and a coffee table I found somewhere. I needed a bed, and someone I worked with was married to an escape artist who had an old casket he used to use in his act. The casket was outfitted with soft cushions, and they assured me it was perfectly comfortable to sleep in. Being the morbid person I was, I leapt at this opportunity. I would sleep with the lid closed, and a book stuffed in the corner for ventilation. I was surprised at how roomy it was inside.

I also had a TV and VCR, and a burgeoning movie collection, so I dove into it – isolating myself once again among fictional onscreen friends. I quit my job and slowly stopped going out socially, my only activity for several months being daily trips to the video store to watch all the horror films in alphabetical order. I started writing fan letters to Dario Argento, and would feebly try to translate them into Italian using an English-Italian dictionary. Convinced that the translations must be terrifically puerile, I claimed to be only 12 years old, so that he would forgive my bad Italian. I watched about 5 movies a day, and any friends who tried to maintain contact with me

were met with frightening comments like "I can't talk to you right now, I'm having dinner with a very famous actor." Eventually I got to the letter F in the horror section, and the film *Fade to Black* (1980) made its way through my VCR seven times in a row before I realized I needed to get out of the house. If I didn't get myself together I was going to be Eric Binford in no time.

I went back to work, and tried getting used to socializing again, but during my isolation I had made myself incredibly paranoid and it took a while before I could last more than 10 minutes in any social setting. However, within a couple months I was back to normal – well, as normal as you can be when you sleep in a coffin.

The coffin became a bit of a curiosity piece in my social circle; everyone wanted to see it, or lie down in it to see what it was like. It was also the foundation for hilarious rumours that I was a teenage necrophiliac.

The coffin wasn't solely responsible; since seeing the 1971 feature *Harold and Maude* I'd been attending funerals recreationally – that is, until I was kicked out of Thompson Funeral Home under the auspices of being a pervert. But the truth was that I wanted to be an undertaker, and I was worried that I secretly might not have the guts to be alone in a room with a corpse. So I would sit at the back at funerals, and after everyone had said their final goodbyes, I would go up to the coffin and just stare at the person to see how long it would take before I was unnerved, which was usually instantaneous.

That isn't to say that necrophilia wasn't a hot topic in my video collection; no boy was ever left alone with me for more than ten minutes without being subjected to Jörg Buttgereit's *Nekromantik* (1987). I was obsessed with Jörg's soft-focus necro-gore masterworks, partially because they were among the first genuine 'underground' horror films I saw, but also because they seemed to upset people so easily – and as always, I liked being able to endure what other people ran from.

Jacques Lacerte's *Love Me Deadly* (1973) is another necrophile film that plays with the trappings of romantic drama. It has a lot of parallels with *Toys Are Not for Children*, as well as the Mimsy Farmer vehicles *The Perfume of the Lady in Black* and *Autopsy* – a young girl who never got over the loss of her father grows up frigid, but with a 'strange' affection for the dead. Lindsay Finch (Mary Wilcox) is beautiful, sexy, socially charismatic and not at all hard up for male attention. She throws swinging parties in her lavishly decorated '70s baroque pad, which she inherited when daddy died, but routinely disappears at orgy time.

Instead, she pours over the obits, looking for recently departed young males. A regular at funerals, she visits the casket after everyone else has gone, and passionately paws the deceased. In one such scene, hilarity ensues when she starts fondling a corpse who's had an extensive reconstructive make-up job on his face, and his visage collapses under her touch. Comedy! As she watches the other women at the funerals cry, she looks on with wonderment, as though she can't relate to their grief – for her, death is not final; she could never accept it as such.

She's not the only pervert on parade in this high melodrama disguised as an exploitation film, though: there's a whole clique of creepy necrophiliacs who hang out at the morgue hoping to cop a feel (or more) of a fresh corpse. She tries to ward off her feelings for the dead by running to sunny blond stud Wade (Christopher Stone, future husband of perennial movie mom Dee Wallace Stone), and then TV heart-throb Lyle Waggoner, but she can't follow through with the physical component of the relationship. She tries to join the others at the funeral home, but is overwhelmed by their ritual sadism and aggression with the bodies.

Necrophilia aside, the sexual politics of the film are confusing. Group sex, public sex and partner-swapping seem to be the norm in this world, even though the protagonist's goal is clearly to achieve monogamy, old-fashioned romance and therefore closure. As such, tension abounds in the film, as 'normalcy' and 'perversion' are not clearly defined opposites, and each threaten to collide with the other in what is certain to be a cataclysmic moment. Lindsay reaches desperately for the status quo, but no matter how handsome and loving her partner, she can't ignore the beckoning of the latest cold one in the morgue. She cries when touched in anything other than a fleeting manner. She likes flirting, but the way a child flirts; innocently, with no sense of what comes after.

Lindsay's emotional problems are multitudinous. Through flashbacks we can see the affection she had for her father, and it is revealed that she accidentally killed him as a child. The trauma left her unable to truly grow up, despite her fervent attempts to adapt to the '70s stereotype of womanhood (sexy, liberated,

above: Mary Wilcox and friends in Jacques Lacerte's **Love Me Deadly** (1973).

promiscuous), and she sneaks off to the graveyard daily, in pigtails and Holly Hobbie dresses, adopting a child's voice when she engages in conversation with her dead father. Her relationship with death is fascinating – a complete denial of death (her daily routine at daddy's grave) co-exists with total physical immersion in it (her necrophilic exploits). As with most necrophilia films, personal issues with power and identity have a hand in Lindsay's neurosis: Lindsay suffers from an intolerable Thanatophobia, but rather than insulating herself from death, her somewhat shaky mandate is to penetrate and expose death so as to camouflage her own stifling frigidity. Her activities are fuelled by her fear of adult relationships and the emotional responsibility they require.

Necrophilia was a unique sexual aberration that fascinated me as a teenager – it seemed to be the greatest sexual transgression there was. I couldn't imagine what the turn-on would be in making love to a rotting corpse, but I remember voraciously reading about 'unrepentant necrophile' Karen Greenlee in Adam Parfrey's seminal tome *Apocalypse Culture* in the late '80s; Greenlee had been the inspiration for the characters in both Buttgereit's 1991 sequel *Nekromantik 2* and Barbara Gowdy's 1992 short story *We So Seldom Look on Love* (which was made into the film *Kissed* in 1996).

In many of these films, the corpses are recently-dead, waxy and made-up – not viscous and putrid like the one in *Nekromantik*. Contrasting the more sanitized versions of necrophilia in films like *Love Me Deadly* or *Kissed*, the characters of Rob and Betty in *Nekromantik* bathe in dirty water and blood and live in complete squalor. During one such bath, Rob reaches his hand out to grasp the blood dripping from a dead cat, its redness in sharp contrast to the withered whiteness of his waiting appendage; he hopes to absorb some life from the dead.

Rob and Betty's lifestyle may be exaggerated (Buttgereit always maintained that the film was a comedy, even though most fans disagree), but it emphasizes the health risks inherent in necrophilic behaviour. Fluids are still being exchanged, but they're the fluids associated with embalming and bodily disintegration. "When you're on top of a body it tends to purge blood out of its mouth", explains Karen Greenlee in the *Apocalypse Culture* interview with Jim Morton. Having sex with a corpse is an easy way to get sick. At the time of the notorious interview, Greenlee had been avoiding necrophilic interaction because of the AIDS scare: "I haven't tried anything lately. I'm sure I'd have found a way to get into one of these funeral homes by now, but the group I find attractive – young men in their twenties – are the ones who are dying of AIDS."

So by extension, it's safe to say that many necrophilia films are also discussing the health risks inherent in sex in general. As Barbara Creed points out in *The Monstrous Feminine*, "the corpse is the ultimate in abjection, it is the ultimate pollution, because it is a body without an identity, and (in religious terms) without a soul. The body protects itself from such bodily wastes as feces, urine, blood, and pus, by ejecting these things from the body, and at the same time, extricating itself from them and the place where they fall so that it might continue to live."[29]

Nekromantik's most salient feature then, is perhaps its refusal to protect the human body from its own waste, by ultimately aligning them so that the imaginary border between them is obliterated. For Rob and Betty in *Nekromantik* to embrace that which threatens their extinction is an act of self-destruction, of *dis*-integration, of nihilism. In general terms, theorist Julia Kristeva (in her 1982 book *Powers of Horror*) defines the 'abject' as that which "does not respect borders, positions, rules" and "disturbs identity, system and order", and describes the place of the abject as "the place where meaning collapses."[30] Rob and Betty live almost entirely in this place.

What enables them to do this is their mutual lack of assurance or concretization about their own respective identities. Rob and Betty aspire to 'normalcy'; they eat together, smiling at each other from across the table while John Boy Walton's unbearably romantic score accompanies their facetious role-playing. But lingering in the background is the dominating presence of the corpse, which serves as a reminder of their transgressions and insecurities. The juxtaposition of the cadaver (the abject) and the meal (indicator of the symbolic order) delineates Rob and Betty's attempt to 'domesticate' death. But death, of course, is the one thing that cannot be domesticated.

As for myself, I did nothing to dispel the rumours about my own fictional necrophilic tendencies. They kept people from hitting on me and diverted attention from a larger problem – I had contracted a sexually transmitted disease of my own.

above: Beatrice M. and Daktari Lorenz in Jörg Buttgereit's **Nekromantik** (1987).

PART SEVEN:
YOU'VE ALWAYS
———— LOVED
VIOLENCE

One of the first books I ever read – I would have been 4 or 5 years old, shortly after The Man with Green Eyes dreams started to occur – was a Hallmark storybook called *Lamont, the Lonely Monster*, about a hideous but timid monster living in fear of the renowned 'Uriah the Heap', who "eats monsters like him for breakfast", but is actually a misunderstood character who really just wants to be loved.[31] This book formed the predominant

philosophy of my childhood: that there was no such thing as a truly evil monster, only people nobody had taken the time to get to know. In between nightmares I often had pleasant dreams of having tea parties with the monsters that lived in the cubbyhole behind my sister's closet.

The book made my recurring dream of The Man with Green Eyes less scary as it became more familiar. The Man with Green Eyes was special to me; I imagined that we were alike.

When I moved into my first apartment as a teenager, I met a boy named Keith. He was alternately angry and despondent and I thought he was beautiful. He had trouble at home and a girlfriend who caused him a lot of grief. But he was as obsessed with her perfection as I was with his; despite my own feelings I routinely helped them patch things up whenever she cheated on him or tried to kill herself in the bathroom at a party. I became the best friend and confidante, convinced that one day he'd realize he was meant for me. When people asked what I saw in him, my answer was always the same: that he was the only guy I knew who was '*real*'. But '*real*' to me, at that time, meant that one was an open, walking wound: I didn't trust people who were happy, I didn't trust people who hadn't been beaten up by their parents or raped, who'd never run away or survived something terrible. I only identified with pain, and Keith exuded pain like no one I'd ever met.

"P-p-p-please, Mr. Heap," Lamont stammered. "I'd make a terrible breakfast. Couldn't we be friends?"
"Friends?" cried Uriah the Heap. "Friends?!? You and me? Friends?!?!"
"Well, that *is* why I came here, Mr. Heap. I want so much to have a friend."

Keith didn't fully reciprocate my feelings though, and they made him increasingly uncomfortable; the more I catered to him, the more his verbal lashings started directing themselves at me. Our once-supportive relationship morphed into one of vitriol and hatred, spotted with occasions of physical violence. We were teenagers, and this was *real love* to me. I tried dating other people, and my attempt at getting over Keith in a 'healthy' way was rewarded with a short-term boyfriend who brought home a long-term disease: I got herpes from a guy who cheated on me with his ex-girlfriend. If this was what normal guys were like, I wanted no part

above: A page from Dean Whalley's book **Lamont, the Lonely Monster** (1970).

opposite: Maribel Martín in Vicente Aranda's **The Blood Spattered Bride** (1972).

of it. Give me the crazy ones and let's make a suicide pact. Eventually Keith went to jail for robbing a 7-11 with a Nintendo gun, and turned into a Hare Krishna upon release. This mellowed him out significantly and I completely lost interest – but only after six years of celibacy and hidden devotion.

While I rationalized my celibacy as being derived from strict honour codes concerning emotional fidelity, the truth is that it shielded me from having to tell anyone that I had a communicable disease. For those who don't know, herpes doesn't go away, and there's always the risk of transmitting it to someone else. Low self-esteem accompanied me through my early 20s as a result, which further fuelled my sympathy for men more monstrous than I perceived myself to be. What I projected onto them was my hidden hope that – like me – they could be proven *not* monstrous with a little patience and love. The disease would also play a continued part in my relationship with horror films, especially those with bodies that were out of control.

There were a few near-relationships in my early 20s, most notably a short-lived fling with a fellow genre fan who would end up penning a now-classic book about Canadian horror films. He worked at the video store I frequented, and after a few months of practically stalking but never speaking to him, a friend dared me to ask him out. So one day I mustered my courage, stormed into the video store, threw a fortune cookie at him and left. Inside the fortune cookie was my phone number. When I got home, the phone was ringing, and we spent the next few weeks dating innocently. But this relationship was better served on a platonic level; ultimately our interests were so similar as to be redundant, and it lacked the maniacal intensity I required at the time.

I first heard of the Stockholm Syndrome when reading about the Patty Hearst case sometime in the mid-'80s, but it had already been my preferred form of fantasy romance for some time before then. The term was coined by psychiatrist Nils Bejerot, and generally refers to a situation in which a hostage or victim develops respect, adulation, sympathy or even love for an aggressor. The syndrome is named after a robbery in 1973 in Stockholm wherein hostages held captive in a bank for six days became emotionally attached to their captors; after their 'rescue', one hostage set up a defence fund for their captors, and another married one of them.

The kind of relationship categorized as fitting the description of Stockholm Syndrome is generally one of Machiavellian kindnesses: while the threat of violence is always there, the victim begins to look upon their oppressor as 'giving' them life merely by not taking it. The victim tends to perceive a lack of blatant abuse as benevolence, and responds with gratitude. Psychiatrists believe that in these situations – which are intensified by isolation – the victim regresses to a state of infancy, and their dependence on their oppressor simulates a primary attachment not unlike that between a baby and a parent.

While the Stockholm Syndrome is now used as a blanket term for any case that involves a victim sympathizing with one's oppressor – and has been used historically to refer almost exclusively to female victims – it is also an easy dismissal of difficult and complex emotions. It is a way to put the blame on an abstract concept without really analyzing the situation. For a woman to love a man who treats her badly, or to build a relationship around a bond of mutual pain, is considered unhealthy. And yet countless mainstream movies and television shows – Steven Soderbergh's *Out of Sight* (1998) comes to mind, or even warm and fuzzy TV fare like *Gilmore Girls* – derive much of their romantic content from situations just like this: rationalizing that the 'bad guy' is really a 'good guy' deep down. It's not an alien concept, and it's not something that only a minority of neurotic women fantasize about. It's a masochistic challenge for sure, but one that is deeply embedded in the romantic chemistry of many women, because in these instances it's a reflection on the 'specialness' of the woman if she can crack the tough outer shell of the reticent male, thus humanizing the monster. When a woman is motivated by the possibility of changing her partner's fundamental makeup – even if she thinks it's for the better – this is a sure sign of encroaching neurosis. But it's more common than we'd like to think.

So much of how women's identities are shaped comes from the way they relate to the men around them, much of it based on the desire for approval of one sort or another. That's not the way it should be, but that's how it is. And when these past experiences are traumatic, look out; identities become muddled as drastic measures are taken in order to cope. In some genre films, women repress the trauma and then identify with their assailants indirectly, such as in Dario Argento's *The Bird with the Crystal Plumage* (1970) and *The Stendhal Syndrome* (1996) – both of which see victimized women taking on the physical identity of their male attackers. As is explained haphazardly in the closing wrap-up, Monica Ranieri in *The Bird with the Crystal Plumage* was raped as a child and in later years came to identify with her killer as a psychological defence mechanism. She demonizes women, especially sexy women, and takes on the role of a man who must punish these women for their sexuality. As a female she is weak and inarticulate, but in the guise of her murderous male doppelganger she is an intimidating and unpredictable antagonist. Stockholm Syndrome is seen as a sturdy example of identification as a defence mechanism. In an 1982 interview in *Playboy* concerning the aftermath of her 1974 kidnapping by the Symbionese Liberation Army, Patty Hearst even said: "It was almost better to think that I had willingly, happily joined them than to think they had been able to play with my mind."[32]

A more traditional approach to the Stockholm Syndrome – one in which a person develops romantic feelings for those who harm or imprison them – can be seen in numerous genre films, which are almost uniformly dismissed as exploitative. But these feelings aren't just the products of male fantasy: they are often the result of pain being 'normalized' through earlier experiences in life, whether through abuse or neglect.

Low self-esteem is often credited as the causal factor in why many women return to abusive relationships in a cyclical fashion. Beaten down physically and emotionally, they cease to imagine the possibility of a relationship without violence or degradation. But sometimes there is an emotional agenda, which rarely gets addressed. When adult women exhibit masochistic behaviour in domestic or sexual relationships, there are a number of reasons for it: a) the women are so used to negative reinforcement or unhealthy relationships from past experiences that they can't take positive steps to escape; b) it can be part of a cycle of power, and a form of manipulation; or c) many women have mastered the art of controlled victimization, often as a means of experiencing pleasure without guilt.

Italian director Mario Bava's violent excesses, and the sexually amoral nature of his films, have historically relegated

his work in the eyes of film scholars to the realm of exploitation. It is only in the last decade that his work has been re-evaluated in an academic arena, and his films recognized for their often progressive (although not always sympathetic) attitude towards gender issues. Although well versed and influential in practically every genre, his seminal work in the area of gender politics remains his 1963 Gothic horror film *The Whip and the Body*. Based on a script by giallo master Ernesto Gastaldi, Bava's *The Whip and the Body* was one of several films that resulted from a flurry of activity at that time (e.g. *Evil Eye, Blood and Black Lace,* and *Black Sabbath*). Forgoing the modern giallo in favour of a return to the Gothic terrain of his breakthrough film *Black Sunday* (aka *The Mask of Satan*, 1960), *The Whip and the Body* is arguably Bava's best and most complex movie.

The film opens with prodigal son Kurt Menliff (Christopher Lee) returning to the family estate after several years of (allegedly debauched) wandering. Hardly welcomed with open arms, he is faced with resentment from every angle – over the suicide of a maid with whom he'd had an affair, over abandoning his invalid father, and most of all from his younger brother Christian, who has in the meantime been married off to a woman (Daliah Lavi) he knows to be in love with Kurt.

When we first see Lavi's character Nevenka, she is playing the piano in the drawing room, staring vacuously and emotionless. But when Kurt glides into the room, it seems she's been resurrected. Everyone in the house – barring Nevenka, whose emotions are more nebulous – loathes Kurt, and resents his return to claim his birthright, which was promised to Christian in his absence. The older maid of the household vows to see him dead, hopefully stabbed in the throat by the same blade her daughter used to kill herself. But Kurt is unfazed by their petty comments. Always quick with a simple but cutting comeback, Kurt seems less cruel than brutally honest. Not a welcome trait in Gothic fiction.

The reunion of Nevenka and Kurt is an odd one; after a bout of suggestively mincing words later that day on the beach, he besets her with her own riding crop, spitting: "You haven't changed, I see. You've always loved violence". And one can hardly argue: when he starts whipping her, the emotions she displays aren't those of protest, but of excitement. She feigns fear, but she immediately turns her back to him, positioning herself for a good beating, and writhes in ecstasy with each lashing. Kurt leaves her lying in the sand, sexually exhausted and unconscious.

Later that night, Kurt is stabbed to death by an unseen assailant in his quarters. The accusations fly, and it looks like the Count or the maid is most likely to be the murderer – although motivation for murdering Kurt plainly exists among every member of the household. As the family unit – already twisted beyond repair by repression – starts to visibly break down, Nevenka starts to have visions of Kurt's ghost, whipping her more violently than ever before. Again, the close-ups reveal her to be in the throes of passion.

above: Christopher Lee and Daliah Lavi in Mario Bava's **The Whip and the Body** (1963).

Matters are further confused by the subsequent murder of the Count – and by Christian's fervent belief that the dead Kurt is somehow responsible. Upon following a cloaked figure one night, believing it to be the sadistic older brother's ghostly apparition, Christian is shocked and surprised to discover that it is in fact Nevenka dressed in her former lover's clothes. Repression and guilt have caused Nevenka's complete mental breakdown, and she oscillates between violence and remorse. She murdered Kurt, but in his absence there was no one to beat her – so she had to take on his identity in order to satisfy her sexual desires. But the conflict continues; convinced that Kurt is still alive and punishing her, she kills him again, by turning the knife on herself. It is a denouement that would be mirrored in Bava's final feature film *Shock* (1977).

Bava's movies were not known for their kind treatment of women as much as for the fetishization of violence directed at them. But although it is a common critical tactic to dismiss female masochism in movies as nothing more than a sexist male fantasy, Nevenka's 'neurosis' is not the product of Bava's sadistic imagination. If anything, Bava's contribution to Nevenka's condition is the *severity* of her beatings; while most masochists desire a certain degree of pain, female masochists tend to use pain symbolically. They interpret the pain inflicted upon them by their lovers as 'desire' and 'attention', whereas male masochists tend to revel in humiliation, degradation and the stripping away of their sexuality. For female masochists, the pain *reinforces* their sexuality. Pioneering sexologist Wilhelm Reich concurred that much of female masochism was a means of dispelling guilt about sex.

Additionally, pain releases endorphins in the body – opium-like chemicals with analgesic qualities – which serve to produce feelings of euphoria. But the same people who may indulge in S/M activities may not experience the same pleasure when they hurt themselves accidentally. S/M may appear outwardly violent, but it is often accompanied by metacommunicative signifiers that indicate a certain safety; the appeal of S/M is less

above: Daliah Lavi turns a knife on herself in **The Whip and the Body**.

about pain than it is about creating a playful relationship with power dynamics. Often what female masochists desire is not 'pain' per se, but – as Theodor Reike wrote in 1941 – "what they can buy with it".[33] Suffering isn't often the goal in itself; rather the tolerance for discomfort or deprivation is used as a means of servicing the ego or ego ideal. Nevenka wants to remain chaste, because chastity is demanded of any woman of good family, and she wants to suppress her desires because women of good family aren't supposed to have any. The attraction of this relationship is that it is guilt-free sex, and the perfect antidote to sexual repression. She concocts a fantasy that robs her of her own volition.

From a 19th century standpoint, enduring pain was likened to self-sacrifice and purification – she is simultaneously aroused, sated and punished for the sin of entertaining sexual thoughts, and purified in the process. It's an amazing package deal. The link between pain and ecstasy is also very prominent in Catholic myth and imagery, and Catholic dogma would have a heavy hand in the development of the Italian horror film – especially as regards their depiction of women. The Italian directors were always struggling against Catholic dogma in their films while inherently informed and corrupted by it (which gives Nevenka's dilemma in *The Whip and the Body* a broader meaning).

While 19th century psychologists promoted the theory that women were masochistic by nature, this theory was invented to encourage the submissiveness of wives and daughters, and to sanction whatever measures (i.e beatings, the refusal of education or political determination) were required to maintain it. Men were taught that being rough with their female partners was not only acceptable, but that the women would cling to them even more fiercely as a result. And women were taught that for a man's passions to be so riled as to beat her were proof of his love.

above: Daliah Lavi in Mari Bava's classic of Gothic romance, **The Whip and the Body**.

This notion was reflected in the literature of the age, one such example being Pierre Louÿs's novel from 1898, *Woman and Puppet*, whose heroine confesses to her abusive lover that if she ever lied to him it was only "to have you beat me, Mateo. When I feel your strength, I love you, I love you so; you cannot imagine how happy it makes me to weep because of you. Mateo, will you beat me again? Promise me that you will beat me hard! You will kill me! Tell me that you will kill me!"[34]

My own relationships have inevitably been affected by my mother's relationships with both of my fathers: on the one hand a promiscuous man who cheated on her, which translated into my own fear of dating men with promiscuous backgrounds out of a fear of infidelity and/or abandonment; and conversely, my stepfather, who was extremely loyal (for years after my mother left him he never accepted that she wasn't coming back) but their relationship – as mine was with him – was founded on repression, anger, and bargaining. After the violence came the presents, making 'violence' a currency of sorts in our house. This created in me an association between turmoil and love. Real love was characterized by endurance tests, and no matter how inappropriate or unmanageable things got, to see it through meant real devotion. I believed that to expect happiness without the turmoil was just shallow. As such, my own concept of love was also influenced by a Catholic upbringing in which dedication was proved through suffering.

So, if being beaten by one's lover was the norm in Victorian society, why would Nevenka in *The Whip and the Body* feel guilt over her relationship with Kurt? The problem lay in the fact that Kurt is not the man to whom she should 'submit'. Kurt is not the marrying type; he is a rascal, a philanderer, and his relationship with Nevenka is purely sexual. Their adulterous relationship, while consensual, violates her betrothal to Christian. That makes her – in the eyes of Victorian society – a whore.

By the time *The Whip and the Body* was released, these values had been reversed; adultery was common, women were scoffing at the idea of marriage, and abusive relationships (sexual or otherwise) came under criminal scrutiny. Analyzing the film from a 20th century standpoint, it is the issue of Nevenka's masochism that was of greater concern – especially to the secular portion of the anti-S/M camp, which tended to be composed of radical feminists. Andrea Dworkin's interpretation of female masochism in her 1976 book *Our Blood: Prophesies and Discourses on Sexual Politics* is typical of this position:

> "For women, the pleasure in being fucked is the masochistic pleasure of experiencing self-negation. Under the male-positive system, the masochistic pleasure of self-negation is both mythicized and mystified in order to compel women to believe that we experience fulfilment in selflessness, pleasure in pain, validation in self-sacrifice, femininity in submission to masculinity. Trained from birth to conform to the requirements of this particular world-view, punished severely when we do not learn masochistic submission well enough, entirely encapsulated inside the boundaries of the male-positive system, few women ever experience themselves as real in and of themselves. Instead women are real to themselves to the degree that they identify with and attach themselves to the positivity of males. In being fucked, a woman experiences the masochistic pleasure of her own negation, which is perversely articulated as the fulfilment of her femininity."[35]

The anti-S/M feminists see S/M as antithetical to feminist goals, and assert that S/M is a repeat of male suppression and therefore incompatible with feminism (Dworkin sees the sexual interaction of males and females as incompatible with feminism *period*). As Darlene Pagano, Jeanette Nichols and Margaret Rossoff write in *Against Sadomasochism: A Radical Feminist Analysis*: "We question the position that sadomasochism is consensual. As we have already suggested, this view ignores all the *pressures* to consent, and parallels the anti-feminist argument that women freely choose or consent to stifling marriages, second-class jobs or spike heels."[36]

Nevenka consents to both a stifling marriage *and* a sadomasochistic relationship. Her confusion over which of these is more harmful no doubt intensifies her mental fragmentation, but within the context of Bava's film it is obvious that for Nevenka to submit to a life she despises (by marrying Christian) is more masochistic than submitting to the corporal punishment she seeks at the hands of Kurt.

One might get the idea that I do not find Nevenka to be neurotic – I do. And I do acknowledge that her society defined certain roles for women that conditioned them to masochistic behaviour. But subjecting oneself to force by a person of your choosing is not tantamount to self-negation; Nevenka experiences fulfilment within an emotional system that works for her. As Molly Haskell famously said in a 1976 article for *Ms.* magazine: "A rape fantasy has nothing to do with having a couple of teeth knocked out. It's when Robert Redford won't take no for an answer."[37] Even though the issue is far more loaded than this simple comment can convey, it succinctly illustrates the difference between wilfully navigating through mock-abuse and expressing self-hatred.

While Nevenka in Bava's *The Whip and the Body* struggles to accept her masochism, the women in many eurotrash films – most notably those of Jess Franco, Alain Robbe-Grillet and José Bénazéraf – surrender to sado-masochistic situations with the conscious mandate of self-fulfilment.

In Just Jaeckin's 1975 film adaptation of Pauline Réage's *Story of O*, a female fashion photographer is taken by her lover Rene to a chateau, where she is to be turned into a slave for members of his private club. In their inaugural speech to her, they say: "You are here to serve your masters... your hands are not your own, neither are your breasts, nor, above all, is any one of the orifices of your body, which we are at liberty to explore and into which we may, whenever we so please, introduce ourselves."

There is complete trust in these relationships – even if the 'deviant' acts are carried out with or by strangers. Some see liberty in this kind of sexual ownership – though its implicit temporary state creates a necessary boundary, on the other side of which lies more conventional agency. Still, debates rage as to a woman's ability to concede to a situation like this in good conscience and sound mind: witness the controversy surrounding *Sex: The Annabel Chong Story* (1999). Annabel Chong became famous in 1995 for starring in the porno film *The World's Biggest Gang Bang*, breaking the world record at the time by engaging in 251 sex acts with 70 different men over the course of 10 hours. She was a 22-year-old gender studies student at USC, and – aside from the practical motivation to participate in pornographic work to cover her tuition – used her porno films as a means of exposing double standards concerning male and female sexuality. But when the documentary *Sex: The Annabel Chong Story*, by her then-boyfriend Gough Lewis, revealed that she had been raped in the past, and that she engaged in cutting, viewers and critics immediately stripped her of her agency, refusing to see her as anything but a victim who was too messed up to realize she was being exploited.

It can be argued that exploitation films address the politics and psychology of exploitation more coherently than 'legit' films, just because by their very crassness they often bring these issues more clearly out into the open. A case in point is Piero Schivazappa's 1969 S/M classic *The Frightened Woman* (whose Italian title, *Femina ridens*, actually translates as 'The Laughing Woman'). Typical of most Italian films of the era, everything is over-sized – big airy rooms are host to giant paintings, sculptures and photographs, whiskey is downed from massive goblets that dwarf and distort the faces of those imbibing. Emotions are heightened; everything is larger than life. The opening scene sees a group of middle-aged men lining up to be devoured by a giant vagina dentata sculpture.

The film begins as an exaggerated male fantasy: a rich playboy (Philippe Leroy, from *The Night Porter*) who hires hookers to satiate his sadistic role-playing games crosses the line into reality when he kidnaps his feisty new assistant (Euro-starlet Dagmar Lassander) with intentions of subjecting her to the punishing regimen he has acted out with hired accomplices so many times before. He drugs her and whisks her off to his modernist, labyrinthine mansion, where she awakens tied to a fence. Her captor examines her closely: the geometrical pattern formed by the curves of her body against the lines, corners and angles of the fence; the fascinating contortions of her face as she is gripped first by confusion, then fear, then despair.

top right: Dagmar Lassander and Philippe Leroy in Piero Shivazappa's **The Frightened Woman** (1969).

centre right: Dagmar Lassander in **The Frightened Woman**.

above: Another image from **The Frightened Woman**, which was originally entitled **Femina ridens (The Laughing Woman)**.

He teaches her to be subservient, to obey, to be afraid. She succumbs – and just when she gets accustomed to any particular punishment, when her fear subsides and she proves durable, he takes it up a notch. He says he is going to kill her, while pontificating about masculine virility and the female conspiracy to obliterate it – but he is having too much fun with his slave to do anything just yet.

His reduction of her to a series of contours and animal instincts doesn't hold – the hired women were caricatures of victims, but this real woman is altogether different. There's something fiery even in her compliance. There's something going on in her mind that he can't reach, which defies his attempts to conquer her. The more he punishes her, the stronger her resolve.

Of course, he falls in love. Our virile antagonist is reduced to a blushing gnome, skipping about, trying to impress her with feats of 'masculinity'. But his happiness is marred by anxiety over his increasing emotional and physical dependence on his prisoner. From the outset he is fighting against female pretensions of control, which is what fuels his perversion – but he has been systematically disarmed, all his work undone by the weakness of love. As she assumes control, he surrenders to her. Images of him walking into the vagina dentata and being swallowed up are intercut with the climactic sex scene that will give him his fatal heart attack. We find that the captive woman is an old hand at this game of putting men in their place. She was in control all along.

So why would she submit to such an absurd punitive regimen? The modern masochist, claims psychologist Roy F. Baumeister, is taking a breather from the increasing burden of selfhood; if one assumes she can get away at any time, her predicament does not seem that undesirable.[38] Feminist Indonesian writer Ayu Utami has likened masochism to parody, in that they both work within the confines of an existing system in order to subvert its representations of power: "Both use politically incorrect language... Parody and masochist fantasies are not kinds of narration toward which we can pose the question: 'what is the meaning of it'? Because the meaning is always deflected. Masochism and parody pursue the impact of such deflection, an endless stream of paradoxical sensations upon pain and pleasure, compliance and rebellion, politeness and sarcasm."[39]

above: Philippe Leroy and Dagmar Lassander in **The Frightened Woman.**

The Frightened Woman portrays the most obvious delineation of the subversion of power positions facilitated by S/M role-play. As in *Story of O*, the woman endures every torture, every humiliation, and emerges the stronger of the two.

It's an old trope of pop psychology that men take great pains to avoid emotional difficulty, while women like to overcome it. Often this means jumping headfirst into challenges, and sometimes implies creating drama where there is none, sabotaging relationships unnecessarily. A neurotic woman will often 'test beyond the breaking point' with the twisted logic that if it can be broken forcibly, then it was always doomed to break. This reinforces the necessary delusion that she comprises the 'stronger' half of the relationship. But it also means that often women flourish in potentially dangerous situations. The notion that endurance is a sign of nobility is a concept that is prevalent in Asian films, and one that is a particularly complex brand of misogyny that women themselves are often complicit in upholding. This can be seen in the incendiary critical response to Kim Ki-duk's *The Isle* (2000) and *Bad Guy* (2001), both beautiful and complex films fairly representative of the Korean New Wave.

The Korean New Wave – ushered in by a sudden surge of young, brash directors and the inauguration of the Pusan Film Festival in 1996 – unleashed a torrent of subversive films that countered the dominance of American imports, starting with features including Kang Je-gyu's *The Gingko Bed* (1996), Kim Ji-woon's *The Quiet Family* (1997 – later remade by Takashi Miike as *The Happiness of the Katakuris*), Park Ki-hyeong's *Whispering Corridors* (1998) and Nam Gee-woong's *Teenage Hooker Became Killing Machine in Daehakroh* (2000).

Kim Ki-duk is among Korea's most ambitious auteurs, and his films have routinely invited controversy while simultaneously securing awards throughout the festival circuit. Kim was a high school dropout who had no formal education in film or the arts before embarking on his first picture *Crocodile* in 1996, which would mark the genesis of his now-signature focus on marginal spaces and their alienated inhabitants.

The Isle concerns a mute, somewhat feral young woman who acts as caretaker to a floating campground. The pastel-coloured fishing shacks that dot the lake are a stunning location for a very dark love story. She sells supplies, coffee and, at times, her own body to the lowlifes that rent the cottages, and seems remarkably self-reliant despite what appears to be her inherent masochism. When a man fleeing the scene of a murder seeks refuge in one of her cottages, a strange and dangerous unspoken bond develops between them. They become partners in mutual degradation.

The arrival of the stranger throws her accepted way of life into turmoil – her emotional detachment is threatened by her obsessive interest in him. His reasons for self-destructive behaviour are fathomable; as relayed in a flashback, he is guilty of murdering his lover after he catches her making love to another man. It appears he has rented the cottage not only as a hideout from the cops, but also as the setting for his own suicide. The silent caretaker intervenes – not with compassion, but with violence. While initially shocked at this strange obstruction, it results in a mutual understanding. She speaks his language.

Her own motivation is decidedly less apparent. Deliberately feral in both her lifestyle and her physical features, she is fascinating, but gives us little to work with. The theatricality of her appearance stresses her exoticism, and her concentrated silence recalls that of Scorpion in the Japanese *Joshü sasori* series. But where Meiko Kaji's Scorpion has been referred to (by Mitch Davis) as "an East estrogen version of Clint Eastwood's Man with No Name",[40] that comparison may be more apt here, since the former shares with Eastwood's character a certain moral ambiguity. There is a mythology behind Scorpion's identity throughout the *Joshü sasori* films,[41] but *The Isle*'s protagonist remains an enigma. We are given only the tiniest of glimpses into her past – most notably the man's clothing she extracts from her bottom drawer, hidden beneath old newspapers like taboo relics.

Despite not exchanging any dialogue, the two outcasts manage to engage in conflict, and on one such occasion, the man throws his hostess to the ground and kicks her square between the legs. She looks at him blankly as her crotch is repeatedly assaulted, mocking his feeble attempts to hurt her. She gives herself to him, whether for love or anger; it is the contact she craves, and she doesn't distinguish between one type or the other. It is only when he tries to leave that she feels real pain.

In the scene that secured the film's infamy, she turns fish hooks on her own genitals in an attempt to convey her growing emotional dependence on him. It is only here that she emits any sound at all: she lets out a loud

above: Suh Jung in Kim Ki-duk's **The Isle** (2000).

animalistic cry that is the closest she comes to verbal communication. The fish hooks are just one part of a larger theme; the film is awash with fish metaphors. The characters flop around like asphyxiating fish on deck, and when the woman falls into the lake with the fish hooks still embedded in her vagina, she is thoughtlessly reeled in with a fishing line. The very real pain of the numerous live fish that were harmed in the making of the film is matched – perhaps mocked – by the couple's histrionic flailing.

In traditional symbolism, fish indicate something repressed bubbling to the surface, but it's clearly not sexual repression, as both characters seem perfectly at ease having sex, with each other or anyone else. However, both are secretive and emotionally reticent, and each acts as a vehicle for the other's pain. What they have repressed are their feelings of loss and guilt.

The lake makes a powerful independent contribution to the film; it functions not only as the place of the action but also as a means of setting the film's dense psychical tone. The characters' emotional isolation is emphasized by the echoing grandeur of the lake, which oversees their dark folly with a blank, noncommittal dominance. The woman creeps about underwater like a predator, marking the lake itself as her 'Isle', her domain – which, like her, can shift unpredictably from placid beauty to murky danger. People are swallowed up into the fog, dumped into the depths; she conspires with the lake to erase them from existence. But traces of them are still there beneath the surface, waiting to expose her.

'The Isle' refers, as the last shot would suggest, to the female realm of experience, and a troublingly opaque one at that. When the man edges into the weeds at the end, the shot pulls back to reveal the patch of weeds as her garishly overgrown pubis. He's been pulled into her, as have all the other visitors to her floating campground – they're all at her mercy, despite their belief that as the customers, they call the shots. Their rules and their money are only tokens of an outside world that doesn't apply to her in the least.

The spider-woman motif pervasive in Japanese folklore (and in Japanese New Wave cinema, most notably in Yasuzo Masumura's 1966 feature *Tattoo*) – a horrific figure that is a dangerous hybrid of the 'prostitute' and the 'princess' archetypes – has a modern counterpart in *The Isle*'s silent protagonist. In the original folk tales, the spider-woman lives in an isolated mountain lair – sometimes a remote castle or mansion – where weary travellers would seek shelter for the night, only to get ensnared in her web and eventually consumed. Interestingly, despite the reciprocal aspects of the male/female relationship in *The Isle*, it's the female character that emerges as the controlling factor, the vortex of the drama. He buries his grief in her, but she carries on like a silent vessel for the anxieties too unbearable for those around her.

If *The Isle* raised a few hackles on the festival circuit, the following year's *Bad Guy* was enough to make most critics condemn Kim Ki-duk for good. A similarly accomplished film, *Bad Guy* was almost universally reviled as morally reprehensible. Critics and audiences alike saw the film as having an irresponsible 'no-means-yes' message: in the FAB Press book *Fear Without Frontiers*, Art Black described the film as a "controversial and misogynistic tale of a lowlife creep who fixates on a total stranger, driving her to prostitution and degradation."[42]

Jack Mathews of the *New York Daily News* proffered that "Kim Ki-duk does a bizarre riff on the twisted macho ethos of abusing women until they learn to love you",[43] while Stephen Whitty of the *Newark Star-Ledger* said: "As a case study of one disturbed woman it might be interesting; presented as some sort of deathless love story, it's merely distasteful."[44]

Only a handful of critics championed the film, able to acknowledge Kim's masterful ability to emotionally manipulate his audience. Black's synopsis is essentially accurate, but the facts and the emotions provide differing opinions of what *Bad Guy* is about. *Bad Guy* is, above all, a love story. A *twisted* love story, but a love story nonetheless. "90% of the female critics gave a negative review about the movie", Kim said in a 2001 interview with Volker Hummel in *Senses of Cinema*, "If you think of my film as Kim Ki-duk creating the misfortune of the woman it depicts, then that's very dangerous. But if you think of it as the depiction of a problem that already existed in society then you cannot really hate *Bad Guy*."[45] While Jang Sun-woo's *Lies* (1999) – about a high school student who engages in a sadomasochistic relationship with an older man – attracted positive reviews even from the feminist camp, *Bad Guy* was not similarly favoured.

A young college student named Sun-hwa is sitting on a sidewalk bench with her boyfriend when she is spotted by a fierce-looking stranger. The stranger approaches her, grabs her and kisses her, refusing to let go even when set upon by a gaggle of army goons. ("A kiss has more shock value than sex here", says Kim, "Being forcefully kissed by a stranger in a crowded public space is very insulting."[46]) The boyfriend flounders around, bashing the undeterred assailant with a garbage bin, but he ultimately fails to put a stop to the violation. When the stranger is finally separated from the girl, he refuses to apologize for his conduct and she spits on him.

Director Kim Ki-duk has claimed to be a frequent victim of random violence. "I see something which I do not understand and then I make a film in order to comprehend it", he said in the interview with Volker Hummel.[47] The narrative springs from this affront, following the assailant onto his own turf to see what informs his antisocial behaviour. As a male counterpart to *The Isle*'s mute protagonist, *Bad Guy*'s Han-gi (also mute) is suitably enigmatic and unpredictable, but he becomes strangely appealing by the film's conclusion. Han-gi is a low-rent pimp in a colourful red-light district (a set piece that nicely compliments the floating shacks in *The Isle*). Both Han-gi and the prostitutes who inhabit his world are outcasts from 'civilized' society, which views the red-light district as a human junkyard. But the hookers and thugs never let on if they yearn for another life.

"I worked in a number of factories for a few years," said Kim Ki-duk in an interview in the Korean magazine *CINE21*, "Although the jobs were not great, I treated them as if they were something natural for me to do. I felt no shame, because I thought factory jobs were my future. As I reflect on the past, I realize that if one accepts a hard life as the only way to live then this reality becomes that life."[48] As with films like *Streetwise* and *Christiane F.*, the prostitutes and petty criminals form their own society, with its own rules, honour codes and mock-family relationships, never questioning the possibility that their lifestyle choices might be dangerous or unhealthy. The money that comes instantly is often enough to override feelings of hardship.

Han-gi takes to following Sun-hwa, and one day while watching her in a bookstore he makes the move that will seal her fate: he has one of his henchmen steal another customer's wallet, take a good chunk of the cash out, and then leave the wallet within eyesight of Sun-hwa. She takes the bait, grabbing the abandoned wallet and quickly exiting the store. The wallet's owner, upon discovering its absence, chases Sun-hwa out into the street, corners her, and holds her responsible for the huge sum that is missing from the wallet. Unable to pay it back – and unwilling to suffer the degradation of being questioned by the

AT THE END OF HIS SIGHT, THERE SHE IS...

Bad Guy
Kim Ki-duk film

police – she reluctantly agrees to accept the services of a loan shark, who demands her body in lieu of delinquent payment. Not prepared for the consequences, and naïve enough to believe that her contract with the loan shark is legally binding, she is forced into prostitution under Han-gi's supervision when she proves unable to pay the debt.

Sun-hwa has clearly led a sheltered life, and is very susceptible to Han-gi's convoluted ruse. But she makes a conscious decision to steal the wallet, and – while she certainly never imagined that the consequences would entail permanent residence on the 'street of shame' – she is not entirely innocent in her demise. This is not to say that she deserves her fate, but only to point out that the film's characterizations are not as black and white as critics made them out to be. In the street-side brothel, each prostitute has her own private room, and Sun-hwa barely ventures out of it for the first half of the film. Han-gi watches her from behind a two-way mirror, and while admittedly an invasion of privacy, it also ensures that she is protected from certain realities of prostitution, like beatings from drunken patrons. Ironically, Han-gi later beats two of his henchmen when he discovers they have been secretly videotaping some of the prostitutes in action. Kim Ki-duk proudly parades these contradictions and double standards, so that any firm conclusions are easily dismantled.

The doppelganger – usually a portent of doom – is a source of reassurance in this film. When Sun-hwa momentarily escapes from the brothel with the help of one of Han-gi's love-struck underlings, her doppelganger passes her in the street, putting a sweater across her shoulders to keep her from catching cold. Later, when Han-gi catches her and the two sit silently on the beach, she sees the doppelganger again, sitting on the sand just in

above: Promotional sales flyer for Kim Ki-duk's **Bad Guy**.

front of them. The doppelganger, only visible to Sun-hwa, rips up something and buries it in the sand before getting up and disappearing into the waves. Retrieving two shredded photographs from the sand that depict a faceless couple posed on that very beach, Sun-hwa tapes them to her mirror back at the brothel.

We know from tradition that the doppelganger is often a 'storehouse' for unwanted feelings and desires; in this case, the doppelganger stands for Sun-hwa's sense of self-preservation and belief in a true love that may be a little aberrant from that of fairy tales and Hollywood movies. The doppelganger is the film's only departure from a low-key realism; it tells Sun-hwa of the future, and she follows peacefully, without reservation.

Han-gi precipitates a radical change in Sun-hwa; he shows her the meaning of pain, and through that, the meaning of 'pure' love as opposed to superficial love. He never makes any sexual advances toward her, although he does make romantic offerings with some regularity, often anonymously. While he is probably not calculated enough to orchestrate such a thing deliberately, his actions are a means of slowly eating away at her sense of shame – the only thing that separates them, and makes it impossible for her to love a thug like him.

Sun-hwa's reciprocation of his love becomes plainly apparent when he faces execution for a crime he didn't commit. She is visibly shaken by his absence and reprimands him on a visit to the jail: "You can't die like this. You ruin me, and die just like that? Come out here! Come out here, you son of a bitch! Hurry and come out here!" What begins as scorn soon turns into pleading, and she has to be carried away, weeping.

Upon his incarceration she is freed from prostitution but refuses to leave. When one of Han-gi's henchmen selflessly engineers Han-gi's release, the two lovers are reunited, but their relationship remains strangely chaste. In an odd twist on the conventional 'happy ending' the two leave the brothel and hit the road – with Sun-hwa continuing to service customers in the back of the truck while a Christian gospel song about redemption plays over the scene. The musical cues (Kim Ki-duk has stated in interviews that the Christian music was not meant to be ironic[49]) would indicate that Sun-hwa comes out okay, after an incredible ordeal that sees her stripped of her false sense of self. Her redemption is shaped and realized by the experience of abject humiliation. In line with Asian literary tradition, Kim subverts the prostitute stereotype that gets trotted out again and again in occidental films: instead of taking a prostitute and transforming her into an 'ideal woman' fit to marry, Han-gi takes his ideal woman and makes her a prostitute.

Kim Ki-duk employs all the emotional cues of a conventional romance picture, and against my better judgement I found myself hoping that Han-gi's love would be requited. Kim brilliantly manipulates the audience so that they overlook the film's brutality in favour of its romantic elements. The guilt that overtakes the audience when they find themselves emotionally responding to the film in this way is probably what caused much of the critical backlash. Is the film meant to be proof that women are only happy when dominated, or a testament to their inherent emotional strength? And whatever the answer, is it meant to be a sweeping generalization about all women, or does it apply to this fictional woman in particular?

It should be pointed out that all women in *The Isle* and *Bad Guy* are prostitutes, among them a single protagonist who stands out as a stoic character with a strong sense of identity, even if that identity is sometimes shaken and transformed by the film's end. Sun-hwa eventually comes out of the 'safety' of her back room, and joins the other prostitutes in their little cubicles facing the street that are designed to look like storefronts. While this type of display is common enough in international red light districts, it has caused some viewers to question whether this is Kim Ki-duk's way of putting these outspoken women 'in their place'. But Kim is clearly putting Sun-hwa through a trial that is meant to reveal her own masochism, and this 'display' reinforces the view that the most common type of female masochism entails forced exhibitionism, or being put on display to be looked at or touched by strangers – which is interpreted as a form of liberation.

The frequent appearance of prostitutes in South Korean film in recent years is meant to be empowering; even in Western culture there was a time when only nuns and whores were considered women with any sort of real agency or independence. Just as the Japanese 'spider woman' was a transitional character that bridged the gap between the feudal ideal of womanhood and the newly emerging 'liberated' woman, the prostitute in recent South Korean films occupies a similar place in the cinematic imagination. "I think of women as being on a higher level than me", says Kim, "They have something to offer that men always need, that they will even pay for."[50]

In the essential Japanese cinema book *Eros Plus Massacre*, Tadeo Sato pointed out that the term 'feminism' has different connotations in Japan than in the West – and this interpretation can be equally applicable here.

above: Cho Jae-hyun (reflected) and Seo Won in **Bad Guy**.

"The image of a woman suffering uncomplainingly can imbue us with admiration for a virtuous existence almost beyond our reach, rich in endurance and courage. One can idealize her rather than merely pity her, and this can lead to what I call the worship of womanhood, a special Japanese brand of feminism."[51]

While many western feminist critics have a problem with Sato's terminology, it's obvious that characters who endure and survive great hardships in the cinema are valued (take your pick of protagonists from Westerns or samurai films, for example), regardless of their gender. The suffering and humiliation of many female characters in Asian cinema – while customarily reduced to misogyny in western interpretation – is meant to be a testament to their unbreakable spirit and will.

It is perhaps the Japanese cinema of the 1960s that informed the characterization and mood of *The Isle* and *Bad Guy* most heartily. Kim Ki-duk was clearly influenced by the films of Kaneto Shindo and Yasuzo Masumura, and most prominently the psychosexual/existential collaborations between Kobo Abe and Hiroshi Teshigahara: *The Isle* is our generation's *Woman in the Dunes*. In *The Isle*, the man is not exactly imprisoned, but is still at her mercy, even more so after they become emotionally involved. All of these films involve powerful, but indirect communication.

In *The Isle* and *Bad Guy*, characters struggle to communicate their pain through muteness, through their faces and nuances. They try to connect. We've been taught that direct speech is the best and most efficient way to communicate. That people can't 'read our minds'. We have to be clear. But still, no matter how verbose and articulate we are, we run the risk of being misunderstood, of things we say being misinterpreted and twisted. Han-gi and the feral woman from *The Isle* have both retreated into silence; perhaps conventional communication has not been kind to them. In doing so, they alienate themselves from most people. But the *right* people – or the right *person* – will be able to see past their silence and understand them. Most of the people who talk have nothing to say anyway. But Han-gi and the feral woman speak volumes, without ever opening their mouths. "The violence that they turn to, I prefer to call a kind of body language", says Kim, "I would like to think of it as more of a physical expression rather than just negative violence. The scars and wounds which mark my figures are the signs of experiences which young people go through, in an age when they cannot really respond to outside traumas." Regarding the character of Han-gi, Kim says, "His silence is a symbol of sincerity."[52]

It is important to distinguish the fantasy relationship in *Bad Guy* – one that explores destructive emotions and behaviour as food for thought – from real relationships in which a partner (or partners) endures abuse. Like Sun-hwa, I wanted a relationship that didn't follow convention; that could never be neutered by banality. For me this always implied traumatic bonding, and Keith – the target of my adolescent affections – with his alternating passion and despondency, was the perfect romantic stimulant for my teenage self. While there were physical altercations, not to mention loud, nasty arguments, any abuse was mutual. I felt proud of the fact that no one would put up with him but me; I knew that to a certain extent, this made him dependent on me. With Keith being so intolerable to anyone else, my fear of abandonment was quelled.

Although I've never been in a one-sided abusive relationship (some of my friends disagree), I have a high tolerance for physical and emotional abuse stemming from my relationships with my two fathers. I always question whether the difference between being abused or not is really just a difference of perception. It's the same as the exploitation debate: I've always felt that if we don't feel exploited, we're not. But emotional psychology isn't so simple – there are all manner of defences we've built up over the years that protect us from pain and turmoil, and some of these defences shield us from even recognizing abuse when we're experiencing it. Like Cenci in Joseph Losey's *Secret Ceremony*, it's emotionally easier for us to be complicit.

Still, I always had a very low tolerance for other people's abusive relationships. When my closest friend Hanna started on a cyclical pattern of alternately living with and breaking up with her abusive boyfriend (and we're not talking mild abuse – aside from frequent physical violence it was absolute emotional terrorism, including death threats), I couldn't understand why she wouldn't leave him, and why over time she wouldn't even talk to me about it. She isolated herself with this complete monster, who gradually cut her off from everything she knew or cared about, until this once-vibrant, creative, beautiful person was just a numb shell living in fear.

But to hear her tell it is different. He loved her; she always believed that he loved her, even to this day, over a decade since finally leaving him. She believed that he was doing his best. But eventually she had to realize that his best was not good enough.

above: Seo Won and Cho Jae-hyun in **Bad Guy**.

During their relationship, my friendship with Hanna was equally on-again, off-again. I couldn't stand her boyfriend, even though I sometimes tried to make the best of it by focusing on whatever interests we had in common, like trashy movies or medieval torture devices. But I routinely abandoned Hanna whenever she got too despondent. I was a shitty friend. But replacing Hanna wasn't easy – we'd lived together in my first apartment, spent weekends dropping acid together and planning elaborate futures, written songs together. She was that friend I always wanted.

In my late teens I started obsessively reading H.P. Lovecraft stories, and became fascinated with the way he romanticized academia through his myriad characters, many of whom had connections to the iconic Miskatonic University in Arkham, Massachusetts. I was convinced that this fabled institution, with its dark towering libraries full of dusty occult texts, was where I belonged. A place where human companionship was a minor concern, and where I could work late into the night, solving ancient mysteries. But I was a high school dropout; by the time I was 18, I'd been to four different high schools and quit all of them in rapid succession. The only way I could make my way into Miskatonic's hallways was to go back to school.

I registered at a new school called Argyle – an alternative school meant for kids who'd been through the system or proven unable to deal with the structure of regular factory-style education – and when I won the Governor General's medal upon graduation, Oates said that the only reason I'd gotten it was because I went to "a school for retards" (as a result of this quip, I threw the medal in the garbage. It was rescued by my friend Val, who still has it to this day). But no matter, I had graduated. Next stop – Miskatonic! You can imagine my disappointment when I called directory assistance from the payphone outside my apartment only to be told that neither Miskatonic University, nor Arkham, Massachusetts, were real places.

But school wasn't a total write-off: I made a new friend named Laura at Argyle, and set about moulding her into my new twin. It would be a long time before I realized how narcissistic my search for the perfect friend really was.

After a year with my new bosom buddy, she announced that she was marrying her estranged (and strange) boyfriend, who had moved away to Vancouver before I met her. After the wedding they were moving to Vancouver together, and she wanted me to come along. I was reluctant, if only because the adage 'three's a crowd' seemed to have some truth in it, but she convinced me that she didn't know anyone in Vancouver and would risk losing her identity without a friend like me there with her. To be mentally associated with another person's sense of identity was an incredibly flattering reaffirmation of my romantic belief in inseparable friendships, and so I agreed. I was living with Hanna again at the time, but we hadn't spoken much since she had gotten back together with the asshole boyfriend a month or so earlier, and they spent all their time camped in front of the television watching cable on my dime.

As I said goodbye to Hanna and hugged her on the sidewalk in front of the rickety van packed full of my stuff, I could sense the worry in her; even though she had stopped reaching out to me with her relationship problems, I suppose I was still some sort of a lifeline, who would now be thousands of miles away.

Needless to say, positing myself as the third wheel in Laura's new married life was a mistake. As had happened every time Hanna and her boyfriend reunited, Laura and her husband became an insular unit; they whispered to each other while I was in the room, gave me the stink-eye when I came home as though I was intruding on their privacy, hid away in their room. I became a persona non grata. Laura had someone else to talk to now, so she stopped talking to me. She also got a credit card and bought an apron to wear in the kitchen – the latter an inexplicable, decidedly un-ironic statement against the socio-political developments of the last 30 years. My nightly sojourns at the local punk bar were looked upon as a threat to the burgeoning *Stepford Wives* existence she was moulding for herself. I had to be gotten rid of, and was I ever. Laura didn't know how to tactfully ask me to move out so that she could transition into her new married life, so she just held things in until one day I got out of the shower and she threatened, out of nowhere, to "knock me down". She was literally shaking with rage. I was stunned. I moved out and never spoke to her again. I've never been great with forgiveness.

Eventually I got over Keith (after six years of celibacy), but only because I became briefly obsessed with a young gutter punk with a facial tattoo who reminded me of him. After a few weeks of pursuing him, he ended up back at my place, and I spent the next two days being annoyed by this punk kid who just wanted to smash everything and spout nonsensical catchphrases about sticking it to the man. I realized what a waste of time it had been saving myself for the violent 18-year-old version of Keith, who didn't even exist any more. And if he had, I'd long since outgrown him.

I spent a few years kicking around Vancouver, hanging out aimlessly and working the graveyard shift at a 24-hour video store run by a sketchy guy who bought stolen videotapes from Blockbuster. Graveyards were the domain of the porno customers, most of whom rented stacks at a time and returned them all reeking of pepperoni sticks. I knew I had to quit when one guy came in and commented on my braids, and then returned from the porno room nearly an hour later with 6 video boxes – all of which featured a girl with braids on the cover. He asked if I wanted to go for ice cream some time. I said no.

In between marathon bouts of movie watching, I was also developing a speed habit. For a person who struggles with shyness, speed was a godsend. Luckily I was able to quit cold after witnessing the paranoid downward spiral of a few friends who'd been doing it longer. Friends of mine were also dropping like flies from heroin addiction, which was rampant in Vancouver. This realization coincided with an opportunity: right before I quit the video store one of the regular daytime customers – a young, handsome GQ-type I would go see movies with on occasion – gave me a pivotal talking-to. He said I was wasting my life; that I should be doing something better than what I was doing. And more importantly, he was going to put his money where his mouth was and offer me the main floor of a house he was renting for free. The house was in a better neighbourhood, and it was by living there that I started to frequent the indie store Black Dog Video, where I would eventually get a job and work for the next seven years. Gabriel Kamen, wherever you are, I owe you one.

Working at Black Dog changed my life. One might even say it saved my life.

I went back to school, inadvertently got a diploma in classical studies, and started self-publishing a horror fanzine called *Cannibal Culture* where I used my reinvigorated academic discipline to write about obscure genre films that I mail-ordered from companies like Revok, Luminous and European Trash Cinema. Craig Ledbetter from ETC in particular was a goldmine of genre knowledge, and I was turned onto him by fellow genre fanatic Sam McKinlay (also known as esteemed noise artist THE RITA) who was a regular contributor *to Cannibal Culture* and my right hand man in programming the inaugural CineMuerte Film Festival in 1999.

The first CineMuerte happened kind of by accident. One of the Black Dog customers complained that he could never see most of the films I wrote about in *Cannibal Culture*. Because of the Canadian ratings policy – which indicates that every film must legally be rated before being made available to the public, and that only a licensed distributor can submit a film for a rating – many of the films I covered in *Cannibal Culture* couldn't be rented out because they didn't come from legitimate distribution sources. I tried explaining to the customer that there was nothing I could do about the availability of these titles, and he issued what I took to be a challenge: he wanted to know why I wasn't doing anything to get these films onto some local screens.

Being completely naïve about how these things worked, I printed out some articles about the new 35mm print of Lucio Fulci's *The Beyond* that Grindhouse Releasing had issued, and went to local arthouse cinemas pleading the case for booking the film into Vancouver. No one would bite on the idea. So I went to The Blinding Light, the local underground/experimental microcinema run by filmmaker Alex MacKenzie, and gave him a list of films that I thought he should look into. And that was the end of that, until a few months later when Alex called me to ask what dates I wanted to rent the theatre for my horror film festival. *What horror film festival?* He had misunderstood my request. But I paused. *Well, how much is it to rent the theatre?* It was cheap. And I had just gotten my student loan.

Thus began the first of seven editions of the CineMuerte Horror Film Festival (later dubbed the CineMuerte 'Fantastic' Film Festival to accommodate its eclecticism), where I had the pleasure of hosting guests as esteemed as Jörg Buttgereit, Jean Rollin, Buddy Giovinazzo, Udo Kier, John Saxon, Richard Blackburn, Jeff Lieberman, Ed Neal, Jack Taylor, Bob Clark, Matt Cimber, Millie Perkins, Jim Van Bebber and more, not to mention screening some amazing films that have never touched any other Canadian screen.

above: Me with Simone and Jean Rollin at CineMuerte, 2000.

One of these films, Jörg Buttgereit's 1987 debut feature *Nekromantik*, which played at the first CineMuerte, was a challenge to get onscreen, most notably because it was banned in British Columbia. Every province in Canada has a separate ratings system, and in 1997 we got a new 'R' rating in BC, which is the equivalent of the American NC-17, reserved for films that contain explicit sexual or violent material that violate the Motion Picture Act's code of decency but are deemed to have sufficient historical, sociological, scientific or educational merit that warrants their accessibility to the public. I petitioned to the BC Film Classification Board that the films of Jörg Buttgereit be moved off the banned list into the new 'R' rating, and was denied, but with notification that a video retailer could formally appeal this decision. Since I was only an employee of a video outlet, my boss Darren Gay agreed to sign any documentation I wanted to submit if I wanted to proceed with the appeal, which I did.

I drafted my first letter to the Appeal board, essentially a 4-page essay delineating the various merits of *Nekromantik*, which was met by a 40-page juggernaut from the BC Film Classification's legal department referencing various precedents and utilizing legal jargon I didn't understand in order to restate their claim that the film belonged on the banned list. This document was completely overwhelming to me, but with the aid of a Black Dog customer who was in law school – who pointed out that their lawyers were using primarily circular arguments and had clearly not even viewed the film – I was able to write up an authoritative response. Most importantly, their lawyers had cited in their defence a sentence from the 1992 Manitoba-based pornography case *R v. Butler* – but conveniently cut off the sentence before the end, which read: "any doubt regarding the community's tolerance of offensive material must be resolved in favour of freedom of expression." Using the same sentence in my follow-up response – the whole sentence – we were able to demonstrate that there was indeed doubt as to the community's tolerance of the material in this film.

The results came in, and we won. Moreover, the appeal board castigated the Film Classification Board for basing their decision to ban the film on their opinion of what constitutes 'good' or 'bad' art, when their job is only to respond to community standards.

In the months leading up to the launch of the first CineMuerte, I was being courted by an invisible stalker who would leave unlabelled video tapes at my door full of random horrific imagery (some of the footage I recognized as being from Pupi Avati's *Zeder* (aka *Revenge of the Dead*, 1983)). One day as I was talking on the phone, there was a loud bang on my door that scared the shit out of me. When I opened the door there was a manila envelope sitting on the stoop, and inside was a photo of a chicken being gutted and a series of broken baby teeth. I poured the teeth out into my hand and went around the corner to the movie theatre where a bunch of my friends worked. "Look!" I bragged, "I'm going to marry the person who left these teeth at my door!"

My friends were less enthusiastic: "Call the police!" they urged. But I was right – while the videotapes turned out to be from someone else, I married the man who left the teeth at my door.

While the grotesque offering at my door was an attempt to get my attention, Johnny was hardly a morbid character. He was just extremely empathic, generous, and willing to embrace my darkness. There was nothing remotely unbalanced or neurotic about him, and he was feisty without being aggressive. He was the kind of guy everyone loved and rooted for. He was an art school kid who had grown up in the good ol' boy culture out in the sticks, and was able to slip easily between the two – equally comfortable holding a paintbrush or a rifle. And while I hold him in the highest regard, I have no idea what made me think a relationship between us would be able to last.

above: Beatrice M. and friend in Jörg Buttgereit's **Nekromantik** (1987).

We were married in September of 2000, at a caveman-style wedding that lasted three days and took place out at a campground we rented several hours from Vancouver. We had a beer sponsor for the wedding, so by the time the wedding actually took place on the second day, I had to step over drunk people as I walked down the aisle (which was actually just a dirt path). My wedding march was a song from *The Wicker Man* soundtrack, but only me and my friend Anthony Timpson knew that – I think everyone just assumed that somebody in the family was Scottish. There was a hot tub in the woods, free paddleboats, unlimited food and beer, and a guy with no pants walking around. I spent a lot of time trying to make sure my grandmother didn't see him, although in hindsight I suppose it would have been easier to tell him to put his pants back on.

Originally I didn't invite my mother to the wedding, because in recent years she'd gone off her meds, left my stepfather and started having nightmares about being raped, which resulted in long, crazy phone calls in the middle of the night that I had little patience for. She sent me letters written in erratic hand, with the words going around in circles and little arrows everywhere. I was worried that she would come to the wedding and embarrass me. This was the beginning of my grandmother thinking I was a horrible person.

Eventually my grandmother convinced me that my mother should be allowed to attend so long as she had a chaperone. Unfortunately that chaperone was my Aunt Velma, who despite being a wonderful, patient person, was going through chemotherapy at the time and was in no shape to keep my mother in check. Throughout the weekend my mother drank like a fish, fell on her face on some rocks, called an ambulance claiming she'd been knocked to the ground by someone and repeatedly tried to kiss my husband's father on the dance floor. Of course, everyone just thought she was kooky and hilarious, but I was mortified and cried all night in my cabin.

It was a brief marriage, lasting less than two years (2000-2002) – our divergent interests becoming painfully apparent on our Eastern European honeymoon when I wanted to visit the concentration camps and he didn't. I won out of course, but when I grabbed a piece of rubble from the gas chamber at Birkenau and stuffed it in my pocket, he didn't speak to me for the rest of the day.

Almost instantly he sublimated his interests to mine, working thanklessly behind the scenes to support me as I stayed up all night writing the magazine, pleaded with stubborn film distributors and argued with overpriced couriers. He did everything – from making sure I ate regularly, to sweeping the floor at the theatre. But as much as his devotion was exactly the thing I'd been fighting for all my life, it only emphasized how selfish that goal really was: there was no way I would do the same for him or anyone else. As the festival took hold, my marriage started to disappear into the background.

It became obvious over time that the only thing we really had in common was an increasing reliance on alcohol. Johnny was a photographer and illustrator who took a gruelling government job when we got married, as a means of supporting his ideals of domestic stability. As much as his new job provided us with the financial resources to live well, eat well, travel and even buy original artwork on a regular basis from our large stable of artist friends, it limited his own creative endeavours, and his small study became an increasingly untouched depository for expensive cameras, charcoals and pencils.

It became a habit for our refrigerator to be freshly stocked with beer each day, which would be consumed throughout the evening as we watched movies in lieu of engaging in conversation. This night-time drinking was

You are invited to witness the marriage of Kier-La K.Janisse and ▓▓▓▓, which will take place at the Coquihalla Lakes Lodge September 15th-17th. The ceremony will begin Saturday September 16th at 1pm followed by dinner, raucous live music, the usual idiocy and drinks. Please join us for the whole weekend of marriage and mayhem, complete with a spectacular lakeside view, paddleboats, and giant trees -- but bring some warm clothes and something to camp in! There is a kitchen where extra food can be stored, and we will help to arrange carpools if required.

RSVP by September 1st:
(604)708-3519

above: My wedding invitation, artwork by Jason R. Wood.

eventually supplemented by daily after-work sojourns at the bar, and it soon became impossible to imagine doing anything without the ever-present prop of a beer bottle. I had always only been a social drinker before this, but with its ready availability, it rapidly became an unconscious crutch. In fleeting moments of self-awareness, I knew I was turning into my mother. But as much as the reliance on alcohol became a problem in and of itself, it was – with her as with me – fuelled by other concerns.

Vicente Aranda's early outing *The Blood Spattered Bride* (1972) is one of my favourite examples of feminist assertion in a horror film, even though it associates feminism with lesbianism (typical of the film's 1970s context) and murder. A just-married couple (Maribel Martín and sketchy eurostaple Simón Andreu, 'Susan' and 'Husband', respectively) drive out to a large country estate for their honeymoon. But their ostensible happiness is a sham: far from eager to consummate the marriage, the young bride imagines being raped on her wedding night. The rapist in this fantasy is her husband, transparently disguised by the black nylon stocking over his head, and while she fights him to some extent, there is a lack of terror, and thus no clear 'code' that the sex is not consensual. Her interpretation of this episode is consistent with her increasing delusion that her husband wants to imprison and humiliate her.

When Susan meets and comes under the spell of the enigmatic Carmila (a variation on Sheridan Le Fanu's famous lesbian vampiress Carmila Karnstein), she slowly comes to realize she is a lesbian, and since there is no place in her world for lesbianism, she is understandably anxious, filled with conflicting emotions – from fear of her husband to homicidal anger at being forced by society to marry against her will. She takes meaning from things where there is none, such as imagining her husband's family to have a centuries-old conspiracy against women, which spurs on her hatred of him even more. Given her time and culture (immediate post-Franco Spain), her lesbianism is not acceptable, so she has to project fantasies of monstrosity onto her husband in order to justify her sexual leanings. In the film's most celebrated (and censored) scene, Carmila urges Susan to emasculate her husband.

Interestingly, most reviews of the film online describe Susan as turning to Carmila because of her husband's insatiable and perverted sexual appetite. However, I always saw the rape scene as imaginary, an opinion bolstered by the husband's character throughout the film – he seems confused and trepidatious, only asserting himself once he realizes that his wife has made him out to be a villain. Director Vicente Aranda would go on to be one of Spain's pre-eminent anarchist directors, but regrettably never ventured into genre territory again. It is due largely to his progressive politics that *The Blood Spattered Bride* stands out as one of the most remarkable examples of the '70s Spanish horror boom.

above: Simón Andreu and Maribel Martín in Vicente Aranda's **The Blood Spattered Bride** (1972).

opposite: Maribel Martín is assaulted by Simón Andreu in **The Blood Spattered Bride**.

overleaf: A tableau of emasculation in **The Blood Spattered Bride**.

When Ashley Fester made her documentary film *Celluloid Horror* about me, I was stunned to see that she had intercut scenes from *The Blood Spattered Bride* with scenes from my own real-life marriage. I felt it invited the viewer to make an unfair comparison, and urged her to re-edit it. Even Jim Van Bebber, who watched the film with us in his living room, stopped the tape halfway through and said to Ashley, "Why are you cutting this guy's balls off?" But over time I came to realize that – although far less dramatic – the comparison was apt to a certain extent. Marriage does strange things to people. There are pressures and expectations that cause previously healthy relationships to implode. I felt trapped by my marriage, and by the pressure associated with suddenly having a new family to consider; the relationship extended beyond us, into our respective families, who were now bound to each other by a decision we had made to get married. I vividly remember the day I decided I wanted out: his sister called me to ask my shoe size, because his mother was going to go shopping for the family and wanted to get me a new pair of winter boots. I immediately started panicking. I didn't know why she needed to buy boots for me – I could buy my own boots! I could do things for myself! I started to feel guilt over the fact that any problems we had within our marriage could potentially reverberate into the lives of these other people, who could then be disappointed or ashamed by me. So I stood my ground, and focused on my career and my own interests. But as I asserted my independence, I did so by emasculating my husband.

I resented my husband because he gave up on so many things that were important to him, but I was the one who had forced him – implicitly or explicitly – to do so. I've always looked at every situation as though there has to be a winner and a loser; at the time I assumed that for one of us to get what we wanted out of life, the other had to submit. For someone so determined to find that perfectly reciprocal, egalitarian relationship, I always did my damndest to make it a competition.

In this light, I think it's safe to say that I won every fight we ever had. But the more he would concede, the more I would just find new things to fight over. Because I really wasn't fighting him – I was fighting myself. Nothing he could do or say was going to quell my fears: my fear of losing my identity, my fear of abandonment, and more specifically, my fear of ex-girlfriends.

As a teenager, a slew of short-term boyfriends either dumped me or cheated on me with their ex-girlfriends. It seemed my role was to be a transitional person for sheltered guys excited by the possibility of going out with a juvenile delinquent, but too cautious to stay the course. It was a dull playing-out of stereotypes. And as much as

above: Joan Fontaine in Alfred Hitchcock's **Rebecca** (1940).

I'd hate to give these guys credit for creating a deep-seated neurosis in me, it's there plain as day: I'm terrified of ex-girlfriends. There was even a huge fight that spanned the month leading up to our wedding because Johnny wanted to invite his long-term ex-girlfriend to the ceremony. I refused to budge on the issue, and as a result, some of his other friends didn't attend out of protest.

It makes sense then, that *Rebecca* is my favourite Hitchcock film. Released in 1940, and based on Daphne du Maurier's 1938 novel, *Rebecca* stars Joan Fontaine as the sheepish paid companion to a boorish old bag with aristocratic pretensions vacationing in Monte Carlo. Out walking one day she sees the suave but brooding widower Maxim de Winter (Laurence Olivier) about to leap to his death from a cliff top, and shouts out to stop him; while he feigns annoyance, he is secretly taken with the young girl and in no time flat sweeps her away to his sprawling English seaside estate, Manderlay, to become his new wife.

Coming up the drive, when she first spies Manderlay she knows she's out of her depth. Tennis matches and picnics on neutral ground are one thing, but walking into a castle where a legion of house staff are openly devoted to your predecessor is something else entirely. You see, the *real* Mrs. de Winter – Rebecca, who drowned a year earlier – was perfection embodied: the most graceful, eloquent creature who ever lived. Industrious, ambitious, witty – her list of talents never end. So what hope does this poor sopping waif have against such a legacy?

To add insult to injury, at no point is Fontaine's character given a name other than "the second Mrs. de Winter", which further emphasizes the film's portrayal of her as a person of no consequence. I mean, even the *house* has a name, not to mention a character that dominates her own. And it doesn't help that Mrs. Danvers, the matronly, totally mental head of staff is determined to keep everything "just as it was". Rebecca had an entire wing of the house to herself, and there it sits, aired out daily, her linens and lingerie carefully looked after by Mrs. Danvers, whose lesbian obsession with Rebecca becomes increasingly obvious as the film progresses towards its fiery conclusion. "Her underwear was made especially for her by the nuns of the convent of St.Claire", Danvers boasts, her eyes growing wide as she fondles the garments. In fact, she is so certain of the second Mrs. de Winter's insignificance that she is openly fanatical around her, even encouraging the young girl to commit suicide rather than live in Rebecca's shadow. In doing so, actress Judith Anderson (who plays Danvers) creates what is probably the most damaging depiction of lesbianism of its time.

Tantamount to the demonic psychosis of Mrs. Danvers is the increasing mental instability of the protagonist, who whimpers, faints and ingratiates her way through every scene like a kicked puppy. It's unbearable to watch. When Maxim suggests that things aren't working out, she pleads: "But our marriage is a success! We're happy, aren't we? Terribly happy??" To which he concedes, "If you say we're happy, let's leave it at that." But leaving things alone doesn't work; the past has a way of coming back until it's bloody well staked and beheaded. And when Rebecca's boat is found at the bottom of the sea with her body locked inside it and evidence of foul play, the second Mrs. de Winter fears that her husband's rekindled grief will ruin their chances of happiness forever. Maxim is shocked; oblivious to the cause for his young wife's debilitating inferiority complex, he sputters, "You thought I loved Rebecca? You thought that? I *hated* her!"

The second Mrs. de Winter is so relieved by this admission that she is willing to overlook the fact that Maxim indirectly caused and deliberately concealed the nature of Rebecca's death. His reluctant confession creates a bond of collaborative deceit, and the second Mrs. de Winter finds strength in this, enough to stand up to Mrs. Danvers, to throw out Rebecca's embroidered napkins and personalized stationery, to address people without lowering her head. Despite Maxim's assertion that "I've known all along that Rebecca would win in the end", Rebecca hasn't won – because to the second Mrs. de Winter, the prize is love, and she's got it.

I always found the ending of *Rebecca* to be reassuring. The terror and dread I associate with ex-girlfriends was allayed somewhat by Maxim's claim that "he never loved her anyway". But watching the film again, I'm amazed that I ever related to this snivelling, frightened character at all. In real life this line would never work on me; I never had the faith that she has. So just as Maxim loves her for her innocence, I envy her for her stupidity; if only it was so easy to erase self-doubt with a single proclamation of love.

Perhaps all these years I've aligned with the wrong character; I'm too spiteful and independent to be the *second* Mrs-anything. And while only Maxim knew how terrible Rebecca really was, my exes can undoubtedly say the same about me.

top right: Joan Fontaine and Laurence Olivier in **Rebecca**.

PART EIGHT:
HEAL ME WITH
HATRED

As my jealousy intensified, my demands upon Johnny's attention became unrealistic. Like Eihi Shiina's character Asami in Takashi Miike's horrifying *Audition* (1999), who unnervingly pleads to her suitor "You must love only me. Only me. Only me..." I managed through the brief aperture of our marriage to gradually isolate Johnny from his female friends. I made him promise, *only me*, and he happily obliged. If I wanted someone who would give up everything to show their complete devotion to me, Johnny was the one person willing to do it. But I would lay into him without provocation. I didn't just scream and yell – I used guilt and manipulation to somehow make it seem like he had really done something wrong, and he felt compelled to make it up to me. He showed up at my work place once with a giant package of bacon (better than flowers, and edible), begging me to forgive him for something he hadn't even done. Aside from a drink problem that sometimes made him a lumbering handful at parties, he was the most easygoing person I ever met, and I did the unthinkable: I made Johnny hit me, so that I would have something tangible to complain about. I deliberately pushed, interrogated, threatened and attacked him until he was so frustrated he kicked me as hard as he could. The bruises were visible on the backs of my legs for weeks. And like I had done with my stepfather years before, I held it over him – knowing that with this kind of currency, I could buy anything.

While I can divide and sub-divide the neuroses in this book into tiny fractions, it remains that every one of them is related to repression. Every problem manifests because we have falsely constructed ideals and cannot meet them. The repeated failure to make decisions based on logic or sound belief and have our emotions follow suit is confusing to us. So we try to force it, or create a façade so watertight that even we fall for it ourselves. That is, until a tiny crack appears and the whole thing comes crashing down on us.

Spanish director José Larraz made four films before he finally hit it big with *Vampyres* (1974) starring Marianne Morris and *Playboy* centrefold Anulka as lusty, lost-in-time vamps with a savage bite. The movie showcased the beautiful English countryside, creating an air of melancholy to accompany the girls' ambiguous plight. On North American soil, Larraz's other films have been all but eclipsed by the success of *Vampyres*, but a feature he made earlier that same year is equally deserving of attention. *Symptoms* follows in the footsteps of Altman's *Images* and Polanski's *Repulsion* in its intense, brooding study of a young woman teetering on the edge of sanity. Angela Pleasence (daughter of Donald) turns in an amazing performance as Helen Ramsay, an odd-looking girl whose social ineptitude makes her seem like a shut-in child trying to impress the world of adults around her. Like the opening of *Rebecca*, *Symptoms* begins with the recollection of a dream:

"Last night I dreamed they had returned. They were here again, just like in other dreams, but this time it was more confused. I have a feeling that something is about to happen, something final in which I will be involved..."

As she is writing, the camera closes in on a photograph of a dark-haired woman, who we later assume to be Cora, a friend of Helen's who is mysteriously absent despite frequent references to her. Helen invites another

above: Angela Pleasance in José Larraz's **Symptoms** (1974).

opposite: Vanessa Redgrave in Ken Russell's **The Devils** (1971).

friend out to her isolated country manor, which she admits she rarely visits any more – most of the rooms are closed off. The two women sit by the fire telling stories ("I like to watch things burn", Helen says, "it calms my nerves"), and go for walks and trips down the river in a rowboat. Everything seems idyllic but for the strange sense of foreboding reflected in Helen's worried stare. As they do for the title character in Juan Antonio Bardem's *The Corruption of Chris Miller*, weather and location act as a trigger for Helen's psychosis: "Sudden changes in the weather upset me", she says, "I don't know why." She seems normal enough until she enters the house, then it's as though something 'sets in' – everything becomes portentous. There's something about quiet that breeds neurosis, as though our imaginations try to fill in the spaces left by the silence. "I can hear things nobody else can", Helen declares to her friend. In addition to pronounced hearing, she also suffers from frequent headaches (as does Catherine Deneuve in *Anima persa*).

Helen changes dramatically when she comes into the realm of her family home. It is as though she passes through a boundary into unreality, where her relationship to the world around her is directly fed through her psyche, giving her a feeling of omniscience: "I know everything that happens in these woods", she says, "Many things happen in these woods." Part of the reason she knows everything that happens in the woods is that she looks at it through binoculars, specifically as a means of spying on Brady, the odd-job man. When the two women pass Brady in the woods one day, Helen's passiveness disappears in favour of a venomous disgust, and she refuses to even glance at the man in her employ. Her friend senses that Helen is troubled, and vows to stay longer to keep Helen company, despite the protestations of her boyfriend, who wants her to return to the city to escape what is obviously a lesbian fixation on Helen's part.

When Helen's madness is fully unleashed, she's like a beast swiping the air with a knife, meting out punishment to all those who dare abandon or betray her. The noises that run through the house at night are none other than the sounds of Helen being sexually ravaged by the ghost of her dead friend Cora – whose corpse is still sitting in a chair in the room with her. Like Cathryn in *Images*, Helen has an isolated house that acts as a very physical counterpart to her madness. But it is not only a place where she can exercise mania – it is also the only place where she can experience love. The house and the woods surrounding them act as a very clear boundary beyond which it is safe for her to act out her repressed fantasies; these include positive things such as love and physical intimacy but also anti-social emotions: jealousy, paranoia, hysteria and homicidal mania.

While it can be supposed almost immediately that Helen had something to do with the 'absence' of her friend Cora, and that the groundskeeper knows her secret (which is why she despises him so), knowing this does not detract from the film; it only gives us a sense of dread, because we know Helen's madness is going to be violently manifested before long. It is not the plot that keeps us riveted to this simple tale, it's the superb direction by Larraz, Brian Smedley-Aston's sharp editing, and Pleasence's incredible performance as the disturbed lead.

Like Mario Bava's *Shock, Symptoms* employs traditional ghost story elements to fragment any purely psychological reading of the story. Helen's visiting friend confides that she thinks they may not be alone in the house; that she is certain someone else is living there. At times we even catch disturbing glimpses of figures in the room with them, in mirrors, outside the windows, enveloped in darkness, but definitely *there*. Because we see these things, and because Helen's friend can supposedly sense them as well, we question whether Helen is inherently mad, or if she is being driven mad by a presence in the house.

Ghosts, like doppelgangers, are a tool for examining mental fracture: even *Rebecca*, which is not a ghost story, uses the trappings of one to create the oppressive sense of dread that lives within the walls of Manderlay. Rebecca 'haunts' the unnamed protagonist, and reminders of her presence are everywhere, but those reminders can be discarded with personal resolve – a capability many of the characters in this book don't have. A central struggle for many of these women is the issue of control. They want to have control over their environments, the people in them, their loved ones – a lack of control threatens them and precipitates a manic attempt to get that control back, even by the most irrational means. Ironically, the one thing they *need* to control, and the only thing they really *can* control, is their own behaviour. And they find this impossible; somehow it seems easier to isolate the object of their desire in a secluded house in the forest away from the threat of competition. This doesn't always work though, since there is always the threat of an interloper who will call attention to the inherent problems in this makeshift system.

In Norman J. Warren's *Prey* (1977), two female lovers live in isolation in a rambling English country house. Josephine (Jo), the more domineering of the two, reveals her desperation almost immediately, and throughout the film will constantly use manipulative tactics to convince her younger lover Jessica that seclusion is necessary to maintain the purity of their relationship. "What we have is real, Jessica", she says when the latter tries to do something as harmless as go for a walk by herself, "We must never lose it – ever."

The hold Jessica has on Jo is not entirely reciprocal though; Jessica's emotions wander and at the start of the film she is already entertaining the idea of going away for a while on her own – which prompts an argument that pretty much encapsulates their relationship:

"Jessica, we can't risk it."
"Can't you imagine that I might want to be with somebody else sometimes?"
"There can be nobody else."
"But Jo, we're not the only people in the world."
"Jessica if you went away and let yourself get screwed up…"
"I might find somebody who could understand, who could share."
"You know I could never let that happen."

As if to prove the futility of Jo's isolationist mandate, they immediately run into a man named Anders, who – unbeknownst to them – is an alien that has adopted the strapping physical form of his most recent victim. Jessica is instantly fascinated by the reticent young man, whose handsomeness is matched only by his evasiveness. "He's a bit weird, don't you think?" Jessica says to Jo in confidence. Jo, whose disdain for men is hardly disguised, says; "No weirder than most males." But Anders isn't the first man to cause a fissure in Jo and Jessica's hermetic existence: when the film opens, Jessica's been awakened by a nightmare, which somehow figures a man named Simon. Later we discover that Simon was a friend who used to visit the two girls until one day he stopped coming around. But that's not exactly true: he just never left.

Despite the fact that both women are convinced that the socially inept Anders is an escapee from a nearby mental hospital, Jessica invites him to stay with them – much to Jo's disdain. "I think that man is contaminating this house", she hisses. When Jessica suggests they have a little party, Jo attempts to emasculate

above: Sally Faulkner in Norman J. Warren's **Prey** (1977).

Anders by dressing him up as a woman "so that they're all the same", and clearly delights in what should be a humiliation. But because he is an alien, the symbolic value of her gesture is lost on him, and he is unaffected. Still, Jo's disgust for men hides a secret longing, as she too starts to feel attracted to the atypical male visitor. She frightens herself by nearly kissing him.

It turns out that Anders is more observant than he seems. "You're like a caged animal", he says to Jessica, who disagrees, claiming that she acts of her own volition. But the suggestion is enough to make Jessica question her living situation, and to throw the intensely threatened Jo over the edge. A fantastic shrieking fight ensues when Jessica bluffs that she might run away to London with Anders. The two women begin slapping each other madly and Jo ends up bashing Jessica's head repeatedly against a wooden planter, knocking her unconscious.

Jo orders Anders to leave and never return, but with Jess unconscious he is less of a threat, and she gives him some money in a revealing moment of sympathy: "I know what it's like to be fleeing from one of those places", she admits. Once she thinks he's gone, she stands over the lifeless Jessica disapprovingly. "You stupid bitch!" she scolds. And then, in a whisper: "You'll never leave me now…"

Assuming Jessica to be dead, she starts digging a grave in the woods, muttering curses and insults beneath her breath as she hollows out the soft ground. But back at the house, Jessica has awoken, and is busy trying to seduce the unresponsive Anders in the hope that he'll take her away from this "nightmare". The ugliness of this situation is about to get very tangible: Jo returns to fetch her girlfriend's corpse and finds the naked and transformed cat-alien Anders hunched over Jessica's bloody body, with chunks of viscera hanging out of his mouth. Typically, he is unperturbed at being caught in the act, but Jo loses her cool and projectile vomits as she makes a hasty exit. She runs screeching and pell-mell into the woods, trips over a shovel and falls, fittingly, into the grave she has just prepared for Jessica. So desperate to stave off loss, she has done everything in her power to speed up its onset.

Jealousy is a nasty emotion. But jealousy doesn't manifest because we want to trap or abuse another person; it's a response to something else, and sometimes what that something is can be surprising. I wasn't always a jealous person. Jealousy first made an appearance in my life in my late twenties, and for a long time I attributed it to being cheated on or dumped for ex-girlfriends in the past, but it doesn't make sense that such insignificant relationships would have left such deep wounds. I didn't start feeling jealousy until I was involved in more serious relationships, and it's regrettable that the people I cared about most got caught in my emotional sewage as I tried to figure it out. All my adult relationships have been painted black by this crap.

It was in these moments of jealousy that I came dangerously close to my teenage nihilism and predilection for violence. My inherent independence was counteracted by a deep-seated need to have my partner completely devoted to me. I would devise tactics to keep them away from other people I found threatening, somehow rationalizing it to myself so that the behaviour seemed less monstrous. When that didn't work, I would lash out, physically and verbally; I felt like Regan in *The Exorcist*, emitting these crude and venomous insults while simultaneously feeling that the words were coming from someone else. I had no control, no filter, just bile spewing out at any person unlucky enough to fall in love with me. It was frightening, and after my divorce I spent many years steering clear of relationships as a means of avoiding this darkness.

Few films, and even fewer horror films, convey the true tragedy of jealous obsession. Jacques Tourneur's original *Cat People* (1942) is almost unique in its sympathetic depiction of a woman haunted by the fear of her own jealousy. French actress Simone Simon plays Irena, a Serbian fashion designer living alone in New York City. One day while sketching the caged panther at the Central Park Zoo, she strikes up an acquaintance with an engineer named Oliver (Kent Smith) and invites him up to her apartment for tea (in interior sets left over from Welles's *The Magnificent Ambersons*), where she confesses that he is the first friend she has ever had. The two find themselves in wedded bliss only a short time later. Despite her declarations of love, however, Irena is hesitant to consummate their marriage; she holds deeply ingrained superstitious beliefs, claiming that her village in Serbia was cursed following a dark period in which its inhabitants engaged in witchcraft and shapeshifting. As a result she has spent her life alone, afraid to contaminate anyone else with this curse that follows her from her distant homeland. Her husband insists that she see a psychiatrist to cure her of these

top left: Sally Faulkner in **Prey**.

beliefs, and for a brief time, she agrees enthusiastically. It is only when she undergoes hypnosis with the psychiatrist Dr. Judd that the true nature of her fears is revealed, as he explains:

> "You told me of your village and the people, and their strange beliefs. And the cat-women of your village too – you told me of them. Women who, in jealousy or anger, or out of their own corrupt passions, can change into great cats, like panthers. And if one of these women were to fall in love, and if her lover were to kiss her and take her into his embrace, she would be driven by her own evil to kill him. That's what you believe, and fear – isn't it?"

After my marriage ended, I needed something else to pour my energy into: having spent years running a festival, I wanted to move up to programming full time. I wanted my own movie theatre. Teaming up with a film distributor friend who'd recently relocated to Vancouver from the U.S., and my boss at Black Dog Video, we started scouring the city looking for viable locations. We settled on what was probably the *worst* possible location imaginable – The Fox Theatre, a ramshackle, barely functioning porno theatre. It was the last remaining porn theatre in North America that still ran 35mm film, which meant that the programming (if you can call it programming) was comprised of authentic '70s porn, including classics like *Deep Throat* and *Behind the Green Door* alongside lesser-known films by exploitation staple Roberta Findlay and completely unknown efforts by Ed Wood and Roger Watkins, the latter of *Last House on Dead End Street* infamy. It was grindhouse in the purest sense: the film turned on in the morning, ran all day, and at 11pm the film was shut off, even if it wasn't finished yet. It didn't matter, because no one went for the movies, they went for the real show: it was a well-known hook-up joint for prostitutes.

There's no delicate way to put it – the place reeked of piss and cum. It was seedy and gross and nothing in there had been cleaned in a decade, other than the cursory sweep-over the owner would give the auditorium at the end of each night. I loved it. I saw past the stench to envision *Streets of Fire* playing on the big screen in what I imagined would be a movie theatre so important they would write about us nationwide. But try as we might, the owners didn't want to give the place up – apparently the shit hole was making them money, much to our surprise. The most we could do was convince them to rent it to us on weekends (for an exorbitant price, but I didn't realize that at the time). Nothing worked, everything was soaked through with scum (despite our attempts at steam-cleaning, which just intensified the smell), and to think anyone would actually buy concessions in such a place was probably proof of our insanity. But we went for it. We christened it The Criminal Cinema, opened with a 35mm print of *Meet the Feebles*, and in the brief period of our existence – a mere three months – we managed to play *Streets of Fire*, *Bring Me the Head of Alfredo Garcia*, *The Kids Are United*, *Smokey and the Bandit*, *El Topo* and *The Holy Mountain*, *Resident Alien*, *Rude Boy*, *Mark of the Devil*, *Border Radio*, *Valley Girl* and whatever else we could pack into our limited schedule. We even played all the *Airport* movies in a marathon, and when the first one arrived dubbed in Italian and the distributor wasn't able to find a replacement in time, I spent 26 hours transcribing the film so that we could do a live translation. There were more of us doing the voices than there were people in the audience. The best part about the translation was that my friend Kelly did the exact same voice for both Burt Lancaster and George Kennedy, so that whenever they shared scenes, you could never tell who was supposed to be talking. But our greatest moment of triumph came with the completion of a mural on the wall of the women's washroom: Aliza Nevarie painted a giant portrait of Scott Baio, with his name posted above in puffy *Creem*-magazine lettering. It was a masterpiece. Sadly, the day it was completed was also the day we realized that we couldn't afford to keep the place open.

top right: Kent Smith and Simone Simon in Jacques Tourneur's **Cat People** (1942).

centre right: Tom Conway and Simone Simon in **Cat People**.

Opening night had been packed, even my dad Oates came (and I saw to my horror that he was sitting on a condom – I managed to get rid of it without him noticing). But all the opening night did was advertise in one fell swoop how bad the place smelled, and every subsequent weekend was dead with the exception of *Cinema Sewer*'s Robin Bougie, artist/performer Robert Dayton and a couple other loyal trash-hunters. Add to this some seriously faulty equipment that was chewing up prints, and my over-stuffing of the schedule resulting in expensive courier charges, and we were done, done, done. We had to cut our losses and get the hell out of there.

It was a brutal blow, and between the failure of my marriage and the failure of my business all happening within months of each other, I was ready to duck out of town for a while. I called Tim League at the Alamo Drafthouse in Austin, Texas and reminded him of a job offer he'd made while drunk at the Sitges film festival. He didn't remember the offer, but he was true to his word, and my resultant time at the Alamo could fill a book of its own. Aside from being a programmer along with invaluable team mates Lars Nilsen, Zack Carlson and Henri Mazza, my main job at the Alamo was being the primary guest coordinator, which involved booking flights and creating contracts for the theatre's many celebrity guests, as well as some serious sleuthing on occasion (such as tracking down the cast of Walter Hill's *The Warriors* for an off-site Rolling Roadshow screening in Coney Island, many of whom had since pursued other career paths). This meant that often my own neuroses would be put on the back burner as I catered to other people's eccentricities. While most of the crazy stories that came out of my Alamo experience lie outside the scope of this book, one situation in particular warrants a mention.

We had long wanted to do a *Beyond the Valley of the Dolls* screening with John Lazar, aka Ronnie 'Z-Man' Barzell, in person. When I phoned his agent, I was told that John, along with co-stars Cynthia Myers (Casey, the Carrie Nations' bass player) and Erica Gavin (Roxanne, Casey's lover) were doing appearances as a group, in celebration of the then-recent release of the *Beyond the Valley of the Dolls* DVD. We decided this was too big of a deal to confine to the Alamo's Downtown theatre (then on Colorado St.) and decided to team up with a local microbrewery who had a big outdoor lot where we could mount an open air screening with a live band covering the Carrie Nations' tunes.

The contracts were signed, the plane tickets bought and we geared up in anticipation of the screening. But when we went to pick them up at the airport, one very important member of the party was missing – Cynthia Myers. Over dinner it was explained that Cynthia had been struck with some kind of food poisoning on the first leg of the flight and that airport security wouldn't let her on the connecting plane in Phoenix. We were disappointed and a little confused, but more concerned for Cynthia being trapped in a strange city with a sudden illness. We were told that Cynthia's husband was flying to Phoenix to get her and that we would be kept abreast of any new developments.

At about 10am the next morning, my phone rang. It was someone from the brewery where we were holding the screening. "I have a woman here who says she's one of your guests – her name is Cynthia Myers." Excited that Cynthia had made it after all (although curious as to how she ended up at the brewery), I asked to speak to her. Cynthia seemed very upset; she told me she had been abandoned in Phoenix and that she had to find her way to Austin on her own. I told her to take a cab to the hotel and we'd reimburse her for the fare.

About an hour later I got a call from the hotel manager who frantically explained that there was a fight going on in the lobby among our guests and that he was going to throw them all out if I didn't get down there and deal with it. Through a conflicting mess of stories spearheaded largely by their somewhat manipulative mutual agent, I was told that Cynthia was a raving, violent alcoholic, that she had been kicked off the plane for causing a disturbance, and that her co-stars would not do the event if they had to share the stage with her. Moreover they would not even stay in the same hotel with her.

We moved Cynthia to another hotel while we tried to sort out what had gone wrong and how to fix it in time for the show that night. But it didn't look good. Although Erica Gavin didn't seem to have any issue with Cynthia, she joined John in threatening to pull the plug on the event if Cynthia Myers went anywhere near her. We pleaded with them that we wouldn't let Cynthia drink if that was the issue but they wanted nothing to do with her.

Cynthia meanwhile, was soft-spoken and polite – far from the psychopath she was being made out to be – and seemed genuinely confused as to why the others had turned against her. We were hardly about to tell this woman she couldn't appear at the event when she was behaving so professionally.

We brought John and Erica to the site early to set up their autograph tables and they had several hours of meeting the fans before the show started. When darkness fell, the lot started to fill up and showtime neared, we brought Cynthia in and set her up on the opposite side of the lot, out of view of the others. Tim went up to introduce our guests John and Erica and explained that Cynthia wasn't able to make it due to an illness – while I kept Cynthia distracted with conversation and non-alcoholic beer – and John and Erica lamented the absence of their beloved co-star. The second they left the stage, Tim broke the news that we'd just found out that Cynthia had made it after all, and invited her to the stage to make an introduction of her own. Seeing Cynthia up there all by herself, Erica eventually relented and joined Cynthia onstage with a welcoming hug. We never found out what the real issue was between them, but – with a collective sigh of relief – we were able to pull off a great event as planned, without the audience noticing that anything was wrong. That was the magic of the Alamo.

My whole time in Austin was spent immersed in work – other than a brief period living with an ill-matched (albeit extremely talented) boyfriend who'd come down with me from Vancouver, I didn't pursue any relationships for the entire time I lived there. I knew that it only caused trouble I wasn't prepared to deal with.

After four years at the Alamo I found myself living in Winnipeg again as the result of an untimely border-related issue. I got a job working part-time at a record store and, deciding that I couldn't hack this desolate prairie town teeming with old ghosts, I started packing up to move to Montreal. About a month away from my move-date, one of the regulars at the store – an obnoxious, clearly obsessive record collector named Jack – passed me a flyer for a punk show happening in a house basement and urged me to go. The place was on my way home, and I'd been nurturing a secret crush on him for a while, so I said I'd do my best.

Like most guys I'm ever attracted to, I assumed he was out of my league, but I went to the show anyway. He was surprised I actually came, and so was I, considering that I was surrounded by 20-year-old punks and I was a 36-year-old in a Dolly Parton T-shirt. But the result of making this effort to step outside of my comfort zone was that I called off my move to Montreal, and within weeks was madly in love with this gorgeous loudmouth whose emotional makeup was as turbulent as my own. He had erratic mood-swings, and there was no middle ground between histrionics and the silent treatment. He was very much like me.

We were together for less than a year, but the relationship was intense. In many ways we were like twins, and as anyone who watches horror movies knows, twins are never a good sign.

The jealousy that I'd tried to guard myself against for years came out in full force with Jack, aided in no small part by his flippant anecdotes about all the women who wanted to have sex with him. Our relationship ended after the visit of an ex-girlfriend who lived out of town. Despite his insistence that their relationship had been brief and meaningless, fuelled only by boredom and complacency, I was obsessed with the idea that there was more to it. His house was a catastrophe: amidst the sea of guitar pedals, expired chocolates, empty boxes and recycling through which there was only a small cow-path, sat her drum set, gathering dust in the basement. Sometimes – like the second Mrs. de Winter snooping around the west wing of Manderlay – I would sneak down and look at it just to make my stomach wrench. I didn't understand why he wouldn't get rid of it – I just saw it as an inability to let go, as monumental proof that their relationship meant more than he had ever let on. But if he couldn't let go, neither could I; I was the one who wouldn't stop talking about her. I yelled, screamed, and once even smashed a pint glass into my own head, resulting in both a bloodbath and an embarrassing hospital visit. Of course, once we were at the hospital the doctors all assumed that I was covering for him by saying I had done it to myself, which we both laughed about later.

Jealousy, like anger, is an *active* emotion, a tangible, visible means of expressing something. But it's a smokescreen. Jealousy isn't the real problem; it's a reaction to the problem. And the real problem is usually being repressed.

How characters in films respond to their own repressive tendencies varies, but typically, internal violence – the mental struggle that tries to reconcile the actual with the ideal – becomes physical violence, or acting out. This struggle is especially effective when played out in a film set within a religious context, because the dogmatic principles offer a definite focus for rebellion. Horror cinema, being subversive by nature, loves religion, and one of the great repressed characters of all time remains Vanessa Redgrave as the hunchbacked Sister Jeanne in Ken Russell's masterpiece, *The Devils* (1971).

In *The Devils* – based on true events that occurred in Loudun, France in the 17th century[53] – screen giant Oliver Reed plays Urban Grandier, a popular Catholic priest who takes control of Loudon after the Governor's passing. His clandestine sexual proclivities come to the attention of Sister Jeanne, who is sexually obsessed with him, and she sets about effecting his ruination.

Sister Jeanne's rapturous fantasies about Father Grandier are a chaotic amalgam of sexual and religious imagery that both confuses and invigorates her. While it's clear that most of the young nuns are consigned

above: U.S. lobby card for Ken Russell's **The Devils** (1971).

to the cloth to ease the financial burden on their families, and none are especially devout, there are appearances to uphold. For many young women up until the last century, convent life actually meant more independence – there was social mobility within the convent, and despite the lip service to a male god, it was a microcosmic society overseen almost entirely by women. Sister Jeanne was in a position of power within the convent, but with that comes the responsibility of being held up as an example. Her lust for Father Grandier threatens her ability to be such an example, and this means that the bombastic priest has to go.

Sister Jeanne confesses to Father Mignon (amazing character actor Murray Melvin) that Father Grandier is involved with witchcraft, and furthermore, has possessed all the nuns in the convent. When the maniacal Father Barré, inquisitor and professional witch-hunter (and arguably the hottest medieval priest ever depicted onscreen), arrives on the scene to investigate Sister Jeanne's allegations, his interrogations prompt mass hysteria that result in the entire convent disrobing, writhing in orgiastic frenzy and eventually desecrating a statue of Christ (the latter being cut out of most prints, as the film has a historically troubled release).

Meanwhile Father Grandier – who is far from innocent, but certainly innocent of witchcraft in this case – is demonized and sentenced to be burned at the stake, the obvious receptacle for the twisted longings of Sister Jeanne and her fellow nuns. After Grandier's execution, Father Barré presents Sister Jeanne with one of Grandier's charred bones, and she masturbates with it (again, this is only suggested in most prints), underscoring the morbid Christian association of sex with death.

Giulio Berruti's giallo *The Killer Nun* (1979) is also supposedly based on a true story, in this case a nun in Brussels who'd been indicted for several murders. Fading glamour-girl Anita Ekberg stars as Sister Gertrude, a stern nurse/nun at a Belgian insane asylum who suffers a protracted mental breakdown following surgery for a brain tumour. Her symptoms include terrible headaches, blackouts, blurred vision and a pronounced persecution complex. Adding to this already debilitating list of ailments is morphine addiction, which hung on after her alleged recovery and acts as a stand-in in for her dwindling faith.

Like most nuns with something to hide, she loudly condemns perceived improprieties among the patients and fellow staff, while engaging in illicit sex with strangers during excursions to the city. After her afternoons of ecstasy she comes back to the hospital teeming with fresh admonitory vigour, and brutal murders occurring on the hospital grounds all seem to point to her as the prime suspect. The patients are all frightened of her, except for the crippled Lou Castel (who probably *should* be) but she has an ally in the lovestruck lesbian Sister Mathieu, who

top left: Orgiastic chaos in **The Devils.**

above: A priest set upon by wanton women in **The Devils.**

conceals any evidence of Gertrude's transgressions out of blind affection. Sister Mathieu even goes so far as to seduce new doctor Joe Dallesandro to divert his attention from Gertrude's increasingly apparent mental illness.

Gertrude's sanity is so delicate that when the inmates collectively accuse her of being insane, she breaks down instantly, suffering necrophilic hallucinations, fragmented memories and flashbacks to her brain surgery. But the story soon becomes Sister Mathieu's – who we realize has used Gertrude's lack of a short-term memory to her advantage. It was Mathieu who confessed at the film's beginning that she wanted to see all men "snuffed out" – the result of childhood molestation at the hands of her grandfather. Since most of the inmates are elderly she "sees his face in every one of them", especially those who are still sexually active.

Gertrude seems to have two problems: firstly her waning faith and her inability to have a normal sexual relationship due to her vocation cause her to have non-committal flings and to be wrought with guilt afterwards; and secondly her brain surgery and dependence on morphine have caused an amnestic disorder that further alienates her from other people, as well as from her own decision-making faculties. Her life is coloured by doubt – spiritually, emotionally, mentally. She lives a cloudy existence and tries too hard to maintain order. She is mean and vulgar as a result of her own self-hatred and because her façade is cracking, making her routine impossible. She accepts herself as the murderer – she is so suggestible that Mathieu's confabulations take the place of real memories.

Intensifying Gertrude's anxiety is that she – like the other characters in this chapter – lives in an atypical environment. While the characters in *Symptoms* and *Prey* live in self-imposed isolation, in the case of both *The Devils* and *The Killer Nun* the protagonist's home and work are in the same place, which forces her to keep up appearances at all times. It's easy to retreat into your own head when it is the only place where you can get any privacy. But living in your own head is dangerous – especially if you've recently had brain surgery!

Horror history has no shortage of 'split personality' or 'double life' films: *A Candle for the Devil, Sisters, Footprints, The Bird with the Crystal Plumage*… the list goes on. Between these two opposing forces – the ideal self versus the actual self – is violence. Often this violence is perceived as nonsensical or arbitrary, when in fact, like any battle, it's strategic. But the strategy is unconscious. There is a goal – some type of fulfilment we seek – and because on a surface level we may not be comfortable with that goal, our brains use different tactics to navigate our emotional obstacles to reach that goal in one way or another. The inability to recognize this is what creates the perception of craziness.

In Tony Richardson's *Mademoiselle* (1966), Jeanne Moreau commits seemingly random acts of vandalism as a means of expressing pent-up sexual desires. Adapted by Marguerite Duras from an original short story by Jean Genet, *Mademoiselle* stars Jeanne Moreau as a visiting schoolteacher in a small French village who is thrown off kilter by the arrival of migrant Italian workers – particularly the beefy Ettore Manni (who would die in 1980 after shooting himself in the groin).

When the film opens she is in the midst of opening the sluice gate on the local water supply, sending a rushing torrent of water into the town that floods all the nearby farms and threatens to kill the livestock. As the destruction spreads, she sneaks off home and sits in silence, waiting. The local animals are poisoned. A fire is set in the town,

top right: Anita Ekberg in Giulio Berruti's **The Killer Nun** (1979).

centre right: Paola Morra in **The Killer Nun**.

bottom right: Ettore Manni and Jeanne Moreau in Tony Richardson's **Mademoiselle** (1966).

TONY RICHARDSON'S

"MADEMOISELLE"

JEANNE
MOREAU

ETTORE MANNI
Scenario by
JEAN GENET
Directed by
TONY RICHARDSON

PANAVISION
A WOODFALL FILM
Distributed by
LOPERT PICTURES CORPORATION

and then another. She returns to the scene of her crimes to soak in the chaos – and to watch Manou (Manni) play the shirtless hero glistening in the firelight. A flashback reveals the first fire to have been an accident, caused by her fumbling grip on a lit cigarette as she spies on the Italian late at night, but now the tally rises with each passing week, as Mademoiselle grows more fixated. No one would suspect her – she is a respected and beloved figure in the town, "a goddess" as one local police officer notes. As with Ken Russell's *The Devils*, the lust object – in this case, Manou – is targeted for the crimes. He's a foreigner, and known to be bedding all the young women in the town, which predisposes the local men to disliking him. Mademoiselle comes to his defence, which may be the only thing that keeps him from being lynched, and even the Italian has a false impression of her as a local humanitarian. He is unaware that her lustful destruction has another casualty – his young son, Bruno.

Mademoiselle forces Bruno (Keith Skinner, who would grow up to become one of the world's foremost Jack the Ripper experts) to go to school with the other children, but ridicules him openly in class for his poor education and lack of proper school attire, calling him a "filthy gypsy" and making him stand in the corner. The confusion of admiration and destruction that characterizes Mademoiselle's behaviour can also be seen in Bruno, who grows so distraught with her treatment of him that he bashes his pet rabbit's brains out. Still, although he knows Mademoiselle to be responsible for the local trouble, he says nothing. He has his own fixation.

Genet's preoccupation with the beauty of evil is everywhere in *Mademoiselle* – Moreau's character tells a story in class that shows how she relates to both the cruelty of Gilles de Rais and the sanctity of Joan of Arc. She sees this duality and revels in its contradictions. But where Genet would have the character of Mademoiselle be singularly sociopathic (he was not known for his sympathetic portrayal of women), Duras's participation brings a romantic longing to the story.

Movies like this teach us that solitude breeds psychosis. Mademoiselle wasn't always a sociopath; she is portrayed through flashbacks as a more carefree person. She wears her hair down. When Bruno first arrived in class she took a special – almost motherly – interest in him. But as her sexual obsession intensifies, it only serves to pronounce her solitude. Her hair gets pulled back tighter, her clothing more restrictive, her movements become jerky and sudden, and her knotted expression ages her unkindly, making her appear

above: One-sheet poster for **Mademoiselle**.

matronly and spinster-like. When she finally consummates her lust for the Italian, spending a wild night out in the fields barking and whimpering like an animal, rubbing herself against his feet surrounded by mud and rain, we know that something terrible is going to happen. There is no way she will allow herself these freedoms in any context other than this one lost night, which she will inevitably try to erase.

Her need to be humiliated – to be laughed at and beckoned like an animal – is a complete reversal of her function in the town. She is the teacher, the mentor, the role model. The one who can be counted on to keep everything orderly and right. Clearly she clings to this role, and her sense of pride depends on it. But her pride is compromised by her feelings for the Italian, which she despises as weakness. Angry that he has caused her to be weak, she behaves violently.

A similar situation unfolds in Michael Haneke's *The Piano Teacher* (2001), based on the novel by Elfriede Jelinek. In what I consider to be the greatest performance of her career, Isabelle Huppert stars as Erika Kohut, a tightly-wound 38-year-old piano teacher at the Vienna Conservatory. She lives in a small apartment with her mother, sharing the same bed even though Erika has her own room and could easily afford an apartment of her own. The two have a reciprocally abusive relationship, their daily dance consisting of verbal abuse, frequent slaps and hair-pulls, deception and manipulation. These outbursts are always followed by a making-up: "That's how it is, we're a hot-blooded family", mother says, but it's an excuse that just allows them both to hide in failure. Erika has no real control in this situation, although she could easily take it. But she only asserts herself in small doses, and inevitably back-pedals into compliance.

In Jelinek's book, Erika is described as clumsy and homely, and her encounters with rejection frequent. As a result, she has created a very carefully-manicured persona in which neither pleasure nor weakness are ever visible. She ceases to strive for her own success or to feel compassion for others, instead spitting abrupt insults at her pupils until they cry. Says Jelinek: "Her innocent wishes change over the years into a destructive greed, a desire to annihilate."[54]

At home, alone in the bathroom, her own body becomes a target for annihilation. In ritualistic fashion, she positions herself on the edge of the bathtub and slowly begins cutting away at her vagina with a razor blade. Through all this, her facial expression remains unchanged; she cleans the bathtub and gets ready for dinner. As in Mark Savage's *Defenceless*, Erika mutilates this part of herself as a means of internalizing feelings of anger and perceived ugliness. Past experience has taught her to deny her womanhood, to despise it, because she feels 'less than'. Her repression isn't just a fear of actualizing sexual desires, it's a fear of rejection – so she rejects herself

above: Benoît Magimel and Isabelle Huppert in Michael Haneke's **The Piano Teacher** (2001).

before anyone else can do it for her. But this is only one aspect of her taboo-blasting routine: she also patrols downtown peep shows, sniffing the used tissues from the wastebasket. Both activities carry the threat of some kind of infection.

Erika's mother dreams of her daughter becoming a great concert pianist, but the most showcasing Erika ever does – either due to a lack of 'what it takes' or deliberate self-sabotage out of spite for her mother's ambitions – is in private recitals put on by wealthy arts patrons. It is at one such recital that Erika meets Walter Klemmer, the young, incredibly handsome and charismatic engineering student who shares her love for Schumann and Schubert. Like Erika, Schumann himself aspired to be a virtuoso pianist – but his career was cut short by a hand injury and he chose to focus on composition instead. Erika doesn't have that excuse, nor the writing talent to fall back on. But it's clear that she relates to him – her eyes light up when she speaks of those compositions created as his mental health was in decline: "He knows he's losing his mind. It torments him, but he clings on, one last time. It's being aware of what it means to lose oneself before being completely abandoned." When Klemmer points out the morbidity in such fascinations, she adds that her own father died in an asylum, making her competent to speak about "the twilight of the mind".

Klemmer (who is easily 20 years her junior) is revealed to be quite talented on the piano himself. But when he – smitten with Erika – decides to drop his engineering pursuits in favour of enrolling at the Conservatory, Erika votes against his application, even though she can recognize his potential. She rationalizes that he is too precocious, a showboat, and suspects that he doesn't take the music seriously enough. She finds it distasteful that he's so socially adept. It hints at fickleness. But her decision is overruled by her co-workers; Walter becomes her pupil, and every insult she hurls at him endears her to him even more. He is certain that she'll give in eventually. Although sceptical of his intentions, she secretly admires his perseverance. She senses possibility.

As with Jeanne Moreau's character in *Mademoiselle*, Erika's fantasy involves being freed from her persona. She wants to pursue a relationship with Walter – on her terms. She spurns his every advance, promising that she will detail all her fantasies in a letter, which he is to read and comply with. The letter is shocking. Walter's simplified view of her neurosis – that she is slightly repressed and with a little love and affection she can be a normal, happy person – couldn't be further off the mark. She watches his face intently as he reads aloud:

> "If I beg, tighten my bonds, please. Adjust the belt by at least 2 or 3 holes. The tighter the better. Then, gag me with some stockings I will have ready. Stuff them in so hard that I'm incapable of making any sound. Next, take off the blindfold please, and sit on my face and punch me in the stomach, to force me to thrust my tongue in your behind... For that is my dearest wish. Hands and feet tied behind my back, and locked up next door to my mother, but out of her reach, behind my bedroom door till the next morning...If you catch me disobeying any of your orders, hit me, please, even with the back of your hand on my face. Ask me why I don't cry out to mother, or why I don't fight back. Above all, say things like that so that I realize just how powerless I am."

She wants to show weakness, but even this detailed register of her fantasies isn't an abdication of control. The letter is just an indication that she wants to determine the form of submission herself. She pulls the box out from under her bed like a little girl sharing her treasures – but instead it's a box filled with rope, bonds, handcuffs, and other instruments of coercion. "Do I disgust you?" she asks him. "That's not necessary. The urge to be beaten has been in me for years." But we can see the fear in her eyes. She has made a mistake.

Bolstering Erika's significant problem with control is her confusion about different kinds of love and pain, which is illustrated by the fact that her mother figures so heavily in her sexual fantasy. Still, her feelings toward her mother are not sexual. Even though she molests her mother later that night, it is the only time in the film

above: Benoît Magimel and Isabelle Huppert in **The Piano Teacher**.

that she shows any real emotion – declarations of her love paired with violent anguish and distress. Where she failed to be liberated in any way through the staged encounter with Walter – a scenario that served only to reinforce her feelings that he was more interested in seducing her than being in love with her – she has a moment with her mother where all her walls lose their footing and a flood of mixed emotions comes rushing out. And the next day, their relationship is unperturbed. She can't say the same about Walter – and this goes a long way in explaining her criteria for love.

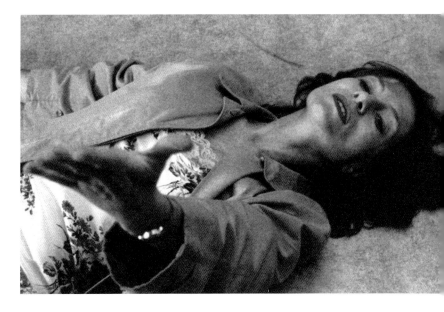

In this light, Erika's attachment to her mother is not that atypical. As David Celani noted in his book *The Illusion of Love*: "...contrary to logic, these 'adults' often end up either living with or constantly visiting their parents while neglecting or avoiding other more appropriate adult relationships. Almost unbelievably, these adults... return again and again to the very parents who failed them in the first place."[55]

Walter asserts that she's sick, that she needs treatment. Furthermore, he states that her sickness is contagious. "You're a witch, a pervert. You want to give everyone your illness, don't you?" He blames her for his own confusion and lack of control.

There are many reasons why I feel an affinity with the character of Erika Kohut, even though it's frightening to admit, given that she's one of the most disturbed and obsessively ritualistic characters I've ever encountered. Her extreme morbid fascinations – smelling used tissues from peep-show wastebaskets, her jealous cruelty and desire to be restrained and beaten – run counter to the rigid and impermeable facade she's constructed. The violence she directs at her own genitals, cutting away at herself as though it's just another of one's daily ablutions, shows how deeply dissociated she is from the emotional frontier she is so precariously perched upon. The way she exposes and retracts, confronts and retreats, the way she ruminates endlessly on impossible scenarios; I have so much love for this character that it's hard to even describe.

Erika's body-hatred also reflected my own residual anxiety about having an incurable sexually-transmitted disease. By my late 20s I had reconciled with the fact that I had contracted it through no fault of my own, but Jack brought back all these self-destructive doubts: he acted like his dick would fall off if he had sex with me (although unlike one would-be partner, he didn't go so far as to actually *spit on the floor* when I told him). The idea that I was sexually transgressive just by virtue of having this disease would rejuvenate my tendencies toward self-loathing behaviour, jealousy and vengefulness. As my fear of rejection grew, I would respond by terrorizing others.

In many ways Walter Klemmer reminds me of Jack (who was also significantly younger than me) – a cocky scenester who goes after the most difficult woman he can find and then blames her when he's not up to the challenge. As though the 'feisty' woman he was attracted to somehow snuck her craziness into the relationship, when in fact her baggage was visible all along. When we were together, Jack and I used to engage in fierce arguments that would escalate to near-violent proportions. On many occasions he had to hold back from punching me, and on one occasion a deliberate shove sent me backwards down a small flight of stairs. He told me that one day I would drive him to murder me. I was easy to fall in love with, he said, but I was impossible to *be* in love with. So he left me, claiming that I made him crazy, that I made him unable to control himself, dumping all responsibility on me for his part in our mutually volatile relationship. Even if it's true that madness is contagious, he was likely crazy already. But clearly some combinations are worse than others, and for some reason, the worst combinations are always my favourite.

above: Isabelle Huppert in **The Piano Teacher**.

PART NINE: PIERCING REALITY

"When we are out of touch, we will resort to violence to restore contact."
– William F. Lynch, *Counterrevolution in the Movies*

"Hysteria, I love this word. I know it by heart now, absolutely."
– Andrzej Zulawski, *Eyeball #5*

When Jack left me, I was distraught. I went to a counsellor and told him that I was going to kill Jack, or I was going to kill myself. I've always had a wavering attraction to suicide, most notably as a teenager, but since then I've had a hard rule about it: I will not kill myself because of how another person makes me feel. It's against my antagonistic nature to commit suicide because of another person, to submit to them by disappearing. It's too easy for them. I'd rather get revenge by living.

But this started a regular curriculum of therapy for me; the counsellor's main priority was to keep me alive, while my priority was to keep from stabbing Jack's new girlfriend in the face. His new girlfriend, who also happened to be his ex-girlfriend. The one with the drum kit.

After our first session, the therapist had me fill out a questionnaire to pinpoint what worked or didn't work for me about her approach. I wrote in the notes section: "You talk too loud. I'm very anxious and you need to speak to me more calmly." She was surprised; said that people usually didn't take the opportunity to be critical. But she also knew that this meant she could trust me to be honest going forward. But as the weeks stretched on, she noticed a pattern: whenever I would talk about something especially painful, I would laugh it off, make a sarcastic remark. "You use very clever turns of phrase", she said, "You're very funny." I smiled. But then her own smile dissipated. "But I'm not here to be amused. We're here to work. So get serious."

It was the first time I'd gone to therapy willingly, and usually a comment like this would have sent me barrelling for the door. Luckily I was able to see that she was right. But this wasn't always the case; being forced, in my youth, to attend individual as well as group therapy in various institutions, I'd developed a significant distrust for the profession. My past experience had been that they oblige you to say things, and then punish you for saying them. They manipulate you for their own egotistical ends. They project their own problems onto you. They posit themselves as parental figures so that now you have one more person to disappoint.

As I was growing up in the '70s, psychiatry underwent a major upheaval with the arrival of the anti-psychiatry movement, which was adopted by professionals and social activists alike. It was especially seized upon by the burgeoning feminist movement. Although many groups had been openly critical of psychiatry for decades (most notably the surrealists), the term 'anti-psychiatry' was first used in 1967 to describe an opposition to conventional methods of analysis and treatment. It was heavily influenced by the writings of Scottish psychiatrist R.D. Laing (although he rejected such categorization), and though it was never a unified movement per se, it gained popularity in its assertion that then-current practices of psychiatry were more damaging than helpful, specifically as regards the power dynamic between doctor and patient (it was this socio-historical context that made *One Flew Over the Cuckoo's Nest* a bestseller).

Jane Arden's *The Other Side of the Underneath* (1972, and remarkably on record as the only British film solo-directed by a woman in the 1970s) is an aggressively shrill film documenting a schizophrenic woman's journey through her own psyche. Even the soundtrack, courtesy of cellist Sally Minford, seems to be stabbing

opposite: Charlotte Gainsbourg in Lars von Trier's **Antichrist** (2009).

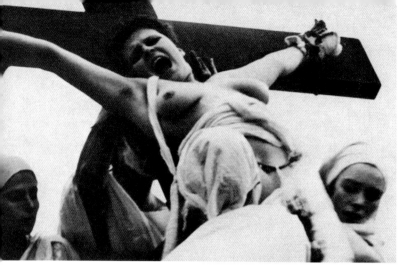

you as you watch it. The film was made by Arden's experimental, radically feminist Holocaust Theatre troupe, and supposedly all the actresses were on LSD throughout filming. Stylistically and structurally, the film has a lot in common with Peter Whitehead's *Daddy* (minus the amazing sculptures of Niki de Saint Phalle). As the film begins, the protagonist is being fished out of the lake and revived from (presumably suicidal) drowning. She is taken to an isolated hospital in the country where histrionic flashbacks and psychological fugues are intercut with group therapy sessions featuring a host of other women dressed in dirty white nightgowns and bare feet (to this day I don't like to be without my shoes on, since they are the first thing taken from you in institutions). The woman and a fellow inmate play a game with broken mirrors – as they move the pieces around in dangerous configurations, their fragmented images are repeated in a ritualistic display. But this is foreplay – revulsion and ecstasy, violence and love are used interchangeably. Funerals masquerade as weddings; women masturbate and vomit in churches; they murder each other with rubber weapons; they are revered as saints while buried alive and crucified.

The film clearly opposes psychoanalytic practices, which are characterized as alienating and antagonistic. Arden herself plays the psychiatrist in the film, and the patients both fear and admire her, fighting fruitlessly for her approval. She hates them, they claim, and try as they might, every question is answered with a question, every cry for affection is met with icy resistance. These are the film's most realistic and wonderful moments, and one suspects they were largely improvised. "I get caught always in this archetypal oppression", one of the patients whimpers. "Caught, caught, caught. But there's always, sometimes, somewhere, a space that I can see through."

Most of the film is an assaultive barrage of violent and/or sacrilegious imagery meant to comprise a complex language of the protagonist's personal symbolism. It's not supposed to 'mean' anything in concrete terms; following on the writings of (reluctant) anti-psychiatrist R.D. Laing, the protagonist's 'madness' is a type of cathartic, shamanic journey – a collapse of the false self is necessary for the real self to emerge. Laing held that schizophrenia and other modes of mental disturbance were manifestations of this kind of collapse, and were actually a societal problem more than a psychological one. His view was that madness should not be dismissed as a type of infirmity. "Strength, little girl, is madness", says the female jester who appears routinely throughout the protagonist's hallucinations, "And madness is the persistent belief in one's own hatefulness. Lightning in the brain signals down the arm… persuading the fingers to conclude that which happened a very long time ago."

If the inability to let go of anger left over from earlier traumatic events in our lives is madness, then a great many of us are insane. Film and psychoanalysis alike are often fundamentally concerned with distinguishing reality from fiction, sanity from insanity. But French playwright Antonin Artaud (an outspoken opponent of psychiatry who would himself be institutionalized on many occasions) maintained that reality was just a 'consensus', and indeed that's how 'normality' is defined. In his book *The Theatre and Its Double* (1938), Artaud compares the suspension of disbelief when one enters a play (or a cinema) to our approach to reality – we agree to accept that certain things are real and certain things aren't. But when we look, it's hard to know if we are all seeing the same thing.

Many of the women in Arden's *The Other Side of the Underneath* could easily be described as hysteric, living in an altered state of consciousness that is, in its strictest definitions, "the bodily expression of unspeakable distress". The term hysteria came into wide use in the 19th century to describe a type of dementia exclusive to women (its origin is from the Greek ὑστέρα 'hystera', which means 'uterus'), but although some patients exhibited the telltale lack of physical control, its symptoms also conveniently included any sign of female protest concerning her role in society. The prognosis was meant to keep her in the house, and the doctor's opinion was so esteemed that if he labelled a woman a hysteric, she would most certainly be ostracized and have no choice but to stay where her husband wanted her.

top left: Mock-crucifiction in Jane Arden's **The Other Side of the Underneath** (1972).

The term had been in use since the 3rd century B.C. and enjoyed incredible popularity throughout the middle ages, but by the turn of the 20th century, physicians had replaced the clergy as moral authorities, and, in the words of lecturer Leslie Anne Merced, "the doctors and hygienists delivered to patriarchy a scientific power-base to reinforce male intellectual superiority".[56] Women were encouraged to follow the moral directives laid out by the physicians lest they be labelled insane and stripped of whatever rights they had.

Let's go back to the official definition of hysteria: "the bodily expression of unspeakable distress". In genre films, this is where things get most interesting. In David Cronenberg's *The Brood* (1979), Art Hindle stars as Frank Carveth, the exasperated husband of Nola (Samantha Eggar), a neurotic woman who's checked herself into the Somafree Institute for experimental therapy with Dr. Hal Raglan (screen titan Oliver Reed, also of *The Devils*). Raglan, the author of a popular self-help book called *The Shape of Rage* is the proponent of an unconventional psychotherapeutic method called "psychoplasmics", in which past traumas, when discussed openly, manifest themselves in the form of sores and abrasions on the patient's body as the trauma is being "expelled". A very literal take on Freud's "talking cure" through which hysterical patients could be cured by confronting the thing making them ill (which is still the foundation for psychological treatment today), and an exaggeration of common stress-induced hives or rashes, psychoplasmics is nonetheless a dangerous game. Because what Nola is expelling from her body during these sessions aren't just toxins – they're repository rage monsters. Faceless children who kill all those who have ever hurt her.

above: Samantha Eggar in David Cronenberg's **The Brood** (1979).

While Frank isn't hoping to reconcile with his estranged wife, he is concerned that her therapy is having a negative emotional effect on their young daughter, Candy, who is becoming increasingly antisocial and despondent following every visit with her mother. After one such visit, Candy comes home with bruises, and Frank becomes more determined to keep the child away from her mother. But, as Dr. Raglan asserts, access to the child is key to Nola's recuperation, and at that time (1979) awarding sole custody to the father without access to the mother was practically unheard of and not likely to occur in Frank's favour. The film is notoriously referred to as "Cronenberg's *Kramer Vs. Kramer*", and is inspired by his own custody battle with his ex-wife, who joined a religious cult in California and was planning to take their daughter Cassandra with her, before Cronenberg kidnapped the child and got a court order that prevented the ex-wife from taking Cassandra away.

As with many of Cronenberg's outlandish ideas, carrying them off often comes down to the performance, and Samantha Eggar pulls it off with gusto, equally threatening and oblivious. The therapy sequences in which Raglan draws out her past trauma are as frightening as the film's more overtly horrific set pieces; reverting to a childhood state, Nola reveals that anger at her husband is not the only thing fuelling her neurosis – beatings by her alcoholic mother have never been addressed. But her real anger is reserved for her father, the parent she loves the most, but who she feels abandoned her at those crucial moments: "You shouldn't have looked away when she hit me. You pretended it wasn't happening. You looked away... didn't you love me?"

above: Art Hindle and Samantha Eggar in **The Brood**.

A brief scene with the abusive mother reveals her to be as lost as anyone else, hiding behind liquid medication and unable to deal with her daughter's feelings toward her: "Thirty seconds after you're born you have a past", she says, "and sixty seconds after that you start to lie to yourself about it." The neurosis handed down from mother to child is passed down a generation further when Candy witnesses the rage-babies savagely murdering her grandmother. The police are concerned that, while outwardly placid, Candy's stress level could be dangerous. As in Nicolas Roeg's ethereal *Don't Look Now* (1973) the threat, or 'monster', takes on the appearance of a child, in this case because Nola's issues stem from her childhood and keep her emotionally stunted there, with both the inexplicable pain and the need to lash out irresponsibly.

After my mother left my stepfather, she moved to a small house in the country, and took up with a greaseball decades her junior who shared her taste for binge drinking. She had completely let go of propriety; she would call me at odd intervals, rambling on incoherently, every once in a while turning away from the phone to shout something like "Mike, put your pants back on!" Sometimes she would hand the phone to him and I would have to listen to him drunkenly slobbering into the phone about how special my mother was. I tried to distance myself from her, as though her craziness could seep through the telephone and into my ear like the killer parasite that chews through Laurence Harvey's brain in 'The Caterpillar' episode of *Night Gallery*. I knew how easy it was to settle into a dark sub-reality and was worried that her lunacy was contagious – that it could hurt me. I wanted nothing to do with her.

Cronenberg is also suspicious of motherhood – even though he shows Nola licking one of the slimy embryos in the manner of a nurturing animal, her brood of children is a compensation for her presumed lack of power in other areas of her life. Likewise her fight for Candy is not motivated by her concern for the child's best interests – she uses Candy as a pawn to get back at Frank: "I'll kill Candice before I let you take her away!"

Part of the suspicion lies in the fact that Nola is on her own trip, something that you typically sacrifice when becoming a mother. She has gone inside, and now her inside is coming out, literally bleeding over into the real world. "I seem to be a very special person", she says with psychotic calm. "I'm in the middle of a strange adventure."

This adventure, the journey that we agree to go on whenever we watch these films, is often a strange and unpleasant one. Artaud's 'Theatre of Cruelty' speaks of a theatre in which horrible truths are exposed to the audience. Things we don't want to see, but which break down the barriers that conceal the truth from our falsely-constructed realities. Horror strives to do this in general, but those films dealing with the abject horror of hysteria are the blackest of them all.

For nearly four decades Andrzej Zulawski has been the most criminally neglected major filmmaker at work in the fantastic genre. His work is rarely cast among retrospectives of Polish or French cinema in English-speaking territories, where his films are also difficult to find on home video format. While this holds especially true in North America – which only in 2012 hosted its first ever serious theatrical retrospective of Zulawski's work – the appreciation of his films even in Europe has not been consistent with their merit.

Zulawski's films are rife with women who are beyond merely neurotic. Whether or not their extreme characterizations are meant to be symbolic (most critics will adamantly assert that they are), the fact remains that rarely has the screen been subject to such awe-inspiring fits of hysteria. From his then-wife Malgorzata Braunek's performance in *Diabel* (aka *The Devil*, 1972) to Iwona Petry's turn in *Szamanka* (1996), Zulawski's women tend toward pre-verbal animalistic horror. While *Possession* (1981) is his most popular film among genre fans, admirers of *Possession*'s distinct mania would do well to seek out his other work.

Possession is a film that confounded critics worldwide upon its release in 1982. Reviled in the U.S. as a result of sloppy re-editing aimed at making the film more linear and 'accessible', (according to Zulawski, the film's original producer, Marie-Laure Reyre, was in full artistic support of the director's cut but was sucked into a bad deal with the American buyers) the film has only enjoyed serious reappraisal Stateside in the new millennium due to release of the director's cut on DVD through Anchor Bay.

The film begins with the homecoming of Marc (Sam Neill) after an extended business trip (the nature of his job is elusive, but Zulawski has stated in interviews that Marc is a spy whose assignments involve frequent trips to

top right: Oliver Reed and Samantha Eggar in **The Brood**.

East Germany). Anna (Isabelle Adjani) waits for him curbside as he gets out of a cab; she offers him no welcoming embrace but only a wild-eyed defensiveness that renders him instantly alarmed and bewildered. She turns and storms back toward the apartment, avoiding the barrage of questions that are hurled at her ("What has happened? You can't just say you don't know. When will you know?"). Thus begins the film's recurring push-pull pattern of her confronting then running away, him chasing her like a forlorn child.

He discovers that Anna has a lover and that she has been neglecting their young son, Bob. Marc pleads with Anna's friend Margit to disclose the lover's identity, citing that this infidelity is "not... proper." 'Propriety' is routinely thrown out the window in Possession – Marc chasing Anna in a restaurant; Anna carrying on an affair with her lover Heinrich (Heinz Bennent) while his mother is in the next room; Margit's clumsy passes at Marc; Anna's trance/screaming fit in the subway; Marc's dismissal of Bob's schoolteacher after spending the night with her; Anna's sex with a tentacled monster that is, in a sense, her own offspring. But the movie takes place in a strange hybrid of private and public reality that in a sense seems fitting for a couple undergoing a major transformation such as a break-up. Everything is exaggerated, everything is obscene, every action is hostile and tactless. In real life, any couple will only let you see what they want you to see, but for Marc and Anna their break-up becomes an apocalyptic spectacle.

Ingmar Bergman's Persona (1966) has parallels to Possession's dichotomy between private and public reality, although in Persona it is through silence rather than vocal hysteria that it exposes its protagonist's loss of faith in direct communication. Liv Ullmann is an actress who has retreated from her family and friends, and while diagnosed as physically and mentally healthy, she has to be hospitalized because of her self-imposed condition. The head doctor, an exacting and cool woman, suggests that Ullmann's character is going through a guilt-inducing identity crisis: "What you are with others and what you are alone. The vertigo and constant hunger to be exposed. To be seen through... maybe even wiped out... But your hiding place is not water-tight. The outside world trickles in, forcing you to react." Her only distinct emotional reaction to anything is a thin smile, but even her smile doesn't render her invisible because it exposes and manipulates others. It is a hostile gesture in itself, and others react violently to its insolence.

Both Adjani's character and Ullmann's live in a private reality that causes violent ripples in the public reality that they are nevertheless a part of, but the interplay between Adjani's two realities in Possession is decidedly less subtle; her extracurricular love life doesn't just include the weird, mystic Heinrich (who, like Oliver Reed's Dr. Raglan in The Brood, acts as a guide through her insanity) but an actual physical monstrosity that she keeps hidden away in a secret apartment across town. Even Heinrich doesn't know how far gone she is.

Although Possession is host to numerous flights of fancy, there is one particular moment that absolutely neuters any straight readings of the film. This scene, which comes right about the halfway mark, is notoriously referred to as 'the subway scene', in which a laughing Anna ascends the escalator of a subway station and then proceeds down a long isolated hallway where she stops to have a fit the proportions of which have never been seen before or since. She laughs, screams, howls, contorts (even smacking her head against the wall at one point – which was real), regurgitates, flails, flops and falls. This scene seems to go on so long that it starts off shocking, switches to ridiculous and lands at truly frightening – but in fact the sequence barely lasts three minutes. It is the scene that often divides viewers because of its unapologetic emotional excessiveness. But for me this was the scene that nailed it: it would forever be one of my favourite films.

What makes the scene 'impossible' as it were, is that in this oozing mess Anna has created in the subway, she appears to be pushing something out of herself, something rather slimy and large. This 'thing' is later discovered to be a tentacled monster (created by FX giant Carlo Rambaldi) that she nurtures like both a child and a lover. She is presented as having an insatiable sexual drive, one that even the sleazy Heinrich can't fulfil, and having incestuous sex with her slippery offspring is the closest thing that connects her to any sense of herself (thus her repetition of "almost... almost..."). This recalls critic Seymour Chatman's description of the women in Antonioni's films, and his assertion that their fervent sexuality is only "a palpable mechanism of neurotic relief." He continues: "It does not itself reflect a deep passion; on the contrary, it is a rejection, even a flight from passion. And it is not a viable means of communication, only a superficial substitute for it."[57] Despite her incessant screaming and muddled exposition, Anna remains unable to communicate or connect.

Anna is a woman divided. This is emphasized not only by the film's numerous doppelgangers, but also in the architecture of the city itself – constantly under construction, with Marc and Anna's modern, claustrophobic apartment located right beside the Berlin Wall and Anna's private apartment a yellowing Gothic monument across town. She shows up at the domicile at odd intervals to put on a transparent front of motherly vigilance. She scurries around the house randomly starting and abandoning wifely chores as Marc desperately follows her from room to room hurling questions at her: "Are you happy? Are you worried I won't like you? Are you worried I'll get mad again and beat you?" When Anna turns an electric knife to her own neck during one of these interrogations, Marc imitates her in a misguided attempt at commiseration. Both agree that it doesn't really hurt.

These sequences are especially important because, aside from providing an emotional context for the tale's fantastical elements, they are the most autobiographical for Zulawski. The director relays verbatim conversations from his own failed marriage to actress Malgorzata Braunek, as well as channeling emotional residue from Zulawski's first wife, artist Barbara Baranowska (The original script for *Possession* even features an additional character: Anna's first husband 'Abe', based on Baranowska's first husband, the writer Adolf Rudnicki).**58** Zulawski imbues these volatile exchanges with a very real life of their own. There is nothing stagy about them despite their reference to actual events – all is pure, frightening emotional recklessness.

I can relate intensely to Anna's disturbing fits. The shaking, tingly feeling that precipitates disassociation, the wringing of hands, the stomping from one room to another, up and down stairs, threatening, daring oneself to act on the threat. When Anna holds the knife to her neck, she is daring to act on the threat of violence. In my house growing up, it was my voice that was a problem. I was told not to talk. As Anna struggles to talk, her whispers become growls, screams and hyperventilating. There is a freedom in this kind of self-obliteration, the collapse of propriety. We all need that place, that window of time to go crazy.

Marc comes home and finds a package at the door – a 16mm home movie lensed by Heinrich, who captures Anna in intense confessional mode. Her monologue does not elucidate the film's events in any tangible sense, but *pieces* of it make sense with other *pieces* of the film, even though when everything is taken as a whole, the film becomes logistically overwhelming.

> "It's like there's two sisters, faith and chance. My faith can't exclude chance, but my chance can't explain faith. My faith didn't allow me to wait for chance and chance didn't give me enough faith. And then I read that private life is only a stage and I play in many parts that are smaller than me and yet I still play them. I suffer, I believe, I am, but at the same time I know there's a third possibility like cancer or madness. But cancer or madness *contort* reality. The possibility I'm talking about *pierces* reality...I can't exist by myself because I'm afraid of myself. Because I'm the maker of my own evil."

It helps the film's mandate that Adjani speaks English as a second language, that her speech is broken and often incoherent. The struggle between words and images in *Possession* (a tactic also used to great effect in Zulawski's 1989 movie *Mes nuits sont plus belles que vos jours*) reveals an insistence that intellect and logic are somehow out of touch with existence, and the film's immediacy has the sense of an aggressive 'action'.

above: Isabelle Adjani in Andrzej Zulawski's **Possession** (1981).

Just as the characters struggle to communicate, Zulawski struggles to communicate with an audience that has trouble accepting the marriage of absurd dialogue and imagery. The film chooses to emphasize words and ideas by means of their noticeable absence. *Possession* does not actually champion interiority; it struggles to break free from it. The film is not against interpretation – my guess is that Zulawski is not that lazy – he just wants to show the seemingly impenetrable barriers that divide people from one another, audience from screen, reality from truth.

When Marc first meets Bob's schoolteacher – the film's first overt doppelganger to appear – he is shocked at her resemblance to Anna. "Is this a joke?" he demands, pulling at her hair as though it's a wig. But the teacher just laughs at his obtuse behaviour. "Have you ever seen my wife?" he asks desperately. "Of course", she says, "every day of the school year" – an indication that her resemblance to Anna may exist only in Marc's mind. The teacher – who is sweet and calm as well as beautiful – soon becomes a channel for Marc's conflicting emotions about Anna. "I'm at war against women", he says. "They have no foresight, there's nothing about them that's stable, there's nothing to trust... they're dangerous." But she shrugs off "these pathetic histories of women contaminating the universe", offering that for Marc, freedom means evil – and that he is demonizing Anna for wanting to be free. But Anna clearly views herself the same way.

Like a mother protecting her deformed child from the prying eyes of judgement, Anna attacks and kills the two detectives that Marc sends out to look for her. As she says to Marc in one of her few moments of stillness: "What I miscarried there was sister faith and what I have left is sister chance. So I have to take care of my faith, to protect it." Marc begins to understand. "So *that's* what you're doing there?" he prompts, referring to her other life in the apartment across town. She nods hypnotically: "Yes."

Faith and spirituality are integral components of *Possession*, especially with regard to inner divinity and wholeness. Anna's search for divinity, which is prompted by her relationship with the faux-mystic Heinrich (who is not at all prepared to face actual divinity, and instead uses guru tactics as a means of control), is not counteractive to the divorce narrative. Her faith – or her effort to cradle and restore her faith – is contagious, and as Marc follows her physically, this pursuit eventually becomes spiritual as well. Heinrich's postcard to Anna, which is what tips Marc off to the affair in the first place, is the first sign of the film's underlying preoccupation with divinity: "I've seen half of God's face here. The other half is you."

There are several references to the creature's divinity. When the two detectives see the creature – Anna's self-conceived child, lover, and the living symbol of her disfigured 'faith' – they both exclaim "mein gott!", and Heinrich experiences temporary blindness after seeing it. The creature's divinity is the 'third possibility' Anna speaks of. Marc concurs: "Perhaps you met God a minute ago and you didn't even realize it!" he says to a bewildered Heinrich, "Now you believe in God certainly, in that great incomprehensible God you reach through *fucking*, or *dope*?"

Anna's hysteria, the creature, the doppelgangers – all suggest a purification process that leads to a higher state of being akin to divinity. The awful other, when we grapple with it, can turn out to be not demonic, but gracious. "Do you believe in God?" she asks Marc. "It's in me!" Though the word 'God' is thrown around a lot in the latter half of the film, conventional religion – at least in any contemporary sense – is a far cry from the

top left: Isabelle Adjani and Sam Neill in **Possession**.

centre left: Heinz Bennent and Isabelle Adjani in **Possession**.

grotesquerie of the creature. Instead, Anna's relationship to divinity is based upon those non-rational elements that informed religion in earlier times – the mysterious, the uncanny, the awesome and terrifying. Just before the subway incident she visits a church, and as she cries out to the crucified figure above her, it lays silent and stationary and does not answer her whimpering pleas. It resists her projections of weakness, fragility, hopes, fears and fantasies. She is left to create her own idol, which becomes a thing both beauteous and monstrous. Barbara Creed's *Monstrous Feminine* is certainly at work here, although Zulawski's universe is not defined or confined solely by staid academic theory. His is a living, breathing, metamorphosing reality.

Like faith or divinity, the feelings that prompt a divorce are in themselves something irreconcilable, inexplicable, incomprehensible. Our decisions in these matters are based on faith – faith in something better. It is a painful mutation. Our faith in what we thought was 'forever' is shaken, and is now fragile and delicate, and relying on chance. A chance has to be taken in order to restore our faith. That Anna creates a monster that transforms into the likeness of her estranged husband is a sign of her faith, her determination to try again, to get things right.

John T. Irwin once wrote an interpretive tome on Faulkner's work called *Doubling & Incest/Repetition & Revenge* (1975) that was cited extensively in Maitland McDonagh's seminal Argento analysis *Broken Mirrors/Broken Minds* (1990). The title of Irwin's book alone is a tidy way of encapsulating what is going on in *Possession*. But its intended application as a Faulkner reader shows just how universal the concept of doubling as a means of righting past wrongs really is. This is something that all people do, whether they are conscious of it or not. We all create doubles, and some of them are monsters.

I think early on I recognized that the character of The Man with Green Eyes from my childhood dreams was more than just the result of having seen a horror film at such an impressionable age. I knew that I was connected to him in some way. As the dreams repeated nightly, in an identical fashion, my fear changed to curiosity, and then acceptance. He had become familiar to me, and even in the dreams themselves, my trepidation eased. When he beckoned, I would go to the closet more and more willingly, knowing that it would always end the same way.

The dreams stopped when I hit adolescence. Years passed, fraught with all manner of chaotic events, including the move back to Winnipeg as a teenager where I got my first apartment, shared with Hanna and a rotating queue of River Heights skater kids who wanted somewhere to smoke up and drink. After about seven months of this (which seemed like *years* in teenager time) a breakfast cereal-related argument prompted a temporary parting of the ways for Hanna and I, and I moved into the main floor of a house with a punk kid who'd been curb-stomped and you could tell. I had just broken up with a boyfriend I found annoying (I was too chicken to actually break up like an adult, so I conveyed my sentiments by throwing a beer bottle at his head instead), and my life was starting to seem hopelessly uninteresting. I'd had enough.

So, armed with the conviction that life just wasn't going to improve, I blew all my hydro bill money on sleeping pills at the corner drug store. Why the guy behind the counter sold a teenager four bottles of sedatives is still beyond me, but in any case, I went home, and started downing them in any way possible. Hanna, whose cereal-related transgressions I had now forgiven, came over and helped me crush up the pills so I could ingest them more efficiently. I was hallucinating wildly within an hour. I only made it through two of the bottles before she put me to bed, monitoring me periodically from the other room.

I sat up in my bed, wide-awake and the room alive with shadows and colours. I heard a scratching sound coming from inside my closet. I sat there staring at the door for what seemed an eternity, not yet recognizing the sound, until the door slowly slid open, grasped from the inside by a white bony hand.

It had been almost six years since this scenario had last been played out in my dreams or my memory. But with the fear came an additional worry: I was *awake*. As The Man with Green Eyes slowly emerged, he did something he had never done before – he left the refuge of the closet and started walking toward me, speaking words I've never been able to recall. This was definitely not the protocol all the other dreams had strictly followed. But here he was, the psychic remnant of *Horror Express* all those years ago, grinning madly and closing in on me as I leaned farther and farther back against the wall with nowhere to go. As his face came up against mine, and I stared into those glowing, soulless orbs, he wrapped his hands around my neck and squeezed.

When Hanna came in to check on me, having heard a banging sound coming from my room, she was shocked to see my hands clasped tightly around my own neck, my face blue and my head cracking against the wall. Like the characters in numerous Mario Bava films – *The Whip and the Body*, *Shock*, and the 'Drop of Water' segment from *Black Sabbath* – the spectral figure was only the manifestation of a crazed and suicidal mind. My room-mate fought to get my hands free, stuffed me into a cab, filled out forms at the hospital, and sat by me as vengeful nurses shoved tubes down my nose and throat (they're not especially compassionate towards suicides). After a few days of hallucinating in the hospital and steeling myself against the inevitable barrage of embarrassing questions from doctors and counsellors, I went home, and thought for a long time about why The Man with Green Eyes had come back.

It is a tradition in the literature of the doppelganger (*William Wilson* and *The Student of Prague*, for example) that while the doppelganger serves a distinct psychological purpose, it soon becomes a menace, a constant, invasive reminder of one's own shortcomings. The protagonist is driven to kill the doppelganger as a means of survival. But as Otto Rank points out, to kill the double is essentially suicide – what he refers to as "the strange paradox of the suicide who voluntarily seeks death in order to free himself of the intolerable thanatophobia".[59] The paradox doesn't end there though: if killing the double, like killing oneself, is an attempt to assert control (a misguided act of self-preservation), then what about the rather significant aspect of suicide that indicates *resignation*?

The suicidal murder of the double is also underscored by a sense of the liebestod, or love-death, a marriage between the ego and its shadow-self though mutual obliteration.[60] As Alfred Hitchcock's double says to him in Johan Grimonprez's film *Double Take* (2009), it was as though "we had scripted this moment together." For a child surrounded by Catholic guilt, abuse, humiliation and terror, The Man with Green Eyes (if you recall, an orthodox priest possessed by a prehistoric creature) was a rather fitting receptacle for dangerous emotions and impulses. But while confrontations with the doppelganger in literature and cinema often follow a similar trajectory in which the protagonist doesn't survive, those 'dangerous' things about me that were personified in the double actually saved my life.

The performances in *Possession* are astonishing all around, but Isabelle Adjani has to be given credit for going perhaps more out on an emotional limb than any actress before or since.[61] "She said to me this memorable sentence", recounts Zulawski in the *Eyeball* interview, "'You don't have the right to put the camera in this way because it looks inside one's soul' – and her soul is dark, I think, and she knows it."[62] Adjani's performance was well-deserving of its French César award, although her characterization is reminiscent of Kathleen Quinlan's in the Anthony Page melodrama *I Never Promised You a Rose Garden* (1977). Both are wide-eyed, shaking messes, clawing out at random, choking on words, speaking unreal languages, and belonging in part to an imaginary, pre-verbal world of alien carnality. Like Adjani in the kitchen with the electric knife, Quinlan's character slits her wrist, but catches all the blood in saucepan, stating, "I didn't want it to go too far." Interestingly, the latter film stars Bibi Andersson, star of *Persona*, as Quinlan's understanding psychiatrist.

Zulawski's work with actors – especially female ones – is infamous. With accusations of emotional cruelty and even physical brutality levelled at him in the past, Zulawski must still be credited as a director who can extract a career-making performance out of any given actor: *Possession* secured Best Actress awards for Isabelle Adjani from the French Césars, Fantasporto and Cannes; Romy Schneider won the César for Best Actress for *L'important c'est d'aimer* (1975); and Valérie Kaprisky earned a César nomination for *La femme publique* (1984).

He has suggested that his means of ensuring such insane performances lies in his use of "voodoo" or hypnosis, which he attributes to the influence of fellow Pole Jerzy Grotowski's ritual theatre experiments in Haiti. Fuelled by the theories of Carl Jung, Grotowski attempted to tap into the sources of ancient expression and thus prompt his actors to reach a higher state of spiritual awareness in which they would see their performances as ritualistic emotional sacrifices. This unorthodox method of directing his actors is another reason some of Zulawski's films have come under critical attack in his native Poland. While he asserts that any neurosis this procedure unearths is already present in the actor's subconscious, critics prefer to see Zulawski as a director who delights in driving women to the brink of insanity due to some deep-seated misogyny. "I like pushing actors to the border", says Zulawski in the *Eyeball* Interview. "I've made exercises with them before, especially with girls because they are so blocked by civilization, you have to open them in a way – I'm not joking – for their own good."[63] Whether or not Zulawski is correct in asserting that the rewards of the trance process are greater with female actresses, one thing is for certain: they make impressive vessels for Zulawski's creative expression.

above: Isabelle Adjani in **Possession.**

Zulawski's 1996 film *Szamanka* is a return to the hyper-intense emotionalism of *Possession*, and 18-year-old first-time actress Iwona Petry who plays the character known only as 'The Italian' had a similarly contentious relationship with Zulawski. Although she has since publicly lauded the film, in the period immediately following the shoot she purportedly had a nervous breakdown and attempted suicide, accusing Zulawski of emotionally abusing her on set.

When synopsized, the film seems disjointed, convulsive and shocking. Take for example Daniel Bird's summary of Zulawski's *Szamanka*, again originally published in *Eyeball*:

> "It concerns the intensely sexual relationship between an anthropology lecturer, Michael (Boguslaw Linda) and a nineteen year old engineering student, The Italian (Iwona Petry). Michael has recently being assigned the remains of an ancient shaman discovered in a peat bog, beside a factory just outside Warsaw. His engagement to an architect by the name of Anna is disrupted by an affair with The Italian. The Italian leaves her home village to study in Warsaw, stealing from her mother. She is drawn back to the village when she accompanies Michael to identify the body of his brother, a priest who had committed suicide because of his homosexuality. The Italian's father beats her before forcing her to work in a meat processing factory (which adds rats to the produce for good measure) to fund her studies in Warsaw. The Italian becomes integral to Michael's obsession with the shaman, who speaks to him during a heavy dope session. The shaman tells Michael that The Italian had destroyed him. Meanwhile, on discovery of Michael's affair with The Italian, Anna, being a good architect, commits suicide by throwing herself through an unfinished sky light. Michael becomes increasingly puzzled by the presence of female semen up the backside of the shaman, and employs The Italian in a practical exercise involving himself to discover how exactly it got there. Eventually Michael gives up, turns to religion and dresses up in his dead brother's smock before being hit on the head with a can of meat which The Italian had probably turned out the night before. The Italian proceeds to ecstatically eat Michael's brains with a spoon before the outbreak of World War Three or Four (don't ask, I don't know...)."[64]

Since Bird is known as one of the most fervent champions of Zulawski's work, it is evident that any synopses of his layered and emotionally complex romances (and I use 'romance' in the fantastical sense of the word) come out seeming dismissive, whether intentional or not. Zulawski has not always been forthcoming with explanations, but neither has the press at large been exactly curious. It is far easier to toss out Zulawski's work as incoherent and misguided than it is to attempt to understand the beauty of his unique chaos. Although written by feminist author Manuela Gretkowska, *Szamanka* was condemned critically for its brutal sexuality and confusing portrayal of beautiful women as alternately moronic and needy or as savage, cannibalistic vampires, and the combination of explicit sex and overtly sacrilegious imagery resulted in the Polish authorities sufficiently limiting theatrical screenings to ensure box office failure.

When we first see The Italian she is spastic and twitchy, clumsily rushing from one place to another, ordering food in a cafeteria (in a bit of foreshadowing, she orders brains), spitting it out and rushing off again. She meets Michael (played by Polish superstar Boguslaw Linda) when he is posting a room for rent. He is brusque and rude, barely making eye contact with her as he shows her the room. She says she likes it, and moves closer to him, at which point he first really looks at her, a dishevelled idiotic beauty, and with his cigarette still firmly planted in his lips he grabs her clothes and starts to remove them, almost mechanically. There is no emotion in him, no passion, and she has done nothing to invite this transaction. She doesn't fight, but stands there stunned in what nevertheless plays out like a rape scene. As he positions her on the bed, her expression betrays her sense of violation, but when his face contorts in that orgasmic moment when he is outside of himself, she smiles.

Both Michael and The Italian already have romantic partners, who prove sexually uninspiring once their affair begins. Initially Michael sees their compulsive relationship as a game, in which he tries to humiliate her, only to have her comply and adapt with enthusiasm. He orders her to spit in his face; he treats her like a feral child; he dresses her as a whore and takes her to a party at his wealthy girlfriend's house. Through everything, she remains loyal and unquestioning – but never controlled. She lives in an almost constant state of hysteria: flailing, screaming, laughing, spitting and generally exhibiting shocking and inappropriate social behaviour.

The two characters of Michael and The Italian, like their predecessors in *Possession*, strive for a spiritual connection, but their attempts to bond through ferocious sexual trysts only emphasize their isolation and incompleteness. Much of the film takes place up close and personal with the two leads, but in those moments of exchange with other characters, it's obvious that everyone lives in their own personal bubble; their experiences of each other are incredibly narcissistic and conversations often seem nonsensical and pointless – just time-killers in between the sexual sacraments. The search for divinity is here, as it is with *Possession*, a major preoccupation

– but again, traditional forms of religion prove unsatisfactory. Like Adjani's Anna, The Italian stands below the image of a religious icon – in this case the Virgin Mary – whimpering, immediately before vomiting and defecating in a public place. When Michael's perfectly-manicured architect girlfriend asks why he's left her to move in with the Italian, he shrugs. "I don't know... she's either a fool or a saint." On more than one occasion he jokingly refers to The Italian as a virgin.

At the halfway point in the film, a change comes over Michael – his sexual trysts with The Italian, once awkward and brutish, become rhythmic and fluid. As he becomes more emotionally engaged, he starts to have a physical reaction, one of extreme anxiety. He starts to see The Italian's naïveté as a fabrication. When his anthropological team discovers the bog-body of an ancient shaman in a nearby construction site, he begins to formulate a connection between the respective mysteries of the shaman and The Italian. "Shamans aren't chosen from among normal people", he argues with his superior at the University (who also happens to be his girlfriend's father), continuing that they are "likely epileptics or hermaphrodites."

The film considers mental illness or disability on numerous occasions – peripheral sequences see The Italian visiting her boyfriend in the hospital where he works with developmentally disabled children, and Michael on a tour through a mental ward. A correlation is being set up between these characters and The Italian, which, to Michael, confirms her shamanic abilities.

After finding female ejaculatory fluid in the shaman's rectum, he goes to pieces, believing this to be a sign of emasculation that he relates to the shifting power dynamic in his relationship with The Italian. He goes home and sodomizes her, as she screams in protest: "Am I crazy? Or have you torn me apart?!" But as they both achieve orgasm, they are bathed in a bright light from above, one of many times in the film that a 'divine light' accompanies an act of destruction. He goes back to the University to smoke a joint and sit in visitation with the shaman's body. He confesses to the shaman that The Italian has gotten under his skin, has taken him

above: Boguslaw Linda and Iwona Petry in Andrzej Zulawski's **Szamanka** (1996).

over from the inside. In what may be a hallucination, the shaman awakens and whispers to him that he was pushed into the bog by a female shaman (thus the film's title, *Szamanka*). "She was love and death for me", says the shaman. "She wanted my power. She got it. She raped me in secret. I loved her and she raped me. The secret is in death." But as the shaman speaks, Michael is saying the lines simultaneously; he is talking to himself.

He comes to believe that The Italian has "possessed" him, that she is a succubus depleting his life force. Michael is correct about one thing: her psychosis seems to be contagious. Her mental instability is apparent from the outset just through its physical manifestations – drooling, jumping, shaking, twitching – while his is only unleashed through his increasing sexual liaisons with her. But she cannot create psychosis in him; it's already there. We rein these things in because the world doesn't allow them – but she allows it, nurtures it, shares in it. He goes crazy *with* her, and this compromise of his mental integrity causes him to be crippled by guilt and shame. He doesn't want to know *why*, he just knows that it didn't happen until he met her, that *she* is the problem. But again, he is being self-centred; he does not take into account that the obsession goes both ways, that the lack of control that accompanies this intense human connection unravels them both equally. He panics and tries to leave her. She is confused: "You bewitch me, and then just make off? I love you. Why?" He shrugs: "You are like death." She has no choice but to prove him right.

Alberto Cavallone was one of many European filmmakers who used surrealism as a socio-political tool. Perhaps most infamous for his 1978 film *Blue Movie*, his 1977 film *Man, Woman and Beast* is equally extreme but rarely seen or commented upon in critical circles. The film has so far not been made available in English; the DVD release in North America has an Italian soundtrack only. Its graphic imagery includes numerous close-ups of female genitalia, defecation and coprophagy. Although the film is a sensory overload in general, of interest here is the mute, feral character Luciana.

From the film's opening, Luciana is clearly mad, kept locked up in the apartment of her emotionally distant husband, a communist artist whose particular fixation is the eroticisation of scientific anatomy. It is festival week in their small town – carnivals, parades, concerts make the tiny streets a flurry of activity which the husband joins while his wife skulks around the apartment in her lingerie, masturbating and self-mutilating. Mentally she exists in a primitive, non-verbal state; she eats off the floor, spilling her food carelessly, drinks water out of the toilet bowl. Left in the care of a nanny at frequent intervals, she is a danger to herself and others, which becomes apparent when she knocks out the nanny with a hairdryer, cuts the unconscious woman's clothes off with scissors and comes close to cutting off the woman's nipples before her husband stumbles in to stop her. But she has no concept of right or wrong, and reprimanding her seems to have no effect. Her character is strikingly

similar to The Italian in Zulawski's *Szamanka*. Both have a limitless sex drive, both are non verbal, both eat like wild animals and both naively confuse the sensations associated with sex and murder respectively.

top right: Boguslaw Linda and Shaman in **Szamanka**.

centre right: French promo-sheet for **Szamanka** under the variant spelling **Chamanka**.

bottom right: Iwona Petry and Boguslaw Linda in **Szamanka**.

She lives in auto-erotic isolation, like a silent extension of her husband's artwork and that of the surrealists whose now-tired showpieces (i.e. Magritte's 'The Rape') adorn the house. Neither is this analogy lost on her – she plays the part effortlessly, she disrobes in front of a mirror and proceeds to make love to her own image, all the while mute and medicated.

As with many films of the period, sex scenes are intercut with scenes depicting the debasement or killing of animals, and using meat as an aesthetic fixture. The use of 'meat as art' coincided with the widespread rise of vegetarianism in the early '70s, which made it an easy shock tactic that many avant-garde filmmakers seized upon. The concept of viscera as art was also promulgated for almost a decade beforehand courtesy of the Vienna Actionists and the Panic Theatre, to which Cavallone's film owes an obvious debt (think Arrabal's films *I Will Walk Like a Crazy Horse* (1973) and *Viva la muerte* (1971) without the over-pronounced humour).

When a homeless teenage boy who has been beaten by a jealous husband is deposited at the artist's apartment to recuperate, he is seized upon by the lustful Luciana, as her husband looks on and photographs. A fevered sex scene is intercut with the bacchanal down in the streets below, with the portentous 'In the Hall of the Mountain King' from Grieg's Peer Gynt playing over the action. Just when it seems things couldn't possibly get more frenzied, Luciana shits in the boy's mouth, suffocating him, then castrates him with scissors and kills him as her husband continues to look on with a detached gaze. But only moments later, he'll be dead too, the corpses lying at Luciana's feet as she reclines on the couch and masturbates like a retarded child.

Man, Woman and Beast's Luciana and *Szamanka*'s The Italian share a bizarre infantilism with a highly charged sex drive, a combination that Freud would happily categorize as hysteria. However, Freud originally dismissed the idea that hysteria was connected to sexuality, and found the concept insulting to his female patients (many of whom had suffered some sort of sexual abuse as children). But by the time of his most famous case, Dora, documented in *Fragment of an Analysis of a Case of Hysteria* (1901) – and after increased pressure from wealthy patrons eager to hide evidence of rampant sexual abuse in the upper class – Freud changed his tune. Instead, he established a theoretical apparatus that proved that hysteria was a woman's inability to reconcile her erotic drives with her conscious self-perception, resulting in an altered state of consciousness known as disassociation. And while the psychological profiles of horror film characters are not laid out so as to match up with the neat categorization of the DS/M IV – neuroses mutate and blend in genre cinema – more often than not they fall in line with Freud's basic observations concerning female sexuality being a source of horror – both for the woman, and for everyone unlucky enough to be around her. A highly sexual woman is one to be feared, because her insatiability is a sign that darker forces are at work within her. In *Possession* it is a physical monster that eats men, in *Szamanka*, a witch who depletes her lover's lifeforce. In many cases the women themselves start to examine their own capacity for evil. If 'the monster' is a warning, a thing that 'points' to something,[65] then in these films the monster is a woman's finger, pointing at herself.

Lars von Trier's *Antichrist* was one of the most hotly-debated films of 2009 due to its examination of a woman's descent into what she perceives to be her own primordially-inspired evil. When the film opens, a married couple played by Charlotte Gainsbourg and Willem Dafoe (referred to in the credits only as 'She' and 'He') are in the throes of passion as their young son accidentally falls to his death through the couple's bedroom window. Her grief in the aftermath of this event is debilitating, and she is hospitalized for an extended period of time, being plied with medication that leaves her asleep for much of it. Her husband is a psychiatrist, and insists that she is being overmedicated – he urges her to lucidly experience her grief, with him as a guide through her recovery. But her reaction – however groggy – establishes him as controlling, condescending and arrogant. Her grief is compounded by the fact that she holds herself responsible for the son's death, and when her husband asserts that he's equally to blame, she denies it – even though she is obviously harbouring resentment against him.

Her doctor has apparently told her that her "grief pattern is abnormal", but her husband disagrees: "Grief is not a disease", he says, insisting that being walled up in a hospital is the worst thing for her recovery. He wants to take her home, but she is reluctant. Her mistrust of him is laid out plainly: she accuses him of always being distant from her, and from their son. "I never interested you until now", she says, "Now you're patient. You're indifferent to whether your son is alive or dead."

Gainsbourg and Dafoe's characters are the only two people in the film, the entirety of which is based on the push-pull relationship between them, and the ensuing arguments that pit them opposite each other in a gender-fuelled contest of power. Like the couple in Nicolas Roeg's *Don't Look Now* (1973), they will each deal

top left: The bathroom floor as dinner table in Alberto Cavallone's **Man, Woman and Beast** (1977).

with their grief and guilt in different ways, but the psychic space here is hers; her husband is an active observer who – while his concern seems genuine – is as emotionally distant from the audience as he is from his wife.

When he finally gets her to come home from the hospital, the relocation prompts a series of intense conversations and mock-therapy sessions – psychological 'exercises' that are meant to help her overcome her fears, but only serve to elucidate the uneven power dynamic in their relationship. Despite her apparent resentment over what she feels is his systematic dismissiveness, their relationship is sexually charged, and her sex drive is intensified by her need to distract herself from crippling grief. He discourages her aggressive advances: "I know it distracts you, but it's not healthy", he says. "You have to have the courage to stay in the situation that frightens you. Then you'll learn that fear isn't dangerous." But she disagrees: "This is physical – it's dangerous", she says; and indeed her anxiety is palpable. Her body responds physically with trembling, quickened pulse, dry mouth, inability to breathe. She bangs her head on the toilet repeatedly – as with most means of self-harm, one pain blots out another. "I want to die too!" she cries. He cradles her, reciting comforting platitudes: "Let fear come if it likes. What the mind can conceive and believe, it can achieve." But by the end of the film, he'll regret saying this.

In their therapy sessions, she is told to close her eyes and imagine herself in the place that most frightens her. She reveals that she is scared of the woods, where they have an isolated cabin called 'Eden', and where she has spent long periods of time working on her now-abandoned thesis. He urges her to picture herself walking through the woods, and she complies – as she moves through the forest in eerie slow motion, everything around her seems to loom large over her small frame, the fog is dense, and she lies down in the grass, her arms outstretched like Ophelia, her equally troubled and suicidal Shakespearean counterpart. He decides that this fear – which he doesn't understand – can only be overcome by going to Eden in person to work through it physically. But doing this involves crossing a divide between public space and private space – a move into the woods will mark a psychic transgression that is, as she has suggested, dangerous. When they cross the footpath into Eden, she becomes hyper-aware and she can sense death everywhere. The woods are full of dead and cannibalistic animals, mothers who eat their children. Even he witnesses the dark magic of the place; again, like Donald Sutherland in *Don't Look Now*, he has clairvoyant experiences that he will try to ignore, to his own detriment. He keeps his cool only through her anxiety and hysteria – it gives him a focus.

above: Charlotte Gainsbourg in Lars von Trier's **Antichrist** (2009).

overleaf: Charlotte Gainsbourg in **Antichrist**.

Once in the cabin, he goes through various interrogative threads trying to isolate the root of her fear, eventually zeroing in on her now-abandoned thesis, about gynocide – she was investigating what makes people do horrible things to women. While doing her research she came to believe that if human nature was inherently evil, then it followed that women were evil too, and this created both a professional and spiritual crisis for her. Furthermore she decided that the vengefulness of women was aligned with the wrath of nature, and that the foreboding atmosphere in the woods at Eden supported this. "Women do not control their own bodies", she says, "nature does." Despite his arguments that nature can't make her do anything she doesn't want to do, she is convinced that she is part of a larger system, acting out some historically encoded evil. And the death of their son was one of the ways this evil has manifested.

After this revealing session with Dafoe's character, an ensuing sex scene is marked by her incessant weeping. She begs him to hit her, hard enough to cause pain, but he doesn't want to. "Then you don't love me!" she shouts, and runs off into the woods, where she starts masturbating beneath a large gnarled tree. He follows and obliges her, and while intense sexual trysts have been frequent in the film thus far, it is here that we see the power dynamic shifting. She is no longer using sex as a means of temporarily obliterating her guilt/doubts/fears – she is communing with nature. With *her* nature – which is wild, fierce, and vengeful.

above: Charlotte Gainsbourg and Willem Dafoe in **Antichrist**.

In the attic of the cabin, he finds the notes from her thesis; as he turns the pages, her handwriting becomes more erratic, the letters get bigger and turn to gibberish. Like my mother's schizophrenic letters to me all those years ago, she is writing in an unrecognizable language informed by fantasy. He starts to acknowledge that she has become frightening, possibly beyond his capacity to help. Still, he encourages her to get in touch in with her emotions, to allow herself to cry and grieve. "The crying woman is a scheming woman", she offers flatly in response. But in asserting that crying is a form of manipulation – a tactic used by women to disarm those around them – she denies herself the grief of losing her child and instead resigns herself to being a villain.

The film goes through many other examples of her wilful maleficence, with increasingly psychotic behaviour that sees her husband fighting for his life. A flashback sequence reveals that she saw their son edging toward the open window, but was too caught up in orgasm to stop it from happening – causing her to equate her sexuality with monstrosity (resulting in a now-infamous depiction of genital mutilation). By the time this flashback occurs, she is so far gone mentally that we don't know whether to trust it as fact, or whether this 'memory' is merely an extension of her self-directed misogyny. But what is interesting is the shifting of responsibility as a result of overwhelming grief. Throughout the course of the film, she moves this responsibility around – from herself, to her husband, to Satan, to nature, and back to herself as a *vehicle* of nature – all the while desperately clutching for someone to blame. Assigning blame is a means of compartmentalizing, and in a film where – as the talking fox says – "Chaos Reigns!", this is her attempt at creating order.

My life has been the arena for an ongoing struggle between order and chaos. All those things I've spent my life fighting against – systems, codes, rules – now have a treasured place in my life. Granted, these are *my* rules, and they often don't make sense to anyone but me. I love honour codes: vows of silence, strictly-defined concepts of fidelity, suicide pacts. I love animals more than people, but I also love the fact that in a cockfight, the birds will not stop fighting until their last breath.

In writing this book, looking back over my greatest periods of upheaval, that's where all the good stories are. As I've gotten older, figured out how to achieve things efficiently and with less risk, gotten *good at what I do*, the chaos dissipates, and the stories disappear. I'm terrified of my life becoming banal, of running out of the stories, those stories I have that make people laugh, make people incredulous, make them proud of me.

I place a lot of stock in my ability to overcome ridiculous obstacles, and the resultant stories that distinguish my life from the tedium that I associate with adulthood. So as the chaos subsides, I have to create chaos in other ways. Always within certain confines, in boxes I can control. These boxes tend to be things called Romantic Relationships. But this tactic is poorly-thought-out: emotionally fraught relationships are nothing new, and are barely interesting. None of these relationships have given me stories worth telling. Pouring my chaos into them is pointless. All these relationships do is give me someone to blame for everything.

This makes my extreme jealousy rather perplexing. That jealousy and hysteria are both forms of 'acting out' some other repressed emotion makes sense to me, but since there wasn't any trauma from my childhood that I hadn't spoken about openly at one point or another, I could never figure out what, exactly, I was repressing that would cause violent or irrational behaviour. When people revert to the same damaging behaviour repeatedly, usually it's because there is some unconscious emotional benefit.

One thing is certain: jealousy always precipitates the demise of my relationships. So as much as I habitually spend years mourning the end of a relationship, it's slowly dawned on me that I don't like being in them. And I take it out on my partner that they've trapped me into a life I don't want. Relationships change me dramatically for the worse, whereas being single gives me the time to obsess over the things that other people think are a waste of time, the things that have, in essence, completely shaped my personality. In this light, my jealousy serves a purpose: it's a violent reminder that I would rather be alone. The problem with this is that we aren't *allowed* to be alone; we're called spinsters and bitches and made to feel as though we're alone because no one wants us. So for me the struggle has been between the person I am – solitary, driven, obsessed – and the person I think I'm supposed to be: a grown-up who has dinner parties and makes a good impression on in-laws. But the truth is, I've never made a good impression, and I hate cooking. In fact, I practically hate *food* because it always becomes the focal point in relationships, and just symbolizes death to me. I don't want a partner to cook food with and get fat with and then go on diets with. I just want to sit on the floor eating cereal and listening to records.

So in a sense my jealousy is a colossal cop-out that keeps me emotionally stunted, so that I can avoid having to redefine myself, which might have to happen if I ever compromised, or ate a vegetable.

Cancelling out romantic relationships altogether isn't the answer though; after all, I've discovered I have pretty intense dependency needs – the kind typical of 'strong' women who are overcompensating for something. To conclude that I'm better off alone is just another in a multi-layered series of escapes, each of them obscuring the real problem. It's almost laughable at this point: The Real Problem! The Key to EVERYTHING!

PART TEN:
YOU CARRY A COFFIN TODAY

In January of 2009, I got a call from my mother. I was in a mall of all places, and I was shocked to hear from her; after all, I hadn't spoken to her in several years and as far as I knew she didn't even have my current phone number, but there she was on the other end, her scratchy voice matter-of-factly explaining that she had six months to live.

"Okay, whatever you say", I offered dismissively, as she continued to list a flurry of ailments, most of them cancerous, which were eating at her from the inside. My mother's relationship with illness was always suspect – she was *always* sick with something – sometimes real and sometimes fictional – that would enable her to play her two favourite roles: angel of the house and survivor of unbearable trauma. But this was one illness she wouldn't survive. She was dead a few weeks later.

This phone call marked the last time I would speak to her. My last words to my mother as she told me plainly she was dying: "Alright, well I hope you feel better. Good luck."

In Andrew Parkinson's *Venus Drowning* (2006), a young woman named Dawn finds out that her long-term boyfriend has succumbed to his protracted battle with cancer, and loses her gestating child to a miscarriage on the same day. After a failed suicide attempt, her psychiatrist advises her to go somewhere that she associates with happy memories, and she opts for the seaside vacation flat where she spent her childhood. She surrounds herself with drawings, dolls, security blankets that she rescues from old dusty boxes in the basement. She arranges them on the kitchen table like an altar to her childhood, a time before the tragedy. But the drawings reveal darker memories – a woman drowning, the alcoholism of her despondent mother – and she soon finds herself at the centre of a one-woman emotional shootout.

Dawn's bereavement fuels hallucinatory visions of her dead boyfriend passing her in the street, and foetuses floating in shallow pools near the beach. She stops to inspect one of these foetal creatures more closely, running her finger across its slimy texture. It's no ordinary foetus: upon closer examination it looks like an aborted mermaid or a disembodied vaginal tract. She carries on her way but can't stop breathing in the peculiar smell it has left on her fingers. Following some bizarre compulsion, she goes back for it, and takes it back to the flat where she washes it like a baby and places it on the kitchen table among her other relics. She fights herself in keeping it; she's always trying to talk herself into or out of things, including her medication ("Diazepam to help me get to sleep. Doxepin for depression. Erotamine for migraine. Ritalin for concentration. Coffee and cigarettes to make me happy.") Eventually she convinces herself to toss the medication, and focuses on resuscitating her newly-adopted stillborn creature.

Initially the creature seems to be a stand-in for her dead baby, but it soon becomes apparent that her connection to this creature runs deeper than a nine-month bond. "This seems like a step backward", she says, cradling and rocking it, "Just when I was about to grow up and accept responsibility, I end up back here. And now I have you." As she smells and licks the intoxicating juices emanating from the creature, there is a regression that has occurred – and it's one of an adolescent masturbation fantasy, where the pulsating, wet vagina is an external being with its own agenda. The lubrication of the creature is directly tied to her own arousal, which she somehow views as monstrous and needs to disassociate herself from.

opposite: Jodie Jameson in Andrew Parkinson's **Venus Drowning** (2006).

This notion of repression, although manifested sexually, is multi-faceted. Her neurosis is also tied to her fear of repeating the familial cycle of alcoholism and her dead boyfriend's cancer. When she got pregnant, he'd had the cancer 'cut out' through surgery. But the operation proved unsuccessful: they didn't completely cut it out; they only bought some more time. Eventually it came back, he went into relapse, and died shortly thereafter. As he relapsed, she regressed. The 'cancer' existed in more ways than one.

Aside from the obvious connection to Cronenberg's *The Brood* (the monstrous child being the physical manifestation of repression), *Venus Drowning* is also reminiscent in many ways of *Mermaid in a Manhole* (1988), the fourth instalment in the notorious Japanese *Guinea Pig* series.

Mermaid in a Manhole tells the story of an artist who spends much of his time traversing the city's sewers looking for inspiration. Upon one such underground excursion, the artist's voice-over informs the audience that a river once flowed where the sewer now lies stagnant and fermenting. Among the remains littered throughout the sewer are Chibi (a dead cat that the artist relates as a childhood pet), a stillborn child, and a mermaid that appears to be suffering from some kind of parasite. "I met you once before, when this place was a river", he says to the mermaid (telepathically), "that was you, wasn't it?" She acknowledges the memory. But soon, her illness starts to pain her and the artist takes her back to his flat and tries to heal her with some goldfish medication.

Curiously, she does not want to be saved, but instead, urges the artist to paint her. While this is going on upstairs, the downstairs neighbours make note of the artist's strange behaviour, and attribute it to the fact that his wife left him some time ago. As the mermaid's illness becomes more pronounced, a variety of worms and seven colours of pus ooze from the disgusting lesions on her body, the latter of which she prompts the artist to use in his painting of her (which grotesquely transforms as she transforms). Eventually she begs him to kill her, and – totally insane by this point – he obliges. He dismembers her body, and is discovered doing so by the aforementioned neighbours. Among the scattered body parts is a stillborn child, not unlike the one seen earlier in the sewer. The neighbours disclose to the police that when they found the artist, he was maniacally hacking away at his wife's lifeless body. The voiceover at the end of the film (this time by the police) confirms that not only was the corpse that of his wife, but that she had been dying of cancer in the apartment for some time. In addition to the cancer, she was also pregnant, but had already lost the child before the artist chopped her up. The final twist is that at the scene of the crime, the police discovered an unidentifiable fish-scale, whose source "remains a mystery".

Both films focus on the interplay between two seemingly distinct types of illness: madness and cancer. Because one is a disease of the body and the other a disease of the mind, it seems the two illnesses would have little in common. But Susan Sontag's essay *Illness as Metaphor* (1978) makes an interesting connection between cancer and madness in that, metaphorically, both are off-shoots of certain notions associated with tuberculosis in the 19th century.

Tuberculosis had a romantic pathos attached to it – it was seen as a disease that strengthened one's character even as it consumed one's vital energy. It thus became known as a disease with a character of its own, which bred the kind of metaphors one can see in much Victorian fiction. Today, the romantic agony once associated with tuberculosis has been transposed to the realm of madness – the stereotype of the 'suffering artist' who loses his grip on reality as his artistic vision becomes clearer is evidence of this.

The repression associated with tuberculosis, on the other hand, has been reassigned to cancer. In Sontag's hypothesis, this is emphasized by the physical symptoms of the disease: "The tumour has energy, not the patient; 'it' is out of control. Cancer cells, according to the textbook account, are cells that have shed the mechanism which 'restrains' growth. Cells without inhibitions, cancer cells will continue to grow and extend over each other in a 'chaotic' fashion, destroying the body's normal cells, architecture, and functions."[66]

top left: Jodie Jameson in **Venus Drowning**.

above: Shigeru Saiki and Mari Somei in Hideshi Hino's **Mermaid in a Manhole** (1988).

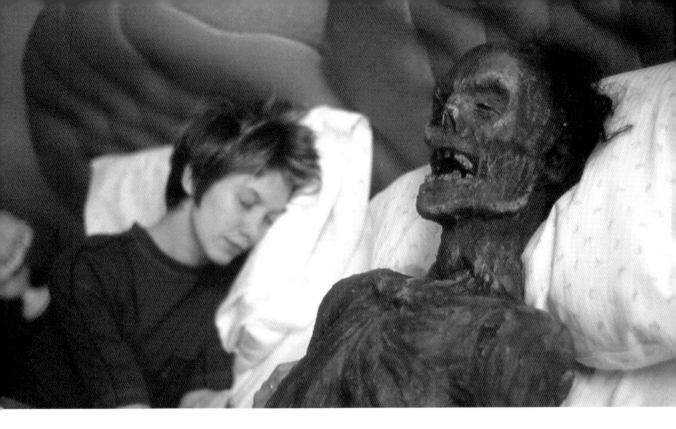

So medication comes into play, as a means of reining in the illness, but medication has another purpose – it is also an acknowledgement of sickness. It's *proof* of sickness. And for Dawn in *Venus Drowning*, there is something attractive about being sick; a push-pull relationship is established between wanting to maintain control and letting the sickness wash over her. The notion that people are made more conscious as they are confronted with imminent death makes the sick more 'interesting' (which is how the word 'romantic' was originally defined, according to Sontag). This is especially relevant in the context of the 19th century, when tuberculosis reigned supreme and was thought to be symptomatic or causal of higher spiritual consciousness.

And again, the formulation of a creature from this messy confluence of regression, repression and rage recalls Anna in *Possession*'s assertion that: "I suffer, I believe, I am, but at the same time I know there's a third possibility like cancer or madness. But cancer or madness contort reality. The possibility I'm talking about pierces reality."

The creature pierces reality – it shouldn't exist. But it exists because Dawn has immersed herself in sickness; she has adopted the creature the way she has adopted all the illnesses around her. Already emotionally unstable, she fabricates connections between her own mental illness and her mother's, between her boyfriend's cancer and the pulsating creature that she both loves and reviles.

Like any grieving person, Dawn is overwhelmed by a range of emotions, including anger at the boyfriend and child who both abandoned her by dying – feelings that are exacerbated by returning home and reliving painful memories of being neglected by her own alcoholic mother. At the intersection of these emotions is where the creature manifests, an all-purpose monster that brings out her maternal, sexual and homicidal instincts. If cancer is seen metaphorically as a disease of repression, what better way to emblematize this than with a dead foetus?

In *Mermaid in a Manhole*, the artist's wife is dying of cancer as the already-dead foetus rots away inside her, while in *Venus Drowning*, Dawn has a miscarriage the same day her boyfriend dies of cancer and ends up adopting a creature that was abandoned on the beach. My own mother's fertility problems – a succession of miscarriages and stillbirths – led to her adopting me.

Sontag claims that "the source for the current fancy that associates cancer with repression is Wilhelm Reich, who defined cancer as 'a disease following emotional resignation, a bio-energetic shrinking, a giving up of hope'."[67]

above: Jodie Jameson in **Venus Drowning**.

By all accounts, my mother faced death calmly, rejecting any medication that could prolong her life. She just wanted painkillers to ease her into it. My mother, who wanted so desperately to survive, who *did* survive so many things for which there is no medication, let go before I could even get there to say goodbye. My plane ticket, which had been purchased too late to facilitate a hospital visit, instead brought me to a funeral.

My brother had phoned me from her bedside as she was starting to sink into delirium. She was right beside him, and I could have spoken to her, but I didn't ask to. It's the kind of inexplicable behaviour you hear about in bad easy-listening pop songs. But my Aunt Velma, the one who had accompanied my mother to my ill-fated wedding all those years ago, insisted that my mother had a conversation with me on her deathbed, that she died happily knowing that everything had been resolved. In my mind, this lets me off too easily.

The day before the funeral there was a meeting at the church to discuss what prayers would be read and what songs would be played at the service. Everyone else seemed prepared, with readings picked out and lists of contemporary Christian music my mother listened to. When it got to me, there was only one song I could think of, and it was 'Yummy Yummy Yummy' by the Ohio Express. Not surprisingly, no one else thought it would be appropriate to play at the funeral.

I sat with my brother and his family in the front row at the funeral, with my mother's weird boyfriend Mike blubbering uncontrollably in the row behind me. This was the first time I'd ever even seen him, and I was struck by how much of a stranger I'd become to my own family. I felt like a spectator, and struggled to keep up with the bizarre routine of sitting, standing, kneeling and call-and-response that forms the basis of any Catholic church service. In the hallway afterwards, both of my fathers came up to me separately and asked if I'd sit with them during the luncheon. I hid in the bathroom, not sure how I could pick between them, especially on a day as emotionally charged as this. Luckily when I emerged they were both sitting at the same table. I did my best to make small talk with relatives and family friends I hadn't seen in decades, but the real shocker came when my mother's boyfriend Mike approached my stepfather Adam – the two of them had never met, and ever since my mother left him, my stepfather had been waiting for her to come to her senses and return. The house they shared was full of yellowing newspapers, grimy knick knacks, rotten food – like Miss Havisham's Satis House in *Great Expectations*, the place remained unchanged, just getting older and falling into disrepair. He had been in denial about Mike. But here he was, holding his hand out in a peace offering. I thought my stepfather was going to have a heart attack – he dropped his plate on the floor and stuttered through an introduction. It was painful to watch.

The next day I went to my stepdad's house to visit, and we ended up drinking for hours in the kitchen talking about my mother and her various eccentricities. The cushioning that surrounded the table, upon which we had folded out a game of *Bonkers* and were playing it half-heartedly, was worn and faded with the habit of decades. This was his favourite spot in the house, and who could argue with well-earned comfort, no matter how blind it might be. As I searched his face for any sign of despair at the previous day's events, I realized that regardless of what may have passed between us long ago, or maybe because of it, he would always be my favourite. When the conversation wound down, I retreated to my old bedroom (which was also my sister's old bedroom – I was finally allowed to move in there at the age of 12) and sat on my bed amidst all the records, books, posters, games and bad '80s clothes. I looked through my closet for the birthday card from Mr. T but couldn't find it, but I did find mountains of dusty old toys, these relics from another life all piled up and obscuring the secret passageway that led to the place where monsters have their tea parties. The closet is full of ghosts, and I slammed the door shut hoping to keep them at bay.

top left: The baby-monster in **Venus Drowning**.

bottom left: My favourite photo of my stepfather.

opposite: The house I grew up in; the den was the room behind the top left window.

EPILOGUE:
THE MONSTER AT THE END OF THIS BOOK

It's funny how easily we can slip. One minute we are lucid, happy, engaged in the opportunities of the world; the next we sit rocking back and forth, staring at our hands, taking in every line and crevice, wondering who they belong to. Whose hands are these that want to strangle and stab? *How are you feeling today?*

I've always felt one step away from violence; it's been a constant struggle not to overreact to the things around me. I make bad choices that illustrate how little willpower I really have, even though the people around me are always quick to tell me how remarkable I am. But I don't feel remarkable. I feel remarkably small and unimportant. When I feel most clearheaded is when I watch horror films; when I see bad behaviour paraded before me, and I shake my head: I don't want to be like *that*. I couldn't possibly be as bad as *that*, could I?

Every movie has a doppelganger. Whether it's a horror film where these dichotomies are explicit, or more innocuous genres like romantic comedies or adventure stories, all characters are battling their own personalities. There's always a shadow, a point of comparison, that other person who is not like us, and who defines us just by their difference. But those characters are us as well, and we can look at our identification with one character or the other as a struggle to define ourselves, to define what we want to be like and what we don't want to be like. How we relate to other people is all a series of fabrications; who we are is mutable depending on what we are compared to, or in many cases, what we compare ourselves to.

As I was working on this book I began to ask both of my fathers a lot of questions, hoping to corroborate my memories, these destructive things that lead me through cyclical patterns of neurosis and self-castigation. I asked them about my mother's attack at the townhouse, and both had interesting things to say: Adam believed that she had been raped, but that it had actually happened years before – although he wasn't sure when – and that by the time I was a kid that event had long since come and gone. He believed that the attack in the townhouse was a fiction, an occasion of violent memory. When I mentioned this to Oates, pointing out that I remembered this event personally, he looked at me worriedly and asked if I had ever heard of the term *confabulation*. He was suggesting that I bonded with my mother over an imagined trauma. But those on my mother's side of the family – my grandmother, my Aunt Velma and my Aunt Pam specifically – remember the court case, where my grandmother was a witness for the prosecution. They claim that the story was deliberately kept out of the paper to save my mother from embarrassment. This is just one example of how all the people in my family remember things differently, each discrediting the other's take on things. So if our own experiences are merely fictions until they are corroborated by someone else, then slap a barcode on me and put me in the horror section.

I'll never know the truth about what happened to my mother and no longer think it's important. What matters is that she was as *like* me as she was *unlike* me; the dark things in her that I didn't want to be near were already ingrained in me from as far back as I can remember. And fictions – whether it's a fiction about a rape in a townhouse somewhere in Southern Ontario, or a Saturday afternoon creature feature, or the prime-time melodrama of a made-for-TV movie – were what we shared, and we shared *something* – and now that's all that matters to me.

opposite: Mylène Jampanoï in Pascal Laugier's **Martyrs** (2008).

When I was a kid I had a book starring neurotic Sesame Street fave Grover, called *The Monster at the End of This Book*. In the story, Grover begs the reader to stop turning the pages, and creates a series of obstacles including ropes and bricks to prevent the reader from reaching the end of the book, convinced that a monster is waiting there. As a kid I would read this story over and over again, each time freshly frightened and anticipating the horrifying ending. But after 24 pages of Grover's pleading, the reader finally turns the last page, only to discover that the monster at the end of the book... is Grover himself.

It took me ten years to write *House of Psychotic Women*. Ten years of procrastinating, circumventing, burying and basically coming up with any excuse imaginable to avoid reaching the end – because, as Grover surmised, there is a monster at the end of this book.

Everything we see onscreen is a fiction that we are asked to believe, and we believe in it because we can find truth in that fiction. There's something there that, for whatever reason, we can grab hold of. So I ask again – *what happens when you feed crazy with more crazy?* It's stepping into a minefield – a place most people will avoid, because to go there means almost certain death. But what if you go into the minefield so much, tracing your steps back and forth, that you memorize where everything is buried so that you can gaze upon the danger and learn to sidestep it at the same time? The hope is that we'll get good at it, and eventually learn to trust our instincts.

When my mother died, I knew I had to finally finish this story, and I knew that it would involve revisiting some unpleasant territory. Because when somebody dies, one thing is certain: like it or not, you have to go back home.

I once told a friend that my life was just a succession of obsessing over the wrong things. "What would your life look like if you ever obsessed over the right thing?" she asked.

It would look like this. Like a book, being finished.

Isabelle Adjani in Andrzej Zulawski's **Possession** (1981).

There was a knife I left behind
I will always search for and never find
A knife I believe was right here in my pocket
And its blade still flashes through my mind
And my fingers will forever be entwined
Around the knife I left behind

There was a knife that would not be found
Though I've searched the whole world round
Spiralling downward, long red ribbons to the ground
Turning smooth as a razor where the skin came all unwound
There was a knife, would not be found

My hand holds a memory, its handle just like ebony
Its blade was beaming, gleaming like a fast blue flame
When it stabs me to the heart I feel the pain
And no other knife could ever be the same

With a heavy heart I drew and snapped the chalk line
That ran between what was yours and mine
In dreams I return to the scene of the crime
For the knife I left behind

– Freakwater, from *Jack the Knife*, 2005

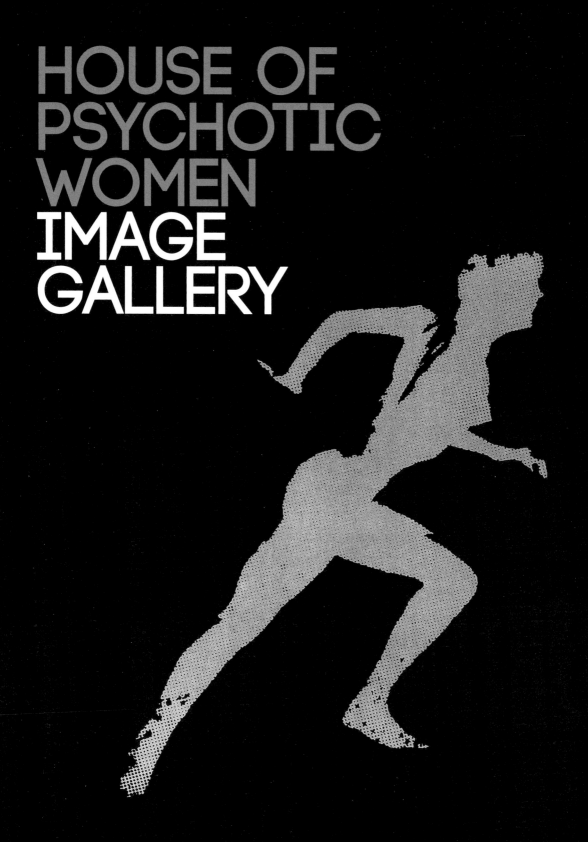

HOUSE OF PSYCHOTIC WOMEN
IMAGE GALLERY

EN NOCHES DE LUNA LLENA EL SEXO SE POSESIONA DE SU CUERPO HASTA CONVERTIRLA EN UNA TERRIBLE BESTIA SEDIENTA DE PLACER...

LA MUJER LOBO

después de satisfacer sus sádicos instintos ¡LOS MATA!

PROTAGONIZADA POR
ANNIK BOREL

...HOWARD ROSS
DAGMAR LASSANDER
TINO CARRARO

DISTRIBUIDA POR
**CINEMATOGRAFICA
ANAHUAC, S.A.**
MONTERREY 104-MEXICO, D.F.

A COLORES

top and bottom left: Annik Borel in Rino Di Silvestro's **The Legend of the Wolf Woman** (1976).
bottom right: Pollyanna McIntosh in Lucky McKee's **The Woman** (2011).

forgive them

forgive them

forgive them

THE MAD ROOM

A COLUMBIA PICTURES presentation starring

STELLA STEVENS · SHELLEY WINTERS

Co-starring SKIP WARD · CAROL COLE · SEVERN DARDEN

BEVERLY GARLAND · MICHAEL BURNS · *introducing* BARBARA SAMMETH · Music by DAVID GRUSIN · Screenplay by BERNARD GIRARD and A.Z. MARTIN

Produced by NORMAN MAURER · Directed by BERNARD GIRARD · A NORMAN MAURER PRODUCTION · COLOR

top: Quad format poster for
Bernard Girard's **The Mad Room** (1969).
right: Béatrice Dalle in Clair Denis's
Trouble Every Day (2001).

PARAMOUNT FILMS PRESENTA

una vela para el diablo

aurora bautista · esperanza roy con

judy geeson y la presentación cinematográfica de blanca estrada

victor alcazar · lone fleming · dirigida por eugenio martin

operador: josé f. aguayo · guión: eugenio martin y antonio fos · eastmancolor

DISTRIBUCION PARAMOUNT

OSUDOVÁ přitažlivost

top: East European poster for Adrian Lyne's **Fatal Attraction** (1987).
right: Glenn Close plays a woman scorned in **Fatal Attraction**.

opposite top: Mexican lobby card for Antonioni's **Red Desert** (1964).
opposite bottom left: Laurence Dubas and Christiane Coppé in Jean Rollin's **The Escapees** (1981).
opposite bottom right: French poster for Robert Wise's **The Haunting** (1963).

above: Daria Nicolodi in Mario Bava's **Shock** (1977).
below: Clint Eastwood and Jessica Walter on lobby cards for Eastwood's **Play Misty for Me** (1971).

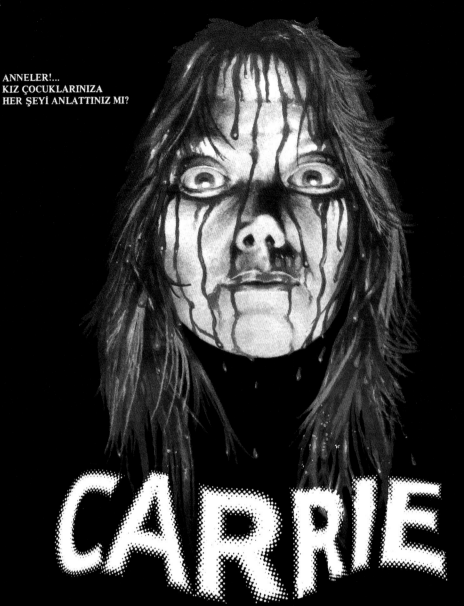

ANNELER!...
KIZ ÇOCUKLARINIZA
HER ŞEYİ ANLATTINIZ MI?

CARRIE
GÜNAH TOHUMU

ÖZENFİLM
United Artists

SISSY SPACEK

JOHN TRAVOLTA
RENKLİ-TÜRKÇE

PIPER LAURIE

Yönetmen
BRIAN De PALMA

Monstrous mothers.
from top: Piper Laurie in Brian De Palma's
Carrie (1976); Samantha Eggar in David
Cronenberg's **The Brood** (1979).

DIABEŁ

SCENARIUSZ & REŻYSERIA:
ANDRZEJ ŻUŁAWSKI
ZDJĘCIA ♠ MACIEJ KIJOWSKI
W ROLACH GŁÓWNYCH:
♠ WOJCIECH PSZONIAK
LESZEK TELESZYŃSKI
MAŁGORZATA
♠ BRAUNEK
PRODUKCJA:
PRF ZF • ZESPÓŁ
FILMOWY X •
1972

WALKVSKI '87

HOUSE OF PSYCHOTIC WOMEN

The Mafu Cage

A film by Karen Arthur

A terrifying love story.

Lee Grant Carol Kane

DARIO ARGENTO

ASIA ARGENTO
THOMAS KRETSCHMANN

LA SINDROME DI STENDHAL

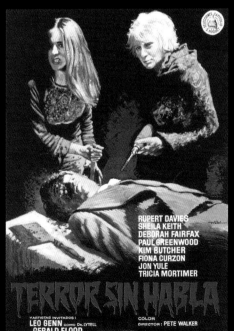

RUPERT DAVIES
SHEILA KEITH
DEBORAH FAIRFAX
PAUL GREENWOOD
KIM BUTCHER
FIONA CURZON
JON YULE
TRICIA MORTIMER

TERROR SIN HABLA

YARTISTAS INVITADOS:
LEO GENN COMO Dr. LYTELL
Y GERALD FLOOD COMO MATTHEW LAURENCE

COLOR
DIRECTOR: PETE WALKER

above: Asia Argento on an Italian fotobusta for Dario Argento's **The Stendhal Syndrome** (1996).
left: Spanish poster for Pete Walker's **Frightmare** (1974).
below: Melissa Sue Anderson and Glenn Ford in J. Lee Thompson's **Happy Birthday to Me** (1981)

Happy Birthday to me

from top:
Mexican lobby cards for Alfred Sole's
Alice, Sweet Alice (1976) and Sergio
Martino's **All the Colors of the Dark** (1972).

Zwei Weltstars in einem der besten Filme des Jahres

JULIE CHRISTIE

DONALD SUTHERLAND

Wenn die Gondeln Trauer tragen

JULIE CHRISTIE DONALD SUTHERLAND
in DAPHNE DU MAURIER'S »DON'T LOOK NOW«
Regie: NICOLAS ROEG
Produziert von PETER KATZ · Drehbuch: ALLAN SCOTT und CHRIS BRYANT
Ausführender Produzent: ANTHONY B. UNGER
Eine Produktion der LION INTERNATIONAL FILMS London

German poster for Nicolas Roeg's **Don't Look Now** (1973).

above: Josie Ho in Pang Ho-cheung's **Dream Home** (2010).
right: Bette Davis on a lobby card for **What Ever Happened to Baby Jane?** (1962).
opposite top: Melanie Lynskey in Peter Jackson's **Heavenly Creatures** (1994).
opposite bottom left: British quad poster for Roman Polanski's **Repulsion** (1965).
opposite bottom right: One-sheet poster for Brett Leonard's **Feed** (2005).

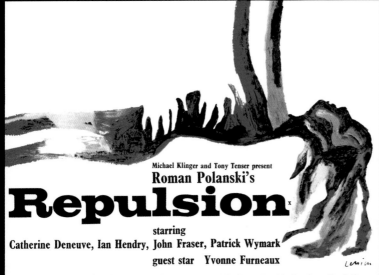

Michael Klinger and Tony Tenser present
Roman Polanski's
Repulsion x
starring
Catherine Deneuve, Ian Hendry, John Fraser, Patrick Wymark
guest star Yvonne Furneaux

screenplay by Roman Polanski and Gerard Brach   directed by Roman Polanski   produced by Gene Gutowski

From the director of 'Lawnmower Man' and 'Man Thing'
FEED
consumption is evolution

BECKER FILMS INTERNATIONAL presents an HONOUR BRIGHT and ALL AT ONCE PRODUCTION
ALEX O'LOUGHLIN PATRICK THOMPSON GABBY MILLGATE and JACK THOMPSON
"FEED" Produced by MELISSA BEAUFORD Written by KIERAN GALVIN Directed by BRETT LEONARD

Polish illustrator Jan Lenica's German commissioned poster for Roman Polanski's **Repulsion** (1965).

from top: Barbara Hershey in
Sidney J. Furie's **The Entity** (1982).
left: Kathleen Byron in Michael
Powell & Emeric Pressberger's
Black Narcissus (1947).

It will never happen again!

Ms❍45

ROCHELLE FILMS INC. PRESENTS **Ms❍45** A NAVARON FILM PRODUCTION
ZOË TAMERLIS · STEVE SINGER · JACK THIBEAU · PETER YELLEN · JOE DELIA · JAMES MOMEL
CHRISTOPHER ANDREWS · DA PRODUCTIONS · NICHOLAS ST. JOHN · ROCHELLE WEISBERG
NAVARON FILMS · ABEL FERRARA · RELEASED THRU ROCHELLE FILMS, INC. **R RESTRICTED**

THRiLLER

CON

CHRISTINA | HEINZ
LINDBERG | HOPF

PRODOTTO DA
BO A. VIBENIUS DIRETTO DA **ALEX FRIDOLINSKI**

SCENEGGIATURA DI
ALEX FRIDOLINSKI·BO A. VIBENIUS   EASTMANCOLOR

A CRUEL PICTURE A UNITED PRODUCERS RELEASE
THROUGH AMERICAN INTERNATIONAL PICTURES

left, from top: Poster for Abel Ferrara's **Ms.45** (1981); Carol Laure in Karim Hussain's **La Belle Bête** (2006).

right, from top: Tuesday Weld in Noel Black's **Pretty Poison** (1968); Poster for Bo Vibenius's **They Call Her One Eye** (1974).

CLINT EASTWOOD

LA NOTTE BRAVA
DEL SOLDATO JONATHAN

GERALDINE PAGE · ELIZABETH HARTMAN

SCENEGGIATURA DI JOHN B. SHERRY E GRIMES GRICE   PRODOTTO E DIRETTO DA DON SIEGEL   PRESENTATO DA JENNINGS LANG   UNA PRODUZIONE UNIVERSAL PICTURES/MALPASO COMPANY   TECHNICOLOR   DISTR. CINEMA INTERNATIONAL CORPORATION

SHE'D HAD A BAD EXPERIENCE-
THE WORST KIND!
SHE WANTED JUSTICE-
THE LAW COULDN'T, WOULDN'T HELP HER...
THERE WAS NOTHING LEFT-
EXCEPT PERSONAL REVENGE!

BUT HOW?

HAND GUN 18

EMI Films presents A **Kestrel** Film **HAND GUN**
Starring **KAREN YOUNG** · **CLAYTON DAY**
Music by **MIKE POST** Co-Produced by **DAVID STREIT**
Written, Produced and Directed by **TONY GARNETT**

top: Karen Young on the UK quad poster for
Tony Garnett's **Handgun** (1983)
right: The futuristic opening shot of Gordon
Willis's **Windows** (1980).

BLACK

NATALIE PORTMAN   VINCENT CASSEL   MILA KUNIS

SWAN

FROM THE DIRECTOR OF **THE WRESTLER** & **REQUIEM FOR A DREAM**

Impressionistic promotional artwork for Noel Black's **Pretty Poison** (1968).

top: Italian fotobusta for Dario Argento's **The Bird with the Crystal Plumage** (1970).
left: Rifka Lodeizen in Esther Rots's **Can Go Through Skin** (2009).

top: Mass hysteria in Juan López
Moctezuma's **Alucarda** (1975).
right: Michael Petrovitch and
Susan Hampshire in Fred Burnley's
Neither the Sea Nor the Sand
(1972).

Mademoiselle
film angielsko-francuski

Jeanne Moreau
Reżyseria: Tony Richardson

produkcja
Woodfall
Londyn
Procinex
Paryż

Fv.B.STAROWIEYSKI '70

Polish poster for Tony Richardson's **Mademoiselle** (1966).

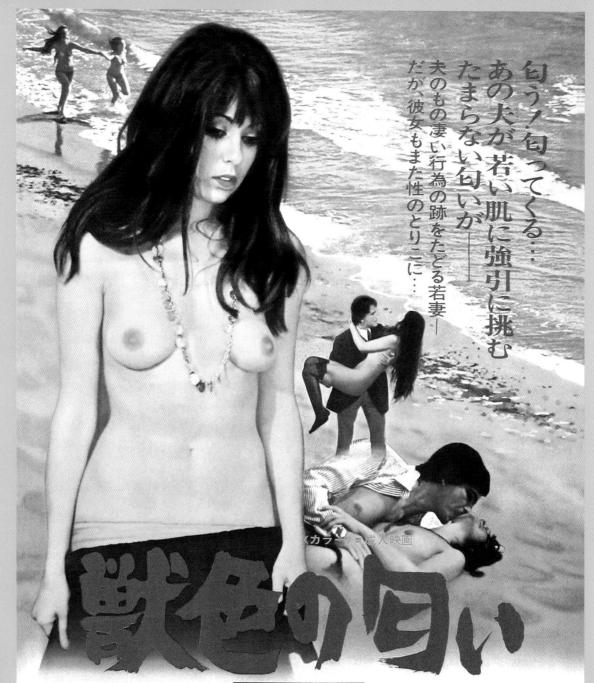

匂う！匂ってくる…
あの夫が若い肌に強引に挑む
たまらない匂いが
夫のもの凄い行為の跡をたどる若妻─
だが、彼女もまた性のとりこに…

獣色の匂い

Le Journal intimate d'une nymphomane

やわ肌ケイレン、のたうつ絶叫！
色情女のすさまじい濡れ場が
続出する直立ポルノ！

アンヌ・リベール／ドリス・トーマス
監督クリフォード・ブラウン／撮影マリオ・リベルト
フランス映画 ■ ミリオンフィルム提供

〔映倫〕

above: Bette Davis and Joan Crawford in a studio promo shot for **What Ever Happened to Baby Jane?** (1962).
left: Lobby card for William Castle's **Strait-Jacket** (1964).

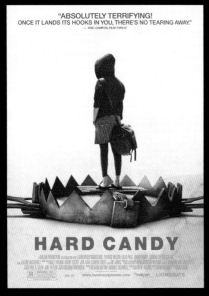

clockwise from top:
Polish poster for Adrian Lyne's
Fatal Attraction (1987);
Australian daybill poster for Uli Edel's
Christiane F. (1981);
U.S. poster featuring Ellen Page as
jailbait predator in David Slade's
Hard Candy (2005).

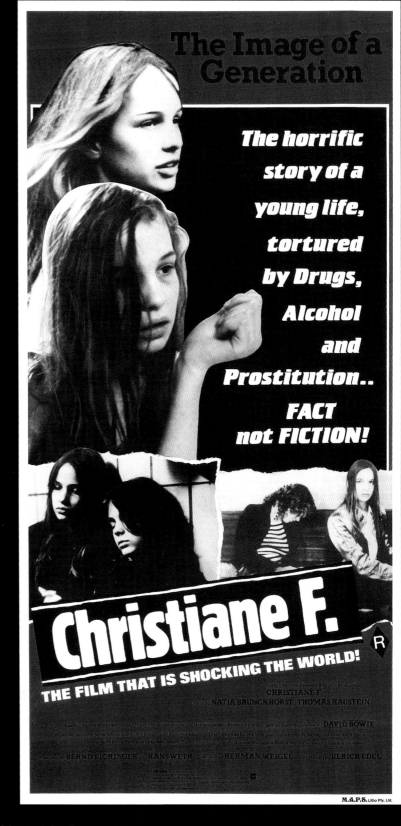

Italian poster for Ingmar Bergman's **Persona** (1966).

CLINT EASTWOOD *w filmie amerykańskim* **OSZUKANY**

W pozostałych rolach:
**Geraldine Page
i Elisabeth Hartman**
Produkcja: **Universal Pictures**

Reżyseria
Donald Siegel

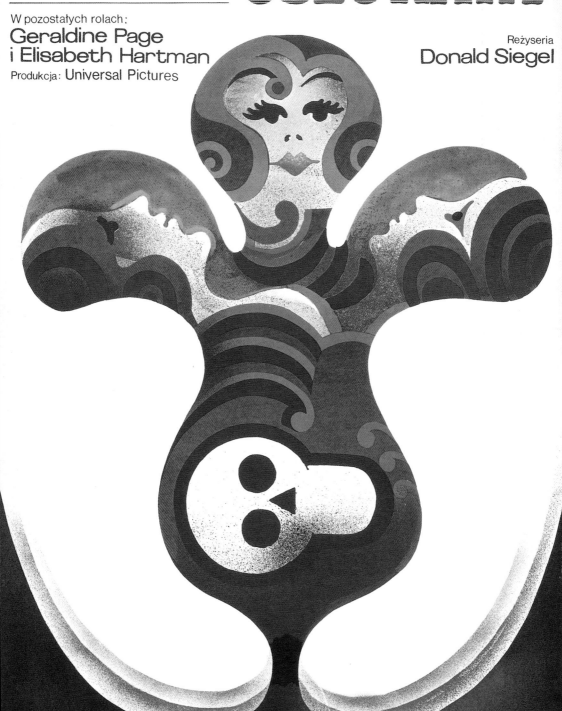

W.GÓRKA 72

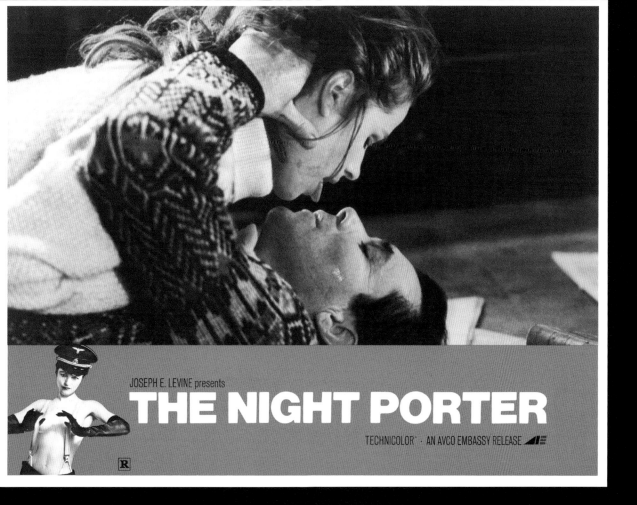

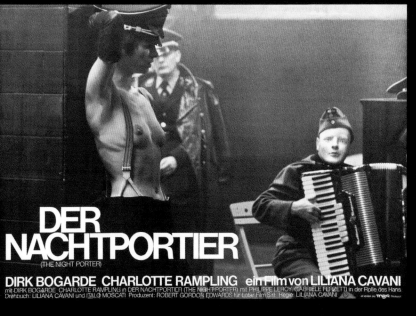

from top: U.S. lobby card and German quad poster for Liliana Cavani's **The Night Porter** (1974).

Angela Bettis in Lucky McKee's **May** (2002).

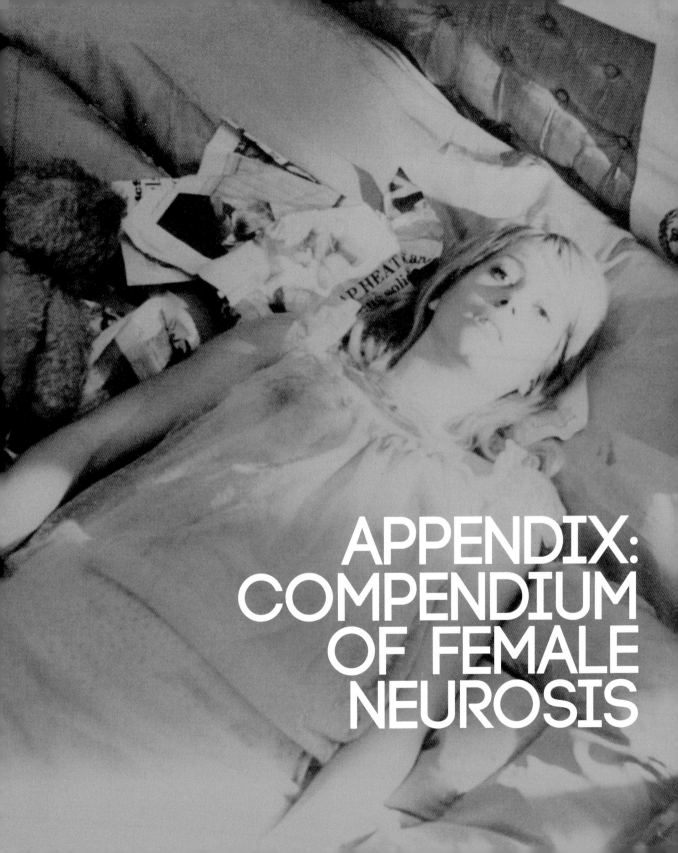

APPENDIX:
COMPENDIUM
OF FEMALE
NEUROSIS

APPENDIX: COMPENDIUM OF FEMALE NEUROSIS

An appendix is, by nature, the thing that comes after the book, an additional gallery or catalogue meant to bolster the expositions of the main text. By that token, the girth of this appendix may be unusual in that it literally fills out half the physical density of the book, even after the book has claimed to reach its end. But it remains an appendix all the same; while by no means comprehensive, this appendix is a cross-section of horror and violent exploitation films that feature disturbed or neurotic women as primary or pivotal characters. This includes capsules of films discussed previously in the narrative as well as other films that are relevant to the book's overarching theme. Admittedly some films stretch genre definitions, and others fall completely outside of the genre but are nonetheless important progenitors for genre characterizations.

Please note that in order to fully examine the themes and content of the films discussed, many of these reviews contain 'spoilers' that reveal key plot elements.

Credits for key production personnel are listed under the following abbreviations:

D: Director
P: Producer
W: Writer / Screenplay
Ed: Editor
M: Music
DoP: Director of Photography / Cinematographer
AD: Art Director
PD: Production Designer

ALICE, SWEET ALICE

1976, USA
Alternative titles: **Communion**; **Holy Terror**
D: Alfred Sole. P: Richard K. Rosenberg. W: Rosemary Ritvo, Alfred Sole. Ed: M. Edward Salier. M: Stephen Lawrence. PD: John Lawless.
Cast: Linda Miller (Catherine Spages), Mildred Clinton (Mrs. Tredoni), Paula Sheppard (Alice Spages), Niles McMaster (Dominick 'Dom' Spages), Jane Lowry (Aunt Annie DeLorenze), Rudolph Willrich (Father Tom), Michael Hardstark (Detective Spina), Alphonso DeNoble (Mr. Alphonso), Gary Allen (Jim DeLorenze), Brooke Shields (Karen Spages)

One of just four directorial efforts from TV production designer Alfred Sole (another being the 1982 horror spoof *Pandemonium*), *Alice*'s legacy has benefited greatly from an early appearance by a cherubic Brooke Shields in her first feature film role, which gave the film renewed marketing cachet after *The Blue Lagoon* was a global hit four years later (her controversial turn in Louis Malle's *Pretty Baby* in 1978 didn't hurt either). The home video boom of the '80s allowed her presence to be exploited on all the box covers despite the fact that she's dead in the first ten minutes.

Attractive single mother Catherine Spages (Linda Miller, Jackie Gleason's daughter, sporting an amazing Mary Tyler Moore hairstyle) visits her local priest Father Tom with her two daughters, Karen (Shields) the younger and clearly favoured one, and Alice (Paula Sheppard, whose only other film role is in cult hit *Liquid Sky*!), her despondent and sociopathic 12-year-old sister. Father Tom also clearly favours Karen, giving her a gold crucifix necklace to wear at her upcoming first communion. Karen doesn't make it though, as she's found burnt to a crisp in a hollow pew during the ceremony. With sister Alice found holding Karen's communion veil, all eyes look to her as the perpetrator – except for her mother, who finally seems to notice and nurture her with the precious Karen now out of the picture.

When Aunt Annie (Jane Lowry) is brutally attacked in the stairwell of their building by a small person wearing a yellow mackintosh and an opaque plastic mask like the one Alice has, Annie is convinced it was Alice, and says as much to the police in hilariously histrionic fashion, despite her sister's threats to never speak to her again. After her Aunt's attack, Alice is found in the basement, cowering; she claims that the dead Karen was the culprit, and a lie detector test shows her to believe this as the truth, but we've seen more of Alice than her parents have, and can easily suspect that she's manipulating them. Her school records indicate disturbed behaviour, and this combined with her intense jealousy of her sister and the hard evidence (such as her possession of her sister's veil and the mask worn by her Aunt's attacker) make her a perfect suspect.

Alice gets dumped in juvie for observation while the parents all speculate on the masked killer's identity, projecting their fears about their own respective children. As the bodies pile up, the real culprit is revealed to be a religious fanatic who lost her own daughter on the day of her first communion, who is trying to protect Father Tom from the corrupting influence of the sinners around him. "Children pay for the sins of their parents", she says, zeroing in on Catherine because she was pregnant with Alice out of wedlock. In the eyes of the killer, Catherine is a whore who doesn't deserve the sympathy or the support of the Church.

While the killer is a stereotypical movie psycho, acting out her own trauma on others and bolstered by religious zeal, Alice is quietly feeding her own neurosis with the images of death enveloping her. When the blame shifts away from Alice, she is again ignored and literally brushed aside by people, leaving us to contemplate whether she wishes she had been the killer after all.

from top: Paula Sheppard; ecclesiastical extra; Alphonso DeNoble being attacked by a masked killer in Alfred Sole's **Alice, Sweet Alice** (1976).

ALL THE COLORS OF THE DARK

1972, Italy/Spain
Original titles: **Tutti i colori del buio**; **Todos los colores de la oscuridad**
Alternative titles: **They're Coming to Get You**; **Day of the Maniac**
D: Sergio Martino. P: Mino Loy, Luciano Martino. W: Ernesto Gastaldi, Sauro Scavolini, Santiago Moncada (story). Ed: Eugenio Alabiso. DoP: Giancarlo Ferrando, Miguel F. Mila. M: Bruno Nicolai. AD: Cubero Galicia [Jaime Pérez Cubero & José Luis Galicia]. Cast: George Hilton (Richard Steel), Edwige Fenech (Jane Harrison), Ivan Rassimov (Mark Cogan), Julian Ugarte (J.P. McBride), Jorge Rigaud (Doctor Burton), Maria Cumani Quasimodo (old woman), Susan Scott [Nieves Navarro] (Barbara Harrison), Marina Malfatti (Celia Morgan, 'Mary Weill'), Dominique Boschero (Jane's mother), Alan Collins [Luciano Pigozzi] (Franciscus Clay)

Taking its cues from *Rosemary's Baby* in the supernatural department, *All the Colors of the Dark* is a unique entry in Martino's oeuvre and easily the most hallucinatory of all his films. This giallo/occult horror hybrid stars Euro-starlet Edwige Fenech as Jane, a woman recovering from the loss of her child in a car accident who lives with her boyfriend Richard (George Hilton) in a posh London high-rise. She is often left to her own devices during Richard's long absences. Plagued by nightmares and convinced that she is being followed by a man (Ivan Rassimov), she is urged by Richard to self-medicate as a means of curbing her 'overactive imagination'. But as terror and loneliness overtake her, she finds herself befriending a new neighbour who introduces her to the world of modern Satanism. Ernesto Gastaldi's script becomes muddled and improbable at times, but the film remains one of the most psychologically interesting of Martino's films.
For more on this film see **Part 3: All Safe and Dead**.

above: Edwige Fenech cowers in Sergio Martino's **All the Colors of the Dark** (1972).

ALUCARDA

1975, Mexico/USA
Original title: **Alucarda, la hija de las tinieblas**
Alternative titles: **Sisters of Satan; Innocents from Hell**
D: Juan López Moctezuma. P: Max Guefen, Eduardo
Moreno. W: Alexis Arroyo, Juan López Moctezuma. Ed:
Maximino Sánchez Molina. DoP: Xavier Cruz.
M: Anthony Guefen. AD: Kleomenes Stamatiades.
Cast: Claudio Brook (Doctor Oszek/the hunchback/old
witch), David Silva (Father Lázaro), Tina Romero (Alucarda/
Alucarda's mother), Susana Kamini (Justine), Lily Garza
(Daniela), Tina French (Sister Angélica), Birgitta Segerskog
(Mother Superior), Adriana Roel (Sister Germana), Antonia
Guerrero, Martín LaSalle (Brother Felipe)

One of the screaming-est of all psychotic women films,
Alucarda is an iconic entry into the genre, thanks in no
small part to a showstopping performance by Tina Romero
as the title character. When the despondent Justine is sent
to live in a rural convent after the accidental death of her
parents, she is immediately set upon by the frizzy-haired,
black-clad Alucarda, a lonely girl who was abandoned
there as a child. Justine is immediately intrigued by the
bizarre girl-in-black, and within minutes they are pledging
an immortal bond to each other, later consummating
their love in a ceremony with Satan. This is a visionary film,
aesthetically and ideologically, based loosely on Sheridan
Le Fanu's *Carmilla*.
For more on this film see **Part 5: Afterschool Special**.

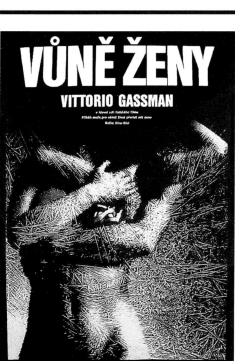

ANIMA PERSA

1977, Italy/France
Alternative title **Ames perdues**
D: Dino Risi. P: Pio Angeletti, Adriano De Micheli. W: Dino Risi,
Bernardino Zapponi, Giovanni Arpino (novel). Ed: Alberto Gallitti.
DoP: Tonino Delli Colli. M: Francis Lai. PD: Luciano Ricceri.
Cast: Catherine Deneuve (Sofia Stolz), Vittorio Gassman (Fabio Stolz),
Anicée Alvina (Lucia), Danilo Mattei (Tino), Ester Carloni (Annetta),
Gino Cavalieri (Versatti), Michele Capnist (Il Duca), Aristide Caporale
(regular at café)

Vittorio Gassman and Catherine Deneuve are stately couple Fabio
and Sofia, who live in Sofia's crumbling ancestral home in Venice.
The arrival of their teenage nephew, who is staying with them while
he attends art school, brings their dysfunctionality to light: Sofia is a
nervous wreck for undisclosed reasons, and her domineering husband
clearly detests her. The revelation that Fabio's insane brother lives shut
in an attic room is unnerving enough – but that's only the beginning of
the horrors that await the young art student. This study of neurosis and
the structures we create around it in order to function is fascinating
and disturbing, and while not focused specifically on female neurosis,
Catherine Deneuve's character is the perfect pallid vision of the 19th
century-style 'Angel of the House'.
For more on this film see **Part 3: All Safe and Dead**.

from top: Tina Romero in Juan López Moctezuma's **Alucarda** (1975); Czech poster for Dino Risi's **Anima persa** (1977).

ANTICHRIST

2009, Denmark
D: Lars von Trier. P: Meta Louise Foldager. W: Lars von Trier. Ed: Åsa Mossberg,
Anders Refn. DoP: Anthony Dod Mantle. M: Kristian Eidnes Andersen.
PD: Karl Júlíusson. AD: Tim Pannen.
Cast: Willem Dafoe (He), Charlotte Gainsbourg (She), Storm Acheche Sahlstrøm (Nic)

A couple (Charlotte Gainsbourg and Willem Dafoe) grieving over the recent loss
of their young son retreat to a cabin in the woods for a psychological showdown
that pits his cold, doctoral inquisitiveness against her passionate belief in her own
evil – an evil that she insists is responsible for the death of their son. A battle of wills
and bodily entanglements that stays the course through some hard questions, von
Trier's magical staging of a relationship in crisis is the most infernal examination since
Zulawski's *Possession*. Played out entirely with its intense cast of two, Gainsbourg's
character in particular is a perfect blend of despondency, anger and sexual greed
that manifests in her mind as a configuration of the all-consuming evil that she sees
as woman's birthright.
For more on this film see **Part 9: Piercing Reality**.

ASYLUM

1972, UK
Alternative title: **House of Crazies**
D: Roy Ward Baker. P: Max J. Rosenberg, Milton Subotsky.
W: Robert Bloch. Ed: Peter Tanner. DoP: Denys Coop.
M: Douglas Gamley. AD: Tony Curtis.
Cast: Barbara Parkins (Bonnie), Richard Todd (Walter), Sylvia
Syms (Ruth), Peter Cushing (Smith), Barry Morse (Bruno), Britt
Ekland (Lucy), Charlotte Rampling (Barbara), James Villiers
(George), Megs Jenkins (Miss Higgins), Herbert Lom (Byron)

In the third segment of Roy Ward Baker's episodic Amicus film
Asylum, Charlotte Rampling stars as Barbara, a recovering
drug addict who, upon her release from rehab, moves back
into the family home with her uptight brother George. She
greatly opposes George's hiring of a live-in nurse to look
after (i.e. spy on) her, and believes that George wants
her committed so that he can have the house and family
inheritance to himself. One day Barbara's friend Lucy (Britt
Ekland) shows up; George has forbidden Barbara from seeing
the free-spirited Lucy, but the latter manages to convince
Barbara to sneak out of the house in defiance of fuddy-
duddy George. Lucy doesn't get Barbara back on drugs;
in fact she expressly forbids Barbara's drug use, threatening
to leave Barbara forever if she continues. But that's not to
say Lucy is on George's side: on the contrary, Lucy has it in
for George. She drugs his tea and eventually murders both
George and the nurse, proclaiming to Barbara; "now you're
free!" When Barbara looks in the mirror, the reflection staring
back at her is Lucy's.

from top: Charlotte Gainsbourg in Lars von Trier's **Antichrist** (2009); Charlotte Rampling and Britt Ekland, and alternate title poster for **Asylum** (1972).

THE ATTIC

1980, USA
D: George Edwards, Gary Graver [uncredited]. P: Ray Dryden, Phillip Randall. W: Tony Crechales, George Edwards. Ed: Derek Parsons. DoP: Gary Graver. M: Hod David Schudson. AD: Tom Rasmussen.
Cast: Carrie Snodgress (Louise Elmore), Ray Milland (Wendell Elmore), Ruth Cox (Emily Perkins), Rosemary Murphy (Mrs. Perkins), Frances Bay (librarian), Fern Barry (Mrs. Mooney), Marjorie Eaton (Mrs. Fowler), Dick Welsbacher (Missing Persons Agent), Joyce Cavarozzi (secretary), Michael Ray Rhodes (sailor)

The only directorial effort of writer/producer George Edwards (regular collaborator of cult director Curtis Harrington), and co-directed/shot by porn director Gary Graver, The Attic stars one-time heavy-hitter Carrie Snodgress as Louise, who is set up as the typical disturbed woman: an alcoholic librarian abandoned at the altar almost 20 years earlier, re-watching old 16mm films of happier days with slit wrists dripping blood all over her stuffed animals.

At only 35 years old, she's already crossed over into spinster territory – she looks remarkably old and skeletal, worn down by years of caring for her emotionally abusive invalid father (Ray Milland). He makes fun of the bandages on her wrists: "Oh, first you want to kill yourself and now you're worried about a little infection? Women. They're all the same: weak, manipulating, vindictive. The only good woman I knew was your poor dead mother. And I'm waiting for some of her to rub off on you." She undergoes this treatment day after day, fuelling her need to drink and fantasize.

But she's aware of all her coping tactics; when she is picked up by a young sailor at a movie theatre, she pretends he is her missing fiancé Robert, and her conversations with Emily – the young girl who is replacing her at the library due to an emotional outburst on duty – allow her to plainly lay out her beliefs and to impart advice that she could do with herself, as though trying to live vicariously through this girl whose whole life is before her. "Have you ever been seized by moods of despondency?" she asks Emily, as she describes being overwhelmed and driven to vandalize the library, causing the fire that resulted in her premature termination of employment. She imagines hurting people, especially her father.

Ray Milland as the curmudgeonly father has many hilarious lines but nothing beats his reaction when Louise brings home a chimpanzee as a pet – "There's an ape in the house! It might try to maul me!" The monkey's appearance marks a shift to a more humorous tone, which will dominate the second act, coinciding with Louise's newfound feelings of fulfilment, both from having a pet to care for, and a new friend in the form of Emily. But her father is irritated by her happiness and will see to it that it is short-lived. A succession of events he orchestrates to rein her in throws her over the edge again just when she is making some constructive progress. She realizes that her father's cruelty over the years exceeds even his overt mistreatment of her; that his every action has been part of a methodical humiliation that will break her completely.

It's worth noting that this is one of Carrie Snodgress's first roles after a near 8-year hiatus from acting in the '70s, after she put aside a promising career to care for a family member – her young son (from musician Neil Young) who was stricken with cerebral palsy. And in the same year The Attic was shot, she was bludgeoned and almost killed by her ex-boyfriend, renowned composer Jack Nitzsche. It's possible that both of these elements play into her intense performance here.

AUDITION

1999, Japan
Original title: **Ôdishon**
D: Takashi Miike. P: Satoshi Fukushima, Akemi Suyama. W: Daisuke Tengan, Ryû Murakami (novel). Ed: Yasushi Shimamura. DoP: Hideo Yamamoto. M: Kôji Endô. PD: Tatsuo Ozeki.
Cast: Ryô Ishibashi (Shigeharu Aoyama), Eihi Shiina (Asami Yamazaki), Tetsu Sawaki (Shigehiko Aoyama), Jun Kunimura (Yasuhisa Yoshikawa), Renji Ishibashi (old man in wheelchair), Miyuki Matsuda (Ryoko Aoyama), Toshie Negishi (Rie), Ren Ohsugi (Shimada), Shigeru Saiki (toastmaster), Ken Mitsuishi (director)

A divorcee gets more than he bargained for when he selects his graceful, shy and obedient new girlfriend through a demeaning cattle-call style open audition process. Although Aoyama, the 'protagonist' of Takashi Miike's breakout film, is posited as a well-meaning dad who has been conditioned to mistreat women through centuries of tradition, this is a revenge story we are only too happy to participate in. When he meets Asami (Eihi Shiina in her first role) he is immediately struck by her demure nature and ethereal beauty. She too, seems taken with him, acting eternally grateful that he would care for her. But Asami is not what she seems. She flits in and out of Aoyama's life like a ghostly apparition, a sensation reinforced by the fact that her given address is a boarded-up dance studio.

This enigmatic woman is revealed in the third act to be fragile and possessive. When they finally consummate their love, Asami lies naked and vulnerable on the bed, pleading with him to "Love only me... only me... only me..." This need to possess comes from a long tradition of Japanese ghost stories where wronged women find a way to keep their beloved with them forever (Kenji Mizoguchi's Ugetsu features a similar exchange: "Now you're mine... from now on you must devote your entire life to me..."), even if it means killing them to keep their love frozen in time. Asami may be acting out within this tradition, and her subsequent violent actions are fuelled in part by past wrongs that have nothing to do with Aoyama, but with its slow-burn approach, Miike's Audition is able to make a commentary on the systematic abuse of women that goes beyond the film's notoriously graphic denouement.

above: Carrie Snodgress in George Edwards's **The Attic** (1980).

AUTOPSY

1975, Italy
Original title: **Macchie solari**
Alternative title: **The Victim**
D: Armando Crispino. P: Leonardo Pescarolo. W: Lucio Battistrada, Armando Crispino. Ed: Daniele Alabiso. DoP: Carlo Carlini. M: Ennio Morricone. AD: Elio Balletti.
Cast: Mimsy Farmer (Simona Sanna), Barry Primus (Father Paul Lennox), Ray Lovelock (Edgar), Angela Goodwin (Daniele), Massimo Serato (Gianni Sanna), Gaby Wagner (Betty Lennox), Carlo Cataneo (Uncle Lello Sanna), Ernesto Colli (Ivo), Leonardo Severini (the caretaker), Eleonora Morana (Eleonora)

Mimsy Farmer plays a forensic pathologist finishing her master's degree. Her thesis: defining the difference between authentic suicides and simulated ones. The subject matter is getting to her – she is experiencing hallucinatory episodes at work, imagining that the dead are popping up from their beds and fornicating with one another. This is the first of many indicators that in poor Mimsy's mind, there is something inseparable about sex and death; some crossed wires in her past have traumatized her. Armando Crispino's film is convoluted at times, full of threads that go nowhere but which make for interesting visual set pieces that bolster Mimsy's debilitating sexual repression.
For more on this film see **Part 4: Secret Ceremonies**.

THE BABY

1973, USA
D: Ted Post. P: Milton Polsky, Abe Polsky. W: Abe Polsky. Ed: Dick Wormell, Bob Crawford Sr. DoP: Michael D. Margulies. M: Gerald Fried. AD: Michael Devine.
Cast: Anjanette Comer (Ann Gentry), Ruth Roman (Mrs. Wadsworth), Marianna Hill (Germaine Wadsworth), Susanne Zenor (Alba Wadsworth), Tod Andrews (Doctor), Michael Pataki (Dennis), Beatrice Manley (Judith), Erin O'Reilly, Don Mallon, David Manzy (Baby)

1973 was a busy year for long-time TV director Ted Post, with three features released in quick succession: *Magnum Force*, the follow-up to Don Siegel's acclaimed *Dirty Harry*; *The Harrad Experiment*, based on Robert Rimmer's bestseller about a free-love experiment in a co-ed dorm, starring a young Don Johnson; and *The Baby* – the runt of the litter. Anjanette Comer (who had the pleasure of starring opposite Hugo Stiglitz in *The Night of a Thousand Cats*) stars as Ann Gentry, a social worker who fights to become the regular caseworker for Baby, a 22-year-old man who has been living in diapers since birth, kept in a crib by his mother Mrs. Wadsworth (the gravely-voiced Ruth Roman) and sisters Germaine (Marianna Hill from *Messiah of Evil*) and Alba (Susanne Zenor). Living with her mother-in-law following the unexplained disappearance of her husband – whose memory she frequently revisits by watching old slideshows depicting their prior bliss – Ann fills the emotional void by pouring all of her affection on Baby, determined to give him the care that she feels he's been deprived of, which she feels is responsible for his stunted development. Convinced that Baby has been forcefully infantilized through negative reinforcement, as punishment transferred onto him through Mrs. Wadsworth's resentment of her own absentee husband, Ann becomes an unwelcome fixture in the Wadsworth home. Her beguilement with Baby transcends her professional capacity, and reflects the conflicting role foisted upon him by his own crooked family: while not always acted upon, it is clear that Baby is sexualized by the women around him. Fearing that Ann is poised to take Baby away from her in one way or another, Mrs. Wadsworth enlists her daughters in a plan to discredit the social worker, prompting a battle of wills in which the two women each fight to make Baby their own.

---

from top: Ray Lovelock and Mimsy Farmer in Armando Crispino's **Autopsy** (1975); poster for Ted Post's **The Baby** (1973).

BAD DREAMS

1988, USA

D: Andrew Fleming. P: Gale Anne Hurd. W: Andrew Fleming, Steven E. de Souza. Ed: Jeff Freeman. DoP: Alexander Gruszynski. M: Jay Ferguson. PD: Ivo Cristante.

Cast: Jennifer Rubin (Cynthia), Bruce Abbott (Dr. Alex Karmen), Richard Lynch (Franklin Harris), Harris Yulin (Dr. Berrisford), Dean Cameron (Ralph), Susan Barnes (Connie), E.G. Daily (Lana), Sy Richardson (Detective Wasserman), Susan Ruttan (Miriam), Charles Fleischer (Ron the pharmacist)

At an isolated farmhouse in the mid-'70s, cult leader Franklin Harris leads a host of his devotees at the 'Unity Fields' commune to self-immolate in a suicide pact. The ensuing explosion kills all but the teenaged Cynthia, who nonetheless falls into a long coma. When she wakes up 13 years later, the psychiatrist assigned to her recommends that she join the resident borderline personality therapy group, along with a dream cast of colourful crazies including Dean Cameron (who played teenage horror fan 'Chainsaw' in *Summer School*), '80s cult staple E.G. Daily, and Susan Ruttan (who is superb in her role as the twitchy, chain-smoking *Weekly World News*-type reporter). While her doctors admit that she doesn't quite fit the personality type to

be in the group, they hope that the sessions may make some headway into restoring her memory, which has a major blank spot in it concerning the events that led up to the explosion.

Jennifer Rubin as Cynthia gives a great, nervous and guarded vocal delivery throughout, her sense of dislocation exacerbated by her fellow inmates' unpredictable mood swings. She suffers from hallucinations of the hideously burnt former cult guru urging her to commit suicide to join her brothers and sisters from Unity Fields, and when others in the psych ward start dropping like flies in alleged suicides, she is convinced that Harris is taking others in her place. While the tale's resolution is improbable and leads away from any reading of Cynthia as mentally ill, there is enough craziness on display here to warrant the film's inclusion. Of course the film's greatest irony that the cult leader is played by character actor Richard Lynch, who himself suffered extensive burns after setting himself on fire in 1967 while on an LSD trip (which he talked about the following year in the educational film *LSD: Trip to Where?*).

BAD GUY

2001, South Korea
Original title: **Nabbeun namja**

D: Kim Ki-duk. P: Lee Seung-jae. W: Kim Ki-duk. Ed: Ham Sung-won. DoP: Hwang Chul-hyun. M: Park Ho-jun. AD: Kim Seon-ju, Salt.

Cast: Cho Jae-hyun (Han-gi), Seo Won (Sun-hwa), Kim Yoon-tae (Yun-tae), Choi Duk-mun (Myeong-su), Kim Jeong-yeong (Eun-hye), Choi Yoon-yeong (Hyun-ja), Sin Yu-jin (Min-jung), Namgung Min (Hyun-su), Rhin Hon-ey, Kwon Hyeok-ho

Kim Ki-duk's controversial follow-up to *The Isle* (2000) is about the Stockholm Syndrome-type relationship that develops between a mute, violent thug and the young student he manipulates into a life of prostitution in Seoul's red light district. College student Sun-hwa is sitting on a sidewalk bench with her boyfriend when the fierce-looking criminal Han-gi suddenly and forcefully kisses her before being beaten away by outraged onlookers. Fixated on this girl who is so out of his league, he orchestrates her debt to vicious loan sharks who will inevitably turn her over to him to work off her debt through prostitution. Set up in a street-side brothel where the women are positioned in windows and doorways to be picked out like merchandise, she goes through various degradations, assaults and humiliations, with Han-gi alternately spying on her through a two-way mirror and offering up revealing moments of tenderness that she, over time, comes to reciprocate. While hardly enthusiastic, Sun-hwa seems to adapt to this new life acceptingly, so much so that most critics castigated the film for nurturing a misogynist stereotype. However, people adapt to abuse easily, every day, in many situations, and Sun-hwa's character brings up many pertinent and complex questions.

For more on this film see **Part 7: You've Always Loved Violence**.

from top: Jennifer Rubin and the house that haunts her in Andrew Fleming's **Bad Dreams** (1988).

BAS-FONDS

2010, France
D: Isild Le Besco. P: Nicolas Hidiroglou. W: Isild Le Besco. Ed: Sylvie Lager.
DoP: Thomas Bataille, Nicolas Hidiroglou, Jowan Le Besco. M: Alain
Chamfort, Léonor Graser, Nils Hiron. PD: Laurence Vendroux.
Cast: Valérie Nataf (Magalie Pichon), Ginger Romàn (Barbara Vidal),
Noémie Le Carrer (Marie-Stéphane Pichon), Gustave de Kervern (lover),
Ingrid Leduc (baker's wife), Benjamin Le Souef (baker), Benjamin Belkhodja
(Barbara's boyfriend), Alain Ollivier (presiding judge), François Toumarkine
(father), Christine Pignet (mother)

French actress/director Isild Le Besco's *Bas-fonds* ('The Dregs') could almost
be seen as a violent, inverse doubling of her debut short feature *Demi-tarif*
– the latter hailed by Chris Marker as the vanguard of a resurgent Nouvelle
Vague[68] – which studies three children left at length in an apartment without
adult supervision, and the self-contained version of a family that they fashion
in isolation. *Bas-fonds* similarly focuses on a tripartite pseudo-family, headed
up by the hulking, explosively-tempered Magalie Pichon (Valérie Nataf) who is
served and sated by the attentions of her petite lover Barbara (Ginger Romàn)
and her borderline-autistic younger sister Marie-Steph (Noémie Le Carrer).

They live together in a squalid apartment – the toilet encrusted with
blood and the wall beside it lined with self-loathing graffiti, the floor littered
with jumbo-sized ravioli cans – and live out their days in a confluence of sexual, vocal and boozy gluttony. Barbara – "the pretty
one" – is seen as the only breadwinner, whose earnings as a janitor allow Mag to lie in bed all day with dirty feet, masturbating to
lesbian porn on TV and yelling viciously at the others from her reposed position in the back bedroom. Occasionally Mag does leave
the bed, if only to stomp to the other room to get beer and to dish out physical and verbal abuse which is so shrill and incessant
that it immediately posits the other two as mentally disturbed just by their ability to tolerate it. But as Le Besco's off-screen narration
of *Psalm 139* suggests (in its reading as a love-letter from a servant to their master), Mag is perceived as some kind of goddess,
despite her monstrosity. Barbara later recounts how she first became drawn to, and fell in love with, this flailing free-spirit, whose
lack of social constraints at one time held a seed of transcendent possibility before it degenerated into hatred and sadism.

When the three girls invade a bakery after hours in a spree of vandalism and thievery, Mag accidentally shoots the baker (a
young good looking man scarcely older than they are) and they escape, but the incident puts further strain on the dynamic in
the apartment. Marie-Steph is seized by nightmares and has to sleep in her sister's bed (with the dog she stole at gunpoint from a
passing pedestrian), displacing Barbara, who is being given the cold shoulder by her sour-faced lover. Barbara and Marie-Steph
begin to aggressively compete for Mag's attention, and when she fails to win back Mag's favour, Barbara takes drastic action that
will spark the irreversible infiltration of the outside world.

from top: French poster and actresses Noémie Le Carrer, Valérie Nataf and Ginger Romàn of Isild Le Besco's **Bas-fonds** (2010).

BEDEVILLED

2010, South Korea
Original title: **Kim Bok-nam salinsageonui jeonmal**
D: Jang Cheol-soo. P: Park Kuy-young. W: Choi Kwang-young.
Ed: Kim Mi-Joo. DoP: Kim Gi-tae. M: Kim Tae-seong. PD: Shim
Jeog-hui.
Cast: Seo Yeong-hee (Kim Bok-nam), Ji Seong-won (Hae-won), Park Jeong-hak (Man-jong), Lee Ji-eun (Yun-hui), Je-Min
(prostitute), Bae Sung-woo (Chul-jong), Jo Duk-je (inspector),
Chae Si-hyun (Mi-ran), Jeong Gi-seop (Choi), Tak Sung-eun
(Ji-soo)

When aggressive overachiever Hae-won (Ji Seong-won) is
reluctantly sent on vacation after an outburst at work, she
goes to visit childhood friend Bok-nam (Seo Yeong-hee) on a
remote, barely populated island outside of Soeul.

Once on the island, we realize that Hae-won is only
present as a witness; this will not be her story. The narrative
shifts from Hae-won to Bok-nam, a desperate, needy woman
who lives like a slave, being beaten and sodomized daily by
her husband. Her one-sided friendship with the emotionally
distant Hae-won is a source of hope at first, but like the other
women on the island, Hae-won becomes yet another who
sees everything and does nothing. The complicity of the
women in their own abuse is infuriating, a complicity that
the audience is asked to share in, since we too are led to
the island as witnesses; interestingly, the establishment of
Hae-won as a false protagonist ensures that we are aligned
with the witness to Bok-nam's
story. The silent witness is a
recurring theme in the film,
even before we get to
the island: back in Seoul,
Hae-won witnesses a
prostitute being beaten
to death by thugs, and
when the police call
her in, she refuses
to cooperate, not
out of fear, but
because she
doesn't see it as
her concern. The
film takes a while
to get where
it's going, and
as such there is
much seemingly-
s u p e r f l u o u s
degradation for
the audience to
behold in the first hour.
However, there is one
transgression Bok-nam
won't tolerate, and
its violation leads to a
bloody and histrionic
third act that is well
worth the wait.

THE BEGUILED

1971, USA

D: Don Siegel. P: Don Siegel. W: Irene Kamp, John B. Sherry,
Thomas Cullinan (novel). Ed: Carl Pingitore. DoP: Bruce
Surtees. M: Lalo Schifrin. AD: Alexander Golitzen.
Cast: Clint Eastwood (John McBurney), Geraldine Page (Martha
Farnsworth), Elizabeth Hartman (Edwina Dabney), Jo Ann Harris
(Carol), Darleen Carr (Doris), Mae Mercer (Hallie), Pamelyn
Ferdin (Amy), Melody Thomas (Abigail), Peggy Drier (Lizzie)

Clint Eastwood plays Union
soldier John McBurney, who
is found injured by the pre-
teen Amy (Pamelyn Ferdin,
later of Dennis Donnelly's
The Toolbox Murders) from
a nearby Confederate
boarding school during
the Civil War. Escorting him
back to the school for aid,
the all-female crew is both
entranced by the interloper
and simultaneously afraid
of him, having heard stories
of Union soldiers pillaging
the area and raping any
woman left vulnerable.
Adding to this trepidation is
their fear of the authorities
finding out that they're
harbouring the enemy, but
his attractiveness to this
household of lonely women
– including capable head-
mistress Martha (screen vet Geraldine Page), nervous prissy
teacher Edwina (Elizabeth Hartman) and seductive student
Carol (Jo Ann Harris of *Rape Squad* aka *Act of Vengeance*),
all of whom vie for his affection – overrides their sense of
patriotic duty.

As John thoughtlessly shares romantic moments with each
of them, taking advantage of their emotional and physical
hunger, he underestimates their retributive potential, especially
in a wartime scenario where few are held accountable for
their actions. When Edwina discovers him in bed with Carol, she
pushes him down the stairs, breaking his leg in three places so
that it (in the opinion of Martha) has to be amputated. His anger
riled by having his leg surreptitiously removed – tantamount,
in his mind, to castration – he besets upon all of them with
verbal abuse, laying bare their secrets and insecurities before
their peers, which includes Martha's past incestuous love affair
with her now-dead brother. With their respectable household
reduced to a conflagration of corrupt thought-crimes and
unspeakable indiscretions, they are forced to take harsh steps
to restore order. An added sense of melancholy comes from
the fact that we know something they don't – that the South
will lose the war, making their systematic efforts rather futile
considering the fate that awaits them.

Actress Elizabeth Hartman, who first made a name for
herself playing the blind girl Selina opposite Sidney Poitier in *A
Patch of Blue*, would later throw herself from a fifth floor window
after many years of depression.

from left: Seo Yeong-hee and Ji Seong-won in Jang Cheol-soo's **Bedevilled** (2010); lobby cards for Don Siegel's **The Beguiled** (1971).

LA BELLE BÊTE

2006, Canada
Alternative title: **The Beautiful Beast**
D: Karim Hussain. P: Anne Cusson, Julien
Fonfrede, Karim Hussain. W: Marie-Claire Blais,
Karim Hussain. Ed: Eric Lavoie. DoP: Karim
Hussain. M: David Kristian. AD: Richard Tassé.
Cast: Carole Laure (Louise), Caroline
Dhavernas (Isabelle-Marie), Marc-André
Grondin (Patrice), David La Haye (Lanz),
Sébastien Huberdeau (Michael), Ludivine
Dubé-Reding [Vénutia-Ludivine Reding]
(Anne), Normand Lévesque (Professor),
Nicolas Girard Deltruc (news-vendor),
Richard Tassé (Hunter)

Adapted by Marie-Claire Blais from her own
scorching 1959 debut novel, Karim Hussain's
La Belle Bête shows remarkable restraint
following on from the visceral excesses of his
earlier *Subconscious Cruelty*, and manages
to explore the dense layers of emotional
decrepitude all the better for it.

Carole Laure stars in the role of Louise,
the widowed matriarch of an incestuously-
charged dysfunctional family consisting of
her two teenage children – Patrice (ubiquitous
Quebecois actor Marc-André Grondin), the
classically beautiful but idiot son, and Isabelle-
Marie, his rebellious, 'ugly' older sister, who live
together in an isolated farmhouse. Louise, an
ageing beauty, lives vicariously through her
son's youthful attractiveness, and dotes on him
to the absurd extent that he is unable to do
anything by himself, while alternately neglecting
and dishing out verbal abuse to his sister.

While best known to exploitation fans from
her role as Miss World in Dusan Makavejev's
Sweet Movie, Carole Laure is a queen in
the world of Franco-Canadian cinema, and
perfectly cast here as the vain mother who
infects her whole family with the decaying force
of her own shallowness. But another interesting
casting choice is Caroline Dhavernas as
Isabelle-Marie. Her character is described in
the book as 'ugly', and her ugliness is a defining
component of her relationship to the other
characters. But Caroline Dhavernas is a well-
known Canadian leading actress and far from
ugly, which only emphasizes the insidious nature
of parental cruelty; Isabelle-Marie believes she
is ugly because she is constantly told so ("Your
ugliness is driving me insane!"). As a testament
to Dhavernas's acting acumen, her jealousy
and resentment actually do make her appear
ugly at times. She fantasizes about murdering
them, determined to bring them down to her
level, to expose their ugliness – but Louise's
despicable behaviour yields its own fruit in the
form of a cancerous blemish that will signal an
apocalyptic end to things as they know it.

above, both images: Caroline Dhavernas in Karim Hussain's **La Belle Bête** (2006).

THE BIRD WITH THE CRYSTAL PLUMAGE

1970, Italy/West Germany
Original titles: **L'uccello dalle piume di cristallo**; **Das Geheimnis der schwarzen Handschuhe**
Alternative title: **The Gallery Murders**
D: Dario Argento. P: Salvatore Argento. W: Dario Argento. Ed: Franco Fraticelli. DoP: Vittorio Storaro. M: Ennio Morricone. AD: Dario Micheli.
Cast: Tony Musante (Sam Dalmas), Suzy Kendall (Julia), Enrico Maria Salerno (Inspector Morosini), Eva Renzi (Monica Ranieri), Umberto Raho (Alberto Ranieri), Raf Valenti (Professor Carlo Dover), Giuseppe Castellano (Monti), Mario Adorf (Berto Consalvi), Pino Patti (Faiena), Rosa Toros (fourth victim)

Dario Argento's debut feature and the film that really kicked off the giallo craze (despite Mario Bava's earlier genre entries), *The Bird with the Crystal Plumage* stars Tony Musante as Sam Dalmas, an American writer staying in Rome who witnesses the attempted murder of Monica Ranieri, the wife of a well-to-do gallery owner. In the film's most memorable set piece, Sam is trapped between two giant glass doors unable to escape the horror or do anything to stop it. Discovering that this attack is the latest in a slew of serial killings targeting young female victims and convinced that he is misremembering the events, he takes on the role of amateur sleuth, which leads him through an unfriendly landscape consisting of art galleries, antique shops, suspicious cops and a cat-eating painter who answers the 'why' to the mystery, if not exactly the 'who'.

The killer's first victim worked in an antique shop, where she sold the murderer an old painting depicting a violent attack on young girl in a park. Sam tracks down the artist, who says that the work was inspired by a true story from years earlier. All roads eventually lead to Monica Ranieri, the supposed gallery victim; the key element confused in Sam's memory was her role in the attack. Assaulted by a madman as a young child, she repressed the horrible memory until seeing the painting in the antique shop brought it all back. Following an immediate mental snap, she took on the persona of her attacker rather than face up to her own victimization. Borrowing the garb from Mario Bava's *Blood and Black Lace* that has since become synonymous with the giallo killer (trench coat, fedora, black gloves), Monica Ranieri in her transformed state is a snarling, spitting, cackling killer, who plays with Musante the way a cat plays with its food. When she is conveniently captured right before meting out Musante's fate, a television talk-show host give us the wrap-up: "Monica Ranieri, hopelessly insane, is in custody at the psychiatric hospital. Her husband who loved her, not wisely, but too well, lost his life in a last attempt to turn suspicion away from his wife." Although a psychiatrist goes onto explain that Monica had suffered severe trauma as the result of a violent attack ten years earlier, the rapidity of the exposition combined with the dismissive term "hopelessly insane" illustrates how attempts to explain bad behaviour usually cease with the word "crazy".

from top: Eva Renzi as Monica Ranieri; Spanish poster for Dario Argento's **The Bird with the Crystal Plumage** (1970).

BLACK NARCISSUS

1947, UK
D: Michael Powell, Emeric Pressburger. P: Michael Powell,
Emeric Pressburger. W: Michael Powell, Emeric Pressburger,
Rumer Godden (novel). Ed: Reginald Mills. DoP: Jack Cardiff.
M: Brian Easdale. PD: Alfred Junge.
Cast: Deborah Kerr (Sister Clodagh), Sabu (Dilip Rai, the
young general), David Farrar (Mr. Dean), Flora Robson (Sister
Philippa), Esmond Knight (the old general), Jean Simmons
(Kanchi), Kathleen Byron (Sister Ruth), Jenny Laird (Sister
'Honey' Blanche), Judith Furse (Sister Briony), May Hallatt
(Angu Ayah)

Powell-Pressburger's *Black Narcissus* isn't an obvious inclusion
in this book from a genre perspective, but it does feature
one of the screen's most notorious and influential mental
unravellings.

Deborah Kerr heads up the cast as Sister Clodagh, the
young Sister Superior for a group of nuns who've relocated to
a previously-abandoned mountaintop palace in the Himalayas
where they plan to open a mission for the local peasants.
Among the handful of nuns selected to service this frontier
– each of whom has been chosen for individual skills that will
be necessary for survival in such a remote place – is Sister Ruth
(Kathleen Byron), an insolent, sickly nun that the Mother of the
Order hopes will be rejuvenated, physically and spiritually, by her
new post. But this is not to be: all the nuns soon find
themselves disturbed and desperate
– "something in the atmosphere"
says one character. Instead of
the promised tranquillity, the wind
and the mountains and valleys
instead have an oppressive
quality, and "the view too
far" enables too much of the
wrong kind of contemplation.
Sister Clodagh herself is
affected, drawn to sudden
reminiscences of her youthful
love for a young man prior to
joining the Order, and Sister
Ruth is worst of all, her former
insolence becoming a
dangerous psychosis
that is all the more
p r o n o u n c e d
through her lust
for the local
h a n d y m a n ,
Mr. Dean.

Jealous of the developing friendship between Mr. Dean and
Sister Clodagh, Ruth soon fixates on Clodagh as a problem that
needs to be gotten rid of.

Black Narcissus is a flurry of shrill voices and clashing wills,
but never does the music swell in exaggerated terror more
than in that pivotal moment where Ruth… puts on a dress and
make-up! Horror of Horrors! "Sister Ruth has gone mad!" the
nuns exclaim, and certainly she has, but that this rebellious act
is treated as proof of her utter hysteria just shows how much
the sisters do their best to live in ignorance. After all, Ruth is
nuts whether or not she's wearing the dress, and that much
has been obvious to the audience ever
since her first moment onscreen.
The film is much darker than
one might expect, and
Byron is outstandingly
creepy as Sister Ruth, who
is likely the inspiration for
countless crazy nuns in
subsequent movies.

top right: Kathleen Byron
as Sister Ruth.

BLACK SWAN

2010, USA

D: Darren Aronofsky. P: Scott Franklin, Mike Medavoy, Arnold Messer, Brian Oliver. W: Mark Heyman, Andres Heinz, John J. McLaughlin. Ed: Andrew Weisblum. DoP: Matthew Libatique. M: Clint Mansell. PD: Thérèse DePrez. AD: David Stein. Cast: Natalie Portman (Nina Sayers), Mila Kunis (Lily), Vincent Cassel (Thomas Leroy), Barbara Hershey (Erica Sayers), Winona Ryder (Beth Macintyre), Benjamin Millepied (David), Ksenia Solo (Veronica), Kristina Anapau (Galina), Janet Montgomery (Madeline), Sebastian Stan (Andrew)

Natalie Portman gives a incredibly overwrought performance as Nina, a young ballet dancer who gets her first shot at a major part when her lecherous ballet instructor Thomas (Vincent Cassel) appoints her the role of The Swan Queen in Tchaikovsky's suicidal tragedy Swan Lake. With the support of her mother (Barbara Hershey), herself a retired dancer with mixed feelings about the profession, Nina has been working toward this all her life – and her mind and body alike are already starting to show the wear and tear of her strict daily regimen before the show even begins. Now Nina's real test is upon her: the Swan Queen is a dual role – she must play both the virginal White Swan, and her evil, lustful twin, the Black Swan, and the latter is where Thomas feels she may not have it in her to perform. But, as her instructor points out, her only obstacle is herself. Constantly pushing her to free herself from

what he adamantly claims is pent up sexual frustration, Thomas plays on her fears, reinforcing her dread of being replaced by suddenly turning his flirtatious eye toward the uncouth, but undeniably talented new student Lily (Mila Kunis).

What begins as a small rash on her back turns into repeated delusions of bodily decay as the pressure on Nina increases. She pulls at her skin, picks at sores, and creates wounds that may or may not be imaginary. She sees doppelgangers everywhere – when she first sees her rival Lily, she is taken aback, thinking that she is looking at herself. Mirror images rebel and transmute. Paintings move and talk (her mother's paintings are, incidentally, all self-portraits or pictures of Nina, further reinforcing the mirror motif). But to see yourself in everything is itself a sign of a deep neurosis, and is indicative of Nina's self-absorption and tragic narcissism.

Nina herself was the reason for the forced early retirement of the former diva Beth Macintyre (an almost unrecognizable Winona Ryder), whom she both idolized and coveted – to the point of stealing small trinkets from Beth's dressing room – earrings, a nail file, a tube of lipstick (ironic, considering Ryder's own tabloid-fuelled psychological history). She was also the reason for her own mother's retirement – her mother gave up a budding career when she became pregnant. So Nina's fears of being replaced are well-founded – after all, she has already replaced two others herself – but the mother is hard to read; at times a fanatical disciplinarian, she's no Margaret White, nor a stereotypical sports mom. She does seem genuinely concerned about her daughter's well-being and doesn't necessarily push her to follow through on obligations that threaten her mental or physical health, but she is also clearly neurotic and conflicted, and sometimes seems like she is setting Nina up for a fall.

Desperate and determined, Nina's neurosis blossoms into madness, and – while the film's rich metaphors have been explored countless times in previous films – how Aronofsky's film views this change in its protagonist is where it provides the most to chew on. Self-destruction is here both a thing of horror and revelry. The film is quick to point out improprieties as a 'cheap' or 'easy' way of being bad, but it equates Nina's true self-destructive darkness with martyrdom, making the film as a whole rather morally ambiguous.

above: Natalie Portman and the mirror's frightening revelations in Darren Aronofsky's **Black Swan** (2010).

THE BLOOD SPATTERED BRIDE

1972, Spain
Original title: **La novia ensangrentada**
D: Vicente Aranda. W: Vicente Aranda, Sheridan Le Fanu (novella). Ed: Pablo González del Amo. DoP: Fernando Arribas. M: Antonio Pérez Olea. PD: Juan Alberto Soler.
Cast: Simón Andreu (Husband), Maribel Martín (Susan), Alexandra Bastedo (Carmila/Mircala Karstein), Dean Selmier (Doctor), Maria-Rosa Rodrigues (Carol), Montserrat Julió (Carol's mother), Angel Lombarte (Carol's father)

A just-married couple (Maribel Martín and Simón Andreu, 'Susan' and 'Husband', respectively) drive out to a large country estate for their honeymoon. Far from eager to consummate the marriage, the young bride imagines being raped on her wedding night, followed by an increasing delusion that her husband wants to imprison and humiliate her. When Susan meets and comes under the spell of the enigmatic Carmila (a variation on Sheridan Le Fanu's vampiress Carmilla Karnstein), she slowly comes to realize she is a lesbian, and since there is no place in her world for lesbianism, she is understandably anxious, filled with conflicting emotions – from fear of her husband to homicidal anger at being forced by society to marry against her will.
For more on this film see **Part 7: You've Always Loved Violence.**

THE BLUE EYES OF THE BROKEN DOLL

1973, Spain
Original title: **Los ojos azules de la muñeca rota**
Alternative title: **House of Psychotic Women**
D: Carlos Aured. P: José Antonio Pérez Giner. W: Jacinto Molina [Paul Naschy], Carlos Aured. Ed: Javier Morán. DoP: Francisco Sánchez. M: Juan Carlos Calderón. AD: Gumersindo Andrés.
Cast: Paul Naschy (Gilles), Diana Lorys (Claude), Eduardo Calvo (Doctor Phillipe), Eva León (Nicole), Inés Morales (Michelle), Antonio Pica (Inspector Pierre), Luis Ciges (René), Pilar Bardem (Caroline), Maria Perschy (Ivette)

This film was marketed in the U.S. as *House of Psychotic Women* and is thus the namesake of this book. Genre icon Paul Naschy stars as Gilles, a drifter who ends up getting handyman work – and so much more – at the rustic home of three strange sisters: Claude, the stern redhead with prosthetic hand; the nymphomaniacal Nicole; and Ivette, who is wheelchair-bound after a mysterious accident. Their mother died insane and their father committed suicide, and the three have shut themselves up in the isolated house, bound to each other through self-loathing and a fear of abandonment but full of resentment toward one another all the same. Naschy has his hands full with these three, but things get worse when a series of murders in the area seem to point to him as the killer.
For more on this film see **Part 2: Broken Dolls.**

BORN INNOCENT

1974, USA
D: Donald Wrye. P: Bruce Cohn Curtis. W: Gerald Di Pego, Creighton Brown Burnham (book). Ed: Maury Winetrobe. DoP: David M. Walsh. M: Fred Karlin.
Cast: Linda Blair (Chris Parker), Joanna Miles (Barbara Clark), Kim Hunter (Mrs. Parker), Richard Jaeckel (Mr. Parker), Allyn Ann McLerie (Emma Lasko), Mary Murphy (Miss Murphy), Janit Baldwin (Denny), Nora Heflin (Moco), Tina Andrews (Josie), Mitch Vogel (Tom Parker)

Linda Blair plays Christine Parker, a 14-year-old soft-spoken runaway who is deposited in a state school for juvenile delinquents when her parents sign her over as a ward of the court. A good girl in a bad situation, Chris undergoes a series of humiliations including aggressive body-searches and de-lousing, but when one of the staff exhibits signs of favouritism toward her, she is punished by the other girls, who rape her in the showers with a toilet plunger. There are many women-in-prison films that depict the transformation of a good girl into a hardened criminal (one of the earliest being the great Academy Award nominee *Caged*, 1950) but for the most part they fall outside the scope of this book. *Born Innocent* is included here for its relevance to my personal trajectory.
For more on this film see **Part 6: The Strange Passenger.**

from top: Alexandra Bastedo in Vicente Aranda's **The Blood Spattered Bride** (1972); Inés Morales in Carlos Aured's **The Blue Eyes of the Broken Doll.**

BOY MEETS GIRL

1994, UK
D: Ray Brady. P: Ray Brady, Chris Read. W: Ray Brady, Jim Crosbie. Ed: Ray Brady, Russell Fenton. DoP: Kevin McMorrow. M: Jim Crosbie, Geoff Southall. PD: Ray Brady.
Cast: Tim Poole (Tevin), Danielle Sanderson (Julia), Margot Steinberg (Anne Marie), Susan Warren (woman in chair), Nathalie Khanna (Tevin's wife), Myuki Smith Khanna (Tevin's child), Pierre Smith Khanna (Tevin's child), Georgina Whitbourne (female victim on monitor), Robert Haynes (branded man), John Reid (hanging man).

In *Boy Meets Girl* the female antagonist suffers from one-dimensional characterization and a lack of any clear motivation; "I'm not a vigilante", she claims, "I am just a casual observer." Her high moral ground would, however, seem to indicate otherwise.

After taking a man home for a supposed one-night stand, she drugs him, and he wakes up naked and tied to a chair in a black room of indeterminate size. While filming him as part of her "ongoing research", she cruelly interrogates and chastises him for everything from smoking cigarettes to not reading enough books. She deflowers his "sacred hole" with a dildo, while making a heavy-handed statement about how "men don't own violence".

This is clearly a man's idea of what a woman's revenge would look like, and although that's the case with many of the films discussed here, the feminist rhetoric being aggressively employed throughout *Boy Meets Girl* in conjunction with nonsensical violence is a means of demonizing the cause rather than exploring its faults, as Auli Mantila's *The Geography of Fear*, Abel Ferrara's *Ms.45* or Todd Morris's *A Gun for Jennifer* do more thoughtfully.

THE BRAVE ONE

2007, USA
D: Neil Jordan. P: Susan Downey, Joel Silver. W: Roderick Taylor, Bruce A. Taylor, Cynthia Mort. Ed: Tony Lawson. DoP: Philippe Rousselot. M: Dario Marianelli. PD: Kristi Zea. AD: Robert Guerra.
Cast: Jodie Foster (Erica Bain), Terrence Howard (Detective Mercer), Nicky Katt (Detective Vitale), Naveen Andrews (David Kirmani), Mary Steenburgen (Carol), Ene Oloja (Josai), Luis Da Silva Jr. (Lee), Blaze Foster (Cash), Rafael Sardina (Reed), Larry Fessenden (Sandy Combs).

Ambiguous cult star Jodie Foster turns in another stellar performance heading up this revenge picture from director Neil Jordan (*The Company of Wolves*). Foster stars as Erica Bain, a middle-aged radio host in love with New York City until she and her fiancé are brutally attacked in Central Park by a gang of hoodlums. The altercation leaves her fiancé dead, and Foster with a burning need for revenge, especially when the police prove incapable of handling her case with either any sympathy or efficiency.

Initially Foster is gripped by fear of her surroundings, and finds it hard to venture outside of her apartment without being enveloped by crippling paranoia. She buys an illegal gun for protection, and finds herself having to use it before long, but with that first taste of inadvertent vigilantism comes a major character transition, as she becomes the voice for all the people who've been affected by violent crime without any closure or justice.

While billed as 'a female *Death Wish*', the film goes deeper into post-trauma psychology than Michael Winner's earlier film dares (or cares) to, and somehow Foster pulls off a series of monologues about fear and dissociation that would have been pure cheese coming from anyone else. Instead she maintains an almost frightening intensity, like a lost, suicidal soul.

Keep your eyes peeled for indie horror hero Larry Fessenden in a small role as a psychopath.

left from top: Danielle Sanderson and Tim Poole in Ray Brady's **Boy Meets Girl** (1994); *right:* Jodie Foster in Neil Jordan's **The Brave One** (2007).

THE BRIDE

1973, Canada/USA
Alternative titles: **The House That Cried Murder; No Way Out**
D: Jean-Marie Pélissié. P: John Grissmer. W: John Grissmer, Jean-Marie Pélissié. Ed: Sam Moore. DoP: Stephen H. Burum, Geoffrey Stephenson. M: Peter Bernstein.
Cast: Robin Strasser (Barbara), John Beal (father), Arthur Roberts (David), Iva Jean Saraceni (Ellen)

This low-budget Canuxploitation oddity, released under a number of titles from *No Way Out* to *The House That Cried Murder*, exhibits its self-awareness right off the bat when Barbara (Robin Strasser) leads her beau David (Arthur Roberts) through a field to her large, isolated modern house, which she has designed using her father's money (who she practically seduces in the process of pitching the project). "They say a house is always the reflection of its builder. This house is me", says Barbara, admiring its skewed angles and jutting terraces. "I could live in it forever." Nearly completed, the house needs only the installation of surface accoutrements to be liveable – paint, fixtures, appliances – and Barbara can't wait for her and David to move in. Clearly humouring her, David says he loves the house, but is obviously intimidated by the level of obsessiveness its construction has required – an obsessiveness that is not limited to the house; we get the sense that when Barbara wants something, she'll stop at nothing to get it. "You know you're the first girl I've known who built a house?" David says. Not missing a beat, she replies: "I'm the last girl you're going to know."

Barbara has plans to marry David, but her father (John Beal, fresh off a stint on *Dark Shadows*), who is also his employer, senses that David is after her family's wealth. He insists that there's something "negative" about David, something he can't put his finger on – "like a bad odour". But like a petulant child she insists that not only is she going to marry him, but daddy's going to pay for the wedding too! Which he does. And of course, daddy's premonitions were spot-on: right in the middle of the wedding David is upstairs in a bedroom making out with his ex-girlfriend Ellen (Iva Jean Saraceni of Romero's *Knightriders* and *Creepshow*), prompting Barbara to stab him with a pair of scissors before peeling out of the driveway in her bloody wedding dress.

From this point on, Barbara will be absent for most of the film, but she makes her presence known through threatening phone calls, skeletons and decapitated chicken heads left at David's house (which he is now sharing with Ellen). "This is a familiar pattern with Barbara", her father explains to David passive-aggressively in a lunch meeting two weeks after the wedding. "But I feel a moral obligation towards you David – you have to be warned… I've had a little more experience with what might be called the 'dark side' of her character."

The notion of an absent protagonist (not that this film necessarily has a protagonist, but if it does, it's the duped bride) lends the film a convincing sense of dread that it might not have if it had played out like a conventional scorned-woman picture. That she remains invisible makes it impossible for her adulterous victims to share their anxiety with anyone but themselves, which proves corrosive to their relationship. We also don't get to spend much time in the titular house (leading us to believe the filmmakers only had access to the house for a very limited time), but as her father says, the house really is a monument to Barbara: it's the constructive flip side to her madness. "Bright windows to let in the light, corners to trap the darkness. And all unfinished… wasted. This is a house of great sorrow, David, don't you feel it?" We feel it, and we empathize, but this is largely due to the great performance by John Beal, who has to carry the film in his movie-daughter's absence, and usher us through the mystery of her disturbed mind.

THE BROOD

1979, Canada
D: David Cronenberg. P: Claude Héroux. W: David Cronenberg. Ed: Alan Collins. DoP: Mark Irwin. M: Howard Shore. AD: Carol Spier.
Cast: Oliver Reed (Dr. Hal Raglan), Samantha Eggar (Nola Carveth), Art Hindle (Frank Carveth), Cindy Hinds (Candice Carveth), Nuala Fitzgerald (Juliana Kelly), Henry Beckman (Barton Kelly), Susan Hogan (Ruth Mayer), Michael McGhee (Inspector Mrazek), Gary McKeehan (Mike Trellan), Robert Silverman (Jan Hartog)

Art Hindle stars as Frank Carveth, the exasperated husband of Nola (Samantha Eggar), a neurotic woman who's checked herself into the Somafree Institute for experimental therapy with Dr. Hal Raglan (screen titan Oliver Reed, also of *The Devils*). Raglan, the author of a popular self-help book called 'The Shape of Rage' is the proponent of an unconventional psychotherapeutic method called 'psychoplasmics', in which past traumas, when discussed openly, manifest themselves in sores and abrasions on the patient's body as the trauma is being 'expelled'. But what Nola is expelling from her body aren't just toxins – they're repository rage monsters: faceless children who kill all those who have ever hurt her.
For more on this film see **Part 9: Piercing Reality**.

above: U.S. poster for Jean-Marie Pélissié's **The Bride** (1973); *opposite:* Karen Black and Bette Davis in Dan Curtis's **Burnt Offerings** (1976).

BURNT OFFERINGS

1976, USA

D: Dan Curtis. P: Dan Curtis. W: William F. Nolan, Dan Curtis, Robert Marasco (novel).
Ed: Dennis Virkler. DoP: Jacques R. Marquette. M: Bob Cobert. PD: Eugène Lourié.
Cast: Karen Black (Marian Rolf), Oliver Reed (Ben Rolf), Burgess Meredith (Arnold
Allardyce), Eileen Heckart (Roz Allardyce), Lee Montgomery (David Rolf), Dub Taylor
(Walker), Bette Davis (Aunt Elizabeth), Anthony James (chauffeur), Orin Cannon
(minister), James T. Myers (Dr. Ross)

Dan Curtis – probably America's most prolific producer/director of made-for-
television horror – turns in one of his few theatrical offerings with this seminal '70s possessed house chiller.

Karen Black and Oliver Reed star as financially-strapped couple Marian and Ben Rolf, who happen upon the deal of a
lifetime when they discover a rambling summer rental house, which its owners, ageing siblings Arnold and Roz Allardyce (Burgess
Meredith and Eileen Heckart) offer to them for a mere $900 for the whole summer. The only catch: their mother Mrs. Allardyce
is extremely old and cannot be moved from her room in the attic, meaning that the Rolfs will need to bring her food and be
available to her in case of an emergency.

Ben finds this condition appropriately strange, and the 37-room house and its sprawling estate is in need of some TLC,
but Marian is in love with the house instantly and is enthusiastic about instilling some life into its crumbling walls. And of course,
this is exactly what she does, since the house is a living, breathing entity that maintains its immortality by draining the life-
force of its enthusiastic inhabitants. Both Ben and Marian are
affected by the house's strange power, but Ben fights
it, whereas Marian embraces it, feeling for the first
time a sense of 'home'.

Like Julie Harris's character in The Haunting,
the house gives Marian a sense of identity, a
purpose that is invigorating – even though the
only real identity here is that of the house; she's
just a vessel. But Marian has a deep need to
be needed, and she caters to the house and its
unseen matriarch in the attic more than she pays
attention to her own son David (Lee Montgomery
of Curtis's Dead of Night), who – while not affected
by the house other than as a victim to his
parents' unpredictable behaviour – just
wants to go back home to their crummy
apartment. As Marian takes on the
persona of the house – obsessed
with cleaning, sitting for
hours looking at the
old photographs that
line the tabletops
of Mrs. Allardyce's
antechamber,
adopting theatrical
vocal mannerisms and
donning the Victorian
wardrobe presumably left behind
by a previous resident – she
concedes to the ruination of her
family, which includes being a
party to their deaths in the service
of the house's rejuvenation.

As an aside for horror fans,
the creepy hearse chauffeur who
figures greatly in Ben's childhood
flashbacks is a progenitor of
the 'Tall Man' character from
Phantasm, which is especially
fitting since Burnt Offerings was
filmed entirely on location at
the historic Dunsmuir House in
Oakland California, which also
served as the funeral home in
Phantasm.

BUTCHER, BAKER, NIGHTMARE MAKER

1981, USA
Alternative titles: **Night Warning**; **Nightmare Maker**;
The Evil Protégé
D: William Asher. P: Stephen F. Breimer. W: Stephen F.
Breimer, Alan Jay Glueckman, Boon Collins. Ed: Ted
Nicolaou. DoP: Robbie Greenberg. M: Bruce Langhorne.
Cast: Jimmy McNichol (Billy Lynch), Susan Tyrrell (Cheryl
Roberts), Bo Svenson (Detective Joe Carlson), Marcia Lewis
(Margie), Julia Duffy (Julia), Britt Leach (Sgt. Cook), Steve
Eastin (Coach Tom Landers), Cooper Neal (Frank), Caskey
Swainz (Phil Brody), Bill Paxton (Eddie)

After a spectacular highway accident (filmed by Jan de
Bont) kills both of his parents, Billy (Jimmy McNichol, brother
of Kristy) is raised by his neurotic, overly-affectionate aunt
Cheryl (Susan Tyrrell). Years later, Billy is a strapping young
basketball star at his high school with a peppy blonde
girlfriend (Julia Duffy of Newhart, in an only slightly less
annoying role). Billy is thinking about going away to college,
and not only does Aunt Cheryl strongly discourage him
from going, but she is certain that the interloping blonde
is to blame for Billy's sudden travel bug. As Aunt Cheryl's
paranoia over losing him intensifies and her behaviour
becomes more erratic, she riles herself into a sexual frenzy
and attempts awkwardly to seduce a chubby repairman,
who she ends up murdering when he rejects her.

Claiming it to be an attempted rape, she leaves Billy
(literally) holding the murder weapon when the cops show
up (led by a jaw-droppingly homophobic Detective Carlson,
played by Bo Svenson, who says the word 'fag' so many
times you could make a drinking game out of it). Carlson's
homophobic vernacular is not happenstance – it turns out
that the murder victim was one half of a gay couple, the
other half being Billy's basketball coach. In Carlson's mind,
this puts Billy in the middle of a homicidal gay love triangle,
and succeeds in diverting police attention away from the
real psychopath here – Aunt Cheryl – who is dangerously
projecting her past abandonment issues onto Billy.

Movies abound with jealous older women whose
homicidal mania is easily triggered, but few have the
panache of Susan Tyrrell, truly one of the greatest character
actors of the last half-century. As Aunt Cheryl, she joins the
ranks of the screen's most iconic cougars (Gloria Swanson in
Sunset Boulevard) and decrepit villains (Bette Davis in What
Ever Happened to Baby Jane?). The film benefits not only
from her insane performance, but also from her libidinous,
larger-than-life personality off-screen, which bleeds over
into her character. She said in a Q+A at Austin's Alamo
Drafthouse that she hates the film and that she and the
other actors would get high in the attic of the house and
try to think of ways to ruin the production.[69] As such, her
showstopping performance is very deliberately bigger than
the film, which Tyrrell was hoping would transform it into a
comedy, since – in her opinion – no one could take the film
seriously anyway. Director William Asher was no stranger
to camp himself, having helmed Johnny Cool in 1963, plus
a handful of well-known beach movies and numerous
television shows, including Bewitched, but it's hard to know
whether he intended for Butcher, Baker, Nightmare Maker to
be as hilarious as it is.

CAN GO THROUGH SKIN

2009, Netherlands
Original title: **Kan door huid heen**
D: Esther Rots. P: Esther Rots, Hugo Rots, Trent. W: Esther Rots.
Ed: Esther Rots. DoP: Lennert Hillege. M: Dan Geesin. AD: Tess Ellis,
Vera van de Sandt, Marije van der Waard.
Cast: Rifka Lodeizen (Marieke), Wim Opbrouck (John), Chris
Borowski (Pizzaman), Elisabeth van Nimwegen (Siska), Tina de
Bruin (Aniek), Mattijn Hartemink (Klaas), Roel Goudsmit (Herfst),
Anita Donk (Herfst's friend), Hans Zuydveld (Taxi driver), Jeroen
van Wijngaarden (Ben)

When the film opens, Marieke (Rifka Lodeizen) has just been dumped
by her long-time boyfriend and makes a series of unsuccessful booty
calls trying to fill the emotional void. When she gives up and goes
to take a bath she is unexpectedly attacked in her home; as the
assailant tries to drown her, her head is bashed on the side of the tub
and she falls unconscious. When she comes to, her female neighbour
is in the house fighting the guy off, and the two women run into the
street – Marieke completely uncovered – screaming for help.

It is uncertain whether Marieke was raped in the attack but
later incidents seem to point in that direction. She makes some
strange decisions: she buys a decrepit, isolated, rat-infested
farmhouse with no shower, and moves in, living in the dark among
piles of garbage. She finds a large cubbyhole behind the wall in the
kitchen and climbs into it, hiding as though she was a rat herself.
Her only connection to her life back in the city (Rotterdam) is the
internet – which she uses almost exclusively to chat on rape forums
– and the court dates related to her attack. She is temperamental
and paranoid, behaves erratically and talks to herself increasingly
as the film progresses.

Aesthetically and emotionally, the film recalls Lynne Ramsay's
Morvern Callar, and with its similarly unlikable protagonist, the film
can be tough going at times.

from top: Susan Tyrrell and Jimmy McNichol in William Asher's **Butcher, Baker, Nightmare Maker** (1981); Rifka Lodeizen in **Can Go Through Skin** (2009).

A CANDLE FOR THE DEVIL

1973, Spain
Original title: **Una vela para el Diablo**
Alternative title: **It Happened at Nightmare Inn**
D: Eugenio Martín. W: Eugenio Martín, Antonio Fos.
Ed: Pablo González del Amo. DoP: José F. Aguayo.
Mª Antonio Pérez Olea. AD: Adolfo Cofiño.
Cast: Judy Geeson (Laura Barkley) Aurora Bautista
(Marta), Esperanza Roy (Veronica), Vic Winner [Víctor
Alcazar] (Eduardo), Lone Fleming (Helen Miller), Blanca
Estrada (Norma), Loreta Tovar (May Berkeley), Julia
Montserrat (Otilla), Fernando Villena (Doctor), Fernando
Hilbeck (Mayor)

Horror Express director Eugenio Martín's *A Candle for the Devil* is a great tale of doomed sibling solidarity that examines the oppressive nature of Catholicism and its effect on the mental health of two women living through the height of the sexual revolution.

Two prim middle-aged sisters run a bed and breakfast service in a Spanish resort town, but are consistently offended by the 'loose' women who gravitate to their place. Both women are gorgeous, not that you would know it, since they dress like matronly schoolmarms, complete with church-collars and clodhoppers. The more dominant (and psychotic) of the two sisters is threatened by the open sexuality of the young boarders, and mentally transforms their every nuance and comment into a sin worthy of serious retribution. She imagines that one of them claws at her clothes in a lesbian frenzy; another shamelessly exhibits her body while tanning on the roof; yet another is deemed an unfit mother. All meet the same grisly fate.

The older sister has abandonment issues stemming from being ditched at the altar years before, turning to religion because it was easier to have faith in a superior entity with a divine plan than it was to accept being alone. Her piety has its fissures though, even aside from her homicidal judgements. The most telling set piece sees her spying on some kids skinny-dipping in a waterhole near the hotel. The camera returns over and over again to the undeveloped penis of a prepubescent boy, as a means of conveying her paedophilic preoccupations. Catching herself in a sin, disoriented and flustered, she fights through a tall mess of weeds to get back to the hotel. The weeds rip at her clothes and hair as she stumbles through them, whipping her into a frenzy that deliberately recalls the ecstasy of religious flagellation.

Whilst the younger sister is an accomplice to her sister's madness as a matter of habit (older sister kills someone, younger sister cleans up the mess), she would rather be elsewhere, living the liberated lifestyle represented by her younger hunky boyfriend, a relationship that is kept secret lest it be seen as a betrayal. When a woman comes looking for her missing sister at the boarding house, the younger sister sees her situation from another perspective; the two sets of sisters are like an inverse mirror of one another. But this fleeting moment of objectivity is not enough – the younger sister is trapped by a sense of familial responsibility, even though her actions are enabling to the older sister's mental illness. Both sisters are stuck in a cycle that will only end when one of them dies.

CARRIE

1976, USA
D: Brian De Palma. P: Paul Monash. W: Lawrence D. Cohen, Stephen King (novel). Ed: Paul Hirsch. DoP: Mario Tosi. M: Pino Donaggio. AD: William Kenney, Jack Fisk.
Cast: Sissy Spacek (Carrie White), Piper Laurie (Margaret White), Amy Irving (Sue Snell), William Katt (Tommy Ross), Betty Buckley (Miss Collins), Nancy Allen (Chris Hargensen), John Travolta (Billy Nolan), P.J. Soles (Norma Watson), Priscilla Pointer (Mrs. Eleanor Snell), Sydney Lassick (Mr. Fromm)

Stephen King's story of an awkward, unliked teenage girl who unleashes her telekinetic powers on all those who have habitually tormented her has to stand as the horror genre's defining statement concerning high school bullying and clique mentality.

Though Carrie White (Sissy Spacek) has her moments of disorientation and blinding anger, she is still portrayed as a normal, shy kid; nothing in her physical or vocal mannerisms conveys that she has mental issues (unlike her direct descendant in *May*). It is really her mother, Margaret White (Piper Laurie) who suffers from mental illness (here equated with religious fundamentalism). What makes Laurie's performance such a showstopper is that she doesn't play the straight-up tyrannical mother. She is like a woman possessed; possessed by a fear of her repressed passions that is channelled into an ecstatic, frightening love for Jesus. Her startling admonitions ("First comes the blood, then comes the boys – trying to figure out where that smell comes from.") and autistically-repeated bible passages ("First sin was intercourse. First sin was intercourse. First sin was intercourse...") are balanced by a calmness that is almost more unnerving because of what it hides.

Margaret White is the most terrifying screen villain there is; her image gives me that same abject terror that staring into a great white shark's open mouth does. It makes me wonder if maybe there's nothing scarier than one's own horrible mother.

above: Sissy Spacek in Brian De Palma's **Carrie** (1976).

LA CASA MUDA

2010, Uruguay
Alternative title: **The Silent House**
D: Gustavo Hernández. P: Gustavo Rojo. W: Oscar Estévez, Gustavo Hernández (story), Gustavo Rojo (story). Ed: Gustavo Hernández. DoP: Pedro Luque. M: Hernán González. PD: Federico Capra.
Cast: Florencia Colucci (Laura), Abel Tripaldi (Néstor), Gustavo Alonso (Wilson), María Salazar (Niña)

A man and his teenage daughter Laura arrive at a decrepit house in the country with the goal of fixing it up so that their family friend Néstor can sell it. The windows are boarded up, there is no electricity, and it lies deep in the South American woods. The first night they are there, Laura hears banging sounds and footsteps on the second floor. She wakes up her father to investigate, and when he does, he promptly turns up dead – leaving her alone in the dark house with only a small lantern and the certainty that her own time is running out. The doors are all mysteriously locked, so she moves around the house looking for an exit and comes across some curious things: a child's nursery; a bedroom plastered with lewd Polaroids of half naked party girls side by side with pictures of herself – pregnant.

What is set up as a ghost story slowly emerges as a revenge scenario, but this twist itself is not as interesting as the way time and space are mutable within the film's framework. While the shaky reality horror-cam and lack of cutaways indicate that events are playing out in real time, there is a sense that they could be happening at any time, or perhaps are playing out over and over again in the liminal space of the abandoned house (all the sounds Laura hears coming from upstairs at the beginning are the same sounds that she will make later when she is on the second floor).

The title of the film translates as 'the silent house', which implies that the house has a story to tell – the truth of which is only known within these walls. On more than one occasion we are reminded of David Lynch's *Twin Peaks: Fire Walk with Me*, not only in terms of the protagonist's name, but also with the titular 'casa' falling somewhere between Leo Johnson's cabin and the Black Lodge. Despite the film's many accolades on the festival circuit declaring it to be some kind of white-knuckle suspense masterpiece, I have to admit I kept expecting a *Scooby-Doo* ending, where some grouchy neighbour would be caught trying to scare them off from selling the house.

above: Florencia Colucci in Gustavo Hernández's **La casa muda** (2010).

CAT PEOPLE

1942, USA
D: Jacques Tourneur. P: Val Lewton. W: DeWitt Bodeen.
Ed: Mark Robson. DoP: Nicholas Musuraca.
M: Roy Webb. AD: Albert S. D'Agostino, Walter E. Keller.
Cast: Simone Simon (Irena Dubrovna Reed), Kent Smith
(Oliver Reed), Tom Conway (Dr. Louis Judd), Jane Randolph
(Alice Moore), Jack Holt ('Commodore' C.R. Cooper), Steve
Soldi (organ grinder) Alan Napier ('Doc' Carver), John Piffle
(The Belgrade proprietor), Elizabeth Dunne (Miss Plunkett),
Elizabeth Russell (cat woman)

Jacques Tourneur's original *Cat People* (1942) is the first of the
Val Lewton-produced cycle of RKO's 'terror' films, and is almost
unique in its sympathetic depiction of a woman haunted by
the fear of her own jealousy.

French actress Simone Simon plays Irena, a Serbian
fashion designer living alone in New York City. One day while
sketching the caged panther at the Central Park Zoo, she
strikes up an acquaintance with an engineer named Oliver
(Kent Smith) and the two find themselves in wedded bliss only a
short time later. But Irena's deeply ingrained superstitious beliefs
concerning the 'cat women' of her village in Serbia – women
who turn into fierce panthers when their passions are riled,
specifically jealous passions – threaten to drive Oliver into the
arms of another woman who is less emotionally challenging.

The film does a wonderful job of melding the usual early-
horror dichotomies of realism/fantasy and good/evil in a way
that invites multiple readings (supported by some beautifully
calculated imagery), but to me its enduring appeal is the
tragic Irena, who takes a chance on love against her better
judgement, and is punished for it.
For more on this film see **Part 8: Heal Me with Hatred**.

LA CÉRÉMONIE

1995, France/Germany
D: Claude Chabrol. P: Marin Karmitz. W: Claude Chabrol, Caroline
Eliacheff, Ruth Rendell (novel). Ed: Monique Fardoulis. DoP:
Bernard Zitzermann. M: Matthieu Chabrol. AD: Daniel Mercier.
Cast: Isabelle Huppert (Jeanne), Sandrine Bonnaire (Sophie),
Jean-Pierre Cassel (Georges Lelièvre), Jacqueline Bisset
(Catherine Lelièvre), Virginie Ledoyen (Melinda), Valentin Merlet
(Gilles), Julien Rochefort (Jeremie), Dominique Frot (Madame
Lantier), Jean-François Perrier (Priest), Ludovic Brillant

Based on British crime writer Ruth Rendell's 1977 novel *A
Judgement in Stone*, Chabrol's fantastically dry tale of a secretly
illiterate woman's retaliation against her employers is both a
curious depiction of female pathology and a class revenge flick
in the vein of Joseph Losey's *The Servant*.

Sandrine Bonnaire (the award-winning lead of Agnès
Varda's *Vagabond*) stars as Sophie, an illiterate woman who
is hired as a live-in domestic at the large, remote home of
the Lelièvre family, headed up by gallery owner Catherine
(Jacqueline Bisset) and her opera-obsessed husband Georges
(Jean-Pierre Cassel). She is immediately so unlikable, unfriendly
and shifty it's hard to believe she would get hired at all, but when
she meets Jeanne, the outspoken receptionist at the post office

(Isabelle Huppert), it's confirmed that they've had trouble finding
someone to take the position. Catherine is instantly enamoured
with Sophie's work ethic, but the daughter Melinda (Virginie
Ledoyen) – who no longer lives at home full time – suggests giving
her a realistic trial period, and also tries to convince her wealthy
parents that it might be uncouth to refer to Sophie as a 'maid'
(her parents don't heed either nugget of advice). Throughout
the film Melinda will seem like Sophie's closest ally in the family,
but even her concern can be read as pity, which Sophie cannot
endure. When Melinda discovers that Sophie is illiterate, and that
she has concocted elaborate (and rather inefficient) schemes
to avoid her secret getting out, Sophie cannot deal with the
potential humiliation and responds like a trapped animal.

Sophie's only release comes from her budding friendship
with the local bad girl, Jeanne, despite gossip that Jeanne killed
her own daughter and got away with it. Sophie immediately
confronts Jeanne about it, and she is surprisingly unruffled at the
accusation. "They couldn't prove anything", Jeanne says, before
revealing that she knows something equally incriminating about
Sophie: that she was charged with starting the house fire that
killed her invalid father. "They couldn't prove anything", Sophie
mimics, laughing. But her employers don't appreciate Sophie's
newfound social bliss; they notice her increased insolence since
she started hanging out with Jeanne, and consequently forbid
Jeanne from entering their house.

While the class revenge scenario is a major part of the
original text and is what initially fuels the girls' friendship in
Chabrol's film (Jeanne wants a place to watch TV since she
doesn't have one, and their TV-watching is shown in contrast to
the 'high' culture enjoyed by the Lelièvres), here the relationship

between the two women
is brought to the forefront,
allowing both actresses
the room to show off their
respective neuroses and
to bond over their past
crimes – the only time
Sophie's smiles seem
genuine. It is hard to
imagine illiteracy causing
homicidal distress, but
even the book's opening line – "Eunice Parchman killed the
Coverdale family because she could not read or write" – states
as fact the degree to which her emotional problems stem from
this (very alterable) intellectual disadvantage. When Sophie is
given the tour of the house, she is brought first to the kitchen,
which is cited as "her domain", and then led to the library – a
cavernous, daunting room for one who is illiterate. She'll get her
revenge on this room later.

Rendell's novel was also filmed as *The Housekeeper*
(aka *A Judgment in Stone*) in 1986, starring '60s odd-duck Rita
Tushingham (whose director and then-husband Ousama Rawi
gets a nod in Chabrol's opening credits) and Canadian cult
queen Jackie Burroughs as the homicidal pair. Rawi's version is
a more by-the-numbers affair that begins with a full backstory
detailing the main character's lifelong mistreatment and the
fallout of her sexual repression, and allows more camp in its
performances. In Chabrol's comparatively straight-faced
retelling, ambiguity is favoured; its characters are sociopathic
types more than raving lunatics, and without the backstory to
create sympathy for his characters, they are rendered needlessly
mean-spirited and destructive – and ultimately more insidious.

above: Isabelle Huppert and Sandrine Bonnaire in Claude Chabrol's **La cérémonie** (1995).

CHILDREN SHOULDN'T PLAY WITH DEAD THINGS

1972, USA
Alternative title: **Things from the Grave**
D: Bob Clark. P: Bob Clark, Gary Goch. W: Bob Clark. Ed: Gary Goch. DoP: Jack McGowan. M: Carl Zittrer. AD: Forest Carpenter.
Cast: Alan Ormsby (Alan), Anya Ormsby (Anya), Valerie Mamches (Val), Jane Daly (Terry), Jeff Gillen (Jeff), Paul Cronin (Paul), Roy Engelman (Roy), Bob Filep (Emerson), Bruce Solomon (Winns), Seth Sklarey (Orville Dunworth)

Bob Clark's early feature is a trash masterpiece about an amateur theatre troupe who head off to an island cemetery to dig up a corpse for use in an ill-fated black magic ritual. When said corpse (the now-iconic zombie 'Orville') is mocked and defiled by the bell-bottomed gang of thesps, his graveyard pals rise from the dead to defend his honour, showcasing Alan Ormsby's budding make-up FX talents (which would later be seen in *Deathdream*, *Deranged*, *Shock Waves* and more).

The film gleefully transcends its bare-bones budget with inspired dialogue (courtesy of writer and star Ormsby) and a bevy of histrionic performances, most notably from Ormsby, Valerie Mamches and – the subject of this entry – Anya Ormsby, (Alan's then-wife) as the gaunt, flaky hippie whose brand of flower-power leans toward funeral bouquets more than sunshine and lollipops. While most of the cast exchanges witty barbs throughout the film, Anya doesn't speak at all until nearly 20 minutes in, when she expresses excitement over the possibility of seeing a real ghost. "Something's going to happen tonight – I can feel it!" she exclaims with wide eyes and a (medication-induced?) grin that rivals Conrad Veidt's in *The Man Who Laughs*. "Poor Anya", Val offers, "Any second now I expect her to float off." This is the only overt address of her mental state, but she's clearly off her rocker and responds inappropriately to nearly every situation, whether by staring off vacuously during scenes of violent horror, or fondling their corpse-friend with necrophilic affection. Her face and limbs contort into exaggerated expressions as she marvels at the wonders of the dead, and the only thing that gets her out of the now-vacated coffin where she lies "gazing at the soul of immortality" is Alan's proposition that they bring Orville back to their crumbling nearby cabin for a "coming-out party". But when the jokes get too hands-on, Anya suddenly fears that they've crossed the line of propriety: "There is great beauty in death – it shouldn't be defiled!" Sensing that something is wrong out in the woods – where the dead have begun to rise – she goes into a hysterical fit and has to be restrained.

This was one of the first films I ever saw as a kid and the lady Ormsby made a lasting impression.

CHRISTIANE F.

1981, West Germany
Original title: **Christiane F. – Wir Kinder vom Bahnhof Zoo**
D: Uli Edel. P: Bernd Eichinger, Hans Weth. W: Herman Weigel, Kai Hermann (book), Horst Rieck (book). Ed: Jane Seitz. DoP: Justus Pankau, Jürgen Jürges. M: Jürgen Knieper.
Cast: Natja Brunckhorst (Christiane F.), Thomas Haustein (Detlef), Jens Kuphal (Axel), Reiner Wölk (Leiche), Christiane Reichelt (Babsi), Jan George Effler (Bernd), Daniela Jaeger (Kessi), Kerstin Richter (Stella), Lothar Chamski (Rolf), Peggy Bussieck (Puppi)

The true-life tale of Christiane Felscherinow, a 13-year-old heroin addict and prostitute at Berlin's notorious Zoo Station, remains one of the most harrowing films of the JD (juvenile delinquent) film catalogue. Based on the best-selling autobiography (which was in fact written by two journalists based on interviews with Christiane, her mother and those in her circle), the film became a sensation among teenage viewers who overly romanticized Christiane's lifestyle and her makeshift street-family, and a source of controversy for its use of underage actors in sex scenes and other adult situations. While this, in common with many other JD films, does not equate drug-induced behaviour with developmental neurosis, the film is included here, like *Born Innocent*, for its impact on me at a pivotal age.
For more historical and anecdotal information on this film see
Part 6: The Strange Passenger.

from top: Newspaper ad for Bob Clark's **Children Shouldn't Play with Dead Things** (1972); Natja Brunckhorst in Uli Edel's **Christiane F.** (1981).

THE COLLECTOR

1997, Finland
Original title: **Neitoperho**
D: Auli Mantila. P: Tero Kaukomaa. W: Auli Mantila. Ed: Riitta Poikselkä. DoP: Heikki Färm.
Cast: Leea Klemola (Eevi), Elina Hurme (Ami), Rea Mauranen (Anja), Henriikka Salo (Helena), Robin Svartström (Jusu), Pekka Kyrö (criminal investigator#1), Marja Packalén (criminal investigator #2), Jari Hietanen (Jake), Tanjalotta Räikkä (dog-trainer), Pekka Halttunen (night guard)

Auli Mantila's debut feature film *The Collector* is an uncompromising glimpse into the mind of a disturbed young woman and her violent response to feelings of social invisibility. Celebrated Finnish theatre actress Leea Klemola plays the awkward, tomboyish Eevi, whose frightening aggression leads to one rejection after another, and to violently unpredictable behaviour through which she alienates herself from her peers, and from society at large. When her sister ejects her from their shared apartment so that her lover can move in, the expulsion takes on a cataclysmic significance for the obsessive-compulsive Eevi, and after trying to set fire to the apartment she hits the road for a 'holiday' that entails petty theft, kidnapping and murder.
For more on this film see **Part 5: Afterschool Special**.

THE CORRUPTION OF CHRIS MILLER

1973, Spain
D: Juan Antonio Bardem. W: Santiago Moncada. Ed: Emilio Rodriguez.
DoP: Juan Gelpí. M: Waldo de los Rios.
AD: Ramiro Gómez.
Cast: Jean Seberg (Ruth Miller), Marisol (Chris Miller), Barry Stokes (Barney Webster), Perla Cristal (Perla), Rudi Gaebel (Luis), Gerard Tichy (commissioner), Alicia Altabella (Adela), Vidal Molina (Ernesto), Maria Bardem (Maria), Juan Bardem (Pedro)

Ruth Miller (Jean Seberg) lives with her exotic-looking stepdaughter Chris in an isolated country house. Chris is recovering from a recent stay in an institution, and the dynamic between them is immediately set up as one of oppression and mistrust. Abandoned by Chris's father, Ruth spouts her hatred for the male gender at frequent intervals, while Chris has no choice but to listen and absorb. Ruth veils her own possessiveness in a guise of concern for Chris's welfare; she lives only for revenge, and isolates herself in a cocoon of man-hating security that manifests itself as an obsession with Chris, who she sees simultaneously as an opportunity and a threat. When a handsome vagrant turns up looking for work, Ruth's calculated power dynamic is thrown out of balance, and extreme measures are requiresd to restore order. *The Corruption of Chris Miller* is one of the pivotal films of the Spanish horror boom of the '70s.
For more on this film see
Part 2: Broken Dolls.

L'ALTRA CASA AI MARGINI DEL BOSCO

con **JEAN SEBERG** - **MARISOL** - **BARRY STOKES** - **PERLA CRISTAL**

Regia: **JUAN ANTONIO BARDEM**   Produzione: JAVIER ARMET XIOL BARCELLONA   Colore della **TELECOLOR**

LES COUSINES

1970, France
Alternative titles: **From Ear to Ear; The French Cousins; The Coffin**
D: Louis Soulanes. P: Claude Capra. W: Louis Soulanes, Fletcher D. Benson (novel). DoP: Albert Susterre.
Cast: Nicole Debonne (Elisa), Robert Lombard (M. Borgo), Solange Pradel (Lucile), Liliane Bert (Béatrice), Danielle Argence (Josine), Jean Genin (Bruno), Alain Doutey (André), Katia Tchenko (Dolly), Marie-Paule Pioli, Katia Bagarry

Louis Soulanes's adaptation of Fletcher D. Benson's novel *The Perverse Women's Night* (which likely takes a cue from Jean Genet's *The Maids*) is a rarely-seen oddity – a bizarre, insular family drama about two demented cousins, Elisa and Josine (Nicole Debonne and Danielle Argence, who look strangely like Mary Woronov and Mimsy Farmer) who entertain themselves by tormenting Elisa's sister Lucile – a wheelchair-bound quadriplegic. The two able-bodied and flimsily-dressed cousins share an incestuous lesbian relationship and delight in torturing Lucile, who can only follow their actions with her darting eyes, but cannot scream or react physically. Their mother is fully aware of the situation but takes no disciplinary or preventative action.

Lucile is a nervous wreck, dreading the next random punishment she'll be dealt by her bored tormentors. A spider crawling up her nightgown is played up for maximum effect, and when Elisa holds a limbless doll in front of Lucile, she watches her paralyzed sister's eyes fill with terror, and then proceeds to listen to her sped-up heartbeat with puerile sadism. When the two indiscriminately promiscuous cousins invite friends over for a free-for-all sex party, they are suddenly seized with the desire to hang one of their male suitors by the neck from the ceiling, shrieking in ecstasy as they raise him up on the rope. This act of murder bonds the cousins further, and their complicity means they now have to get rid of the body together.

While the two cousins are having their Thana-tastic sex party in the other room, Lucile somehow finds the skeletal remains of a baby, and the nature of her disability becomes clear: after the death of her illegitimate child years earlier, her body seized up with grief; a traumatic event that manifested as a very real physical disability (not unlike Camille Keaton in *What Have You Done to Solange?* or Carroll Baker in *Knife of Ice*).

Inexplicably released in the U.S. as *From Ear to Ear*, Vincent Canby said of the film in his *New York Times* review: "Although it is unpleasant, it is without importance, like bad breath, greasy food, junk mail or a slight fever."[70] Maybe it can't stand up next to the great masterworks of cinema, but for those surveying representations of female neurosis onscreen, it is absolutely essential.

"CRIMINALLY INSANE"

1975, USA
D: Nick Philips [Nick Millard]. P: Frances Millard. W: Nick Philips. Ed: John Lincoln. DoP: Karil Ostman. AD: Charles R. Fenwick.
Cast: Priscilla Alden (Ethel Janowski), Michael Flood (John), Jane Lambert (Mrs. Janowski), Robert Copple, C.L. LeFleur [George 'Buck' Flower] (detective), Gina Martine (Mrs. Kendley), Cliff McDonald (Dr. Gerard), Charles Egan (drunk man), Sandra Shotwell (nurse), Lisa Farros (Rosalie)

This amazing cheapie from sexploitation director Nick Philips remains one of few examples of a rotund horror psycho (only Shirley Stoler from *The Honeymoon Killers* comes to mind) who, in this case, sees her enforced diet as a declaration of war in which she will take no prisoners.

We are introduced to our obese protagonist Ethel Janowski (Priscilla Alden) with images of her being restrained, drugged and straitjacketed in a mental hospital. Her doctor lays it all out for her inquiring grandmother ("Severe paranoid manifestations, long periods of depression, violent outbursts – frankly, it's against my better judgment that she's being released."), before prescribing weekly electroshock visits and encouraging grandma to put Ethel on a diet. The generally disinterested Ethel only comes alive when preparing a sumptuous meal of 7 eggs and a pan full of greasy bacon, commenting sardonically that, "That goddam jew doctor gave them orders not to give me enough to eat!" (This is not the film's only instance of head-shaking racist dialogue!) When grandmother hides all the food in the house, Ethel responds by viciously stabbing her, and gives the same treatment to the grocery delivery boy (whose '70s coif is superb) when he demands $80 and Ethel only has $4.50. When Ethel misses her electroshock appointments, the doctor comes calling and meets the same fate.

Ethel's prostitute sister Rosalie comes to stay with her for a few days, but mainly uses the house as a means of entertaining her tricks. When her boyfriend John shows up trying to get Rosalie to take him back after a detour in Vegas with some floozie, Rosalie is reluctant because John used to slap her around. His response is one of the film's many examples of grade-A dialogue (to match the grade-A ketchup used as blood throughout): "You need a good beating once in a while. All women do. And you especially."

When Rosalie and her greasy beau start complaining about the stench emanating from grandma's room, Ethel eschews the (logical) decision of getting rid of the corpses in favour of adding to the bodycount. While psychedelic sequences portray the extent to which Ethel's mania has taken over, no real attempt is made to locate the source of her neurosis, although one can speculate that she is acting out against pressures to conform to traditional standards of beauty.

What gives *"Criminally Insane"* its lingering entertainment value is really Priscilla Alden, who performs her part with a nihilistic fuck-you attitude that's admirable in its refusal to go over-the-top, as many would be tempted to do in a role like this. She would reprise her role 12 years later in the sequel, *Crazy Fat Ethel 2* (1987).

top right: Priscilla Alden in Nick Philips's **"Criminally Insane"** (1975).

THE CURSE OF THE CAT PEOPLE

1944, USA

D: Robert Wise, Gunther von Fritsch. P: Val Lewton. W: DeWitt Bodeen. Ed: J.R. Whittredge. DoP: Nicholas Musuraca. M: Roy Webb. AD: Albert S. D'Agostino, Walter E. Keller.
Cast: Simone Simon (Irena), Kent Smith (Oliver Reed), Jane Randolph (Alice Reed), Ann Carter (Amy Reed), Eve March (Miss Callahan), Julia Dean (Julia Farren), Elizabeth Russell (Barbara Farren), Erford Gage (captain of guard), Sir Lancelot (Edward), Joel Davis (Donald)

This has been described as an 'unrelated' sequel to Jacques Tourneur's *Cat People*, but in fact it's completely related, in terms of both its returning characters and predominant themes. Kent Smith and Jane Randolph return as Oliver and Alice Reed, now married and living in Tarrytown, NY (the site of the tale of *Sleepy Hollow*) with their young daughter Amy, who has trouble making and keeping friends – most of her classmates don't like her, due primarily to her tendency to daydream. Lacking any real companions, Amy invents one – in the form of her father's deceased first wife – who plays with her in the garden. Amy has this friend prior to hearing anything about Irena, but it is only after seeing a photograph of Irena and hearing her name aloud that she imbues her invisible friend with these characteristics.

The most glaring distinction between *The Curse of the Cat People* and its predecessor is that the sequel almost entirely forgoes the terror elements in favour of a psychological study of childhood loneliness – the same loneliness that had afflicted Irena in the first film and caused her own folkloric 'delusions'. While childhood fantasy only crosses over into neurosis in extreme circumstances, and would be better served outside the scope of this book, it is

assumed by Amy's father Oliver that his daughter has either behavioural problems – making her invisible friend an act of defiance – or that she is deeply troubled and could end up completely mad just like his first wife. The spectre of Irena's 'madness' hangs heavily over the film and, as in the original *Cat People*, is seen as contagious and something that must be reined in – occasionally with violence. After refusing to concede to her father that her friend Irena is a fiction, Amy suffers her first instance of corporal punishment ("a first spanking is an important event!" says the girl's teacher in encouragement of the disciplining).

An underdeveloped but important subplot involves Mrs. Farren, the ageing actress who lives in the mansion down the street – whom Amy likes to visit on occasion – and the sultry woman who takes care of her (Elizabeth Russell, who briefly appeared as Irena's 'sestra' – as in, fellow cat-sister – in the first film). Mrs. Farren is convinced that this woman is trying to harm her, but Russell's character, alternately threatening and vulnerable – claims to be Mrs. Farren's daughter Barbara, tormented by the fact that her own mother won't acknowledge her. Mrs. Farren maintains that Barbara died as a child, and the 'impostor' Barbara gets seethingly resentful when young Amy – a veritable stranger – visits and is showered with affection. Delusion again comes into play here, as we are never told for certain whether the woman really is Barbara or just a conniving woman hoping to cheat an old woman out of her fortune. Either way, there are many lonely people in this film who will beg, borrow or steal for affection. Amy is so desperate for love that she imagines Irena's face over that of Barbara's, and few moments in cinema are more heartbreaking than the little girl walking towards a woman who wants to kill her saying, "my friend, my friend..."

235

HOUSE OF PSYCHOTIC WOMEN

a film by douglas buck

CUTTING MOMENTS

"...an extremely disturbing cinematic experience..."
-Abel Ferrara, director
"Body Snatchers", "King of New York"

"...sure to leave even the most stalwart viewer cringing"
-SHOCK CINEMA magazine

"...the sickest film I've ever seen..."
-Tom Savini, director
Night of the Living Dead (1990)

CUTTING MOMENTS

1996, USA
D: Douglas Buck. P: Douglas Buck. W: Douglas Buck.
Cast: Nicca Ray (Sarah), Gary Betsworth (Patrick), Jared Barsky (Joey)

Douglas Buck's shocking short film *Cutting Moments* took the festival circuit by storm in 1996, and was re-released theatrically in 2004, as part of a feature entitled *Family Portraits: A Trilogy of America*. Nicca Ray (daughter of Nicholas Ray) stars as the mother of a young boy who is being taken away by Child and Family Services after being molested by his father. The woman blames herself, not only for her silence, but also for not being 'appealing' enough to her husband. She knows that the daily grind of suburban life has worn her down, made her tired, and that her marriage has been reduced to a shallow role-play. She tries to win over her husband's attention by putting on a sleek red dress and matching lipstick, but he responds with only confusion and indifference. Retreating to the bathroom, she starts scrubbing off her lipstick, and then her lips, and then reaching for the scissors... *Cutting Moments* is an absolutely essential film that goes beyond its shock value.
For more on this film see **Part 5: Afterschool Special**.

top left: Sell-sheet for Douglas Buck's **Cutting Moments** (1996).

DADDY

1973, UK/France
D: Peter Whitehead, Niki De Saint Phalle. P: Tom G. Neuman, Peter Schamoni. W: Niki De Saint Phalle. Ed: Peter Whitehead. DoP: Peter Whitehead.
Cast: Niki de Saint Phalle, Rainer von Diez (Daddy), Mia Martin (daughter's friend), Clarice Rivers, Marcel Lefranc, Jean-Pierre Raymond, Sere Inhof

Counterculture documentarist Peter Whitehead and his onetime lover, sculptress Niki de Saint Phalle, collaborated on this bizarre sexual revenge picture in which Saint Phalle's character, a statuesque art-star, returns to her childhood chateau in France after receiving a telegram that her father has died. She starts to ruminate on her childhood, with a combination of flashbacks (revealing her obsession with the inappropriate game called 'Blindman' that she and her father used to play together in the garden) and fantasy scenarios wherein she and her mother team up to humiliate and reject the father.

A very theatrical (and seemingly therapeutic) film, one of Whitehead's only forays into fiction, full of perverse sexual imagery and Saint Phalle's gorgeous sculptures.
For more on this film see **Part 4: Secret Ceremonies**.

DEAD CREATURES

2001, UK
D: Andrew Parkinson. W: Andrew Parkinson. Ed: Andrew Parkinson. DoP: Jason Shepherd. M: Andrew Parkinson. AD: Jennifer Clapcott.
Cast: Beverley Wilson (Jo), Antonia Beamish (Ann), Brendan Gregory (Reece), Anna Swift (Sian), Bart Ruspoli (Christian), Fiona Carr (Zoe), Eva Fontaine (Fran), Sam Cocking (zombie youth), Lindsay Clarke (Ali), Hilary Sesta (Grandma Penny)

Expanding on the themes and social-realist aesthetic of his debut feature *I, Zombie: The Chronicles of Pain*, Parkinson's sophomore feature is, on the surface, a story about a group of female zombie-cannibals in London who are being hunted by an unidentified man with a rather nasty impalement weapon. London doesn't seem to be overrun with zombies – although radio news reports are audible at times, debating vague issues relating to genetic experimentation and environmental hazards – so this is far from a zombie apocalypse film. While Britain is depicted as desolate and in ruins, it is in fact filmed just as it is – which is telling when we consider our preconceived notions of what constitutes an 'apocalypse'.

All of these women were, at one time or another, normal living humans. As they in turn found themselves alone, disoriented and ravenously hungry after a zombie attack, they were taken in by Ali, who formed a loose-knit group with new 'rules' of moral and safety conduct to keep them all alive and healthy for as long as possible before decay inevitably sets in. At the opening of the film, Ali herself is on the verge of death, unable to walk or feed herself, her flesh rotting off. The other girls cater to her with affection and patience – they know it could be their turn next. They try to remember what their lives used to be like before they had to unlearn the rules of socialization (i.e. that eating people is wrong). "Memories are important", says Ann (Antonia Beamish), "They keep things in perspective. Make things straight."

There are many gruesome, stomach-turning scenes of these everyday zombies devouring raw flesh from distinctly human carcasses, but through its many domestic conversations – the film takes place mostly in a series of small apartments – the film is instead revealed as a study of the bond that could develop between women in a crisis situation. Cut off from their families, they try to persevere and to maintain hope despite a daily regimen that consists of seducing food sources through prostitution and murder, watching TV talk shows, decorating and re-decorating as apartments change, and being on the lookout for the strange self-appointed zombie-hunter who stalks them. They maintain their daily ablutions – "wishful make-uping" – and are able to pass for human, but they are rotting away inside (foul breath and bloody urine among the signs of encroaching decrepitude).

The film has been described as an AIDS allegory and as a Ken-Loach-meets-Romero hybrid, but at its heart it's existential horror with a female face.

DEFENCELESS: A BLOOD SYMPHONY

2004, Australia
D: Mark Savage. P: Mark Savage, Susanne Hausschmid.
W: Mark Savage. Ed: Mark Savage.
DoP: Mark Savage.
M: George Papanicolaou.
Cast: Susanne Hausschmid (the woman), Bethany Fisher (the girl), Colin Savage (the husband), Erin Walsh (the lover), Max Hopkins (the son), Yvette Johansson (unhappy wife), Mitchell Turner (developer), George Gladstone (developer), Anthony Thorne (developer), Richard Wolstencroft (the stepfather)

Stylistically pared-down – even to a complete lack of dialogue – Australian director Mark Savage's *Defenceless* is a woman's revenge story brimming with vaginas and viscera, and is not for the weak of stomach. Genitals don't last long in this movie. Aside from the graphic and repeated castrations that colour the film, Savage also has some interesting things to say about female space.

The story is simple: an environmental activist (Susanne Hausschmid, who also co-produced) takes on some rather relentless and seemingly untouchable developers with horrific results. One by one, the most important things in her life are taken away from her – her husband, her lover, her child – and in mythological fashion, she is led to exact a primal, bloody revenge.

For more on this film see **Part 4: Secret Ceremonies** and **Part 5: Afterschool Special**.

opposite from top: Mia Martin and Niki de Saint Phalle in **Daddy** *(1973); Susanne Hausschmid in Mark Savage's* **Defenceless: A Blood Symphony** *(2004).*

DEMENTIA

1953, USA
Alternative title: **Daughter of Horror**
D: John Parker. P: John Parker. W: John Parker. Ed: Joseph Gluck. DoP: William C. Thompson. M: George Antheil. PD: Ben Roseman. Cast: Adrienne Barrett (the gamine), Bruno Ve Sota (the rich man), Ben Roseman (the law enforcer/father), Richard Barron (the evil one), Lucille Howland (the mother), Edward Hinkle (the butler), Gayne Sullivan (the wino), Jebbie Ve Sota (the flower girl), Faith Parker (nightclub dancer)

John Parker's masterpiece of the surreal was – until a re-release in 2000 – known for decades only in its edited form, which was retitled *Daughter of Horror* and narrated by Ed McMahon, who functioned as the verbal 'square-up'. Considered too obscene by the pre-MPAA censor board, the distributors were forced to add McMahon's voice of doom to both explain surreal set pieces and to ensure that the film was not perceived as condoning any of the behaviour it portrayed.

The film is littered with stock B-movie characters – pimps, prostitutes, fat wealthy johns, crooked cops, jazz musicians – who all weave their way through the loose narrative, which basically takes place entirely in the demented mind of a very sick young woman. With bad skin and a worse demeanour, this stiletto-heeled psychocat has no problem bopping to the latest jazz grooves or severing human body parts with equal vigour. Suffering from a bizarre electra complex, her scene is man-hating in the first degree, and she is forced to re-enact the murder of her abusive father in her nightly excursions into the alleyways of psychosis. Black-hooded beings, not unlike the kuroko of traditional Japanese puppet theatre, act as the Greek Chorus, leading her through the events of her past and pointing her to her fate.

The woman wakes up from a nightmare, grabs her switchblade, and heads out for a night roaming the streets of shame, as her bruised neighbour's abusive husband is hauled away by the police. After being nearly attacked by a drunk, a stranger offers to pimp her to a john who looks suspiciously like Orson Welles, and she accepts, hoping to get her sadistic rocks off. She pushes him out of a window, then severs his hand when it refuses to let go of the pendant it ripped form her neck on the way down. Securing the pendant, she deposits the hand in a sickly flower-seller's basket and heads off to a basement jazz club for some serious bugging out.

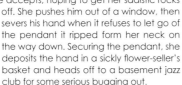

Pursued by a policeman (played by Ben Roseman, the same actor who plays her father), the woman becomes increasingly paranoid, and her world violently turns on her. There is no dialogue in the film; the only human sounds emitted are either insane laughter or grunts of distress. (It's worthy of note that Shorty Rogers of onscreen jazz band 'Shorty Rogers and His Giants' later wrote the score for the *Partridge Family* TV series). The eerie score and jarring jazz interludes have the effect of muting everyday sounds and emphasizing violent ones, which act as a fitting soundscape for the girl's psychosis. The film claims to be "the first Freudian Motion Picture". Freudian it is; the first it is most certainly not.

DESCENT

2007, USA
D: Talia Lugacy. P: Rosario Dawson, Morris S. Levy, Talia Lugacy. W: Talia Lugacy, Brian Priest. Ed: Frank Reynolds. DoP: Jonathan Furmanski, Christopher LaVasseur. M: Alex Moulton. PD: Tristam Steinberg. AD: Joel Custer. Cast: Rosario Dawson (Maya), Chad Faust (Jared), Marcus Patrick (Adrian), Vanessa Ferlito (Bodega girl), Jonathan Neil Schneider (Archeology Professor), James A. Stephens (Professor Byron), Nicole Vicius (Melanie), Paul Sado (downstairs guy), Scott Bailey (upstairs guy), Tracie Thoms (Denise)

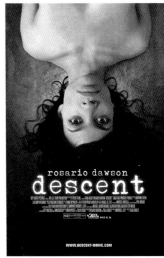

Maya (Rosario Dawson, who also co-produced) is a level-headed, romantically tentative college student on the path to academic success when she meets a football player named Jared (Chad Faust) who charms her into going on a date with him. After a candlelit dinner she ends up at his rooftop hideaway, trapped beneath him as he assaults her, whispering racial slurs (that the actor is clearly not comfortable with, and his performance suffers for it) in place of sweet nothings. She doesn't tell anyone; she just withdraws socially and loses her emotional footing.

In some ways the film follows the typical rape-revenge structure (Dawson's character cuts her hair short after the incident and stops wearing make-up, followed by a period of seductive hypersexuality) but because this is a date-rape film (like *Handgun*, discussed elsewhere in this appendix) the film's trajectory isn't allowed to be as cleanly retributive as it might when the rape is an act of random violence. The 'he said/she said' aspects of a date-rape case mean that a lot more is at stake when choosing to report the crime, which further compounds the humiliation.

Descent is also as much an examination of the safety of racial stereotypes as it is a rape-revenge film – after the incident it seems that Maya – who is of mixed descent – withdraws from white people altogether, as though the rape wasn't just a statement about the powerlessness/disposability of her gender but of her race as well. Over summer break she falls in with a beefy black/Latino nightclub DJ and his circle of acolytes, and it is while in this circle – with its mutable power dynamics, and games of bullying and manipulation – that she refuels, and hatches a plan to get revenge on her attacker.

While the film's violent climax betrays a sadistic shift in Maya's character that would seem more at home in a blatant exploitation film, rather than the realistic character study *Descent* posits itself as up to this point, it is unique on many levels – including its rare examination of interracial date-rape and its rather novel means of revenge.

left from top: Adrienne Barrett and her neck pendant in John Parker's **Dementia** (1953); Right: poster for Talia Lugacy's **Descent** (2007).

THE DEVIL'S WIDOW

1970, UK
Original title: **Tam Lin**
Alternative title: **The Ballad of Tam Lin**
D: Roddy McDowall. P: Alan Ladd Jr., Stanley Mann. W: Gerald Vaughan-Hughes. Ed: John Victor Smith. DoP: Billy Williams. M: Stanley Myers. PD: Donald M. Ashton. AD: John Graysmark. Cast: Ava Gardner (Mrs. Michaela 'Mickey' Cazaret), Ian McShane (Tom Lynn), Stephanie Beacham (Janet Ainsley), Cyril Cusack (Julian Ainsley), Richard Wattis (Elroy), David Whitman (Oliver), Madeline Smith (Sue), Sinead Cusack (Rose), Joanna Lumley (Georgia), Bruce Robinson (Alan)

Ava Gardner stars as a beautiful and mysterious older woman known affectionately as Mickey (abbreviated from Michaela) who uses her vast wealth as a means of luring young bohemians to her country estate for company. They are told they can stay as long as they like (or until she tires of them), and they spend their days leisurely playing games in the garden and being served cocktails while the men among them vie for the coveted spot as 'man of the hour'. The latest of Mickey's conquests is a young, dashing Ian McShane who vows his eternal love to her but then promptly falls for the local vicar's daughter (Stephanie Beacham, a genre regular throughout the '70s). This betrayal brings out Mickey's maniacal possessiveness: she tells McShane he has one week to get away before she will hunt him down and kill him.

This was a bit of a doomed film, and the only directorial effort of Roddy McDowall (who turned down his role in *Beneath the Planet of the Apes* because of his obligations here). Also known as *The Ballad of Tam Lin*, the film is based on a Robbie Burns poem which, in turn, is based on a Scottish folk legend about a young man named Tam Lin (adapted to Tom Lynn here) whose true love must rescue him from under the spell of an evil Faerie Queen.

Ava Gardner plays the ageing but charismatic Mickey with a perfect blend of grace, fierce sexuality and vulnerability. Surrounding herself with young people to help maintain her own sense of youthful vivaciousness inevitably only exaggerates her age, making her more self-conscious and vengeful. Her power dissipates as she loses herself in a savage revenge fantasy.

As an aside, many of the young hangers-on are played by then-emerging British actors including Madeline Smith, Joanna Lumley, Sinead Cusack and even Bruce Robinson, later to direct the cult classic *Withnail & I*.

above: Ava Gardner in Roddy McDowall's **The Devil's Widow** (1970).

THE DEVILS

1971, UK
D: Ken Russell. P: Ken Russell, Robert H. Solo. W: Ken Russell, Aldous Huxley (novel), John Whiting (play). Ed: Michael Bradsell. DoP: David Watkin. M: Peter Maxwell Davies, David Munrow. AD: Robert Cartwright.
Cast: Vanessa Redgrave (Sister Jeanne), Oliver Reed (Father Urbain Grandier), Dudley Sutton (Baron de Laubardemont), Max Adrian (Ibert), Gemma Jones (Madeleine), Murray Melvin (Father Mignon), Michael Gothard (Father Barre), Georgina Hale (Phillipe), Brian Murphy (Adam), Christopher Logue (Cardinal Richelieu)

Based on true events that occurred in Loudun, France in the 17th century, Ken Russell's notoriously-censored *The Devils* stars screen giant Oliver Reed as Urbain Grandier, a popular Catholic priest who takes control of the walled town of Loudon after the Governor's passing. His clandestine sexual proclivities come to the attention of Sister Jeanne (Vanessa Redgrave), who is sexually obsessed with him, and she sets about effecting his ruination. Sister Jeanne confesses to a fellow priest that Father Grandier is involved with witchcraft, and furthermore, that he has possessed all the nuns in the convent. When the maniacal Father Barre, inquisitor and professional witch-hunter, arrives on the scene to investigate Sister Jeanne's allegations, his interrogations prompt mass hysteria.
For more on this film see **Part 8: Heal Me with Hatred**.

DIABEL

1972, Poland
D: Andrzej Zulawski. W: Andrzej Zulawski. Ed: Krzysztof Osiecki. DoP: Maciej Kijowski. M: Andrzej Korzynski. PD: Jan Grandys.
Cast: Wojciech Pszoniak, Leszek Teleszynski (Jakub), Malgorzata Braunek (Jakub's fiancée), Iga Mayr, Wiktor Sadecki, Michal Grudzinski (Ezechiel), Maciej Englert, Monika Niemczyk (nun), Bozena Miefiodow, Marian Zdenicki

Andrzej Zulawski's second film opens in an insane asylum in 18th century Warsaw with the onset of the Prussian invasion. A small, black-clad man arrives at an asylum with the missive to lead one of its political prisoners – a man named Jakub, who had made an attempt on the life of the Prussian King – back to his home after a recent pardon. The asylum is a madhouse in more ways than one – not only are the inmates raving and filthy, but even the nuns who are meant to be tending to them have clearly gone mad. "I have never touched a human body before!" says one stout nun, her hands drenched in the blood of a dying combatant.

The weaselly escort puts the partially-mad Jakub on a horse with a completely mad young nun (for compassionate company) and then pops up routinely throughout Jakub's disturbing journey, in which he will find that his father has committed suicide, his mother has become a rich prostitute, his sister has gone mad after being the victim of repeated incestuous rape, and his beloved – played by Zulawski's then-wife Malgorzata Braunek – has also gone mad and married his best friend. It is revealed that her body was used as payment in exchange for Jakub's freedom, but her mind did not come out of the experience unscathed. She has the vacuous gaze of the Angel of the House, pregnant and sickly, her arms flailing and her mouth unable to annunciate. Jakub, tainted by the chaos that has enveloped his country and his loved ones, has no choice but to go mad as well, and with his impish guide leading him on (thus revealing himself to be the Devil of the title – albeit a snivelling and relatively powerless one) he commits a series of bloody murders.

While ostensibly an allegory for a particular event in the 1968 student riots, where *Diabel* is interesting to me as a genre fan is in its direct performative ties to Zulawski's later, more well-known works. *Diabel* is absolutely the prototype for the hysteria of Zulawski's *Possession*, and their respective characters mirror each other in type as well as in bodily mannerisms: anyone who's seen both films may recognize Jakub in *Possession*'s Marc (Sam Neill), Malgorzata Braunek's character in Anna (Adjani), The Devil in Anna's mystical lover Heinrich (Heinz Bennent), and the calm, placating nun in Anna's doppelganger, the schoolteacher. While these connections are obvious throughout, Malgorzata Braunek's performance here in particular is such a specific physical precedent for Adjani's in *Possession* that it makes me wonder if Zulawski's claims of hypnotizing his actresses are true.

Like many of Zulawski's films, this is a surreal journey that Zulawski scholar Daniel Bird has likened to Alejandro Jodorowsky's *El Topo* – while also pointing out its deep connection to the tradition of Polish Romanticism that accompanied the partitioning of Poland.[71] 19th century Polish Romantic literature is rife with the kinds of situations that seem to contemporary audiences like masturbatory excess in *Diabel*: heightened emotionalism, a respect for the irrational, fantasy and folktales, Messianism, female sexuality and hysteria. Without a country,

HOUSE OF PSYCHOTIC WOMEN

left: Vanessa Redgrave in Ken Russell's **The Devils** (1971).

seemingly abandoned by God and nurturing a deep mistrust of authority, the apocalyptic landscape of *Diabel* makes sense. And like Zulawski, many of the Polish Romantics developed their work and their idea of a Polish identity while exiled in Paris;[72] it was because of the banning of *Diabel* in Poland that Zulawski moved to Paris for the first time.

In the Australian SBS broadcast of the film (which is how I saw it), the host states that the Church banned *Diabel* on moral grounds. However, Daniel Bird clarifies that "The governing bureaucrats claimed *The Devil* was just too depraved. Zulawski, however, maintains that the decision to [ban] the film was political rather than moral."[73]

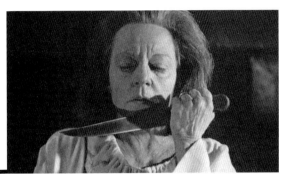

DIE! DIE! MY DARLING

1965, UK
Alternative title: **Fanatic**
D: Silvio Narizzano. P: Anthony Hinds. W: Richard Matheson, Anne Blaisdell (novel). Ed: John Dunsford. DoP: Arthur Ibbetson. M: Wilfred Josephs. PD: Peter Proud.
Cast: Tallulah Bankhead (Mrs. Trefoile), Stefanie Powers (Patricia Carroll), Peter Vaughan (Harry), Maurice Kaufmann (Alan Glentower), Yootha Joyce (Anna), Donald Sutherland (Joseph), Gwendolyn Watts (Gloria), Robert Dorning (Ormsby), Philip Gilbert (Oscar), Diana King (talkative woman shopper)

Stefanie Powers plays Patricia Carroll, a young woman about to get married, who decides to pay a courtesy visit to the mother of her former betrothed, Steven – who died in a car accident years earlier. Hoping to close an old chapter of her life, Patricia is naïvely frank with her would-be mother-in-law Mrs. Trefoile (Tallulah Bankhead in her last feature film role), who is driven over the edge by Pat's disclosures.

Under the auspices of inviting Pat to spend the night to attend mass together the next morning, Mrs. Trefoile traps her in the house, where she is subjected to a strict regimen of bible readings and fasting, locked in a small attic room and constantly chastised for her sinful life. However, Mrs. Trefoile is projecting her own sense of guilt onto her would-be daughter in law, as she doubtlessly did to her son, indirectly causing his suicide. Convincing herself (superficially) that Steven died an accidental death as a virginal innocent, she sets about redeeming his 'trampy' ex so that the two might

live together in purity when the judgement day comes. Mrs. Trefoile obviously sacrificed a great deal when she married her husband, who is long-since dead when the film opens, and lives vicariously through the 'sin' of others, only to punish herself by punishing them. She clearly admires her son for escaping, but has to maintain that he was a good Christian boy in order to keep from judging herself and the mistakes she might have made in her own life. With him dead, he cannot contradict her ideals, and he is raised in her mind to the level of martyrdom.

The psychotic matriarch Mrs. Trefoile doesn't fear her dead son outright, but she fears what he represents: freedom, culture, sin. Once a glamorous entertainer, she married a staunch religious man and became a frighteningly uptight old woman (an early prototype for Piper Laurie's Margaret White in *Carrie*), but she keeps a locked room in the basement filled with decadent fabrics, luridly coloured costumes, nude paintings, old theatre posters – all surrounding a portrait of her dead son Steven (wearing a collar-up pink shirt) like a shrine to his escape from their rigid Christian existence. In a moment of weakness she even reveals a hand-mirror, lipstick, and a bottle of hooch buried in her closet – but mirrors in general are not allowed in the house lest they encourage the sin of vanity.

Even more despicable than the domineering Mrs. Trefoile is the housekeeper Anna (Yootha Joyce), whose self-esteem is so non-existent that she allows her husband to cheat on her, and to be bullied into being a criminal accomplice to Mrs. Trefoile's imprisonment of the young visitor. Even when she finally takes action, she does so off-screen, so we never see her as a character with any agency whatsoever.

from top: Malgorzata Braunek (centre) in Andrzej Zulawski's **Diabel** (1972); Tallulah Bankhead in Silvio Narizzano's **Die! Die! My Darling** (1965).

THE DINNER PARTY

2009, Australia
D: Scott Murden. P: Brad Diebert, Brendan Sloane. W: Scott Murden. Ed: Greg Evans. DoP: Brett Murphy. M: Oonagh Sherrard. PD: Peta Black.
Cast: Lara Cox (Angela King), Ben Seton (Joel), Sam Lyndon (Matts), Mariane Power (Sky), Jessica Turner (Maddy), Kai Harris (Freddy), Jerome Pride (Derek), Brendan Sloane (Blake), Paul J. Murphy (Kell), Graham Gall (Police Officer)

A dinner party is a perfect place for dysfunction to come to light, but this particular dinner party brings its participants together for a sinister reason: to celebrate the pending suicide of its hosts, Angela and Joel. The only problem: Joel doesn't know that he's committing suicide, even though all the guests do.

Australian TV actress Lara Cox turns in what should have been a career-making performance as the psychotically unstable Angela. For the first ten minutes we only hear people talk about her – that she's beautiful but insecure, that she's drugged Joel with Rohypnol in the past and isolated him from his friends and relatives. Through flashbacks related via police interviews, it is shown that just prior to the party, Angela and her enabling friend Maddy purchased enough heroin for two people to overdose, which is how Angela plans to go out. But Maddy isn't the only enabler here; Joel himself is a nice guy who has allowed himself to become imprisoned in their relationship, and all the dinner guests, who wrestle with their moral obligations, nonetheless shrink from them. They are there for the food and the spectacle, and when things get uncomfortable, they all leave, abandoning Joel to his fate.

People comment on Angela's two-faced behaviour ("sweet and polite to your face but twisted behind your back") but her conflicting messages are not calculated, they are innate – she really is divided as a person. She treats Joel as though she resents him, but frequently pleads that she can't live without him; she wants to possess more than she understands how to love, but Angela's problems run deeper than jealousy. She is in a drama all her own (the moody score by Oonagh Sherrard contributes significantly to the creation of Angela's interior world) with Joel as an interchangeable appendage. It's frightening how, despite her aggressively neurotic behaviour, no one at the dinner table wants to do anything to curb the evening's inevitable climax.

above: Lara Cox in Scott Murden's **The Dinner Party** (2009).

DIRTY WEEKEND

1993, UK

D: Michael Winner. P: Michael Winner, Robert Earl. W: Michael Winner, Helen Zahavi. Ed: Michael Winner. DoP: Alan Jones.
M: David Fanshawe. PD: Crispian Sallis.
Cast: Lia Williams (Bella), Ian Richardson (Nimrod), David McCallum (Reggie), Rufus Sewell (Tim), Miriam Kelly (Marion), Sylvia Syms (Mrs. Crosby), Jack Galloway (David), Shaughan Seymour (Charles), Michael Cule (Norman), Christopher Ryan (Small One).

"This is the story of Bella, who woke up one morning and decided she'd had enough."

Death Wish director Michael Winner returns to vigilante territory with this rape-revenge picture adapted by Helen Zahavi from her own book. Lia Williams stars as Bella, a bookish London woman who moves to Brighton after her boyfriend cheats on her, and gets a low-paying job as a temp secretary. This leaves her little money for added security when the creep in the apartment opposite the courtyard from her (a pasty-looking Rufus Sewell) starts making threatening phone calls, pledging to rape and mutilate her. When she turns to the police, the officer on the case refuses to help when she spurns his inappropriate sexual advances.

With her would-be killer closing in – he starts approaching her in the open, out on the streets – she is convinced by a clairvoyant to take action on her own. She buys an illegal handgun, breaks into the neighbour's house and kills him in his sleep – waking him up just long enough to be aware of the vengeful nature of her visit. After killing her tormenter, Bella becomes a highly sexualized predator herself. She gets a "burning sensation" that has to be satiated by sex with a sleazy stranger who she will kill afterward.

As with many of the genre's most challenging films (and admittedly this one is challenging in part because of its over-the-top hammy performances), what often begins as a sympathetic plight transforms into severe anti-social behaviour. An ongoing criticism of rape-revenge films is the uncomfortable relationship between an ostensibly feminist political agenda and the context of an exploitation film. Once the women decide on a retributive course of action, they often utilize seductive prowess as part of the plan: they adopt the role of the femme fatale in order to lure their offenders into humiliating situations – which implies manipulation, deceit and entrapment. "You're going to die because you're unlucky", she whispers sweetly to her rotund victim, Norman. "Because the rules have changed and no one let you know."

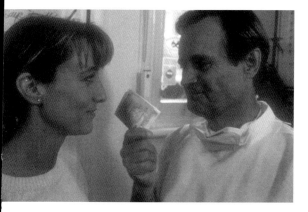

Lia Williams and David McCallum in **Dirty Weekend** (1993).

DR. JEKYLL AND HIS WOMEN

1981, France
Original title: **Dr. Jekyll et les femmes**
Alternative title: **The Blood of Dr. Jekyll**
D: Walerian Borowczyk. P: Robert Kuperberg, Jean-Pierre Labrande. W: Walerian Borowczyk, Robert Louis Stevenson (novella). Ed: Khadicha Bariha. DoP: Noël Véry. M: Bernard Parmegiani. PD: Walerian Borowczyk. Cast: Udo Kier (Dr. Henry Jekyll), Marina Pierro (Miss Fanny Osbourne), Patrick Magee (General), Gérard Zalcberg (Mr. Hyde), Howard Vernon (Dr. Lanyon), Clément Harari (Reverend Donald Regan), Jean Mylonas, Eugene Braun Munk, Louis Michel Colla, Catherine Coste

One of the neglected auteurs of the European fantastic, Walerian Borowczyk was known for his bizarre erotic tales that depicted women as creatures with an all-consuming sexuality (most notably in *The Beast* (1975), which included among its many 'perversions' a woman enjoying her rape at the paws of the famed Beast of Gévaudan). By the time *Jekyll* was released, Borowczyk had been all but dismissed by serious critics as a pornographer even though, by his own standards, *Jekyll* seems tame in that regard. It is also the closest he came to making an outright horror film.

Jekyll takes place entirely in one night, during a dinner party celebrating the engagement of Henry Jekyll (Udo Kier) and Fanny Osbourne (Borowczyk regular Marina Pierro). A heavy-handed philosophical debate between the eccentric Dr. Jekyll and a fellow doctor (eurotrash staple Howard Vernon) occurs at the dinner table, and when the guests retire following the meal, the mysterious Mr. Hyde shows up and upsets the household with a spree of rape, sodomy and murder – with a 35cm penis his weapon of choice. Fanny receives a note from her betrothed advising her to keep away from him until he contacts her, but she hides in the lab and witnesses Jekyll's transformation into the diabolical Mr. Hyde, by means of bathing in a tub of red liquid. Hyde discovers her and tries to kill her, but as he starts to revert back to Jekyll he realizes what he's done, and carries her off to the lab in hopes of healing her wounds. To his shock and surprise, she leaps into the bath, immersing herself in the mutative potion.

The film belongs to Jekyll and his well-endowed alter-ego, but the previously unassuming Miss Osbourne surprises us all in the last act with her dip into Jekyll's bath – knowing full well what the result will be. With moist red eyes denoting her transformation, she beckons the bewildered Jekyll into the bath with her. Since he has no more of the reverse elixir, he knows this journey will be the final one, with no turning back. With this, they give themselves over to their most primal instincts, both lustful and homicidal. The two set off on a massacre in the bourgeois household, dripping wet, manic, insatiable. The image of Pierro licking Udo's wounds as they escape the scene in their carriage is one of the most striking in Borowczyk's oeuvre. Pierro so aptly captures the unsullied naïveté of her character that her metamorphosis seems that much more savage and violent. Most of Borowczyk's films are concerned with Victorian repression and its inevitable undoing, and *Jekyll* is no exception.

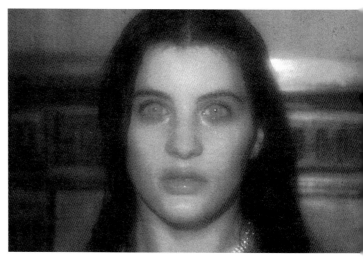

from top: Three faces of Marina Pierro in Walerian Borowczyk's **Dr. Jekyll and His Women** (1981).

DON'T DELIVER US FROM EVIL

1970, France
Original title: **Mais ne nous délivrez pas du mal**
D: Joël Séria. P: Bernard Legargeant. W: Joël Séria.
Ed: Philippe Gosselet. DoP: Marcel Combes. M:
Dominique Ney, Claude Germain. AD: Jac Adam.
Cast: Jeanne Goupil (Anne), Catherine Wagener
(Lore), Jean-Pierre Helbert (The Count), Véronique
Silver (The Countess), Henri Poirier (Mr. Fournier),
Nicole Mérouze (Mrs. Fournier), Gérard Darrieu
(Emile), René Berthier (Gustave), Michel Robin
(Léon), Serge Frédéric (Priest)

Inspired by the real life story of 1950s teenage
murderesses Pauline Parker and Juliet Hulme (who
also formed the basis for Peter Jackson's *Heavenly Creatures* in 1994), the duo of delinquent girls in *Don't Deliver Us from Evil* are
expert mischief-makers who spend their weekdays in a Catholic boarding school, and weekends and vacations with their oblivious
parents in the French countryside. Anne, the more dominant of the two girls, gets a kick out of evil-doing, whether it's confessing
to sins of impurity that she didn't commit just to embarrass the priest, reading dirty books, seducing simpletons, torturing animals,
or spitting out her communion wafers to save them up for a Black Mass. Her sweet-faced companion Lore is less of a criminal
mastermind, but enthusiastically partakes in Anne's campaigns to traumatize nearly everyone who comes into contact with them.
Both are careful to feign innocence around their parents, lest they be forbidden from seeing one another. The two girls determine
that they can never be apart, and make a drastic decision that will keep them together in hell for eternity.
For more on this film see **Part 5: Afterschool Special.**

DON'T LOOK NOW

1973, UK/Italy
Alternative title: **A Venezia… un dicembre rosso shocking**
D: Nicolas Roeg. P: Peter Katz. W: Alan Scott, Chris Bryant,
Daphne du Maurier (story). Ed: Graeme Clifford. DoP:
Anthony Richmond. M: Pino Donaggio. AD: Giovanni Soccol.
Cast: Julie Christie (Laura Baxter), Donald Sutherland (John
Baxter), Hilary Mason (Heather), Clelia Matania (Wendy),
Massimo Serato (Bishop Barbarrigo), Renato Scarpa
(Inspector Longhi), Giorgio Trestini (workman), Leopoldo
Trieste (hotel manager), David Tree (Anthony Babbage), Ann
Rye (Mandy Babbage)

One of the most stunning, elegiac horror films ever made,
Nicolas Roeg's film of the Daphne du Maurier short story stars
Donald Sutherland and Julie Christie as John and Laura, a
couple grieving the recent loss of their young daughter who
drowned in the pond behind their rural English home. With John
summoned to Venice to oversee the restoration of a crumbling
church, the couple attempt to have a working vacation in this
watery, cold and somewhat inhospitable place.

Laura meets two sisters, one of them a blind psychic who claims that she has seen their little girl, sitting between them and
laughing. Laura faints, but she is swiftly reinvigorated by the idea that the blind seer offers a line of communication between herself
and her dead daughter, and the aggressive pursuit of this idea is where she crosses the line into neurotic behaviour, something her
husband John is quick to point out. "My daughter is dead, Laura. She does not come peeping back with messages from behind
the fucking grave. Christine is dead, she is dead! Dead, dead, dead, dead, dead!" "You must think I'm ill then", she whispers,
practically cowering from him. He nods: "Yeah." She starts questioning herself and her relationship with the two women. Her
physicality changes abruptly from a confident, enthusiastic woman to one hunched over with shame and guilt. John encourages
her to self-medicate, jumping up to fetch her a glass of water when she suggests that maybe she should start taking her pills again.
But ultimately this film is about his neurosis, not hers. Laura is going through varying stages trying to deal with grief, trying out different
things to see what works, and naturally some methods of healing seem crazier than others – whereas John is in a state of denial
that will blind him to his own inevitable fate.

from top: Teen temptresses in Joel Séria's **Don't Deliver Us from Evil** (1970); Julie Christie in Nicolas Roeg's **Don't Look Now** (1973).

DON'T TORTURE A DUCKLING

1972, Italy
Original title: **Non si sevizia un paperino**
D: Lucio Fulci. W: Lucio Fulci, Roberto Gianviti, Gianfranco Clerici. Ed: Ornella Micheli. DoP: Sergio D'Offizi. M: Riz Ortolani.
Cast: Florinda Bolkan (Maciara), Barbara Bouchet (Barbara, 'Miss Patrizia'), Tomas Milian (Andrea Martelli), Irene Papas (Aurelia Avallone), Marc Porel (Alberto Avallone), Georges Wilson (Francesco), Antonello Campodifiori (police lieutenant), Ugo D'Alessio (Captain Podesti), Virginio Gazzolo (commissioner)

It has often been said that the stringent Catholicism of Italy and Spain contributed greatly to the luridness of their horror films, the sleaziness of their comedies, the predatory nature of their thrillers. It's no surprise; the Catholic religion is a staunch advocate of repression and self-denial, which usually just results in exactly the kind of sexually transgressive behaviour they are trying to warn against.

A case in point: the murderous priest Don Alberto (Marc Porel) in Lucio Fulci's *Don't Torture a Duckling* has been strangling pre-pubescent boys to death as a means of preserving their 'sexual innocence'. He is accused of paedophilia and leaps to his death from a cliff, even though it's left unclear whether or not he has acted on his sexual inclinations. Conversely, Barbara Bouchet's character Patrizia is overtly paedophilic, but this issue is glossed over in the film; it is depicted as a 'quirk' in her personality that is not worthy of condemnation. Meanwhile the priest is both publicly condemned and racked with sexual confusion. While his actions are interpreted as repressed pederasty (even if there are no signs of actual sexual abuse), Patrizia's brazen exhibitionism and manipulation of little boys is seen as totally acceptable within the framework of the film.

It's no secret how Fulci felt about the Church, but the homophobia apparent in his differing treatment of the two paedophiles is suspect. Why isn't Bouchet subject to the same scrutiny? It's a typical European response to the notion of an inexperienced boy receiving sexual attention from an older, more experienced woman; in Italian cinema, this is often the stuff of farce. Don Alberto fetishizes the boys' innocence – but perhaps Fulci is merely using Bouchet's character as a means of showing that the kids were never innocent to begin with.

DOPPELGANGER

1993, USA
D: Avi Nesher. P: Donald P. Borchers. W: Avi Nesher. Ed: Tatiana S. Riegel. DoP: Sven Kirsten. M: Jan A.P. Kaczmarek. PD: Ivo Cristante. AD: Ken Larson.
Cast: Drew Barrymore (Holly Gooding), George Newbern (Patrick Highsmith), Dennis Christopher (Doctor Heller), Leslie Hope (Elizabeth), Sally Kellerman (Sister Jan), George Maharis (Mike Wallace), Peter Dobson (Rob), Carl Bressler (Larry Spaulding), Dan Shor (Stanley White), Jaid Barrymore (Mrs. Gooding)

One of Israeli director Avi Nesher's few U.S.-based outings, and one of the first dramatic roles of Drew Barrymore's post-recovery renaissance, *Doppelganger* stars Barrymore as Holly Gooding, a young woman with a murderous double. After beating a murder charge following the bloody death of her mother (played with an ironic wink by Barrymore's real-life mother Jaid Barrymore), Holly packs up and heads to L.A., where her brother Fred is in a mental hospital. She takes up a room in the apartment of struggling screenwriter Patrick Highsmith (George Newbern), who quickly becomes enamoured with Holly's various personalities – the sweet, naïve Holly and her hyper-sexualized animalistic other. Before he knows it, he's caught up in a mystery more exciting and convoluted than anything he could have dreamt up in a script.

With both parents dead, Holly and her brother Fred stand to inherit a great deal of money, which – according to the police – makes Fred a target for the murderous attentions of Holly's doppelganger. Soon enough, Fred is the victim of a brutal attack that he barely survives, but Fred's not talking – he hasn't spoken a word since he was committed at the age of 11, under suspicion of killing their father by tossing him from a window in their large Gothic family home. You see, Holly not only believes that she has a doppelganger shadowing her, but believes that Fred has one too – that their family is 'cursed'. With the encouragement of Holly's blasé long-time shrink (Dennis Christopher of *Fade to Black*, characteristically hamming it up), George soon buys into the whole doppelganger theory and vows to help Holly defeat it.

"If you're good you must never blame yourself for misfortunes that come your way", Holly says to George, opening herself up to the inevitable question: "Did you blame yourself when your parents died?" and thus blowing the lid on the whole doppelganger phenomenon – namely that a doppelganger is a repository for repressed desires and a means of escaping responsibility for things that might otherwise rack us with guilt. When you have two siblings accused of murdering two separate parents and an opening credit sequence that plays over a music box inscribed with the words "To Holly, Love Daddy", it doesn't take a genius to figure out that Holly is repressing something horrible related to dear old dead dad.

The film is incredibly goofy and the only standout in the cast is Leslie Hope as Patrick's motor-mouthed, lovelorn writing partner, but the film at least attempts to play out textbook doppelganger theory to the best of its limited abilities, through imagery as well as through long sequences of exposition. This is ironic in itself given psychology's emphasis on the 'talking cure' – since if the characters are so willing to lay everything on the table there likely wouldn't be a doppelganger in the first place.

DRACULA'S DAUGHTER

1936, USA
D: Lambert Hillyer. W: Garrett Fort, John L.
Balderston, Bram Stoker (story). Ed: Milton Carruth.
DoP: George Robinson. M: Heinz Roemheld
(uncredited). AD: Albert S. D'Agostino.
Cast: Otto Kruger (Jeffrey Garth), Gloria Holden
(Countess Marya Zaleska), Marguerite Churchill
(Janet Blake), Edward Van Sloan (Professor Von
Helsing), Gilbert Emery (Sir Basil Humphrey), Irving
Pichel (Sandor), Halliwell Hobbes (Sergeant
Hawkins), Billy Bevan (Albert, police constable),
Nan Grey (Lili), Hedda Hopper (Lady Esme
Hammond)

"The strength of the vampire lies in the fact that
he is unbelievable", says Von Helsing to Sir Basil
Humphrey at Scotland Yard, when he is charged
with the murders of Count Dracula and his imbecilic
henchman Renfield in this sequel to Universal's 1931
Dracula. Requesting the famed psychiatrist Dr.
Jeffrey Garth to defend him in court will begin the
film's exploration of the science vs. folklore debate
that will posit the supernatural as a symptom of
mental illness.

Dracula's daughter, Countess Marya Zaleska
(Gloria Holden in a truly spellbinding performance),
certainly knows how to enter a room: wrapped
completely in a black shroud with only her pleading
yet baleful eyes peering through, she hypnotizes the
jailhouse minder in order to steal her father's body
and set it aflame, in the hope that it may cure her
hereditary blood-drinking illness. With her father
dead and his supernatural grip on her supposedly
dissipated, she celebrates her transference into the
realm of 'normality' by sitting down at the piano to
play a happy song as a 'free woman', but even her
lullaby transforms into an ominous dirge. "That music
doesn't speak of release", says her imposing servant
Sandor, who urges her to own up to what she is. "That
music tells of the dark. Evil things. Shadowy places."
When he looks into her eyes and claims to see only
death, Marya realizes that the curse is not lifted. Like
Irena would do in *Cat People* six years later, Marya
turns to psychiatry to help free her from her folkloric
beliefs, which those in the scientific community would
claim have been bred into her through conditioning.
"Sympathetic treatment will release the human mind
from any obsession", says Von Helsing's protégé Dr.
Garth, attempting to convince her that her 'illness'
can be cured with therapy and willpower.[74]

The primary influence on Michael Almereyda's
revisionist vampire film *Nadja* (1994), starring Elina
Löwensohn as the equally exotic counterpart to
Gloria Holden's Countess Marya Zaleska, both
films see their tragic protagonists abandon hope,
relinquishing themselves to their damned fate,
seeking instead to take a mate with them into the
liminal realm of the undead. But in giving up, Marya
ceases to be sympathetic, and resigns herself to the
role of the villain.

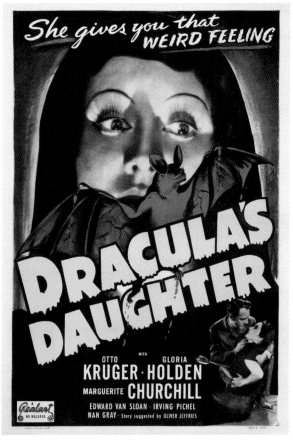

above: Gloria Holden features in a still and poster for Lambert Hillyer's **Dracula's Daughter** (1936).

DREAM HOME

2010, Hong Kong
Original title: **Wai dor lei ah yut ho**
D: Pang Ho-cheung. P: Pang Ho-cheung, Conroy Chan, Josie Ho, Leung Kai-yun. W: Pang Ho-cheung, Derek Tsang, Jimmy Wan. Ed: Wenders Li. DoP: Yu Lik-wai. M: Gabriele Roberto. PD: Man Lim-chung.
Cast: Josie Ho (Cheng Lai-sheung), Eason Chan (Siu To), Derek Tsang (Cheung Jai), Lawrence Chou (On Jai), Juno Mak (Cop Fat), Michelle Ye (flat 8A female owner), Norman Chu (Sheung's father), Paw Hee-ching (Sheung's mother), Lo Hoi-pang (Sheung's grandpa), Wong Ching (security guard)

Singer/actress Josie Ho stars in and exec-produced this Hong Kong slasher film inspired by the audacity of notorious category III film *Riki-Oh*. Ho stars as Cheng Lai-sheung, a bank telemarketer who moonlights in retail in a desperate attempt to save funds for an expensive waterfront apartment. The film flits back and forth between the present – in which Ho's character graphically maims and dismembers the residents of her much-coveted high rise community – and the past, which shows her repeated failures to get ahead financially despite her work ethic.

At her day job, she is one of few employees with any empathy towards debt-ridden customers, and her initial motivation to purchase the expensive housing property is to care for her family, who have habitually lived in crowded tenements and been the victims of triad harassment as these areas were targeted for gentrification. But as she becomes more obsessed with her goal, her altruistic concern for her family dissipates, and repeated seemingly catastrophic disappointments cause her to dissociate (this process rendered beautifully through a sequence in which the background moves shakily in a different speed and direction from the character). While the film does its best to convey a rationale for Cheng Lai-sheung's homicidal turning point, the severity of her crimes – which include asphyxiating a pregnant woman with a vacuum hose – doesn't make sense without establishing some kind of long-time sadistic streak.

As such, tonally the film is rather schizophrenic, its gorgeous visuals and colour palette (including lighting from Wong Kar-wai main man Wong Chi-ming) contrasting awkwardly with over-the-top gore and cruelty. The opening credits indicate that it is based on a true story, but the 'truth' here refers less to the lead character's exploits than to the brutal statistics laid out in the film's preamble, which indicate the shocking discrepancy between the cost of living and the income of the average citizen. Still, despite its flaws, *Dream Home* was a much-needed kick for Hong Kong horror at the time of production.

above: Josie Ho in Pang Ho-cheung's **Dream Home** (2010).

THE ENTITY

1982, USA
D: Sidney J. Furie. P: Harold Schneider. W: Frank De Felitta.
Ed: Frank J. Urioste. DoP: Stephen H. Burum. M: Charles
Bernstein. PD: Charles Rosen.
Cast: Barbara Hershey (Carla Moran), Ron Silver (Dr. Phil
Sneiderman), David Labiosa (Billy Moran), George Coe
(Dr. Weber), Maggie Blye (Cindy Nash), Jacqueline Brooks
(Dr. Elizabeth Cooley), Richard Brestoff (Gene Kraft), Michael
Alldredge (George Nash), Raymond Singer (Joe Mehan), Alex
Rocco (Jerry Anderson)

In this controversial film based on a true story, director Furie
explores the domestically-abused-woman-as-masochist
stereotype by veiling it as a supernatural horror film. Carla
Moran (Barbara Hershey) is a single mother whose struggle
to get by is aggravated by the presence of an extremely
violent, foul-smelling and distinctly masculine ghost. The
entity threatens her body as much as her sanity; it repeatedly
and brutally rapes her, in one instance in front of her children,
and another while she is fast asleep. Her boyfriend Jerry
(Alex Rocco) is talked about more than seen; he is away on
business trips for most of the film.

    As the entity's attacks intensify, Carla assumes the role
of the abused housewife, which is especially fitting since the
absence of a patriarch in the home leaves room for the entity
itself to function as a sort of drunk, violent husband. Furthermore,
the entity attacks her in a friend's home, and in her car, which
causes her to retreat into the physical and emotional isolation
that is characteristic of many victims of domestic abuse.
Close-ups of her increasingly vacant, detached gaze signify
her resignation to the violence. When she visits a psychiatrist
and later invites a team of parapsychologists in to monitor her
home, the two opposing schools of thought clash, with Carla
as the defeated victim in the middle.
For more on this film see **Part 1: Walking Wounded**.

THE ESCAPEES

1981, France
Original title: **Les paumées du petit matin**
Alternative title: **Les échappées**
D: Jean Rollin. W: Jean Rollin, Jacques Ralf. DoP: Claude
Bécognée. M: Philippe D'Aram.
Cast: Laurence Dubas (Michelle), Christiane Coppé (Marie),
Marianne Valiot (Sophie), Patrick Perrot (Pierrot), Louise Dhour
(Mme Louise), Jean-Louis Fortuit, Jean Hérel, Claude Lévèque,
Patricia Mercurol, Brigitte Lahaie

Rollin's elegiac tales are often
populated by lost women
in the midst of a physical
or emotional journey, but
in this case the approach
is more literal, with its two
protagonists recent escapees
from a mental hospital in
the French countryside.
18-year-old Marie has been
hospitalized on numerous
occasions for "incurable
inability to communicate
with the outside world". But
there must be something in
the world that she wants,
because she leaves the
staid care of the hospital for
the unpredictable outside
in the company of Michelle,
the hysterical, strait-jacketed
fellow inmate who kicks,
screams and communicates in all the ways that Marie can't.
"They say I'm sick. Very sick", Marie explains to Michelle when
they first meet. "But I try to find out what's wrong and I can't.
I'm afraid of everything. Sometimes my whole body shakes."
On their journey they hook up with a travelling exotic theatre
(resulting in the great set piece of a vintage fairground stage set
up in a junkyard), a confident leather-clad petty thief named
Sophie (who repeatedly extols the virtues of life on the margins),
a matronly barkeep and some sleazy yuppies (including Rollin
regular Brigitte Lahaie) who will prove their undoing.

    Marie becomes instantly and inexplicably bound to
Michelle, clinging to her as though her only hope for sanity
rests in this one relationship. Michelle finds the girl's needy
behaviour annoying, but something in her must appreciate
being needed, because despite her threats to turn the girl
away, she always relents and consoles her. Marie goes
through circles of existential crisis and – like the characters
in Rollin's La nuit des traquées of a year earlier (reviewed
elsewhere in this appendix) – she finds re-affirmation of her
identity in Michelle. "I no longer exist", she says. "I slide into
a world of wonder. Everything is a reflection. Everything is
still. Frozen. Everything is silence. I'm in a swirl of laughter. I
am sunshine. I am light. I am Marie." Brigitte has the same
relationship with her boyfriend Pierrot – but these relationships
are doomed, because the characters can't figure out how
to let go and to hold on tight simultaneously. In the pseudo-
supernatural world of Rollin perhaps this paradox can work,
but in real life it can only implode.

left: Barbara Hershey enveloped by chaos in **The Entity** (1982); right: Christiane Coppé and Laurence Dubas in Jean Rollin's **The Escapees** (1981).

HOUSE OF PSYCHOTIC WOMEN

EYES OF A STRANGER

1981, USA

D: Ken Wiederhorn. P: Ronald Zerra. W: Mark Jackson [Ron Kurz], Eric L. Bloom. Ed: Rick Shaine. DoP: Mini Rojas. M: Richard Einhorn, Red Neinkirchen. AD: Jessica Sack.

Cast: Lauren Tewes (Jane Harris), Jennifer Jason Leigh (Tracy Harris), John DiSanti (Stanley Herbert), Peter DuPre (David), Gwen Lewis (Debbie Ormsley), Kitty Lunn (Annette), Timothy Hawkins (Jeff), Ted Richert (Roger England), Toni Crabtree (Mona), Robert Small (Dr. Bob)

A brutal classic of the early slasher craze from the director of underwater Nazi zombie flick *Shock Waves* (which is seen playing on television in the film).

When a young woman's defiled body is found in the swamps on the outskirts of Miami, news anchor Jane Harris (Lauren Tewes of TV's *The Love Boat*) makes a special point of warning women in the audience to report any suspicious behaviour to the police. Her overzealousness on the air is a response to her own sister Tracy's rape as a child, which left the girl (Jennifer Jason Leigh in her first feature film role) psychosomatically blind and deaf.

While the story revolves around Tewes's amateur investigation of the murders (she is convinced that her creepy

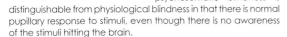

neighbour is the killer), and she becomes fixated on solving the crime herself through questionable means, the neurotic woman in the film is technically Tracy, even though she exhibits no sign of trauma other than her psychosomatic disorders. Once referred to as a type of hysteria (now know as a 'conversion disorder'), psychosomatic blindness is distinguishable from physiological blindness in that there is normal pupillary response to stimuli, even though there is no awareness of the stimuli hitting the brain.

These symptoms are a means of concealing a painful message; they can be cured through confronting the repressed trauma. In real life this is done through hypnosis and biofeedback, but in films this often means reliving the trauma through a repeated attack – which makes for a spectacular climactic sequence that shows off Leigh's acting chops.

FATAL ATTRACTION

1987, USA

D: Adrian Lyne. P: Stanley R. Jaffe, Sherry Lansing. W: James Dearden, Nicholas Meyer (uncredited). Ed: Michael Kahn, Peter E. Berger. DoP: Howard Atherton. M: Maurice Jarre. PD: Mel Bourne. AD: Jack Blackman.

Cast: Michael Douglas (Dan Gallagher), Glenn Close (Alex Forrest), Anne Archer (Beth Gallagher), Ellen Hamilton Latzen (Ellen Gallagher), Stuart Pankin (Jimmy), Ellen Foley (Hildy), Fred Gwynne (Arthur), Meg Mundy (Joan Rogerson), Tom Brennan (Howard Rogerson), Lois Smith (Martha)

Although its A-list cast and mainstream popularity (it was nominated for 6 Oscars) pushes it outside the realm of interest for a lot of genre fans, *Fatal Attraction* was a pivotal film for a number of reasons: it's an erotic thriller (that *most* '80s of genres, next to the BMX/skateboard saving-the-clubhouse dance-off movie) that functioned simultaneously as an AIDS allegory, a consumerist manifesto, a testament to the ubiquitousness of the self-improvement industry, and most of all, a giant billboard-sized advertisement for the sanctity of marriage. But what concerns me here is its more face-value depiction of the single woman as fundamentally unable to exist without male commitment and the subsequent mental unravelling of a particular woman when she is spurned by her weekend fling (that said, the plot is taken directly from Clint Eastwood's earlier *Play Misty for Me* and Reagan-ized so that Eastwood's bohemian bachelor is now a yuppie family man).

There is no doubt about it: Glenn Close as Alex Forrest is terrifying in this film, and a very palpable threat to married men who can't keep it in their pants. When she and Dan Gallagher (Michael Douglas) first lock eyes at the book launch for 'Samurai Self-Help', she is already determined to get him – wife or no wife. "I guess you better run along", she says when she spies Dan's (incredibly fit, gorgeous, patient, capable and compassionate) other half Beth (Anne Archer), as though the old ball-and-chain has come to drag him away from all the fun. And this will be Alex's primary tactic – over their subsequent weekend together she is determined to show him all the fun she thinks he must be missing: sex in elevators, sex on countertops, late-night dancing, Madame Butterfly at full volume. And just in case that all seems too superficial and unsustainable, she can also cook, play catch in the park with the dog, and manage a high-level exec job at a publishing firm. She's the perfect woman! So, needless to say, she's surprised when he won't suddenly up and leave his wife after their weekend of Tantric fulfilment. But Dan lays it all out: they had an agreement; no strings attached; she knew the score. She assured him she was 'discreet', but of course she's not discreet, and she's not able to let go after one weekend – it was all a trick (because no woman really wants to be alone, right?). When she sees him with his family, enjoying their new suburban house, she vomits. This is her body telling her that she *doesn't want that kind of life*, but she doesn't listen. She just keeps barrelling toward the impending train wreck.

Alex lies, manipulates and plays whatever mood she has to – alternating freely between soft-spoken and calm to knife-wielding maniac – depending on his reaction. She'll slit her wrists, boil his pet rabbit, kidnap his daughter (this is where the AIDS allegory kicks in, as Dan's promiscuity 'contaminates' the rest of his family); whatever it takes. When he tries to strangle Alex, she says disturbingly "Go ahead hit me! If you can't fuck me, then hit me!" She wants to be bound to him through whatever means necessary, whether through shared guilt, abuse, pregnancy or death. The most amazing scene in the film intercuts scenes of Dan and friends at the bowling alley, living out the 'lifestyle' of married grown-ups, with Alex slumped against a wall in her apartment, switching a lamp off and on repeatedly in mechanical dissociation while Madame Butterfly swells on the cassette player, creating a parallel between Alex and the opera's jilted lover who commits suicide – which is how *Fatal Attraction* was supposed to end before test screenings demanded a less peaceful demise for its villain.[75]

above: Jennifer Jason Leigh and John DiSanti in Ken Wiederhorn's **Eyes of a Stranger** (1981).

FEED

2005, Australia

D: Brett Leonard. P: Melissa Beauford. W: Kieran Galvin, Alex O'Loughlin (story), Patrick Thompson (story). Ed: Mark Bennett. DoP: Steve Arnold. M: Gregg Leonard, Geoff Michael. PD: Jessamy Llewelyn.
Cast: Alex O'Loughlin (Michael Carter), Patrick Thompson (Phillip Jackson), Gabby Millgate (Deidre), Jack Thompson (Richard), Rose Ashton (Abbey), Matthew Le Nevez (Nigel), David Field (Father Turner), Sherly Sulaiman (Mary), Marika Aubrey (Jesse), Adam Hunt (German cannibal)

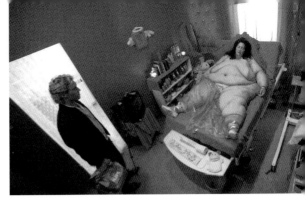

Based on a story co-written by its leads Alex O'Loughlin and Patrick Thompson (the son of actor Jack Thompson, who also stars), *Feed* is unique in its examination of the unusual sexual fetishes of 'feeding' and 'gaining' within a fictional horror film context.

O'Loughlin stars as Michael Carter, a demented serial killer who runs a website where he streams live video footage of himself feeding fat women to death and taking bets from online members as to how long they will hold out. But the obese women being fed to death are there voluntarily; while they lay immobile as they are stuffed with food, they clearly derive immense sexual pleasure out of the acts they perform. This is not because they are grateful to Michael and their online 'fans' for accepting their weight as beautiful, because they are *not* accepted per se; they are coerced into becoming more fat, *lethally* fat. The women are dehumanized through this process (which is emphasized further by the fact that people are betting on their mortality), and while the film is supremely interesting it definitely calls for further investigation into their real-life counterparts.

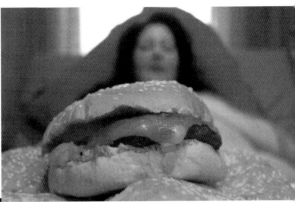

FIVE ACROSS THE EYES

2006, USA

D: Greg Swinson, Ryan Thiessen. P: Rick Stroud, Greg Swinson, Ryan Thiessen. W: Greg Swinson, Marshall Hicks. Ed: Ryan Thiessen. DoP: Ryan Thiessen. M: Shannon McDowell, David Risdahl.
Cast: Sandra Paduch (Isabella), Danielle Lilley (Jamie), Mia Yi (Melanie), Angela Brunda (Caroline), Jennifer Barnett (Stephanie), Veronica Garcia (driver), Dave Jarnigan (store clerk), Keith Smith (dead body in SUV), Abby Vessell (dead body in SUV), Jane Swinson (dead body in SUV)

If you ever wondered what it would be like to spend 90 minutes in a car with 5 screaming teenage girls, *Five Across the Eyes* is the film for you. Shot entirely within the confines of a vehicle – even when the action takes them outside of the van, the camera stays behind – this gimmick is one of the only noteworthy elements of this otherwise by-the-numbers film about a group of girls who take a shortcut on the way home from a football game and find themselves terrorized on an isolated back road by a psychotic woman in a business power suit.

While there is no overt sequence of exposition, it's clear that the woman sees this group as representative of the kinds of young girls who might steal her husband away – she keeps calling them "homewreckers", admonishing them that "older men are not available" and is insistent that the girls have "hurt her babies". In fact the only contact the girls have had with her is in accidentally dinging her car in a parking lot and knocking out one of her headlights. But the Driver (as she is credited) fixates on them and decides that they are responsible for her misfortunes, whatever they may be.

The Driver is utterly hysterical, waving a shotgun around and screaming, jumping on their car, grabbing frantically through their windows, smashing at them with hammers, violating their genitals (off-screen) with various tools – but it never transcends a predictable 'crazy person' performance into truly believable frenzy. There's no real sense of the layers of trauma that converge into the kind of craziness the actress is trying to channel here.

The most uniquely neurotic behaviour exhibited in the film is by one of the victims, who shits in her own hand so that she can throw it at the Driver's windshield.

from top: Alex O'Loughlin and Gabby Millgate in Brett Leonard's **Feed** (2005); Artwork for Greg Swinson and Ryan Thiessen's **Five Across the Eyes** (2006).

FOOTPRINTS

1975, Italy
Original title: **Le orme**
Alternative title: **Primal Impulse**
D: Luigi Bazzoni. P: Luciano Perugia. W: Mario Fenelli, Luigi Bazzoni. Ed: Roberto Perpignani. DoP: Vittorio Storaro. M: Nicola Piovani. AD: Pierluigi Pizzi.
Cast: Florinda Bolkan (Alice Campos), Peter McEnery (Henry), Caterina Boratto (boutique owner), Evelyn Stewart [Ida Galli] (Mary), Lila Kedrova (Mrs. Heim), Klaus Kinski (Professor Blackmann), Nicoletta Elmi (Paola Burton), John Karlsen (Alfredo Rovelli), Myriam Acevedo (Alice's supervisor), Rosita Toros (Marie Leblanche)

In this bizarre giallo from the director of *The Fifth Cord*, Florinda Bolkan stars as Alice, a well-paid foreign translator living in Italy. Her lack of connection to her surroundings combined with memories of an old sci-fi movie (starring Klaus Kinski) that made "a terrible impression" on her in her youth inform her fantasy life in the present – which includes alternate identities, false histories, and even murder.

Her adventure begins when – after waking from a bizarre nightmare inspired by a memory of the sci-fi film – she shows up for work and is reprimanded for having been absent the previous three days. Realizing she has no memory of this 3-day period, and assuming it must be due to an accidental overdose of the tranquilizers she routinely ingests due to general anxiety, she is nevertheless faced with a series of inexplicable tokens that hint at a forgotten adventure: an unfamiliar blood-stained dress in her closet; and a ripped up postcard from a place called Garma. Drawn to the place in the postcard, she goes to investigate – and finds out some startling things about herself.
For more on this film see **Part 6: The Strange Passenger**.

FORBIDDEN PHOTOS OF A LADY ABOVE SUSPICION

1970, Italy/Spain
Original titles: **Le foto proibite di una signora per bene**; **Días de angustia**
D: Luciano Ercoli. P: Alberto Pugliese, Luciano Ercoli. W: Ernesto Gastaldi, Mahnahén Velasco. Ed: Luciano Ercoli. DoP: Alejandro Ulloa. M: Ennio Morricone. AD: Juan Alberto Soler.
Cast: Dagmar Lassander (Minou), Pier Paolo Capponi (Peter), Simón Andreu (blackmailer), Osvaldo Genazzani (Commissioner Poletti), Salvador Huguet (George), Susan Scott [Nieves Navarro] (Dominique)

An atypical giallo in the sense that it focuses on the pathologized characterizations of the giallo without any of the habitual murder set pieces. That's not to say the film is short on sleaze; it revels in potentially offensive gender politics.

Dagmar Lassander plays Minou, the bored housewife of a rich businessman who spends her days in a haze of booze and sedatives. One day while walking on the beach at night she is accosted by a stranger (Simón Andreu) who teasingly molests her at knifepoint while he tells her that her husband Peter (Pier Paolo Capponi) has murdered one of his business associates – and then abruptly splits, leaving her with a weird feeling of unfulfilled violation. When she tells her husband about the incident, he dismisses it since she wasn't "actually attacked". "I'd have adored being violated!" says her sexually confident friend Dominique (giallo regular Susan Scott), who proceeds to show Minou a slideshow of pornographic photos that pique the interest of the admittedly repressed housewife – especially when she spies her attacker in one of the shots.

When Minou reports the incident to the police, the detective tells her "You were very smart to play along like that", which gives her license to co-operate guilt-free when he inevitably shows up again. Realizing that Andreu's character is a blackmailer, she agrees to meet him to pay him off in exchange for a cassette recording incriminating her husband. But the repeated meetings with the blackmailer are only a convenient cover for an exciting sexual game that she is too ashamed to experience without force:

> "I can still feel his hands on me. I've washed myself a hundred times and I still feel dirty."
> "But you did it for Peter. You don't have to feel guilty about it."
> "I don't know anymore."

When she comes clean and tells Peter about her meetings with the blackmailer, there's no evidence that the blackmailer ever existed, and both Peter and the police think she imagined the whole thing. Minou becomes more and more anxious after her confession doesn't bring any comforting resolution, and her unravelled mental state makes room for her conspirator(s) to close in. While Minou is almost a stock giallo character, rarely is that character given as much room to move as in this Ernesto Gastaldi-scripted treat.

above: Dagmar Lassander and Pier Paolo Capponi in Luciano Ercoli's **Forbidden Photos of a Lady Above Suspicion** (1970).

FOUR FLIES ON GREY VELVET

1971, Italy/France
Original titles: **4 mosche di velluto grigio**;
Quatre mouches de velours gris
D: Dario Argento. P: Salvatore Argento. W: Dario Argento, Luigi Cozzi (story), Mario Foglietti (story). Ed: Françoise Bonnot. DoP: Franco Di Giacomo. M: Ennio Morricone. PD: Enrico Sabbatini.
Cast: Michael Brandon (Roberto Tobias), Mimsy Farmer (Nina Tobias), Jean-Pierre Marielle (Gianni Arrosio), Bud Spencer [Carlo Pedersoli] ('God' Godfrey), Aldo Bufi Landi (coroner), Calisto Calisti (Carlo Marosi), Marisa Fabbri (Amelia), Oreste Lionello (the professor), Fabrizio Moroni (Mirko), Corrado Olmi (gay porter)

Roberto Tobias (Michael Brandon) is an emotionally vacant drummer in an Italian prog band. After discovering that he's being followed by a sinister fellow in a trench coat, Roberto confronts the man and accidentally stabs him, only to be photographed in the act by a witness wearing an androgynous plastic face mask. Reluctant to report the incident to the police lest he be jailed for murder, Roberto goes home and tries to ignore it, but the mysterious masked figure makes a threatening appearance there as well. As the investigation gets closer to a revelation and witnesses threaten to come forward, the bodies start to pile up. Roberto, still convinced that going to the police isn't an option, becomes a prisoner in his own home, waiting in the dark with a gun pointed at the door.

When the murderer is revealed through a (fictional) scientific process to be his own wife, Nina (Mimsy Farmer), she lays it all out in a confessional monologue: "I wanted so badly to see you die slowly… painfully. Because you're so much like him… My pig father – he made me suffer! Do you know he brought me up as a boy? He treated me like a boy – he beat me. He beat me! He said I was crazy. My mother – she died in an asylum. He brought me there too. Then my father died – before I could kill him! When I met you, I couldn't believe it. It was like a miracle. You look just like him. I knew I would kill you."

Maitland McDonagh pointed out in *Broken Mirrors / Broken Minds* that the desire to marry the twin of her father acts as some kind of incestual wish-fulfilment on Nina's part, but I think that – like many of the characters in this book – the issue is more one of approval, acceptance and encouragement. Sadly Roberto is not a nurturing character, and any chance he had of reversing Nina's trauma with affection is undermined by his own obliviousness.
For more on this film, and actress Mimsy Farmer, see **Part 4: Secret Ceremonies**.

When the flies start to crawl, so will your flesh...

If you dare to see it alone, make sure someone escorts you home.

FREEZE ME

2000, Japan
Alternative title: **Freezer**
D: Takashi Ishii. P: Takashi Ishii, Nobuaki Nagae.
W: Takashi Ishii. DoP: Yasushi Sasakibara. M: Goro Yasukawa. PD: Teru Yamazaki.
Cast: Harumi Inoue (Chihiro), Shingo Tsurumi (Kojima), Kazuki Kitamura (Hirokawa), Shunsuke Matsuoka (Nogami), Naoto Takenaka (Baba), Daisuke Iijima, Yôzaburô Itô, Ken Nakayama, Kyoko Muramatsu, Satsuki Natsukawa

Despite the implications of his background in pinku eiga (or softcore Japanese sex films), Takashi Ishii (*Angel Guts: Red Vertigo, Gonin 2, Black Angel*) has been celebrated as a 'feminist' director who makes heroes of his various female characters. While not an entirely new topic for Ishii, *Freeze Me* is a condemnation of the stigma attached to rape victims, and an examination of the destructive potential of the accompanying shame.

Chihiro (Harumi Inoue) is a young bank worker who was accosted and raped by three assailants while still in high school. Having never recovered from the shame of her victimization, she moved to the city to start a new life, keeping her past a secret from everyone (including her fiancé) and extracts herself from her own family, who only serve as reminders of the trauma. When one of her attackers is released from prison, the three use the occasion to pay her a visit, and she endures several days of mental, physical and social torment from them before finally murdering each of them in turn.

As a long-time fan of rape-revenge films, one of the things that frustrated me to no end about *Freeze Me* was that despite a few brief moments of well-warranted aggressiveness, its protagonist remains speechless and passive, she doesn't utilize available support systems, and even once she has dispatched her attackers, she keeps their bodies in various freezers in her home, containing them – and what they represent to her – in a place where they continue to endanger her. But as James R. Alexander has pointed out in issue #36 of the online journal *Senses of Cinema*, wherein he places *Freeze Me* in the larger context of the Japanese pink film: "Rarely in pink films did a rape victim struggle throughout the ordeal of her rape – "fighting to the end", as it were – but rather always reverting to a resigned catatonic state – passively waiting for the ordeal to be over and her attackers to leave. That passivity then became her permanent state, signifying her shame, and resignation to it reflected an overt acceptance of the presence of rape aggression as a random act in the public world."[76]

While Alexander and others have acknowledged Ishii's film as a hybridized form of political exposé concerned with the social status of women in Japan, it doesn't change the fact that Chihiro is more concerned with her reputation than with her own safety, which makes her a difficult character to sympathize with. The rape scenes are devoid of fetishism (when they even appear onscreen at all), but Chihiro's revenge becomes so cartoony that it negates the gravity of the events and removes the audience emotionally from the crime.

above: Detail from poster art for Dario Argento's **Four Flies on Grey Velvet** (1971).

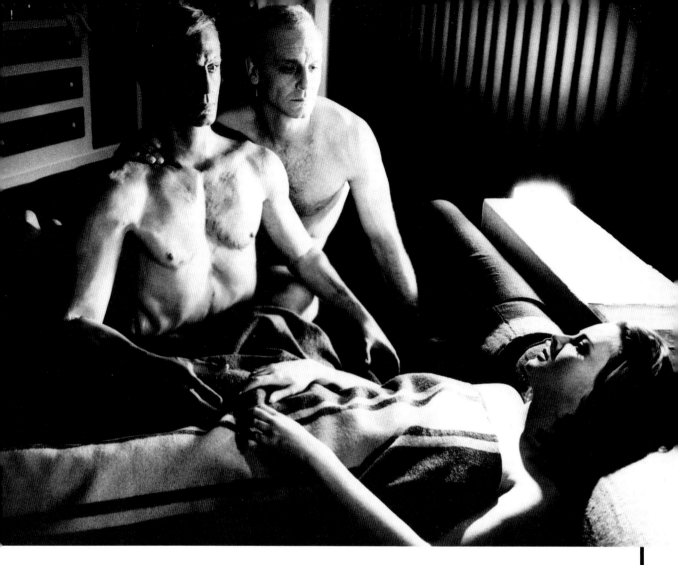

THE FRIGHTENED WOMAN

1969, Italy
Original title: **Femina ridens**
Alternative title: **The Laughing Woman**
D: Piero Schivazappa. P: Giuseppe Zaccariello. W: Piero Schivazappa. Ed: Carlo Reali. DoP: Sante Achilli. M: Stelvio Cipriani.
AD: Francesco Cuppini.
Cast: Philippe Leroy (Doctor Sayer), Dagmar Lassander (Mary), Maria Cumani Quasimodo (Sayer's secretary), Mirella Panfili (streetwalker), Lorenza Guerrieri (Gida), Varo Soleri (administrator)

The Italian title for this film directly translates as 'The Laughing Woman', which reveals more about its psychology than the victimizing American counterpart. A rich playboy (Philippe Leroy) hires hookers to satiate his sadistic role-playing games, and crosses the line into reality when he kidnaps his feisty new assistant (Euro-starlet Dagmar Lassander) with the intention of subjecting her to the punishing regimen he has acted out with hired accomplices so many times before. He teaches her to be subservient and obedient, and finds it remarkable how well she adapts to each new humiliation. At times, she almost seems to be enjoying herself, which both fascinates and confuses him.
For more on this film see **Part 7: You've Always Loved Violence**.

above: Philippe Leroy and Dagmar Lassander in Piero Schivazappa's **The Frightened Woman** (1969).

FRIGHTMARE

1974, UK

D: Peter Walker. P: Pete Walker. W: David McGillivray, Pete Walker (story). Ed: Robert Dearberg. DoP: Peter Jessop. M: Stanley Myers. AD: Chris Burke.

Cast: Rupert Davies (Edmund Yates), Sheila Keith (Dorothy Yates), Deborah Fairfax (Jackie), Paul Greenwood (Graham), Kim Butcher (Debbie), Fiona Curzon (Merle), Jon Yule (Robin), Tricia [Trisha] Mortimer (Lillian), Pamela Farbrother (Delia), Edward Kalinski (Alec)

"It's such fun being night people, isn't it, Jackie?"

The second of five collaborations between director Pete Walker and former 'television granny' Sheila Keith, *Frightmare* stars Keith as Dorothy Yates, an insane cannibal woman who is put into an asylum following a series of grisly murders she committed with her husband Edmund (Rupert Davies). With the help of her other half and their now-grown daughter, she resumes her anthropophagous habits once released from the asylum 15 years later.

They install themselves in an isolated farmhouse, where Edmund's daughter from a previous marriage, Jackie (who works as a make-up artist for the BBC), shows up once a week to deliver parcels of animal brains in the hope of curbing her stepmother's craving for human flesh. Jackie tries to live a normal social life but is plagued by nightmares of Dorothy's ghoulish exploits. However, neither Jackie nor Dorothy's enabling husband know that Dorothy has been advertising as a fortune-teller in order to lure new victims to eat. Since they are all such "lonely people", Dorothy convinces herself that she is doing them a favour.

Meanwhile, Jackie's teenage half sister Debbie (born in the asylum just after her parents were committed) is proving to be an insufferable delinquent sociopath likely to follow in the footsteps of her murderous mother, who she's never met. Jackie's new beau Graham, a budding psychologist, is convinced that Debbie is suffering from an identity crisis as a result of having no knowledge of where she came from. But Jackie refuses to talk about their parents, which leads Graham to conduct a private investigation of his own, with bloody results.

Walker goes knee-deep into the viscera for this one, and Keith brings a certain charm to her blood-soaked, power drill-wielding villainess, looking quite at home amidst all the animal guts and human body parts. Keith proved similarly maleficent in Walker's *House of Whipcord* (1974), *House of Mortal Sin* (1976), *The Comeback* (1978) and *House of the Long Shadows* (1983), but it's in *Frightmare* that she really gets the spotlight to herself. She plays the part to the hilt, embodying both the kindly tea-time granny and frothing madwoman with equally unnerving vigour.

above: Sheila Keith and Kim Butcher in Pete Walker's **Frightmare** (1974).

FUNERAL HOME

1980, Canada
Alternative title: **Cries in the Night**
D: William Fruet. P: William Fruet. W: Ida Nelson. Ed: Ralph Brunjes. DoP: Mark Irwin. M: Jerry Fielding. PD: Roy Forge Smith. AD: Susan Longmire.
Cast: Lesleh Donaldson (Heather), Kay Hawtrey (Maude Chalmers), Barry Morse (Mr. Davis), Dean Garbett (Rick Yates), Stephen Miller (Billy Hibbs), Harvey Atkin (Harry Browning), Alf Humphries (Joe Yates), Peggy Mahon (Florie), Jack Van Evera (James Chalmers)

When teenaged Heather (Canadian tax shelter-era scream queen Lesleh Donaldson) comes to small town Ontario to help her grandmother Mrs. Chalmers (Kay Hawtrey) turn their former funeral home into a bed-and-breakfast, her stocky Grandma isn't a fan of the idea, knowing that her husband (who just "disappeared one day, just like he vanished into thin air") wouldn't have approved of the transition. Heather is certain they'll "make a million bucks" though, and Grandma is only too happy to have some fresh air in the house courtesy of the plucky teen, even though she dreads what her husband will have to say about it, if and when he returns.

While primarily friendly and accommodating, Mrs. Chalmers has a bit of a fundamentalist slant (that is brought out when an obnoxious adulterous couple checks in to the B&B), and late at night she can be heard arguing with her departed spouse, who appears to be inexplicably hiding in the basement. Every development that brings the house closer to its target as a tourist destination seems to result in a newly-discovered cadaver in the area, and when Heather's summertime beau recounts a tale that depicts her grandfather as a mean-spirited alcoholic, everything starts to point to the missing septuagenarian as the culprit.

Heather starts to worry that her grandmother is dangerously stuck in the past and too heavily influenced by her husband ("She really doesn't have a mind of her own!"), an intuition that proves right on the money when she discovers her grandmother in the basement, conversing with herself in the guise of Grandpa, who she killed years earlier when he was found drunkenly cavorting with another woman. After years of abuse it seems she snapped, and with her Christian beliefs preventing her from taking responsibility for the crime, she repressed the entire incident and took on his vile persona in clandestine late-night meetings in order to keep the truth from herself.

Written by Ida Nelson (co-writer of seminal Canadian holiday TV special A Cosmic Christmas) and clearly a reverse-gender riff on Psycho, Funeral Home is a modest early slasher with a slow pace and little blood. Unfortunately, even though Hawtrey makes a fearsome villain, this failure to exploit the red stuff at such a pivotal time in the genre's development saw it overshadowed in the history books by the likes of Canuxploitation classics My Bloody Valentine and Happy Birthday to Me (both 1981).

GENTLY BEFORE SHE DIES

1972, Italy
Original title: **Il tuo vizio è una stanza chiusa e solo io ne ho la chiave**
Alternative titles: **Excite Me**; **Your Vice Is a Locked Room and Only I Have the Key**
D: Sergio Martino. P: Luciano Martino. W: Ernesto Gastaldi, Adriano Bolzoni, Sauro Scavolini, Edgar Allan Poe (story). Ed: Attilio Vincioni. DoP: Giancarlo Ferrando. M: Bruno Nicolai. AD: Giorgio Bertolini.
Cast: Edwige Fenech (Floriana), Anita Strindberg (Irina Rouvigny), Luigi Pistilli (Oliviero Rouvigny), Ivan Rassimov (Walter), Angela La Vorgna (Brenda), Enrica Bonaccorti (hooker), Daniela Giordano (Fausta), Ermelinda De Felice (bordello owner), Franco Nebbia (Inspector), Riccardo Salvino (Dario)

The Italian title for Sergio Martino's Gently Before She Dies (aka Excite Me) translates directly as "Your vice is a locked room and only I have the key" – a line from the previous Ernesto Gastaldi/Sergio Martino collaboration The Strange Vice of Mrs. Wardh (aka Next!). In a script freely adapted from Edgar Allan Poe's The Black Cat, Gently Before She Dies stars Anita Strindberg as Irina, the anorexic, humiliated and abused wife of philandering failed writer Oliviero (Luigi Pistilli) who gets caught up in a murder rap. When Oliviero's promiscuous niece Floriana (Edwige Fenech) shows up to stay with them, Irina is thrown even more off guard by the girl's sexual advances and suggestions that she bump off her loutish husband. "He's a brute, an alcoholic and a drug addict", Floriana insists, pointing out that he's also rumoured to have slept with his own mother. When Floriana suggests that Irina should leave him, Irina says he would never allow it: "To lose his plaything, his victim? Never." For more on this film see **Part 3: All Safe and Dead**.

above, from left: Kay Hawtrey and Lesleh Donaldson; Kay Hawtrey in William Fruet's **Funeral Home** (1980).

THE GEOGRAPHY OF FEAR

2000, Finland/Denmark/Germany
Original title: **Pelon maantiede**
D: Auli Mantila. P: Tero Kaukomaa. W: Auli Mantila, Anja Kauranen [Anja Snellman] (novel). Ed: Kimmo Taavila. DoP: Heikki Färm.
M: Hilmar Örn Hilmarsson. AD: Jukka Uusitalo, Tiina Tuovinen.
Cast: Tanjalotta Räikkä (Oili Lyyra), Leea Klemola (Maaru Tang), Pertti Sveholm (Rainer Auvinen), Kari Sorvali (Eero Harakka),
Anna-Elina Lyytikäinen (Laura Lyyra), Elsa Saisio (Riikka Malkavaara), Eija Vilpas (Saara Tanner), Kaarina Hazard (Kristiina
Kukkonen), Maaria Rantanen (Leenakaisa Sukunen), Irma Junnilainen (Johanna Louhimies)

Based on Anja Kauranen's controversial bestseller *Pelon maantiede*, Auli Mantila's *The Geography of Fear* won best screenplay
at Cannes in 2001, and continues on the theme of female violence that was explored in Mantila's earlier film *The Collector* (1997).
The film opens with the investigation of a drowned man drifting ashore near Helsinki. Oili Lyyra is the forensic dentist assisting in the
case who discovers that the man's death may be connected to her sister Laura's new circle of friends – a group of radical female
vigilantes. When Laura is brutally raped and left for dead, she finds herself infiltrating this circle, first out of curiosity and later out of
a shared bond of resentment over the way a woman's world is limited by the aggressiveness of male interests.
For more on this film see **Part 4: Secret Ceremonies**.

THE GIRL NEXT DOOR

2007, USA
D: Gregory Wilson. P: William M. Miller,
Andrew van den Houten. W: Daniel
Farrands, Philip Nutman, Jack Ketchum
(novel). Ed: Michael Fiore. DoP: William
M. Miller. M: Ryan Shore. PD: Krista Gall,
Jeff Subik.
Cast: William Atherton (adult David
Moran), Blythe Auffarth (Meg Loughlin),
Blanche Baker (Ruth Chandler),
Kevin Chamberlin (Officer Jennings),
Dean Faulkenberry (Kenny), Gabrielle
Howarth (Cheryl Robinson), Benjamin
Ross Kaplan (Donny Chandler), Spenser
Leigh (Denise Crocker), Daniel Manche
(David Moran)

In the placid suburban summer of 1958,
12-year-old David pals around with the
three boys next door, enjoying typical
prepubescent activities like catching
crawfish, playing hide and seek and
teasing the local girls. That is, until the
boys' beautiful teenage cousin and her
younger invalid sister come to live with
them after being recently orphaned in
a horrible car crash. As David befriends the older of the two girls and starts to feel the pangs of first love, he begins to notice that
the girls' presence in the house next door seems to elicit inexplicable jealousy and resentment on the part of the boys' mother
Ruth, a crass single woman that all the kids in the neighbourhood look up to. As Ruth's hostility towards her two charges escalates
into open verbal and physical abuse, she finds willing accomplices in the local children, who are eager participants in the girls'
humiliation in exchange for peer approval and the clandestine privilege of drinking the beer Ruth routinely plies them with. As the
situation gets more sordid and evolves into a gruesome routine of group torture, David is forced to join in or find himself the next
target for this sexually-fuelled aggression.

    The performances are incredible all round – most notably from the young lead Daniel Manche, whose first love and lost
innocence are so effectively conveyed, to its central villain Ruth, played by Blanche Baker (best known as the spoiled older sister
in *Sixteen Candles* and daughter of '50s pinup/giallo regular Carroll Baker) – who masterfully balances comedic, cynical likeability
with horrifying misanthropy taken to atrocious extremes. It's these performances that save the film from just being an exercise in
sadism and elevate it to shattering emotional drama about personal ethics and the ugliness often buried beneath a squeaky
clean veneer. This is a difficult film in every sense of the word – difficult to watch, but even more difficult to ignore.

above: Daniel Manche and Blanche Baker in Gregory Wilson's **The Girl Next Door** (2007).

THE GLASS CEILING

1971, Spain
Original title: **El techo de cristal**
D: Eloy de la Iglesia. W: Antonio Fos,
Eloy de la Iglesia. DoP: Francisco Fraile.
M: Angel Arteaga.
Cast: Carmen Sevilla (Martha), Dean
Selmier (Richard), Emma Cohen (Rosa),
Fernando Cebrián (Charles), Patty
Shepard (Julie), Encarna Paso (Rita),
Rafael Hernández (Padre), Javier De
Campos (clerk), Patricia Cealot, Hugo
Blanco (delivery man)

Eloy de la Iglesia (*Cannibal Man*) wrote
and directed the effective Spanish
giallo *The Glass Ceiling*, starring Carmen
Sevilla as Martha, a loyal housewife
whose husband goes away on business
way too often, leaving her isolated
and alone with her imagination. Her
boredom leads her to eavesdrop on
her neighbours and speculate on
what their lives are like – and on what
it means when she hears a loud thump
in the middle of the night followed by
scurrying footsteps. When she notices
the extended absence of the man
upstairs, she comes to the conclusion
that his wife Julie (stunning Euro-
starlet and Barbara Steele-look-alike
Patty Shepard) and an alleged lover
murdered him. She becomes obsessed
with the idea, and her days are filled
with trying to solve the 'mystery' of
Victor's disappearance.
For more on this film see
Part 3: All Safe and Dead.

GOODBYE GEMINI

1970, UK
Alternative title: **Twinsanity**
D: Alan Gibson. P: Joseph Shaftel, Peter Snell. W: Edmund Ward, Jenni Hall (novel).
Ed: Ernest Hosler. DoP: Geoffrey Unsworth. M: Christopher Gunning. PD: Wilfred
Shingleton. AD: Fred Carter.
Cast: Judy Geeson (Jacki Dewar), Peter Jeffrey (Detective Inspector Kingsley),
Freddie Jones (David Curry), Alexis Kanner (Clive Landseer), Martin Potter (Julian
Dewar), Mike Pratt (Rod), Michael Redgrave (James Harrington-Smith), Marion
Diamond (Denise), Terry Scully (Nigel Garfield), Daphne Heard (Mrs. McLaren)

Emotionally-stunted twins Jacki (Judy Geeson, *To Sir, with Love*) and Julian (Martin Potter,
Fellini Satyricon) arrive in London with their teddy bear Agamemnon and get involved
with a shady hustler named Clive (Canadian-British actor Alexis Kanner, sporting the
weirdest hybrid accent ever) in the seedy underbelly of swinging London. Everyone's
obsessed with these enchanting blond newcomers, who have an unnatural, barely-
disguised incestuous affection for one another. Various hipsters contrive to wean them
off of each other as a means of seducing one or the other, but this only strengthens
their resolve to build a wall around themselves. When Clive gets Julian involved in a
compromising situation involving a gang of licentious transvestites, and then tries to
blackmail him in order to get the 400 quid he owes to a burly gangster, the twins initiate
him into one of their fatal games.
　　Suddenly Jacki is on her own, screaming through the streets and unable to recall
what just happened or where Julian has gone. As the newspaper headlines reveal that
the twins are sought in connection with the murder, a TV journalist (Michael Redgrave,
The Innocents) – who frequently hangs out with the kids to stay on top of the youth
movement – reluctantly gives shelter to Jacki while he urges her to fess up about what
happened. Meanwhile the boho
crowd makes their own speculations.
"Clive may have been the original
kinky kid, but those two twins of yours
wouldn't have taken any prizes for
normality", says ageing libertarian David
Curry (Freddie Jones, who played Dr.
Frankenstein in the flopped Harry Nilsson
vehicle *Son of Dracula*). But when
Jackie locates Jules it's clear that his
obsession with her is the fuel for their
shared neurosis and she must come to
terms with her own part in the insanity
(that is, *twin*sanity!)

Artwork from **Goodbye Gemini.**

A GUN FOR JENNIFER

1997, USA
D: Todd Morris. P: Deborah Twiss. W: Todd Morris, Deborah Twiss. Ed: Rachel Warden, Todd Morris. DoP: David Tumblety, Joe di Gennaro, Eliot Rockett.
Cast: Deborah Twiss (Jennifer/Allison), Benja Kay (Detective Billie Perez), Rene Alberta (Becky), Tracy Dillon (Grace), Freida Hoops (Jesse), Veronica Cruz (Priscilla), Sheila Schmidt (Trish), Beth Dodye Bass (Annie), Joseph Pallister (Grady), Arthur J. Nascarella (Lt. Rizzo)

A female vigilante gang headed up by the aggressively unstable Jesse operates out of a collectively-operated strip club through which the women frequently turn the tables on their sexist customers by humiliating them. Co-writer Deborah Twiss plays Allison, who is attacked by two men shortly after arriving in New York City and then falls in with the vigilantes, who, aside from their activities at the strip club, have also been systematically castrating and killing known rapists, pimps and child-sex traffickers.
For more on this film see **Part 4: Secret Ceremonies**.

HANDGUN

1983, USA
Alternative title: **Deep in the Heart**
D: Tony Garnett. P: Tony Garnett. W: Tony Garnett. Ed: Bill Shapter. DoP: Charles Stewart. M: Mike Post. PD: Lilly Kilvert.
Cast: Karen Young (Kathleen Sullivan), Clayton Day (Larry Keeler), Suzie Humphreys (Nancy), Larry Corwin (Jim), Ben Jones (Chuck), Kenneth Garner (William Masters), Helena Humann (Miss Davis), Joe Bowman (trick shooter), Kitty Harlen (Mrs. Sullivan), Robert Hibbard (Detective Dave Farmer)

One of two great (but commercially unsuccessful) directorial efforts from influential British producer Tony Garnett (the other being *Prostitute*, 1980), *Handgun* takes a hard look at America's love of weaponry with this story of a petite schoolteacher named Kathleen (Karen Young in a stunning screen debut) who finds herself date-raped at gunpoint by a charismatic man she had invited to her classroom as a guest-lecturer. The rape scene, while not graphic, is utterly horrific in part due to the rapist's genuine belief that he has

only coaxed out of her desires that were repressed. As they lie in bed afterward (Kathleen staring in terror at the ceiling and strategizing her getaway), he is all cuddles and sweet-nothings, and tells her that he really cares for her and will do whatever she needs to help her get over whatever trauma has caused her to be so repressed. The speech he gives is mind-boggling and infuriating, and quite frankly I couldn't wait for him to get his balls shot off.

Apparently, neither can Kathleen. After cutting off her long hair into a boyish short-cut and replacing her breezy summer dresses with flannel shirts and jeans, she joins the very gun club where her rapist spends his weekends, and learns how to be efficient and deadly on the weapon she previously abhorred. Her transformation follows the standard rape-revenge trajectory – she disassociates from her usual social reality and is only able to care about familiarizing herself with various forms of weaponry, practicing both on the range and in her own home in front of the mirror. Establishing her "destructive potential", as Rita Mae Brown (the feminist screenwriter of slasher parody *The Slumber Party Massacre*) calls it,[77] Kathleen becomes the noble avenger, spreading a clear message through her violent actions that the rapist's behaviour will not be tolerated. But of course, in taking on this avenging role, she loses her old self, and sacrifices her sanity.

As an aside, Harry Nilsson, my favourite singer-songwriter and virulent anti-gun activist, performs the closing theme song 'Lay Down Your Arms'.

above: Promotional artwork for Tony Garnett's **Handgun** (1983).

HAPPY BIRTHDAY TO ME

1981, Canada
D: J. Lee Thompson. P: John Dunning, André Link. W: Timothy Bond, Peter Jobin, John C.W. Saxton. Ed: Debra Karen. DoP: Miklós Lente. M: Bo Harwood, Lance Rubin. PD: Earl G. Preston. Cast: Melissa Sue Anderson (Virginia Wainwright), Glenn Ford (Dr. David Faraday), Lawrence Dane (Hal Wainwright), Sharon Acker (Estelle Wainwright), Frances Hyland (Mrs. Patterson), Tracy E. Bregman (Ann Thomerson), Jack Blum (Alfred Morris), David Eisner (Rudi), Lisa Langlois (Amelia), Lesleh Donaldson (Bernadette)

One of the best films of the Canadian tax shelter era, the Cinepix-produced *Happy Birthday to Me* stars Melissa Sue Anderson (of TV's *Little House on the Prairie*) as Virginia, the 'new girl' at the exclusive Crawford private school, who falls in with the cliquey Crawford 'Top Ten' whose nightly exploits involve causing trouble at the Silent Woman Inn and playing 'The Game' – a dangerous match of chicken with the local drawbridge. Soon the Top Ten start to go missing, and though the teachers suspect it's all part of some elaborate practical joke, the audience is privy to their colourful murders (the film was an early proponent of the '80s 'creative killing' craze), including a giallo-esque straight-razor attack, a weightlifting 'accident', a motorcycle engine mishap, and a slippery shish-kebab impalement. A handy red herring is provided by the character of Alfred, a 'Bad Ronald'-esque creep with a pet rat and a knack for gruesome make-up FX (Jack Blum, best known for playing 'Spaz' in *Meatballs*).

During science lab, Virginia has a sudden flashback of being probed with electrodes whilst on a slab. Her therapist Dr. Faraday (Glenn Ford) explains that she is recovering her memory piece by piece after being the pioneering recipient of experimental brain surgery, meant to restore damaged brain tissue – in this case, after the car accident that killed her mother and left Virginia temporarily brain dead.

Virginia's increasing flashbacks coincide with blackouts that all seem timed to the disappearances of her friends. When she has a delusion of her friend Ann's lifeless body in the bathtub she calls her therapist for help, thinking she's blacked out and killed her. Dr. Faraday is convinced that there is a link between Virginia's trauma and her new friends, and urges her to remember what happened before the car accident. It seems that she isn't new in town at all, but in fact lived in Crawford as a high school wallflower who went unnoticed by the popular kids. When the Top Ten don't show up for her birthday celebration in favour of their own exclusive party (to which Virginia is not invited), Virginia's alcoholic mother goes ballistic, seeing it as an extension of her own ostracization in the community years earlier. She crams Virginia into the car on a stormy night hoping to crash the rich kids' party, but crashes the car instead.

The convoluted plotting – there are more twists even beside what's mentioned here – is compounded by a Scooby-Doo ending, but somehow it all works, helped in large part by a memorable slasher cast that includes character actor Matt Craven (*Jacob's Ladder*), Tracey Bregman, Lesleh Donaldson, David Eisner (of Canadian sitcom *Hangin' In*), Canuxploitation goddess Lisa Langlois (*Class of 1984*, *Deadly Eyes*), and props to Melissa Sue Anderson, who plays the delusional teen with gusto, amply conveying her total mental breakdown.

HARD CANDY

2005, USA
D: David Slade. P: Michael Caldwell, David Higgins, Richard Hutton. W: Brian Nelson. Ed: Art Jones. DoP: Jo Willems. M: Harry Escott, Molly Nyman. PD: Jeremy Reed. AD: Felicity Nove. Cast: Patrick Wilson (Jeff Kohlver), Ellen Page (Hayley Stark), Sandra Oh (Judy Tokuda), Gilbert John [G.J. Echternkamp] (Nighthawks clerk), Jennifer Holmes [Odessa Rae] (Janelle Rogers)

A 14-year-old girl named Hayley (Ellen Page in her breakout role) turns the tables on an internet predator (Patrick Wilson) in a meticulously plotted revenge scenario, but Hayley doesn't just usurp his role as predator – she's a herself predator from frame one of the film. She deliberately entraps him, supposedly out of loyalty to "all the little girls he ever looked at, touched, hurt or killed", but she has no direct personal motivation for stalking and torturing him. When she finds child pornography in his house, she manages to tie him to a chair and can easily call the police and have him over along with the evidence, but toys with him relentlessly instead. No background is given for the girl that might shed light on her actions, and she doesn't even flinch or falter in carrying out her punishments, as the vigilantes in *The Geography of Fear* or *The Ladies Club* do. The character of Hayley in *Hard Candy* is clearly a sociopath, already hardened long before the opening of the film.

The film was criticized upon release for its sympathetic portrayal of the paedophile. Interestingly, Wilson's character is not actually portrayed in a sympathetic light – it's just that we side with him by default because Hayley is the more threatening of the two. Even though Hayley is trying to teach the paedophile a lesson in responsibility, she does not assess her own actions in those terms. She does not assume responsibility for baiting the paedophile because she's a minor and her actions don't count as 'adult' actions, either in her own eyes or in the eyes of society. She knows she can get away with anything, and even admits that the worst she'll get if she kills him is "two years of community service and a star-studded Hollywood biopic".

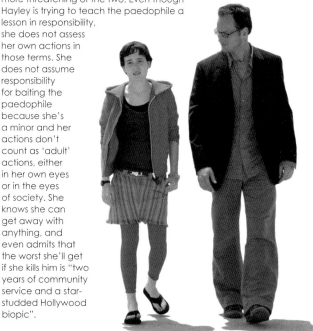

bottom right: Ellen Page and Patrick Wilson in David Slade's **Hard Candy** (2005).

THE HAUNTING

1963, USA/UK
D: Robert Wise. P: Robert Wise. W: Nelson Gidding, Shirley Jackson (novel). Ed: Ernest Walter. DoP: Davis Boulton. M: Humphrey Searle. PD: Elliot Scott.
Cast: Julie Harris (Eleanor 'Nell' Lance), Claire Bloom (Theo), Richard Johnson (Dr. John Markway), Russ Tamblyn (Luke Sannerson), Lois Maxwell (Grace Markway), Fay Compton (Mrs. Sannerson), Valentine Dyall (Mr. Dudley), Rosalie Crutchley (Mrs. Dudley), Diane Clare (Carrie Fredericks), Ronald Adam (Eldridge Harper)

Based on Shirley Jackson's beloved horror story, Wise's film is – along with Jack Clayton's *The Innocents* two years prior – one of the quintessential 'Gothic breakdown' films that provides the foundation of this book's subject matter. Julie Harris gives one of her many swooning performances as Eleanor 'Nell' Lance, a naïve and neurotic young woman who sleeps on her dismissive sister's couch after being left homeless since their mother's demise. Nell spent her life caring for her bedridden mother, and suffers from guilt over the fact that she ignored her mother's call one night – and the old woman died as a result. Although the mother left her meagre belongings to both children, Nell does not assert her right to the property, instead allowing her sister to treat her as an irritating boarder.

Anxious for something – *anything* – that will give her a sense of purpose, she agrees to participate in Dr. John Markway's paranormal investigation of the reputedly haunted 'Hill House' as one of a circle of volunteers with psychic abilities. The 90-year-old Hill House has a history of death, murder and insanity, and its most recent caretaker was found hanging from the spiral staircase in the library.

The concept of the haunted house as psychic space is key to the genre, but is illustrated beautifully in Nell's relationship to the house, which film scholar Kristopher Woofter has referred to as an inverse of the typical hero's journey – instead of individuation, the hero *dis*-integrates by the end.[78] The haunted house film is usually coloured by issues of ownership – a new owner trying 'take possession' of a house that is already possessed and paying for it in the end – but Nell doesn't want to own the house, she wants it to own *her*. As the house's supernatural attacks start to centre on her, it's clear that the house wants her to stay forever, and she melts into the only welcoming embrace she's ever known.

THE HAUNTING

2009, Spain
Original title: **No-Do**
D: Elio Quiroga. W: Elio Quiroga. Ed: Luis Sánchez-Gijón. DoP: Juan Carlos Gómez. M: Alfons Conde. AD: Gabriel Carrascal.
Cast: Ana Torrent (Francesca), Francisco Boira (Pedro), Héctor Colomé (Miguel), Miriam Cepa (Rosa), Rocío Muñoz (Jean), Sonia Lázaro (girl), Francisco Casares (Gabriel), María Alfonsa Rosso (Blanca), Alejandra Lorenzo (girl), Cristina Rodríguez (girl)

A paediatrician (Ana Torrent of *Thesis*) moves with her husband and four-month-old son to a huge country mansion that once was a school run by the local clergy. Suffering from paranoid delusions concerning the safety of her newborn child, and bothered by strange noises in the house, she has difficulty sleeping. With her increased weariness, her husband Pedro starts to worry that moving to the house was a mistake. On temporary leave from work as a result of personal trauma causing unprofessional behaviour, she spends her days in quiet conversation with her daughter Rosa, who died accidentally ten years earlier.

In her fragile mental state, burdened by parental guilt and hyper-aware of danger, she becomes a ready receptacle for the otherworldly messages being sent to her by the legion of ghosts who live in the house. However, further investigation into her mental health is sidestepped by a mystery involving the Church's cover-up of a massacre during the Franco regime, which is connected to the current manifestation of spirits in the house and revealed through old film reels of the state-controlled Spanish Documentary News (or No-Do, which is also this film's original title).

above, both images: Julie Harris in Robert Wise's **The Haunting** (1963).

THE HAUNTING OF JULIA

1977, UK/Canada
Alternative title: **Full Circle**
D: Richard Loncraine. P: Peter Fetterman, Alfred Pariser. W: Dave Humphries, Harry Bromley Davenport (adaptation), Peter Straub (novel). Ed: Ron Wisman. DoP: Peter Hannan. M: Colin Towns. AD: Brian Morris.
Cast: Mia Farrow (Julia Lofting), Keir Dullea (Magnus Lofting), Tom Conti (Mark), Jill Bennett (Lily), Robin Gammell (David Swift), Cathleen Nesbitt (Mrs. Rudge), Anna Wing (Rose Flood), Edward Hardwicke (Captain Paul Winter), Mary Morris (Greta Braden), Pauline Jameson (Claudia Branscombe)

Mia Farrow plays the distraught mother of a child she has accidentally killed while performing an emergency tracheotomy. When Julia emerges from the hospitalization that ensues, she immediately leaves her husband Magnus (Keir Dullea) and goes looking for a house of her own, to be alone with her grief. Augmenting pressure from her aggressive husband and his meddling sister to return to her unhappy marriage is the fact that Julia's new home is the kind of immense, sinister house that undoubtedly fuels nightmares and paranoia. Julia decides to investigate the former inhabitants of the house, and discovers that a little girl named Olivia once lived there, a girl so beautiful that she could get away with anything – including the murder of another child. Julia starts to feel the presence of this little girl in the house with her, but is not threatened; she identifies with the child's murderous guilt, playing the roles of both child and the child's redeemer. She is going to help the terrible child find peace.
For more on this film see **Part 3: All Safe and Dead**.

HAUTE TENSION

2003, France
Alternative title: **Switchblade Romance**
D: Alexandre Aja. P: Alexandre Arcady, Robert Benmussa.
W: Alexandre Aja, Grégory Levasseur. Ed: Baxter, Al Rundle, Sophie Vermersch. DoP: Maxime Alexandre. M: François Eudes.
PD: Renald Cotte Verdy, Tony Egry. AD: Grégory Levasseur.
Cast: Cécile De France (Marie), Maïwenn (Alexia), Philippe Nahon (the killer), Franck Khalfoun (Jimmy), Andrei Finti (Alex's father), Oana Pellea (Alex's mother), Marco Claudiu Pascu (Tom), Jean-Claude de Goros (police inspector), Bogdan Uritescu (policeman), Gabriel Spahiu (man in the car)

A milestone in the development of the new wave of French horror, Alexandre Aja's breakout film follows two female friends, Marie and Alexia, on a road trip through the French countryside while a brutal madman (the fearsome Philippe Nahon of Gaspar Noé's *Carne* and *I Stand Alone*) follows close on their trail.
    The film opens with Marie, damaged and scarred on a hospital bed, repeating to herself "I won't let anyone come between us anymore..." after being picked up on a rural road, bleeding and pleading for help. She wakes up in the back seat of her friend Alexia's car, apparently conveying the previous sequence as a dream. When Alexia inquires about the pursuer in the dream, Marie says: "It was me – it was me running after me." This is the first indication of what will turn out to be the film's (disastrous) twist ending and the reason for its inclusion in this book.
    Shortly after the two girls arrive at Alexia's family home in the country, Nahon's hulking unnamed character closes in on the house and wastes no time in hacking up the family (Giannetto De Rossi, well known as creating some of the most memorable images of the heyday of Italian horror, provides the film's gruesome FX) with the exception of Alexia, who the killer takes as a hostage, and Marie, who overhears the mayhem in time to hide.
    For the bulk of the film, Marie is posited as a final girl-type character, alternately baiting and being pursued by the killer in her attempts to rescue her friend. The killer catches her momentarily and questions her at knifepoint: "Why do you care so much about Alexia? She turns you on, doesn't she? She does the same thing to me." We are led to read this as him projecting a lesbian fantasy onto the girls; after all, any hints that might convey Maria's unhealthy obsession with her friend are brief and subtle, and easily explained away without casting suspicion. But with less than ten minutes left in the film's running time, it is revealed that Maria has been the killer all along, and suddenly her split personality is totally obvious, as she chases Alexia down in the guise of her bloody male alter-ego.
    The ending is unforgivable, not only because it trips up what, to that point, had been a bold, seemingly perfect exercise in sheer terror, but also because it is so blatantly tacked on with no consideration for its own trajectory, let alone how effectively mental illness can be utilized in a horror film when done right.

above: Maïwenn and Cécile De France in Alexandre Aja's **Haute tension** (2003).

HEAVENLY CREATURES

1994, New Zealand
D: Peter Jackson. P: Jim Booth. W: Peter Jackson, Frances Walsh. Ed: Jamie Selkirk. DoP: Alun Bollinger. M: Peter Dasent. PD: Grant Major. AD: Jill Cormack.
Cast: Melanie Lynskey (Pauline Parker), Kate Winslet (Juliet Hulme), Sarah Peirse (Honora Parker Rieper), Diana Kent (Hilda Hulme), Clive Merrison (Dr. Henry Hulme), Simon O'Connor (Herbert Rieper), Jed Brophy (John/Nicholas), Peter Elliott (Bill Perry), Gilbert Goldie (Dr. Bennett), Geoffrey Heath (Rev. Norris)

Based on the true story of 1950s teenage murderesses Pauline Parker and Juliet Hulme, Peter Jackson's Oscar-winning film (which launched the career of Kate Winslet) uses the real Pauline Parker's diary entries as a narrative guide through this lovely and horrific tale of a consuming friendship that results in both emotional and physical casualties.

When the outspoken, world-travelled Juliet (Winslet) is admitted as a new student at the Christchurch Girls' High School, misfit fellow student Pauline (Melanie Lynskey) immediately takes a liking to her, and the two become fast friends, bonding over their respective childhood illnesses and flights of fancy. Pauline in particular is woken out of her previous despondency by Juliet's effervescent nature, and in between frantic bouts of social obstinacy, pushing aside all the normal boring people who obstruct their wilding ways, they create their own fictional kingdom of Borovnia, which Jackson brings to life in elaborate fantasy sequences that are as vivid for us as they become for the two dramatic teens.

Juliet's cheery, freewheeling nature has its dark side, fuelled by the tuberculosis that has seen her shipped off to various corners of the globe in search of an accommodating climate. This, combined with the transient nature of her father's work and her mother's affair with a client (later to become Juliet's stepfather, Bill Perry) has left her feeling unbalanced, like an appendage or after-thought in her parents' lives. As the mythology of Borovnia starts to get more violent, and their parents question the propriety of their girls' relationship – noticing their sociopathic irritability toward all other people – the elders contrive to keep them apart, "to avert trouble before it starts". But the girls have other plans, most notably for Pauline's mother, who they see as their greatest obstacle to being together. In her diary, Pauline details their plan to murder her, which proves their undoing after they bludgeon her to death in the woods.

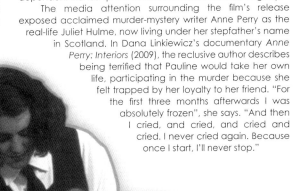

The murder itself takes up a tiny fraction of the film's running time, but its spectre haunts the proceedings, imbuing the girls' co-dependent friendship with an irreconcilable sense of tragedy.

The media attention surrounding the film's release exposed acclaimed murder-mystery writer Anne Perry as the real-life Juliet Hulme, now living under her stepfather's name in Scotland. In Dana Linkiewicz's documentary *Anne Perry: Interiors* (2009), the reclusive author describes being terrified that Pauline would take her own life, participating in the murder because she felt trapped by her loyalty to her friend. "For the first three months afterwards I was absolutely frozen", she says. "And then I cried, and cried, and cried and cried. I never cried again. Because once I start, I'll never stop."

from top: Kate Winslet; Melanie Lynskey and Kate Winslet in Peter Jackson's **Heavenly Creatures** (1994).

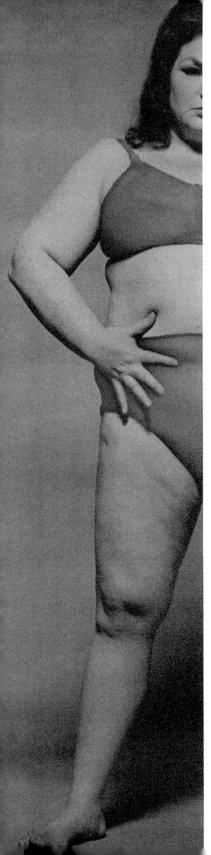
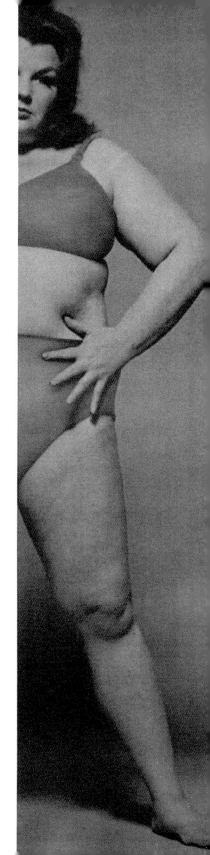

THE HONEYMOON KILLERS

1969, USA
D: Leonard Kastle. P: Warren Steibel. W: Leonard Kastle.
Ed: Richard Brophy, Stan Warnow. DoP: Oliver Wood.
M: Selections from work by Gustav Mahler.
Cast: Shirley Stoler (Martha Beck), Tony Lo Bianco (Ray Fernandez), Mary Jane Higby (Janet Fay), Doris Roberts (Bunny), Kip McArdle (Delphine Downing), Marilyn Chris (Myrtle Young), Dortha Duckworth (Mrs. Beck), Barbara Cason (Evelyn Long), Ann Harris (Doris Acker), Mary Breen (Rainelle Downing)

Based on the true story of 'Lonely Hearts Killers' Raymond Fernandez and Martha Beck, who killed an alleged 20 women between 1947 and 1949, Leonard Kastle's stark serial killer picture (originally meant to be helmed by Martin Scorsese, before he was fired) made the career of Tony Lo Bianco and set in motion a string of cult hits for imposing actress Shirley Stoler (*Klute*, *Seven Beauties*, *Frankenhooker*, *Pee-wee's Playhouse*).

Stoler plays Martha Beck, a portly spinster and supervising nurse who lives with her mother and takes out her anger on the co-workers whose amorous backroom trysts emphasize her own lack of companionship. She meets swarthy playboy Raymond Fernandez (Lo Bianco) through a lonely hearts dating service, but even after she realizes that he's been romancing and swindling a number of women, she still loves him, and vows that she would kill herself without him (in the film she is presented as a woman who has never experienced affection before, whereas in real life she had been married). She is willing to give everything up to be with Ray. When her employer fires her from the hospital after finding her torrid love letters on her desk, she's happy to be rid of the place ("I'm not so sure Hitler wasn't right about you people!" she barks at him), and when Ray tells her she can't bring her mother to come live with them in New York, she dumps her mother at an old folks' home without a second thought. Being with Ray involves other compromises too, though: she has to share him with the other women he marries for money; marriages that usually get severed during the honeymoon – figuratively or otherwise.

They jump from one crime to the next, never financially or criminally sated; their mutual crookedness fuels their passion, and they steal moments together behind locked doors while their cuckolded victims sign cheques and flash cash just to see their young Latin lover smile. Martha surprises Ray by emerging as the more forceful of the two, carrying out most of the murders herself while he looks on impotently, increasingly stunned by her emotionlessness. Her eye-rolling impatience and bitchy sarcasm with Ray's conquests (who believe that she's Ray's overprotective sister) imbues the film with its few moments of humour; although camp runs through the film due to its low budget, its pointed use of Gustav Mahler's dramatic compositions and – quite frankly – its uncommonly overweight lead, there is much about the film to be celebrated as high art (there's even a nod to *Battleship Potemkin* in one of the murder scenes). Oliver Wood's cinematography and deliberately blown-out lighting in particular lends the film a level of class that contrasts magically with its more exploitive elements.

Shirley Stoler in Leonard Kastle's **The Honeymoon Killers** (1969).

A HORRIBLE WAY TO DIE

2010, USA
D: Adam Wingard. P: Simon Barrett, Kim Sherman, Travis Stevens. W: Simon Barrett.
Ed: Adam Wingard. DoP: Chris Hilleke, Mark Shelhorse. M: Jasper Justice Lee.
Cast: AJ Bowen (Garrick Turrell), Amy Seimetz (Sarah), Joe Swanberg (Kevin),
Brandon Carroll (Rusty), Lane Hughes (Reed), Michael J. Wilson (Jones), Melissa
Boatright (Jessie), Whitney Moore (Daphne), Holly Voges (Carla), Jen Huemmer
(dark-haired woman)

AJ Bowen (*The Signal*, *The House of the Devil*, *You're Next*) turns in a career-
making performance as guilt-stricken, strangely compassionate serial killer Garrick
Turrell who, after breaking out of prison during a facility transfer, sets out across
the southern States in pursuit of the girlfriend he betrayed. The film is full of tragic,
fragile characters, but the most breakable of all is Sarah (Amy Seimetz, one of the
busiest actresses on the indie scene). A recovering alcoholic crippled by guilt over
the fact that her routine drinking blinded her to her boyfriend's bloody nocturnal
endeavours, Sarah meets awkward nice-guy Kevin (mumblecore staple Joe Swanberg) in her AA group. He seems unthreatening
enough for her to test the relationship waters again, but as she and Kevin get closer, the circle of bodies left by her troubled ex's
murderous compulsions starts to close in.

It could be argued that Sarah is more cautious than neurotic, that she repeatedly makes bad choices and consequently
trusts her own judgment less and less, but Seimetz brings so much apprehension to the character that it's breathtaking; the simplest
communication resonates with Herculean effort, and when she radiates pain, we feel it. It is a brilliant performance.

The story's elliptical reconstruction through out-of-order sequences where the present is frequently interrupted by the past
has an almost ghostly effect. Where Wingard's earlier film *Pop Skull* employed overt ghost story elements, *A Horrible Way to
Die* uses the concept of haunting as a memory that won't let go; like any entity, Garrick Turrell is one that Sarah won't be rid of
easily. Underscored by sadness and regret, *A Horrible Way to Die* is not only a dazzling achievement in genre cinema, but also a
meditation on the baggage that keeps each one of us ultimately alone.

I NEVER PROMISED YOU A ROSE GARDEN

1977, USA
D: Anthony Page. P: Daniel H. Blatt, Michael Hausman, Terence F. Deane. W: Gavin
Lambert, Lewis John Carlino, Hannah Green [Joanne Greenberg] (novel). Ed: Garth
Craven. DoP: Bruce Logan. M: Paul Chihara. PD: Toby Carr Rafelson.
Cast: Bibi Andersson (Dr. Fried), Kathleen Quinlan (Deborah Blake), Sylvia Sidney
(Miss Coral), Ben Piazza (Jay Blake), Lorraine Gary (Ester Blake), Darlene Craviotto
(Carla), Reni Santoni (Hobbs), Susan Tyrrell (Lee), Signe Hasso (Helene), Norman
Alden (McPherson)

While not a horror film, AIP's adaptation of Joanne Greenberg's best-selling
semi-autobiographical novel (using the pseudonym Hannah Green) warrants
a mention due to its tentative connection to other work discussed in this
book, namely Ingmar Bergman's *Persona* (via their shared actress Bibi Andersson), Peter Jackson's *Heavenly Creatures* and
Karen Arthur's *The Mafu Cage*, as well as the fantastical means of exploring the voices that plague its cantankerous young
protagonist.

Deborah Blake is a 16-year-old girl recently admitted to an institution after a suicide attempt ("Do you have any hobbies,
Deborah?" one of the counsellors asks. "Sure", she says, "Didn't they tell you? Suicide.") and an unwillingness to be touched
or to emotionally connect with the world around her. She is shut in with mostly irreverent staffers and a mountain of crazies –
including rambunctious character faces Susan Tyrrell and Sylvia Sidney – who harass and manhandle her, only encouraging
her to retreat further. But she routinely directs her anger at herself; when she attempts suicide again while in the asylum, she
confesses to Dr. Fried (Andersson) that she had to do it because she's "poisonous".

As with her real-life counterpart, Deborah underwent surgery for urethral cancer during childhood, a painful and stigmatized
experience after which she started to dissociate, creating the fictional, primitive kingdom of 'Yr' as a place she could escape
to in times of anguish (which is depicted in fantasy sequences throughout the film, utilizing members of Oingo Boingo among its
extras). While Yr was originally a place of comfort, over time it came to be no less threatening than the real world.

Although Greenberg was not consulted on the adaptation and has dismissed its characterization of mental illness, actress
Kathleen Quinlan gives a remarkable performance as a disturbed young woman struggling to reconcile her real and fantasy
lives within the confines of formal institutionalization.

from top: Amy Seimetz in Adam Wingard's **A Horrible Way to Die** (2010); Kathleen Quinlan in **I Never Promised You a Rose Garden** (1977).

IMAGES

1972, Ireland/USA
D: Robert Altman. P: Tommy Thompson. W: Robert Altman. Ed: Graeme Clifford. DoP: Vilmos Zsigmond. M: John Williams. PD: Leon Ericksen.
Cast: Susannah York (Cathryn), Rene Auberjonois (Hugh), Marcel Bozzuffi (René), Hugh Millais (Marcel), Cathryn Harrison (Susannah), John Morley (old man)

The second film in Altman's 'Feminine Quartet', *Images* stars Susannah York as Cathryn, a children's writer with a husband, two houses, and a split personality. Her disconnection from the world outside of her own mind is conveyed straight away through her tentative relationships, and the film plays freely with dream-logic and 'condensation', whereby people and things transform, duplicate and replace one another. Connected to this condensation process is the appearance of a double; in Cathryn's case, the double exists as an outlet for her adulterous desires. There are two Cathryns (often distinguished by black/white costuming), just as there are two homes, and the camera will follow one and then the other without warning, so that the viewer comes to accept the simultaneous existence of both. For more on this film see **Part 2: Broken Dolls**.

IN MY SKIN

2002, France
Original title: **Dans ma peau**
D: Marina de Van. P: Laurence Farenc.
W: Marina de Van. Ed: Mike Fromentin.
DoP: Pierre Barougier. M: Esbjorn Svensson Trio. AD: Baptiste Glaymann.
Cast: Marina de Van (Esther), Laurent Lucas (Vincent), Léa Drucker (Sandrine), Thibault de Montalembert (Daniel), Dominique Reymond (female client), Bernard Alane (male client), Marc Rioufol (Henri), François Lamotte (Pierre), Adrien de Van (intern)

Lanky François Ozon regular de Van stars in her directing debut as the upwardly mobile marketing assistant who accidentally cuts her leg open while stumbling through the backyard at a business party. She walks into a series of obstacles in the dark yard, but, feeling no sensation of pain, thinks she's only ripped her trousers – until she notices the trail of blood staining the carpet behind her. She takes to probing the wound, digging into her stitches in dark corners at work, in the bathroom, in restaurants. After an initial period of bodily disorientation, she falls in love with her own skin – and wants to see what lies beneath. For more on this film see **Part 5: Afterschool Special**.

from top: Hugh Millais and Susannah York in Robert Altman's **Images** (1972); Marina de Van in her film **In My Skin** (2002).

THE INNOCENTS

1961, UK
D: Jack Clayton. P: Jack Clayton. W: William Archibald, Truman Capote, Henry James (novel). Ed: Jim Clark. DoP: Freddie Francis.
M: Georges Auric. AD: Wilfred Shingleton.
Cast: Deborah Kerr (Miss Giddens), Peter Wyngarde (Peter Quint), Megs Jenkins (Mrs. Grose), Michael Redgrave (The Uncle),
Martin Stephens (Miles), Pamela Franklin (Flora), Clytie Jessop (Miss Jessel), Isla Cameron (Anna), Eric Woodburn (coachman)

Jack Clayton's adaptation of Henry James's fright classic *The Turn of the Screw* remains one of the most rich and monumental depictions of a woman's mental deterioration to ever hit the big screen. With a careful screenplay by Truman Capote, the lush cinematography of Hammer mainstay Freddie Francis and unnerving performances all around, *The Innocents* is a truly powerful film, within and without its genre designation.

Deborah Kerr plays Miss Giddens, who goes to see a wealthy, jet-setting bachelor (Michael Redgrave) about a post as governess to the two orphaned children in his care. The children are installed at his sprawling country estate Bly, where she is to live with them and a small cadre of servants. Her prospective employer tells her that, should she accept the post, she is not to ever call or write to him, but to take full responsibility for all decisions relating to the children.

Giddens is enchanted with the young Flora (future scream queen Pamela Franklin), who insists that her brother Miles (Martin Stephens, who also plays the knowing alien child in *The Village of the Damned*) is coming home soon from boarding school – and sure enough the next day a letter arrives announcing that Miles is being sent home under vague charges of being a 'bad influence' on the other boys. When Miles arrives – charming and overly mature for his young age – Miss Giddens can't imagine how the child could have done anything so dastardly as to get himself thrown out of school. However, her enthralment with the children gradually turns to unease when she finds them sharing secrets and begins to suspect that they are manipulating her. When the housekeeper Mrs. Grose tells Giddens disturbing stories about the past governess Miss Jessel and her abusive, indiscreetly passionate relationship with the former chauffeur Quint – both now mysteriously dead – Giddens comes to believe that the children's questionable behaviour is being informed by these licentious ghosts. "So far these monsters have kept their distance", she confides to Mrs. Grose. "Only been seen in high places, through windows, across the lake. But they intend coming closer." She is certain that they mean harm to the children. And she resolves, at all costs, to save them.

While James's original novella is ambiguous regarding the story's supernatural aspects, the film is more so, and though we are treated to unobscured images of the spectres, it is still always conceivable that these images are all in Giddens's mind. An equally possible projection is what Giddens perceives as Miles's calculated sexual fixation on her. After a scolding one night, Miles asks for a kiss, and kisses her long and squarely on the lips, which she takes as an erotically-charged gesture that both disturbs and possibly excites her. As her obsession intensifies and she makes a crusade of getting the children to tell the truth about the entities that are shadowing them, she becomes an abuser herself, shaking, pushing and frightening the children to the point of hysteria. In a finale that originally won the film an X rating from the BBFC, she proves herself a true pastor's daughter; she believes in "helping even when it hurts", and in the process, makes martyrs of them all.

above: Eerie artwork for Jack Clayton's **The Innocents** (1961).

INSIDE

2007, France
Original title: **À l'intérieur**
D: Alexandre Bustillo, Julien Maury. P: Vérane Frédiani, Franck Ribière. W: Alexandre Bustillo. Ed: Baxter. DoP: Laurent Barès.
M: François Eudes. PD: Marc Thiébault.
Cast: Béatrice Dalle (the woman), Alysson Paradis (Sarah), Nathalie Roussel (Louise), François-Régis Marchasson (Jean-Pierre),
Jean-Baptiste Tabourin (Matthieu), Dominique Frot (the nurse), Claude Lulé (the doctor), Hyam Zaytoun (the policewoman),
Tahar Rahim (policeman), Emmanuel Guez (policeman)

After her husband is killed in a head-on auto collision, a pregnant woman retreats into a state of general misanthropy, caring neither for herself nor the baby she is carrying. Four months later, it is Christmas Eve, and she is preparing for her impending delivery the next day. Eschewing the company offered by her mother, she chooses to remain alone. She falls asleep and has a nightmare in which her baby forces its way out through her mouth, one of the film's many indications that she resents – possibly even *hates* – her unborn child.

She is awoken by a strange visitor: a severe-looking black-clad woman (Béatrice Dalle) appears at the door asking to use the phone to call for help, but Sarah denies the request, claiming that she doesn't want to wake her husband. "Your husband is not sleeping, Sarah", the woman says. "Your husband is dead."

Thus begins a bloody game of survival that will bring out Sarah's dormant will to live, and test her devotion to her baby. Dalle plays the role like a classic giallo killer, brutal and unrelenting, her black Victorian dress strangely anachronistic and her imposing stature emphasized by the fact that she's often too tall for the frame. If there is a Monstrous Mother here, Dalle's character seems like a prime candidate, but the square-off between the two women questions this facile categorization; in The Woman's mind, Sarah has violated the pact of motherhood – she doesn't care whether her baby lives or dies. "You don't need this baby anymore. I'll take care of him", The Woman says, her scissors poised over Sarah's exposed belly. She'll rip the child out if she has to.

As Sarah cowers in the bathroom, getting bloodier every time she opens the door to see what's happening outside, The Woman kicks, stabs, punches, screams, coerces and hyperventilates. Cut-frames and sudden intense sound design are meant to convey her fractured mental state, but Dalle manages just fine without the help of these tricks, which are often distracting and unnecessary.

While the gore is abundant (and probably shouldn't be viewed by any pregnant women), *Inside* is a tight debut from Julien Maury and Alexandre Bustillo – a well-acted Francophone bloodbath whose foetal transgressions are the most extreme since Joe D'Amato's *Anthropophagous the Beast*.

above: Béatrice Dalle and Alysson Paradis in Alexandre Bustillo and Julien Maury's **Inside** (2007).

THE ISLE

2000, South Korea
Original title: **Seom**
D: Kim Ki-duk. P: Lee Eun. W: Kim Ki-duk. Ed: Kyung Min-ho.
DoP: Hwang Seo-sik. M: Jeon Sang-yoon. AD: Kim Ki-duk.
Cast: Suh Jung (Hee-jin), Kim Yu-seok (Hyun-shik), Park Jeong-gi (Eun-A), Cho Jae-hyun (Mang-Chee), Jang Hang-sun (middle-aged man), Seo Won, Son Min-seok, Han Ji-seon, Kang Chung-sik, Choe Hui-gyeong

Kim Ki-duk's films routinely deal with marginal spaces and their inhabitants, and *The Isle* concerns a mute, feral young woman who acts as caretaker to a floating campsite, where

the pastel-coloured fishing shacks that dot the lake offer a stunning location for a very dark love story. She sells supplies, coffee and at times, her own body to the lowlifes that rent the cottages, and seems remarkably self-reliant despite what appears to be an inherent masochism. When a man fleeing the scene of a murder seeks refuge in one of her cottages, a strange and dangerous unspoken bond develops between them. They become partners in mutual degradation.
For more on this film see **Part 7: You've Always Loved Violence**.

JULIE DARLING

1982, West Germany/Canada
Alternative title: **Daughter of Death**
D: Paul Nicolas. P: Ernst von Theumer, Monica Teuber, Maurice Smith. W: Paul Nicolas, Maurice Smith. Ed: Alfred Srp. DoP: Miklós Lente. M: Joachim Ludwig. AD: Lindsey Goddard.
Cast: Anthony Franciosa (Harold Wilding), Sybil Danning (Susan), Isabelle Mejias (Julie), Paul Hubbard (Weston), Cindy Girling (Irene), René Kolldehoff (Lt. Rossmore), Michael Tregor (Kirby), Natascha Rybakowski (Michelle), Benjamin Schmoll (Dennis), Elizabeth Paddon (Shirley)

Julie (Isabelle Mejias) isn't a normal teenager. She's morbid, disinterested in boys, and listens to classical music on her headphones (the sure sign of a budding psychopath). She's also perversely fixated on her father (Anthony Franciosa, best known to genre fans as Peter Neal from *Tenebrae*), which creates a competitive relationship with her mother that is exacerbated when Mother pays the grocery delivery boy to release Julie's pet snake into the wild. When her mother is attacked and murdered in front of her (by the same grocery boy), Julie takes no action to intervene, and further, she tells the police she didn't see a thing – allowing the killer to go free.

The night her mother is killed she can hardly contain her giddy relief at having her father all to herself. Feigning a fear of the killer-at-large, she asks if she can sleep with Daddy. He obliges, not realizing that her interest goes beyond a desire for quality time with ol' dad. When he plans to remarry almost immediately – to exploitation stunner Sybil Danning – Julie is not thrilled. This new threat intensifies her obsession, and when she overhears her father and new stepmother having sex, she imagines herself in Danning's place.

When she notices her father giving Danning's son the same degree of affection she thought was reserved for her, Julie's bond with her father is called into question; feeling she has nothing left to lose, she becomes more overt in her bad behaviour. This includes thinking of various ways to get rid of her new kid brother, which Danning catches onto pretty swiftly, promising Julie that she'll go to any lengths to guarantee the safety of her child. Reading this as a challenge, Julie tracks down the guy who killed her mother and says she'll turn him in if he doesn't kill her new mother too – adding "you can rape her all you want before you kill her."

Also known as *Daughter of Death*, this is a disturbing, surprisingly unknown film whose young star Isabelle Mejias would go on to be nominated for a Best Actress award at the Genies (the Canadian Oscars) two years later for *Unfinished Business*.

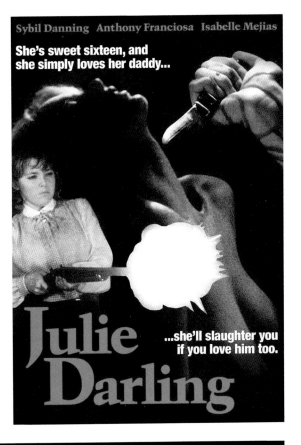

Sybil Danning   Anthony Franciosa   Isabelle Mejias

She's sweet sixteen, and she simply loves her daddy...

...she'll slaughter you if you love him too.

Julie Darling

top left: Suh Jung in Kim Ki-duk's **The Isle**; *above:* Promotional artwork for Paul Nicolas's **Julie Darling** (1982).

KICHIKU

1997, Japan
Original title: **Kichiku dai enkai**
D: Kazuyoshi Kumakiri. P: Kazuyoshi Kumakiri, Tomohiro Zaizen. W: Kazuyoshi Kumakiri. Ed: Kazuyoshi Kumakiri. DoP: Kiyoaki Hashimoto. M: Akainu. AD: Satoko Yasui.
Cast: Sumiko Mikami (Masami), Syunsuke Sawada, Shigeru Bokuda (Kumatani), Toshiyuki Sugihara (Sugihara), Kentaro Ogiso (Fujiwara), Tomohiro Zaizen (Yamane), Yuji Hashimoto (Aizawa)

Translated as either 'Satanic Banquet' or 'Banquet of the Beasts', *Kichiku* was Kumakiri's student film (which was, incidentally, *not* well-received at the graduation screening) based on the true story of a group of student revolutionaries whose infighting causes them to brutally murder one another in the mountains. "I remember that I saw a TV program featuring the incident, in which a picture of how they were lynched was shown", he said to Sam McKinlay in *CineMuerte Magazine #10*. "I was only a small child at the time, but was strongly shocked by the picture, and it is still in my mind like a trauma. This memory became the core of *Kichiku*."

While Aizawa, the leader of a radical student group, is in prison, his girlfriend Masami takes over, and the group degenerates into a scattered collection of do-nothings who find an identity in their designation as 'radicals' but do little to deserve the title. Masami sexually manipulates the men in the group to keep them allied with her until Aizawa is released. When word gets back that Aizawa has committed suicide in his cell, the interim community they've created is suddenly like a hydra without a head; in grasping for something concrete they start to question each other's loyalties, and paranoia mounts, most notably in Masami who feels an incredible pressure to prove herself a worthy successor to Aizawa. Her emotional fragility manifests as power-tripping and she exhibits increasingly sadistic and dictatorial behaviour over the group, leading to beatings, torture and ultimately murder – all done in the kind of graphic detail that is usually reserved for splatstick. But despite a level of gore on par with *Braindead* or *Story of Ricky*, there's nothing funny about *Kichiku*. While various characters can be held responsible for the onscreen violence, it is really Masami whose madness seems to be infecting all of them. "She was a member of a small troupe at my college, but was completely amateur as far as playing in movies", Kumakiri said of Sumiko Mikami, who played Masami. "At first, she was very embarrassed, so we had to make her drink alcohol or make her shout before acting. I wanted something extreme in her acting, so I tormented her any way I could. By the way, she is now an ordinary office-worker."

THE KILLER NUN

1979, Italy
Original title: **Suor omicidi**
D: Giulio Berruti. P: Enzo Gallo. W: Giulio Berruti, Alberto Tarallo. Ed: Mario Giacco. DoP: Antonio Maccoppi.
M: Alessandro Alessandroni.
Cast: Anita Ekberg (Sister Gertrude), Joe Dallesandro (Dr. Patrick Roland), Alida Valli (Mother Superior), Massimo Serato (Dr. Poirret), Daniele Dublino (director), Laura Nucci (Baroness), Alice Gherardi (nurse), Ileana Fraja, Paola Morra (Sister Mathieu), Lou Castel (Peter)

Fading glamour-girl Anita Ekberg stars as Sister Gertrude, a stern nurse/nun at a Belgian insane asylum who suffers a protracted mental breakdown following surgery for a brain tumour. Her symptoms include terrible headaches, blackouts, blurred vision and a pronounced persecution complex, all of which are exacerbated by morphine addiction.

She loudly condemns perceived improprieties among the patients and fellow staff, while engaging in illicit sex with strangers during excursions to the city.

Following her afternoons of ecstasy she comes back to the hospital teeming with fresh admonitory vigour, and brutal murders occurring on the hospital grounds all seem to point to her as the prime suspect.
For more on this film see **Part 8: Heal Me with Hatred**.

from top: Sumiko Mikami in Kazuyoshi Kumakiri's **Kichiku** (1997); Paola Morra in Giulio Berruti's **The Killer Nun** (1979).

KISSED

1996, Canada
D: Lynne Stopkewich. P: Dean English, Lynne Stopkewich. W: Angus Fraser, Lynne Stopkewich, Barbara Gowdy (story). Ed: John Pozer, Peter Roeck. DoP: Gregory Middleton. M: Don MacDonald. PD: Eric McNab. AD: Darryl Dennis Deegan.
Cast: Molly Parker (Sandra Larson), Peter Outerbridge (Matt), Jay Brazeau (Mr. Wallis), Natasha Morley (young Sandra), Jessie Winter Mudie (Carol), James Timmons (Jan), Joe Maffei (biology teacher), Robert Thurston (detective), Annabel Kershaw (mother Larson), Tim Dixon (father Larson)

For way too long I had a hate-on for this film because the British Columbia Film Classification Board always used it as the reason *Nekromantik* should remain on the banned list. But in all honestly, *Kissed* was a groundbreaking film; somehow Lynne Stopkewich managed to get government funding for a feature about necrophilia, and to have enough success with the film to reinforce that this was a good decision, thereby paving the way for future Canadian genre films (provided their makers were handy with creative grant writing).

In this film based on Barbara Gowdy's short story *We So Seldom Look on Love*, which was inspired in turn by the true story of unrepentant necrophile Karen Greenlee, Molly Parker plays Sandra Larson, a young woman who, since childhood, has been obsessed with the rituals surrounding death. Her elaborate ceremonies for the dead animals she finds throughout her small town border on orgiastic, enough so to frighten away the only friend she has. "For the first time, I saw myself the way others might."

Transported emotionally by the smells and textures of death, she is moved to become an embalmer's assistant at the local funeral home. "Cutting into the body seemed dangerous, and destructive. But I had to get inside. To see the order, understand the perfection." After hours she shares tender moments with the recently departed young men, claiming to see "a light" during their closest moments, recalling the Victorian belief that being close to the dead allowed for a glimpse into the afterlife.

Unlike her counterparts in *Nekromantik*, Sandra is able to conceal her morbid interests behind a front of social acceptability, which is aided in no small part by the fact that she is gentle and ethereally beautiful. When she confesses to a handsome acquaintance that she sleeps with the corpses, he is unruffled, and more determined than ever to get to know her romantically. Even taking this chance is an act of social integration on her part though, and it serves to emphasize the film's somewhat fantastical envisioning of the life of a necrophile. As they get closer, he suggests that she may have a schizophrenic imagination, projecting fictional lives onto the corpses so that she can have control over them, but she maintains that, "each of them has its own wisdom, its own innocence, its happiness, its grief. I feel everything from the body, OK? I see it. It's like looking into the sun without going blind. I'm consumed."

A beautifully composed movie directed with a very Canadian sense of tastefulness, *Kissed* may not be the most realistic portrait of a necrophile, but until there is such a thing, *Kissed* stands as the most thoughtful filmed consideration of the subject.

KNIFE OF ICE

1972, Italy/Spain
Original titles: **Il coltello di ghiaccio**; **Detrás del silencio**
D: Umberto Lenzi. P: Salvatore Alabiso. W: Umberto Lenzi, Antonio Troisio. Ed: Enzo Alabiso. DoP: José F. Aguayo Jr. M: Marcello Giombini.
Cast: Carroll Baker (Martha Caldwell), Evelyn Stewart [Ida Galli] (Jenny Ascott), Eduardo Fajardo (Marcos, the chauffour), Silvia Monelli (Mrs. Britton, the housekeeper), George Rigaud (Uncle Ralph), Franco Fantasia (Inspector Durand), Lorenzo Robledo (Sgt. Mallow, Durand's assistant), Consalvo Dell'Arti (the mayor), Rosa María Rodríguez (Christina), Alan Scott (Doctor Laurent)

Former pinup and Lenzi favourite Carroll Baker plays Martha, who has been psychosomatically mute since seeing her parents killed in a railway accident as a young teenager. She lives with her occult-obsessed Uncle Ralph in a large house in the small country town of Montseny, Spain and communicates through a mix of tapping, writing and charades. Her cousin Jenny (Evelyn Stewart), a jet-setting singer, arrives for a visit and presents Martha with an old reel-to-reel recording of Martha giving an oral presentation at a recital as a child – which terrifies Martha not only because is prompts painful flashbacks but also due to the uncanny nature of hearing her own alien voice. Jenny winds up murdered shortly thereafter.

In typical giallo fashion, the befuddled police think there's a "sex maniac" at large, due to the mysterious death of another young girl in the area just before, and the subsequent deaths of Martha's housemaid Mrs. Britton and Christina, the inquisitive little girl she baby-sits (Rosa María Rodríguez of *The Blood Spattered Bride*). Martha's paranoia mounts as the numerous red herrings include her forgetful physician (Alan Scott of Jacques Demy's *Lola*), her creepy chauffeur Marcos (genre regular Eduardo Fajardo) and Uncle Ralph himself (George Rigaud). Rigaud's casting here is especially telling considering his role as the suspect physician in Sergio Martino's *All the Colors of the Dark* (also 1972) with which this film shares many striking similarities, including a female protagonist considered by those around her to be 'especially vulnerable', parental trauma that causes debilitating flashbacks, the blending of 'paranoid woman's film' tropes with supernatural elements, and a lurking peripheral character with demonically weird blue eyes.

In the climactic sequence, Martha is pursued into an underground cavern and frightened into screaming aloud, her voice returning as the result of extreme stress that reverses the initial traumatic trajectory. But on the heels of this breakthrough comes the revelation that the killer is Martha herself – the flimsy explanation is that she resented Jenny for having "the one thing she doesn't… a voice" – with the other superfluous murders meant to cover up the initial crime. Given that the film has followed Martha subjectively, and seen her terrorized by various silhouetted pursuers, it's hard to accept this leap, especially since no attempt is made to connect it to the death of her parents, which caused her psychosomatic illness in the first place. As such, the ending is sloppily tacked-on and invalidates much of the fog-and-shadow-laden dread that the film tried heavy-handedly to create.

top left: Promotional artwork for Lynne Stopkewich's **Kissed** (1996).

THE LADIES CLUB

1986, USA
Alternative Titles: **The Sisterhood**; **Violated**
D: A.K. Allen [Janet Greek]. P: Paul Mason, Nick J. Mileti.
W: Fran Lewis Ebeling, Paul Mason, Betty Black (novel), Casey
Bishop (novel). Ed: Marion Segal, Randall Torno. DoP: Adam
Greenberg. M: Lalo Schifrin. PD: Stephen Myles Berger.
Cast: Karen Austin (Joan Taylor), Diana Scarwid (Lucy
Bricker), Christine Belford (Dr. Constance Lewis), Bruce
Davison (Richard Harrison), Shera Danese (Eva), Beverly
Todd (Georgiane), Marilyn Kagan (Rosalie), Kit McDonough
(Carol), Arliss Howard (Ed Bricker), Randee Heller (Harriet)

Janet Greek's *The Ladies Club* – released under the
pseudonym A.K. Allen due to a dispute over marketing
tactics – deals in female vigilantism of a calculated sort: Diana
Scarwid stars as an average housewife whose teenage sister
is catatonic after being raped. After receiving more than 100
letters from women who'd been raped or whose friends or
family members had been raped, Scarwid and her doctor
(whose daughter had also been raped and murdered) form
a support group that soon morphs into a vigilante group
aimed at surgically castrating male repeat-sexual offenders.
For more on this film see **Part 4: Secret Ceremonies**.

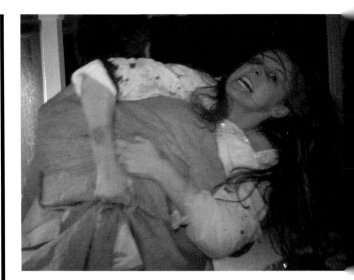

THE LAST EXORCISM

2010, USA
D: Daniel Stamm. P: Marc Abraham, Thomas A. Bliss, Eric
Newman, Eli Roth. W: Huck Botko, Andrew Gurland. Ed: Shilpa
Sahi. DoP: Zoltan Honti. M: Nathan Barr. PD: Andrew W. Bofinger.
Cast: Patrick Fabian (Cotton Marcus), Ashley
Bell (Nell Sweetzer), Iris Bahr (Iris Reisen),
Louis Herthum (Louis Sweetzer), Caleb
Landry Jones (Caleb Sweetzer),
Tony Bentley (Pastor Manley),
John Wright Jr. (John
Marcus), Shanna
Forrestall (Shanna
Marcus), Justin
Shafer (Justin
Marcus),
Carol Sutton
(shopkeeper)

A Necessary Death director Daniel Stamm teams up with
a team of producers including Eli Roth, and writer Andrew
Gurland (*Mail Order Wife*) for this subjectively-shot vérité horror
about a lifelong priest (inspired in part by former child-preacher
Marjoe Gortner) out to expose the exorcism racket as a fraud
before leaving the faith for good.

Cotton Marcus is a likable and charismatic reverend
whose father shanghaied him into the biz as a child, an act that
went over especially well in the doom-and-gloom southern
states. As an adult, a medical emergency with his only child
that coincided with news reports of children dying during
contemporary exorcisms caused a crisis of faith that he's never
shaken. He decides to participate in a tell-all documentary
that goes behind the cloth to expose the hucksterism and the
perils of exorcism in an enlightened era. He makes a deal with
the filmmakers: the next letter he opens requesting an exorcism
will be filmed, with Cotton revealing all the tricks he uses to
deceive those in need of ecclesiastical reinforcement for what
he believes are essentially psychological problems.

Their mandate is thwarted when they encounter a rather
frightening case of hysteria: a young home-schooled farm
girl, the naïve daughter of a fundamentalist bible-thumping
widower, has started mutilating livestock in her sleep, breaking
her own fingers, throwing her body into inhuman contortions
and, of course, speaking Latin.

What's most interesting about the film is that they subtly
touch on every possible reason for the girl's predicament: the
murky spiritual terrain of the south, where numerous
religions (both established and peripheral) 'rub up
against each other' in an isolated, lost-in-time
environment; sibling abuse; possible incestual
sexual abuse; and schizophrenia resulting from
debilitating shame. The film is convincing until
the last act dumps an unnecessary twist on us,
soiling what could have been an important genre
offering – if its questions concerning religious fanaticism, child
exploitation and female repression had been left to steep on
their own.

Ashley Bell in Daniel Stamm's **The Last Exorcism** (2010).

THE LEGEND OF LYLAH CLARE

1968, USA

D: Robert Aldrich. P: Robert Aldrich. W: Hugo Butler, Jean Rouverol, Robert Thom, Edward DeBlasio. Ed: Michael Luciano. DoP: Joseph F. Biroc. M: Frank De Vol. AD: George W. Davis, William Glasgow.

Cast: Kim Novak (Lylah Clare/Elsa Brinkmann/Elsa Campbell), Peter Finch (Lewis Zarken), Ernest Borgnine (Barney Sheean), Milton Selzer (Bart Langner), Rossella Falk (Rossella), Gabriele Tinti (Paolo), Valentina Cortese (Countess Bozo Bedoni), Jean Carroll (Becky Langner), Michael Murphy (Mark Peter Sheean), Lee Meriwether (young girl)

This campy high melodrama from the director of *What Ever Happened to Baby Jane?* stars Peter Finch as Lewis Zarken, a megalomaniacal director who, in an attempt to make a comeback after a 20 year hiatus, hires unknown actress Elsa Campbell (Kim Novak) to play the Hollywood screen legend Lylah Clare (a brash fictional mix of Jean Harlow and Marlene Dietrich).

Lylah was an enchanting, opinionated and reputedly promiscuous starlet to whom Zarken was briefly married before her tragic death 20 years earlier, and Campbell suspects going into the job that Zarken and his entourage (including giallo regular Rossella Falk as a heroin-addicted lesbian dialogue coach) will project Lylah's image onto her as some twisted form of therapy. She plays along with the illusion; adopting Lylah's mannerisms and loud, condescending laugh, she drops her vocal register and dons Lylah's seductive German accent. People who knew Lylah are all too willing to accept this perfect replica, and soon no one – including Elsa herself – can tell the difference. Elsa becomes so consumed by Lylah's overpowering personality – a sharp contrast to her own mousy timidity – that she is willing to die to maintain the illusion.

It's possible to read the film as a 'possession' story, but it holds more weight as a histrionic criticism of the star-making machine (that riffs heavily on Hitchcock's *Vertigo*). The acerbic dialogue is a treat (co-written by Corman regular Robert Thom, who also wrote the original DuPont Show of the Week episode upon which it was based) and revels in its jabs at the industry through heartless and sexually frustrated characterizations of well-worn Hollywood types. Ernest Borgnine is terrific as the grouchy studio head, who barks at his assistant: "*Films?* Whatever happened to MOVIES?? What are ya, in the *art* business? I make movies, not FILMS!"

right: U.S. poster for **The Legend of Lylah Clare** (1968).

Overnight she became a star. Over many nights she became a legend.

THE STRANGE WOMAN-
She rules the mansion where Lylah lives!

THE DIRECTOR-
Overnight, he can make or destroy a sex-goddess.

THE STUDIO BOSS-
He was known for his clean pictures and his dirty deals.

METRO-GOLDWYN-MAYER PRESENTS
AN ASSOCIATES AND ALDRICH COMPANY PRODUCTION

★The LEGEND of LYLAH CLARE★

KIM NOVAK · PETER FINCH · ERNEST BORGNINE

THE LEGEND OF THE WOLF WOMAN

1976, Italy
Original title: **La lupa mannara**
Alternative title: **Werewolf Woman**
D: Rino Di Silvestro. P: Diego Alchimede. W: Rino Di Silvestro. Ed: Angelo Curi. DoP: Mario Capriotti. M: Coriolano Gori.
AD: Arrigo Breschi, Rino Di Silvestro.
Cast: Annik Borel (Daniela Messeri), Frederick Stafford (Inspector Monica), Dagmar Lassander (Irena), Tino Carraro (Count Corrado Messeri), Elio Zamuto (Doctor Trevell), Osvaldo Ruggeri (Fabian), Andrea Scotti (Alivi), Howard Ross [Renato Rossini] (Luca Mondini), Felicita Fanni (Doctor Savelli), Isabella Rosa

In Rino Di Silvestro's *The Legend of the Wolf Woman*, the werewolf story conveniently allows the protagonist to act opposite to her social obligations while in a transformed state, rendering her irresponsible for any transgressions in reality.

Most werewolf stories feature undercurrents of sexual repression, but few are as shamelessly in-your-face as *The Legend of the Wolf Woman* (aka *Werewolf Woman*). There's no stretched-out characterization that builds up to the obligatory metamorphosis; in a naked frenzy, the titular lycanthrope is transformed before our eyes before the opening credits are even finished rolling. Annik Borel (who has a hilarious role in *Truck Turner* and is no stranger to onscreen nudity) plays the pasty wolfwoman in human form. Flashbacks indicate that she spent some time in an institution after being raped as a child, and now as an emotionally delicate adult, she lives in a provincial home with her father. Everything seems fine until her glamorous sister (Dagmar Lassander) comes to visit with new husband Fabian in tow, and the wolfwoman's repressed sexual urges come to the fore.

Between the pull of the full moon and the sexual freedom it represents for her, the wolfwoman is in a practically hypnotized state – transfixed by her desires (which are directed at her sister's husband Fabian) and characterized by her glazed-over expression of masturbatory excess. She watches her sister and Fabian making love and masturbates just outside their bedroom door before running naked into the woods to transform into her 'real' self – the self that takes what she wants, which will ultimately include Fabian. Having heard a suspicious noise, Fabian gets up to investigate and ends up following the wolfwoman into the forest where he is molested and then devoured by the hairy-breasted she-beast. Satiated, the wolfwoman throws Fabian's limp body over a ravine and howls in triumph.

Hospitalized again as a result of allegedly 'witnessing' the murder of her brother-in-law by a mad dog, the wolfwoman becomes more hysterical than ever. Bound to her bed by restraints, medicated frequently and covered in a disturbing rash, she spits out a torrent of obscenities at the doctors, nurses and her visiting sister that rivals anything in *Magdalena, Possessed By the Devil* or *The Exorcist*. And there's no shortage of vagina in this movie either – one wonders how a U.S. print of this film managed to stay intact, even on the drive-in circuit. Borel lifts her nightgown at every opportunity, lest we forget the sight of her pubic triangle. But that's not a criticism; Borel's defiant refusal to keep her vagina tucked away is one of the things that makes this movie great.

The scenes of hysteria are the high points of this film (although the first time you see her hairy wolf-breasts, that's pretty great too). The narrative itself is secondary: she escapes from the hospital, hooks up with stuntman Howard Ross and embarks on a healthy relationship only to be raped again and set backward by a gang of construction workers. The real concern is with Borel's assertion and acceptance of her sexuality, which is hampered by a mental association between sex and violation.

To cope, she creates a framework for her sexuality, a fictional story through which she can distance herself from sexual responsibility. Described as an "ancestral complex" by her psychiatrist, the wolfwoman believes she is the reincarnation of a distant ancestor from the 18th century, a beautiful, high-born woman whose lycanthropy saw her burned at the stake. Folk tales are rife with witches and werewolves, which we now recognize as stories of societal transgression grotesquely modified to take on an admonitory purpose. But the wolfwoman identifies with this person whose exaggerated story has taken on a very real meaning for her.

It's possible that to admit enjoying sex would, in her own mind, make her complicit in her own rape, and so she has to re-imagine herself as 'monstrous' in order to accept sexual pleasure. While superficially manifested as a series of exhibitionist psychotic episodes spurred on by the lunar cycle, her problem is a long-running identity disorder stemming from an incident of childhood abuse. Her primary, passive identity gives way to her hostile, aggressive identity (complete with the bodily illusion of lycanthropic transformation) when a situation arises that reminds her of her trauma. Although for a brief time she is able to enjoy a healthy relationship with Howard Ross, she – like Monica Ranieri in Argento's *The Bird with the Crystal Plumage* – subconsciously relates to sex the same way her attackers do – as a non-consensual means of domination.

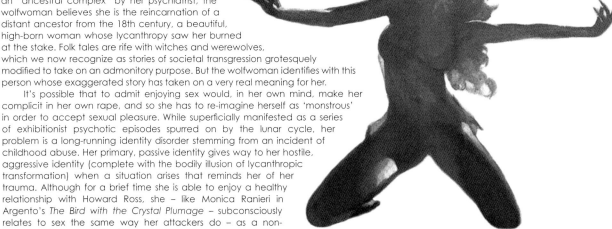

right: Annik Borel in Rino Di Silvestro's **The Legend of the Wolf Woman** (1976).

LET'S SCARE JESSICA TO DEATH

1971, USA
D: John D. Hancock. P: Charles B. Moss Jr.
W: Ralph Rose [John Hancock], Norman Jonas
[Lee Kalcheim]. Ed: Murray Solomon. DoP: Bob
[Robert M.] Baldwin. M: Orville Stoeber.
Cast: Zohra Lampert (Jessica), Barton Heyman
(Duncan), Kevin O'Connor (Woody), Gretchen
Corbett (girl), Alan Manson (Sam Dorker),
Mariclare Costello (Emily)

One of the most subtle masterpieces of '70s
genre cinema is John Hancock's moody,
ethereal *Let's Scare Jessica to Death*, starring
Zohra Lampert as a young woman recently
released from a mental institution. Her husband's
bright idea is to move to a new home so that his
wife can 'get better' – in this case an imposing,
labyrinthine house on a remote apple farm, far
removed from New York City. While he brings
along his pal Woody as added company, there
is no escaping the fact that Jessica's husband
has brought her into a very limited environment
in which she has to be dependent solely upon
him. The nearby townspeople – all hostile and
intimidating old men wearing weird bandages
– will prove no help to Jessica either.

Jessica is fascinated by rumours in the
town about the house's previous inhabitants,
the Bishop family, whose 20-year-old daughter
Abigail drowned in her wedding dress in the
cove behind the house. Abigail's body was
never recovered, and the townsfolk believe
that she is still alive, roaming the country as a
vampire. When a transient hippie named Emily
comes to say with them, these vampiric myths
intertwine with Jessica's increasing view of Emily
– a spitting image of the 'missing' Abigail Bishop
– as a predator who wants to steal away her
husband and keep Jessica a prisoner on the
farm. As Jessica's visions intensify, and Emily/
Abigail gets more aggressive with both Jessica
and the men in the house, Jessica finds it harder
and harder to maintain any front of normality.
For more on this film see
Part 3: All Safe and Dead.

A LIZARD IN A WOMAN'S SKIN

1971, Italy/Spain/France
Original titles: **Una lucertola con la pelle di donna**; **Una lagartija con piel de
mujer**; **Carole**
Alternative title: **Schizoid**
D: Lucio Fulci. P: Edmondo Amati. W: Lucio Fulci, Roberto Gianviti, José Luis
Martínez Mollá, André Tranché. Ed: Vincenzo Tomassi, Jorge Serralonga.
DoP: Luigi Küveiller. M: Ennio Morricone. AD: Maurizio Chiari.
Cast: Florinda Bolkan (Carol Hammond), Jean Sorel (Frank Hammond), Stanley
Baker (Inspector Corvin), Leo Genn (Edmond Brighton), Silvia Monti (Deborah),
Anita Strindberg (Julia Durer), George Rigaud (Dr. Kerr), Alberto de Mendoza
(Sergeant Brandon), Penny Brown (Jenny), Edy Gall (Joan Hammond)

Florinda Bolkan plays Carol, the prim, upright and repressed wife of an
ambitious young lawyer who neglects and cheats on her. At night she dreams
of her promiscuous next door neighbour Julia (Anita Strindberg), who Carol
is secretly excited by despite her apparent disgust with Julia's excessively
hedonistic lifestyle. She routinely attends therapy and discusses her dreams with
a psychiatrist who is only too happy to interpret them as typical doppelganger
fare: in her dreams, the neighbour becomes the depository for her shameful
desires. When the dreams escalate to include the murder of the neighbour,
the psychiatrist proclaims this to have been "a liberating dream... you killed
the part of yourself that is attracted to degradation". But if the neighbour is a
doppelganger, we know that means one thing: one of them is about to die for
real. Carol soon finds herself at the centre of a murder investigation, and her
ability to distinguish between dream, memory and reality gradually crumbles.
For more on this film see **Part 6: The Strange Passenger**.

LOVE ME DEADLY

1973, USA
Alternative title:
Secrets of the Death Room
D: Jacques Lacerte. P: Buck
Edwards. W: Jacques Lacerte.
Ed: Leo H. Shreve. DoP: David
Aaron. M: Phil Moody.
Cast: Mary Wilcox (Lindsay
Finch), Lyle Waggoner (Alex
Martin), Christopher Stone (Wade Farrow), Timothy Scott (Fred McSweeney),
I. William Quinn (Billy-Jo), Michael Pardue (Lindsay's father), Dassa Cates
(housekeeper), Terri Anne Duvalis (Lindsay as a child), Louis Joeffred
(McSweeney's colleague), Bruce Adams (McSweeney's colleague)

Jacques Lacerte's only film is a necrophilic oddity that plays with the trappings
of romantic drama. Lindsay Finch (Mary Wilcox) is beautiful, sexy, socially
charismatic and not at all hard up for male attention. She throws swinging
parties in her lavishly decorated '70s baroque pad, which she inherited when
daddy died, but routinely disappears at orgy time. Instead, she pours over the
obits, looking for recently departed young males. A regular at funerals, she visits
the casket after everyone else has gone, and passionately paws the deceased.

As with most necrophilia films, personal issues with power and identity have
a hand in Lindsay's neurosis: Lindsay suffers from an intolerable Thanatophobia,
but rather than insulating herself from death, her somewhat shaky mandate is
to penetrate and expose death so as to camouflage her own stifling frigidity.
Her activities are fuelled by her fear of adult relationships and the emotional
responsibility they require.
For more on this film see **Part 6: The Strange Passenger**.

from top: Mary Wilcox in Jacques Lacerte's **Love Me Deadly** (1973); Zohra Lampert and Mariclare Costello in **Let's Scare Jessica to Death** (1971).

Tasmanian director Sean Byrne's narrative feature debut has some stunning production design, bathed in pink and blue hues, decked out in satin and glitter. And this slick appearance goes a long way in preventing the audience from noticing that the film is actually quite shallow and underdeveloped, especially regarding the female psycho at its centre.

Brent (Xavier Samuel) is a teenager who was behind the wheel in the car accident that killed his father, and copes by getting high and cutting himself to ease the mental anguish. He has a girlfriend who loves him despite his despondency and commitment-phobia, and a mother who has shrivelled up into a fragile shell of worry and dread, while another girl – a quiet classmate named Lola – is secretly fixated on him. When he politely turns down Lola's invitation to the end of year dance, Brent finds himself forcibly whisked away into the makeshift high school prom fantasyland she and her enabling, twisted father have concocted back at their house – complete with disco ball lighting, paper crowns and torture devices to use on this latest fool who gets to be king for a day. A series of 'loved ones' have preceded him, and his road towards the same dehumanizing fate sees him stabbed, injected, cut, carved, and drilled into submission as Lola gets to act out her most gleefully psychotic fantasies like a spoiled bloody princess. Her father, with whom she has a borderline incestuous relationship, is only too happy to oblige her, and not only participates in the torture but has also been led to zombify his own wife – nicknamed 'Bright Eyes' – as a result of his obsessed daughter's desire to have Daddy all to herself.

Robin McLeavy plays the role of Lola with gusto, but her character is woefully underdeveloped. From her approximately one minute of screen time before the criminal activities commence, we're supposed to assume that she is socially invisible and that perhaps this has led to her psychosis. She's clearly stunted in pre-adolescence, but is also highly sexual in her interactions with her latest captive. Overall, the lack of character development is an oversight that just makes the film indistinguishable from a legion of other tortured-prey films, its candy-coloured design (and the more charismatic but ultimately useless side character Jamie, played by Richard Wilson) the only things that keep one's eyes stuck to the screen.

THE LOVED ONES

2009, Australia
D: Sean Byrne. P: Michael Boughen, Mark Lazarus. W: Sean Byrne. Ed: Andy Canny. DoP: Simon Chapman. M: Ollie Olsen. PD: Robert Webb. AD: Robert Webb.
Cast: Xavier Samuel (Brent), Robin McLeavy (Lola 'Princess'), Victoria Thaine (Holly), Jessica McNamee (Mia), Richard Wilson (Jamie), John Brumpton (Daddy), Andrew S. Gilbert (Paul), Suzi Dougherty (Carla), Victoria Eagger (Judith), Anne Scott-Pendlebury (Bright Eyes)

MACABRE

1980, Italy
Original title: **Macabro**
D: Lamberto Bava. P: Gianni Minervini, Antonio Avati. W: Pupi Avati, Roberto Gandus, Lamberto Bava, Antonio Avati. Ed: Piera Gabutti. DoP: Franco Delli Colli. M: Ubaldo Continiello.
Cast: Bernice Stegers (Jane Baker), Stanko Molnar (Robert Duval), Veronica Zinny (Lucy Baker), Roberto Posse (Fred Kellerman), Ferdinando Orlandi (Mr. Wells), Fernando Pannullo (Leslie Baker), Elisa Kadigia Bove (Mrs. Duval).

Allegedly inspired by a true story brought to the director's attention by co-writer Pupi Avati (*The House with Laughing Windows*), Lamberto Bava's first solo feature sees actress Bernice Stegers, fresh off Fellini's *City of Women*, throwing all the class out the window as an adulterous woman who goes over the edge when her lover is decapitated in front of her in a car accident.

When Jane Baker's husband goes away for a while she wastes no time in scurrying over to her love shack across town to cavort beneath the sheets with her lover Fred (exploitation bit player Roberto Posse), while her homicidal pre-teen daughter Lucy drowns her little brother in the bathtub back home. When Jane gets a phone call bearing news of the 'accident', she and Fred race off in the car, and her frantic behaviour causes a collision. After recuperating in a mental hospital for a year, and now estranged from her husband, she moves into her former part-time pad, upstairs from the blind landlord Robert Duval (Croatian actor Stanko Molnar, also of Bava's A *Blade in the Dark* and *Demons 5*).

Despite her outwardly 'cured' appearance, Jane has a secret — she keeps her lover's head in the freezer — and is so preoccupied with night-time necrophilia that she doesn't notice the blind babe from downstairs trying to romance her. And while he may be blind, he's not deaf; he can hear her making love with her imaginary visitor all night long, which both torments him and piques his curiosity. His own investigation into what lies behind her locked doors is matched by that of Jane's manipulative daughter Lucy, who pops by uninvited to leave 'gifts' in her mother's room in an effort to drive her mad and hopefully see her locked up for good.

While Steger's wide-eyed performance leaves much to be desired and the sociopathic daughter's role is underdeveloped, *Macabre* is an economic first feature, limited to a handful of actors in mostly a single location, and is loaded with enough camp and grotesquerie to warrant its current fan base.

above: Bernice Stegers in Lamberto Bava's **Macabre** (1980).

THE MAD ROOM

1969, USA
D: Bernard Girard. P: Norman Maurer. W: Bernard Girard, A.Z. Martin, Garrett Fort (original screenplay), Reginald Denham (original play and screenplay), Edward Percy (original play). Ed: Pat Somerset. DoP: Harry Stradling Jr. M: Dave Grusin. AD: Sydney Z. Litwack.
Cast: Stella Stevens (Ellen Hardy), Shelley Winters (Mrs. Armstrong), Skip Ward (Sam Aller), Carol Cole (Chris), Severn Darden (Nate), Beverly Garland (Mrs. Racine), Michael Burns (George), Barbara Sammeth (Mandy), Jennifer Bishop (Mrs. Ericson), Gloria Manon (Edna)

A somewhat goofy re-imagining of Charles Vidor's 1941 eerie melodrama *Ladies in Retirement*, Bernard Girard's *The Mad Room* has the neutered quality of a TV production, and indeed this is where most of Girard's previous experience lay. One gets the sense that a 1969 film could be more daring than this, especially considering the gruesome potential of its subject matter.

The opening credits flash over a barrage of newspaper headlines detailing a Toronto crime case where two small children (4 and 6 years old) murdered their parents. The oldest sister Ellen, who witnessed the crime, is put into foster care while the young children are institutionalized indefinitely. Years later, the adult Ellen (Stella Stevens, a far cry from Ida Lupino in the original) is working as a live-in secretary to a wealthy, self-indulgent woman named Mrs. Armstrong (Shelley Winters) on Vancouver island, and is also poised to marry Mrs. Armstrong's son Sam, despite the elder woman's misgivings. But when Ellen is forced to take custody of her now-teenaged siblings following the death of their uncle, she flies back to Toronto to retrieve them from the institution, clearly unnerved by stepping foot inside the place. As she wanders through the classroom at the asylum waiting for her siblings to join her, she is disturbed by a hanging mobile of disembodied hands pointing in different directions (a telling piece of set-dec considering later developments).

She brings the teenagers, George and Mandy, home to the Armstrong's estate, admonishing them to withhold the truth about their past from their new patrons. Having spent half their lives in an institution learning to accept responsibility for their crime, they find this to be a misguided request and a possible step backward emotionally, but Ellen is adamant that their secret can only be shared with time for the family to get to know and care for them. Even their doctor tells Ellen that she is the only one who refuses to deal maturely with the past. Despite her status as a caregiver, Ellen's refusal to grow up and face change is illustrated through her anachronistic aesthetic: she looks like a Barbie doll in Pollyanna curls, totally out of it for the film's 1969 setting, in contrast to the housekeeper Chris (Carol Cole) who listens to loud rock music – courtesy of the Nazz – which sometimes makes her oblivious to events in the house.

"George and I are going to need a 'mad room'" says Mandy, quite seriously, and they convince Ellen to covertly give them access to the late Mr. Armstrong's private study in the attic, which is off limits to everyone in the house. When Winters catches Mandy in the verboten room, she interrogates Ellen and finally gets her to fess up about her siblings' homicidal past – but then Mrs. Armstrong doesn't want them in the house anymore. Before long, she ends up dead, hacked to pieces in the mad room.

Late at night Ellen and George throw her body over a suspension bridge, not realizing that the dog has absconded with one of Mrs. Armstrong's severed hands and hidden it. Through this process, Ellen's lack of emotional response and need to pretend that nothing has happened alarms the kids, who start to wonder if maybe they're not the crazy ones after all…

MADEMOISELLE

1966, France/UK
D: Tony Richardson. P: Oscar Lewenstein. W: Marguerite Duras, Jean Genet (story). Ed: Antony Gibbs. DoP: David Watkin. M: Antoine Duhamel. AD: Jacques Saulnier.
Cast: Jeanne Moreau (Mademoiselle), Ettore Manni (Manou), Keith Skinner (Bruno), Umberto Orsini (Antonio), Jane Beretta (Annette), Mony Reh (Vievotte), Georges Douking (the priest), Rosine Luguet (Lisa), Gabriel Gobin (police sergeant)

Adapted by Marguerite Duras from an original short story by Jean Genet, *Mademoiselle* stars Jeanne Moreau as a visiting schoolteacher in a small French village who is thrown off kilter by the arrival of migrant Italian workers – particularly the beefy Ettore Manni. She commits seemingly random acts of vandalism as a means of expressing pent-up sexual desires, including setting fires, flooding the local farmlands and poisoning the animals. No one in town would suspect her; she is the teacher, the mentor, the role model. The one who can be counted on to keep everything orderly and right. Clearly she clings to this role, and her sense of pride depends upon it, but her pride is compromised by her feelings for the Italian, which she despises as weakness. Angry that he has caused her to be weak, she behaves violently. For more on this film see **Part 8: Heal Me with Hatred**.

from top: Stella Stevens in Bernard Girard's **The Mad Room** (1969); Jeanne Moreau *(centre)* in Tony Richardson's **Mademoiselle** (1966).

MADHOUSE

1974, UK
Alternative title: **The Revenge of Dr. Death**
D: Jim Clark. P: Max J. Rosenberg, Milton Subotsky. W: Greg Morrison, Ken Levison, Angus Hall (novel). Ed: Clive Smith. DoP: Ray Parslow. M: Douglas Gamley. AD: Tony Curtis.
Cast: Vincent Price (Paul Toombes), Peter Cushing (Herbert Flay), Robert Quarry (Oliver Quayle), Adrienne Corri (Faye Carstairs Flay), Natasha Pyne (Julia Wilson), Michael Parkinson (himself), Linda Hayden (Elizabeth Peters), Barry Dennen (Gerry Blount), Ellis Dayle (Alfred Peters), Catherine Willmer (Louise Peters)

In Jim Clark's giallo-inspired Amicus/AIP co-production *Madhouse*, Adrienne Corri plays the mad wife of a film director played by Peter Cushing, who is hidden away in a crumbling basement (recalling *Jane Eyre*'s 'wife in the attic') after an accident leaves her scarred and disfigured. She is bald, bloody and living in filth, surrounded by tarantulas she calls her 'babies'.

It is insinuated that her madness is the result of sublimating her needs to her husband's. She married Cushing out of pity, and gave up her career as an actress to be by his side through a difficult time. Inevitably, she started to resent him for it, her resentment manifesting itself in careless, adulterous behaviour. Ignoring the danger inherent in casual sex with strangers, one night she picked up a few guys who beat her "for fun", then got scared of being reported, so, as she explains it: "They set the car on fire and pushed it down the hill. When I came out of it, I wasn't pretty anymore." So instead, she hides in the basement with her spiders and her old phonographs, waiting to die.

above: Adrienne Corri in Jim Clark's **Madhouse** (1974).

MADHOUSE

1981, USA/Italy
Alternative title: **There Was a Little Girl**
D: Ovidio G. Assonitis. P: Peter Shepherd, Ovidio G. Assonitis.
W: Stephen Blakely, Ovidio G. Assonitis, Peter Shepherd,
Robert Gandus. Ed: Angelo Curi. DoP: Roberto D'Ettorre
Piazzoli. M: Riz Ortolani. AD: Stefano Paltrinieri.
Cast: Trish Everly (Julia Sullivan), Michael MacRae (Sam Edwards),
Dennis Robertson (Father James), Morgan Hart (Helen), Allison
Biggers (Mary Sullivan), Edith Ivey (Amantha Beauregard),
Richard Baker (Sacha Robertson Jr.), Don Devendorf (Principal),
Jerry Fujikawa (Mr. Kimura), Doug Dillingham (Golden)

Julia Sullivan (Trish Everly) is a teacher of deaf students who
hasn't seen her identical twin sister Mary in almost a decade.
When she is summoned to visit
Mary in the hospital by their
uncle James (Dennis Robertson)
– a priest determined to bring
the two sisters together again
– she is filled with trepidation.
"Nobody knows what she
did to me", Julia says, but
Uncle James prods her into
the hospital room where her
sister – now horribly disfigured
by a degenerative virus – lies
in wait. As Julia crosses the
doorway, the room becomes
dark, barely illuminated by
blue light, with sheets of plastic
lining makeshift hallways that
eventually lead to her sister's
bed. Time has not healed the
rift between them; if anything it
has intensified in Mary's mind,
whose madness has manifested
as physical deformity. She
grabs Julia and threatens her,
shrieking that she'll make Julia
suffer like she's suffered. Julia
recalls their mutual childhood
birthdays, which Mary would
seize upon to mete out special
punishments, often using her
loyal, bloodthirsty Rottweiler
to paralyze Julia with fear.
Mary resented having to share
her life with this twin whose
innocence only emphasized her own internal ugliness. When
Julia's doctor boyfriend questions why she never resisted or
told anyone, she replies: "I was completely under her power –
it was almost as if I were doing it to myself."

It is clear that Julia's decision to cut her sister out of her
life – a healthy survival tactic – has made her susceptible to
guilt, which her Uncle James exploits at every opportunity. In
church, he gives a sermon detailing the wrath of God upon
those who neglect their familial bonds, using sisters who are
close in age, appearance and background as an example.
When Mary escapes from the hospital on the eve of their
birthday and Julia's closest allies start turning up dead – most

the victims of mysterious dog attacks – she realizes that the
chapter on her troubled childhood is not ready to be closed.
There will be one more birthday party, where Julia must cease
to be the silent victim. When push comes to shove, Julia
proves herself quite handy with an axe, hacking away at her
tormentor so viciously that her boyfriend questions her sanity.
As she twitches off-screen, we wonder if she's gone mental
from the horror of this event or whether this madness was
always there, waiting to get out.

A sharp, colourful film with a few standout performances
(most notably Dennis Robertson as Uncle James, who seems
to be channelling the dark alter ego of tragic folksinger
Phil Ochs), *Madhouse* is stylistically impressive – but the plot
lags and the denouement suffers from its similarity to J. Lee
Thompson's superior *Happy Birthday to Me*, which came out
the same year.

JULIA THINKS
SHE LIVES
ALONE...
SHE DOESN'T !

MANY PEOPLE VISIT...FEW EVER LEAVE

OVIDIO G. ASSONITIS PRESENTS "MADHOUSE"
STARRING TRISH EVERLY • MICHAEL MACRAE • DENNIS ROBERTSON
MORGAN HART CO-STARRING JERRY FUJIKAWA
DIRECTOR OF PHOTOGRAPHY ROBERTO D'ETTORRE PIAZZOLI A.I.C. MUSIC COMPOSED AND CONDUCTED BY RIZ ORTOLANI PUBLISHER BY CA
EXECUTIVE PRODUCER OVIDIO G. ASSONITIS
EXECUTIVE IN CHARGE OF PRODUCTION JACQUES GOYARD PRODUCTION SUPERVISOR PETER SHEPHERD
SCREENPLAY BY STEPHEN BLAKELY • OVIDIO G. ASSONITIS • PETER SHEPHERD and ROBERT GANDUS
PRODUCED AND DIRECTED BY OVIDIO G. ASSONITIS

MADNESS

1994, Italy
Original title: **Gli occhi dentro**
Alternative titles: **Occhi senza
volto**; **Eyes Without a Face**
D: Herik Montgomery [Bruno
Mattei]. P: Mimmo Scavia.
W: Lorenzo De Luca. Ed: Bruno
Mattei. DoP: Luigi Ciccarese.
AD: Alterio Angela.
Cast: Carol Farres [Monica Seller]
(Giovanna Dei), Gabriele Gori
(Nico Mannelli), Emy Valentino
(Emy), Anthony Berner [Achille
Brugnini] (Marzio Mannino),
Carlo Granchi, Antonio Zequila
(Amedeo Callistrati), Fausto
Lombardi (Lorenzo Calligari)

In Bruno Mattei's *Eyes Without a
Face* (no connection to Georges
Franju's film of the same name),
Carol Farres (aka Monica Seller)
plays Giovanna, a comic book
artist whose popular character
'Doctor Dark' murders babysitters
and steals their eyes. When a
string of murders emulating the
comic start happening, the clues
lead to Giovanna herself. It seems she is 'reinterpreting' events
from her childhood in an attempt to symbolically rectify them: as
a child her babysitter would lock her in the dark as a punishment,
telling her to look out for the Man in Black, who would come and
steal her eyes away. To overcome her fear, she would identify with
the Man in Black, eventually dictating his actions and feelings by
making him a character in her comic book. Unfortunately the
fixation didn't end on the page – in attempting to exorcise this
source of anxiety from her past, she created a sinister double life
for herself. In one of the hammiest performances of the giallo
canon, Farres oscillates between the innocent, confessional
Giovanna and the sadistic eyeball-collector, Doctor Dark.

above: Promotional artwork for Ovidio Assonitis's **Madhouse** (1981).

everything to Cissy – her work, her personal life – she even hates animals and yet she repeatedly acquiesces to Cissy's demands for a large unruly pet that will inevitably be buried in the backyard before long. But hints at a past incestuous relationship illustrate why the bond between the two sisters is difficult to shake. When a co-worker courts Ellen, Cissy's bubble is threatened and the interloper finds himself at the centre of a violent sacrificial ceremony.

Although she's an award-winning television director, this is one of Karen Arthur's few ventures onto the big screen (her first feature, 1975's Legacy also had a neurotic woman as its focus), and aside from the lush, exotic production design, the performance by Carol Kane as Cissy is particularly jaw-dropping.

THE MAFU CAGE

1978, USA
Alternative titles: **Deviation; My Sister, My Love; The Cage; Don't Ring the Doorbell**
D: Karen Arthur. P: Diana Young. W: Don Chastain, Eric Westphal (play). Ed: Carol Littleton. DoP: John Bailey. M: Roger Kellaway. PD: Conrad E. Angone.
Cast: Lee Grant (Ellen Carpenter), Carol Kane (Cissy Carpenter), Will Geer (Zom), James Olson (David Eastman), Budar (Mafu), Will Sherwood (Will)

One of the most compelling and uniquely dark films of the psychotic woman subgenre, Karen Arthur's adaptation of Eric Westphal's play You and Your Clouds stars Lee Grant as Ellen, an astronomer who lives with her feral sister Cissy (Carol Kane) in the large house left to them by their now-deceased anthropologist father. The distinction between the two sisters – one a caregiver with social responsibilities, the other an angry pet – is illustrated through aural cues: weird harpsichord music accompanies Ellen's limited private life while pounding tribal percussion underscores Cissy's fanciful existence alone in the house, which is decked out in exotic African textiles, pelts and artefacts. Cissy herself prefers to go around unclothed, or to wear ceremonial African vestments brought back from her father's many expeditions. The centrepiece of their living room is a large cage, where Cissy keeps her rotating queue of 'mafus' (monkeys) who live as long as she will let them before she loses patience and sentences them to death.

Cissy is not just a 'wild thing', she's completely nuts: she hyperventilates and screams like a dangerous child (the amount of high-pitched screaming here ranks with Alucarda's fits of hysteria), and when Ellen refuses to get her another mafu on account of the fates of the previous ones, Cissy is alternately spiteful and conciliatory, demanding "You get me what I want or I will assassinate myself right now!" (slicing her wrists open to emphasize the point). When Ellen concedes and procures a new mafu from an old friend of their father's (Will Geer of The Waltons, in one of his last roles), Cissy role-plays with the large orangutan, positing herself as 'Ellen' and the mafu as 'Cissy' the uncivilized creature, trying to impose order and obedience upon it. When the mafu fails to comply, she beats it to death with a chain, which is how she perceives Ellen to treat her.

As much as Ellen wants Cissy to be normal, 'normalcy' is relative: Ellen is an enabler, and things only get this far out of hand because she allows them to. She sacrifices

MAN, WOMAN AND BEAST

1977, Italy
Original title: **L'uomo, la donna e la bestia: Spell (Dolce mattatoio)**
D: Alberto Cavallone. W: Alberto Cavallone. Ed: Alberto Cavallone. DoP: Giovanni Bonicelli. M: Claudio Tallino. PD: Joseph Teichner.
Cast: Jane Avril [Maria Pia Luzi], Martial Boschero, Paola Montenero (Luciana), Giovanni De Angelis, Angela Doria, Emanuele Guarino, Macha Magall, Aldo Massasso, Mónica Zanchi, Josiane Tanzilli

Although Alberto Cavallone's film is a sensory overload in general, of interest here is the mute, feral character Luciana. From the film's opening, Luciana is clearly mad, kept locked up in the apartment of her emotionally distant husband, a communist artist whose particular fixation is the eroticisation of scientific anatomy. Mentally she exists in a primitive, non-verbal state; she eats off the floor, spilling her food carelessly, and drinks water out of the toilet bowl. Left in the care of a nanny at frequent intervals, she is a danger to herself and others, which becomes apparent when she knocks out the nanny with a hairdryer, cuts the unconscious woman's clothes off with scissors and comes close to cutting off the woman's nipples before her husband stumbles in to stop her. She she has no concept of right or wrong, and reprimanding her seems to have no effect. When a homeless teenage boy who has been beaten by a jealous husband is deposited at the artist's apartment to recuperate, the lustful Luciana seizes upon him in a frenzy of sex and death.
For more on this film see **Part 9: Piercing Reality**.

above, from left: Carol Kane and Lee Grant; Carol Kane in Karen Arthur's **The Mafu Cage** (1978).

MARTYRS

2008, France/Canada
D: Pascal Laugier. P: Richard Grandpierre, Simon Trottier.
W: Pascal Laugier. Ed: Sébastien Prangère. DoP: Stéphane
Martin, Nathalie Moliavko-Visotzky, Bruno Philip. M: Alex
Cortés, Willie Cortés. PD: Jean-Andre Carriere.
Cast: Morjana Alaoui (Anna), Mylène Jampanoï (Lucie),
Catherine Bégin (Mademoiselle), Robert Toupin (father),
Patricia Tulasne (mother), Juliette Gosselin (Marie), Xavier
Dolan (Antoine), Isabelle Chasse (creature), Emilie Miskdjian
(torture victim), Mike Chute (executioner)

Laugier's ambitious and controversial *Martyrs* is a heady
fusion of sibling and doppelganger horror. It is the tale of
two abused children who grow up haunted: Lucie, a young
woman determined to murder the strangers who tortured her
as a child, dogged by the spectre of a fellow victim who never
made it out, and Anna, Lucie's protectress and enabler. The
two women met at a home for orphans and disturbed children,
following Lucie's escape from her captors. Visibly traumatized,
Lucie is reticent and secretive, and only Anna knows about
Lucie's nightly visits from the grotesque, crawling white-skinned
woman that functions equally as a physical manifestation of
her guilt over having abandoned another child in escaping,
and also as a doppelganger that fills her with homicidal rage.
As she grows into a young woman, Lucie is still being followed
by the doppelganger, and she believes the only way she can
get rid of it is to seek revenge on the people who captured and
tortured her almost 20 years earlier.
For more on this film see **Part 2: Broken Dolls**.

MARNIE

1964, USA
D: Alfred Hitchcock. P: Alfred Hitchcock. W: Jay Presson Allen,
Winston Graham (novel). Ed: George Tomasini. DoP: Robert
Burks. M: Bernard Herrmann. PD: Robert F. Boyle.
Cast: Sean Connery (Mark Rutland), Tippi Hedren (Marnie
Edgar), Diane Baker (Lil Mainwaring), Martin Gabel (Sidney
Strutt), Louise Latham (Bernice Edgar), Bob Sweeney (Cousin
Bob), Alan Napier (Mr. Rutland), S. John Launer (Sam Ward),
Mariette Hartley (Susan Clabon), Bruce Dern (sailor)

Tippi Hedren plays the title character, a compulsive thief, liar
and identity swapper, whose ongoing MO is to get a job with a
large firm, gain their confidence, and then raid the safe. With a
new dye-job, a new social security number and a new name,
she then moves onto the next job. Occasionally she reassumes
her natural identity to visit her ailing, emotionally distant mother
in Baltimore, and her beloved horse Foreo at a rural stable. The
horse is her only real outlet for affection; her mother, on the
other hand, is a dour Christian woman who shows Marnie no
affection whatsoever. Marnie finally meets her match in the
blue-blooded Mark Rutland (Sean Connery), her dashing new
employer, who incidentally knows exactly who she is and what
she's up to. He's a former zoology major who sees Marnie as
a beautiful, trapped animal, observing her as though studying
predatory animal behaviour. He knows she's dangerous, but
he wants to tame her, to solve her mystery.
For more on this film see **Part 6: The Strange Passenger**.

top left: Tippi Hedren and Louise Latham in Alfred Hitchcock's **Marnie** (1964); *bottom right:* Mylène Jampanoï in Pascal Laugier's **Martyrs** (2008).

MASKS

2011, Germany
D: Andreas Marschall. P: Tim Luna. W: Andreas
Marschall. Ed: Andreas Marschall. DoP: Sven Jakob.
M: Sebastian Levermann, Nils Weise. PD: Tim Luna.
AD: Brendan Flynt, Bitto Graciano.
Cast: Susen Ermich (Stella), Magdalena Ritter (Roza
Janowska), Julita Witt (Cecile), Stefanie Grabner
(Lenka), Sonali Wiedenhöfer (Valeri), Michael Siller
(Florian), Dieter-Rita Scholl (Kasper), Teresa Nawrot
(Yolanda), Norbert Losch (Mateusz Gdula), Michael
Balaun (Dr. Braun)

Beginning with the saturated monochromatic credit
sequence of '60s giallo/krimi films and a soundtrack to
match (a hybrid of bombastic prog and a De Angelis
Brothers-esque guitar-driven score), *Masks* wears its
influences on its sleeve. While it has been dismissed
by some critics as wholly derivative, the homage
in *Masks* – largely to Dario Argento's *Suspiria* (and
director Andreas Marschall does it much better than Aronofsky's *Black Swan*, which came out a year earlier) – taps into that
overwrought sense of the surreal that characterized many golden-era giallo films, and the equation of culture and spirituality
that we see in later Argento films like *Opera* and *The Stendhal Syndrome*.

After giving an unimpressive audition, a young actress named Stella is handed a pamphlet for the obscure acting school
of deceased polish instructor Mateusz Gdula, whose methods, she is told, may help her. As with the beginning of *Suspiria*, a
distraught woman is running away just as Stella arrives, and as she passes through the long hallways painted in rich blues and
reds, hearing whispers behind closed doors, we are again reminded of *Suspiria*'s long tracking shots and colour palette (at one
point there is even a still from *Suspiria* sitting among a pile of various documents). When she loses her temper in the audition, it is
this quality – this lack of control – that makes them accept her; the potential they see "behind that beautiful mask".

She becomes obsessed with part-time classmate Cecile, a shy, cautious girl who has private lessons in Gdula's method
of "orgiastic potency", lessons you have to be specially selected for, and whose secrets must never be spoken of. In Stella's
eyes, Cecile "shines like an angel" even though she keeps coming to class with bizarre cuts, bruises and welts. Curious about
the method, Stella finds an old documentary on Gdula in which it is explained that in his brand of theatre there is "no more
normality... everything is extreme. We live on emotions."

When Cecile goes missing, Stella has an outburst in class that simultaneously gets her expelled and wins her an invitation to
take Cecile's place in the private lessons. She must hand over her phone, cease all communication with the outside world and
"give over her soul" to this intense field of study. Led to a dilapidated part of the building where she is left in the dark with few
amenities, she will begin a ritualistic regimen of abuse from which her acting will benefit, but her sanity will not.

It could be argued that most giallo films have protagonists, or at least pivotal characters, that work in the arts (while *Masks*
is not a giallo per se, it is clearly well versed in the form), which allows for the film to create a visual obsessiveness to match its

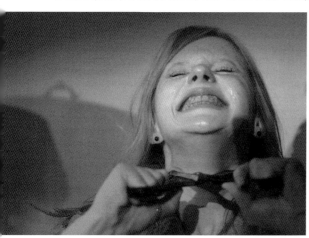

protagonist's journey into the mysterious. Here, the setting is the
exclusive acting school of controversial Polish instructor Mateusz
Gdula, who is likened to famed theatre director Jerzy Grotowski
(mentioned in **Part 9: Piercing Reality** in the discussion on Zulawski's
films), known for inducing primal trance-like states in his tight-
knit group of actors in order to explore the deep connection
between emotion and physicality.[79] A highly influential and
unorthodox alternative to Stanislavski's system of method acting
(later popularized by Lee Strasberg), Grotowski's methods are
exaggerated and made horrific through their reinterpretation
here, supplemented by the administration of hallucinogenic drugs
and a version of Arthur Janov's Primal Therapy, wherein repressed
trauma is deliberately recalled and re-experienced rather than
merely 'talked out'. They are encouraged to go crazy, to go into
the Pain. "The Pain – it will make you shine", assures her instructor,
but despite her subsequent magical performances, what she
realizes too late is that they are not teaching her to act – they are
teaching her to be insane so that she doesn't have to act. In the
hermetic world of *Masks*, insanity is seen as its own reward, given
to Stella like a precious gift.

from top: Susen Ermich and Magdalena Ritter; an early victim of the Gdula method in Andreas Marschall's **Masks** (2011).

MAY

2002, USA
D: Lucky McKee. P: Marius Balchunas, Scott Sturgeon. W: Lucky McKee.
Ed: Debra Goldfield, Rian Johnson, Chris Sivertson. DoP: Steve Yedlin.
M: Jaye Barnes-Luckett. PD: Leslie Keel. AD: Charlie Gonzales.
Cast: Angela Bettis (May), Jeremy Sisto (Adam), Anna Faris (Polly),
James Duval (Blank), Nichole M. Hiltz (Ambrosia), Kevin Gage (Papa),
Merle Kennedy (Mama), Chandler Hecht (young May)

May is an essential component of the recent indie horror resurgence. It stars
Angela Bettis as May, a girl who doesn't fit in. Her trajectory to neurosis is fuelled
by a damaging relationship with her mother, who is obsessed with perfection
and passed her unattainable standards down to the impressionable and
unassertive May. As a result, May grows up socially isolated, over-analytical
and awkward, detachedly scrutinizing people in search of the elusive
'perfection' her mother trained her to value. Taking her mother's advice to
heart ("if you can't find a friend, make one"), May decides to 'make' a friend
by combining the 'perfect' parts of all the people who've rejected her.
For more on this film see **Part 5: Afterschool Special**.

MISERY

1990, USA
D: Rob Reiner. P: Andrew Scheinman, Rob Reiner. W: William Goldman, Stephen King (novel). Ed: Robert Leighton.
DoP: Barry Sonnenfeld. M: Marc Shaiman. PD: Norman Garwood. AD: Mark Mansbridge.
Cast: James Caan (Paul Sheldon), Kathy Bates (Annie Wilkes), Richard Farnsworth (Sheriff Buster), Frances Sternhagen (Virginia),
Lauren Bacall (Marcia Sindell), Graham Jarvis (Libby), Jerry Potter (Pete), Thomas Brunelle (anchorman), June Christopher
(anchorwoman), Julie Payne (reporter)

Paul Sheldon (James Caan) is a romance novelist whose Victorian-era
heroine 'Misery Chastain' has been good to him financially but left him feeling
artistically bankrupt. After completing a challenging new book about kids
in the slums (although if you look at the pages up close it's actually a press
release about Cameron Crowe), he hits the road to meet with his publisher
(Lauren Bacall) in New York. On the way he gets caught in a blizzard and his
car overturns. He is found and pulled out of the car by a stranger, and wakes
up days later in the home of Annie Wilkes, a big, bubbly nurse who claims
to be his number one fan. She also claims that all the phones are out and
the roads are closed due to the storm, and with several broken bones he is
trapped in the bed and completely dependent on her.

When Paul offers to let her be the first to read his latest manuscript in
exchange for saving his life, she is horrified to discover the thematic departure
from his previous romance novels – not to mention the amount of profanity
in the text. Her colourful outburst is the first indication Paul has that he should
start to be more proactive about getting the hell out of there. Then, when Annie comes home excitedly with the latest *Misery* novel
– in which (unbeknownst to her) he kills off his long-time protagonist – he starts to fear for his life.

Aside from a background investigation by the local sheriff (Richard Farnsworth), this is a two-man show, with the incapacitated
Sheldon squaring off against his considerably larger foe in a series of squirm-inducing confrontations. Annie, like Paul, needs to
have things done a certain way. In many ways he can relate to her need for order, routine and tradition. And by figuring out what
her needs are, he is able to manipulate her.

Kathy Bates (who won a Best Actress Oscar for her role here) believably shifts from chipper Annie to psychotic Annie (her
made-up swear words like "cockadoody", "christing" and "dirty birdie" bridging the two). She also falls in line with the behavioural
patterns exhibited by celebrity stalkers: most notably, an imaginary sense of importance in their lives, and alternating depression
and cruelty. Moreover, her history of abusing those in her care does not begin with Paul Sheldon – an old scrapbook reveals that
several times throughout her life, her professional mobility coincided with the mysterious deaths of co-workers, and that she was
the subject of an inquest concerning a rash of infant deaths, for which she did jail time.

While entertaining and well-acted, the only problem with the film is that regardless of how mental Annie gets, the character
seems written for comedy. This is psychotic women-lite, for people who can't handle a movie like *Possession*.

---

from top: Angela Bettis in Lucky McKee's **May** (2002); Kathy bates in Rob Reiner's **Misery** (1990).

MORRIS COUNTY

2009, USA
D: Matthew Garrett. P: Thomas R. Rondinella. W: Matthew
Garrett. Ed: Daniel Brown, Apryl Lee, Arin Sang-Urai. DoP: Jeff
Powers, Daniel Watchulonis. M: David Kristian. PD: April Hodick,
Clarissa Shanahan.
Cast: Darcy Miller (Ellie), Marc Donovan (Mitch), Maren Perry
(Rachel), Jeff Zorabedian (Kevin), Christian Davidock (Scott),
Robert Peters (Joshua), Peter Ganim (Benjamin), Alice Cannon
(Iris), Pamela Stewart (Ms. Jacobs), Erik Frandsen (Elmer)

Starring indie regular Pamela Stewart (Hal Hartley's *Trust*
and *Amateur*) alongside powerhouse performances from
newcomers Alice Cannon and Darcy Miller, Matthew Garrett's
debut feature is a triptych of subtle terror tales set in the
bleeding underbelly of suburban New Jersey. While all three
stories pack a nasty punch, the tales that bookend the feature
– *Ellie* and *Elmer & Iris* – are of specific interest here.

In *Ellie* (which first played the festival circuit as a stand-
alone short film in 2006), Darcy Miller plays the title character,
a high school girl on an enigmatic path of self-destruction.
The film takes place over a single day, and expertly withholds
expository information so that we experience the transience
of identity that Ellie feels in what we suspect is the aftermath
of some sort of debilitating trauma. When the film opens, Ellie is
vomiting (that the film's title appears on a black screen to the
tune of the toilet flushing is a nice touch), and after packing
off for school she instead takes a detour to a park bench for
an unwanted cigarette before hitting up the convenience
store for a bottle of whiskey. When she is denied due to her
age, she desperately states that she "needs it", prompting one
of the two store employees to offer it to her in exchange for
sexual favours. She obliges, but once in the back storeroom
she shrieks when touched, which freaks out one of the boys
but doesn't rattle the other, who has no qualms about taking
advantage of this clearly troubled young girl. While he doesn't
ask any questions, we as the audience are full of them: *why is
she doing this?* Unlike other film characters who are reacting
to an emotional disturbance, Ellie is not jaded; we can tell
through Miller's distressing performance as well as through tiny
hints carefully planted that her behaviour is inconsistent with
what came before. Even the fact that she does sit-ups in the
morning before embarking on a terrible day where she will
prompt her gag reflexes by forcing herself to smoke and drink
indicates that her self-damage is a recent development. But
this mystery, and the fact that Garrett is able to contain it so
compellingly, is part of what makes *Ellie* a special film.

After emerging from the storeroom tryst in a daze,
Ellie walks into the woods where she meets up with some
stoners who are surprised to see her skipping school to drink
alone in the woods (their response indicates that she is
thought of as a 'good girl'). She agrees to smoke up with
them – apparently a first for her – before they pair off, and
Ellie awkwardly makes out with obnoxious Kevin – until he
puts his hand down her pants and it emerges covered with
blood. It's a horrifying spectacle, partly because we are as
confused as he is, and partly because he reacts with such
disgust that we can only guess at how devastating this must
be for Ellie. His reaction is to slap her, smearing her own blood
on her face while yelling expletives: "What the fuck is wrong
with you, you fucking bitch?!!"

She runs off, and finds
her way to a Christian youth
after-school meeting. She's
a mess, her clothes dirty
and dishevelled, dried
blood on her face – but
she's not there for support,
she's there to confront.
Because this day will have
a bodycount.

The closing story,
Elmer & Iris, begins on a
sad note with the elderly
Iris (Alice Cannon) forced into retirement because she can't
keep up with technological advancements in the workplace.
Her husband Elmer is a curmudgeon whose contribution to
conversation consists of a few grunts here and there, in sharp
contrast to Iris's unnaturally chipper personality. But the smile
plastered on her face becomes more heartbreaking with
every scene; not only has she lost her job, but when she
wakes up the next morning she finds Elmer dead in front of
the TV. When she goes out the door to get the morning paper
after finding Elmer dead, she looks around and goes back in,
where she pretends everything's fine, like looking through a
window after a dream and having it dissipate.

Over the next 6 days, as Elmer's body starts
decomposing, she piles up the bowls of potpourri, and loads
up on room sprays and flytraps. She still enjoys sitting next
to him to watch TV – she tunes into *Reali-date* religiously,
a superficial romance program – and appreciates the
opportunity to be more affectionate with Elmer than she
could when he was alive.

This isn't the first time she's been in denial about something.
She confides shocking truths to her former employer (Pamela
Stewart), the one who
was adamant to see
her go. Ms. Jacobs is
condescending (she
talks loudly and over-
annunciates) but being
put in the position of
a confidant is visibly
alarming to her. She's
a power office woman
and the sentimentality
of this elderly woman
with her homemade
cookies and butterfly
brooches is really what
the office environment

doesn't have room for anymore. While being let go was a
pivotal moment for Iris, she hasn't had anything to live for in
a while other than a multi-layered fantasy where people love
her. But for Iris, each new development in her story will be more
undignified than the last.

Bolstered by grotesque FX from Brian Spears (*I Sell the
Dead*, *Stake Land*, *The Innkeepers*) and a diverse score
by electronic musician David Kristian (who also scored
Karim Hussain's *La Belle Bête* and Doug Buck's *Sisters*, both
reviewed elsewhere in this appendix), *Morris County* exposes
suburbia's dark heart and the self-destructive compulsions
that fester within.

from top: Marc Donovan and Darcy Miller; Alice Cannon and Erik Frandsen in Matthew Garrett's **Morris County** (2009).

MORVERN CALLAR

2002, UK/Canada
D: Lynne Ramsay. P: Robyn Slovo, Charles Pattinson, George Faber. W: Lynne Ramsay, Liana Dognini, Alan Warner (novel). Ed: Lucia Zucchetti. DoP: Alwin Küchler. PD: Jane Morton. AD: Philip Barber, James David Goldmark. Cast: Samantha Morton (Morvern Callar), Kathleen McDermott (Lanna), Raife Patrick Burchell (boy in room 1022), Dan Cadan (Dazzer), Carolyn Calder (Tequila Sheila), Steve Cardwell (welcoming courier), Bryan Dick (guy with hat's mate), El Carrette (gypsy taxi driver), Andrew Flanagan (overdose), Desmond Hamilton (Him)

After her boyfriend's suicide over the Christmas holidays, Morvern Callar (Samantha Morton in an extension of her breakout role in 1997's *Under the Skin*) leaves his body on the floor and unwraps their Christmas presents, which include a mix-tape he's made for her that will become the soundtrack to the film. His suicide note, which he's left impersonally typed on the computer, informs her that he's left enough money in their bank account to cover the funeral and urges her to send his recently completed novel to a publisher for consideration.

Her eyes wide and fixed on nothing, she disassociates; she paints her nails, paints her face, sits, waits, then takes money out of his pocket to pay for a night out partying. Instead of telling anyone about his death, she says only that he's left her, gone "to another country". In a telling scene that exemplifies her disassociation, she lifts her dress to expose herself to a passing boat (creating a parallel between vulnerability and freedom that is also used to great effect in Steven Shainberg's *Fur: An Imaginary Portrait of Diane Arbus*, 2006) before engaging in a three-way makeout session with her best female friend and another male acquaintance.

The combination of Morton's performance and Lynne Ramsay's careful composition also allows for a great depiction of female private time; the way she moves through space when she's alone, the way she sees things and chooses to imbue them with importance.

Back home, she steps over her boyfriend's dead body to cook a frozen pizza. She decides to erase him; dismembering his body and burying him in a remote field, she takes his novel as her own and starts on a bizarre elegiac journey that will alternate between Gen-X directionlessness and intoxicating rediscovery of herself and the world around her. But in disposing of her boyfriend's body and identity – the only remnant of which remains the mix-tape – she has become an accessory. Like Lady Macbeth, her hand won't stop shaking – the film's only real cue that she feels any sense of responsibility for her actions.

both images: Samantha Morton in Lynne Ramsay's **Morvern Callar** (2002).

MOTHER'S DAY

1980, USA
D: Charles Kaufman. P: Michael Kravitz, Charles Kaufman.
W: Charles Kaufman, Warren Leight. Ed: Daniel Loewenthal.
DoP: Joseph Mangine. M: Phil Gallo, Clem Vicari Jr. PD: Susan
Kaufman. AD: Sandy Hamilton.
Cast: Nancy Hendrickson (Abbey), Deborah Luce (Jackie),
Tiana Pierce (Trina), Holden McGuire [Frederick Coffin] (Ike),
Billy Ray McQuade [Michael McCleery] (Addley), Rose Ross
[Beatrice Pons] (Mother), Robert Collins (Ernie), Karl Sandys
[Peter Fox] (Brad 'the Dobbler' Dobson), Marsella Davidson
(Terry), Kevin Lowe (Ted)

After spending the day bonding at a mushy self-help seminar,
an old lady (Beatrice Pons of *Car 54, Where Are You?*, using the
pseudonym Rose Ross) offers two sketchy 20-somethings a ride
home via a back country road. Their exchanged glances lead
us to believe they're up to no good, but when the car suddenly
stalls, the tables turn: the septuagenarian reveals herself to
be the eponymous 'mother' whose hick sons – two of the
most visually distinctive sicko siblings in the backwoods horror
canon – carry out dirty deeds at her bidding (actors Michael
McCleery and Frederick Coffin both use fake names in the
credits, seemingly predicting how the film would be received
by their more 'legit' industry peers at the time).

Cut to the 'Rat Pack', a trio of likeable gal pal pranksters
– Jackie the hard-luck tomboy (Deborah Luce), Abbey the
bookish caretaker to her squealing bedridden mother (Nancy
Hendrickson) and Trina the Hollywood glamour girl (Tiana Pierce)
– old college roommates who reunite for a camping trip in the
country. Against the admonishments of the obligatory inbred
creep who works at the convenience/fishing tackle store, they
head off into the remote area known as Deep Barons.

The girls easily establish themselves as some of the best
female characters to emerge from the early slasher-craze era,
with a believable friendship that liberates them from the more
oppressive aspects of their
daily lives. But in the middle
of a serious heart-to-heart
around the campfire, they
are jumped and accosted
by the two brothers who
drag them back to
Mother's house in their
sleeping bags (harking
back to an earlier prank
in which one girl was
smuggled out of the
dorm in a sleeping
bag for an after-
curfew date).
There, they are
bound, gagged and
utilized as unwilling
participants in the
boys' role-
playing and
rape-games
while Mother
looks on with
pride.

**"I'm so proud of my boys –
they never forget
their mama."**

While the Troma tag infers a certain scatological juvenilia,
Mother's Day is one of their first productions, and tonally is
more along the lines of the original *Last House on the Left*, with
seriously disturbing imagery (such as the barely-alive Jackie
being kept in a dresser drawer) and human savagery side by
side with inappropriately-placed humour that makes the whole
picture that much more potent. The boys mock-fight and bicker
("You're dumb, you like punk!" one says to the other) and
Mother plays out certain grandmotherly affectations at odds
with her family's chaotic tendencies (insisting that the boys wipe
their shoes at the door or play backgammon with her). Sadism
aside, Mother's real goal is to school her boys in being efficient
protectors (complete with an '80s training montage!) against
a possible attack from Queenie, her 'evil' sister who allegedly
roams the woods living a feral existence. While the boys suspect
that there is no 'Queenie', that it's a story Mother's made up to
keep them from leaving, they wouldn't dream of abandoning
her – especially when she indulges their most perverse fantasies
while allowing them to remain essentially children.

Ms.45

1981, USA
Alternative title: **Angel of Vengeance**
D: Abel Ferrara. W: N.G. St. John
[Nicodemo Oliverio]. Ed: Christopher
Andrews. DoP: James Momèl [James
Lemmo]. M: Joe Delia. AD: Ruben
Masters [Bonnie Constant].
Cast: Zoë Tamerlis [Zoë Lund] (Thana),
Albert Sinkys (Albert), Darlene Stuto
(Laurie), Helen McGara (Carol), Jimmy
Laine [Abel Ferrara] (1st rapist), Nike
Zachmanoglou (Pamela), Peter Yellen
(burglar, 2nd rapist), Editta Sherman
(Mrs. Nasone), Vincent Gruppi (heckler
on corner), S. Edward Singer (photographer)

Ms.45 is the most enjoyable and fulfilling rape-revenge film of
those that follow the standard genre trajectory. Zoë Tamerlis
stars as Thana, an innocent mute girl who works as a seamstress
at an independent fashion studio in NYC's garment district. Her
innocence is stressed through her relationship with others: her
nosy landlady checks in on her; her boss pats her on the head;
her co-workers look out for her – they all see her muteness
as a 'severe handicap'. When she is raped twice by *two*
unconnected assailants as she returns home from work one
day, she kills the second in her apartment, severs his limbs and
deposits suspicious paper bags in random dumpsters around
town. The murder weapon is an iron – her primary tool at work.
As such, her anxiety is constantly triggered and she becomes
irritable and subject to flashbacks of the event. She starts to
lack concentration, stops short of finishing tasks and gets in
trouble for inattentiveness. She becomes hyper-aware of
male aggression, is suspicious of others' concerns for her and
is averse to being touched. She knows she's alone and has to
take care of her problem alone. There's no therapy for Thana –
but there is disassociation, withdrawal and revenge.
For more on this film see **Part 4: Secret Ceremonies**.

MUMSY, NANNY, SONNY & GIRLY

1970, UK
Alternative title: **Girly**
D: Freddie Francis. P: Ronald J. Khan. W: Brian Comport,
Maisie Mosco (play). Ed: Tristam Cones. DoP: David
Muir. M: Bernard Ebbinghouse. AD: Maggie Pinhorn.
Cast: Ursula Howells (Mumsy), Patricia Heywood
(Nanny), Howard Trevor (Sonny), Vanessa Howard
(Girly), Michael Bryant (New Friend), Hugh Armstrong
(Friend in Five), Robert Swann (Soldier), Imogen Hassall
(Girlfriend), Michael Ripper (Zoo attendant)

Based on Maisie Mosco's stage play
Happy Family, the satirical horror film
Mumsy, Nanny, Sonny & Girly sees its
dysfunctional family living in a semi-
permanent state of infantilism in a
Victorian fantasy world. Sonny and
Girly are teenagers, but dress and
act like oversexed five-year-olds.
The teens habitually pick up
strangers (all uniformly named
"New Friend") and bring them
to the house for deadly games.
Michael Bryant plays the latest
"New Friend" – a male prostitute who
is lured into their role-playing game and
held prisoner until the time when
he will inevitably be "sent to the
angels". But when Girly tries to play
a new game called "Mothers and
Fathers" with New Friend, it upsets
the dynamic of the household and
will inevitably prove their undoing.
For more on this film see **Part 2: Broken Dolls**.

NABI: THE BUTTERFLY

2001, South Korea
D: Moon Seung-wook. P: Park Jina, Kim
Chang-hyo. W: Moon Seung-wook, Jeong
Hye-ryeon. Ed: Kim Deok-yeong, Lee Jang-uk.
DoP: Gwon Hyeok-jun. M: Jeong Hoon-young.
Cast: Kim Ho-jung (Anna), Kang Hae-jung
(Yuki), Jang Hyun-sung (K), Byeon Sin-hong,
Kim Byeong-su, Bae Jin-man, Kim Dong-hwa, Yun Jong-hun,
Heo Jong-su, Hong Seong-hyeon

A Korean woman named Anna arrives in Seoul after a long time
abroad in Germany. A young girl locates Anna, introducing
herself as Yuki. She will be her guide through the 'Oblivion Virus'
– an elusive virus that infests the city's construction sites and
promises a clean slate to all who catch it. While discovered
inadvertently, it has become a popular industry, and 'travel
agencies' have been set up to exploit the power the virus holds
for those who want to permanently erase painful memories
from their lives and start over.
For more on this film see **Part 6: The Strange Passenger**.

top left: UK Admat; *above:* Sonny and Girly with 'New Friend' Michael Bryant in **Mumsy, Nanny Sonny & Girly** (1970); *right:* **Nabi: The Butterfly** (2001).

NEIGHBOR

2009, USA
D: Robert A. Masciantonio. P: Charles Smith. W: Robert A. Masciantonio. Ed: R. Emmett Sibley.
DoP: Jeff Schirmer. M: Kurt Oldman. PD: Michael Crenshaw. AD: Rob Nemeth.
Cast: America Olivo (The Girl), Christian Campbell (Don Carpenter) Lauren Rooney (Elizabeth
Hitchcock), Pete Postiglione (Mike Hodder), Joe Aniska (Sam Landis), Sarah McCarron (Nancy
Baker), Amy Rutledge (Jenn Crawford), Mink Stole (Mrs. Spool), Meredith Orlow (Sophia Kane),
Giovanna Guldi (Laurie Leigh)

An unnamed woman prowls the streets of an upper middle class neighbourhood, letting herself
into people's homes and offering them her company, but things don't usually end well for her hosts.

The girl is spunky, beautiful, and unnaturally happy. Especially when she's having slumber parties
with dead teenagers, causing old ladies to have heart attacks, and drilling holes through the limbs
of unsuspecting bachelors. She's a sociopath who's mastered the art of charm; she's destructive and
anarchistic, simultaneously random and calculated.

As with many sociopaths, the girl is host to some idiosyncrasies: she panics at the sight of her own
blood, hyperventilating at the slightest cut, but the blood and pain of others has no effect on her
other than inciting a morbid scientific curiosity (exemplified by her overt reference to the dentist in
Marathon Man, jokingly asking the protagonist "Is it safe?" as she revs up a power drill). But the
movie references don't end there: her dialogue incorporates quotes from *Misery*, *Jaws* and
more, leading us to believe that she's spent a fair amount of time in front of a screen, lapping
up imagery and behavioural reinforcement from classic horror films.

Neighbor features some innovative, shocking gore, but there's nothing fun about
it, despite how much fun our villain seems to be having; it's nasty stuff. Where most films
would cut away, *Neighbor* keeps going, revelling in the bloody details. The film has invited
comparisons to Takashi Miike's *Audition*, but it's less obvious here why the girl chooses
this particular neighbourhood, or these particular victims, and we also don't know how
long she's been there – we only know it's been more than a few weeks. There are hints of
jealousy – she comments on the bachelor having a big house all to himself, and in every
home she plays house – making tea and food, showering, watching TV, with no worry of
being caught.

TV news reports indicate that there is a killer on the loose – another killer, not our girl – an
escapee from a nearby institution, and the whole community is buzzing about it, but it still
doesn't make them lock their doors. People are so willing to trust a pretty face.

Neighbor is also a movie about masculinity, and how women defeat men in one way
or another – whether castrated by marriage, punished with physical torture, or haunted by
memories and regrets. The film also points out – through interesting structural techniques –
that the fear of being dominated by a woman, or having one's identity compromised by
commitment to a relationship, are symbolic fears that pale in comparison to meeting a
torture-happy stranger with a toolbox.

from left: Christian Campbell and America Olivo in Robert A. Masciantonio's **Neighbor** (2009).

NEITHER THE SEA NOR THE SAND

1972, UK

D: Fred Burnley. P: Jack Smith, Peter Fetterman. W: Gordon Honeycombe. Ed: Norman Wanstall. DoP: David Muir. M: Nachum Heiman. AD: Michael Bastow.

Cast: Susan Hampshire (Anna Robinson), Frank Finlay (George Dabernon), Michael Petrovitch (Hugh Dabernon), Michael Craze (Collie), Jack Lambert (Dr. Irving), Betty Duncan (Mrs. MacKay), David Garth (Mr. MacKay), Tony [Anthony] Booth (Delamare)

Susan Hampshire of *Malpertuis* plays Anna, a young woman who is on vacation on the Isle of Jersey while she considers whether or not to leave her husband. Her answer comes easily when she meets Hugh, the broodingly handsome lighthouse keeper (Michael Petrovitch) and the two fall passionately in love. Hugh comes from an old, distinguished family, and his brother George (Frank Finlay, whose marquee value was used to sell the film despite his small role) does not approve of Hugh's sudden wantonness with this strange woman. Leaving George to his tsk-tsking, the two lovers set off for a whirlwind trip to Scotland, where Hugh suddenly ups and dies of a heart attack on the beach. While much of the film happens in a fantasy space, this scene in particular is upsetting for its realism: one minute he's there, the next minute he's gone (director Fred Burnley also died suddenly at the age of 41, a few years after completing this picture), with Anna left scrambling to find help in the middle of nowhere. The local doctor pronounces him dead and has little sympathy for Anna's pleas that "he can't die! He said he'd be with me forever!"

Hugh keeps that promise, coming back from the dead later that night. Judging from her reaction, Anna seems to expect him, but all is not right with Hugh – he no longer speaks (not that he spoke much to begin with), and barely moves, with only his eyes following Anna everywhere she goes. His brother George instantly suspects that Hugh is dead, and proves it by setting him on fire to illustrate that Hugh has no reaction to the pain. Soon enough though, George will be out of the picture and Anna can set up house with her cadaverous lover.

It is in these moments that Anna's psychosis – possibly a temporary response to grief – is apparent. She coddles and compliments Hugh, but won't often look him in the face. She does the cooking, shopping, and tries to act wifely – in fact the very fate she just clamoured to escape from by ending her relationship with her husband back home – but pays no heed to the fact that Hugh isn't eating his food or moving about of his own volition, because that would force her to acknowledge that something is wrong. When a nosy neighbour starts irritatingly checking in on her, she keeps insisting that "nothing's wrong, nothing's wrong…" But when Hugh kisses her, it's inescapable: she can taste death on him. She starts to notice how much he's decaying. She becomes terrified of him and beats him with a candlestick, begging him to leave, to "stop loving her". It's incredibly sad. And I find Michael Petrovitch's performance – which has been almost unanimously dismissed as wooden and lifeless (even before he's meant to be a zombie) – to be terribly affecting. He does a lot with a little, and aptly conveys a man enchanted – and his enchantment is enchanting in itself. It's easy to see how she would fall for him.

The coastal settings, with their greys and blues, the mountainous waves, the lonely lighthouse separated from land by the changing tide – all contribute to the epic nature of this very special love story. It implies a nature bigger and more enduring than us; as Hugh says twice in the film, pointing out past the rocks: "It all begins again out there." The film's themes and aesthetics intersect the decaying Gothic and sublime Romantic; while Hugh's human body is disintegrating, his immortality – and that of his love for Anna – will be carried on in the wind and the waves. When Anna rejects him, he is like Frankenstein's monster, cast out and drawn to the tide. A financial and critical flop for Tigon, the film pretty much suffered the same fate.

from top: British quad poster and actress Susan Hampshire from Fred Burnley's **Neither the Sea Nor the Sand** (1972).

NEKROMANTIK

1987, West Germany
D: Jörg Buttgereit. P: Manfred O. Jelinski. W: Jörg Buttgereit, Franz Rodenkirchen. Ed: Manfred O. Jelinski, Jörg Buttgereit. DoP: Uwe Bohrer. M: John Boy Walton, Hermann Kopp, Daktari Lorenz.
Cast: Daktari Lorenz (Robert Schmadtke), Beatrice M. [Beatrice Manowski] (Betty), Harald Lundt (Bruno), Susa Kohlstedt (Vera), Henri Boeck (J.S.A. employee), Clemens Schwender (J.S.A. employee), Jorg Buttgereit (J.S.A. employee), Heike S. [Heike Surban] (prostitute), Collosseo [Colloseo Schulzendorf] (Joe), Holger Suhr (J.S.A. employee)

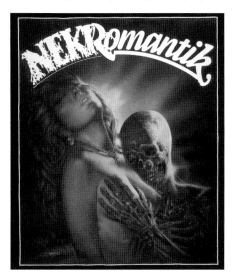

Jörg Buttgereit's infamous necrophilic love-in remains as squalid and disgusting today as it did back in 1987 when it was the subject of controversy, gorehound adulation, bans and police raids.

Rob and Betty's romance is on the rocks. Rob works for a street-cleaning agency that picks up dead bodies, and he occasionally takes one home for a ménage-a-trois with his domineering girlfriend, who seems to like the corpses more than she likes him. Complemented by John Boy Walton's romantic score, the love scenes are filmed with the soft-focus Vaseline glow of old Hollywood melodramas, which contrasts cleverly with the gross-out spectacle of Betty writhing against the slimy corpse while Rob sucks out its putrid eyeball. The film is a mockery of stereotypical domesticity, with Betty bathing in stale blood and watching TV nature shows while Rob is out looking for a new friend to bring home as an after-dinner treat. However, it was the film's follow-up, *Nekromantik 2*, that really examined necrophilia from an exclusively female perspective…
For more on this film see
Part 6: The Strange Passenger.

NEKROMANTIK 2

1991, Germany
D: Jörg Buttgereit. P: Manfred O. Jelinski. W: Jörg Buttgereit, Franz Rodenkirchen. Ed: Jörg Buttgereit, Manfred O. Jelinski. DoP: Manfred O. Jelinski. M: Hermann Kopp, Peter Kowalski, Daktari Lorenz, John Boy Walton, Mark Reeder, Monika M.
Cast: Monika M. (Monika), Mark Reeder (Mark), Lena Braun (porno-synch girl), Jörg Buttgereit (cinema audience), Carola Ewers (Nekro-gang member), Astrid Ewerts (Nekro-gang member), Florian Koerner von Gustorf (drunk at bar), Käthe Kruse (actress in film playing at cinema), Eva-Maria Kurz (Nekro-gang member), Beatrice M. [Beatrice Manowski] (Betty)

Nekromantik 2 opens with the fresh grave of the first film's hapless hero being dug up by female necrophile Monika M. (in a dress and heels, no less). When Betty (Beatrice M.) shows up to reclaim Rob's corpse, she's too late.

It's a cleaner-looking film than its predecessor, which makes its visual transgressions that much sharper, even though the multiple exposures of the first film's love scenes are employed here as a continuing stylistic motif (as an added touch, a drawing by real-life necrophile Karen Greenlee is on the wall behind Monika as she has sex with Rob's corpse). On the verge of orgasm, she rushes to the bathroom and vomits – a rarity in the necrophile film genre but possibly a realistic comment on the health risks inherent in this particular sexual proclivity. Contrary to her unsanitary pastime, Monika's apartment is exceptionally tidy; after their first lovemaking session sickens her, she spends time scrubbing the body, which is already in an advanced state of decay (To emphasize this, the flowers she places next to it are seen wilting instantly).

She goes to the movies one night and, by chance, meets Mark, whose day job is dubbing porn films. The two begin a whirlwind romance, and Monika tearfully opts to let go of her corpse-love, dismembering him in the bathtub with a saw for easy disposal. Except the head, that is. Oh, and the shrivelled penis, which finds a new home in the refrigerator. A later shot of the blue garbage bags sitting in Rob's coffin back at the gravesite is almost sad, like a rejection. But when Monika and Mark share their first moments of intimacy, he just can't turn Monika on. He moves and talks too much. He grabs at her. He's too concerned with his own pleasure. As he comes, she looks at him with disgust.

Although some known female necrophiles, such as Karen Greenlee and Leilah Wendell, have admitted an attraction to the odours and rituals surrounding death (often their own rituals, not necessarily traditional religious rituals), the commonly-held belief among psychologists is that the unpredictable nature of life in other people is a threat to the level of control a necrophile needs. Eventually Monika requests of Mark that he not move during intercourse, and he reluctantly agrees, even though he finds it "perverse".

If Monika's interests are a rejection of life, however, she is not alone. An unusual scene in the film sees Monika and her female friends sitting around eating bon bons and watching a graphic video of a seal being butchered,

with Rob's decomposing head lying openly in the middle of the coffee table, implying that she is only one of a community of women with such morbid tastes. But when she tries to share the video with Mark, the risk doesn't pay off. While his day job propagates an 'accepted' means of perversion, he can't think outside of that well-worn box, which prompts Monika to retreat into her world of the dead – with unexpected results.

left: Promotional artwork for Jörg Buttgereit's **Nekromantik** (1987); *bottom:* Monika M. In **Nekromantik 2** (1991).

NEXT OF KIN

1982, Australia
D: Tony Williams. P: Robert Le Tet. W: Michael Heath, Tony Williams. Ed: Max Lemon. DoP: Gary Hansen. M: Klaus Schulze.
AD: Richard Francis, Nick Hepworth.
Cast: Jackie Kerin (Linda Stevens), John Jarratt (Barney), Charles McCallum (Lance), Gerda Nicolson (Connie), Alex Scott (Dr. Barton), Bernadette Gibson (Aunt Rita/Mrs. Ryan), Vince Deltito (Nico), Robert Ratti (Kelvin), Debra Lawrance (Carol), Tommy Dysart (Harry)

New Zealand-born TV commercial director Tony Williams's only foray into the genre is also his last film, an unfortunate fact considering how unnerving and accomplished it is (including a much-lauded one-take climactic scene).

Linda (Jackie Kerin) comes back to smalltown Australia to inherit the sprawling retirement home 'Montclare' that her now-deceased mother had operated for more than 30 years. Still deliberating whether or not to sell the property, she takes over as directress, with the help of her mother's helping hand Connie and the local physician, Dr. Barton. The shadow of her mother looms over the house – Linda describes her as "unreliable, unpredictable, crazy", and also as an expert keeper of secrets. Now that her mother is dead, those secrets can be found in the wealth of personal diaries she left behind, so Linda spends nights poring over them. They describe a woman terrorized by strange noises in the house, unable to sleep, lights going on and off, taps left running in the bathrooms. Dr. Barton says she died as the result of stress and anxiety over finances, but Linda soon finds out otherwise.

The delusions plaguing her mother start to affect her as well – she is convinced that someone is watching her, that people are dying around her, and that a macabre conspiracy is afoot (in this sense the film has much in common atmospherically with Gary Sherman's Dead & Buried, 1981). The camerawork (by award-winning DP Gary Hansen, who died on the job a year later) and the pounding, anarchic score (by krautrock wunderkind Klaus Schulze) frame Linda as mentally disturbed, with slow-motion and alternately low- and high-angle shots that show her as a body out of control, engulfed by the threatening space of the house. Her boyfriend Barney (Ozploitation fave John Jarratt) has to shake her out of a hysteric, hyperventilating fit. The film plays a great deal with perception, casting doubt on its characters and its events so that one is always questioning whether the film's morbid occurrences are real, or the product of an insane mind. And if the latter, just whose insane mind is it?

It's interesting that Dr. Barton has a reproduction of Andrew Wyeth's famous painting Christina's World in his office (it also appears in Nobuhiko Obayashi's Hausu) – I always thought this was a painting of a woman in the aftermath of an attack, crawling toward a house for help. I later found it's a painting of a polio victim who would regularly crawl to get around, and was not meant to be sinister at all. This misperception shows how we project our own anxieties onto things, a sentiment that ripples throughout the film.

above: Bernadette Gibson in Tony Williams's **Next of Kin** (1982).

THE NIGHT PORTER

1974, Italy
Original title: **Il portiere di notte**
D: Liliana Cavani. P: Robert Gordon Edwards. W: Liliana Cavani, Italo Moscati, Barbara Alberti (story), Amedeo Pagani (story). Ed: Franco Arcalli. DoP: Alfio Contini. M: Daniele Paris. AD: Nedo Azzini, Jean Marie Simon.
Cast: Dirk Bogarde (Maximilian Theo Aldorfer), Charlotte Rampling (Lucia Atherton), Philippe Leroy (Klaus), Gabriele Ferzetti (Professor Hans Vogler), Giuseppe Addobbati (Stumm, the cleaning man), Isa Miranda (Countess Erika Stein), Nino Bignamini (Adolph, the porter), Marino Masé (Anthony Atherton), Amedeo Amodio (Bert Behrens), Piero Vida (The day porter)

Liliana Cavani's film about the mutual obsession between an ex-Nazi officer and the young girl he favoured in a concentration camp is both brave and controversial; while sadomasochistic relationships were common onscreen at the time in both arthouses and the exploitation circuits, Cavani was criticised for placing her story of sexual transgression within the context of the Holocaust.

Vienna 1957: Maximilian Theo Aldorfer (Dirk Bogarde), a former SS officer, is working as a night porter in a Viennese hotel and trying to remain inconspicuous. The quiet life he has tried so hard to build for himself after the war is interrupted when a famous conductor checks into the hotel with his lovely wife

Lucia (Charlotte Rampling) in tow – Max's former prisoner and lover. As her eyes lock with Max's, terror strikes each of them. Memories come flooding back: he shoots at her for fun as she scurries around a small room, naked and shaven; he buys her a sleek, peach-coloured dress; she performs a Marlene Dietrich song in Nazi regalia; he presents her with another prisoner's head on a platter.

Back in the present, she's afraid of him because he makes her afraid of herself. She can turn him into the police – she's a witness to countless war crimes – but she's gripped by something she can't explain. She sends her husband on ahead and says she'll meet him in a few days at his next concert date. Alone in the hotel where Max works, she has only to wait. Propriety is literally discarded when they reunite – he takes off her expensive earrings one by one and tosses them on the floor. Their love is violent, vicious, primal. She was a young girl when they met – this is the only way she has learned how to love; with the ferocity of an only chance before death.

Max's fellow Nazis are none too happy about the existence of this resurgent witness, and order him to give her up. Instead he sequesters them in his apartment, draws the blinds, orders in food. While he's at work one of the Nazis, Dr. Vogler, drops in on Lucia, to try to convince her that Max needs to confess and be formally acquitted so that he can truly be 'cured' like the rest of his brethren. She scoffs: "There is no cure." But Dr. Vogler disagrees:

> Vogler: "It is you who are ill. Otherwise you wouldn't be with somebody who made you…"
> Lucia: "That's my affair."
> Vogler: "But nevertheless your mind is disturbed. That's why you're here, fishing up the past."
> Lucia: "Max is more than just the past."

The cyclical nature of trauma demands that we constantly poke at our wounds in an attempt to reassert control over them. Lucia is a wealthy, glamorous woman married to a famous conductor, and yet she has allowed herself to be chained up in an ex-Nazi's apartment, eating rationed food with her bare hands. Eventually her motor functions cease altogether – he has to take her to the toilet, as she becomes too weak to move. Max, whose life is now threatened by the Nazis, can no longer go out, and must quit his job to stay with Lucia. There is something damnably romantic about this Stockholm Syndrome tale, but both lovers will soon find themselves spiritually as well as physically malnourished. The bond of bad behaviour will not keep them immortal.

from left: Provocative poster art and Dirk Bogarde with Charlotte Rampling in Liliana Cavani's **The Night Porter** (1974).

A NIGHT TO DISMEMBER

1983, USA
D: Doris Wishman. P: Doris Wishman. W: Judith J. Kushner. Ed: Lawrence Anthony. DoP: C. Davis Smith. M: Danny Girlando. Cast: Samantha Fox (Vicki Kent), Diane Cummins (Mary Kent), Saul Meth (Adam Kent), Miriam Meth (Blanche Kent), Bill Szarka (Billy Kent), Chris Smith (Sam Kent), Dee Cummins (Vicki Todd), Norman Main [Larry Hunter] (Larry Todd), Mary Lomay (Ann Todd), Rita Rogers (Aunt Bea Todd)

Exploitation queen Doris Wishman's last film before a long hiatus, *A Night to Dismember* is most famous for the fact that it had to be cobbled together from inferior sources when much of its footage was lost or destroyed at the lab, resulting in a hilariously disjointed narrative about a young woman named Vicki (porn actress Samantha Fox), recently released from a mental hospital, who questions her recovery when bodies start to pile up around her. Her siblings are anxious to return her to the funny farm and go about driving her mad in any way they can, which includes making her believe she's responsible for the sudden influx of corpses. Wishman tried to salvage the film by adding surreal narration by Tim O'Malley to 'explain' plot developments that may have been obscured by the lack of footage, but these snippets of off-screen exposition that burst in with a jarringly different sound mix don't manage to make any sense of the proceedings. Despite the fact that the protagonist is a mental patient, and Samantha Fox tries to take her role seriously, there is no effort here to engage with any complex discussion on female neurosis, so to put forth such an analysis would be moot. That said, *A Night to Dismember*, while inept in every way, is odds-defyingly entertaining, and Wishman's bizarre, Dada-esque editing warrants a look.

NIGHTBIRDS

1968, UK
D: Andy Milligan. W: Andy Milligan. DoP: Andy Milligan.
Cast: Julie Shaw (Dee), Berwick Kaler (Dink), Bay White (Dee's mother), Elaine Shore (Mabel), Bill Clancy (Ginger), Johnathan Borkai (shopkeeper), Felicity Sentance (first girl), Susan Joyce (second girl), Susan McCormick (Rosie), Tom Houlden (Tom)

While filmmaker Andy Milligan is persistently associated with his usual playground of Staten Island, with a regular stable of actors who participated in his ramshackle pictures and theatre projects, he did spend a year and a half in London from 1968 to early 1970, where he made five films with the production company Cinemedia. As with his arrangement with 42nd St. theatre owner William Mishkin, who served as both producer and exhibitor of his films in New York, Cinemedia was owned by the same parent company that ran the Soho theatres where Milligan's films habitually played in London. The first of these five films was *Nightbirds* (originally called *Pigeons*), which was long

thought lost until Milligan biographer Jimmy McDonough sold the only known 35mm print to filmmaker and exploitation movie champion Nicolas Winding Refn, who set about restoring it for a BFI Flipside release.

Nightbirds stars Berwick Kaler in his screen debut (although he would go onto four more Milligan pictures before eventually landing on such popular British TV shows as *Coronation Street* and *Auf Wiedersehn Pet*) as the unfortunately-named Dink, a downtrodden former spoiled momma's boy who's run away from home and has been living on the streets. He is approached by a looker named Dee (Julie Shaw), who he dubs a "Florence Nightingale of the streets" when she offers to take him home and give him something to eat. Set in a squalid section of London's East End, the two hole up in Dee's one-room apartment and embark on a co-dependent sexual relationship. But this relationship reveals itself to be rather one-sided, as he bares his soul to her, telling her of his troubled family life while she evades his questioning about her own background. As their relationship intensifies they become more and more afraid of anything intruding on their bubble - or their 'castle' as they call it – and she is especially opposed to their going out during the daytime. Jealousy becomes rife on both fronts: Dee is jealous of Dink's friend Mabel, a crass former prostitute who adopts a somewhat maternal relationship to Dink (despite her obvious sexual attraction to him), and Dink is none too pleased when he discovers Dee's "arrangement" with her sleazy Irish landlord. They both want to isolate each other from friends and other outside influences, but Dee is clearly the dominant party; it turns out Dink's gone from one domineering woman (his mother) to another, but one with infinitely more power since she's introduced him to sensual pleasures and the illusion of love.

And while these kinds of sexual and emotional conflicts are familiar terrain to Milligan viewers, the tell-tale Milligan stamp is that Dee's predatory games are syphilitic in nature. Much is made of Milligan's 'love him or hate him' reputation, but apologetic admonitions aside, Milligan is like a Stateside Jean Rollin, revisiting certain themes over and over throughout a singularly visionary career, with whatever minuscule budget may be available to him. As with many of his films, predominant themes here include co-dependence, psychic vampirism, jealousy and bad blood. With its two leads commanding almost every scene together in a contained environment, the film also seems like an extension of Milligan's theatrical background.

Although Milligan's films are routinely categorized as horror, *Nightbirds* is not a horror film so much as a dishevelled nouvelle vague-type drama somewhere between *Breathless* and *Last Tango in Paris*, and a predecessor to genre-defying films like Simon Rumley's *Red White & Blue*. And since the rambling nouvelle vague approach implies an inseparability from its historical, geographical and social context, it's interesting to note that the London of *Nightbirds* isn't swinging as much as clinging desperately to life. Sure, Dee might have white lipstick and Dink a sideswept part, but aside from these visual signifiers of the era's fashions, clearly London wasn't swinging for everyone.

from left: Samantha Fox in Doris Wishman's **A Night to Dismember** (1983); Julie Shaw and Berwick Kaler in Andy Milligan's **Nightbirds** (1968).

NIGHTMARES

1980, Australia
Alternative title: **Stage Fright**
D: John D. Lamond. P: John D. Lamond, Colin Eggleston. W: Colin Eggleston, John Michael Howson (story). Ed: Colin Eggleston. DoP: Garry Wapshott. M: Brian May.
Cast: Jenny Neumann (Helen Selleck), Gary Sweet (Terry Besanko), Nina Landis (Judy), Max Phipps (George D'alberg), John Michael Howson (Bennett Collingswood), Briony Behets (Angela), Adele Lewin (Sue), Edmund Pegge (Bruce), Sue Jones (Fay), Maureen Edwards (Mother)

After seeing her parents having sex, a little girl and her mother drive off in a car. Once the girl is asleep in the back seat, the mother picks up another man along the way for a quick extra-marital romp. The child, who wakes up and thinks the stranger is attacking her mother, shouts suddenly – causing the car to swerve and crash. Finding her mother lying halfway out the front window, the girl grabs her legs to try to pull her back into the car, but in doing so, she slits her mother's throat on the glass from the broken windshield, killing her. When the girl comes to in the hospital, she overhears the doctors saying that she caused the accident, and even her own father unsympathetically accuses her of being responsible for her mother's death.

The grown-up Helen is a neurotic stage actress appearing in a sub-sub-sub-standard play by an asshole director. She has a young boyfriend she won't sleep with, as images of sex are equated in her mind with images of glass slitting throats. Which coincidentally is exactly what happens when anyone in the film has sex.

Some jokes about theatre superstition are so stupid they're kind of funny – "Don't whistle, it's bad luck! You're wearing a green shirt. Never do it again!" – but the majority of the dialogue is hopelessly lame. *Nightmares* is very disappointing considering it was written by Colin Eggleston, who directed the amazing *Long Weekend*.

LA NUIT DES TRAQUÉES

1980, France
Alternative title: **The Night of the Hunted**
D: Jean Rollin. P: Monique Samarcq. W: Jean Rollin. Ed: Gilbert Kikoïne. DoP: Jean-Claude Couty. M: Gary Sandeur [Philippe Bréjean].
Cast: Brigitte Lahaie (Elisabeth), Vincent Gardère (Robert), Dominique Journet (Véronique), Bernard Papineau (Dr. Francis), Rachel Mhas (Solange), Catherine Greiner [Catherine Stewart] (Catherine), Natalie Perrey (mother), Christiane Farina (Christiane), Véronique Délaissé [Élodie Delage] (Marie), Alain Plumey [Cyril Val] (Alain)

Rollin's *La nuit des traquées* focuses on a group of people (including Rollin regular Brigitte Lahaie) who are being held in an experimental research facility, bound together by a mutual and total loss of memory, requiring that their object of attention be directly in front of them at all times lest it be immediately forgotten. The surreal and desolate atmosphere of the facility – more akin to the alienated urban centres of Rollin's *The Escapees* than his usual craggy rocks and country chateaux – exacerbates the patients' bewildering state of anxiety. This anxiety is only alleviated by the presence of other people, to whom they develop an immediate and intense attachment that more often than not, comes to fruition in the form of a lengthy sex scene. While there are male patients, Rollin's camera lingers on the women, who cling to each other pleadingly, the perfect picture of mental distress. Many of Rollin's films play with time, but *La nuit des traquées* directly questions the possibility of an eternal present, of an existence without memory. For more on this film see **Part 6: The Strange Passenger**.

from top: Over-eager video art for John Lamond's **Nightmares** (1980); Brigitte Lahaie and Dominique Journet in Jean Rollin's **La nuit des traquées** (1980).

DE MIEDO TAMBIEN SE PUEDE MORIR...
¡¡¡ ESTAIS ADVERTIDOS !!!
ENTRAR SOLO LOS
QUE TENGAIS VALOR

FRANCA CARLO
STOPPI · DE MEJO EN

TERROR
EN EL
CONVENTO

THE OTHER HELL

1981, Italy
Original title: **L'altro inferno**
Alternative titles: **Terror en el convento**; **The Presence**
D: Bruno Mattei. P: Arcangelo Picchi. W: Claudio Fragasso.
Ed: Liliana Serra. DoP: Giuseppe Bernardini. M: Goblin.
Cast: Franca Stoppi (Mother Vincenza), Carlo De Mejo (Father Valerio), Francesca Carmeno (Elisa), Susan Forget (Sister Rosaria), Frank Garfeeld [Franco Garofalo] (Boris), Paola Montenero (Sister Assunta), Sandy Samuel, Andrew Ray [Andrea Aureli] (Father Inardo)

There's so much mental disturbance on display in the first five minutes of this film that it feels like you're watching the confessional climax rather than the set-up. Crazy Mother Vincenza (Bruno Mattei regular Franca Stoppi) stabs the crotch of a dead nun she's embalming, explaining to her mortified assistant: "There! That's the place – the evil starts there, the evil grows and consumes everything, even the spirit. The Devil enters a woman there and devours her. The genitals are the door to evil... Here in the convent, the demon lives and feeds on good, suckling at the breasts of nuns like this one here!" She reveals the mummified corpse of the previous Mother Superior – who committed suicide – then starts grunting and convulsing before stabbing the other nun to death. All this before the opening credits!

Set in the 20th century, Father Inardo has a hard time convincing his male colleagues that they should sanction an exorcism in the convent, which is overrun with hysterical cases and suicides. Setting up an opposition between religion and psychology, a younger

priest (Carlo De Mejo of *City of the Living Dead*) proclaims, "the Devil exists all right, but he exists in the heart and the mind... in the dark recesses of the subconscious."

The mass hysteria in the convent stems from Mother Vincenza, who terrorizes and traumatizes the other nuns as a result of repressing a terrible secret of her own. When the young priest comes to investigate, and the source of Vincenza's neurosis is brought to light, it launches a bloody freak-out of biblical proportions.

THE OTHER SIDE OF THE UNDERNEATH

1972, UK
D: Jane Arden. P: Jack Bond. W: Jane Arden. Ed: David Mingay. DoP: Jack Bond, Aubrey Dewar. M: Sally Minford. AD: Penny Slinger, Liz Danciger.
Cast: Sheila Allen (Meg the Peg), Jane Arden (Therapist), Liz Danciger, Elaine Donovan, Susanka Fraey, Ann Lynn, Jenny Moss, Penny Slinger

Jane Arden's *The Other Side of the Underneath* is an aggressively shrill film documenting a schizophrenic woman's journey through her own psyche. As the film begins, the protagonist is being fished out of a lake and revived from (presumably suicidal) drowning. She is taken to an isolated hospital in the country where histrionic flashbacks and psychological fugues are intercut with group therapy sessions with a host of other bare footed women dressed in dirty white nightgowns. The woman and a fellow inmate play a game with broken mirrors – as they move the pieces around in dangerous configurations, their fragmented images are repeated in a ritualistic display. But this is foreplay – revulsion and ecstasy, violence and love are used interchangeably. Funerals masquerade as weddings; women masturbate and vomit in churches; they murder each other with rubber weapons; they are revered as saints while being buried alive and crucified.
For more on this film see **Part 9: Piercing Reality**.

from top: Spanish poster; Actors Carlo De Mejo and Franca Stoppi in **The Other Hell** (1981); Clowning around in **The Other Side of the Underneath** (1972).

OUT OF THE BLUE

1980, Canada
D: Dennis Hopper. P: Leonard Yakir, Gary Jules Jouvenat. W: Leonard Yakir, Brenda Nielson. Ed: Doris Dyck. DoP: Marc Champion. M: Tom Lavin. PD: Leon Ericksen. AD: David Hiscox.
Cast: Linda Manz (Cindy 'Cebe' Barnes), Dennis Hopper (Don Barnes), Sharon Farrell (Kathy Barnes), Raymond Burr (Dr. Brean), Don Gordon (Charlie), Eric Allen (Paul), Fiona Brody (Carol), David Crowley (Anderson), Joan Hoffman (Jean), Carl Nelson (Cabby)

A young tomboy named Cebe (Linda Manz) turns to the chaotic dogma of punk rock when her hero Elvis dies. Cebe's love of Elvis comes from her alcoholic father (Dennis Hopper), who's been in prison for five years after a drunk driving accident that caused the deaths of a busload of schoolchildren. While her father is in jail, Cebe is left living with her promiscuous junkie mother. She doesn't have any friends, is constantly hit on by her mother's gross male companions and idealizes her relationship with her absent father.
  As with Kristy McNichol's traumatizing turn in the same year's *Little Darlings*, *Out of the Blue*'s teenage awkwardness comes across as very real. Cebe is constantly observing and assimilating, and there are times in the film when she seems genuinely happy, but her faith in people keeps being shaken by the shitty adults around her – most notably when her father's release from prison brings up some bad memories that she's not equipped to deal with. For more on this film see **Part 5: Afterschool Special**.

PARANOIA

1969, Italy/France
Original titles: **Orgasmo**; **Une folle envie d'aimer**
D: Umberto Lenzi. P: Salvatore Alabiso. W: Ugo Moretti, Umberto Lenzi, Marie Claire Solleville. Ed: Stan Frazen, Enzo Alabiso, John Shouse. DoP: Guglielmo Mancori. M: Piero Umiliani. AD: Giorgio Bertolini.
Cast: Carroll Baker (Kathryn West), Lou Castel (Peter Donovan), Colette Descombes (Eva), Tino Carraro (Brian Sanders), Lilla Brignone (Teresa), Franco Pesce (Martino), Tina Lattanzi (Kathryn's Aunt), Jacques Stany (Police Inspector), Gaetano Imbró, Calisto Calisti

Paranoia is often the subject of confusion due to the other Umberto Lenzi film known as *Paranoia* made the following year – aka *A Quiet Place to Kill*. Both films star Carroll Baker, and this one is also known as *Orgasmo*, which should not to be confused with Lenzi's later *Spasmo*!
  This weakly-plotted but sleazy giallo stars Baker as the recently widowed Kathryn West, whose oil baron husband left her more than 200 million dollars in loot before dying in a mysterious auto accident. Kathryn buries herself in pills and (J&B) whiskey, much to the disdain of her worried lawyer Brian, and shuts herself away in a large villa on the outskirts of Rome. She is subject to fainting spells and delusions, brought on by her substance abuse more than any lingering grief over her husband's death, and spends her nights in loneliness until the sudden appearance of a baby-faced stranger (actor, filmmaker and anarchist activist Lou Castel), who seduces her and moves in shortly thereafter. But he's no ordinary kept man; seemingly disinterested in her money, he wants only to dominate her – which she initially enjoys until she detects an underlying class-revenge motivation. When his pixie-ish 'sister' Eva comes to join them, Kathryn finds herself at the mercy of these two manipulative, petulant children, who make her a prisoner in her own home, drugging her drinks and increasing her mental instability to the point where suicide seems a happy alternative.
  While not the most engaging mystery, *Paranoia* is worthwhile as a deconstruction of Carroll Baker herself; Lenzi seems to delight in putting her on a pedestal and then pulling it out from beneath her.

PARANOIA sucks you into a whirlpool of erotic love!

from top: Linda Manz in Dennis Hopper's **Out of the Blue** (1980); Promotional artwork for Umberto Lenzi's **Paranoia** (1969).

PARANORMAL ACTIVITY

2007, USA
D: Oren Peli. P: Jason Blum, Oren Peli. W: Oren Peli. Ed: Oren Peli. DoP: Oren Peli.
Cast: Katie Featherston (Katie), Micah Sloat (Micah), Mark Fredrichs (Psychic), Amber Armstrong (Amber), Ashley Palmer (Diane)

Katie and Micah are a young couple who invest in a home video camera to record the nightly paranormal occurrences that have been plaguing them since they moved in together: banging and scratching sounds coming from the walls and the hallways, the movement of small objects, an odorous breath coming from an invisible source. But as Micah becomes more fascinated with the possibility of capturing a haunting on tape, Kate becomes increasingly agitated and fearful that the camera is antagonizing the entity and inviting more intense attacks. It is revealed that Kate is no stranger to these incidents; they've been happening to her intermittently since she was a child. She becomes listless and withdraws into emotional vacancy, resigning herself to a lack of control as her boyfriend and the demon engage in a dangerous battle of wills over her life.
For more on this film see **Part 1: Walking Wounded.**

THE PERFUME OF THE LADY IN BLACK

1974, Italy
Original title: **Il profumo della signora in nero**
D: Francesco Barilli. P: Giovanni Bertolucci. W: Francesco Barilli, Massimo D'Avack. Ed: Enzo Micarelli. DoP: Mario Masini. M: Nicola Piovani. AD: Franco Velchi.
Cast: Mimsy Farmer (Silvia Hachermann), Maurizio Bonuglia (Roberto), Mario Scaccia (Mr. Rossetti), Donna Jordan (Francesca Vincenzi), Orazio Orlando (Nicola), Jho Jhenkins (Andy), Nike Arrighi (Orchidea), Daniela Barnes [Lara Wendel] (young Silvia), Alexandra Paizi (Ms. Cardini), Renata Zamengo (Marta, Silvia's mother)

Mimsy Farmer stars as Silvia, a well-paid and workaholic scientist who lives alone in a large apartment in Italy. Her boyfriend of four months (played by Maurizio Bonuglia) is a geologist named Roberto who is often out of town on work assignments, but despite his own occupational commitments, he has no patience for hers, and childishly threatens to dump her whenever she puts her work before him. After one such argument, she goes to his house to apologize and is frightened by the image of her dead mother in the mirror. She screams for Roberto, but when he arrives the apparition is gone. She starts to have flashbacks of traumatic events from her childhood, and when she has sex with Roberto, her pleasure is interrupted by images of her mother having sex with a man who molested her as a child. As these memories intensify, mirrors start to become omnipresent – with reflections duplicated, distorted or broken – their purpose revealed one stormy night by the sudden appearance of a little girl at Silvia's door, who she suspects to be her doppelganger.
For more on this film see **Part 4: Secret Ceremonies.**

PERSONA

1966, Sweden
D: Ingmar Bergman. P: Ingmar Bergman. W: Ingmar Bergman. Ed: Ulla Ryghe. DoP: Sven Nykvist. M: Lars Johan Werle. AD: Bibi Lindström.
Cast: Bibi Andersson (Nurse Alma), Liv Ullmann (Elisabeth Vogler), Margaretha Krook (doctor), Gunnar Björnstrand (Mr. Vogler), Jörgen Lindström (Elisabeth's son)

While it warrants far more attention than can be given here, the relationship at the centre of *Persona* is a template for many of the others described in this book.

Elisabeth Vogler (Liv Ullmann) is an actress who has retreated from her family and friends and stopped speaking altogether. While diagnosed as physically and mentally healthy, she has to be hospitalized because of her self-imposed condition, which has already lasted several months at the start of the film. Alma (Bibi Andersson) is the young nurse assigned to care for Elisabeth, even though

she is intimidated by the fact that Elisabeth's 'illness' is in fact wilfulness that she may not have the experience to break through. After only a short time, Elisabeth initiates a change in Alma even without saying anything: Alma projects integrity and nobility onto Elisabeth's silence, and admires her greatly, which causes Alma to question her beliefs, and the superficiality of her own life.

Feeling that the hospital setting is not helping Elisabeth, the head doctor urges Alma to take Elisabeth to her country house. It is here, with uninterrupted time together, that Alma starts to manufacture a bond between herself and her silent charge. With this captive audience, and perhaps feeling pressure to fill the silence, she prattles on endlessly, specifically about a past indiscretion that has clearly troubled her for some time. She drunkenly suggests that she and Elisabeth are alike, and could easily switch roles. Through all these confessions, Elisabeth's only distinct emotional reaction is a thin smile; but even her smile doesn't render her invisible, because it exposes and manipulates others. It is a hostile gesture in itself, and Alma reacts violently to its insolence once she discovers that Elisabeth has been secretly mocking her.

Elisabeth's psychic vampirism is illustrated though a dream sequence that has her drinking Alma's blood from a slit forearm, while flashing sequences of crucifixions, self-immolations and slaughtered lambs indicate Alma as the sacrificial offering to Elisabeth's stubborn narcissism. Alma imagines that Elizabeth has bewitched her in the night, creating some kind of transcendental fugue in which their personalities have merged, but this is only Alma's desperation to connect, an obsession that she must ultimately ride out alone.

above: European poster for Ingmar Bergman's **Persona** (1966).

PHENOMENA

1985, Italy
Alternative title: **Creepers**
D: Dario Argento. P: Dario Argento. W: Dario Argento, Franco Ferrini. Ed: Franco Fraticelli. DoP: Romano Albani. M: Simon Boswell, Goblin. PD: Maurizio Garrone, Nello Giorgetti, Luciano Spadoni, Umberto Turco.
Cast: Jennifer Connelly (Jennifer Corvino), Daria Nicolodi (Frau Brückner), Dalila Di Lazzaro (school director), Patrick Bauchau (Inspector Rudolf Geiger), Donald Pleasence (Professor John McGregor), Fiore Argento (Vera Brandt), Federica Mastroianni (Sophie), Fiorenza Tessari (Gisela Sulzer), Mario Donatone (Morris Shapiro), Francesca Ottaviani (nurse)

Jennifer Connelly plays the somnambulistic daughter of a famous actor who has recently been installed at a snobby private girls' school in Switzerland. Having moved around frequently due to her father's profession, her only real friends are insects, with whom she shares a psychic affinity. With her talents called upon to help solve a string of murders, it is eventually revealed that the deformed child of headmistress Frau Brückner (Daria Nicolodi) is the culprit, with Brückner – who is seriously disturbed herself – adding to the bodycount in order to cover up her son's crimes.

Although the 'psychotic woman' element of *Phenomena* seems like a tack-on to the film's numerous other plot tangents, Nicolodi's performance here is typical of the hysterical mania that follows a long period of repression and denial. Brückner's child is of special interest because he is the product of his mother's rape by a lunatic. It is here that we see evidence of the monstrous child (who is physically monstrous in *Phenomena* rather than just behaviourally, as in Mario Bava's *Shock*) as the product of the monstrous female imagination. As with the id-children of David Cronenberg's *The Brood*, the child in *Phenomena* acts out his mother's homicidal impulses. Argento uses the deformed child as the physical manifestation of the deformed mind of his parent, and in doing so, reverts to the medieval interpretation of the aberrant child as the signifier of sin and madness.

THE PIANO TEACHER

2001, Austria/France/Germany
D: Michael Haneke. P: Veit Heiduschka. W: Michael Haneke, Elfriede Jelinek (novel). Ed: Monika Willi, Nadine Muse. DoP: Christian Berger. AD: Christoph Kanter.
Cast: Isabelle Huppert (Erika Kohut), Annie Girardot (the mother), Benoît Magimel (Walter Klemmer), Susanne Lothar (Mrs. Schober), Udo Samel (Doctor Blonskij), Anna Sigalevitch (Anna Schober), Cornelia Köngden (Mrs. Blonskij), Thomas Weinhappel (baritone), Georg Friedrich (man in drive-in), Philipp Heiss (Naprawnik)

Isabelle Huppert gives the performance of a lifetime as the tightly-wound 38-year-old piano teacher Erika Kohut in Michael Haneke's adaptation of Elfriede Jelinek's semi-autobiographical novel.

Erika teaches at the Vienna Conservatory and lives with her mother, with whom she has a reciprocally abusive relationship. Failing to become the great concert pianist her mother had always hoped for, Erika's professional ambitions are satisfied by giving private recitals in the salons of wealthy arts patrons. It is at one such recital that Erika meets Walter Klemmer, the young, incredibly handsome and charismatic engineering student who shares her love for Schumann and Schubert.

Walter becomes her pupil, and though she hurls insults at him, he is determined to win her. She spurns his every advance, promising that she will detail all her fantasies in a letter, which he is to read and comply with. The letter is shocking. Walter's simplified view of her neurosis – that she is slightly repressed and with a little love and affection she can be a normal, happy person – couldn't be further off the mark.
For more on this film see **Part 8: Heal Me with Hatred**.

above: Jennifer Connelly and Daria Nicolodi in Dario Argento's **Phenomena** (1985).

PIGS

1972, USA
Alternative titles: **Daddy's Deadly Darling; Roadside Torture Chamber; The Strange Exorcism of Lynn Hart; The Killer**
D: Marc Lawrence. P: Marc Lawrence. W: F.A. Foss [Marc Lawrence].
Ed: Irvin Goodnoff. DoP: Glenn R. Roland Jr. M: Charles Bernstein.
Cast: Marc Lawrence (Zambrini), Toni Lawrence (Lynn), Jesse Vint (Sheriff Dan Cole), Walter Barnes (doctor), Katharine Ross (Miss Macy), Jim Antonio (man from hospital), Erik Holland (Hoagy), Paul Hickey (Johnny), Iris Korn (Annette), William Michael (deputy)

Following an abrupt montage detailing the committal of a young woman named Lynn to a mental hospital for murdering her incestuously abusive father, a fantastic bubblegum pop song (written and sung by composer Charles Bernstein, and later sampled by death-rapper Necro) kicks in and a spaghetti western font announces this über-low-budget oddity as *Pigs* – directed by and starring blacklisted cinematic tough guy Marc Lawrence (*The Asphalt Jungle*, *Key Largo*) as a vehicle for his daughter Toni Lawrence, who plays Lynn.

Lynn escapes from the hospital in a stolen VW and winds up at the desolate country café of Zambrini (Marc Lawrence) a beyond-sketchy, pock-marked lurker who is looking for a pretty new waitress to mind the place while he feeds human corpses to his bloodthirsty pigs in an enclosed pen out back. The poor pigs are vilified by the camera and the sound design, as well as by Zambrini's nosy neighbour Miss Macy, who continually phones the sheriff (Jesse Vint of *Macon County Line* and *Bobbie Jo and the Outlaw*) to complain: "The pigs are loose, they've been snorting around the house! He feeds those pigs dead people – and then he eats the pigs!" She urges Sheriff Cole to arrest Zambrini, but he says he can't because, "It seems as though dead people just have no civil rights at all."

Lynn seems to be getting along fine in her new digs, until one of the regular customers tries to molest her and she is forced to slice him up with a razorblade before hiding under a table in infantilized shock. Zambrini walks in on the bloody scene and his paternal instincts kick in – long considered 'not right in the head', he can relate to outcasts and crazies, and he cleans up the mess (with the help of the pigs) and covers for her with the increasingly curious sheriff.

After this incident, Lynn's psychosis becomes apparent. She becomes flighty and unable to socialize, and repeatedly phones a disconnected number trying to get a hold of her (dead) father. She runs through the country roads screaming uncontrollably. She dances provocatively to the jukebox. And she flat-out ignores the stunningly good-looking Jesse Vint, which is the true indication of how crazy she must be. But when an investigator sent by the hospital shows up to take her back, Zambrini will show just how much he wants this deadly darling for his very own, with tragic results.

from top: Actress Toni Lawrence and misleading alternative title artwork for Marc Lawrence's **Pigs** (1972).

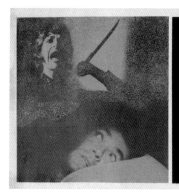

CLINT EASTWOOD
IN
"PLAY MISTY FOR ME"

TECHNICOLOR® 　　　　A UNIVERSAL PICTURE

PLAY MISTY FOR ME

1971, USA
D: Clint Eastwood. P: Robert Daley. W: Jo Heims, Dean Riesner. Ed: Carl Pingitore. DoP: Bruce Surtees. M: Dee Barton. AD: Alexander Golitzen.
Cast: Clint Eastwood (Dave Garver), Jessica Walter (Evelyn Draper), Donna Mills (Tobie Williams), John Larch (Detective Sergeant McCallum), Jack Ging (Frank Dewan), Irene Hervey (Madge Brenner), James McEachin (Al Monte), Clarice Taylor (Birdie, the maid), Don Siegel (Murphy, the bartender), Duke Everts (Jay Jay)

Shot in the picturesque bohemian community of Carmel-by-the-Sea (where he later became mayor) with the Monterey Jazz Festival as a partial backdrop, Eastwood stars in his directorial debut as Dave Garver, an easy-listening radio DJ at KRML (the real local radio station). He has a reputation with the ladies, but is hung-up on one in particular – sensible multi-media artist Tobie (Donna Mills). Foreshadowing the horror to come, Tobie explains her reasons for leaving him: "The thing I hate the most in the whole world is a jealous female, and that's what I was getting to be. I was starting to become one of my most un-favourite people. I hated it."

After the familiar request "play Misty for me" comes in from an anonymous woman on the call-line, Garver closes up shop and goes to his favourite watering hole, where he meets a woman named Evelyn Draper (Jessica Walter, unrecognizable from her more recent incarnation on *Arrested Development*) who's looking for a fling, no strings attached. Garver is only too happy to oblige. But he gets a surprise when she shows up at his house the next day, barging in to cook them dinner, calling him "darling" and generally setting off every warning bell imaginable.

Whenever he tries to call her on her presumptuous behaviour (which includes swiping his keys to make copies), she plays the sympathy card, and if that doesn't work, she does something to publicly humiliate him, her behaviour even costing him an important job possibility at a bigger station. She soon turns homicidal when she realizes that Garver's old flame Tobie is back in the picture.

The film is obviously the prototype for Reagan-era stalker hit *Fatal Attraction*, right down to the referencing of Madame Butterfly, the post-break-up suicide attempt and the insinuation into his girlfriend's life under false pretences. The morality is not quite the same – it's a different era with different values – but similarly, the independently-minded chosen partner is a sharp contrast to the delusional stalker. Evelyn is always at Garver's house, invading his space, while Tobie – his actual girlfriend – never steps foot in the place throughout the whole film.

In light of Don Siegel's *Dirty Harry*, which would come out the same year (and using some of the same crew), *Play Misty for Me* is a similar indictment of the justice system: Evelyn delivers multiple stab wounds to Garver's housemaid, nearly killing her, but after a short stint in a sanatorium,

she's out on the streets again and right back on Garver's trail, with the police placing more emphasis on questioning Garver than on looking for the homicidal lunatic.

Since the 1990s stalking has been recognized as a legit charge in most places and the authorities know how rampant it is, so it is frustrating to watch these events unfold from this privileged position. But in the context of 1971, at the height of the sexual revolution, it is frightening how much Evelyn has to ruin Garver's life before the authorities will take action.

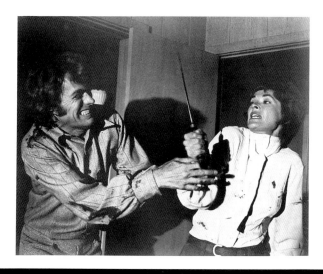

clockwise from top: Ad strip for Clint Eastwood's **Play Misty for Me** (1971); Jessica Walter solo and with Clint Eastwood.

POSSESSION

1981, France/West Germany
D: Andrzej Zulawski. P: Marie-Laure Reyre. W: Andrzej Zulawski, Frederic Tuten. Ed: Marie-Sophie Dubus, Suzanne Lang-Willar. DoP: Bruno Nuytten. M: Andrzej Korzynski. AD: Holger Gross. Cast: Isabelle Adjani (Anna/Helen), Sam Neill (Marc), Heinz Bennent (Heinrich), Margit Carstensen (Margit Gluckmeister), Michael Hogben (Bob), Johanna Hofer (Heinrich's mother), Shaun Lawton (Zimmermann), Carl Duering (Detective), Maximilian Rüthlein (man with pink socks), Gerd Neubert (subway drunk)

Possession is a film that confounded critics worldwide upon its release. Reviled in the U.S. as a result of sloppy re-editing aimed at making the film more linear and 'accessible', the film has only enjoyed serious reappraisal stateside in the last decade due to the belated release of the director's cut on DVD. The film begins with the homecoming of Marc (Sam Neill) after an extended business trip to find that his wife Anna (Isabelle Adjani) has a lover and that she has been neglecting their young son, Bob. But Anna's extracurricular love life doesn't just include the weird, mystic Heinrich (Heinz Bennent), but an actual physical monstrosity that she keeps hidden away in a secret apartment across town.

Heavily inspired by the real-life break-up of Zulawski and his wife Malgorzata Braunek, the film takes place in a strange hybrid of private and public reality that in a sense seems fitting for a couple undergoing a major transformation such as a break-up. Everything is exaggerated, everything is obscene, every action is hostile and tactless. A logistically and emotionally overwhelming film, *Possession* remains one of the most flawless examples of a woman losing her mind onscreen. For more on this film see **Part 9: Piercing Reality**.

PRETTY POISON

1968, USA
D: Noel Black. P: Marshall Backlar, Noel Black. W: Lorenzo Semple Jr., Stephen Geller (novel). Ed: William Ziegler. DoP: David Quaid. M: Johnny Mandel. AD: Jack Martin Smith, Harold Michelson. Cast: Anthony Perkins (Dennis Pitt), Tuesday Weld (Sue Ann Stepanek), Beverly Garland (Mrs. Stepanek), John Randolph (Morton Azenauer), Dick O'Neill (Bud Munsch), Clarice Blackburn (Mrs. Bronson), Joseph Bova (Pete), Ken Kercheval (Harry Jackson), Don Fellows (detective), George Ryan's Winslow High Steppers [George Ryan] (drillmaster & team)

In Noel Black's feature debut (with a terrific screenplay by Lorenzo Semple Jr., later of *Papillon* and *The Parallax View* fame), Anthony Perkins continues the typecast set in motion by *Psycho* as he plays Dennis Pitt, a recently-released mental patient who did time for setting his aunt's house on fire as a teenager (with her in it). Installed at a new job at a lumber yard while still on probation, he spies local schoolgirl Sue Ann Stepanek (Tuesday Weld) and decides to woo her by pretending to be a CIA operative who needs her help.

Perkins has his hands full with his new gal-pal, though: Sue Ann is the perfect lip-smacking sex kitten, beautiful, bubbly and seemingly dumb (although she is purportedly at the top of the honour roll); it's not until the halfway point that we realize Sue Ann is sociopathic herself, and sees her new CIA gig as a means of getting away with matricide. "I feel like we're married now, don't you Dennis? Like really married?" she says after plugging a couple into her wise-mouthed ma (Beverly Garland). But Dennis isn't quite as elated – he has to rush to the bathroom to throw up. So while originally he was leading her down the garden path with his bogus CIA story, he soon finds himself doing Sue Ann's dirty work.

left: Marital strife in **Possession** (1981); *right from top:* Japanese poster for **Pretty Poison** (1968) and its stars Anthony Perkins and Tuesday Weld.

PREY

1977, UK
Alternative title: **Alien Prey**
D: Norman J. Warren. P: Terence Marcel, David Wimbury. W: Max Cuff. Ed: Alan Jones. DoP: Derek V. Browne. M: Ivor Slaney. AD: Hayden Pearce.
Cast: Barry Stokes (Anders), Sally Faulkner (Josephine), Glory Annan (Jessica), Sandy Chinney (Sandy), Eddie Stacey (first policeman), Jerry Crampton (second policeman)

Two female lovers live in isolation in an English country house. Josephine (Jo), the more domineering of the two, reveals her desperation almost immediately, and throughout the film will constantly use manipulative tactics to convince her younger lover Jessica that seclusion is necessary to maintain the purity of their relationship. As if to prove the futility of Jo's isolationist mandate, they immediately run into a man named Anders, who – unbeknownst to them – is an alien that has adopted the strapping physical form of his most recent victim. Jessica is immediately fascinated by the reticent young man, whose handsomeness is matched only by his evasiveness. Jo's response to the interloping menace is to become more maniacally possessive of Jessica; like the uninvited guests of Pasolini's *Teorema* or Miike's *Visitor Q*, the alien will expose the fragility of their relationship, and prove its undoing in a suitably violent manner.
For more on this film see **Part 8: Heal Me with Hatred**.

from top: Glory Annan, Barry Stokes and Sally Faulkner; Sally Faulkner and Barry Stokes in Norman J. Warren's **Prey** (1977).

PSYCHO GIRLS

1985, Canada
D: Jerry Ciccoritti. P: Robert Bergman, Michael Bockner, Jerry Ciccoritti. W: Michael Bockner, Jerry Ciccoritti. Ed: Robert Bergman. DoP: Robert Bergman. M: Joel Rosenbaum. AD: Craig W. Richards.
Cast: John Haslett Cuff (Richard Foster), Darlene Mignacco (Sarah Tusk), Rose Graham (Mrs. Foster), Agi Gallus (Victoria Tusk), Silvio Oliviero [Michael A. Miranda] (Kazma), Pier Giorgio DiCicco (Tony), Michael Hoole (Dr. Dekker Wilson), Dan Rose (Dr. Hippocampus), Kim Cayer (Wendy Fields), Dorin Ferber (Femme Wilson)

The hard-boiled narration of its pulp-writer protagonist Richard Foster (John Haslett Cuff, who later helmed a documentary about Canada's premiere vérité filmmaker Allan King) opens up this $15,000 tongue-in-cheek revenge thriller from the director of vampire oddity *Graveyard Shift* (1987). Little does Foster know, he'll soon get to live out a sordid adventure to rival anything in his detective books.

After killing her parents with rat poison in 1966, Sarah Tusk spends the next 15 years in the Lakeview Asylum for Mental Disease, but when the asylum is about to be condemned, her doctor offers to release her under the guardianship of her posh sister Victoria. Victoria has other plans: "I want her to die here", she says, "I'm never going to sign these release papers." Instead, she tells the asylum staff to transfer Sarah to a new institution and throw away the key.

Four years later, Sarah escapes from the asylum by biting the throat of one of the nurses (they wouldn't let her have any sharp objects), with two male inmates in tow (in keeping with their admitted celebrity obsession, one looks like Freddie Mercury, the other like Huntz Hall with an eye patch). She tracks down Victoria, who is now working as a chef for the pulp writer and his sarcastic wife (with whom he shares a bizarre sweat-soaked sex scene following a [very '80s] competitive bicep-curling marathon). Sarah, whose derangement has calcified with institutionalization, knows more than she's let on to the doctors about who really killed their parents. "You thought you could get rid of me in this place", she says to Victoria, "but instead, you just turned me into you. Isn't that great?"

While she reserves special hatred for the medical and psychological professions due to her barbaric treatment inside, her sister needs some payback first.

Sarah takes Victoria's place serving dinner at the anniversary party of Victoria's employers, serving them Victoria's brain on a platter, disguised as steak tartar and laced with a sedative that knocks them all unconscious. They awake later at the abandoned asylum, gagged and tied, with their new hostess made up like Siouxsie Sioux and pontificating in front of a garishly-lit altar to Sigmund Freud, whose image hangs on the wall.

This film is an example of the pre-occupation with mind-control in post-MKULTRA Canadian horror films. As Canadian film historian Paul Corupe has pointed out extensively,[80] the non-consensual mind control experiments that proliferated in Canada during the 1950s – most notably at Montreal's Allan Memorial Institute, which was given extensive funding for these experiments by both the CIA and the Canadian Government – have left an unmistakable imprint on our nation's horror films, which demonize and play out revenge scenarios upon the medical profession. "Psychologists, psychiatrists, you're all charlatans", says Foster to Dr. Wilson, one of his dinner party guests, "You're always toying with our brains, you're trying to turn us into zombies or fucking guinea pigs or something just to justify your experiments."

With the tables turned, and Dr. Wilson strapped in a chair with the psychotic Sarah acting as makeshift shrink, she probes him with the usual questions: "Did you have a happy childhood? Was your mother a shrew? Were you jealous of your brother? Were you a spoiled child? Come, come, Dr. Wilson, you're a doctor, you know how important it is to cooperate. Well then, if you won't let me help you with psychoanalysis, I'm simply going to have to revert to modern methods."

The film's overwrought acting and deliberately ham-fisted dialogue are assets to the film's kitsch value (and in fact prefigure much of indie Canadian horror today), but once most of the characters are gagged and the focus shifts to Sarah and her psychotic sideshow, it loses steam for about 20 minutes, becoming mired in its own psychobabble. Fortunately it gets back on track once actor John Haslett Cuff takes care of business in the bloody climax.

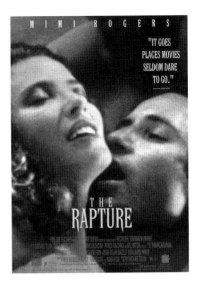

THE RAPTURE

1991, USA
D: Michael Tolkin. P: Nick Wechsler, Nancy Tenenbaum, Karen Koch. W: Michael Tolkin. Ed: Suzanne Fenn. DoP: Bojan Bazelli. M: Thomas Newman. PD: Robin Standefer. AD: Kathleen M. McKernin.
Cast: Mimi Rogers (Sharon), David Duchovny (Randy), Patrick Bauchau (Vic), Kimberly Cullum (Mary), Terri Hanauer (Paula), Dick Anthony Williams (Henry), Carole Davis (Angie), Will Patton (Foster), Darwyn Carson (Maggie), Marvin Elkins (bartender)

This is probably the only movie in this book where a woman's craziness is manifested as happiness. After some ominous sound design ushers in the opening scene in a noisy information call centre, the camera pans over a sea of grey cubicles before settling on the protagonist Sharon (Mimi Rogers): telephone operator by day, swinger by night. She attempts to dispel the numbness of her daily routine by having unconventional (and probably unsafe) sexual encounters with unfamiliar couples she and her friend Vic pick up in bars and airports. She's seen it all, done it all, and remains unmoved by these trysts that test her unknowable limits. Post-coitus conversations with semi-regular lover Randy (David Duchovny, sporting an abominable mullet) reveal an amorality that nevertheless plagues her with its emptiness. "If we weren't taught that killing is bad, would I still feel this bad?" Randy asks, after admitting that he once killed someone for a paltry thousand dollars. Just *conditioning*, she says – a notion that will play out repeatedly in different ways throughout the film, whether referring to morality, socialization, professional obligations, or the end-of-the-world religious cult she will soon find herself at the centre of. The conversations between Sharon and Randy – who reveals himself to be more insightful than we suspect – lay bare the film's philosophy; there's not much to read into it beyond what is spoken out loud, but this lack of mystery does show how forced and contrived a turn toward organized religion (in this case Christianity) can be. "There has to be something more", she muses. "I'm tired of the pain in my life. I'm tired of feeling empty all the time." Like Florinda Bolkan's character in *Footprints* (which is reviewed elsewhere in this book), her job is to facilitate communication between other people, even though she feels entirely disconnected herself.

A series of events happen to Sharon successively that prompt her change of heart: she overhears some co-workers talking about The Rapture; she is visited by door-to-door evangelists; she and Vic pick up a girl with an enormous back tattoo depicting a giant pearl being handed down from heaven – apparently a common portentous symbol for those who have been saved (referred to in The Gospel of Matthew as 'the Pearl of Great Price'). She starts to yearn for religious fulfilment, or whatever it is that makes these other people

so certain they're on the right track. Determined to gain favour into their ranks, she starts obsessively following the commandments, bathing in scalding water, flossing vigorously, proselytizing. More than their religion, what she really covets is their conviction, although she doesn't know this yet.

Feeling increasingly lost, she holes up in a hotel room and points a gun at her chin, disappointed that she can't find the courage to pull the trigger. Prefiguring the events to come, the Velvet Underground song 'I'll Be Your Mirror' is playing in a distant room, Nico's deep voice singing: "I'll be your mirror, reflect what you are, in case you don't know... I'll be the wind, the rain and the sunset, the light on your door to show that you're home..." As she puts the gun in a drawer with her cigarettes and booze, taking out the Gideon's bible for comfort instead, she falls asleep... and dreams of The Pearl. She has been saved.

She falls in with a group of believers led by a child prophet and for six years she and the now-converted Randy prosper as a happy Christian family awaiting their ascendancy to heaven, until one day he is gunned down in an office shooting. Shortly thereafter, Sharon has a vision that leads her to the desert with her young daughter in tow. Believing that they'll be taken up to the divine kingdom in short order, she brings a minimum of supplies and soon they are starving. Their daughter, brainwashed into believing the cult's visions, keeps begging to die so that she can be in heaven where everything is fine, and Sharon obliges by shooting her in the back of the head – but stops short from shooting herself after she remembers that suicides don't get into heaven. But when God doesn't come for her, and she's just left there – a mother holding a gun staring at her dead daughter in the desert – her faith goes out the window. Incarcerated for child-murder, she ironically finds herself in a cell with a proselytizing born-again Christian – the same woman whose back tattoo set her on the quest for the Pearl of Great Price in the first place. And what a great price it was.

To hammer home this irony, once she's given up on it, the Rapture actually happens. And now, she finally has the conviction she wanted all along: she stands right before heaven, she sees it, it's *real*, and all she has to do to get in is say she loves God. But she refuses. She will not kiss the ass of a god responsible for so much suffering, even though it would be so easy, and the alternative is to stay in purgatory forever. As the others around her are swept up into the afterlife, she is determined to stand alone in a black void. It's a great fuck-you finale that makes all the cheesy apocalyptic effects worth enduring.

from top: Mimi Rogers; ominous tattoo depicting 'The Pearl of Great Price' in Michael Tolkin's **The Rapture** (1991).

THE RATS ARE COMING! THE WEREWOLVES ARE HERE!

1972, USA
D: Andy Milligan. P: William Mishkin. W: Andy Milligan.
Ed: Gerald Jackson [Andy Milligan]. DoP: Andy Milligan.
Cast: Hope Stansbury (Monica Mooney), Jackie Skarvellis (Diana), Noel Collins (Mortimer Mooney), Joan Ogden (Phoebe Mooney), Douglas Phair (Pa Mooney), Ian Innes (Gerald), Berwick Kaler (Malcolm Mooney), Chris Shore (Mr. McHarbor), George Clark [Andy Milligan] (Gunsmith), Lillian Frit (Rebecca)

Staten Island filmmaker Andy Milligan's UK-shot *The Rats Are Coming! The Werewolves Are Here!* centres on the Mooneys, an eccentric family living in a decrepit Victorian household who are stricken with hereditary lycanthropy. Although the family has a dying patriarch as their focal point, the men in the family (including middle-brother Mortimer and youngest son Malcolm) are subject to the whims of the three distinctly-typed females: Phoebe, the eldest sister and self-appointed 'mother' figure; Monica, the sadistic and attention-starved middle sister; and Diana, the youngest and only educated sister, who is also the most emotionally stable, and born of a different mother than the others. Sent to medical school abroad so that she could continue her father's delicate genetic experiments, any hope of cleansing the family bloodline lies in Diana's hands.
For more on this film see **Part 2: Broken Dolls**.

above: Lycanthropic adventures in Andy Milligan's **The Rats Are Coming! The Werewolves Are Here!** (1972).

REBECCA

1940, USA
D: Alfred Hitchcock. P: David O. Selznick. W: Robert E. Sherwood, Joan Harrison, Philip MacDonald, Michael Hogan, Daphne du Maurier (novel). Ed: W. Donn Hayes. DoP: George Barnes. M: Franz Waxman. AD: Lyle R. Wheeler.
Cast: Laurence Olivier (Maxim de Winter), Joan Fontaine (Mrs. de Winter) George Sanders (Jack Favell), Judith Anderson (Mrs. Danvers), Nigel Bruce (Major Giles Lacey), Reginald Denny (Frank Crawley), C. Aubrey Smith (Colonel Julyan), Gladys Cooper (Beatrice Lacey), Florence Bates (Edythe Van Hopper), Leo G. Carroll (Dr. Baker)

Based on Daphne du Maurier's 1938 novel and an integral component of the 'paranoid woman's film' of the 1940s, *Rebecca* stars Joan Fontaine as the sheepish paid companion to an older society woman vacationing in Monte Carlo. Out walking one day she sees the suave but brooding widower Maxim de Winter (Laurence Olivier) about to leap to his death from a cliff top, and shouts out to stop him; while he feigns annoyance, he is secretly taken with the young girl and in no time flat sweeps her away to his sprawling English seaside estate, Manderlay, to become his new wife. But she can't escape the ghost of the first Mrs. de Winter, Rebecca, to whom all the house staff – most notably the menacing Mrs. Danvers – are still fervently devoted. Tantamount to the demonic psychosis of Mrs. Danvers is the increasing mental instability of the protagonist, who shrinks in Rebecca's domineering shadow.
For more on this film see **Part 7: You've Always Loved Violence**.

RED DESERT

1964, Italy/France
Original titles: **Il deserto rosso**; **Le désert rouge**
D: Michelangelo Antonioni. P: Antonio Cervi. W: Michelangelo Antonioni, Tonino Guerra. Ed: Eraldo Da Roma. DoP: Carlo Di Palma. M: Giovanni Fusco, Vittorio Gelmetti. AD: Piero Poletto.
Cast: Monica Vitti (Giuliana), Richard Harris (Corrado Zeller), Carlo Chionetti (Ugo), Xenia Valderi (Linda), Rita Renoir (Emilia), Lili Rheims (worker's wife), Valerio Bartoleschi (Valerio, Giuliana's son), Aldo Grotti (Max), Emanuela Paola Carboni (girl in the fable), Giuliano Missirini (radiotelescope worker)

As mentioned in the introduction to this book, Giuliana (Monica Vitti) in Antonioni's *Red Desert* has been labelled 'the neurotic personality of our time'. This story of a woman who was left with severe feelings of alienation and terror following a car accident has proven a significant influence on cinematic representations of female neurosis ever since, regardless of genre definition. Her physical mannerisms – shaking, jerking, collapsing and trying to get out of her own skin – betray Giuliana's struggle to connect with others, her terror of her surroundings and her feelings of separation from her own body. The truth is that she sees herself as poisonous, just like the factories that surround her, with their belching yellow gases and grey facades. Her sexuality is palpable through her pronounced physicality – which draws her husband's employer Corrado (Richard Harris) to her – but it is also awkward and repellent. She asks Corrado if he loves her, and when he asks why she wants to know, she responds: "I really don't know. I never get enough. Why do I always need other people?... I'd like all the people who ever loved me to be here, all around me, like a wall." Although the film has been discussed at length elsewhere, and does not fit the scope of this book in genre terms, it remains a potent point of comparison for films like *Possession*, *In My Skin*, various Jean Rollin films and numerous others.

from top: Joan Fontaine and Judith Anderson in Alfred Hitchcock's **Rebecca** (1940); Monica Vitti in Michelangelo Antonioni's **Red Desert** (1964).

RED SUN

1969, West Germany
Original title: **Rote Sonne**
D: Rudolf Thome. P: Rudolf Thome. W: Max Zihlmann. Ed: Jutta Brandstaedter.
DoP: Bernd Fiedler.
Cast: Marquard Bohm (Thomas), Uschi Obermaier (Peggy), Diana Körner (Christine),
Gaby Go (Isolde), Sylvia Kekulé (Sylvie), Peter Moland (Wenders), Don Wahl
(Howard), Hark Bohm (leftist student), Henry van Lyck (Lohmann)

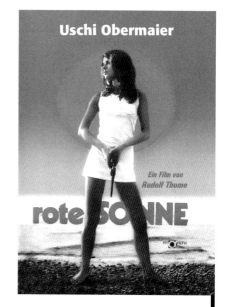

Rudolf Thome's *Red Sun* is inseparable from the socio-political context in which it was created. In 1968, model and groupie Uschi Obermaier was at the inaugural Song Days Rock festival at Essen with Krautrock band Amon Düül 1 when she met political activist Rainer Langhans and the two became a couple. Langhans was one of early members of Berlin's Kommune No. 1 (also known as K1), an outgrowth of the student revolts which saw its members living together in a single bedroom and engaging in satirical 'actions', which eventually alienated them from other revolutionaries who saw their provocative activities as ego-driven (although they were an inspiration for the founding of the left-wing terrorist group The Red Army Faction). This activist-as-hedonist stereotype was reinforced by the arrival of Uschi Obermaier, who signalled a new era in the K1 that was more in line with the free-love goals of the sexual revolution, with she and Langhans posited as the German 'John and Yoko' (although Obermaier was more politicized by her relationship[81] than she was inherently political).

During this time, Obermaier met Rudolf Thome – initially considered a major new German talent alongside Fassbinder, Wenders and Herzog but nearly forgotten now – and starred in his first two feature films: the nouvelle vague-inspired counterculture krimi *Detektive* (1968) and *Red Sun* (1969), whose ethics are a violent exaggeration of K1's radical mandate and an examination of the emptiness of fad-driven politics. Widely acclaimed in its time, *Red Sun* is critical of the political zeitgeist that gripped the youth of its day, a sentiment that is especially poignant in its use of Uschi Obermaier as a lead.

Slacker leech Thomas (Fassbinder regular Marquard Bohm) comes back to town to find that his old flame Peggy (Obermaier) has hooked up with a radical group of women who have a policy of killing their lovers after five days as a means of discouraging long term relationships. They steal and order supplies to manufacture their own weapons and explosives, which they use to facilitate random destruction. Unlike the K1, they have several bedrooms (the doors to which always remain closed), but don't claim ownership over any of them, moving around to sleep wherever they fall. Their apartment is sparsely decorated, emphasizing this transient lifestyle. But the arrival of Thomas threatens the girls' secretive bubble, as well as Peggy's political conviction. Even

though Peggy encourages him to leave, and frequently ignores him in the hopes of accelerating his departure, he has nowhere else to go, and insinuates himself into their lives. When a friend of one of the missing 'boyfriends' approaches Thomas with his suspicions about the girls, and the admonition that Thomas is going to be next, Thomas dismisses it, saying that one of the girls favours him (referring to Isolde, the tiniest of the four girls and the most opposed to their homicidal agenda). But the man shakes his head: "Watch a vampire film some time."

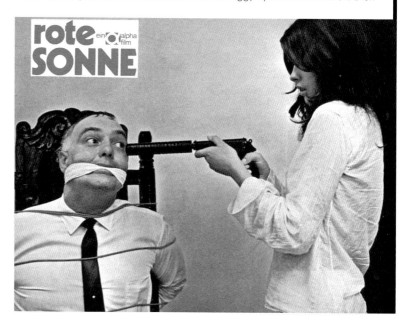

Isolde admits to Thomas that the killing spree began with Sylvie's unfaithful lover, and when the police believed it was a suicide, the girls decided to continue, believing that to be with a man for more than 5 days was dangerous, as one risked falling in love and becoming susceptible to manipulation. As such, their political mandate is a sham that exists only to cover up fears about being in adult relationships – but being in a relationship with each other brings its own dangers and betrayals.

from top: Model/activist Uschi Obermaier on a DVD cover and a lobby card for Rudolf Thome's **Red Sun** (1969).

RED WHITE & BLUE

2010, USA
D: Simon Rumley. P: Bob Portal,
Simon Rumley. W: Simon Rumley.
Ed: Robert Hall. DoP: Milton
Kam. M: Richard Chester.
PD: Josh Crist. AD: Brad Mathis.
Cast: Amanda Fuller (Erica),
Marc Sentor (Franki) Jon
Michael Davis (Ed), Nick Ashy
Holden (Alvin), Patrick Crovo
(Carl), Mary Mathews (Marj),
Noah Taylor (Nate), Julian
Haddad (Lil' Alan), Ernest James
(nightclub pick-up), Jenny
Gravenstein (druggie rock girl)

Simon Rumley blew minds in 2006 with his debut genre feature *The Living and the Dead*, which swept up awards all over the festival circuit and established him as a major international talent. Despite the fact that he already had a healthy back-catalogue of indie films prior to *The Living and the Dead*, the response it received assured that he's been at home in genre films ever since.

Red White & Blue is an equally devastating film in which three emotionally disfigured people find themselves at the centre of a multi-tiered revenge triangle. Amanda Fuller plays Erica, a troubled young woman who spends her nights indiscriminately and compulsively bar-hopping and bed-hopping with the goal of self-obliteration. She's not just racing towards death, she's also determined to take others with her; she's been diagnosed HIV positive and has made no effort to share this information with her numerous sexual partners (including Marc Senter of Chris Sivertson's *The Lost* and *Brawler*). While this can be viewed as thoughtlessness and self-absorption more than direct malice, the fact is that she's so unable to connect to other people that life and death cease to hold meaning for her. It's just a shallow routine that she engages in to numb the pain, but we get to see the lives she's affecting – she doesn't. She engages in sex with strangers the way a cutter takes to their arms with razors – it's a form of self-destructiveness that only makes sense to the person who's doing it.

When she meets Nate (Noah Taylor), an equally battle-scarred individual who claims to be ex-military, she detects a crack in her hardened shell and decides to accept it, opening herself up to the possibility of love. But her past indiscretions will catastrophically catch up with them all.

THE REINCARNATION OF PETER PROUD

1975, USA
D: J. Lee Thompson. P: Frank P. Rosenberg. W: Max Ehrlich. Ed: Michael F.
Anderson. DoP: Victor J. Kemper. M: Jerry Goldsmith. AD: Jack Martin Smith.
Cast: Michael Sarrazin (Peter Proud), Jennifer O'Neill (Ann Curtis), Margot Kidder
(Marcia Curtis), Cornelia Sharpe (Nora Hayes), Paul Hecht (Dr. Samuel Goodman),
Tony Stephano (Jeff Curtis), Norman Burton (Dr. Frederick Spear), Anne Ives (Ellen
Curtis), Debralee Scott (Suzy), Jon Richards (newspaper custodian)

A bizarre and morally disturbing film, *The Reincarnation of Peter Proud* stars Michael Sarrazin as the title character, who is haunted by recurring dreams that convince him he is reliving scenes from a past life. The dreams lead him to a small lakeside town where, 30 years earlier, he was murdered by his wife Marcia (Margot Kidder) in a staged drowning incident. The more he delves into his past life the more he realizes what a reprehensible character his 1940s counterpart was – aside from myriad adulterous indiscretions, he sexually humiliated and abused his wife, prompting the 'accident'. With her dead husband's doppelganger suddenly reappearing in her life, Marcia comes apart, her routine drinking becoming more of a crutch as she suffers horrifying flashbacks of the abuse that led her to kill. Like Carla Moran in *The Entity*, she struggles with the concept of blame, believing she deserves the torment because of her inability to reconcile her need for individuality and respect with her sexual appetite toward an abuser.
For more on this film see **Part 3: All Safe and Dead**.

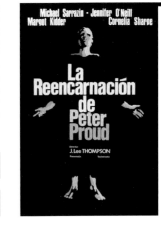

top: Amanda Fuller in Simon Rumley's **Red White and Blue** (2010).

above: Michael Sarrazin; *right:* French poster for J. Lee Thompson's **The Reincarnation of Peter Proud** (1975).

REPULSION

1965, UK
D: Roman Polanski. P: Gene Gutowski. W: Roman Polanski,
Gerard Brach, David Stone (adaptation and additional
dialogue). Ed: Alastair McIntyre. DoP: Gilbert Taylor.
M: Chico Hamilton. AD: Seamus Flannery.
Cast: Catherine Deneuve (Carol), Ian Hendry (Michael),
John Fraser (Colin), Patrick Wymark (Landlord), Yvonne
Furneaux (Helen), Renee Houston (Miss Balch), Valerie
Taylor (Madame Denise), James Villiers (John), Helen
Fraser (Bridget), Hugh Futcher (Reggie)

Carol (Catherine Deneuve) is a withdrawn manicurist who
lives in London with her sister Helen. Right from the start of
the film she's unresponsive to conversation, and shudders
or recoils when touched, indicating some past trauma
that she has struggled to bury. At home she sits alone,
mesmerized by her own distorted reflection, kissing her own
hand, surveying the apartment's childlike knick knacks and
watching the nuns at the school down below her window. At night in bed, she can hear her sister loudly having sex down the hall,
oblivious to Carol's distaste – the stem of which is hinted at when the camera lingers on a family photograph in which she stares
aggressively at an unidentified male relative.

"I must get this crack mended", Carol says of a split in the kitchen wall, and as if to hammer the point home further, she later stops
to inspect a crack in the sidewalk, planting herself on a bench to stare at it as though gazing into the abyss. The crack signifies a pending
breakdown in her own carefully-manicured façade, and when her sister goes to Italy, Carol is left alone with her damaged psyche and
all the predatory images that lurk within. The crack in the wall that grows loudly and violently as the film progresses is only the first in a
series of spatial or textural transformations the apartment will undergo as she retreats into her frightening inner world.

Her most obvious issue (to which the other characters are somehow oblivious) is that men are repellent to her; they are
brutes and violators of personal space. Even the man who's positioned as her would-be love interest breaks down her door
when she won't answer the phone, despite there being no indication that they have any relationship whatsoever other than
his desire for her. When she discovers the toothbrush, straight razor and shaving brush of Helen's boyfriend Michael in the
bathroom, she moves them to the opposite side of the shelf so as to not contaminate her things, and eventually throws them
out, which earns her a scolding from Helen. Later, when she finds one of Michael's
soiled undershirts on the bathroom floor, she vomits.

This is only one facet of Carol's delusions about cleanliness; she is constantly
wiping invisible dirt from her clothes, her face and the objects she touches. Meanwhile
the rabbit her sister meant to cook for dinner but never did has been left out to rot
and attract flies, the dirty dishes pile up, the potatoes grow roots, and she makes no
attempt to clean the increasingly filthy apartment. She fails to show up for work, and
when she does, she gets a warning for looking dishevelled and is sent home after
absent-mindedly maiming one of the clients.

The frequent use of mirror shots and reflections also convey that the film takes
place in a mental space where images are split and doubled. The mirror shot did not
begin with Repulsion, nor did it begin in the '60s (there are mirror shots at least as early
as Edison's Frankenstein (1910) and they are a staple of the film noir), and neither was
Lewis Carroll's Alice in Wonderland – which this film references – the first to posit the
mirror as a magical, liminal space. But the mirror shot is one of the hallmarks of 1960s
cinema, with its anxiety concerning the breakdown between reality and artifice, and
rarely has a film been made since that does not utilize it. The mirror shot marks an
ontological rupture, and Repulsion is full of them, but reconciling her inner and outer
worlds is too much for Carol, and after violently dispatching the male predators who
encroach upon her space, she ends up catatonic – she's completely gone inside. As
the film closes, the camera returns to the family photograph (a shot that would be
mimicked in Francesco Barilli's The Perfume of the Lady in Black), reasserting it as the
source of Carol's anxiety.

From today's perspective, Repulsion is a virtual catalogue of the tell-tale
trappings of the 'neurotic woman' horror film – the insular plot, the dis-integrated
characterization, stylistic flourishes such as repeated mirror shots, disembodied hands
that grope the protagonist, the actual or optical enlargement of sets to create
disorientation, the low-angle shots of the woman swiping maniacally at her victim –
but Repulsion is perhaps the godmother of them all.

from top: Catherine Deneuve in Roman Polanski's **Repulsion** (1965) and an Argentinean poster for the film.

ROAD TO SALINA

1970, France/Italy
Original titles: **La route de Salina**;
Quando il sole scotta
D: Georges Lautner. P: Robert
Dorfmann, Yvon Guézel. W: Georges
Lautner, Pascal Jardin, Jack Miller,
Maurice Cury (novel). Ed: Michelle
David, Elisabeth Guido. DoP: Maurice
Fellous. M: Bernard Gérard, Christophe,
Clinic. AD: Jean d'Eaubonne.
Cast: Mimsy Farmer (Billie), Robert
Walker Jr. (Jonas), Rita Hayworth
(Mara), Ed Begley (Warren), Bruce
Pecheur (Charlie), Sophie Hardy
(Linda), David Sachs (Sheriff), Marc
Porel (Rocky), Ivano Staccioli, Albane
Navizet (Pat)

Robert Walker Jr. plays Jonas, a drifter who stops at an isolated house on the way to Salina, and the lady of the house, Mara (Rita Hayworth), is convinced that he's her long-lost son Rocky, who disappeared four years earlier without a trace. Tired, broke, and with nowhere else to go, he decides to play along with the ruse. When Rocky's sister Billie (Mimsy Farmer) comes home, he's sure he'll be found out, but Billie acknowledges him as Rocky too, as does the neighbour Warren (Ed Begley, in his last film role). He knows he should move on rather than dragging out a lie, but the combination of Mara's desperation to have her son back and Billie's unnatural affection towards her (alleged) brother keeps him in place. His attraction to Billie is reciprocated and the two begin a sordid love affair, much to the dismay of Mara, who has seen this scenario play out before and is worried that it may result in Rocky running away again. Jonas is confused by Billie's incestuous tendencies but his infatuation with her is too strong to overcome. With the three of them in relative isolation and few visitors to intrude upon their fantasy world, Jonas is happy to play whatever game these doting females want him to, even though it's obvious that they're both seriously deluded.

Jonas can't stop wondering what happened to the real Rocky, and eventually he sees a photo of Rocky (tragic Euro-star Marc Porel) and realizes they look nothing alike. His investigation into Rocky's life – including a visit to Rocky's ex-girlfriend Linda – spawns jealousy in Billie, who redirects Jonas's attention to herself by admitting that she's known he's not really Rocky all along. Still, his curiosity isn't quelled, so Jonas pushes Billie to tell him the truth about what happened that last fateful day when Rocky disappeared. She explains tearfully that Rocky was planning to elope with Linda and she couldn't let him go; hopelessly in love with her own brother, she followed him and begged him not to leave, killing him when he refused to listen to her pleas. Once she's confessed to Jonas, she suddenly can't stand the sight of him; she becomes spiteful and mean. "I wanted you to be Rocky... I believed you were him... but you weren't satisfied, you had to know everything – you had to kill him again!"

Although director Georges Lautner originally wanted Pink Floyd to provide the film's rock soundtrack (likely inspired by their soundtrack to Barbet Schroeder's sun-soaked *More* a year earlier, which also features Farmer as an enigmatic young woman), they were unavailable, prompting him to take up French-Canadian-British band Clinic in their place – and the soundtrack is one of few things that places the film in the 1970s. The story itself has both proto-noir (1943's *Ossessione*) and neo-noir elements and could easily have been an influence on Juan Antonio Bardem's *The Corruption of Chris Miller* (1973) and Nikos Nikolaidis's 1990 *Singapore Sling* (both reviewed elsewhere in this appendix), most notably the latter, which similarly features a man destroyed by the corrupt fantasies of two isolated women. *Road to Salina* also helped solidify the Mimsy-Farmer-as-head-case typecast that would be played out in many of her subsequent films.
For more on actress Mimsy Farmer see **Part 4: Secret Ceremonies**.

top: Mimsy Farmer and Robert Walker Jr.   *above:* Mimsy clings to Marc Porel in George Lautner's **Road to Salina** (1970).

SANTA SANGRE

1989, Italy/Mexico
D: Alejandro Jodorowsky. P: Claudio Argento. W: Alejandro Jodorowsky, Roberto Leoni, Claudio Argento. Ed: Mauro Bonanni. DoP: Daniele Nannuzzi. M: Simon Boswell. PD: Alejandro Luna. Cast: Axel Jodorowsky (Fenix), Blanca Guerra (Concha), Guy Stockwell (Orgo), Thelma Tixou (tattooed woman), Sabrina Dennison (Alma), Adan Jodorowsky (young Fenix), Faviola Elenka Tapia (young Alma), Teo Jodorowsky (pimp), Maria de Jesús Aranzabal (fat prostitute), Jesús Juárez (Aladin)

While *Santa Sangre* is admittedly the most accessible and linear of Jodorowsky's epic surrealist films, it is too thematically, culturally and symbolically dense to do the film justice in a few paragraphs.[82]

Loosely inspired by the crimes of Mexican serial killer Goyo Cárdenas, 'the strangler of Tacuba', the story begins in an asylum where 20-something Fenix (Axel Jodorowsky, the director's son) is living in a feral state, before illustrating through flashbacks how he was placed there as a child (all the other inmates have Down's Syndrome, implying that the asylum is a depository for people with various mental or developmental disorders) following a violent incident involving his parents.[83]

Fenix is a child magician in the 'Circus del Gringo', run by his corpulent father Orgo the knife-thrower (U.S. TV actor Guy Stockwell, brother of AIP regular Dean Stockwell) and his mother Concha (Mexican actress Blanca Guerra), the latter of whom is a devotee of a controversial fringe 'saint' whose temple is being threatened with destruction by the city. While Orgo is getting intimately familiar with the limber Tattooed Lady at the circus, Concha is leading a demonstration protesting the demolition of her church, which houses a large pool of 'holy blood' miraculously left by their martyred figurehead, whose armless effigy adorns the apse of the small building. As Concha leads a visiting Bishop through the temple hoping to win his support, he is horrified by the story of the martyr – a young girl who was raped and had her arms cut off by her attackers – as told through illustrations that line the walls like a perversion of the Christian Stations of the

ROMAN'S BRIDE

2010, USA
D: Michael Paul. P: Anne Paul. W: Anne Paul. Ed: Michael Paul, Anne Paul.
DoP: Michael Paul. M: Mark Nadolski. Cast: Anne Paul (Lily Heller), Michael Rennat (Roman), Otis Wilson (The Rev), Stanley Massey (Amos), Elmer Chalmers (Rusty), Lisa Rennat (Angela), Lee Rennat (Dayna), Elyse Rennat (Zoe), Jim Siokos (Gary), Jennifer Galbraith (Lindsey)

Iowa-based writer/producer Anne Paul stars as Lily, a reclusive, highly religious woman who has been nurturing an unrequited obsession for her lifelong neighbour Roman since they were kids. Alone in the old farmhouse where she lived with her venomously punishing mother – until her mother had an unfortunate 'accident' – Lily spends her days self-medicating and creating bizarre floral arrangements with weeds and sticks that her lovelorn friend Amos orders in bulk in order to 'keep her busy'. But Amos isn't the only one maintaining Lily's delusions – Roman himself doesn't clearly demarcate the boundaries in their relationship until he's on the verge of getting married to his live-in girlfriend, which sends Lily spiralling over the edge. Her strict sense of religious propriety contradicts her own deeply inappropriate behaviour – following Roman around through the woods and fields, violating his privacy, molesting him when he's incapacitated by frequent drinking binges – and the appearance of her disapproving mother's ghost doesn't help things. She takes up her mother's punitive regimen: in several squirm-inducing sequences, she responds to rejection by punishing herself for having the kinds of feelings that would prompt rejection in the first place.

Paul's performance as Lily starts off overly affected, but her creepiness becomes more authentic as the film wears on: her long red hair hanging over pasty white skin; her feet and fingers noticeably dirty; her eyes betraying a gradual dissociation that will allow her homicidal impulses to bear out horrific results for men, women and children alike. Two standout sequences include Lily trying to figure out how to use a power-saw in front of its intended victim, and a rather large farm implement being utilized to its maximum potential (and I'm not talking about farming).

above, both images: Anne Paul in Michael Paul's **Roman's Bride** (2010).

Cross. He calls her a 'crazy woman' and proclaims the 'holy blood' to be mere paint, riling Concha's maniacal religious fervour. Shouting that the temple is a heretical abomination, the Bishop gives the city workers the go-ahead to raze the place. Seeing his mother willing to die for her saint, Fenix rushes to her side, and his distress causes her to choose him, abandoning the site – a humanity that she will rarely exhibit in the film going forward.

Concha's maniacal energy will only be channelled elsewhere, and when she catches Orgo with the Tattooed Lady, she pours acid on his crotch and laughs hysterically, prompting him to cut off her arms in one fell swoop before slitting his own throat. It's a fantastic sequence, and one of many graphic, hyper-stylized death scenes in the film. From this point on Concha becomes the armless saint of her devoted son Fenix, but as he will discover, she is thankless and tyrannical, and demands bloody retribution for what she has suffered.

Fenix escapes from the asylum to live with her, literally becoming her arms so that she can gesticulate, put on make-up, play piano, and perform bizarre renditions of Marcel Marceau pantomimes for plebeian audiences. While Fenix is the film's subjective soul, he is a passive vehicle for Concha's murderous desires, and she urges him to kill any woman that arouses corrupt lustful passions in him that might lead him away from the only woman he should care for, namely his mother. But her attachment to him – as literal as it is, with her clothing containing armholes so that their bodies merge into one – is also incestuous, and having inappropriate sexual desires is especially dangerous in those subject to religious fanaticism. To mask her unnatural affection for her son, she is rude and brusque with him, unsympathetic to his troubled conscience ("You can't atone for your sins with nightmares!") and frequently verbally abusive.

In due course it is revealed that Concha died of haemorrhaging years ago when her arms were cut off, and she has only been alive in Fenix's mind, making all of our suppositions about Concha to be projections from her mentally ill son. And while this can easily be guessed at from her first re-appearance outside the asylum, we are deliberately led by Jodorowsky to explore and revel in the diseased mind of a fanatical woman until the film's climax removes her from the equation.

from top: Blanca Guerra solo and with co-stars Axel Jodorowsky and Sabrina Dennison in Alejandro Jodorowsky's **Santa Sangre** (1989).

SCHIZO

1976, UK
D: Pete Walker. P: Pete Walker. W: David McGillivray. Ed: Alan Brett. DoP: Peter Jessop. M: Stanley Myers. AD: Chris Burke. Cast: Lynne Frederick (Samantha Gray), John Leyton (Alan Falconer), Stephanie Beacham (Beth), John Fraser (Leonard Hawthorne), Jack Watson (William Haskin), Queenie Watts (Mrs. Wallace), Trisha Mortimer (Joy), Paul Alexander (Peter McAllister), Colin Jeavons (Commissionaire), Victoria Allum (Samantha as a child)

After a disembodied voice expounds an outmoded definition of schizophrenia (which equates it with split personality), the camera pans over North-East England before resting on a newspaper headline announcing the pending society wedding of figure skater Samantha Gray and rich factory-owner Alan Falconer. Seeing the headline, craggy-faced creep William Haskin (character actor Jack Watson) gets on a train for London, and begins a relentless program of terrorizing Sam: placing a bloody knife beside her wedding cake, breaking into her house and lurking outside her shower, pressing his face up against her windows. Her initial paranoia becomes hysterical distress as the stranger gets closer and closer to her, but when he addresses her by another name over the phone, her startled response indicates that he may not be a stranger after all.

Lynne Frederick (known to genre fans from *Vampire Circus* but perhaps most famous as the highly-criticized inheritor of the entire Peter Sellers estate) stars as Sam, who has clearly been withholding information about her past from her increasingly suspicious new hubby. Alan's jealousy is stoked further when she turns to her lecherous shrink friend Leonard (John Fraser of *Repulsion*) for advice instead of him, but the scene does allow for both an economical explanation of what's been troubling Sam and also gives Leonard the opportunity to wax on with Freudian rhetoric. Sam confesses that as a child she witnessed her mother's murder at the hands of the mother's lover Haskin – the man who has been threatening her – but shortly after she leaves, Leonard is brutally attacked in his car.

Her surprisingly blasé response to Leonard's murder is the first indication that something's not right with Sam (considering she has more of a reaction to a plastic spider on the countertop), as are her inconsistent responses to the various murders that follow. Overall, *Schizo* is a rather transparent whodunit in the krimi/giallo vein, and with all the obligatory trappings: a gloved killer, a neurotic woman, a sleazy psychiatrist, a too-obvious red herring, some really ugly wallpaper and an O. Henry ending (that we can unfortunately see coming a mile away).

While Stephanie Beacham (returning from Pete Walker's *House of Mortal Sin* a year earlier) holds her own as Sam's sophisticated friend Beth, the film suffers from the absence of a powerhouse like Sheila Keith, who appeared in most of Walker's horror pictures; ultimately Lynne Frederick has the same screen presence as Samantha Fox in Doris Wishman's *A Night to Dismember*, which is to say, none.

*above, both images: Lynne Frederick in Pete Walker's **Schizo** (1976).*

SCISSORS

1991, USA
D: Frank De Felitta. P: Don Levin, Mel Pearl, Hal W. Polaire.
W: Frank De Felitta, Joyce Selznick (story). Ed: John F.
Schreyer. DoP: Anthony B. Richmond. M: Alfi Kabiljo.
PD: Craig Stearns. AD: Randy Moore.
Cast: Sharon Stone (Angie Anderson), Steve Railsback (Alex
Morgan/Cole Morgan), Ronny Cox (Dr. Stephan Carter),
Michelle Phillips (Ann Carter), Vicki Frederick (Nancy
Leahy), Larry Moss (Mr. Kramer), Austin Kelly (Folger), Jesse
Garcia (Counterman), Will Leskin (Billy), Ivy Jones (Mother)

This overly melodramatic erotic thriller from the writer of *The Entity* and *Audrey Rose* stars a pre-*Basic Instinct* Sharon Stone as Angie Anderson, a repressed, 20-something virgin who can't stand to be touched and spends her time fixing broken antique dolls. As a testament to her resignation concerning her sexual potential, she has even given up her bedroom, sleeping on the couch so that her doll workshop can have its own room instead. One doll – a pink pig hand-puppet – is a particular menace.

Returning to her apartment one day, she is attacked in the elevator by a man with a red beard, who tries to rape her. She stabs him in the arm with a pair of scissors from her bag and he takes off at another floor, while she curls up against the back wall until the door opens at the top floor and she is discovered by her neighbour Alex (Steve Railsback), who takes her to his apartment while he calls the police. There she discovers that Alex is a semi-famous actor who portrays a psychotherapist on a daytime soap, and meets his identical twin brother Cole (also Steve Railsback), a wheelchair-bound artist who makes expressionistic paintings of naked faceless women spreading their legs and holding birdcages. When Alex invites her to a party at their house shortly thereafter, she is horrified to learn that Cole has painted a portrait of her, cowering nude in the elevator and being menaced by a man with a red beard. He confesses shamelessly that her nude likeness was informed by his frequent habit of watching her undress through the window. When Alex tries to comfort her, she allows him to touch her, even getting partially disrobed before she notices her pig doll staring at her and she recoils in horror.

Carrying over *The Entity*'s suspicion of the psychiatric profession, Stone's sessions with her shrink Dr. Carter (Ronny Cox) – which involve hypnotherapy – are uncomfortable, often inappropriate, and don't seem to be doing anything to help her other than regurgitating clichés that pronounce her frustration (visually the film regurgitates these same clichés, wracked with obvious Freudian symbolism that make it seem like a bad, bloodless late-'80s giallo)

At some point a temp job assignment lands in her in a practically empty warehouse building being converted into high concept lofts. She finds herself locked in, discovers a corpse in the back bedroom (stabbed in the back with her own pair of red scissors), and is terrorized by mechanical toys and talking ravens that keep repeating "You killed him! You killed him!" The film spends a lot of time in this apartment and things just get stupider and stupider to the point that we no longer care why she's there or who the man with the red beard is, although we will most assuredly find out in an abrupt, tacked-on ending.

SCREAM 4

2011, USA
D: Wes Craven. P: Wes Craven, Iya Labunka, Kevin Williamson.
W: Kevin Williamson. Ed: Peter McNulty. DoP: Peter Deming.
M: Marco Beltrami. PD: Adam Stockhausen. AD: Gerald Sullivan.
Cast: Lucy Hale (Sherrie Marconi), Shenae Grimes (Trudie Harrold),
Roger Jackson (The Voice), Dane Farwell (Ghostface), Anna Paquin
(Rachel Milles), Kristen Bell (Chloe Garrett), Brittany Robertson
(Marnie Cooper), Neve Campbell (Sidney Prescott), David Arquette
(Dewey Riley), Courteney Cox (Gale Weathers-Riley)

In an era overflowing with unwanted sequels and remakes, *Scream 4*'s honchos try to re-establish their place as the progenitors of the previous decade's slasher renaissance with their most annoyingly meta-cinematic stab-fest yet. Although the series has its occasional psycho woman (Laurie Metcalf as Mrs. Loomis in *Scream 2* comes to mind), my interest in *Scream 4* stems from a single line of dialogue.

Neve Campbell appears again as Sidney Prescott, who has reluctantly returned to the accursed town of Woodsboro to launch her new book about overcoming victimization. Reunited with nice-guy deputy Dewey (now sheriff, played by genre champion David Arquette) and her former nemesis Gale Weathers (Courteney Cox) – who has since married Dewey and sunk into a matrimonial slump complete with writer's block and a full-on existential crisis of confidence – Sidney just can't seem to keep the ghosts (or in this case, 'ghostface') at bay, and the bodies start piling up (in rather unimaginative ways) as soon as she hits town.

"You're a victim for life – embrace it", says Sidney's unsympathetic, go-getting publicist. This one line, while played flippantly for laughs, is the key to the whole film – and the key to the continuing trend of female victimization in genre films even in a post-feminist era. The fact remains that the female victim carries a weight that male victims can't. *Scream 4* acknowledges this, and both begs a redefinition of the term 'victim', and simultaneously posits victimization as currency.

That's not to say these characters are incapable. They can fight (Neve Campbell even gives the killer a roundhouse kick to the head at one point), they can deduce, rationalize, and make hard decisions about who to trust. But the film makes a connection between victimization and survival that is interesting. Sidney Prescott proves increasingly harder to kill with each *Scream* film, and yet she views herself as a victim, and hopes to escape this history by writing an autobiography and starting anew. According to the textbook definition of the word victim, Sidney is one, no question: she is routinely targeted for terror, injury and death by another person(s). But the word victim is loaded. Being a victim is now considered a matter of personal perspective; you're only a victim if you feel like one. By getting 'used to' being a victim, Sidney has adapted accordingly and learned to survive in a permanent mode of controlled victimization. While for the most part a dismissible film – it has been disowned even by Craven – its paradoxical politics make it worth a look.

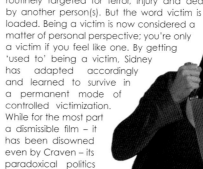

above: Neve Campbell in Wes Craven's **Scream 4** (2011).

SÉANCE ON A WET AFTERNOON

1964, UK
D: Bryan Forbes. P: Richard Attenborough, Bryan
Forbes (uncredited). W: Bryan Forbes, Mark
McShane (novel). Ed: Derek York. DoP: Gerry
Turpin. M: John Barry. AD: Ray Simm.
Cast: Kim Stanley (Myra Savage), Richard
Attenborough (Billy Savage), Nanette Newman
(Mrs. Clayton), Patrick Magee (Superintedent
Walsh), Mark Eden (Charles Clayton), Gerald Sim
(Detective Sergeant Beedle), Marian Spencer
(Mrs. Wintry), Lionel Gamlin (man at seances),
Judith Donner (Amanda Clayton), Margaret
Lacey (woman at first seance)

In this subtly eerie kitchen-sink horror (remade
by Kiyoshi Kurosawa in 2000 as *Séance*), middle-
aged couple Myra (Kim Stanley) and Billy (Richard
Attenborough, who also produced) are grieving
the loss of their son Arthur. They live in the large
Victorian house left to Myra by her family, where Myra holds séances for people trying to connect with their departed loved ones,
claiming that her 'special gift' is assisted from beyond by Arthur's spirit. Despite the comfort implied by the grand appearance of
the house, Billy and Myra are financially and emotionally unstable.

Billy questions Myra's powers as a medium, but supports her endeavours because he recognizes them as a necessary funnel
for her grief, and that of the people she 'helps'. In fact, he is aware that she's quite mad, but his love for her drives him to tolerate
and enable her madness; the best he can do is to try not to contradict or upset her. When she turns off the radio, and then accuses
him of turning it off only moments later, we see the resignation in his
face. As she condescends to him, it is clear that he has been a victim
of emotional abuse for some time, and he is completely shrunken and
worn down as a result.

> Myra: "Oh Billy, why did I ever marry you?"
> Billy: "I don't know, dear, why did you?"
> Myra: "Because you're weak. And because you need me."

He lives only to serve her, and when she concocts a plan to
kidnap a wealthy couple's child so that she can prove her psychic
abilities and gain recognition by 'finding' the child, he's the one
sent out to carry out the abduction (of course leaving witnesses
and fingerprints all over everything). "I'm not a master criminal", he
says to Myra, and indeed the film derives much of its tension from
Billy's capacity for error. Like the enabling husband in Pete Walker's
Frightmare, he gets wrapped up in crimes that are not of his own
imagining, while his wife sees everything as a sign that they are doing
the right thing.

The script by Bryan Forbes (based on the book by mystery writer Mark McShane) gives Kim Stanley plenty to work with
psychologically ("You know what I sometimes wish? I sometimes wish I were ordinary like you. Dead ordinary. Ordinary and
dead like all the others."), but the actress's girlish expressions and her sad, lost eyes are where her madness is conveyed most
poignantly. In the film's climactic séance, her vocal register shifts dramatically
and she commands the scene as a woman possessed – not by the spirits of
the dead, but by her own damnable soul. After a chilling, Oscar-nominated
performance like this it's surprising that Kim Stanley didn't go on to a more prolific
film career, but in fact other than a handful of television appearances she didn't
appear on the big screen again until her role as Frances Farmer's domineering
mother in *Frances* (1982), which also earned her an Oscar nomination (and
featured a score by John Barry, who also provided the suitably nerve-wracking
score for *Séance on a Wet Afternoon*).

Actor/director Bryan Forbes again delved into the realm of female delusion in
The Whisperers (1967) but perhaps his most recognizable genre credit is as director
of *The Stepford Wives* (1975), which would count as a neurotic woman film if not
for the science fiction elements.

---

from top: Kim Stanley with Richard Attenborough, lost in a séance and following the light in Bryan Forbes's **Séance on a Wet Afternoon** (1964).

SECRET CEREMONY

1968, UK
D: Joseph Losey. P: John Heyman, Norman
Priggen. W: George Tabori, Marco Denevi (story).
Ed: Reginald Beck. DoP: Gerry Fisher. M: Richard
Rodney Bennett.
PD: Richard MacDonald. AD: John Clark.
Cast: Elizabeth Taylor (Leonora), Mia Farrow
(Cenci), Robert Mitchum (Albert), Pamela Brown
(Hilda), Peggy Ashcroft (Hannah)

In Joseph Losey's underrated *Secret Ceremony*,
an ageing but still glamorous Elizabeth Taylor
stars as Leonora, a prostitute grieving over the
death of her daughter in a drowning accident.
Travelling to the graveyard for a visit one day,
she is accosted on a city bus by a waifish weirdo
named Cenci (Mia Farrow), who insists that
Leonora is her 'missing' mother. Cenci's pleading
eyes remind Leonora of her dead daughter, and
she concedes to follow the girl to her giant London
house, where she immediately spies a picture
of the mother in question and understands the
confusion – the two women are nearly identical. But in all the family photos, the image of the father is suspiciously blackened out.
Leonora sizes up the situation: a young girl alone in a big house who wants her dead mommy back, and a childless mother
living in poverty who could get quite used to being doted on by a young daughter-figure and living a life of opulence. Within
minutes the two are playing out a scenario of domestic damage, wherein Cenci recounts the events that led up to her father's
absence: he was caught doing something 'scandalous' to Cenci in the kitchen – something that left her permanently deranged.
Leonora has to decide whether or not to use the girl's neurosis to her own advantage, knowing that to get sucked into Cenci's
perverse game could mean risking her own sanity as well.
For more on this film see **Part 4: Secret Ceremonies**.

THE SECRET LIFE OF SARAH SHELDON

2006, USA
D: Annette Ashlie Slomka, Joseph Dodge. P: Annette Ashlie Slomka. W: Annette Ashlie Slomka.
Ed: Joseph Dodge. DoP: Igori Kamoevi. M: Denis DeFrange.
Cast: Annette Ashlie Slomka (Sarah Sheldon), Max Phyo (Alex), Patty McCollim (Jenny), Brenda
Lamberty (Cindy), Dana Fares (Cherrie), Rylan Williams (Dylan), Lyndsay Brill (Julia), Marten Borg
(Jonathon), James Casey (Luke), Lainnie Felan (Lisa)

After being kicked out of med school, Sarah Sheldon embarks on a series of population control
experiments that involve endowing an Asian man with a giant 'appendage' – namely, an organic
penis with an appetite for destruction. As the attachment grows (and growls), it produces teeth meant
to disable a woman's ovaries during intercourse as a means of sterilization, but instead, its eats their
insides entirely and the unfortunate subjects die of massive haemorrhaging. The male subject begs to have the penis removed,
and the aggressive appendage is deposited in a jar where it bangs its head against the glass and generally misbehaves. This results
in punishment, by way of it not being allowed out in the sunshine (it loves the sunshine).
This is a fully vulgar, misanthropic and highly original film with atrocious acting – but to keep a straight face through this
remarkably absurd plot is a feat in itself. The actors stagger through mostly emotionless lines like "What ever happened to (pause)
profound conversations and (pause) the (pause) discovery of inner truth and spirituality?" and "You haven't experienced the
stallion until you've felt this Italian sausage."
Sarah is obsessed with sex, but clearly loathes sex with men (although she engages in it frequently). When one of her pick-ups
beats her, she laughs, hissing at him: "You think you're the first guy to beat me up?" Ultimately she has to admit that she wants the
penis attached to herself. After trying it out with her naïve girlfriend, she cuts her hair (symbolic transformative act) and tracks down
the guy that beat her so that she can rape him with her giant toothed dick. This is not the last of the film's many strange twists.
Although I have seen films with better writing, better acting and better production values, I have never forgotten this film.
In the catalogue of this book, *The Secret Life of Sarah Sheldon* is one of a kind.

from top: Mexican lobby card for Joseph Losey's **Secret Ceremony** (1968); poster for Annette Ashlie Slomka's **The Secret Life of Sarah Sheldon** (2006).

SHOCK

1977, Italy

Alternative title: **Beyond the Door II**

D: Mario Bava. P: Turi Vasile. W: Lamberto Bava, Francesco Barbieri, Paolo Brigenti, Dardano Sacchetti. Ed: Roberto Sterbini. DoP: Alberto Spagnoli. M: I Libra [Walter Martino, Alessandro Centofanti & V. Cappa]. AD: Francesco Vanorio. Cast: Daria Nicolodi (Dora Baldini), John Steiner (Bruno Baldini), David Colin Jr. (Marco), Ivan Rassimov (Dr. Aldo Spidini), Nicola Salerno (Carlo), Paul Costello (man at party), Fred Bava (boy with balloon), Christian De Sica (Paolo)

Released in the U.S. as *Beyond the Door II*, *Shock* sees Daria Argento's spouse Daria Nicolodi as a woman returning to a former site of tragedy, in the hope of emotional closure. When her abusive junkie ex-husband Carlo dies under mysterious circumstances (officially labelled a suicide), Dora (Nicolodi) suffers a nervous breakdown and is admitted to a mental institution. Released and remarried seven years later, she follows the (ill) advice of her new husband Bruno (classy Euro-star John Steiner) to move back into her old house, with over-attached son Marco in tow.

Upon unpacking, Dora spies a strange figure peeping out from beneath some cushions on the sofa – it is a large sculpture of a disembodied hand that seems to stir some fragments of memory for her. Unable to nail down the memory, she dismisses it and dusts off the sculpture, adding it to the décor. The accoutrements of the house in general indicate a more arty and emotionally-charged counterpart to her now-conventional domestic life with Bruno. Although Dora is happy with Bruno, and looking forward to her new life with him, her attachment to the excitement associated with her chaotic former life will not dissipate so easily.

The family enjoys a few days of tranquillity before weird things start to happen – most notably to the boy Marco, who is Dora's son from her previous marriage. He starts talking to an imaginary friend and develops a strange hostility toward his new father-figure, accompanied by an overtly sexual obsession with his mother. After a disturbing incident during which Marco tries to hump her, Dora avoids the issue by trying to divert his attention with a trip to the park, where they sit in on a puppet show. Marco is enamoured with the puppet show, although Dora insists that the story – about a spirit who tries to take a living woman away with him to the land of ghosts – is too scary for him.

When Bruno returns, they have a party to settle in to the new house. Among the guests is her former psychiatrist (the creepy Ivan Rassimov) who is still concerned about her recovery. He is right to be: after a particularly upsetting comment by her young son ("Mamma, I have to kill you") Dora is hurled into a distressing hallucinatory flashback involving a ticking metronome and a laughing piano. She sees her hands playing the piano, but she can't control them as they thrash about noisily. This is just one example of the recurring 'disembodied hand' motif that permeates the film, beginning with the hand sculpture at the film's opening. The hand is a signifier of responsibility, and the hand's disembodiment is the refusal of that responsibility. She is trying to hide from herself – or repress – something she has done, as signified by the hand sculpture being hidden beneath the cushions and releasing locked memories when unearthed. Similarly, she imagines being groped by her dead husband Carlo's zombified hand as she is asleep in the garden.

Soon Marco's sexual fascination with his mother becomes more violent: Dora finds deliberately mutilated photos of her and Bruno, and some of her lingerie hidden in one of Marco's drawers, slashed to ribbons. Her protests to Bruno are answered with medication, which he supplies to her without her knowledge. In a sense her situation hasn't really changed much from one marriage to the next: her first husband Carlo was a junkie who turned her onto the needle. Bruno insists, "You're lucky to be without him – you were living with a monster! You were only a victim!" He says this without irony, as he feeds her medication without her knowledge that only serves to unhinge her completely.

Dora takes Marco to the psychiatrist Dr. Spidini, but both he and Bruno think she is overreacting, and that Marco is just acting up as a means of getting attention. "If you can accept the past," says Spidini, "then you can face the future peacefully with your husband and child." But Dora can't accept the past – because she can't remember it. Her psychiatrist's revelation that she was administered electroshock treatment (making it especially fitting that the film is entitled 'Shock') answers a lot of questions concerning her amnesia. It is not only psychological repression she is suffering from – shock treatment is a very physical mental eraser. "That period is a complete void inside of me", Dora says, "My mind seems to have cast it out – cancelled it completely… Only now in that house, in my house, I'm starting to remember things… it's strange, it's as if my own son is a go-between."

When Dora's nervousness starts to get out of control, Bruno responds by feeding her more medication to calm her down, which only fuels her frightening hallucinations. She starts to fear that her son is possessed by the spirit of her dead ex-husband, who is haunting her with accusations of his murder. The accusations turn out to be true – Dora killed her husband in a fit, then sank into a coma remembering none of it, while the lovelorn Steiner covered up for her and made it look like a suicide. Dora doesn't take this news well. "If you love me, how could you bring me back to this house?" she shrieks, "You left me alone in this house – maybe you wanted me to go crazy!" Completely berserk by the time of this revelation, Dora kills Bruno too, then turns a razor to her own neck, imagining it to be Carlo's dead hand in control of the deed. Both *Shock* and Bava's earlier *The Whip and the Body* (1963) – and to a certain extent William Fruet's *Funeral Home* – have female protagonists who murder their villainous ex-lovers and then inflict physical punishment on themselves, imagining it to be the spirit of the dead men.

Although being subjected to rehabilitation, her return to the house was a mistake that only served to ignite repressed memories. An odd choice for Bruno, who since her release has only wanted Dora to forget about her past and look forward to a bright future with him. Her psychiatrist also encourages her to forget rather than deal with her trauma. So when she returns to the house, she's not at all equipped to deal with the inexplicable fear that suddenly grips her. Everything in the house is predatory – the furniture, the artwork, and most notably, young Marco. The film is probably unique in its use of a five-year-old as a sexual predator, even though Marco's erratic behaviour is later revealed to be the product of Dora's guilty imagination. But by imagining the child to be sexualizing her, she is in fact sexualizing the child (as is the audience), which makes *Shock* – and Nicolodi's role in it – that much more disturbing.

opposite: Daria Nicolodi and Nicola Salerno (in doorway) in Mario Bava's **Shock** (1977).

SINGAPORE SLING

1990, Greece
D: Nikos Nikolaidis. P: Marie-Louise Bartholomew. W: Nikos Nikolaidis. Ed: Andreas Andreadakis. DoP: Aris Stavrou. PD: Marie-Louise Bartholomew.
Cast: Meredyth Herold (daughter/Laura), Panos Thanassoulis (Singapore Sling), Michele Valley (mother)

In this depraved take on Otto Preminger's *Laura*, a man searching for his lost love stumbles upon an isolated villa where two women play out a perverse identity game. Barely conscious upon arrival, he is quickly adopted into the fold as both plaything and patriarch. Substitution, and the role-playing that results from it, is discernible throughout *Singapore Sling*. The two women act out their mother/daughter fantasy – wherein they are lovers as well as kin – and the younger woman confesses also to a sexual relationship with her absent 'father' before the two women killed him. But at the heart of the film and its bizarre trajectory of torture and manipulation is the visiting man's belief that the younger woman is actually his missing girlfriend, Laura. For more on this film see **Part 2: Broken Dolls**.

SINNER

1973, France
Original title: **Le journal intime d'une nymphomane**
Alternative title: **Diary of a Nympho**
D: Jess Franco.
P: Robert de Nesle.
W: Jess Franco, Elisabeth Ledu de Nesle (adaptation and dialogue). Ed: Gilbert Kikoïne. DoP: Gérard Brisseau. M: Jean-Bernard Raiteux, Vladimir Cosma. Cast: Jacqueline Laurent (Rosa), Montserrat Prous (Linda Vargas), Anne Libert (Countess Anna de Monterey), Doris Thomas (Mrs. Schwartz), Howard Vernon (Doctor), Gaby Herman [Kali Hansa] (Maria Toledano), Gene Harris [Francisco Acosta] (Alberto), Manuel Pereiro (Mr. Ortiz)

top: Monserrat Prous with Anne Libert, and with knife (*bottom right*) in Jess Franco's **Sinner** (1973).

Jess Franco's film reconstructs the events that led to a young woman's compulsive nymphomania and eventually, her own suicide. Underlying this film's colourful blend of sleaze and kitsch, however, is Franco's characteristic commentary on alienation.

In the opening sequence, a prostitute named Linda picks up an older man at a bar, gets him wasted and leads him down the street to a hotel room. After hasty sex, the older man lies passed out and spent, and she calls the police to report a murder. She then slits her own throat, giving herself just enough time to put the knife in his hand before collapsing lifeless on top of him. The police bust in and arrest the bewildered man for murder. His wife, convinced of his innocence (at least in regard to the murder charges) starts her own investigation into the girl's life, which leads to a barrage of garish, sex-filled flashbacks detailing the girl's search for intimacy and her subsequent descent into debauchery – including posing for pornographic pictures and heavy drug use.

As related by her closest friend and first lover, Linda's first sexual experience with a man was getting molested on a Ferris Wheel by the balding man that she later frames for murder. Confused, she runs away from home and has a succession of affairs with both men and women, trying to turn her abandonment issues and fear of (real) intimacy into something she wrongly perceives as positive: indiscriminate sexual activity. Another of Linda's close friends (and another wanton exhibitionist) has possession of Linda's diary, and reads part of it aloud to the wife, relating Linda's bizarre interpretation of her actions as humanitarian: "I wanted to give my body, my feelings, my sex, to my sisters and brothers, those who have known only pain, only humiliation."

In the diary, Linda continues to describe one of her greatest fantasies – that a man will be trying as hard as he can to pleasure a woman to no avail – and that Linda would be able to make the woman "come just by touching her. That's my revenge on them for the humiliation and pain they caused me when they raped me." Interestingly, she refers to the man who raped her as plural, as though she holds all men responsible for what happened to her – and yet her self-esteem issues keep her seeking their approval through sexual gratification. She uses sex as a thinly veiled escape tactic, but each escapade only feeds her depression, no matter how much she tries to reinforce through her diary entries that her sexual behaviour is positive and healthy.

She gets taken in by a mysterious doctor (Jess Franco staple Howard Vernon) who whisks her off to a rest home in the country, to reform her into "a healthy, clean young woman again". He makes her realize that everything reverts back to the incident on the Ferris Wheel, but his efforts are in vain; she runs away from the rest home because she can't stop having sex compulsively: "My body was longing to be caressed, to be kissed, to be penetrated." She decides that her situation is hopeless: "When I'm buried, they can write on the stone: 'One Who Wanted Too Much'."

The coincidence of her rapist coming in to the bar provided perfect closure for her, as she was feeling suicidal anyway, but the story is primarily driven by her depression and her staggering alienation rather than by her desire for revenge. Unlike Dagmar Lassander's character in *The Frightened Woman*, Linda has no control, no direction, and her aggressive attempts at intimacy only create further distance between herself and the rest of the world.

SISTERS

1973, USA
Alternative title: **Blood Sisters**
D: Brian De Palma. P: Edward R. Pressman. W: Brian De Palma, Louisa Rose. Ed: Paul Hirsch. DoP: Gregory Sandor. M: Bernard Herrmann. PD: Gary Weist.
Cast: Margot Kidder (Danielle Breton/Dominique Blanchion), Jennifer Salt (Grace Collier), Charles Durning (Joseph Larch), William Finley (Emil Breton), Lisle Wilson (Philip Woode), Barnard Hughes (Arthur McLennen), Mary Davenport (Mrs. Collier), Dolph Sweet (Detective Kelley)

In Brian De Palma's horror debut, Margot Kidder plays Danielle, one half of a pair of French Canadian twins, who submerges herself in pills and alcohol to escape from a terrible secret. After spending the night with a man she just met, he wakes up to hear her arguing with her sister Dominique, who wants to spend the day – their shared birthday – without male accompaniment. He attempts to reconcile this by bringing them a joint birthday cake, and when he returns with it, he is viciously stabbed and killed by a maniacal, spasming woman who is the spitting image of Danielle, minus the coquettish charm. The murder is overseen through a window by Grace Collier, a journalist working for the Staten Island paper. She desperately wants a real story to write about, but when she gets the police involved, they find no evidence that a crime has taken place.

As Grace continues to investigate on her own, she is sucked into a bizarre story of Siamese twins – one passive and charming, the other belligerent – who were the subject of a botched separation attempt that left Dominique dead long ago. Danielle suffered an accompanying split in personality, taking on the role of her dangerous sister, a role that will soon be filled by Grace herself.
For more on this film see **Part 2: Broken Dolls**.

from top: Lobby card for Brian De Palma's **Sisters** (1973); Margot Kidder in the guise of Dominique.

SISTERS

2006, USA/Canada
D: Douglas Buck. P: Alessandro Camon,
Cathy Gesualdo, Edward R. Pressman.
W: Douglas Buck, John Freitas, Brian De
Palma (original story and screenplay),
Louisa Rose (original screenplay).
Ed: Omar Daher. DoP: John J. Campbell.
M: Edward Dzubak, David Kristian.
PD: Troy Hansen. AD: Michael Corrado.
Cast: Chloë Sevigny (Grace Collier),
Stephen Rea (Dr. Philip Lacan), Lou Doillon
(Angelique/Annabelle Tristiana), Dallas
Roberts (Dylan Wallace), JR Bourne (Larry
Franklin), William B. Davis (Dr. Bryant),
Gabrielle Rose (Dr. Mercedes Kent), Serge
Houde (Detective Kalen), Alistair Abell
(Detective Connors), Talia Williams (Lily)

Following the same basic plot outline as De
Palma's film (see previous entry) – including
the emulation of certain key scenes –
Buck's film takes innovative liberties with
the characters that significantly bolster
their sympathetic qualities. Dominique and
Danielle have been renamed Angelique
and Annabelle, and where De Palma
treats his female characters as experiments – just as his Dr. Breton does – Buck allows them to develop a kinship with one another throughout the narrative.

In Buck's version of events (set in Vancouver, Canada), reporter Grace Collier (Chloë Sevigny) is onto Dr. Lacan (Stephen Rea) from the outset, and has been tracking his "improper procedures on children" in the years since he was indicted on related charges. She approaches Angelique (Lou Doillon, daughter of Jane Birkin and director Jacques Doillon), Lacan's ex-wife and one-half of famed Siamese twins, and offers an escape route from his controlling influence: "Help me, and maybe I can help you", she says, but Lacan's influence will be hard to shake – especially as Angelique relies on him to furnish her with addictive experimental drugs that allegedly keep her darker half at bay. Still, Angelique finds relief in allowing herself to tell Grace how she and her sister came into Lacan's care via her mother, a love-struck French woman who allowed herself to be experimented on by Lacan. This leads Grace to another woman, Dr. Mercedes Kent (Canuck staple Gabrielle Rose), who served as a nurse for Lacan at the time the twins were born. Grace and Dr. Kent bond over a cigarette (an illicit act in Vancouver, where smoking was banned in 2000) as they watch an old 16mm film of the twins' birth, and Dr. Kent relates stories of arranging sneak meetings between the babies and their mother because visitation was formally denied. The footage continues to document the conjoined sisters just prior to separation as teenagers. It is here that Grace learns that Annabelle, the despondent 'other' sister, died in that operation.

As Grace gets more entwined with the twins' story, memories of her own mental instability, and that of her mother – whose death left Grace with a debilitating financial burden – start to cloud her objectivity. We start to recognize female doubling deliberately happening all over the film, making its title extend beyond Angelique and Annabelle; and the actualization of this psychic mirroring will occur in the climactic scene at Dr. Lacan's Institute, where Grace is re-appropriated as Angelique's other half in a dream-like surgical sequence. Lacan wants to kill Annabelle all over again, as a means of cementing his bond with Angelique ("Let's share our guilt and be together again.") But Angelique doesn't want to share her guilt with Lacan – she wants to share it with Grace, her new sister.

While De Palma's film had its experiments partially set at the fictional Loisel Institute in Quebec, Buck's film goes further (albeit unconsciously) in exploring the implications of this French-Canadian connection. Canada has a well-documented history with non-consensual human experimentation, most notably with its part in the MKULTRA brainwashing program at Montreal's Allan Memorial Institute (see review of *Psycho Girls* elsewhere in this appendix as well as **Part 4: Secret Ceremonies** for more details), but in the case of Buck's *Sisters*, the emphasis on Lacan's experiments also points to the Duplessis Orphans – a program in which Quebec Premiere Maurice Duplessis authorized the certification of thousands of orphans (most of whom were not even orphans, but were taken away from unwed mothers) as mentally ill, in a scheme to secure Federal funding to (a) support their daily existence and (b) justify 'psychological' experiments on them. As such, from the 1940s through the 1960s, thousands of innocent children were subjected to electroshock and other medical horrors (not to mention sexual abuse), including fatal experiments that resulted in unmarked mass graves that are still being discovered across Quebec to this day.

Of course, in Buck's version, the twins are not French-Canadian, they are from France (largely to accommodate the casting of Lou Doillon), so this connection is not deliberate, but it is an uncanny thread that runs from one film to the next. And coincidentally, Doug Buck has resided in Montreal, Quebec since 2005.

above: Lou Doillon and Stephen Rea in Douglas Buck's **Sisters** (2006).

SLAUGHTER HOTEL

1971, Italy
Original title: **La bestia uccide a sangue freddo**
Alternative title: **Cold Blooded Beast**
D: Fernando Di Leo. P: Tiziano Longo. W: Fernando Di Leo, Nino Latino. Ed: Amedeo Giomini. DoP: Franco Villa.
M: Silvano Spadaccino. AD: Nicola Tamburro.
Cast: Klaus Kinski (Doctor Francis Clay), Margaret Lee (Cheryl Hume), Rosalba Neri (Anne Palmieri), Jane Garret (Mara), John Karlsen (Professor Osterman), Gioia Desideri (Ruth), John Eley [Giangiacomo Elia] (the gardener), Fernando Cerulli (Alfred), Sandro Rossi, Giulio Baraghini (special squad policeman)

The giallo's obsession with mentally unstable women gets a virtual smorgasbord of neurosis in Fernando Di Leo's sleazy thriller (which would seem like a giallo *parody* if it didn't come so early in the cycle). You know exactly what to expect when Klaus Kinski is the doctor at an asylum full of suicidal nymphos. In true giallo fashion all the women are beautiful, wealthy and lazy, and the hospital is a labyrinthine old country house full of openly accessible vintage medieval weapons, as well as an iron maiden (not actually a medieval invention but often catalogued as such), making it the perfect setting for a bodycount movie. And what bodies they are.

There's Mara (Jane Garret in her only known role), the agoraphobic orphan who responds more to the lesbian advances of her weird nurse than to her electroshock treatments; Ruth, the homicidal housewife (Gioia Desideri, who surprisingly never played a transvestite in a Nazi exploitation film); Cheryl (Margaret Lee), the suicidal industry magnate who longs for a 'connection' and finds it in dodgy doctor Klaus Kinski (who shared the screen with Lee in at least 12 films); and Anne (Rosalba Neri), the nymphomaniacal sexpot who asserts to head Doctor Osterman that, "I'm not one of those mad people who need you. I just want to make love. Make love, that's all", to which Osterman replies: "It's just that your desire to make love is obsessive, compulsive. Go and take a shower." In the ensuing shower scene, she throws herself against the walls and writhes on the floor. She's been rejected by her one true love, Peter, and pours herself into meaningless sexual trysts trying to fill the emptiness left by this rejection. Comedy music plays when she enthusiastically attempts to seduce two male nurses, who struggle to keep a straight face as she throws herself at them in a histrionic fit of sex mania.

This is not the only hilarity to be had; the killer's belaboured breathing as he trudges up the steps and through the halls trying to decide where to go in pursuit of his victims seems like something out of *Student Bodies*, endless hardcore masturbation inserts shamelessly flaunt the film's aesthetic appeal, and the mop-topped killer attacks an entire room of nurses with a mace in a bloody massacre!

Slaughter Hotel is the most plotless Di Leo film I've seen; the three components – the women, the asylum, the killer – functioning without a script to connect them. Ironically, it's based on the 1968 book *The Castle of the Blue Bird* by popular post-war German writer Heinz G. Konsalik, but completely drops the narrative involving the head doctor's medical experimentation (which is meant to be its focus) in favour of slobbering over a bevy of bodacious babes. I know many people who love this film. I'm not one of them.

above: Rosalba Neri in Fernando Di Leo's **Slaughter Hotel** (1971).

THE SNAKE PIT

1948, USA
D: Anatole Litvak. P: Anatole Litvak, Robert Bassler. W: Frank Partos, Millen Brand, Mary Jane Ward (novel). Ed: Dorothy Spencer. DoP: Leo Tover. M: Alfred Newman. AD: Lyle R. Wheeler, Joseph C. Wright.
Cast: Olivia de Havilland (Virginia Stuart Cunningham), Leo Genn (Dr. Mark H. 'Kik' Kensdelaerik), Mark Stevens (Robert Cunningham), Celeste Holm (Grace), Glenn Langan (Dr. Terry), Helen Craig (Miss Davis), Leif Erickson (Gordon), Beulah Bondi (Mrs. Greer), Lee Patrick (asylum inmate), Howard Freeman (Dr. Curtis).

This is neither a horror film nor an exploitation film, but it is essential viewing for anyone interested in the subject of mental health on film. One of the prototypical and taboo-breaking 'madwoman' films, Anatole Litvak's adaptation of the Mary Jane Ward novel stars Olivia de Havilland in an Oscar-nominated turn as Virginia Cunningham, a woman in an asylum who has no recollection as to how or why she got there. Clearly lost and disoriented, she tries to keep it together, while her interior monologue betrays her suspicion about the staff and other patients. As her husband and the sympathetic Dr. Kik try to figure out what triggered her psychosis, she is forced to undergo electroshock treatment and is moved through different wards filled with a diverse slate of crazies, shriekers, cacklers, speed-talkers and zombies. De Havilland purportedly threw herself into the role, visiting many such institutions and even sharing in dinners and social functions as part of her intensive research. While far from a glamorous take on life inside an asylum – de Havilland looks convincingly greasy throughout – it does make an effort to humanize the patients, the most poignant example being the co-ed dance where a fellow inmate (played by Jan Clayton) performs a tear-jerking rendition of 'Going Home' (from Dvorak's New World Symphony) and the entire populace stops in their tracks to sing along.

Various forms of therapy reveal that de Havilland's character feels responsible for the deaths of both her father and her first boyfriend, who was essentially a substitute for her father. An early example of Freudian theory at work on film, Dr. Kik concedes that Virginia identifies most men with her father, and relives the trauma of his death whenever she gets too close to anyone. This tidy Freudian resolution might seem trite now, but it was a powerful example of early pop-psychology given the film's massive exposure, and helped usher in legislation in many states that saw improved living conditions in mental hospitals nationwide.

SOMBRE

1998, France
D: Philippe Grandrieux. P: Catherine Jacques. W: Philippe
Grandrieux, Pierre Hodgson, Sophie Fillières. Ed: Françoise
Tourmen. DoP: Sabine Lancelin. M: Alan Vega. PD: Gerbaux.
Cast: Marc Barbé (Jean), Elina Löwensohn (Claire), Géraldine
Voillat (Christine), Coralie (first woman), Maxime Mazzolini
(child) Alexandra Noël (second woman), Annick Lemonnier
(third woman), Sadija Sada Surcevic (Claire's mother)

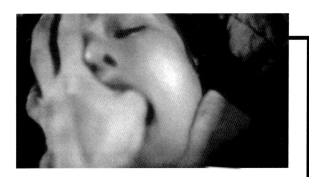

The view from inside a car at dusk: the sun setting; darkness
enveloping the forest; the forest enveloping the car. Moody
nature scenery transitions to the interior of a theatre as children
scream, terrified and invigorated by something unfolding before
them, and again cuts abruptly to a woman being strangled,
as Suicide's Alan Vega provides a sparse score that builds and
threatens. This is our introduction to the strange personal space
of *Sombre*, Philippe Grandrieux's French serial killer film that owes
as much of a debt to Chris Petit's *Radio On* as to Gerald Kargl's
Angst or Lodge Kerrigan's *Clean, Shaven*.

With a grainy, schizophrenic aesthetic, the camera jumps
and shakes as serial killer Jean (Marc Barbé) traverses the
countryside, roughly following the route of the Tour de France,
stopping occasionally to pick up hookers or other amorous
women so that he can rape and kill them. Characteristic of all
the relationships that will be depicted here, we are never given
any conventional emotional cues and often wonder whether a
rape or murder is even occurring.

When, by chance, Jean picks up a stranded woman named
Claire (otherworldly '90s indie staple Elina Löwensohn) in the
middle of a rainstorm, she proves to be more trouble than Jean
bargained for – not because she resists him, but because she
doesn't. Her willing collapse into the arms of death completely
freaks him out, and it is he who tries to run away. As he is drawn
into her life, he discovers from her promiscuous sister that Claire
is a virgin, and his murderous compulsions are confused by this
dichotomous choice of victims. But when he traps them both in a
hotel room, fondling them each in turn, it is Claire he chooses to
take out into the night, leaving her sister tied up on the bed.

He takes Claire to a loud, chaotic party and watches as
she gets drunk, dances, laughs, and makes out with strangers
in front of him. The more she sheds the virginal, stoic image
that attracted him, and uses him as an excuse to release her
animalistic urges, the more he becomes changed and possibly
stabilized – a transformation that frightens him. Her inappropriate
emotional reaction to her situation is messing with his head; does
she want to die, or does she think she can quell his homicidal
itch? When he abandons her on a country road, demanding
that she go back to her life, she adopts a fantasy where he
plays the role of a lost love, while he continues to collect victims,
burying his face in their battered crotches as though desperate
to scramble back inside and escape a world where one of his
victims could fall in love with him.

While the film is deliberately paced and certainly, as its
title suggests, sombre, it stands next to *Angst* as one of the most
effective depictions of a serial killer. For fans of the macabre,
the film is not especially nasty; its violence lies largely in its
camerawork and editing, which are also at times prone to
moments of serene stillness. A review I read once described the
film as being devoid of human emotion; on the contrary, I found
it so full of emotion – often conflicting emotions – that what

results is an intense catalogue of emotional responses without
a definite narrative context to identify them. For those who can
tune in to its atmospheric pace, *Sombre* will leave a lasting and
dizzy chill that only gets better with age.

SPIDER BABY

1968, USA
D: Jack Hill. P: Paul Monka, Gil Lasky. W: Jack Hill. Ed: Jack Hill.
DoP: Alfred Taylor. M: Ronald Stein. AD: Ray Storey.
Cast: Lon Chaney Jr. (Bruno), Carol Ohmart (Emily Howe),
Quinn Redeker (Peter Howe), Beverly Washburn (Elizabeth
Merrye), Jill Banner (Virginia Merrye), Sid Haig (Ralph Merrye),
Mary Mitchell (Ann Morris), Karl Schanzer (Mr. Schlocker),
Mantan Moreland (Messenger), Carolyn Cooper (Aunt Clara)

Setting the tone with its campy *Mad Monster Party*-style credit
sequence, exploitation director Jack Hill's breakout film launches
into psychiatric exposition that details 'The Merrye Syndrome'
– so-called for its prevalence among the members of a single
inbred family, and signified by a developmental regression that
sets in at one's tenth year. "It is believed that eventually the
victim of the Merrye Syndrome may even regress beyond the
pre-natal level, reverting to a pre-human condition of savagery
and cannibalism", reads the narrator, who will also play a part in
the story to unfold. With this mock square-up, we jump headfirst
into 80 minutes of gleefully maniacal behaviour courtesy of
the latest descendents of the Merrye family – siblings Elizabeth
Merrye (Beverly Washburn), Virginia Merrye (Jill Banner) and the
completely infantile Ralph Merrye (Sid Haig) – along with their
put-upon caretaker Bruno (Lon Chaney Jr.) who attempts to
keep them under control after their father's death.

They live together in a large dilapidated house, which
allows for several 'Old Dark House' tropes to play out – from
goofy humour, creaking floors and trap doors to the cowardly
black characters typical of the genre. Virginia's favourite game
is 'Spider' – wherein she ensnares unwanted visitors in her web
and carves them up with butcher's knives – and when distant
family members arrive to make a claim on their father's estate
and assert legal guardianship over them, the other kids want in
on the fun. With their guests spending the night, the increasingly
dishevelled Merrye sisters slink around the house being sexually
as well as homicidally predatory, their repressed distant aunt
Emily ('50s starlet Carol Ohmart of *House on Haunted Hill*) giving
an unwitting eyeful to the imbecilic Ralph before succumbing to
the animalistic teens.

opposite: Olivia de Havilland in scenes from Anatole Litvak's **The Snake Pit** (1948). *above:* Elina Löwensohn in Philippe Grandrieux's **Sombre** (1998).

THE STENDHAL SYNDROME

1996, Italy
Original title: **La sindrome di Stendhal**
D: Dario Argento. P: Dario Argento, Giuseppe Colombo.
W: Dario Argento, Franco Ferrini, Graziella Magherini (novel).
Ed: Angelo Nicolini. DoP: Giuseppe Rotunno. M: Ennio Morricone.
AD: Antonello Geleng.
Cast: Asia Argento (Assistant Inspector Anna Manni), Thomas
Kretschmann (Alfredo Grossi), Marco Leonardi (Marco Longhi),
Luigi Diberti (Chief Inspector Manetti), Paolo Bonacelli (Doctor
Cavanna), Julien Lambroschini (Marie Bale), John Quentin (Mr.
Manni, Anna's father), Franco Diogene (victim's husband), Lucia
Stara (Viterbo shop assistant), Sonia Topazio (victim in Florence)

Inspired by the 1989 book of the same name by psychiatrist Graziella Magherini, who coined the term to describe the psychosomatic disorder involving the disorienting or hallucinatory effects of great works of art (named after the 19th century writer Stendhal, who first reported the symptoms), Dario Argento's late-period giallo stars his daughter Asia Argento as Detective Anna Manni, who is in Florence on the trail of a serial rapist-murderer. When she experiences the syndrome while visiting the Uffizi Gallery, it is Bruegel's *Landscape with the Fall of Icarus* that makes her faint, and when revived, she has momentarily lost her memory – and it is the rapist himself who hands her back her purse. As he ushers her into a taxi, she rolls the window up, revealing the image of his reflection fused with her own.

Later that night he attacks her in her room and though she passes out from the trauma, she awakens in a car where he is raping another woman. He gets away (with her gun), and she is forced to endure the typical bureaucratic response to this kind of violation – the interrogation, the probing medical examinations – and exhibits the standard behaviour of the rape-revenge heroine: she cuts her long hair short, adopts gender-neutral clothing and returns to her childhood hobby of boxing, dismissing her boyfriend Marco's sexual advances. When she eventually responds to Marco by becoming aggressively sexual with him, putting him in a submissive position, it is the first sign of a transference in which she identifies – like Monica Ranieri in *The Bird with the Crystal Plumage* – with her attacker.

After a second attack – in which she kills the rapist and throws his body into the river – Anna becomes obsessed with him, convincing herself that he's still alive and is going to come for her. He's "left his mark on me", she says, referring to a scar on her cheek, which she now covers with a long blonde wig – the film's third phase of her physical transformation. "I feel myself changing", she confesses to the psychiatrist her superiors have ordered her to see. Like the paintings in the film, Anna becomes a mutable canvas that changes styles and effects on her intended audience (as if to emphasize this, part way through the film she takes up painting, covering herself with the oily substance and writhing on a canvas on the floor – effectively making herself a part of her own painting). And like Thana in *Ms.45* she adopts a noirish vamp persona, and is framed as such by highly stylized lighting that accentuates her elusive and threatening nature. By adopting this third persona, Anna is able to use the trappings of male desire to become a destructive force poised against patriarchy itself. Her issues with male control pre-date her rape; her father is stern and unloving (he is even dismissive of the incident and doesn't see why therapy is necessary, as though it's a shame to the family), and her need to control the thing that incapacitated her results in

her becoming romantically involved with an art history professor with a gender-neutral name (Marie) who is punished for his interest in her. Her now-dead attacker becomes her other; 'he' kills Marie because he must have Anna for himself – which allows Anna to be desired, to have control, and to be free of responsibility all at the same time.

Because Argento traditionally fetishizes his scenes of violation, something must also be said for Asia Argento being lensed in this fashion by her own father. Asia Argento has stated that she only took up acting to win her father's attention, and that he only became her father when he was her director,[84] which adds troublesome import to the fact that she is raped repeatedly onscreen with murderous hands grabbing at her that are – as in most of Argento's films – his own hands.

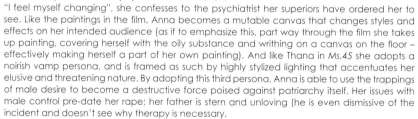

above: The many hairstyles of Asia Argento in Dario Argento's **The Stendhal Syndrome** (1996).

STRAIGHT ON TILL MORNING

1972, UK
D: Peter Collinson. P: Peter Collinson. W: John Peacock.
Ed: Alan Patillo. DoP: Brian Probyn. M: Roland Shaw.
AD: Scott MacGregor.
Cast: Rita Tushingham (Brenda Thompson), Shane Briant
(Peter Price), Tom Bell (Jimmy Lindsay), Harold Berens (Mr.
Harris), James Bolam (Joey), John Clive (newsagent), Claire
Kelly (Margo Thompson), Annie Ross (Liza), Mavis Villiers
(Indian princess), Katya Wyeth (Caroline)

In Peter Collinson's disquieting Hammer thriller, Shane
Briant (*Demons of the Mind*) is the psychopath in question,
but British kitchen-sink staple Rita Tushingham enables
his psychosis with her malleability and deep desire for a
human bond, whatever the cost. Tushingham stars as
Brenda Thompson, a dowdy young woman who leaves
her provincial home for the city, where she hopes to
get pregnant. Desperate for a baby who will love her
unconditionally, she moves in with a slutty co-worker she
dislikes in the hope of meeting more men. She allows herself
to be mocked and used as a trade-off for her roommate's
party life, where her mating needs might be met.

One day she meets and becomes taken with a
striking homicidal maniac named Peter (Briant) who
agrees to give her a baby if she plays housewife to him.
He calls her Wendy, fancying himself as Peter Pan (even
the dog's name is Tinker), and she allows her identity (what
little there is) to be sublimated to his fantasies. They're both
like children, living in a hermetically sealed fantasy world
(reflected in the use of frequent intense close shots). That
she is seemingly oblivious to his true nature betrays her
own deep instability; she feels so unworthy of a healthy
reciprocal relationship that she's willing to turn a blind eye
to Peter's murderous extracurricular activity – as well as the
likelihood that his homicidal attentions will eventually turn
toward her.

STRAIT-JACKET

1964, USA
D: William Castle. P: William Castle. W: Robert Bloch.
Ed: Edwin H. Bryant. DoP: Arthur E. Arling. M: Van Alexander.
PD: Boris Leven.
Cast: Joan Crawford (Lucy Harbin), Diane Baker (Carol
Harbin), Leif Erickson (Bill Cutler), Howard St. John (Raymond
Fields), John Anthony Hayes (Michael Fields), Rochelle
Hudson (Emily Cutler), George Kennedy (Leo Krause), Edith
Atwater (Mrs. Fields), Mitchell Cox (Dr. Anderson), Lee Yeary
[Lee Majors] (Frank Harbin)

One of the essential hagsploitation films that followed in the
wake of Billy Wilder's *Sunset Boulevard*, *Strait-Jacket* was the
first of two features written for exploiteer William Castle by
Psycho scribe Robert Bloch (the other being the 'paranoid
woman' film *The Night Walker* of the same year).

Sentenced to 20 years in an asylum for the axe-murder of
her husband (an uncredited Lee Majors, in his screen debut)
and his mistress, Lucy Harbin (Joan Crawford, in a hilariously
overwrought performance) returns home to her brother's
farm after her release and tries to repair her relationship
with her daughter Carol (Diane Baker of *Marnie*), who was a
witness to the murder. But the tough, confident woman who
went into the asylum is not the same woman that comes out,
and people tiptoe around her, afraid of the things that might
set her off – photographs, gleaming knives, children's songs,
visions of decapitated heads. When the creepy farmhand
(George Kennedy) offers her an axe to let her slaughter a
chicken she nearly has a nervous breakdown.

This reticent, shamed woman is inexplicably transformed
into a drunken flirt when Carol's fiancé stops by for a drink –
possibly buying into her daughter's dream to have everything
'just as it was' 20 years ago – and is snapped out of it only
by a surprise visit from her doctor, who feels she's become
unbalanced again and threatens to take her back to the
asylum. When bodies start piling up, all evidence suggests
that Lucy's murderous impulses have returned.

left: Rita Tushingham in Peter Collinson's **Straight On Till Morning** (1972); *right:* Joan Crawford tries to appear sane in William Castle's **Strait-Jacket** (1964).

THE STRANGE POSSESSION OF MRS. OLIVER

1977, USA
D: Gordon Hessler. P: Stanley Shpetner. W: Richard
Matheson. Ed: Frank Morriss, Jerry Garcia. DoP: Frank
Stanley. M: Morton Stevens.
Cast: Karen Black (Miriam Oliver/Sandy), George
Hamilton (Greg Oliver), Robert F. Lyons (Mark), Lucille
Benson (housekeeper), Jean Allison (Mrs. Dempsey),
Gloria LeRoy (saleslady), Burke Byrnes (bartender at
beach), Asher Brauner (dance partner in bar), Charles
Cooper (Mr. Logan), Danna Hansen (Mrs. Logan)

Curiously, I watched this back to back with Dan Curtis's
Trilogy of Terror, and not only does it have the feel
of a Curtis production, but it also employs his staple
scriptwriter (Richard Matheson) and stars Karen Black in a
dichotomous 'hair up/hair down' dual role not unlike the
one she played in *Trilogy of Terror*'s 'Millicent and Therese'
segment, as well as Curtis's theatrical feature *Burnt
Offerings*. While traces of camp follow her from one film to
the next, she *is* a diverse actress, and these 'role-within-a-
role' parts certainly give her a lot of room to play.

Black stars as Miriam, the stuffy, uptight wife of a self-
absorbed lawyer (George Hamilton) who pressures her to
stay at home and prepare for motherhood. Things that
would be subtext in other films are laid right out on the
table from the opening scenes; after a dream in which
she witnesses her own funeral, Miriam verbalizes her
feelings of being 'trapped' and accuses her husband of
controlling her by not letting her have a job, go to school
or even do volunteer work. "I thought we agreed..." he
begins every sentence, as though Miriam is not allowed to
change her mind or have inconsistent feelings. Of course,
he's a lawyer, and he treats his wife like he has her under
contract.

One day at the mall, she spies a low-cut red sweater
and a blonde wig, and is drawn to try them on. She glows
as she stares at herself in the mirror, transformed. "You look
like a new woman!" exclaims the shop girl, which seems
to be some sort of trigger for Miriam to put everything
back and deny herself these frivolous pleasures. But the
shopkeeper convinces her to at least buy the sweater,
and the next day, Miriam can't resist – she returns to the
shop for the wig, some lipstick and a pair of large hoop
earrings. When she surprises her husband with her new get-
up, he is horrified. "It's just not *you*", he explains. But Miriam
seems to be having some sort of identity crisis – compelled
to change her appearance while assuring her husband
that she's "the same woman you always approved of."

Freewheeling fashions aren't Miriam's only
compulsion; she suddenly rents a beach-house (against
her husband's wishes) where she goes when she wants
to wear her new clothes. Like Cathryn in *Images* or Anna
in *Possession* she has another house where she explores
forbidden aspects of her personality. But when people
in the seaside village start to recognize her as a woman
named 'Sandy', Miriam starts to panic. Why does she keep
seeing images of a burning house? How is it connected
to her dreams, and is she possessed by a dead woman?
Is she a dead woman? Somehow for a film that's been
so obvious about its psychology, the twist still comes as a
surprise, with another quick expository wrap up for anyone
who couldn't put the Freudian two-and-two together from
the flashbacks.

THE STRANGE VENGEANCE OF ROSALIE

1972, USA
D: Jack Starrett. P: John Kohn. W: Anthony Greville-Bell, John
Kohn, Miles Tripp (novel). Ed: Thom Noble. DoP: Ray Parslow.
M: John Cameron. AD: Roy Walker.
Cast: Bonnie Bedelia (Rosalie), Ken Howard (Virgil), Anthony
Zerbe (Fry)

Jack Starrett was an incredible character actor (best known for
playing three versions of the same unruffleable cop character
in Richard Rush's *Hell's Angels on Wheels*, Tom Loughlin's *Born
Losers* and Bruce Kessler's *Angels from Hell*) but also the director
of some of the most idiosyncratic films of the counterculture
indie heyday (my favourite being the Terrence Malick-scripted
The Gravy Train, 1974).

The Strange Vengeance of Rosalie is an odd genre hybrid
that sees travelling salesman Virgil (Ken Howard) duped into
becoming the prisoner of a love-starved teenaged Native
American girl (Bonnie Bedelia, looking shockingly young) at
her remote shack in the California desert. After an eerie
opening scene in which she ceremonially buries her dead
grandfather, backlit by the twilight and effectively scored by
sporadic percussion (the only really appropriate use of music
in the entire film), her loneliness becomes unbearable and
the inhospitable landscape frightens her into trying to find
company. But she's young and unsocialized, having never
been to school, and only going into town occasionally to get
supplies. As she points out later in the film, "no one knows about
this place", and consequently, no one knows about her; she is
not only a marginalised person, she's practically invisible. In a
sense, she's like Kobo Abe's *Woman in the Dunes* – now all she
needs is a mate.

Out on the road hitchhiking, she gets picked up by Virgil,
who is on his way to Los Angeles to catch a flight for a long-
anticipated vacation. As the sky turns dark, he agrees to take her
down the dusty unmarked road that leads to her grandfather's
'ranch' (although it's really a tiny, filthy shack with no doors or
windows), where she proceeds to let the air out of his tyres, and
break his leg with the butt of an axe in order to incapacitate him
(this scene in particular has led many viewers to compare it –
unfavourably – to Stephen King's *Misery*). With Virgil immobilized
and bedridden, she begins a bizarre game of courtship in which
she tries to convince him to fall in love with her, and he tries to
manipulate her to get the hell out of there.

But where *Misery*'s Annie Wilkes tries to hide her motivation
from writer Paul Sheldon, deceptively telling him that the roads
are closed and the telephones are out, once Rosalie lures Virgil
to her ramshackle abode he knows flat out that she's nuts and
that she plans to keep him there as a prisoner until such time as
he wants to stay with her of his own free will. He begs her to get
a doctor, warning her that he could get gangrene and his leg
could fall off ("and then how would you feel?"), but she's satisfied
with the splint she's fashioned for him. "What do you know about
broken legs?" he challenges. She shrugs, unconcerned: "I fixed
a chicken leg like that once" (thus referencing the source
material, Miles Tripp's 1966 book *The Chicken*). Virgil's vitriol for
his captor is blatant – he calls her "a dumb half-breed Indian
squaw" among other niceties, but their interplay is interesting
because it borders on jovial bickering and at times one wonders
if perhaps Stockholm syndrome isn't setting in.

They are rousted out of their insular game by the
appearance of a nosy no-gooder named Fry (squinty screen
villain Anthony Zerbe) who – expanding on the plotline of
Starrett's earlier *Cry Blood, Apache* (1970) – has been hanging

First she loves, then she kills— then she goes out to collect the next victim!

The Strange Vengeance of Rosalie

Palomar Pictures International, Inc. presents "The Strange Vengeance of Rosalie" Bonnie Bedelia · Ken Howard Anthony Zerbe screenplay by Anthony Greville-Bell and John Kohn · produced by John Kohn · executive producer Peter Katz directed by Jack Starrett · A Cinecrest Films Inc. Production · released by 20th Century-Fox Films · COLOR BY DE LUXE

PG

around Rosalie's grandpa trying to find out where he hid his rumoured stash of gold. Hearing of the old man's demise, Fry gets rough with Rosalie in an attempt to pry the gold's whereabouts out of her, and Virgil comes to her defence (even if all he can do in his current state is threaten Fry and offer to pay him off). But as much as the audience – and Virgil – comes to sympathize with this disturbed girl, one can't forget that she is dangerous, and she will do what she needs to in order to survive.

SYMPTOMS

1974, UK
Alternative title: **The Blood Virgin**
D: Joseph Larraz [José Ramón Larraz]. P: Jean L. Dupuis.
W: Joseph Larraz [José Ramón Larraz], Stanley Miller.
Ed: Brian Smedley-Aston. DoP: Trevor Wrenn. M: John Scott.
AD: Kenneth Bridgeman.
Cast: Angela Pleasence (Helen Ramsey), Peter Vaughan (Brady), Lorna Heilbron (Anne), Nancy Nevinson (Hannah), Ronald O'Neill (John), Marie-Paule Mailleux (Cora), Michael Grady (Nick), Raymond Huntley (Burke)
Made the same year as Larraz's better-known *Vampyres*, *Symptoms* follows in the footsteps of Altman's *Images* and Polanski's *Repulsion* in its intense, brooding study of a young woman teetering on the edge of sanity. Angela Pleasence (daughter of Donald) turns in an amazing performance as Helen Ramsey, an odd-looking girl whose social ineptitude makes her seem like a shut-in child trying to impress the world of adults around her. Helen invites a friend out to her isolated, rarely visited country manor and everything seems idyllic but for the strange sense of foreboding reflected in Helen's worried stare. She seems normal enough until she enters the house, then it's as though something 'sets in' – everything becomes portentous. Helen changes dramatically when she comes into the realm of her family home. It is as though she passes through a boundary into unreality. Like Cathryn in *Images*, Helen has an isolated house that acts as a very physical counterpart to her madness, and her visiting friend will soon experience the extent of Helen's madness first-hand.
For more on this film see **Part 8: Heal Me with Hatred**.

SZAMANKA

1996, Poland/France/Switzerland
Alternative title: **Chamanka**
D: Andrzej Zulawski. P: Jacky Ouaknine. W: Manuela Gretkowska.
Ed: Wanda Zeman. DoP: Andrzej Jaroszewicz. M: Andrzej Korzynski. PD: Tomasz Kowalski.
Cast: Iwona Petry (Wloszka 'The Italian'), Boguslaw Linda (Michael), Agnieszka Wagner (Anna), Pawel Delag (Juliusz), Piotr Machalica (Anna's father), Alicja Jachiewicz, Piotr Wawrzynczak (Priest), Wojciech Kowman, Zdzislaw Wardejn, Jolanta Grusznic

Andrzej Zulawski's *Szamanka* is an explosive return to the hyper-intense emotionalism of *Possession*, aided in no small part by the primal performance of 18-year-old first-time actress Iwona Petry. Petry plays a character known only as 'The Italian' who embarks on a violently sexual relationship with an anthropology professor named Michael (Polish superstar Boguslaw Linda) who abuses and humiliates her, only feeding her increasing sexual obsession with him. As she acts with abandon – flailing, spitting, regurgitating food – she disavows the commonality of language in favour of physical expression (like Anna in *Possession*). When Michael's anthropological team discovers the bog-body of an ancient shaman in a nearby construction site, he begins to formulate a connection between the respective mysteries of the shaman and The Italian – believing that The Italian is a succubus depleting his life-force.
For more on this film see **Part 9: Piercing Reality**.

from top: Poster for Jack Starrett's **The Strange Vengeance of Rosalie** (1972); Iwona Petry in Andrzej Zulawski's **Szamanka** (1996).

a park bench; when he is still there several hours later, she invites him up to get warm and dry. He doesn't speak a word, doesn't nod or gesture or give her any indication of mental apprehension other than an occasional smile. He takes everything she gives, and she fills the emptiness left by his silence with words, stories, food, gifts and deluded hope. As the days pass and an unspoken contract is developed in which she is the caregiver and he the kept man, the companionship stimulates her long-repressed sexual impulses – but she dreads his inevitable boredom, and takes to locking him in his room at night.

It's not until he sneaks out the window one night that we know for certain he can speak. He lives partially at home with his family, and partly at the crash-pad of his sister and her draft-dodging drug-dealing boyfriend, where he brags about how much better life is at this strange lady's house – even though she never stops talking and seems "a little mixed up". With no better option, he returns to Frances's company.

Frances's society obligations – tea time and lawn bowling – suddenly seem incredibly spinsterish and tedious, and whenever errands take her out of the apartment, she's anxious to get back to her enigmatic prisoner. One of her bowling companions confesses his affection for her – intercut with scenes of her in a gynaecological examination earlier that day, emphasizing her discomfort with the subject – and she halts the conversation, partially because the man represents everything 'old' that she's afraid of, but also because she's got her heart set on the 19-year-old in the other room, a boy who could be both lover and son to her (an incestuous confusion mirrored by that of his sister, who repeatedly tries to seduce him).

With the same kind of sexual and class manipulation that we see in films like Umberto Lenzi's *Paranoia* (also 1969), this story has a simple trajectory; basically the whole thing is about waiting to see who will break first. Although terrifically unsettling, Dennis's characterization does nothing to assuage negative stereotypes about middle-aged single women (that they get mean and possibly psychotic without a man), but this is only one of the many headcase roles she would excel at throughout her career.

THAT COLD DAY IN THE PARK

1969, USA/Canada
D: Robert Altman. P: Donald Factor, Leon Mirell. W: Gillian Freeman, Peter Miles (novel). Ed: Danford B. Greene. DoP: László Kovács. M: Johnny Mandel. AD: Leon Ericksen. Cast: Sandy Dennis (Frances Austen), Michael Burns (the boy), Susanne Benton (Nina), John Garfield Jr. [David Garfield] (Nick), Luana Anders (Sylvia), Edward Greenhalgh (Dr. Charles Stevenson), Doris Buckingham (Mrs. Ebury), Frank Wade (Mr. Ebury), Alicia Ammon (Mrs. Pitt), Rae Brown (Mrs. Parnell)

Based on the novel by actor/writer Peter Miles (under the pseudonym Richard Miles) and the first film of Altman's 'feminine quartet' (the others being *Images*, *3 Women* and *Come Back to the Five and Dime Jimmy Dean, Jimmy Dean*), *That Cold Day in the Park* is a dreary, desperate film about the lengths to which a person will go to alleviate their emotional solitude.

Stage and screen dynamo Sandy Dennis stars as Frances Austen, a lonely woman who lives in a luxurious apartment overlooking Vancouver's Stanley Park. One day during a downpour she notices a teenage boy (Michael Burns of *The Mad Room*, reviewed elsewhere in this appendix) sitting on

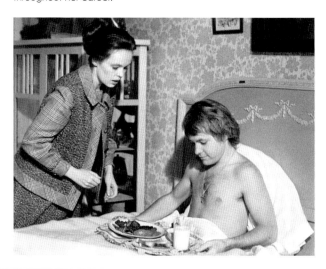

THEY CALL HER ONE EYE

1974, Sweden
Original title: **Thriller – en grym film**
Alternative title: **Thriller – A Cruel Picture**
D: Bo Arne Vibenius. P: Bo Arne Vibenius. W: Bo Arne Vibenius. Ed: Brian Wikström. DoP: Andreas Bellis. M: Ralph Lundsten.
Cast: Christina Lindberg (Frigga/Madeleine), Heinz Hopf (Tony), Despina Tomazani (lesbian), Per-Axel Arosenius (Frigga's father), Solveig Andersson (Sally), Björn Kristiansson, Marie-Louise Mannervall (woman in village), Hildur Lindberg (mother's friend), Stig Lokrantz, Olle Nordlander

Perhaps the most celebrated of Swedish softcore goddess Christina Lindberg's salacious exploitation roles, *They Call Her One Eye* stars Lindberg as Madeleine, a naïve farm girl who has been mute since being sexually assaulted by an old man in the woods as a child. One day on the road she is offered a ride by a sleazebag named Tony who kidnaps her and forces her into a life of prostitution at his brothel, addicting her to heroin in the process. When she refuses to service one of the clients, he has her eye gouged out and this eye-patched beauty becomes an exotic favourite of the brothel's gross clientele (as well as becoming one of the most iconic images of the rape-revenge canon), who see her 'disability' as a turn-on. But the greatest affront in her eye(s) is that Tony has sent a fake letter to her beloved parents, expressing seething hatred toward them that allegedly prompted her to run away from home. When her parents get the letter, they are distraught and commit suicide. Finding out about their death, Madeleine solidifies her plan for revenge. After praying for forgiveness in church (as Max von Sydow did in *The Virgin Spring*, and which prefigures similar sequences in *Ms.45* and *Possession*) she goes through the rape-revenge film's standard self-improvement trajectory – learning how to drive, how to shoot, and practicing martial arts – before donning her famous black trench coat and shotgun and dispatching Tony's accomplices, while subjecting him to a particularly nasty fate.

The film was controversial for its mixing of real and fantasy footage: the sex/violence scenes in most prints include hardcore inserts – predating Virginie Despentes and Coralie Trinh Thi's equally controversial *Baise-moi* – the ammunition was live, and the 'special effect' used to create the eye-gouging scene involved a real cadaver. It was also criticized for its aesthetic inconsistency (despite many ugly, clunky sequences, Vibenius worked with Ingmar Bergman on both *Hour of the Wolf* and *Persona* and the master's influence can be felt in moments of austere beauty), but Lindberg's anguished performance is what makes the film of lasting interest. She is believable, tragic, and shoots with the silent rage of generations.

3 WOMEN

1977, USA
D: Robert Altman. P: Robert Altman. W: Robert Altman. Ed: Dennis M. Hill. DoP: Charles Rosher Jr.
M: Gerald Busby. AD: James Dowell Vance.
Cast: Shelley Duvall (Mildred 'Millie' Lammoreaux), Sissy Spacek (Mildred 'Pinky' Rose), Janice Rule (Willie Hart), Robert Fortier (Edgar Hart), Ruth Nelson (Mrs. Rose), John Cromwell (Mr. Y.R. Rose), Sierra Pecheur (Ms. Vivian Bunweill), Craig Richard Nelson (Dr. Graham Maas), Maysie Hoy (Doris), Belita Moreno (Alcira)

Armed with powerhouse performances by Shelley Duvall and Sissy Spacek, *3 Women* is a film whose provocative schizophrenia is both gripping and contagious. While its horror elements are atmospheric more than overt, the film is a literal sea of doubles that involves a persona-switching trio of women. Spacek plays Pinky Rose, the obtuse new girl working at a surreal geriatric water-therapy centre where she meets her soon-to-be roommate Millie Lammoreaux (Duvall). Millie is everything Pinky isn't: glamorous, confident, in Pinky's words, "perfect". But Millie's projected confidence is a sham, and in Pinky, Millie finally receives the captive audience she needs in order to keep up her illusion of social adeptness, while Pinky gets a role model, however questionable. Millie longs for male attention and finally gets it in the form of their lecherous landlord Edgar, whose pregnant wife Willie (Janice Rule, the third woman) spends her days wordlessly painting serpentine murals along the walls of the compound's pool. When Pinky tries to drown herself in the pool, bewitched by the murals that line its sides, she ends up in a coma, and emerges as a new woman, the first of many transformations through which the three women transgress the laws of identity and come to exist as three parts of the same mind. For more on this film see **Part 2: Broken Dolls**.

from top left: An eye-patched Christina Lindberg with Despina Tomazani, and in her icon get-up in Bo Vibenius's **They Call Her One Eye** (1974).

which sent her over the edge. "You're crazy!" Clara exclaims, rather obviously. "No – I used to be crazy. I tried to solve it by placing puppets all over the house... but now it's different. Now there's life in the apartments... Real life." But the bureaucratic machinations aren't the only thing ailing her; she also lives vicariously through the young couples because her own kid didn't turn out so normal. Ultimately because she's the villain, we only get this pat version of her psychology, but Spanish TV regular Nuria González gives it her all as the blood-soaked landlady from hell.

TO LET

2006, Spain
Original title: **Para entrar a vivir**
D: Jaume Balgueró. P: Álvaro Augustín, Julio Fernández. W: Jaume Balagueró, Alberto Marini. Ed: Frank Gutiérrez. DoP: Pablo Rosso. M: Roque Baños, Mariano Marín. AD: Alain Bainée.
Cast: Macarena Gómez (Clara), Adrià Collado (Mario), Nuria González (letting agent), Ruth Díaz (girl), Roberto Romero (agent's son), David Sandanya (child)

Part of Filmax's *Films to Keep You Awake* series (inspired by Narciso Ibáñez Serrador's *Twilight Zone*-esque 1960s show *Historias para no dormir*), *[Rec]* director Jaume Balagueró turns in this tight thriller about a crazy woman who keeps young couples prisoner in her dilapidated apartment building.

Young expectant couple Clara and Mario are looking for a new home to raise their child, and options are running out. When Mario finds a flyer in their post-box advertising a cheap apartment that seems too good to be true, they drive out to a distant neighbourhood that is practically vacant as it undergoes a major redevelopment by the city. The apartment is roomy but run down, creepy and far too isolated for their liking, even though the real estate agent is aggressively insistent that the place is 'perfect' for them. As they get ready to call it quits on the tour (especially unnerved by the woman's comment about Clara's not-yet-visible pregnancy, which they haven't disclosed to her), they notice some of their own things in the apartment – a photograph, a pair of shoes they threw away – and realize they've been targeted by a madwoman. She violently prevents them from leaving, and – to their horror – they discover that there are others in the building who have suffered the same fate.

"I'm not doing anything bad", the woman assures, "I'm getting my life back – I have the right to do that." She explains that the city condemned her building and evicted all the tenants in order to transition the neighbourhood,

TOYS ARE NOT FOR CHILDREN

1972, USA
D: Stanley H. Brasloff. P: Stanley H. Brasloff, Samuel M. Chartock. W: Macs McAree, Stanley H. Brasloff (story). Ed: Jerry Siegel. DoP: Rolph Laube. M: Cathy Lynn. Cast: Marcia Forbes (Jamie Godard), Fran Warren (Edna Godard), Peter Lightstone (Phillip Godard), Harlan Cary Poe (Charlie Belmond), Evelyn Kingsley (Pearl Valdi), Luis Arroyo (Eddie), Tiberia Mitri (Jamie as a child), Jack Cobb (blindfolded 'john'), N.J. Osrag (Max Geunther), Sally Moore (elderly neighbour)

One of the most revered exploitation films of the '70s among true trash connoisseurs, Stanley Brasloff's *Toys Are Not for Children* is a thoroughly demented Electra-complex tale with plenty of meat and no morals to speak of. Jamie is a teenaged girl who idolizes her absentee father (who her grouchy mother frequently refers to as lecherous scum) and stays emotionally stunted in childhood as a result. Her affection for toys is considered 'unnatural', but it isn't half as unnatural as her sexual longing for her own father. When she meets an ageing prostitute named Pearl, who she suspects is an acquaintance of her estranged father, Jamie finds herself attracted to this seedy lifestyle and becomes a prostitute herself, specializing in older johns who like it when girls call them 'daddy' while she awaits the long-anticipated reunion.
For more on this film see **Part 4: Secret Ceremonies**.

top left: Ruth Díaz and Macarena Gómez in **To Let** (2006); *bottom right:* Marcia Forbes and Evelyn Kingsley in **Toys Are Not for Children** (1972).

TRANCE

1982, West Germany
Original title: **Der Fan**
D: Eckhart Schmidt. P: Barbara Moorse, Martin Moszkowicz. W: Eckhart Schmidt. Ed: Patricia Rommel, Eckhart Schmidt. DoP: Bernd Heinl. M: Rheingold. AD: Joerg Neumann. Cast: Désirée Nosbusch (Simone), Bodo Staiger ('R'), Simone Brahmann (secretary), Jonas Vischer (father), Helga Tölle (mother), Klaus Münster (postman), Ian Moorse (youth), Wilfried Blasberg (man with dog), Sabine Kueckelmann (B), Claudia Schumann (girl)

Eckhart Schmidt's *Der Fan* (renamed *Trance* for both its obscure Canadian and UK video releases) remains one of the most chilling portrayals of female delusion I have ever witnessed onscreen. More art film than exploitation film, *Der Fan* is a deliberately paced but fascinating study of fan-obsessiveness.

German television star Désirée Nosbusch (only 17 years old at the time) plays an alienated and uninvolved teenage girl whose only emotional attachment is to a new wave singing star known only as 'R' (played by Bodo Staiger of the real-life Krautrock band Rheingold, who also provide the soundtrack). She feverishly writes him letters that go unanswered, and considers suicide an alternative if he doesn't write back. When she finally meets him and realizes that he does not fit the idealized version of him that exists in her head, she responds with shocking, violent behaviour.
For more on this film see
Part 5: Afterschool Special.

TRILOGY OF TERROR

1975, USA
D: Dan Curtis. P: Dan Curtis. W: Richard Matheson, William F. Nolan. Ed: Les Green. DoP: Paul Lohmann. M: Bob Cobert. AD: Jan Scott.
Cast: Karen Black (Julie Eldridge/Millicent Larimore/Therese Larimore/Amelia), Robert Burton (Chad Foster), John Karlen (Thomas Amman), George Gaynes (Dr. Chester Ramsey), Jim Storm (Eddie Nells), Gregory Harrison (Arthur Moore), Kathryn Reynolds (Anne Richards), Tracy Curtis (Tracy), Orin Cannon (Motel Clerk)

TV terror titan Dan Curtis – whose film *Burnt Offerings* is covered elsewhere in this appendix – turned in this terrific horror anthology for ABC's *Movie of the Week* series, and although the Richard Matheson-scripted segment 'Amelia', featuring the pint-sized Zuni fetish doll, is the most beloved of the three tales, it's the second story, William F. Nolan's 'Millicent and Therese' that bears mentioning here.

Karen Black (the lead in all three stories, as well as in *Burnt Offerings*) plays both prim, uptight Millicent Larimore and also her promiscuous blonde bombshell sister Therese, who live together in their large family home despite their loathing of one another. When one of Therese's suitors comes calling (John Karlen of Curtis's TV soap *Dark Shadows*), Millicent tells him that Therese has already ditched him to go to a party, before scathingly informing him of Therese's foul habits, occult preoccupations and perverse desires in an attempt to scare him off permanently. But when she starts detailing Therese's sexual seduction of their father, who was buried only that day, Karlen cuts her short, saying: "Miss Larimore, I'm afraid you're the one that really needs help."

George Gaynes (later known for comedy roles in *Police Academy* and TV's *Punky Brewster*) plays the psychiatrist who's been treating Millicent for many years in an attempt to get her to reconcile with Therese. However, the ending reveals that this is a textbook case of split personality, in which the child creates a doppelganger as a means of simultaneously denying and indulging unwanted desires (specifically those directed at her own father). Using Therese's own occult texts against her, she makes a voodoo doll in Therese's likeness and sticks a pin through it – which will turn out to be a suicidal move.

above: Young star Désirée Nosbusch in various scenes, and Bodo Staiger surrounded by mannequins in Eckhart Schmidt's **Trance** (1982).

TROUBLE EVERY DAY

2001, France/Germany/Japan
D: Claire Denis. P: Georges Benayoun,
Philippe Liégeois, Jean-Michel Rey.
W: Claire Denis, Jean-Pol Fargeau.
Ed: Nelly Quettier. DoP: Agnès Godard.
M: Tindersticks. PD: Arnaud de Moleron.
AD: Etienne Rohde.
Cast: Vincent Gallo (Shane Brown),
Tricia Vessey (June Brown), Béatrice
Dalle (Coré), Alex Descas (Léo
Semeneau), Florence Loiret Caille
(Christelle), Nicolas Duvauchelle
(Erwan), Raphaël Neal (Ludo), José
Garcia (Choart), Hélène Lapiower
(Malécot), Marilu Marini (Friessen)

A surprising genre entry from Claire
Denis, *Trouble Every Day* both averts
and indulges the spectacle of the genre
in its story of an enigmatic illness and
the people whose lives are doomed
by it. It takes some time before we can
fathom the connection between the
characters introduced: Coré (Béatrice
Dalle), the cannibalistic wife of Dr.
Léo Semeneau (Alex Descas), whose
radical brain research saw him exiled
from the scientific community; American
newlyweds Shane and June Brown
(Vincent Gallo and Tricia Vessey); and
Christelle (Florence Loiret Caille), the
young chambermaid at the newlyweds'
hotel who will become a pawn in
Shane's degeneration.
 Shane is a scientist at a leading
U.S. laboratory who has brought
his pixie-ish wife to Paris under the

auspices of it being their honeymoon;
but his mandate is primarily to seek
out Semeneau, whose experiments
have some connection to Shane's
bloody hallucinations and his inability
to have a consummate relationship
with his increasingly frustrated young
bride. Meanwhile Coré, locked up in
a farmhouse just outside the city and
refusing to take her medication, finds
ways to escape so that she can prey on
strangers in the road before Léo comes
to collect her and take her home. This
will prove a common routine for Coré –
despondency is followed by mania and
then decompression, and Léo comes to
wash it all away at the end of every day.
He delicately wipes her skin clean, gets
rid of the bodies, reassembles destroyed
furniture, fortifies the house further.

The film blends starkness and excess,
with very little dialogue other than a
few moments of stilted exposition (and
you can tell Denis really hates to give
you any at all) contrasted with scenes
of Grand-Guignol horror that spill more
blood than even your average slasher
film. When some neighbourhood boys try
to break in to save her after seeing Coré
banging on the windows, she seduces
one of them through the slats of wood
that have been nailed up outside her
bedroom door to keep her in. Yanking
the planks free, he embraces her, and
she nibbles at him playfully before riling
herself into a state of frenzy and ripping
a hole in his throat. As he shrieks with pain
and gurgles on his own blood, she slaps
him excitedly, rubbing her face on him
like a pet and chewing off bits of his flesh
in graphic detail. Later, she paces back
and forth in front of a wall painted with
his blood, like an expressionistic souvenir
of her day's work.
 Like Luciana in Alberto Cavallone's
Man, Woman and Beast (reviewed
elsewhere in this appendix), Coré's sexual
hunger manifests as violent physical
appetite, and whatever illness she has,
has also afflicted Shane from some long-
ago experiments his wife knows nothing
about. We are never told what the
experiments were about (although the
imagery ties it to a sexually transmitted
disease) or who experimented on
whom, but we know that Shane fears the
advancement of the illness in himself, as
he starts exhibiting primal, irresponsible
behaviour and edging close to violence.
For most of the film, Shane is a passive
predator – but we can see through
Coré's monstrous gluttony what he is
going to become.

from top: Béatrice Dalle's bloody satiation; Vincent Gallo preys upon Florence Loiret Calle in Claire Denis's **Trouble Every Day** (2001).

TWIN PEAKS: FIRE WALK WITH ME

1992, USA
D: David Lynch. P: Francis Bouygues,
Gregg Fienberg. W: David Lynch,
Robert Engels. Ed: Mary Sweeney.
DoP: Ron Garcia. M: Angelo
Badalamenti. PD: Patricia Norris.
Cust: Kyle MacLachlan (Special
Agent Dale Cooper), Sheryl Lee
(Laura Palmer), Ray Wise (Leland
Palmer), Chris Isaak (Chester
Desmond), Moira Kelly (Donna
Hayward), Dana Ashbrook (Bobby
Briggs), Harry Dean Stanton (Carl
Rodd), Grace Zabriskie (Sarah
Palmer), James Marshall (James
Hurley), Pamela Gidley (Teresa Banks)

David Lynch's feature film follow-up
to his acclaimed television series is a
prequel that examines the events that
led up to the murder of the enigmatic
and tragic Laura Palmer, beginning with
the murder of Teresa Banks (the crime
that led Special Agent Dale Cooper
to believe the Laura Palmer case was
the work of a repeat killer) and then
jumping a year ahead to the last seven
days of Laura Palmer's life.

Laura is the all-American high
school girl – homecoming queen,
community volunteer, recreational drug
user and lover of a bevy of admirers,
including the supernatural predator
Bob, who – as she confides in her
agoraphobic friend Harold – "has been
having her since she was twelve". At
the film's halfway point Laura's already
figured out Bob's identity, and she
spends the second half accelerating
her own obliteration, falling farther

and farther towards the mythical Black
Lodge like its many other lost and
secret souls. She is unable to hold it
together, crying in class, her vision blurry,
desperate for drugs to blot out her
grief. Her chain-smoking mother Sarah
Palmer (Lynch regular Grace Zabriskie)
self-medicates, leaving her witless and
unavailable for emotional support.

While it is revealed in the second
season of the show that Leland Palmer,

'possessed' by a demonic entity known
as 'Bob' was his daughter's murderer,
Twin Peaks: Fire Walk with Me allows
Laura's story to be told from her own
perspective rather than through the
(often conflicting) accounts of others
who thought they knew her. In retelling
the tale, the film becomes much more
of an honest, horrific examination of
incestual sexual abuse and subsequent
trauma than the television show allowed.

above: Sheryl Lee in the film's climax, and the poster art for David Lynch's **Twin Peaks: Fire Walk with Me** (1992).

THE UNINVITED

2003, South Korea
Original title: **4 Inyong shiktak**
D: Lee Soo-youn. P: Oh Jung-wan, Jeong Hoon-tak. W: Lee Soo-youn. Ed: Kyung Min-ho. DoP: Cho Yong-gyu. M: Jang Young-kyu.
AD: Jeong Eun-yeong.
Cast: Park Shin-yang (Kang Jung-won), Jun Ji-hyun (Yun), Yoo Seon (Hee-eun), Kim Yeo-jin (Jung-sook), Jeong Wook (Kang Jae-sung), Park Won-sang (Park Moon-sub), Kang Ki-hwa (Young-suh), Lee Seok-jun, Lee Joo-sil, Jeong Hyeon

It takes a while to figure out what this film has to do with female neurosis, but once it gets there, its imagery is overpowering and creates the melancholic thread that ties the narrative together. A brief-period buzzfilm on the fest circuit due in part to its repeated images of shocking infant trauma (some of which has been trimmed for DVD release), *The Uninvited* seems, at first, not much different from many 'noughties' Korean genre films: stylistically competent, with an emphasis on overt lighting contrasts, communication clouded by proprietary issues, and a ghost story at its centre. But the ghosts are just the gatekeepers of the real story.

Interior decorator Jung-won falls asleep in a subway car, and when he jarringly awakens and jumps off the train at the last stop, he notices two little girls asleep on the train with no adult accompaniment. Instead of alerting the subway officials, or phoning the police, he ignores the incident and goes home. The next morning he hears on the radio that the two girls were poisoned and left on the train by their mother. He starts to see them at his house, asleep in the chairs of his new dining room set. Again he tries ignoring them, staying away from the house as much as possible. But when he inadvertently meets a narcoleptic woman named Yun and has to take her home when she suddenly faints, she is able to see the children too, and this is where the very female component of the film comes into play. Yun is severely lethargic and medicated after her best friend Jung-sook threw both of their infant children over a balcony railing a year earlier. Jung-won is subject to hallucinations and nightmares – most involving a child being run over by a garbage truck and then hidden in a sewer well – and now that he has ghosts hanging around his house, it seems like time to step up and figure out what it all means. Since Yun can see the ghosts, he figures she may be a conduit for whatever revelation he seeks, and he starts following and pestering her until she finally comes to trust him.

During one of the film's many languid periods of confession, she reveals that her mother was a shaman, and the two developed a deep bond as a result of their shared visions and the fact that they both felt socially ostracized due to the mother's supernatural abilities. "I don't know why people don't believe things just by experiencing them", she laments, referring not just to her mother but also to the doubt that plagued her own failed marriage; her husband is convinced that it was she who tossed their baby overboard, and for most of the film strives to have her committed.

So much of the film is concerned with witnessing and empathy; throughout the film, Jung-won witnesses without connection (he leaves the children in the subway train, drives past Yun fainting in the street and takes no action when he sees a suffering cat in the lying road after being mangled by a car), whereas Yun witnesses with an empathic connection (during her friend's MRI examination, she feels the claustrophobic terror of being trapped in a tunnel, and in one of the film's most exceptional scenes, she is standing on her balcony and makes eye contact with a woman who has just jumped from one of the floors above). This kind of empathy is presented as distinctly female, with the male characters struggling to understand it or to do anything other than dismiss it as nonsense or hysteria.

When replaying the events that led to Jung-sook's infanticidal crime – through statements made in court as well as through Yun's memories – Jung-sook's husband describes how she was afraid of her own child, and would not breast-feed for fear that the child would bite her (even though it had no teeth yet). It is through a psychic connection with Yun that Jung-sook is able to realize the source of her fear: abandoned as a child, she survived by eating her own mother. But after being granted this repressed knowledge, Jung-sook is never the same, and slowly becomes unable to function in society, as a mother, or as a friend, killing Yun's child as well as her own. Despite this, Yun's empathy for her friend never diminishes, which obstructs her grieving process and fills her with suicidal guilt.

A confident, remarkable debut feature from female director Lee Soo-youn (and a major award-winner at the Sitges and Fantasia Film Festivals), it's a true shame she's never made another, her only follow-up being a commissioned short for Seoul's International Women's Film Festival in 2008.

above: Jun Ji-hyun and Park Shin-yang haunted by childhood ghosts in Lee Soo-youn's **The Uninvited** (2003).

VENOM

1971, UK
Alternative title: **The Legend of Spider Forest**
D: Peter Sykes. P: Michael Pearson, Kenneth
F. Rowles. W: Donald Ford, Derek Ford,
Christopher Wicking (additional dialogue),
Stephen Collins (story). Ed: Stephen Collins.
DoP: Peter Jessop. M: John Simco Harrison.
AD: Hayden Pearce.
Cast: Simon Brent (Paul Greville), Neda
Arneric (Anna), Derek Newark (Johann),
Sheila Allen (Ellen), Gerard Heinz (Huber),
Gertan Klauber (Kurt), Bette Vivian (Frau
Kessler), Terence Soall (Dr. Lutgermann),
Sean Gerrard (Rudi), Ray Barron
(young man)

> "They say I'm dangerous.
> If anyone touches me, the
> spiders come. Does that
> frighten you?"

Somewhere in the middle of a convoluted
story of Nazi scientists and stolen paintings
is the tale of a feral girl in a forest who
believes she's cursed – any man who
touches her will be set upon by incredibly
venomous spiders and killed instantly. As
such, whenever she gets close to anyone
they die a horrible death, which has caused
her to adopt an increasingly outcast life
that strengthens the superstitious feelings
of the local townspeople. Like a female
version of *Martin*, she has become a self-
fulfilling prophecy, preferring to die with
her mad doctor father in a laboratory
fire than to escape with the chance of a
normal life. This is the debut feature (if you
don't count the hour-long psychedelic
satire *The Committee*) of Peter Sykes, who
subsequently made *Demons of the Mind*
and *To the Devil a Daughter*.

VENUS DROWNING

2006, UK
D: Andrew Parkinson. P: Andrew Parkinson. W: Andrew Parkinson. Ed: Andrew Parkinson. DoP: Jason Shepherd. M: Andrew Parkinson.
Cast: Jodie Jameson (Dawn), Frida Show [Frida Farrell] (Milla), Brendan Gregory (psychiatrist), Bart Ruspoli (John), Ellen Softley
(Dawn's mother), Andrew Parkinson (man with metal detector)

In Andrew Parkinson's *Venus Drowning*, a young woman named Dawn (Jodie Jameson, also of Parkinson's segment in *Little Deaths*)
finds out that her long-term boyfriend has succumbed to his long battle with cancer, and loses her gestating child to a miscarriage
in the same day. After a failed suicide attempt, she is advised by her psychiatrist to go somewhere that she associates with happy
memories, and she opts for the seaside vacation flat where she spent her childhood. She surrounds herself with drawings, dolls,
security blankets that she rescues from old dusty boxes in the basement. She arranges them on the kitchen table like an altar to
her childhood, a time before the tragedy. But the drawings reveal darker memories – a woman drowning, the alcoholism of her
despondent mother – and she soon finds herself at the centre of a one-woman emotional shootout.
For more on this film see **Part 10: You Carry a Coffin Today**.

above: Neda Arneric in Peter Sykes's **Venom** (1971).

THE WASHING MACHINE

1993, Italy/France/Hungary
Original title: **Vortice mortale**
D: Ruggero Deodato. P: Corrado Canzio, Alessandro Canzio.
W: Luigi Spagnol. Ed: Gianfranco Amicucci. DoP: Sergio D'Offizi.
M: Claudio Simonetti. AD: Francesca Pintus, Csaba Stork.
Cast: Philippe Caroit (Inspector Alexander Stacev), Ilaria Borrelli
(Mary 'Sissy' Kolba), Kashia [Katarzyna] Figura (Vida Kolba),
Barbara Ricci (Ludmilla Kolba), Laurence Bruffaerts (Nikolai,
Stacev's assistant), László Porbély (music teacher), Claudia
Pozzi (Irina, Stacev's girlfriend), Yorgo Voyagis (Yuri Petkov),
Vilmos Kolba, Károly Medriczky

Following up tangentially on the home appliance theme set
in motion by his 1988 killer-phone thriller *Dial: Help*, this absurd
sleazefest features three neurotic, manipulative sisters who live
in a house together in post-Eastern bloc Budapest, and whose
washing machine is at the centre of a convoluted murder
investigation.

The antagonistic yet co-dependent relationship
between the sisters Vida (Kashia Figura), Ludmilla (Barbara
Ricci) and Maria aka 'Sissy' (Ilaria Borrelli) is established in the
opening sex scene between the busty Vida and her pimp/
boyfriend Yuri (Yorgo Voyagis of *Garter Colt*), which takes place
in the open doorway of a refrigerator (perhaps riffing on *9 1/2
Weeks*) while Ludmilla looks on from the spiral staircase above,
with her legs spread and clanging on an orchestra triangle (she's
a percussionist in a local orchestra but otherwise this makes no
sense). This scene also sets up how preposterous the next hour
and a half will be, offering up a catalogue of sex scenes in similarly
awkward places with all the cheesy eroticism of a bad '80s music
video (Gino Vannelli's *Black Cars* comes to mind). When Ludmilla
discovers Yuri's dismembered body in the washing machine later
that night, the police are called, and they send over Inspector
Alexander Stacev (Philippe Caroit of Max Pécas's sex comedy
Deux enfoirés à Saint-Tropez); but when he arrives there is no
corpse and no trace of a crime. "So we wasted all this time on
the hallucinations of an alcoholic", says Stacev's partner Nikolai,
referring to Ludmilla, the alleged drunk of the family (though her
alcoholism is talked about more than seen). According to the
two younger sisters, Yuri was really in love with Sissy, which could have prompted Vida to fly into a jealous homicidal rage. But with no
body, Stacev is inclined to walk away from any further investigation. "I'm not wasting my time over childish rivalry!" he tells Ludmilla
sternly. But he will, and so will we.

Stacev's ineffectual investigation leads him to bed all three
sisters in succession after their various hilarious acts of seduction
(Ludmilla throws a salad on his crotch to get attention, Vida
handcuffs him in a stairwell and Sissy makes out with him in a
room full of blind people). When his grouchy girlfriend Irina
confronts him about his infidelities, he accidentally punches her
in the face before proclaiming, "Irina, I don't have a lover – I
have three! And each is more deranged than the next! They're
sucking the life out of me!!"

That the girls are sexually ostentatious and emotionally
inconsistent is certain, but the lack of psychological investigation
presents them more as villainous succubi, who may have 'invented'
the corpse in the washing machine as a means of ensnaring a
new sex slave to fuel their interpersonal competition. *The Washing
Machine* is so over-the-top ridiculous that I must confess I spent
days researching it afterward to determine whether the seemingly
superficial flourishes were in fact secret codes that I was too stupid
to grasp. In the end, I'm still at a loss.

---

from left: Barbara Ricci discovers a mess; Kashia Figura, Ilaria Borelli and Barbara Ricci in Ruggero Deodato's **The Washing Machine** (1993).

WHAT EVER HAPPENED TO BABY JANE?

1962, USA
D: Robert Aldrich. P: Robert Aldrich.
W: Lukas Heller, Henry Farrell (novel).
Ed: Michael Luciano. DoP: Ernest Haller.
M: Frank De Vol. AD: William Glasgow.
Cast: Bette Davis (Jane Hudson), Joan Crawford (Blanche Hudson), Victor Buono (Edwin Flagg), Anna Lee (Mrs. Bates), Maidie Norman (Elvira Stitt), Marjorie Bennett (Mrs. Flagg), Barbara Merrill (Liza Bates), Dave Willock (Ray Hudson), Anne Barton (Cora Hudson), Julie Allred (Baby Jane)

Although the hagsploitation genre likely owes its genesis to *Sunset Boulevard*, Robert Aldrich's film – pairing up over-the-hill screen greats Joan Crawford and Bette Davis – set the template that would cement the genre and give a plethora of talented over-50 A-listers a reinvigorated shelf life. And none of the horrible movie dames can come close to the grotesquerie of Baby Jane Hudson.

1917: Popular but petulant child star Baby Jane Hudson performs one of her sold-out song-and-dance shows while her neglected sister Blanche looks on from the shadows. Blanche is rightly jealous of the indiscriminate attention her sister gets, her schmaltzy numbers lapped up by the adoring crowd. But Blanche's jealousy is passive; unlike her sister, she doesn't act out, and as a result even her humility results in a scolding from their father, who doesn't want anybody showing up his little favourite.

1935: Baby Jane (Bette Davis) is washed up and struggling to make it as a B-actress, while former wallflower Blanche (Joan Crawford) has become an A-list movie star, sparking the jealous ire of the alcoholic Blanche, who runs her over with a car, crippling her – and effectively terminating her acting career.

The Present (1962): The wheelchair-bound Blanche is stuck in a state of depency upon her lush sister, who keeps her tucked away in a room on the second floor while forging Blanche's signature to order cases of Scotch and imitating Blanche's voice in her efforts to deter any inquisitive visitors. When a retrospective of Blanche's films plays on television, Jane's behaviour becomes increasingly hostile and overtly violent – she sends away the housekeeper, Blanche's only lifeline, and ensures that Blanche will starve by serving her a dead rat and her own pet bird for dinner.

Decades of simmering jealousy and corrosive guilt come out in amazing verbal tirades from Davis, who turns in one of the best performances of her career as the psychotic, powder-faced hag Baby Jane. Verbal abuse turns into physical abuse, with Jane kicking and beating her dying sister between bouts of deluded nostalgia; Jane imagines herself on the verge of a comeback, donning her ringlets and baby-doll lace in a monstrous spectacle that speaks to the horrors of ageing and the sadness of knowing that your best days are long past.

from top: Joan Crawford calls for help; Bette Davis and Joan Crawford; Bette Davis and Victor Buono in **What Ever Happened to Baby Jane?** (1962).

THE WHIP AND THE BODY

1963, Italy/France
Original titles: **La frusta e il corpo**; **Le corps et le fouet**
Alternative titles: **Night Is the Phantom**; **What!**; **The Whip and the Flesh**
D: Mario Bava. P: Tom Rhodes [Federico Magnaghi]. W: Julian Berry [Ernesto Gastaldi], Roberto Hugo [Ugo Guerra], Martin Hardy [Luciano Martino]. Ed: Rob King [Roberto Cinquini]. DoP: David Hamilton [Ubaldo Terzano]. M: Jim Murphy [Carlo Rustichelli]. AD: Dick Grey [Ottavio Scotti].
Cast: Daliah Lavi (Nevenka), Christopher Lee (Kurt Menliff), Tony Kendall [Luciano Stella] (Christian), Isli Oberon [Ida Galli] (Katia), Harriet White [Harriet White Medin] (Giorgia), Dean Ardow [Gustavo De Nardo] (old Menliff), Alan Collins [Luciano Pigozzi] (Losat), Jacques Herlin (the priest)

Foregoing the modern giallo in favour of a return to the Gothic terrain of his breakthrough film *Black Sunday* (1960), *The Whip and the Body* is very likely Bava's best and most complex film. The film opens with prodigal son Kurt (Christopher Lee) returning to the family estate after several years of (allegedly debauched) wandering. Hardly welcomed with open arms, he is faced with resentment from every angle: over the suicide of a maid with whom he'd had an affair; over abandoning his invalid father; and most of all from his younger brother Christian, who has in the meantime been married off to a woman (Daliah Lavi) he knows to be in love with Kurt. When Kurt besets upon Nevenka with her own riding crop, eliciting moans of delight, it is revealed that their previous relationship had been one of sadomasochistic pleasures that have proven a source of great shame to Nevenka. When Kurt is mysteriously murdered, Nevenka starts to have visions of Kurt's ghost, whipping her more violently than ever before. When the patriarch is suddenly murdered as well, Christian believes the ghost of his recently-departed brother to be responsible, but finds that it is in fact Nevenka, dressed in Kurt's clothing. With the death of her beloved, she had to assume his identity in order to keep him alive, and thus satisfy her unconventional sexual desires without guilt.
For more on this film see **Part 7: You've Always Loved Violence**.

above: Daliah Lavi in Mario Bava's **The Whip and the Body** (1963).

WHOEVER SLEW AUNTIE ROO?

1972, UK
Alternative title: **Who Slew Auntie Roo?**
D: Curtis Harrington. P: Samuel Z. Arkoff, James H. Nicholson.
W: Robert Blees, James [Jimmy] Sangster, Gavin Lambert
(additional dialogue), David Osborn (story). Ed: Tristam
Cones. DoP: Desmond Dickinson. M: Kenneth V. Jones.
AD: George Provis.
Cast: Shelley Winters (Rosie Forrest), Mark Lester (Christopher
Coombs), Chloe Franks (Katy Coombs), Ralph Richardson
(Mr. Benton), Lionel Jeffries (Inspector Ralph Willoughby),
Hugh Griffith (Mr. Harrison), Rosalie Crutchley (Miss Henley),
Judy Cornwell (Clarine), Michael Gothard (Albie), Charlotte
Sayce (Katherine)

Adding to the catalogue of Grand Dame Guignol films (and
carrying on their titular tradition) Curtis Harrington's *Whoever
Slew Auntie Roo?* is a 1920s re-imagining of Hansel and Gretel
set in England. Harrington, whose canon careened fascinatingly
through avant-garde short films, melodramatic horror and
episodic television, was no stranger to bat-shit crazy women,
most of them older – Piper Laurie in *Ruby*, Simone Signoret
in *Games*, Ann Sothern in *The Killing Kind*, Gloria Swanson in
Killer Bees, Debbie Reynolds and Shelley Winters in *What's the
Matter with Helen?* – and Winters carved out a second career
in these kinds of roles, returning to Harrington's campy world of
decaying glamour with *Roo* in '72.

Winters plays Rosie Forrest, a wealthy former cabaret star
whose magician husband disappeared mysteriously
after their daughter Katherine plummeted to her
death from a staircase. Unwilling to accept her
daughter's death, she reported the child missing
and hid her corpse in a nursery in the attic, where
she sings to it in bed each night with blind motherly
devotion. Lonely and depressed, she frequently employs
the medium Mr. Benton (Sir Ralph Richardson) to conduct
séances to try to contact Katherine's spirit, but Benton
is in cahoots with her maid (Judy Cornwell) and
butler (Michael Gothard of *The Devils*) in a ruse to
cheat the grieving woman out of her riches. This,
combined with Rosie's annual tradition of inviting
10 lucky orphans to her large estate to be spoiled
over Christmas weekend, makes her out to be a
sympathetic, if somewhat pathetic character who
tries any way she can
to find an outlet for
her nurturing instincts.
The weird cabaret
pantomime she performs
in black lace for the
children only reinforces
this picture of desperation.

This Christmas is not
like the others, because
siblings Christopher and
Katy Coombs (pouty
child star Mark Lester of
Melody and *Oliver!*, and
Chloe Franks of the 1972
version of *Tales from the
Crypt*) sneak their way

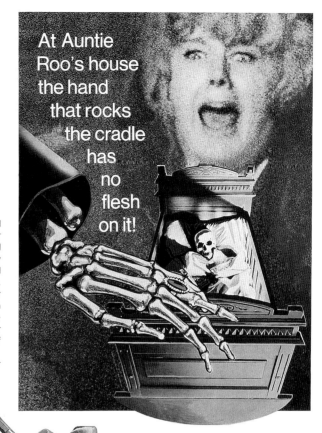

into the festivities, only to have
Rosie convince herself that Katy
is Katherine reincarnated. She
immediately offers to adopt Katy,
but is so obsessed with this new little
girl that she ignores the bond that the
two children have with each other
and doesn't consider that it may be
painful for them to be separated. She
conspires to keep Katy locked away in
Katherine's room in the attic, and while
Katy is enamoured with the array of toys
and luxuries, Christopher is certain that
Rosie – who the children have taken to
calling 'Aunt Roo' – is a witch, fattening
them up to eat them (and in case you
missed the reference, Mark Lester narrates the famous folktale
in snippets of voiceover throughout the film).

When the children try to escape, she falls over
herself trying to block their way, shouting: "I will not be
abandoned! Everybody tries to abandon me!"; while
originally characterized as a sad, mournful widow, through
the children's eyes she becomes a tyrannical witch with
emphatic vocal mannerisms to match. Slowly losing her mind
in the midst of this perceived betrayal, she embraces her
daughter's corpse, whose skull crumbles in her hands as she
whimpers, "I have nothing, I have nothing…"

from left: Shelley Winters armed for a pint-sized fight; promotional artwork for Curtis Harrington's **Whoever Slew Auntie Roo?** (1972).

HOUSE OF PSYCHOTIC WOMEN

WINDOWS

1980, USA
D: Gordon Willis. P: Mike Lobell. W: Barry Siegel.
Ed: Barry Malkin. DoP: Gordon Willis. M: Ennio Morricone.
PD: Mel Bourne. AD: Mel Bourne, Richard Fuhrman.
Cast: Talia Shire (Emily Hollander), Joseph Cortese (Bob
Luffrono), Elizabeth Ashley (Andrea Glassen), Kay Medford
(Ida Marx), Michael Gorrin (Sam Marx), Russell Horton (Steven
Hollander), Michael Lipton (Dr. Marin), Rick Petrucelli (Obecny),
Ron Ryan (Detective Swid), Linda Gillen (policewoman)

The only directorial effort of cinematographer Gordon Willis (*The Godfather* trilogy, Woody Allen's long-time DoP from *Annie Hall*, *Manhattan*, *Interiors* and more), *Windows* is a camp classic that is only starting to be appreciated alongside early '80s voyeuristic thrillers like *The Fan*, *Eyes of a Stranger* and De Palma's *Dressed to Kill* and *Body Double*. Opening with a stunning Antonioni-esque long-shot down the futuristic neon-encircled tunnel at the Brooklyn Children's Museum, we are introduced to Emily (Talia Shire), a mousy and quiet woman – the latter trait due to a stuttering problem – in the middle of a divorce.

Walking into her dark apartment, she is immediately grabbed from behind and thrown down on the couch by a man with a knife. The room is dark (in some moments completely black so that we can only hear what is happening) and his face is mostly obscured save for large protruding lips and a big nose. He puts the knife in her mouth and tells her to lift up her shirt, and then demands that she moan with pleasure repeatedly while he records it to micro-cassette. The next morning as she is filing the police report, her imposing friend Andrea (gravelly voiced character actress Elisabeth Ashley, the shrink from *Vampire's Kiss*) stops by and discourages Emily from telling the police anything, saying they're never going to catch the person that did it anyway. Andrea's motive isn't concern for Emily's comfort level though – she has a lesbian fixation on Emily and paid the attacker to get the recording, which she listens to repeatedly when she is home alone.

It's while she's in a cab on her way to work that Emily recognizes the cabbie's voice as that of the man who attacked her (Rick Petrucelli, best known as the star-struck idiot outside the theatre in *Annie Hall*), and his identity card matches what

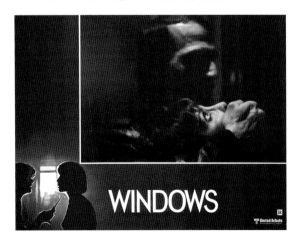

little she was able to see of his face. She asks him to stop at a payphone momentarily, saying she had forgotten she was supposed to meet a friend, and calls the police – getting back in the cab to continue until the cops can catch up with her. With the man arrested he confesses that he was paid to do the job – but won't reveal his accomplice without the charges being dropped. The cops think he's bluffing.

After the attack, Emily moves into a large high rise on the waterfront in Brooklyn, and Andrea gets an apartment directly across the river so that she can watch her through a telescope. But when Emily starts getting romantically involved with the detective assigned to her case (Joseph Cortese), Andrea starts to get itchy for something to happen. The extent of her madness comes out in her therapy sessions, where she feels she can express herself most freely, even though she clearly sees her shrink as an antagonist. Her therapist tries to make her see that her 'relationship' with Emily is one-sided, and that any romantic potential is in her head, but Andrea responds with spurts of anger, alternately whispering and shouting, physically hunched and tense. That her therapist won't indulge her fantasies infuriates her. He makes arrangements for her to be admitted so that she can work through her fantasies in a 'safe' environment like a hospital; he obviously thinks she's dangerous. And he's right.

While we get glimpses of her mental state in her therapy sessions, it's when Andrea finally has Emily alone, late at night, that her craziness is most physically manifested. She shakes, her voice cuts in and out, mirroring Emily's stutter, and she gives Emily a frightening play-by-play of her rape, having memorized it by rote by listening to the recording. Through this verbal replay in combination with the film's many references to scopophilia, *Windows* also comments on the dissociative qualities of fandom in general – there's a thin line between Andrea's hysterical 'performance' and that of fans who recite back their favourite lines to the directors, writers or actors who created them.

The film did not fare well upon release – being nominated for 5 Razzie Awards, including those for acting and directing – ensuring that Gordon Willis would never sit in the director's chair again, which is a shame. As a cinematographer, Willis's composition is meticulous (most notably his hallmark lighting choices) and he succeeds in building and maintaining tension, even though the film's plotting is fairly safe. And while Shire's acting is understated to the point of being lacklustre, to call Elizabeth Ashley's psycho performance worthy of a Razzie is nonsense. The film also suffered negative criticism for its depiction of a gay character as psychotic, but like William Friedkin's *Cruising* (which suffered the same fate), time has endeared the film to some factions of the gay community.

from top: Elizabeth Ashley and Talia Shire; Rick Petrucelli assaults Shire in Gordon Willis's **Windows** (1980).

THE WITCH WHO CAME FROM THE SEA

1976, USA
D: Matt Cimber. P: Matt Cimber. W: Robert Thom. Ed: Bud Warner. DoP: Ken Gibb. M: Herschel Burke Gilbert.
Cast: Millie Perkins (Molly), Lonny Chapman (Long John), Vanessa Brown (Cathy), Peggy Feury (Doris), Jean Pierre Camps (Tadd), Mark Livingston (Tripoli), Rick Jason (Billy Batt), Stafford Morgan (Alexander McPeak), Richard Kennedy (Detective Beardsley), George 'Buck' Flower (Detective Stone)

Monte Hellman alumna Millie Perkins (most famous for playing the title role in George Stevens's 1959 *The Diary of Anne Frank*) plays Molly, whose father was a seafaring man who molested her repeatedly as a child. She loves her father desperately, and is acquiescent throughout the abuse out of love for him, even though she senses that what he is doing to her is wrong. As an adult she mythologizes him, her adamance concerning her father's moral perfection hiding her deeply repressed anxiety over her his incestuous transgressions. She grows up to be an alcoholic, drinking excessively to quell the flashbacks that haunt her and living out a fantasy life in which she seduces and murders men.
For more on this film see **Part 4: Secret Ceremonies**.

THE WOMAN

2011, USA
D: Lucky McKee. P: Andrew van den Houten, Robert Tonino.
W: Jack Ketchum, Lucky McKee. Ed: Zach Passero. DoP: Alex Vendler.
M: Sean Spillane. PD: Krista Gall. AD: Jeff Subik.
Cast: Pollyanna McIntosh (The Woman), Sean Bridgers (Chris Cleek), Angela Bettis (Belle Cleek), Lauren Ashley Carter (Peggy Cleek), Carlee Baker (Genevieve Raton), Alexa Marcigliano (Socket), Zach Rand (Brian Cleek), Shyla Molhusen (Darlin' Cleek), Tommy Nelson (Walter), Frank Olsen (Will Campbell)

Lucky McKee's *The Woman*, based on a story he wrote with author Jack Ketchum as a spin-off to Ketchum's *Offspring/Off-Season* feral family characters was one of the most uncomfortable viewing experiences I'd had in a while. A young woman raised by wolves lives deep in the American wilderness, trapping and hunting her food in pre-verbal isolation. Meanwhile, in a small leave-it-to-beaver town nearby, we are introduced to the all-American family at a neighbourhood BBQ – Chris Cleek (Sean Bridgers), the charming and successful law clerk, his unconfrontational Betty Crockeresque wife (Angela Bettis), their angsty, reticent teenage daughter (Lauren Ashley Carter), the adolescent son who worships his father (Zach Rand), the gleefully unmannered three-year-old girl. But this superficial vision of 'the people next door' will be shaken when dad comes home after a hunting trip to reveal his latest trophy: The Woman – who he chains up in the cellar in order to initiate a torturous program of 'civilization'. He brings the family down to the cellar to show them the new 'surprise' and none of them reacts with the appropriate horror. Instead, he gives them all little jobs to do, to help him turn this wild beast into a proper woman, and they obey him without protest (the son with more sadistic enthusiasm than the others).

The teenage daughter's feelings about what is happening manifest in physical illness, despondency, faltering grades, anxiety. The wife's rebellion is all in her eyes. Angela Bettis says so much with so little, just through the story she tells through her face: a story of lifelong systematic abuse, and complicity in that abuse. Conversely, the woman in the cellar is a growling beast seething with the rage of centuries. It would seem that the film's title refers to the feral character trapped and chained up by the husband – but in fact it extends to the entire gender, the role of 'the woman', in the home, and in society. The feral character is a mirror held up to these staid roles. Like the unsocialized youngest daughter who is reprimanded at the film's opening party for kissing all the little boys, the feral woman is the untamed outlaw. She is loudly imprisoned, screeching and pulling at her chains, but the other women are imprisoned by their own fear and silence.

The abuse turns graphic in the last act, and while the film's first audience at Sundance was subject to fainting spells and outraged rants that were captured on video, the upsetting thing about the film isn't the violence against women (which is abundant, both physically and verbally), but the complicity of the female characters in that violence. The women watch each other being abused, they exchange code-like glances that plead for action, but none does a thing to help the other.

A thoroughly upsetting and loaded film that expounds upon the microcosmic view of unhealthy gender dynamics explored in McKee's earlier film *May*.

from left: The Woman feeds; the dysfunctional family meets their captive in Lucky McKee's **The Woman** (2011).

WOMAN TRANSFORMATION

2006, Japan
Original title: **Yôkai kidan**
D: Tôru Kamei. W: Tôru Kamei, Yûji Nagamori (story), Kenji Matsui (idea).
Ed: Tôru Kamei. DoP: Masato Nakao.
Cast: Mariko Miyamitsu (Michiko Yamane), Tôru Tezuka (Oosako), Anri Ban (Mihiro Iwasaki), Haruki Ichikawa (Mana Saeki), Akiko Monô (Iioka), Gô Ayano (Shingo), Hachirô Ika, Hijiri Sakurai, Chiyoko Asami, Miyuki Tanigawa

Michiko is an unhappy young model whose body is going through some bizarre changes. She checks into the hospital where she is diagnosed with a highly unusual spinal-cord disorder that manifests itself in a superhuman elasticity, allowing her to stretch her neck to fantastic heights. In a subsequent story, a teenage girl obsessed with her expensive fake nails starts noticing that her real nails are growing at an alarming rate, to the point where she can't work, can't eat, can't function. Cutting her nails proves futile, as well as intensely painful. Eventually she is driven to drastic measures. In the last of three tales, Mana is a cruel and thoughtless high school student whose transformation involves a bizarre loss of identity.

While anthology films have a bad rep, these three grim tales of female bodily transformation co-exist through peripherally connected characters, imbuing the film with a fluidity that allows it to bypass the patchiness that plagues efforts at a similar structure. The Japanese title *Yôkai kidan* translates directly as 'Strange Story of Monsters', a title that deliberately conjures images of classic Japanese monster movies like *100 Monsters* and *Spook Warfare* (both of which also feature the mythological long-necked woman). But what sets this film from director Tôru Kamei (*Double Suicide Elegy*, 2005) apart is his use of the 'yôkai' concept to externalize the inner ugliness and turmoil of his characters.

While it recalls the suspicion of femininity espoused in classic horror films like *Cat People*, *The Wasp Woman* and *The Reptile*, the sombre tone of this film is all its own. Each girl is forced to undergo her respective transformation alone; the film emphasizes their physical and emotional isolation with a solemn score, moody lighting and the distinct lack of helpful authority figures. In this particularly terrifying reference to female puberty, each woman is driven to despair over her bodily changes – which, at such an image-conscious age, can be deadly.

WOUND

2010, New Zealand
D: David Blyth. P: Andrew Beattie, David Blyth. W: David Blyth.
Ed: Eddie Larsen, Samantha Sperlich. DoP: Marc Mateo. M: Jed Town.
Cast: Kate O'Rourke (Susan), Te Kaea Beri (Tanya), Campbell Cooley (Master John), Sandy Lowe (Mistress Ruth), Brendan Gregory (Neil), Ian Mune (Dr. Nelson), Maggie Tarver (Dr. Alice Weaver), Chrystal Ash (Rosie), Matt Easterbrook (Mark), Christina Cortesi (catwoman)

David Blyth burst onto the scene with the one-two punch of controversial sexual satire *Angel Mine* in 1980 and revenge thriller *Death Warmed Up* four years later, and despite some detours into mainstream territory since (*Mighty Morphin Power Rangers*?), he remains dedicated to exploring bizarre sexual peccadilloes through the lens of surrealism, leaning on turn-of-the-century dream work as well as citing the work of Buñuel as a primary influence.

Wound is a visually arresting film full of weird, memorable imagery, but it rarely makes rational sense, which is important to keep in mind going in. Even the many video cameras that appear to be monitoring events throughout the film do not act as an objective, reliable eye through which the truth can be gleaned.

A closed-circuit camera system inside an Auckland house flashes from room to room as our protagonist Susan (Kate O'Rourke) answers the door to reveal her estranged father standing there, returning home from a stage career that has kept him abroad in London (in a later dream sequence he's shown in silhouette reciting from Shakespeare's *The Tempest*). She's left everything just how he left it, but as he wanders through the hallway thumbing dusty old paperbacks and knicknacks, he doesn't feel any connection to all this 'stuff' – and it's clear to Susan that she's in that category of 'unwanted stuff' that weighs him down. With a grave already dug for him in the backyard, she bashes him with a baseball bat

from top: Manicure gone mad in Tôru Kamei's **Woman Transformation** (2006); Kate O'Rourke in David Blyth's **Wound** (2010).

and ties him up in her dead mother's former bondage chamber (her mother – it will be revealed – was a dominatrix, until Susan set her on fire nearly a decade earlier). Donning a plastic mask emulating a doll's face (recalling Blyth's earlier fetish films *Bound for Pleasure* and *Transfigured Nights* and even, strangely, Devo's Boogie Boy) she confronts him about sexually abusing her as a child ("you wanted it!" he argues) before strangling and castrating him. But she can't let him go that easily; after all, she has a lifetime invested in reacting to this trauma. This is the problem with closure – it doesn't work; we become attached to the problem.

She buries him in the yard, surrounded by tiny foil-wrapped packages containing her own faeces (the ritualistic nature of this was admittedly my favourite aspect of the film). She sits on the toilet having phone conversations with her dead mother, and then puts the resultant turd in a big freezer in the hallway that houses hundreds of others like it, all neatly and individually wrapped in foil. "I'm taking the pills like Dr. Nelson said", she assures her mother, "but the blackness just keeps creeping in. I can't breathe. It's choking me. It's consuming me."

Susan has an ongoing BDSM sexual relationship with a man she addresses only as 'Sir' who fancies himself not only her master but also her therapist, humiliating her on camera for an internet audience but also requiring that she submit detailed 'condition reports' conveying her innermost thoughts and feelings (the analogy of therapy and BDSM role-play is everywhere in the film). Playing out simultaneously is the story of the juvenile delinquent Goth girl Tanya, whose introduction also comes via a video-recorded session with a condescending high school counsellor. Tanya is adopted, and the records identifying her birth mother have just come in; of course her mother turns out to be none other than Susan, which isn't going to be much help to a girl struggling with emotional problems. Tanya seeks her out, and the result is a relationship that flits in and out of doubling and the dream-condensation of characters and locations.

Susan's medical records indicate that her child (an incest baby) was stillborn in the same year as her mother's death by fire. While there has already been an assumption that everything Susan sees may not be real, things are confused by the fact that the film spends a significant amount of time with Tanya individually, which in cinematic language is supposed to be a grounding technique. When Tanya suckles at Susan's breast and drinks her menstrual blood off the floor, we know it may be a delusion, but when the camera goes with Tanya through school hallways, to a Goth nightclub, and to a train yard to see out a suicide pact, we are left wondering who this character is and whether her image has just crossed Susan's vision peripherally somehow, adopting her into Susan's disturbing familial fantasy (like Amy Reed in *The Curse of the Cat People*).

Susan tells her psychiatrist Dr. Nelson (Antipodean screen vet Ian Mune) that her daughter is inside her, trying to take over her life. She dreams that they are bound together in plastic wrap, like one body with two heads (echoed by the two-headed doll Susan finds in her father's grave) and then cut asunder like Siamese twins being separated. "She's real, she wants to kill me!" she pleads. But the therapist's cold response is that it's all in her head and he can change her medication – and would she address the camera directly please? Or, better yet, he can call the crisis team to come pick her up and admit her. Yes, that seems like a good idea. End of session. "But I want to talk about my father", she insists. "Yes of course, but not now. We have to stabilize you first. Would you please wait in the waiting room?" She sighs. "I'm sick of the waiting room. I've spent my life in the waiting room."

As her delusions accelerate, and various ghosts return for a final act, Susan submits – one last time.

Be not afeard. The isle is full of noises,
Sounds and sweet airs that give delight and hurt not.
Sometimes a thousand twangling instruments
Will hum about mine ears, and sometime voices
That, if I then had waked after long sleep,
Will make me sleep again; and then, in dreaming,
The clouds methought would open, and show riches
Ready to drop upon me, that when I waked,
I cried to dream again.

– William Shakespeare, *The Tempest*

above: Sandy Lowe as Mistress Ruth in David Blyth's **Wound** (2010).

FOOTNOTES

1   Chatman, Seymour Benjamin. *Antonioni, or The Surface of the World*. Berkeley, CA: University of California Press, 1985, p.84.

2   ibid, p.83.

3   Ortega, Javier. *The Entity Haunting: The True Story of Doris Bither*. www.ghosttheory.com, 2008.

4   Curtis, Barry. *Dark Places: The Haunted House in Film*. London, UK: Reaktion Books, 2008, p.24.

5   Burrell, Nigel. *Ten Years of Terror: British Horror Films of the 1970s*, edited by Harvey Fenton and David Flint. Surrey, UK: FAB Press, 2001, p.44.

6   Irwin, John T. *Doubling and Incest / Repetition and Revenge: A Speculative Reading of Faulkner*. Baltimore, MD: The John Hopkins University Press, 1980 (first pressing 1975), p.33.

7   Nicholls, Peter. *The World of Fantastic Films: An Illustrated Survey*. New York: Dodd, Mead & Co., 1984, p.71.

8   Denzin, Norman K. *Hollywood Shot by Shot: Alcoholism in American Cinema*. Piscataway, New Jersey: Aldine Transaction, 2004, p.4.

9   Shainess, Natalie. *Sweet Suffering: Woman As Victim*. Indianapolis, Indiana: Bobbs-Merrill Co., 1984.

10   Perkins Gilman, Charlotte. 'The Yellow Wallpaper', in *Great American Short Stories*, edited by Paul Negri. Mineola, NY: Dover Publications, 2002, p.115.

11   Lippe, Richard. 'Full Circle: A Circle of Deception', in *The American Nightmare*, edited by Robin Wood and Richard Lippe. Toronto, Ontario: Festival of Festivals, 1979, p.65.

12   Palmerini, Luca M. and Mistretta, Gaetano. *Spaghetti Nightmares: Italian Fantasy-Horrors as Seen Through the Eyes of their Protagonists*. Key West, Florida: Fantasma Books, 1996, p.46.

13   McDonagh, Maitland. *Broken Mirrors/Broken Minds: The Dark Dreams of Dario Argento*. New York: Citadel Press, 1994, p.84.

14   Valentine, Gill. 'The Geography of Women's Fear' in *Area*, Vol.21, No.4. Oxford, UK: Blackwell Publishing, 1989, p.386.

15   Griffin, Susan. 'Rape: the All-American Crime' in *Ramparts*, Vol.10. San Francisco, CA: Sept. 1971, p.35.

16   Twiss, Deborah. Personal correspondence with the author, 21 August 2011.

17   Jensen, Jørn Rossing. 'The Geography of Fear', February 2000. http://www.filmfestivals.com/berlin_2000/parallel/_forum_film_pelon.htm

18   Janisse, Kier-La. 'Truly Savage Cinema' in *Fangoria* #256, New York: Starlog Publications, September 2006, pp.72–77.

19   In very simplified terms, Clover's theory held that the survivor of most slasher films was a woman, often one who had traditionally masculine qualities (and sometimes an androgynous name), which allowed for a predominantly young male audience to identify with the character.

20   Laxness, Halldór. *Independent People*. Trans. J.A. Thompson. New York: Alfred A. Knopf, 1946, p.233.

21   Quoted in Brake, Mike. *The Sociology of Youth Culture and Youth Subcultures*. London, UK: Routledge & Kegan Paul Ltd., 1980, p.66.

22   Fetters, Sarah Michelle. 'Drawn to the Odd: Getting Weird with Angela Bettis' on Moviefreak.com, 2003. http://www.moviefreak.com/features/interviews/may1_a.htm

23   Janisse, Kier-La. 'Truly Savage Cinema' in *Fangoria* #256, New York: Starlog Publications, September 2006, pp.72–77.

24   de Van, Marina. Interview in the press release material for *Dans ma peau*, 2002, pp.7–10.

25   Marina Abramovic is a New York-based Serbian performance artist active since the 1970s and known for her confrontational pieces that challenge both audiences and the limits of her own physical body.

26   Jeffries, Stuart. 'In the Cut' in *The Guardian*. London: 15 September 2004. http://www.guardian.co.uk/film/2004/sep/15/features.stuartjeffries

27   Didion, Joan. *The White Album*. New York: Noonday Press, 1990 (first pressing 1979), p.11.

28   Audience Q&A, Vancouver International Film Festival, 27 September–12 October 2001.

29   Creed, Barbara. *The Monstrous Feminine*. New York: Routledge, 1993, p.9.

30   Kristeva, Julia. *Powers of Horror: An Essay on Abjection*. New York: Columbia University Press, 1982, pp.2–4.

31   Whalley, Dean. *Lamont the Lonely Monster*. Kansas City, MO: Hallmark Children's Editions, 1970, p.19.

32   Hearst, Patricia. 'Playboy Interview' in *Playboy* magazine, Vol.29, No.3. Chicago, IL: March 1982, p.69.

33   Quoted in Caplan, Paula J. *The Myth of Women's Masochism*. Bloomington, Indiana: iUniverse, 2005, p.85.

34   Quoted in Dijkstra, Bram. *Idols of Perversity: Fantasies of Feminine Evil in Fin-de-Siècle Culture*. Oxford, UK: Oxford University Press, 1986, p.103.

35   Dworkin, Andrea. 'The Root Cause' in *Our Blood: Prophecies and Discourses on Sexual Politics*. First publication New York: Harper & Row, 1975. Online: http://www.nostatusquo.com/ACLU/dworkin/OurBloodIII.html

36   Pagano, Darlene R., Jeanette Nichols and Margaret Rossoff. 'Is Sadomasochism Feminist?' in *Against Sadomasochism: A Radical Feminist Analysis*, edited by Robin Ruth Linden, Darlene R. Pagano, Diana F.H. Russell and Susan Leigh Star. San Francisco: Frog in the Well, 1982, p.144.

37   Quoted in Caplan, Paula J. *The Myth of Women's Masochism*. Bloomington, Indiana: iUniverse, 2005, p.154.

38   Baumeister, Roy F. 'Masochism As Escape from Self' in *The Journal of Sex Research*, Vol.25, No.1. Oxfordshire, UK: Taylor & Francis, February 1988, pp.28–59.

39   Utami, Ayu. 'On Masochism and Parody' presentation at 'Schule für Dichtung' at 'Alte Schmiede', Vienna, Austria, October 2002.

40   Davis, Mitch. *Fantasia Film Festival Programme*. Montreal, Quebec: July 1999.

41   The 'Female Convict Scorpion' films starring Meiko Kaji are listed below, although the series was revived with other actresses for two further films in 1976 and 1977, as well as a handful more in the 1990s:
– *Female Prisoner #701: Scorpion* (1972) [aka *Joshuu 701-gô: Sasori*]
– *Female Convict Scorpion Jailhouse 41* (1972) [*Joshuu sasori: Dai-41 zakkyo-bô*]
– *Female Prisoner Scorpion: Beast Stable* (1973) [*Joshuu sasori: Kemono-beya*]
– *Female Prisoner Scorpion: #701's Grudge Song* (1973) [*Joshuu sasori: 701-gô urami-bushi*]

42   Black, Art. 'Coming of Age: The South Korean Horror Film' in *Fear Without Frontiers*, edited by Steven Jay Schneider. Surrey, UK: FAB Press, 2003, p.202.

43   Mathews, Jack. *Bad Guy* review in *New York Daily News*, 18 February 2005: http://www.imdb.com/title/tt0307213/criticreviews

44   Whitty, Stephen. *Bad Guy* review in *Newark Star-Ledger*, 24 February 2005: http://www.rottentomatoes.com/m/nabbeun-namja-bad-guy/

45   Hummel, Volker. 'Interview with Kim Ki-duk' in *Senses of Cinema*, issue 19, 13 March 2002. http://www.sensesofcinema.com/2002/feature-articles/kim_ki-duk/

46   Jung, Seong-il. 'Interview with Kim Ki-duk' in *Cine21 magazine issue #339* (5–19 February 2002): http://alternatecontradictions-pidamarthy.blogspot.com/

47   Hummel, Volker. 'Interview with Kim Ki-duk' in *Senses of Cinema*, issue 19, 13 March 2002: http://www.sensesofcinema.com/2002/feature-articles/kim_ki-duk/

48   Seong-il, Jung. 'Interview with Kim Ki-duk' in *Cine21 magazine issue #339* (5–19 February 2002): http://alternatecontradictions-pidamarthy.blogspot.com/

49   ibid.

50   Hummel, Volker. 'Interview with Kim Ki-duk' in *Senses of Cinema*, issue 19, 13 March 2002: http://www.sensesofcinema.com/2002/feature-articles/kim_ki-duk/

51   Desser, David. *Eros Plus Massacre: An Introduction to the Japanese New Wave Cinema*. Bloomington, Indiana: Indiana University Press, 1988, pp.109–110.

52   Jung, Seong-il. 'Interview with Kim Ki-duk' in *Cine21 magazine issue #339* (5–19 February 2002): http://alternatecontradictions-pidamarthy.blogspot.com/

53   These events had also been depicted in Polish director Jerzy Kawalerowicz's *Mother Joan of the Angels* a decade earlier, in 1961.

54   Jelinek, Elfriede. *The Piano Teacher*. Translation by Wheatland Corporation. London, UK: Serpent's Tail, 1989, p.82.

55   Celani, David P. *The Illusion of Love: Why the Battered Woman Returns to Her Abuser*. New York: Columbia University Press, 1994, p.6.

56   Merced, Leslie Anne. 'The Treatment of Female Hysteria in Fin de Siecle Spain: The Discipine of Medical Control'. Oral lecture: *University of Illinois Graduate Symposium on Women's and Gender History*, 2003. Published online: http://www.history.uiuc.edu/hist%20grad%20orgs/WGHS/merced.pdf

57   Chatman, Seymour Benjamin. *Antonioni, or The Surface of the World*. Berkeley, CA: University of California Press, 1985, pp.59–60.

58   Bird, Daniel. 'Devil's Games: Surrealism in Polish Emigre Cinema' in *Dzieje grzechu: Surrealizm w kinie polskim (Story of Sin: Surrealism in Polish Cinema)* edited by Kamila Wielebska and Kuba Mikurda; Korporacja Halart, Krakow 2010.

59   Rank, Otto. 'Narcissism and the Double' in *Essential Papers on Literature and Psychoanalysis*, edited by Emanuel Berman. New York: NYU Press, 1993, p.127.

60   ibid.

61   Thrower, Stephen and Bird, Daniel. 'Cinema Superactivity' in *The Eyeball Compendium*, edited by Stephen Thrower. Surrey, UK: FAB Press, 2003, pp.62–63.

62   ibid, p.66.

63   Bird, Daniel. 'Zulawski and Polish Cinema' in *The Eyeball Compendium*, edited by Stephen Thrower. Surrey, UK: FAB Press, 2003, p.149.

64   A favourite expression of Professor and genre writer Mario DeGiglio Bellemare.

65   Sontag, Susan. *Illness as Metaphor*. New York: Vintage Books, 1979, p.62.

66   ibid, p.22.

67   Adjani has excelled at playing disturbed characters; see also François Truffaut's *The Story of Adele H.* (1975), Jean Becker's *One Deadly Summer* (1983), Bruno Nuytten's *Camille Claudel* (1988), Jeremiah Chechik's *Diabolique* (1996 – a remake of Clouzot's *Les Diaboliques*) and even to a certain extent Werner Herzog's *Nosferatu* (1979).

68   Foundas, Scott. Qtd. in "Wildlife: The Marginal Cinema of Actress-Turned-Auteur Isild Le Besco" in *Film Comment Online* http://www.filmlinc.com/film-comment/article/wildlife

69   Tyrrell, Susan. Audience Q+A, Alamo Drafthouse Cinema Downtown Austin TX. June 27, 2007.

70   Canby, Vincent. "From Ear to Ear is Without Importance" in *The New York Times*. January 16, 1971. http://movies.nytimes.com/movie/review?res=980CEFDF1131E73BBC4E52DFB766838A669EDE

71   Bird, Daniel. Qtd in "Outsiders, Shamans and Devils, Part 1: A Discussion of Central European New Wave Cinema with Film Writer Daniel Bird" in *Slant Magazine* online. March 2, 2009. http://www.slantmagazine.com/house/2009/03/outsiders-shamans-and-devils-part-1-a-discussion-of-central-european-new-wave-cinema-with-film-writer-daniel-bird/

72   Szaruga, Leszek. Polish Literature from 1795. University of Glasgow website. http://www.arts.gla.ac.uk/Slavonic/staff/Polishlit.html

73   Bird, Daniel. Qtd in "Outsiders, Shamans and Devils, Part 1: A Discussion of Central European New Wave Cinema with Film Writer Daniel Bird" in *Slant Magazine* online. March 2, 2009. http://www.slantmagazine.com/house/2009/03/outsiders-shamans-and-devils-part-1-a-discussion-of-central-european-new-wave-cinema-with-film-writer-daniel-bird/

74   The treatment of vampirism in this film as a mental illness foreshadows theories popular in the '70s and '80s that linked vampirism to porphyria, a largely hereditary illness that shares some of its symptoms, including mental disturbance, iron deficiency and sensitivity to light. These theories have since been debunked as they don't acknowledge changes in vampiric folklore over time, notably that a sensitivity to light was an invention of fiction writers that came much later, not to mention the unwarranted stigma it attaches to sufferers of porphyria.

75   Hays, Matthew. "Screening the Epidemic" lecture at the 24th image+nation lgbt film festival, Montreal, Canada, Nov. 6, 2011.

76   Alexander, James R. "The Maturity of a Film Genre in an Era of Relaxing Standards of Obscenity: Takashi Ishii's Freeze Me as a Rape-Revenge Film" in *Senses of Cinema*, Issue 36, 2005. http://www.sensesofcinema.com/2005/36/freeze_me/

77   Brown, Rita Mae. *Rita Will: Memoir of a Literary Rabble-Rouser*. Random House Digital, Inc. New York: 2009. Pg. 45

78   Woofter, Kristopher. "The Haunted House" lecture for *The Miskatonic Institute of Horror Studies*. Montreal, February 1, 2011.

79   As an added bit of meta-cinema, cast member Teresa Nawrot joined Grotowsky's experimental acting troupe in the 1970s, and later opened her own acting school in Berlin.

80   Corupe, Paul. "Echoes From the Sleep Room: Medical Terror in Canadian Horror Cinema" lecture for *The Miskatonic Institute of Horror Studies*. Montreal, November 19/20, 2011.

81   Quoted. In Rosenacker, Gerd. ""Ich wollte kein Opfer werden" in *Spiegel Online*, Dec. 27, 2006. http://www.spiegel.de/kultur/gesellschaft/0,1518,456284,00.html

82   There are many articles and books by or about Jodorowsky that go much further into depth about his philosophies than I can here, including *Anarchy and Alchemy: The Films of Alejandro Jodorowsky* by Ben Cobb and Stephen Barber, and Jodorowsky's own *The Spiritual Journey of Alejandro Jodorowsky* and *Psychomagic: The Transformative Power of Shamanic Psychotherapy*.

83   Interestingly, one of the first voices you hear in the film is that of Nick Alexander, the dubbing director familiar to many exploitation fans for his work on the Italian exploitation films of the 1970s and '80s.

84   Crawford, Travis. "Dangerous Beauty" in *Filmmaker Magazine* http://www.filmmakermagazine.com/issues/fall2000/features/dangerous.php

ADDITIONAL BIBLIOGRAPHY

In addition to those sources listed in the footnotes, below are books and web or print articles that provided insight during the creation of this book.

American Psychiatric Association. *Diagnostic and Statistical Manual of Mental Disorders, Fourth Edition*. Washington, DC: 1994.

Allison, David B. and Mark S. Roberts. *Disordered Mother or Disordered Diagnosis?* Analytic Press, New Jersey. 1998.

Artaud, Antonin. *The Theatre and Its Double*. Trans. Victor Corti. London, UK: Calder Publications Ltd, 1970.

Azundris, Tatiana. "Pretty in Pain: Beauty and the Art of Female Destruction" http://www.azundris.com/output/femme/#assholes

Barton-Fumo, Margaret. "Film Comment Interview: Andrzej Zulawski" in *Film Comment Online*, March 6, 2012. http://www.filmlinc.com/film-comment/entry/film-comment-interview-andrzej-zulawski

Battaglia, Emily. "A Short History of Female Addiction in America" in *Drug and Alcohol Addiction Recovery Magazine*. Online: http://www.drugalcoholaddictionrecovery.com/?p=52

Baumeister, Roy F. "Masochism: His and Hers" in *Spectator vol. 23, no. 19*. San Francisco, CA: 1990.

Boyle, Michael Shane. "Aura and the Archive: Confronting the Incendiary Fliers of Kommune 1" in *A Tyranny of Documents: The Performing Arts Historian as Film Noir Detective*. New York: Theatre Library Association, 2011.

Blum, Harold P. "Masochism, the Ego Ideal and the Psychology of Women" in *Female Psychology: Contemporary Psychoanalytic Views*, edited by Harold P. Blum. New York: International Universities, 1977.

Brownmiller, Susan. *Against Our Will: Men, Women & Rape*. New York: Simon & Schuster, 1975.

Burston, Daniel. "R. D. Laing and the Politics of Diagnosis" in *Janus Head Vol. 4, No. 1*, Spring 2001. Online: http://www.janushead.org/4-1/burstonpol.cfm

Campo, Giuliano and Zygmunt Molik. *Zygmunt Molik's Voice and Body Work: The Legacy of Jerzy Grotowski*. Oxford, UK: Taylor & Francis, 2010.

Davis, Colin. *Trance review* in *Shock Xpress Vol. 2*, edited by Stefan Jaworzyn. London, UK: Titan Books, 1994.

Davis, Colin. "True to His Own Obsessions: The Films of Walerian Borowczyk" in *Shock Xpress Vol. 2*, edited by Stefan Jaworzyn. London, UK: Titan Books, 1994.

Dijkstra, Bram. *Idols of Perversity: Fantasies of Feminine Evil in Fin-de-Siècle Culture*. Oxford, UK: Oxford University Press, 1986.

Dyck,Erika. "Hitting Highs at Rock Bottom': LSD Treatment for Alcoholism, 1950-1970" in *Social History*.

Grajales, Monica. "Gender Differences and Correlation Between Adult Sadomasochistic Sexual Arousal and Child Abuse". Online: http://groups.yahoo.com/group/criminalminds/message/2668

Green, Brian "Hot Rods, Sunny Roads and Flies on Velvet" in *Shindig!* #14. London, UK: Jan/Feb 2010.

Haskell, Molly. "Rape Fantasy: The 2,000 Year Old Misunderstanding." in *Ms. Magazine*. November 1976.

Herman, Judith. *Trauma and Recovery: The Aftermath of Violence from Domestic Abuse to Political Terror*. New York: Basic Books, 1992.

Howarth, Troy. *The Haunted World of Mario Bava*. Surrey, UK: FAB Press 2002.

Kagan, Norman. *American Skeptic: Robert Altman's Genre Commentary Films*. Ypsilanti, MI: Pierian Press, 1982.

Kessyar, Helene. *Robert Altman's America*. Oxford, UK: Oxford University Press, 1991.

Levenkron, Stephen. *Cutting: Understanding and Overcoming Self-Mutilation*. New York: Lion's Crown Ltd., 1998.

Lovejoy, Alice. "Space Invaders: Avant-garde filmmaker Peter Tscherkassky remakes *The Entity*" in *Film Comment* , 38:3, New York: May/June 2002.

Newman, Kim. *Trance review* in *Shock Xpress Vol. 2*, edited by Stefan Jaworzyn. London, UK: Titan Books, 1994.

Robertiello, Robert. "Masochism and the Female Sexual Role" in *Journal of Sex Research Vol. 6*. Oxford, UK: Taylor & Francis, 1970.

Rotzkoff, Lori. *Love on the Rocks: Men, Women, and Alcohol in Post-World War II America*. Chapel Hill, NC: University of North Carolina Press, 2002.

Slater, Jason J. "One Eyed Hacks" in *Dark Side #95*. Plymouth, UK: Stray Cat Publishing, 2002.

Snyder, Scott. "Personality Disorder and the Film Noir Femme Fatale' in *The Journal of Criminal Justice and Popular Culture*, 8: 3. Albany, NY: State University of New York at Albany Press, 2001.

Tombs, Pete and Cathall Tohill. *Immoral Tales*. New York: St. Martin's Press, 1994.

Vasuveda, Vikrant Narayan. "Implications of the Anomie and Sub-Cultural Theories of Deviance in Criminology" in *IndMedica Journal Vol. 7, No. 3*. New Delhi, 2007. http://www.indmedica.com/journals.php?journalid=9&issueid=97&articleid=1316&action=article

Zalcock, Bev. *Renegade Sisters: Girl Gangs on Film*. Creation Books, 1998.

INDEX

Page references in bold refer exclusively to illustrations, though pages referenced as text entries may also feature relevant illustrations.

More Cult Cinema Books published by FAB Press

FrightFest Guide
volume 3 – Ghost Movies

Limited edition hardcover also available, exclusively direct from FAB Press!
Spirits have appeared on film worldwide from the earliest days of cinema, all the way to the contemporary boom of on-screen supernatural horrors. Like many horror fans, award-winning filmmaker Axelle Carolyn (Soulmate and Tales of Halloween — both of which feature spectres) has been obsessed with haunted houses and revenants for as long as she can remember. In this volume, she surveys the last 120 years of the genre and reviews the 200 most memorable titles from across the globe. From timeless classics to recent blockbusters, quirky indies to international sensations, hidden gems to oddities, each of these movies has contributed to the development of the ghost movie as we know it, in all its incarnations and cultural variants. Welcome, foolish mortals, to The FrightFest Guide to Ghost Movies.

ISBN 978-1-903254-97-4
UK: £16.99   –   US: $24.95

FrightFest Guide
volume 2 – Monster Movies

Limited edition hardcover exclusively direct from FAB Press!
Cinema has provided a venue to visualize monsters in all their fearsome, threatening and, sometimes, strangely sympathetic glory.
Now the entire spectrum of screen creatures is gathered in one volume. In The FrightFest Guide to Monster Movies, celebrated writer and editor Michael Gingold starts in the silent era and traces the history of the genre through to the present day. From Universal Studios legends to the big bugs, atomic mutants and space invaders that terrorized the '50s, to the kaiju of Japan and the full-colour Hammer fiends, to the ecological nightmares of the '70s and '80s, to the CG creatures and updated favourites of recent years – they're all here. Dare you confront the beasts within?

ISBN 978-1-903254-94-3
UK: £16.99   –   US: $24.95

FrightFest Guide
volume 1 – Exploitation Movies

Limited edition hardcover exclusively direct from FAB Press!
FrightFest, the UK's biggest horror and fantasy film festival, has joined forces with FAB Press to launch The FrightFest Guide to Exploitation Movies. The inaugural volume is an informative celebration of the grindhouse film industry in all its diverse sex, horror and violence glory. From Blaxploitation and Nunsploitation to Godsploitation and Hixploitation, acclaimed critic, broadcaster, author, and FrightFest co-director, Alan Jones takes a wildly illustrated look at 200 of the most infamous, obscure and bizarre movies ever made. Plus there is a scene-setting introduction by controversial exploitation movie director Buddy Giovinazzo.

ISBN 978-1-903254-87-5
UK: £16.99   –   US: $24.95

FrightFest Guide
volume 4 – Werewolf Movies

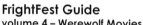

Limited edition hardcover exclusively direct from FAB Press!
The crimson eyes of the werewolf have stalked us across the centuries. We are now most familiar with the wolfman courtesy of Hollywood. Over the past century, a diverse pack of lycanthropes has manifest on the silver screen – in big-bucks blockbusters and zero-budget B-movies – each revealing a little more of the nature of the beast. Within these colorful pages we encounter reluctant wolfmen and shapeshifting sadists, big bad fairytale wolves and lycanthropic nymphomaniacs. Our guide is acclaimed author, broadcaster, occult historian – and lifelong werewolf obsessive – Gavin Baddeley. By finding fresh perspectives on established classics, uncovering neglected gems, and even examining a few howlers among the definitive selection of werewolf movies reviewed, Baddeley shows how the myth has adapted and transformed. Providing our foreword is the award-winning director, writer and producer Neil Marshall, whose brilliant debut feature Dog Soldiers reinvigorated the werewolf movie for the 21st Century. The moon is full, the wolfsbane is in bloom... Time to brave the fogbound moors to find out who – or what – is responsible for that baleful howling... all is revealed in the FrightFest Guide to Werewolf Movies.

ISBN 978-1-913051-01-3
UK: £16.99   –   US: $24.95

More Cult Cinema Books published by FAB Press

Satanic Panic
Pop Cultural Paranoia in the 1980s

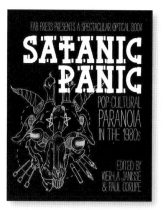

"An electrifying descent into '80s-era cultural terror."
– Mike McPadden, author of Heavy Metal Movies

In the 1980s, it seemed impossible to escape Satan's supposed influence. Everywhere, there were warnings about an evil conspiracy to indoctrinate the vulnerable. This cultural hysteria, now known as the "Satanic Panic" created a cultural legacy of Satan-battling VHS tapes and literature. Satanic Panic: Pop-Cultural Paranoia in the 1980s explores how a culture war played out, from the publication of the memoir Michelle Remembers in 1980 to the end of the McMartin "Satanic Ritual Abuse" Trial in 1990. Satanic Panic addresses the ways the widespread fear of a Satanic conspiracy was propagated through almost every pop culture pathway, from heavy metal music to Dungeons & Dragons RPGs, Christian comics, VHS scare films, pulp paperbacks, children's cartoons, TV talk shows and even home computers. From con artists to pranksters and moralists to martyrs, the book explains how the Satanic Panic was fought on the pop culture frontlines and the serious consequences it had for many involved.

ISBN 978-1-903254-86-8
UK: £19.99 – US: $29.95

Beyond Terror
The Films of Lucio Fulci

An additional 80,000 words of all new writing, plus major revisions to the look of this epic book made possible through the availability of a mass of new colour illustrations!
Italy's Master of the Macabre Lucio Fulci is celebrated in this lavishly illustrated study of his extraordinary films. From horror masterpieces like The Beyond and Zombie Flesh-Eaters to erotic thrillers like One On Top of the Other and A Lizard in a Woman's Skin; from his earliest days as director of manic Italian comedies to his notoriety as purveyor of extreme violence in the terrifying slasher epic The New York Ripper, his whole career is explored. Featuring a foreword by Fulci's devoted daughter Antonella, and produced with her blessing and full co-operation. Featuring COMPLETE FILMOGRAPHIES for ALL the major actors and actresses ever to appear in Fulci films, the appendices alone are a unique, breathtakingly detailed reference source in their own right. Without doubt, by far and away the largest collection of Fulci posters, stills, press-books and lobby cards ever seen together in print. We have scoured the Earth to find the most stunning, rare and eye-catching Fulci images. Everything worth seeing is here. This is a truly beautiful book.

ISBN 978-1-903254-90-5
UK: £39.99 – US: $59.95

Scala Cinema 1978-1993

WINNER of the Kraszna-Krausz Moving Image International Book Award 2019!
The most infamous and influential UK cinema, the Scala's iconic programmes tell their own unique story about culture and society between 1978-1993. The Scala was founded on the site of an ancient theatre in London's Fitzrovia district. In 1981, the Scala moved to the Primatarium, a former picture palace and one-time rock venue close to King's Cross station. An exceptionally atmospheric repertory cinema with its mysteriously rumbling auditorium and resident cats, over a million people went through the doors of the Scala to have their minds blown by its alchemical mix of Hollywood classics and cult movies, horror, Kung Fu, LGBT+, animation, silent comedy, and unclassifiable films, combined with live gigs and music club nights. A lone operator, the Scala closed down in 1993 following a perfect storm of lease expiry, the ravages of the recession… and a devastating court case. Written by Scala programmer Jane Giles, and with an introduction by Scala founder and film producer Stephen Woolley, Scala Cinema 1978-1993 takes stock of a legacy which includes many of today's most exciting filmmakers, who've credited the Scala's influence on their work. This over-size format 424-page coffee table book features the complete collection of all 178 monthly programmes plus photographs and ephemera. It's also an often outrageous time-travelling history taking readers behind the scenes of the Scala. This is a must-have for fans of the legendary cinema, with appeal to anyone interested in film or the story of the 1980s.

ISBN 978-1-903254-98-1
UK: £75.00 – US: $100.00

www.fabpress.com

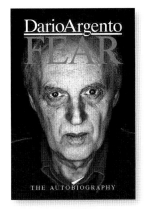

FEAR
The Autobiography of Dario Argento

For many years Argento's ground-breaking shockers like The Bird with the Crystal Plumage, Deep Red, Suspiria, Inferno, Tenebrae and Opera meant box-office gold. Now the maverick auteur, lauded as the Italian Hitchcock and the Horror Fellini, has written his autobiography, revealing all about his fascinating life, his dark obsessions, his talented family, his perverse dreams, and his star-crossed work. With candour and honesty, Fear lifts the lid on the trials and tribulations of Argento's glittering career during the sensational Golden Era of Cinecittà. From his childhood mixing with glamorous Italian movie stars thanks to his noted photographer mother and his film industry father to his start in the fledgling field of cinema criticism, Argento shares compelling anecdotes about his life growing up in La Dolce Vita Rome. Adapted from the Italian translation, annotated by world-renowned Argento expert Alan Jones, and illustrated with numerous rare photographs from his collection, the award-winning and critically acclaimed Master of Terror tells all. So put on your black leather gloves and start turning the pages of Fear for the answer to every question you've ever wanted to ask about the weird and wonderful world of Dario Argento. Dario Argento is a maverick auteur who managed to capture his personal demons on celluloid. At last, his fascinating life story can be told: his passions, his loves, his fears. In this candid autobiography, alongside the tale of an inspirational film director making his mark on the world, one glimpses the anxieties of a driven but shy man, in love with cinema and life itself.

ISBN 978-1-913051-05-1
UK: £20.00 – US: $30.00

The Ghastly One
The 42nd Street Netherworld of Director ANDY MILLIGAN

"I devoured this book – an appalling pocket of cinematic history, delightfully explored and obsessively researched. Andy Milligan is one scary man."
– John Waters (who has named THE GHASTLY ONE as one of his favourite books)

Andy Milligan, the most compelling lone wolf in cinema history, gets his due in this definitive work. Milligan cranked out titles like Bloodthirsty Butchers and The Body Beneath on threadbare budgets. Due to their many limitations, his movies made Milligan a laughingstock. Author Jimmy McDonough changed all that by providing the necessary context and pathos, allowing these chaotic yet highly personal movies (and their creator) to be seen in a new and sympathetic light. Starring a cast of unforgettable, elusive characters, the gripping narrative of THE GHASTLY ONE is told with unflinching honesty. This extraordinary new coffee table art book edition is full of rare images and memorabilia. THE GHASTLY ONE finally gets the presentation it deserves in this lavish production, which has been overseen by Nicolas Winding Refn and is done in the same oversized format as his stunning poster book, THE ACT OF SEEING.

ISBN 978-1-903254-99-8
UK: £75.00 – US: $100.00

American Exxxtasy
My 30-Year Search for a Happy Ending

An Autobiographical Journey from Porn to Primetime by John Amero

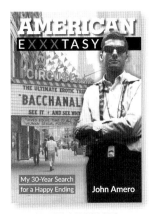

How does a young man from a small New England town become one of the most influential makers of exploitation films in the 1960s? How does the same filmmaker come to be a pioneer of hardcore sex movies in the 1970s and 1980s, including groundbreaking gay features? And how does that very same director move into mainstream productions for television networks like NBC in the 1990s? In American Exxxtasy, John Amero charts his remarkable life and career at the forefront of the sexual revolution, while sharing what it was like to be a gay man living in the heart of New York City through the eras of Stonewall, LGBTQ rights and AIDS. It's a memoir that depicts his close bond with his brother Lem, with whom he formed a thirty-year filmmaking partnership. It details his friendship and collaboration with notorious exploitation director Michael Findlay and his wife Roberta. And it explores John's relationships with notable names such as Andy Warhol, Montgomery Clift, Anthony Perkins, and Olympia Dukakis. American Exxxtasy is an engaging personal story told with frankness, emotion and humour, and a portrait of an industry and a city that were rapidly changing. And it's the only first-person account that provides intimate insight into a singularly unique journey from porn to primetime.

ISBN 978-1-913051-06-8
UK: £20.00 – US: $30.00